SELECTED BIBLE

(Revelation and Word of God)

CREACIONES MONAR
EDITORIAL, S.A.
BARCELONA
(Spain)

Nihil Obstat: The Censor
JOSEP M.ª SOLÉ ROMÀ, cmf.
Barcelona, September 13 1991

JOSEP M.ª SUREDA CAMPS, cmf.
Provincial Superior

Imprímatur:
By order of the Vicar-General

JOSEP RAMON PÉREZ, Chancellor-Secretary

Assessors:
RAFAEL SERRA BOVER, cmf.
    Graduate in Holy Scripture
    Prof. in Rome
JOSEP SOLÉ, cmf.
    Prof. New Testament
CÁNDIDO PALACÍN, cmf.
    Prof. of Modern Languages

© CREACIONES MONAR EDITORIAL, S.A.
Escorial, 26-28
08024 BARCELONA (Spain)

First edition: 1994
Printed in Spain
I.S.B.N. 84-89068-75-5
D.L. B-24.009/2001

FOREWORD OF THE PUBLISHER

In recent years the reading of the Bible has achieved so large a difussion that it cannot be compared to any other bestseller of all times.

In ancient times books were written in longhand, and a multitude of manuscripts spread across all the Christian world. Most of them came out of monasteries richly illustrated.

The earliest manuscripts are: the so-called Vatican manuscript and the Sinaitic. Recently some scrolls containing some parts of the Old Testament have been found in caves at Qumran, near the Dead Sea. They had been hidden by the sect of the Esenians in the Jewish war against the Romans in the year 68.

Since Gütenberg's invention of the print, bibles have spread throughout the world in all the existing languages.

The reading and study of the Bible has always been the purest and richest source of wisdom and inspiration for scholars and experts. Piety and religious vocation have led them to search for the union with God in their mystic elevations. In general, it has also been so for the Christians of all times who have endeavoured to achieve their spiritual perfection.

But there is a very important group of Christians who want to become regular readers of the Bible but their duties do not allow them to do so, or it may be that they find its reading tedious, or even its print may be too small. To those people who would like to know the contents of the Revelation and the Word of God, as also to all the rest, we address this Selected Bible. It is nothing but a selection of the most important texts of the Bible. For that purpose we have selected the best pieces, those which illustrate better the Revelation and the Word of God. We have left out some chapters and paragraphs, as the Church usually does in its reading, in order to offer a text which is clear and faithful to the Word of God.

With this edition of the Selected Bible we are honored to offer our service to the Christian piety and to all those who want to know the Word of God.

We are very grateful to those who have helped us to make this work. We also thank our readers in advance for their acceptance.

THE PUBLISHERS

INTRODUCTION

The Bible is made up of several holy books which contain the Word of God, because it is a fact that God has spoken to men, first through his Prophets in the Old Testament, and later through his Son Jesus Christ. Therefore it is mainly a religious book, which contains the messsage of the salvation of men since the beginning to the coming of Jesus Christ.

Without the Bible we would not know anything about the origins of the world and the universe, of the great civilizations of Mesopotamia, where the first people on the Earth settled, nor would have been located the cities of Ur, Nineveh of Assyria, Babylon, Memphis and so many others, which today are a pile of ruins under the sand of the desert. Religion and science are two different fields, temporal and sensitive is the field of science, and spiritual and trascendental is that of the Faith, but they complement each other as in man do soul and body.

The history of the People of Israel begins with the election of Abraham by God, father of the believers to whom God promised a descendancy countless as the stars in the sky. That elected people had as a misson to prepare the coming of the Messiah, Saviour of the world. He is the Son of God, the most amazing event in the history of Man.

A look at the history of the people of Israel and its environments will enable us to locate it in time and space.

Palestine is situated between the Mediterranean Sea and the deserts of Saudi Arabia, East Jordan and Siria, and to the south of Lebanon. The Jews came originally from Mesopotamia, todays Irak. In its beginnings they were a nomadic people, in the Patriarch's times, then they were slaves in Egypt, and after the crossing of the Red Sea they made a pilgrimage across the desert which lasted forty years. Once they crossed the Jordan they settled down in the Promised Land, except for its coastal line, where the Philistines built their cities. From them comes the name Palestine for the whole country.

Joshua divided the conquered country into the twelve tribes. It was ruled by Judges until the time of King Saul. The monarchy knew its golden period with David and Solomon. With the death of the latter the Northern tribes split up and formed the kingdom of Israel, whose capital was Samaria, and the kingdom of Judah, with the tribe of Benjamin, whose capital was Jerusalem.

The kingdom of Samaria was destroyed by the Assyrians. Its inhabitants were deported to Nineveh and disappeared. The inhabitants of the kingdom of Judah, after Jerusalem was destroyed by Nebuchadnezzar, were taken as prisoners to Babylon until they were set free. God did not foresake what was left of Israel. He sent them Prophets until Babylon collapsed, and Cyrus the conqueror set them free. They came back to their country.

The city of Jerusalem was built again, and they formed a people, the kingdom of Judah, which, thanks to the battles of the Maccabees to keep their religion, could stood firm until the coming of Jesus Christ the Saviour in the Roman's times.

The Jews always lived surrounded by idolatrous nations, and, despite their deviations and disloyalties, which God punished, and despite having broken the terms of their Covenant several times, they never lost the conscience of being the People of God, nor the hope in the promises of a Saviour Messiah.

Thus developed the process of history of the people of Israel under the authority and providence of God. When they parted from him He punished them, but when they were faithful to him he gave them luck and performed miracles for them. The Lord was, actually, their God, and they were His people. The political regime of their monarchy was the theocracy, and their religious and moral beliefs were maintaned by the Prophets, sent by God. He was their guide and protector, and his ways were the Commandments of the Law of the Lord given in Mount Sinai.

Another source of strength of the Jews were the holy books, the Bible. They believed that they were inspired by god, the same as the Church. The holy books do contain the Word of God, that is, the Revelation of the eternal Truth, God gave his commands to Moses and the Prophets, and they passed on his oracles to the People. Most of them kept a written record of them. The same happened with the Apostles and the Evangelists; they preached the doctrine of Jesus, eyewitness as they were, according to Jesus's command: "Go and preach the Gospel to all the nations."

But what is the actual inspiration of the Holy Books? Saint Thomas Aquinas, the Prince of the theologians says, "The Saint Spirit is the main author of the Holy Books. Men were its means." (Quodl. VII Art. 24). God is the main agent, for that reason we say Word of God. But the writer is a human being and leaves his personal print, because he has been given intelligence and will, and he is influenced by the culture of his time, his personal capacity, his own style, character, and so on and so forth. From there comes the diversity of genres and literary styles, although the message is the same. The genres are different, the historical genre is not the same that the prophetic or poetic genre. Besides, Western language uses more images than reason, and is plainer. Jesus Christ used it in the Gospel too.

Words have usually different meanings, and in order to know its true meaning we need a guide. When the matter is as important as our eternal salvation, God cannot leave us without a guide, an authority, nor leave to everyone's judgement, as it happens among the Protestans and their "free examination". That authority is the Catholic Church, the Pope, who is, by the will of Christ, the guardian and keeper of the Faith as the successor or Peter... "I shall give your the keys of the Kingdom of Heaven" (Mathew, 15, 13-20). "...Graze my flock" (John, 20, 15-24). "No Holy Scripture —says Saint Peter (II.20-21)— may be the object of personal interpretation, because it was never written by human will, but men wrote messages of God moved by the Saint Spirit." "There are obscure points (in the Scriptures) which are often misread and misunderstood for the evil (id. 3-16)." "Philip the deacon told the miniser of Candaces his reading of the Bible (Acts of the Apostles, 8,35). The right interpretation of the Bible belongs to the Church. For this reason it has to grant its approval and writes explanatory notes in the Catholic Bibles as a sign of authenticity.

The Bible and the Tradition are the two sources of the Revelation. The Apostolic and Patriarchal Tradition advise the Pope, and both of them have been the guides of the Church which has led them through the centuries. The need for a tradition is obvious, for Saint John says at the end of his Gospel "There are many things that Jesus did which are not recorded, and that if were to be written there would not be space for them in the world." (John 21,25). Therefore tradition is very valuable to understand the Scriptures and the Revelation, not only the Apostolic tradition, but also that of the Saint Fathers and of the scholars of the Church.

The knowing of the true meaning of words is of prime importance, and there are many. The main of them are three: the Literal meaning, the Figurative and the Acquiescent. The Literal meaning is that which words convey, and when it is clear we should not look for another sense, for it corresponds to reality. The Spiritual or Figurative meaning, also called allegorical or symbolic, is, for intance, to say that a person is a lion because of his strength. There is also the so-called typical style, for instance, David is the typical figure of Jesus.

In history there have been two trends: the Literal School of Antioch and the Alegorical School of Alexandria. Each one of them has had great scholars and saints. The Church has moderated both tendencies. The Acquiescent meaning is usually employed by mystics and Saint Fathers in their spiritual elevations and pastoral writings. The Church recommends moderation when using this sense, for it is not safe. In any case the Bible must not be read like a novel, because it is a religious book which contains the Word of God, and it must be thought over and enjoyed as the spiritual food it is, with the same aim with which it was written by the holy authors. The Pope Pius XII says in the "Divino Afflante", "Theologians should bear in mind that they must first see and determine the Literal sense of the biblical words... In the same way they must discuss the spiritual sense if it is clear that God wants it to be discussed, for only God can know this meaning and reveal it."

As for the possibility of miracles, it is obvious that they exist. God is the author of the natural laws and he can change them and even cancel them at will. It is the case that they are real facts, rigurously historical, but only God can make them. Also the saints can perform miracles. God rewards their faith. "If you had faith —said Jesus— you would say to this mountain, 'stand up and throw yourself into the sea', and it would do as you say." (Mat. 17-20). But the saints perform miracles on behalf of God.

It is not reasonable to deny the miracles as a rule.

The acts of God are present throughout history, from the beginning ot the world until the end of times, throughout the Old and New Testaments, and after the Church, follower of the work of Christ, the kingdom of God or of Heaven, as he said, which begins in this world and lasts for the whole eternity. The Bible cannot be understood without taking into account these three fundamental points: the Creation, the Incarnation and the Redemption on the Cross. All the Old Testament is directed to the person of Christ, who came to save us from the slavery of the kingdom of the devil, of sin and death.

Jesus Christ, the Son of God, is the only target and the real author of the New Testament. The texts tell us his doctrine, his life and his message: the Good News of the Gospel and the Kingdom of God under the law of Love.

Saint Paul exhorts us to read it because it is useful for our religious upbringing. It teaches us the great truths which are more interesting for the men of today and of the future: the trascendental truths of man on earth: pain, where do I come from?, what is beyond this world?, why am I here? There the science does not reach. Science does not even explain the origin of life. We are in this world to know, love and serve God, and then to enjoy his company in heaven for ever. This is only taught by the Revelation, the Bible, the Word of God. But to understand it and enjoy it it is necessary to love and think about it as the Virgin Mary did. Everything that she saw in Jesus she "thought over it in her heart."

Therefore we wish that the reading of this Bible is useful spiritually for all of us, as well as for so many millions of Christians who made of the Bible their everyday' spiritual food in prayer and in our love of God and our brothers.

BOOKS OF THE HOLY SCRIPTURES

OLD TESTAMENT

HISTORICAL

(Gen.) Genesis
(Exod.) Exodus
(Lev.) Leviticus
(Num.) Numbers
(Deut.) Deuteronomy
(Josh.) Joshua
(Judg.) Judges
(Sam.) Samuel, I-II
(Kgs.) Kings, I-II
(Chr.) Chronicles, I-II
(Ezra) Ezra
(Neh.) Nehemiah
(Tob.) Tobit
(Jud.) Judith
(Esther) Esther
(Mac.) Maccabees, I-II

RELATED TO WISDOM

(Job) Job
(Ps(s).) Psalm(s)
(Prov.) Proverbs
(Eccles.) Ecclesiastes
(S. of S.) Song of Songs
(Wis.) Wisdom
(Ecc.) Ecclesiasticus

PROPHETIC

(Amos) Amos
(Hos.) Hosea
(Isa.) Isaiah
(Mic.) Micah
(Nahum) Nahum
(Jer.) Jeremiah
(Bar.) Baruk
(Hab.) Habakkuk

(Zeph.) Zephaniah
(Ezek.) Ezekiel
(Dan.) Daniel

(Obad.) Obadiah
(Joel) Joel
(Jonah) Jonah

NEW TESTAMENT

EVANGELISTS

(Mat.) Matthew
(Mark) Mark
(Luke) Luke
(John) John

LETTERS OF PAUL

(Thes.) Thessalonians
(Gal.) Galatians
(Cor.) Corinthians

(Rom) Romans
(Eph.) Ephesians
(Phil.) Philippians
(Col.) Colossians
(Phile.) Philemon
(Tit.) Titus
(Hebr.) Hebrews
(James) James
(Peter) Peter
(John) John
(Jude) Jude
(Rev.) Revelation

OLD TESTAMENT

GENESIS

PART ONE

PRIMITIVE HISTORY

1. THE CREATION AND THE FALL

The tale of the Creation. The Universe. In the beginning[1] God made[2] heaven and earth[3]. The earth was loneliness and chaos[4], and it was dark over the abyss, but the spirit of God swept over the waters[5]. Then God said, "Let there be light", and there was light[6].

God saw that the light was good, and he separated it from darkness. He called the light day, and the darkness night. It was the first day[7].

God said, "Let there be a vault[8] between the waters, to separate water from water", and it was so. And God made the

---

1. Of time.
2. Out of nothing.
3. The Cosmos, Universe.
4. Void, nothingness.
5. God is the pure spirit.
6. The light turns into cosmic energy.
7. The days of the Creation are ages.
8. For the Jews the sky had the form of a vault.

vault, and separated the water that was under him from the water above; and God called the vault heaven. It was the second day.

Then God said, "Let the waters under heaven be gathered into one place, so that dry land may appear", and so it was. God called the dry land earth, and he called the mass of waters seas. And God saw that it was good[1].

And God said, "Let the earth produce growth, and plants with seeds and fruit-trees that bear fruit upon the earth, all of them with seed according to its kind[2]." And so it was. The earth produced growth and plants with seeds according to their kind. And God saw that this was good. It was the third day.

God said, "Let there be lights[3] in the vault of heaven to separate day from night and that can be used as signs to distinguish the seasons, the days and the years, and let them shine in the vault of heaven to give light on earth". And it was so. Thus, God made two great lights, the greater to govern the day and the lesser to govern the night and the stars. God put them in the vault of heaven to give light on earth, govern day and night and separate light from darkness. And God saw that this was good. It was the fourth day.

God said, "Let the waters teem with countless living creatures, and let birds fly above the earth facing the vault of heaven." And, in this way, God made the great sea animals, and all those living creatures that move and swarm in the waters according to their kind, and birds according to their kind too. And God saw that it was good. And God blessed them and said: "Grow up and be fruitful, and fill the waters of the sea, and let the birds multiply on earth." It was the fifth day.

And then God said, "Let the earth produce living animals according to their kind: cattle, reptiles and wild animals, all according to their kind. And it was so. God created

---

1. This is an antropomorphism.
2. They are born, grow and multiply within each kind. The mixture of kinds is not a natural phenomenon. Vegetal, organic world.
3. The condensation of gases produced the galaxies, nebulas, the sun and the moon.

animals on earth, cattle and reptiles, all according to their kind. And God saw that this was good.

Creation of Man. Then God said, "Let us make man in our likeness and image. Let him rule over the fish in the sea, over the birds in the sky, over the cattle, over the wild animals and the reptiles of the earth."

Then God created man out of the dust of the earth[1], and breathed into his nostrils a breath of life and made him a living creature.

God created man in his image[2],
in God's image he was created,
male and female he created them.

God blessed them and said to them, "Be fruitful, fill the earth and subdue it; rule over the fish in the sea, over the birds in the sky, and over all those living creatures that move over the earth." And it was so. And God saw everything that he had made, and it was very good. It was the sixth day.

Thus heaven and earth were completed with all their mighty throng. God finished his work on the seventh day, and that day he ceased from all his work. God blessed that day and made it holy, because on it he had ceased all his creative activity. This was the origin of heaven and earth when they were created.

Paradise, destiny of Man. God planted a garden in Eden, to the East, and in it he put the Man that he had created. God made all kind of trees grow from the earth, all of them pleasant to look at and good for food, as well as the tree of life, in the middle of the garden, and the tree of knowledge of good and evil.

Thus God took the Man and put him in the garden of Eden to keep it and cultivate it. And he gave man the following commandment: "You may eat from every tree in the garden, but

---

1. Man is a rational animal. Material body and spiritual soul make him different from the rest of the animal world.

2. Similar to God, who is spirit. Spiritual soul, intelligent and immortal. Besides, it has the supernatural life of the grace.

do never eat of the tree of knowledge of good and evil, for the day in which you eat from it, you will certainly die."

Creation of Woman. Then God said, "It is not good for man to be alone; I will make a partner for him that is similar to him." And then God put the man into a trance, and while he was sleeping, he took one of his ribs, putting flesh in its place; and with this rib which he had taken out of the man he made the woman, and showed her to the man, and the man said:

"This is truly bone from my bones,
        and flesh from my flesh."

That is why a man leaves his father and mother and is united to his wife, and they become one flesh[1]. They were both naked, the man and his wife, but they were not ashamed of each other.

Temptation, fall[2] and Primary Gospel. The snake was more crafty than any other wild creature that God had made. And God said to the woman, "Is it true that God told you, 'Do not eat from every tree in the garden'?" The woman answered the serpent, "We may eat the fruit of any tree in the garden. He has only forbidden us to eat from the tree which is in the middle of the garden. 'Do not eat or even touch it, or else you will die', God had said." Then the snake said to the woman, "No, you will not die. God knows that as soon as you eat it, your eyes will be opened and you will be like gods, and you will know good and evil."

Meanwhile the woman saw that the tree was good to eat, pleasant to the eye and tempting to attain knowledge. Therefore, she took its fruit and ate it; she gave some to her husband and he ate it too. Then their eyes were opened and they saw that they were naked; so they stiched fig-leaves together and made themselves loincloths.

---

1. And thus they became an inseparable matrimony.

2. Before he was favourable to them he tested their obedience, as he had done with the angels. The rebel angels were turned into devils and expelled from heaven. The Devil, in the form of a snake, temped our first fathers. They were tricked and learnt sin, the knowledge of evil. Primary Gospel: Promise of the Redemptor. Fight and victory of the Woman (Mary and his descendant, Jesus, and his sons). Except for her we all get the Original Sin.

They heard the steps of God walking in the garden in the evening breeze, and the man and his wife hid from him among the trees of the garden. Bud God called the man, saying, "Where are you?", and he replied, "I have heard yoo walking in the garden, and I was afraid, for I was naked, and then I hid myself." God continued, "Who let you know that you were naked? Have you eaten from the tree which I forbade you?" The man answered, "The woman that you gave to me as my companion gave me to eat from the tree, and I did." God said to the woman "What have you done?" And the woman answered, "The serpent tricked me, and I ate." Then God said to the serpent:

"Because of what you have done,
you are cursed among all the cattle and wild animals.
I will put enmity between you and the woman, between your
        brood and hers; he will smash your head as you
        approach her heel[1]."

Then he said to the woman: "I will increase your labour in pregnancy. You shall bear children with pain, and, however, you shall be eager for your husband, and he will be your master."

To the man he said: "Because you have listened to your wife, and because you have eaten from the tree which I forbade you:

Cursed is the ground on your account.
With labour you will grow on it your food for the rest of your
        life.
She will give you thorns and thistles, and you shall eat the
        wild plants from the ground.
You shall eat your bread with the sweat of your brow until
        you return to the ground, for from it you were taken.
        Dust you are and to dust you shall return."

---

1. Adam and Eve lose their Supernatural Life of the Grace, and were doomed to suffering and Death. They rebelled against God, and their passions rebelled against themselves. Good against evil.

The man called his wife Eve because she was the mother of all those who lived. God made for the man and his wife tunics of skins, and he clothed them. Afterwards, he said: "There he is, the man who has become one of us because of the knowledge of good and evil". So he drove him out of the garden of Eden, so that he would till the ground from which he had been taken. He casted him out, and in front of the garden of Eden he placed the cherubin and the flame of a flashing sword to guard the way to the tree of life.

2. HISTORY OF THE CULTURE

Cain and Abel. The first murder. The man lay with his wife, and she conceived and gave birth to Cain, and said, "I have had a man, thanks to the Lord". Then she gave birth to Abel, Cain's brother. Abel became a shepherd, and Cain a tiller of the soil. Some time later, Cain offered the Lord some of the fruits of his labour. Abel offered him the best first-born of his flock. The Lord received Abel and his gift with favour, but he did not receive Cain and his gift so. Cain was very angry and his face fell. The Lord said to him, "Why are you so angry? If you do well, you would carry your head high, but if you do wrond the sin is at your door. Sin is after you, but you can prevent it."

Then Cain said to his brother Abel, "Let us go into the country". Once there, Cain attacked his brother and killed him. The Lord asked him, "Where is your brother?", and he answered, "I do not know. Am I his keeper?" Then the Lord said to him, "What have you done? The sound of the blood of your brother is shouting up to me from the ground. Thus, you are cursed, and you shall be casted out of the ground, which has opened its mouth to receive your brother's blood, which you have shed. When you till the ground, it will not longer give you its fruits. You shall be a vagrant and a wanderer on earth."

Descendants of Adam. When God created the man he did so in his own image. He created them male and female, he blessed them and gave them the name of "man" on the day of their creation. Adam, when he was one hundred and thirty years old, had a son, and named him Set. After the birht of Set Adam still lived eight hundred years, and had other sons and daughters. Adam lived nine hundred and thirty years, and then he died[1].

3. THE FLOOD

As the Lord saw that the evil of mankind over the earth was great, and that every thought of their heart was evil, he was sorry that he had created man upon earth, and his heart was so sad that he said, "I will wipe off the face of the earth the man I have created, both men and animals." But Noah had the Lord's favour.

Noah was in his time a fair man, righteous and afraid of God. He had three children: Shem, Ham and Japheth. Then the Lord said to Noah, "The end opf the flesh has come, for the earth is full of iniquity because of man. Thus, I am going to destroy them, together with the earth. Make yourself an ark with resin woods, divide it into compartments in the inside, and coat it with pitch inside and outside. These shall be its measures: three hundred cubits long, fifty cubits wide, and thirty cubits high. You shall make a roof for the ark, and give it a fall of one cubit when complete. On one side you will make the door, and the ark shall have three decks. I intend to bring the waters of the flood over the earth to destroy every being under heaven that is under the spirit of life. Everything that is on earth shall perish. With you, however, I will make a covenant. You shall go into the ark, together with your three sons. You will bring into the ark two of every kind of all living creatures, male and female, to save them with you. Two of every kind of birds, and reptiles shall come with you to be saved. See that you take everything that can be used as food for them and for you." Noah did as God commanded him.

---

1. The longevity of the first Patriarchs is a mistery. Maybe the Lord did it so to increase the expansion of the first settlers. They did not count time as we do.

Then, the Lord said to Noah, "Go into the ark with all your family, because only you are chosen in this generation. In seven day's time I will send rain over the earth during forty days and forty nights, and I will wipe off its face every living creature that I have made." Noah did everything as he was told by God.

Thus, Noah, with his wife, sons, and his sons's wives, went into the ark to escape the waters of the flood. And in the ark with him went animals in pairs, clean and unclean, birds and reptiles, male and female, as the Lord had commanded. At the end of the seven days the waters of the flood came upon the earth.

In the year when Noah was six hundred years old, on the seventeenth day of the second month, all the springs of the great abyss broke through, and the windows of the sky were opened. And the rain fell upon the earth.

It rained for forty days upon the earth, and the waters, always increasing, and lifted the ark upon the ground, floating on the waters. They increased more and more; meanwhile, the the ark went on floating on the surface of the waters. They increased so much upon the earth that they covered all the highest mountains under the sky. The waters covered fifteen cubits over the highest mountains. Every living creature that moved on the earth died; birds, cattle, wild animals and reptiles, and every human being[1]. Everything which had the breath of life and lives on dry land died. All the living creatures that existed upon the surface of the earth were wiped off, men and wild creatures, reptiles and birds disappeared from the earth. Only Noah and those who were with him in the ark survived. The flood of the waters upon the earth lasted one hundred and fifty days.

End of the Flood. God thought of Noah[2], and of all those creatures that were with him in the ark. He made a wind blow over the earth and the waters subsided. The springs of the abyss

---

1. The Cainites and their descendants represented the blood of the snake because of their iniquity and idolatry. The Setites, Noah and his family, on the contrary, were the elected part of humanity.

2. Noah was a man of faith among the usual corruption.

and the windows of the sky were closed, and the rain stopped falling. Then, the waters withdrew gradually from the earth, and after one hundred and fifty days they began to get dry. On the seventeenth day of the seventh month the ark grounded on a mountain in Ararat. The waters continued receeding until the tenth month, and on the first day of this month the peaks of the mountains could be seen. Forty days afterwards Noah opened the window that he had made in the ark[1] and released a raven that flied over the waters, to and fro, until the waters on the earth had dried up. Noah then released a dove to see if the waters on the earth had already dried up, but the dove did not found any place to settle and came back to the ark, for the waters were still covering the surface of the earth. Noah stretched out his hand, caught the dove and took her into the ark. He waited for seven days more, and again he released the dove out of the ark. In the evening the dove came to him with a newly plucked olive leaf on her beak. Thus, Noah knew that the waters did not cover the surface of the earth any longer. However, he waited seven days longer, and again he released the dove, that would never come back to him.

When Noah was six hundred and one years old, on the first day of the first month the waters over the surface of the earth had dried up. Noah removed the hatch and looked up, and the surface of the earth was dry. By the twenty-seventh day of the second month the earth was completely dry.

Out of the ark. Then God said to Noah, "Come out of the ark, you and your wife, your children and the wives of your children. Also the animals of any kind that you have with you, birds, cattle and reptiles. Fill the earth, be fruitful and increase there." Noah went out with his sons, his wife and the wives of his sons. And all the creatures, cattle, birds and reptiles came out of the ark by kinds[2].

---

1. The ark measures were: 156 m long, 26 m wide, 16 m high, with a capacity of 64,896 m.

2. The Babilonic chronology counts 10 kings before the flood. The existence of the flood is confirmed by the Sumerian, Asirian and Babilonic traditions. Its universality is not clear.

Noah erected an altar to the Lord. He took clean beasts and birds and offered whole-offerings on the altar. The Lord smelt the sweet odour, and said within himself, "I will not curse the earth because of man again, for the impulses of the heart of man are inclined to evil since his youth; I will never punish the living creatures as I have just done."

Covenant of the Lord and Noah. God blessed Noah and his sons, and said to them, "Be fruitful, multiply and fill the earth. All the animals, birds, fishes, and everything that crawls upon the surface of the earth shall have fear and dread of you. They are all in your hands. Every creature that moves and lives upon the earth shall be food for you.

This shall be my covenant with you: Never again shall any creature be murdered by the waters of the flood. Never again shall there be another flood over the earth." And the Lord added, "This will be the sign of my covenant with the earth, you and every living creature, for all the future generations. I set my bow in the clouds, and it will be the signs of the covenant between myself and the earth; whenever I see the bow I will remember my covenant, and the waters will never again be a flood to destroy all living creatures on the earth."

4. FROM THE FLOOD UNTIL ABRAHAM

Noah's sons. The sons of Noah who came out of the Ark were Shem, Ham and Japeth. Ham was the father of Canaan. These were the sons of Noah, and they spread over the whole earth.

After the flood Noah still lived three hundred and fifty years. When he died he was nine hundred and fifty years![1]

The tower of Babel. Once upon a time all the world spoke a single language and used the same words. As men journeyed in the east, they came to a plain in the land of Shinar and settled there. And they said to one another, "Come, let us make bricks and bake them hard." They used bricks for stone and bitumen

---

1. The dove of the ark is the symbol of peace.

for mortar. Then they said, "Come, let us built ourselves a city and a tower with its top in the heavens[1], and make a name for ourselves, or we shall be dispersed all over the earth." But the Lord came down to see the city and tower which mortal men had built, and he said, "Here they are, one people with a single language, and now they have started to do this; henceforward nothing they have a mind to do will be beyond their reach. Come, let us go down and confuse their speech, so that they will not understand what they say to one another." So the Lord dispersed them from there all over the earth, and they left off building the city. That is why is called Babel, because the Lord confounded there the speech of all the people in the earth and scattered them all over the face of the earth.

Descendants of Abraham. This is the descendancy of Shem: when he was one hundred years old he begot Arphadax, two years after the flood. After the birth of Arphadax Shem lived five hundred years, and he begot other sons and daughters.

Terah was seventy years old when he begot Abraham, Nahor and Haran.

---

1. So that the earth was wedded to the god of heaven, Marduk, a maid was sacrified every year from the ziggurats.

PART TWO

HISTORY OF THE PATRIARCHS

1. HISTORY OF ABRAHAM

Abraham's Vocation[1]. The Lord said to Abraham, "Leave your own country, your family and your father's house, and go to the country which I will show you. I will make you into a great nation, I will bless you and make your name so great that it will be used in blessings. All the nations of the earth shall be blessed for you."

And so Abraham set out as the Lord had told him, and with him he took Lot. Abraham was seventy-five years old when he left Harran. He took his wife with him, Sarai, and Lot, his nephew. He took all their property and the servants they had acquired in Harran. And so they set out to the land of Canaan[2]. When they arrived there, Abraham crossed the country as far as the holy place of Shechem, up to the terebinth-tree of Moreh. At that time the Canaanites inhabited the country. Then the Lord appeared to Abraham and said, "I will give this land to your descendancy." And there Abraham built an altar to the Lord who had appeared to him. From there he went on to the hill-country east of Bethel and pitched his tent between Bethel on the west and Ai on the east. There he built an altar to the

---

1. With Abraham begins the history of the Hebrews. God chose him as the father of the first People of God and father of all the believers.

2. Nowaday's Palestine.

Lord as well, and invoked the Lord by name. Thus he journeyed by stages towards the Negeb[1].

Lot, who accompanied Abraham, also had sheep, cattle and tents. The land could not support them both, their livestock was so numerous that they could not settle in the same district. There were quarrels between Abraham's herdsmen and Lot's. Abraham, then, said to Lot, "Let there not be quarrels between your herdsmen and mine, for we are kinsmen. The whole country is there before you. Let us part company: If you go left, I shall go right, and if you go right, I shall go left. Then Lot looked up and saw all the well-watered plain of the Jordan —that was before the Lord had destroyed Sodom and Gomorrah[2]— and that plain till Zoar was like the garden of the Lord, like the land of Egypt. Lot chose the valley of the Jordan, and set out for the east. In this way they parted company. Abraham settled in the land of Canaan[3], and Lot moved on to live in the cities of the valley. His tents arrived to the Sodom. The inhabitants of Sodom were wicked and great sinners against the Lord.

The Lord said to Abraham, once Lot had parted from him, "Look up and from where you are look north and south, east and west. All the land you can see I will give to you and your descendants for ever. I will make your descendancy countless as the dust of the earth; if anyone could count the dust of the earth, then he could count your descendants. Go through the length and width of the land, for I give it to you." Abraham moved his tents and moved to the terebinths of Mamre at Hebron; and there he built and altar to the Lord.

Melchizedeck. On Abraham's return from his defeat of Kedorlaomer and his confederate kings, the king of Sodom came out to meet him in the valley of Shaveh, which is now the King's Valley. Melchizedeck king of Salem brought bread and

---

1. To the south of Palestine.
2. Two cities in the Pentapolis, on the sea-shore of the Dead Sea, in the valley of the river Jordan.
3. Their origins are in Phoenicia. The Canaanites worshipped Baal, Bel-Marduk in form of a bull, and Ashtaroth.

wine. He was the priest of God Most High, and he blessed Abraham and said,

"Blessed be Abraham of God Most High, who created heaven and earth, and blessed be God Most Hight, who has delivered your enemies into your hands."

And Abraham gave him a tithe of everything[1].

Divine promises and covenants. After these events the Lord spoke to Abraham and said to him, "Do not be afraid from me, Abraham, I am your shield. Your reward will be great." And Abraham answered, "Oh Lord, my God, what are you going to give me? I am going to die without any children, and heir to my household is Eliezer of Damascus. You have not given any descendancy to me, and now one of my servants will be my heir." Then the Lord spoke to him and said:

"No, he shall not be your heir. Your heir shall be a child of your own body." Then he brought him outdoors and said to him, "Look up into the sky and count, if you can, the stars." and added, "So many shall your descendants be". Abraham believed the Lord and the Lord counted that faith to him as righteousness[2].

Then the Lord said to him, "I am the Lord who brought you out of Ur of the Chaldees to give you this land to occupy. From now on you shall know that your descendants will live as foreigners in a strange land[3], in which they shall be slaves and shall be oppressed for four hundred years; but I shall judge the people to which they will have served, and they shall leave it with great possessions. But you must go with your fathers, and will be buried at a very old age. The fourth generation of your descendants shall come back here, because the iniquity of the Amorites has not increased enough yet."

The Covenant and the Circumcision. When Abraham was ninety-nine years old the Lord appeared to him and said, "I am God Almighty, live always in my presence and be perfect. I

---

1. Melchizedeck was a priest who worshipped the truly God at Salem (Jerusalem). He offered a sacrifice of bread and wine.
2. Because of his faith he is recorded as Father of the believers.
3. Egypt.

shall set my Covenant between myself and you and I shall multiply your descendancy greatly." Abraham postrated on the ground and the Lord went on saying, "I set my covenant between myself and you and your descendancy after you, down from generation to generation. An everlasting Covenant, so that I am your Lord and your descendancy's, that shall follow after you."

The Lord said to Abraham, "You shall keep my Covenant, you and your descendancy after you for generations. The Covenant that must be kept between myself and your generations after you, is this: every male among yourselves shall be circumcised at the age of eight days. You shall circumcise the flesh of your foreskin, both of those children born in your house and any foreigner, not of your blood but bought with your money. Thus shall my Covenant be marked in your flesh as an everlasting Covenant[1]."

Sarai is promised a son. The Lord said to Abraham, "You shall not call your wife Sarai any more, her name shall be Sarah. I will bless her and she will bear you a son, and with my blessing she shall become mother of nations, and even kings of peoples shall spring from her. Your wife Sarah shall give you a son, and you shall name him Isaac. I will set my Covenant with him, as an everlasting Covenant, to be his God and his descendancy's after him. As for Ismael, I have also heard him. But my Covenant shall be set with Isaac, whom Shara will bear to you at this season next year[2]."

The Lord appears at Mamre. The Lord appeared to Abraham by the terebinths of Mamre. As Abraham was sitting at the opening of his tent in the heat of the day, he looked up and saw three men standing in front of him. When he saw them, he ran from the opening of his tent to meet them, bowed low to the ground, and said to them, "Sirs, if I have deserved your favour, do not pass by my humble house without a visit. Let me send for some water so that you may wash your feet and rest

---

1. The circumcision is the external sign which indicates that the Jews are sons of Abraham for ever. This Covenant is more perfect than Noah's.

2. The old Abraham believed the promise.

under a tree; and let me fetch a little food so that you may refresh youselves a little. Afterwards you can continue the journey which has brought you my way." They answered, "Do as you say." Abraham hurried to Sarah's tent and said to her, "Take three measures of flour quickly, knead it and make some cakes." Then Abraham ran to the cattle, chose a fine tender calf and gave it to a servant, who hurriedly prepared it. He took curds and milk and the calf he had prepared, set it before them, and waited on them himself under the tree while they ate. They asked him, "Where is Sarah, your wife?" And he answered, "She is in her tent." The stranger said, "About this time next year I shall come back to you. By then your wife shall have a child." Sarah was listening at the entrance of the tent behind the man who was speaking. Abraham and Sarah were very old, and Sarah was past the age of child-bearing. Sarah laughed to herself and thought, "Now that I am old shall I bear a child, being my husband old too?" But the Lord said to Abraham, "Is there anything difficult to the Lord? I shall come back here for certain in a year's time, and Sarah shall have a son[1]."

Abraham intercedes. The men stood up and headed for Sodom. Abraham accompanied them. The Lord then said, "There is a great outcry over Sodom and Gomorrah, and their sin[2] is certainly great. I shall come down to them and see if they have done as I have heard they have; I will know the truth."

When the men turned and went towards Sodom, Abraham was still before the Lord. He came near him and said, "Are you really going to sweep away good and bad together? Suppose there are fifty good men in the city, will you really sweep them away, and not pardon the place because of the fifty good men? Far it from you to do this! To kill good and bad together; for then the good would suffer with the bad. Far be it from you. Shall not the judge of all earth do what is just?" The Lord answered, "If I find in the city of Sodom fifty good men, I shall pardon the whole place for their sake." Abraham replied, "I am certainly dary, I, dust and ashes. Suppose there are five short of

---

1. Abraham spoke to God in the three people.
2. Idolatry, human sacrifices, sodomy, and so on.

the fifty good men. Are you going to destroy the whole city for those five men?" "No, I will not destroy it if I find forty-five good men." Abraham went on and said, "There might be only forty." And He answered, "I will not do it for the sake of the forty." Abraham insisted, "Oh Lord, do not be angry if I speak again, but there might be only thirty." And the Lord replied, "I will not do it for the sake of the thirty." "My Lord, may I presume to insist, there might be only twenty." And the Lord said, "I will not do it for the sake of the twenty." And Abraham said, "I pray you not to be angry, oh Lord, if I speak just once more: suppose ten can be found there." And the Lord answered, "I will not do it for the sake of the ten."

When the Lord had finished talking to Abraham, he left, and Abraham came back to his place.

Sodom's perversion. The two Angels came to Sodom in the evening, and they met Lot sitting at the gate of the city. When he saw them he stood up and came to meet them. He prostrated on the ground and said to them, "Sirs, I pray you to come to my humble home, spend the night there and wash your feet; you can rise early and continue your journey." But they answered, "No, we will spend the night in the street." But he insisted so much that they went with him, and spent the night at his house. He prepared a meal for them, baking unleavened cakes, and they ate them.

Sodom's destruction. At dawn the Angels hurried Lot and said to him, "Be quick, take your wife and your two daughters who are here, or wou will be swept away when the city is punished." And as he hesitated, those men took him by the hand, him and his wife and daughters, and took him outside the city because the Lord had spared them. Once they were outside the city, one of the Angels said, "Flee for your lives; do not look back and do not stop anywhere in the Plain. Flee to the hills or you will be swept away."

As soon as it was dawn Lot reached Zoar. Then the Lord rained down fire and brimstone from the skies on Sodom and Gomorrah. And he destroyed these cities and everything that grew on the land. But Lot's wife looked back and turned into a pillar of salt.

Birth of Isaac. The Lord visited Sarah as he had said, and he did as he had promised. And so, Sarah begot a son to Abraham, in his old age, at the time when the Lord had said. And Abraham named the son who Sarah had had Isaac, Abraham circumcised Isaac, his son, when he was eight days old, as the Lord had commanded him. When his son Isaac was born Abraham was one hundred years old.

The boy grew up, and on the day of his weaning Abraham gave a feast.

Sacrifice of Isaac. It happened that after this event the Lord wanted to test Abraham, and he called him, "Abraham, Abraham!" He answered, "Here I am." And God said to him, "Take your beloved son, the only one you have, Isaac, and go to the land of Moriah. There you shall offer him as a sacrifice on one of the hills which I will show you."

Abraham rose early in the mornig, saddled his ass, took his two servants and his son Isaac; he split the firewood for the sacrifice and set out for the place of which God had spoken. On the third day Abraham looked up and saw the place in the distance. He said to his men, "Stay here with the ass while the boy and I go over there. When we have worshipped we will come back to you." Abraham then took the firewood for the sacrifice and put them on the shoulders of his son Isaac. Then he took the fire and the knife in his hand, and they went together. Isaac said to his father, "Father!" And he answered, "Here am I, my son." Isaac said, "We have the fire and the wood, but, where is the young beast for the sacrifice?" Abraham answered, "God will provide himself with a young beast for the sacrifice, my son", and they went on their way[1].

When they arrived to the place which the Lord had shown him, Abraham built an altar, prepared the firewood and binded his son Isaac to the altar over the firewood. Then he stretched out his hand and took his knife to kill his son. But the Angel of the Lord called him from heaven and said to him, "Abraham! Abraham!" He answered, "Here am I." And the Angel said to

---

1. It was a heroic sacrifice that God was asking him in his own child to test his faith in his promise. God was satisfied.

him, "Do not stretch your hand over the boy, nor do him any harm. I see that you are a God-fearing man because you did not deny me your only son." Then Abraham raised his eyes and saw behind him a ram caught by its horns in a thicket. He took the ram and offered it as a sacrifice instead of his son. Abraham named that place "The Lord provides."

The Angel of the Lord called Abraham a second time, and said to him, "I swear by my own self, word of the Lord, that in as much as you have done this and have not denied to me your only son I shall bless you infinitely, and I will multiply your descendants so much that they shall be like the stars in heaven and like the sand in the sea-shore, and your descendancy shall possess the gates of your enemies. The nations of the earth shall be blessed because your descendancy is blessed, for you have obeyed my voice." Abraham came back to where his servants were and they returned to Beersheba[1], and there Abraham remained[2].

The graves of the Patriarchs. Sarah lived one hundred and twenty-seven years. She died in Kiriath-arba, which is Hebron, in the land of Canaan. Abraham came to mourn and weep for her. Then he buried her in the cave in the plot of land at Machpelah to the east of Mamre, which is Hebron, in Canaan.

Marriage of Isaac. Abraham was very old and the Lord had blessed him in all that he did. He said to his oldest servant, the one who was in charge of all his possessions, "Put, I pray you, your hand under my tight. I want you to swear by the Lord, God of heaven and earth, that you will not take for my son a wife among the daughters of the Canaanites among whom I live. On the contrary, you shall go to my own country, to the country of my kinsmen, to find a wife for my son Isaac." The servant[3] answered, "What if the woman is unwilling to come with me to this country, shall I take your son to the country from which you came?" Abraham replied, "On no account are you to take my son back there. The Lord, God of heaven and earth, who

---

1. Southern Canaan.
2. In the liturgy the sacrifice of Isaac is celebrated.
3. Eliezer (God is help).

brought me out of the house of my father and of the country of my kinsmen, spoke to me and swore to me, saying, "I will give this land to your descendants", he will send and Angel to you and you will take there a wife for my son. And if she is not willing to come with you, then you will be released from your oath to me, but on no account will you take my son there." The servant put his hand under Abraham's tight, his master, and swore and oath on those terms.

Then the servant took ten camels of his master and set out carrying with him every kind of goods of his master. On his way, he arrived at Aram-naharaim, the city of Nahor. Towards the evening, when the women come out to draw water, he made the camels kneel down outside the city, and said, "Oh Lord, God of my master Abraham, give me good fortune today; keep faith with my master Abraham. I shall stand by the spring while the women of the city come out to draw water. Let it be like this: I shall say to a woman, 'Please lower your jar so that I may drink', and if she answers, 'drink and I shall water your camels too' that will be the girl whom you intend for your servant Isaac; In this way I shall see that you have kept faith with my master[1]."

Before he had finished praying, Rebecca, daughter of Bethuel[2], son of Milcah, the wife of Abraham's brother Nahor, came out of the city with her water-jug on her shoulder. The woman was very beautiful, and a virgin, who had not had intercourse with a man. She came down to the spring, filled her jug and, as she was going to come up, the servant came to meet her and said, "Give me, please a sip of water from your jar." She answered, "Drink, sir" and rapidly she lowered the jar from her shoulders to let him drink. And when he finished drinking she said, "Now I shall draw water for your camels too until they have had enough." She quickly emptied her jar into the through, run to draw some more water and watered the camels.

---

1. God would listen to his prayer.
2. Bethuel, father of Rebecca and Laban, and brother of Abraham in the country of the Arameans.

Meanwhile the man was watching her silently, wondering if the Lord had guided his journey or not.

Once the camels had finished drinking he said to her, "Tell me, whose daughter are you? And please, tell me if there is no place in your father's house for me to stay over." She replied, "I am daughter of Bethuel, the son who Milcah bore to Nahor." And then she added, "We have straw and fodder and also room for you to spend the night." Then the servant prostrated himself to the Lord and worshipped Him, saying, "Blessed be the Lord, God of my master Abraham, who has not failed to keep faith and truth with my master; for I have been guided by the Lord to the house of my master's kinsman." The girl ran to her mother's house and told them what had happened. Rebecca had a brother called Laban, and he run out to the servant by the spring. When he saw the ring[1] and the bracelets that his sister was wearing and as he heard his sister say, "This and that is what the man has told me.", he approached him, for he was still with his camels by the spring, and said, "Come in, whom the Lord has blessed, why should you stay outside? I have prepared the house, and there is a place for the camels." So the man came into the house. Laban unloaded the camels and provided straw and fodder for them, and to the servant and his men he brought water so that they could wash their feet.

Then they brought them some food, but he said, "I will not eat until I have said what I have come here to say.", and Laban replied, "Speak." He began, "I am Abraham's servant. The Lord has blessed my master and has made him rich; he has provided him with flocks and herds, gold and silver, male and female servants, camels and asses. Sarah, my master's wife, had a child when she was old, and to him he has given everything he owns. My master made me swear an oath, saying, 'You shall not take a wife for my son from the women of the Canaanites[2] in whose land I live; but you shall go to my father's house and to my family to find a wife for him.' Today I stand by the spring; and I have said: 'Lord, God of my master Abraham, let the woman

---

1. Golden ring of half a siclum weight. Golden bracelets also as gifts.
2. The Canaanites were idolaters; their house and blood was Aramean, though.

that comes out to draw water, to whom I say, 'Give me some water from your jug', and replies, 'Drink and I shall water your camels too', be the woman that the Lord intends for my master's son. I had not finished praying and I saw Rebecca coming out with her water-jug on her shoulder. She came down to the spring and drew some water, and I said to her, 'Give me some water to drink.' Quickly, she lowered her jug from her shoulder and said, 'Drink, and I shall water your camels too.' I drank and she watered my camels. Then I asked her, 'whose daughter are you?' To which she answered, 'I am the daughter of Bethuel, the son who Milcah bore to Nahor.' Immediately afterwards I put the ring in her nose and the bracelets on her wrists. Then I bowed down and worshipped the Lord[1], and I blessed the Lord, God of my master Abraham, who had led me by the right road to take my master's niece for his son. Now, then, tell me if you want to keep faith and truth with my master or not. If not, say so, and I will turn elsewhere."

Laban and Bethuel said, "This is from the Lord, we cannot say anything for or against. Here is Rebecca; take her and leave; she shall be the wife of the son of your Master, as the Lord has said." When the servant of Abraham heard these words he prostrated himself on the ground before the Lord. He brought out gold and silver ornaments, and clothes which he gave to Rebecca. He gave costly gifts to her brother and to her mother. He and his men ate and drank, and spend the night there.

Next morning, when they rose, he said, "Let me come back to my Master". But the brother and the mother of Rebecca replied, "Let us call the girl and see what she says." So they called Rebecca and said to her "Do you want to go with this man?" and she answered, "Yes." Thus, they let her sister Rebecca and her nurse go with Abraham's servant and his men. And they blessed her, and said,

"You are our sister,
may you be the mother of myriads."

---

1. Thanksgiving because he had showed him the way to the woman chosen for his master's son.

Then Rebecca and her servants stood up, mounted their camels and followed the man immediately. And the servant, taking Rebecca with him, went his way.

Meanwhile Isaac, who by then was living in the Negeb, had moved on as far as the well of Lahai-roi[1]. In the evening he had gone out into the open country. He looked up and saw some camels drawing near. Rebecca looked up too and saw Isaac. She slipped from her camels and said to the servant, "Who is that man who comes to us walking across the country?" And the servant answered, "It is my master." Then she took her veil and covered her face[2]. The servant told Isaac everything he had done. Isaac conducted her into Sara's tent, and took her as a wife. He loved her and was consoled for the death of his mother.

Death of Abraham. Abraham lived one hundred and seventy five years, and then he died. He died at a good old age, after a very long life, and was gathered to his father's kin. His sons, Isaac and Ishmael, buried him in the cave at Machpelah, on the land of Ephron, son of Zohar the Hittite, near Mamre. It is the land that Abraham had bought from the Hittites. There were buried Abraham and Sarah, his wife. After Abraham's death God blessed Isaac, his son, and the latter settled close by the well of Lahai-roi.

2. ISAAC AND JACOB

Birth of Esau and Jacob. This is the story of Isaac, son of Abraham:

Abraham had a son, Isaac, who, when he was forty years, married Rebecca, daughter of Bethuel, the Aramean from Mesopotamia, and sister of Laban. Isaac appealed to the Lord on behalf of his wife, who was barren. The Lord listened to his words, and her wife, Rebecca, conceived. The children pressed

---

1. In the old times its name was Layis, city of the tribe of Dan, and it meant place of lions.

2. It was a custom to present oneself before the groom covered with a veil that he had to remove.

hard on each other in her womb, and she said, "If it is how it is with me, what will be?" And she went to seek the guidance of the Lord. And the Lord said to her,

"In your womb there are two nations;
two peoples shall go their own way from birth;
one shall be stronger than the other, and the older shall be
        servant to the younger[1]."

One day she gave birth, and there were indeed twins in her womb. The first came out fair, hairy like a hair-cloak, and they named him Esau. Immediately afterwards his brother was born, grasping with his hand Esau's heel, and they named him Jacob. When Rebeca gave birth Isaac was sixty years old. The children grew up; Esau became a skilful hunter and a man of the plains, whereas Jacob was a quiet man and stayed among the tents. Isaac favoured Esau because he kept him supplied with venisons, but Rebecca favoured Jacob.

Esau sells his first-born rights. One day Jacob prepared a broth, and Esau, who came back from the fields feeling very tired, said to Jacob, "Let me eat some of that red broth, please, I am exhausted." Jacob answered him, "Then sell me your rights as first-born right now[2]." Esau said, "I am dying, what use is my birthright to me?" Jacob insisted, "Not till you swear." He did so and sold his birthright to Jacob. Then Jacob gave him bread and some lentil broth; he ate and drunk, stood up and left. In this way Esau showed how little he valued his birthright.

Isaac blesses Jacob. Isaac had grown old, and his eyes became so dim that he could not see. Then he called his elder son Esau and said to him, "My son!" "Here I am", he answered. "As you see", Isaac went on, "I am an old man and I do not know when will I die. Take, then, your hunting gear, you quiver and your bow, and go into the country and get me some venison. Then make me a savoury dish of the kind I like, and bring it to me to eat so that I may give you my blessing before

---

1. The fight of the children in their mother's womb forecasted the hostility of the two peoples.

2. The first-born rights were sacred. The first-born had a double part on it.

I die." Rebecca had overheard what Isaac had said to Esau, and
as soon as he was off into the country to find some venison for
his father, she called her son Jacob and told him, "I have just
heard your father talking to your brother, and he said to him,
'Bring me some venison and prepare a savoury dish for me, so
that I may eat and bless you before I die.' So, my son, listen to
me and do as I tell you. Go to the flock and bring me two fine
young kids, and I will make them into a savoury dish for your
father of the kind he likes. You shall take it in to him so that he
may eat it and bless you before he dies." But Jacob replied to
Rebecca, his mother, "You know that my brother Esau is a hairy
man, and my skin is smooth. If by any chance my father would
feel me, he would think I am tricking him, and he would curse
me instead of blessing me." But his mother said, "Your curse
shall fall upon me, my son, but do as I say. Go and bring me the
kids." He went to fetch the kids and brought them to his mother,
who prepared the venison of the kind that his father liked. Then
Rebecca took Esau's clothes, her elder son, the best she had at
home, and put them on Jacob, her younger son. She covered his
hands and the nape of his neck with the goatskins, and handed
him the savoury dish that she had prepared[1].

Jacob came to his father and said to him, "My father! Here I
am!" His father answered, "Who are you, my son?" And Jacob
replied to his father, "I am Esau, your elder son. I have done as
you told me; now, stand up and eat your venison so that you
may bless me afterwards." Isaac said to his son, "What is this
that you found so quickly?", and he answered, "Because the
Lord, you God, has handed it in to me." Isaac said to Jacob,
"Come close, my son, and let me feel you, so that I can see if
you are my son Esau or not." Jacob came closer to his father
Isaac, who, after having felt him, said, "This is the voice of
Jacob, but these are the hands of Esau." And he did not
recognise him because his hands were as hairy as his brother
Esau's. Then he said, "Bring me some of your venison so that I

---

1. The trick was prepared by Rebecca and Jacob. It is unacceptable for the
   evangelic moral. A good end did not justify the means. The author tells the
   fact, but does not approve of it. The promise goes through Jacob before time.

may eat and bless you afterwards." Jacob came close and his
father ate. He brought him wine too, and he drank. Then Isaac,
his father, said to him, "Now come closer and kiss me, my son."
He came near and kissed him. And when Isaac smelt the smell
of his clothes, he blessed him and said,

"Oh, the smell of my son is like the smell of a fruitful earth,
that has been blessed by the Lord.
God give you dew from heaven and richness from earth,
and plenty of corn and new wine.
Peoples shall serve you, nations bow down to you.
Be lord over your brothers; may your mother's sons bow
    down to you.
A curse upon those who curse you, and a blessing over those
    who bless you[1]."

When Isaac had finished blessing Jacob, and as soon as he
left his father's Isaac presence, his brother Esau came back from
hunting. He prepared a savoury dish as well, and brought it in to
his father, saying, "Father, sit up and eat some venison of your
son so that you may bless me." But Isaac, his father, said to
him, "Who are you?" And Esau answered, "I am Esau, your
elder son." Isaac became very agitated, and said, "Then who
was it that hunted and brought me venison? I have eaten from it
before you came, and I have blessed him, and blessed he will
stand." When Esau heard his father's words he shouted with
strenght and bitterness and said to his father, "Bless me too, my
father[2]." But he answered, "Your brother has come to me
treacherously and taken away your blessing." Esau insisted, "He
is rightly called Jacob, this is the second time he has supplanted
me. He got my birthright and now he has taken away my
blessing." And he added, "Have you kept back any blessing for
me?" Isaac answered Esau, "I have made him lord over you,
and I have given him all his brothers as servants. I have

---

1. Although the blessing of Esau and Jacob has an agricultural character, it marks
   already the rivalry between the Israelites and the Edomites.
2. The fatherly blessing was irrevocable. The Blessing and the Promise passed on
   to Jacob.

provided him with corn and wine, what can I do for you now, my son?" Then Esau said to his father, "Have you then only one blessing father?" And he cried bitterly. Then his father said,

"Your residence shall be without richness,
without the dew that falls from heaven.
You shall live by your sword, and you shall serve your
          brother,
but when you grow restive you will break off his yoke from
          your neck[1]."

From then on Esau bore a grudge against Jacob because of the blessing that his father had given him, and he said to himself, "The days in which my father will be mourned are near; then I shall kill my brother Jacob." Rebecca was told the words of her elder son. She called her younger son Jacob, and said to him, "Look, Esau, you brother is threatening to kill you. Slip away at once to my brother Laban's, to Harran. Stay there for a time, until your brother's anger cools and he forgets what you have done to him. Then I shall send someone for you. What should I lose you both in one day?"

Isaac farewells Jacob. Isaac called Jacob, blessed him and gave him this instruction: "You must not marry one of these women of Canaan. Go at once to the house of Bethuel, your mother's father, in Paddam-aram, and there find a wife, one of the daughters of Laban, your mother's brother. God Almighty bless you, make you fruitful and increase your descendants until they become a host of nations. May he bestow on you and your descendants the blessing of Abraham, so that you may possess the land of your pilgrimages, the land which God gave to Abraham." In this way Isaac sent Jacob away, and he set out for Paddam-aram, to Laban's house, son of Bethuel, the Aramean, and brother of Rebecca, mother of Esau and Jacob[2].

---

1. Rebecca had shown her hatred for the Hittite and Canaanite women. It may be for that reason that she sent his son to the land of her elders. As Esau, the Edomites, his descendants, shall live by the sword and the plunder.

2. After a long journey Jacob came to the country of his antecessors in Mesopotamia, Aram.

Jacob at Laban's. Jacob set out and came to the land of the sons of the West. There he saw a well in the open country and three flocks of sheep lying beside it, because the flocks were watered from that well. Over its mouth was a huge stone, and all the herdsmen used to gather there and roll it off the mouth of the well and water the flocks; then they would put it back in its place over the well. Jacob said to them, "Where are you from, my brethen?" And they answered, "We are from Harran." He continued, "Do you know Laban, son of Nahor?" And they answered, "Yes, we do." And he said to them, "Is he all right?" "Yes", they answered, "he is well. Here is his daughter Rachel, coming with the flock[1]."

He was still speaking with them when Rachel came up to them with her father's flock, for she was a shepherdess. When Jacob saw Rachel, daughter of Laban, his uncle, with Laban's flock, brother of his mother, he came closer, removed the stone from the well's mouth and watered the flock of his uncle Laban. Then Jacob kissed Rachel and was moved to tears. Then he told Rachel that he was her father's nephew, because he was son of Rebecca, and she ran to tell it to her father. As soon as Laban heard about Jacob's arrival, his sister's son, he ran to meet him, embraced him, kissed him and showed him into his house. Jacob told Laban the whole story. And Laban said, "Yes, you are my flesh and blood." And Jacob stayed with him.

One month later, Laban said to Jacob, "Why should you work for me for nothing simply because you are my nephew? Tell me what your wages ought to be." Laban had two daughters. The elder was called Lea, and the younger Rachel. Lea's eyes were dull, but Rachel was beautiful and graceful. Jacob loved Rachel, and said, "I will work seven years for your younger daughter Rachel." Laban replied, "It is better to give her to you than to a stranger, so stay with me." And so Jacob worked seven years more for Rachel, and they seemed like a few days, so much did he love her. Then Jacob said to Laban, "Give me my wife, it is time for me to sleep with her. I have

---

1. The relatives of the patriarchs Abraham and Nahor, grandfather of Abraham, earned their living as shepherds.

served you seven years." Then Laban invited all the people in the place and gave a feast.

Jacob's return to Palestine. Laban woke up early in the morning, kissed his grandsons and his daughters and blessed them. Then Laban set out and came back to his place[1].

Jacob meets Esau. Jacob looked up and saw Esau coming with four hundred men. Then he divided the children between Lea, Rachel and the two slave-girls. He put the slave-girls with thir children in front, Lea with her children next, and Rachel at the end. He went on ahead of them and bowed down to the ground seven times before as he approached his brother[2]. But Esau ran to meet him, embraced him, threw his arms round his neck and kissed him, and both of them cried. Then Esau looked up, and when he saw the women and the children he said, "Who are these with you?" Jacob answered, "They are the children whom God has graciously given to your servant." Then the servants with their children came near and bowed low to the ground, and Lea did the same with her children, and then Rachel with Joseph. Esau asked, "What was all those herds that I met?" Jacob answered, "It was meant to win favour with you, my lord." Then Esau said, "I have enough, my brother, keep what is yours." But Jacob insisted, "No, please, if I have won your favour, then, I pray, accept this gift from me, for, you see, I come into your presence as into that of a god, and you receive me favourably. Accept, then, the gift that I bring you; for God has been gracious to me, and I have all I want." So he urged him, and Esau accepted.

On his journey from Paddam-aram, Jacob came safely to the city of Shechem[3] in Canaan and pitched his tent to the east of it.

Again, the Lord appeared to Jacob on his way back from Paddam-aram, and he blessed him and said[4] to him: "Your

---

1. Jacob, as he came near the country where Esau had settled down, took his precautions.
2. This meeting shows the character of each brother. Jacob, humble and wise, and Esau, aggresive.
3. Old Canaanite city between the mountains Garizim and Ebal. Trading and historical centre of Israel. Joseph's grave is there.
4. In Bethel he changed his name for that of Israel.

name is Jacob, but it shall not longer be Jacob; your name shall be Israel." So he named him Israel. And the Lord said to him, "I am God Almighty; be fruitful and multiply. A host of nations shall come from you, and kings shall spring from your back. The land which I gave to Abraham and to Isaac I give it to you and your descendancy after you." And the Lord left him.

Jacob built a sacred pillar in the place where God had talked to him. On it he made a drink-offering and poured out some oil. And Jacob named the place where the Lord had talked to him Bethel.

Birth of Benjamin and death of Rachel. Ephrata was already near when Rachel was in labour and her pains were severe. While her pains were upon her, the midwife said, "Do not be afraid, you shall have this son." With her last breath, for she was dying, she called him Ben-oni, but his father called him Benjamin. Rachel died and was buried on the way to Ephrata, that is, to Bethlehem. Jacob built a sacred pillar over her grave, the sacred Pillar of Rachel's Grave, which still exists nowadays.

Death of Isaac. Jacob came to Isaac's house, his father, at Mamre by Kiriath-arba, that is, Hebron, where Abraham and Isaac had lived. Isaac lived one hundred and eighty years, and then he expired. He died and was gathered to his father's kin at a very old age. His sons Esau and Jacob buried him.

3. JOSEPH'S STORY

Joseph's dreams. Jacob lived in the land, the country in which his father had made pilgrimage, the land of Canaan.

These are the descendants of Jacob:

Joseph was seventeenth years old; he was still very young when he was in charge of the flock with his brothers. But Joseph brought their father a bad report of their brothers. Israel loved Joseph more than the other sons, because he was born when he was old, and he made him a long, sleeved robe. His brothers saw that their father loved him more than any other, and they hated him and could not speak a kind word to him.

Joseph had a dream[1] and told it to their brothers. He said to them: "Listen, I pray you, to this dream I have had: we were in the field binding sheaves, and then my sheaf rose on end and stood upright, and your sheaves gathered round and bowed low before mine." His brothers answered him, "Are you going to be our king or lord?" And they hated him even more because of his dreams and words. But Joseph had still another dream, and he told it to his brothers too. He said, "Listen, I have had another dream: The sun, the moon and eleven stars were bowing low to me." He told this to his father and brothers, and his father took him to ask, "What is this dream of yours? Must we come to you and bow low to the ground before you, I, your father, your mother and your brothers?" And his brothers hated him, while his father was thinking it over and over.

Joseph is sold by his brothers. His brothers had gone to mind their father's flocks in Sechem. Israel said to Joseph, "Your brothers are minding the flock in Sechem. Come, I want to send you to them." And he answered, "Here I am." And his father said, "Go, then, to see if all is well with you brothers and the flock and bring me an answer." Then Joseph left in search of his brothers and he found them in Dothan[2]. When they saw him coming in the distance, they plotted to kill him. They say to one another, "See, here comes the dreamer. Let us kill him and throw him into one of these pits[3]. We can say that he has been devoured by a wild beast, and so we will se what comes of his dreams." When Reuben heard this, he wanted to save him from their hands and said, "no, do not kill him!" And he added, "Do not spill his blood, just throw him into that pit in the wilderness, but do him no bodily harm." He wanted to save him from their hands and take him back to their father. Thus, when Joseph came to his brothers, they stripped him of the long, sleeved robe which he was wearing[4], took him and threw him into the pit. The pit was empty, there was no water in it. Then they sat to

---

1. Joseph's dreams were not natural.
2. Old Canaanite place north of Sechem.
3. Desert pits digged in the rock to collect rainwater.
4. Weaved by his own father.

have lunch. When they looked up they saw an Ishmaelite caravan coming in from Gilead. Their camels were carrying gum tragacanth, balm and myrrh, which they were carrying to Egypt. Then Judah said to their brothers, "What shall we gain by killing our brother and concealing his blood? Let us sell him to the Ishmaelites. Let us do him no harm, for he is our brother and has our own flesh." His brothers agreed. Meanwhile the Midianite merchants passed by[1], and they drew Joseph up out of the pit. They sold Joseph to the Ishmaelites and they took him to Egypt.

His brothers took his robe, killed a goat and dipped it in the goat's blood. Then they brought the long, sleeved robe to their father, and said, "Look what we have found; see if this is your son's robe or not." He looked at it and said, "It is my son's robe!" A wild beast has devoured him. Joseph has been torn to pieces.' Jacob tore his clothes, put on sackcloth and mourned his son for many days. Meanwhile the Midianite merchants had sold him in Egypt to Potiphar, one of Pharaoh's eunuchs, the captain of the guard.

Joseph in Egypt. Joseph had been taken to Egypt. Potiphar, the Egyptian, was one of Pharaoh's eunuchs[2] and the captain of the guard. He bought him[3] from the Ishmaelites who had brought him there. But the Lord was with Joseph and he prospered, so he stayed in his master's house, the Egyptian. As his master saw that the Lord was with him and was giving him success in all that he undertook, Joseph found favour with him, and became his personal servant. He put him in charge of his household, and entrusted him everything he had. And from the time that he put him in charge of his household and all his property, the Lord blessed the Egyptian's house for Joseph's sake.

Joseph was handsome and goodloking. After this it happened that his master's wife[4] took notice of him and said to

---

1. Nomadic Arabian traders.
2. Minister or courtier.
3. At the slave market.
4. Blind with passion, she tried to seduce Joseph.

him, "Come and lay with me." But Joseph refused, and he said to his master's wife, "With me my master does not worry about his house, and he has entrusted me all he has. How can I do something so wicked, and sin against God?" And although she insisted every day, Joseph refused to lay with her. But one day Joseph came into the house to do his work and none of the men of the household were indoors. She caught him by his cloak, saying, "Come and lay with me." But he left the cloak in her hands and ran out of the house. As she saw that he had left his cloack in her hands and ran out of the house, she called his servants and said to them, "Look, he has brought a Hebrew to us to make a mockery of us. He came to me to lay with me, but as I screamed for help he has left his cloak in my hands and run away[1]." She kept his cloak until his husband came back home. Then she told the same to her husband, "The Hebrew slave whom you brought to us has come to me has tried to lay with me, but as I screamed he left his cloack with me and run away." As the husband heard his wife saying, "Look what your slave has done to me", he was furious. He took Joseph and jailed him with the prisoners of the king. And there he stayed in jail[2].

Joseph, in jail, interprets dreams. But the Lord was with Joseph, and he won the favour of the governor of the dungeon. He put him in charge of all the prisoners in the dungeon.

Pharaoh was angry with two of his eunuchs, the chief butler and the chief baker, and he put them in custody in the house of the captain of the guard, in the dungeon where Joseph was imprisoned. The captain of the guard put them in charge of Joseph, who served them. And so they were in prison for a time. One night they both had dreams, each needing its own interpretation. "We have had a dream and there is no one to interpret it for us." Joseph said to them, "It is God who interprets; however, tell me your dream."

So the chief butler told his dream to Joseph, saying, "I have dreamed that I had a vine before me, and in it there were three branches; the vine, scarcely open, blossomed and its clusters

---

1. Enraged, she slandered him.
2. But the Lord was with him and did not abandon him.

ripened into grapes. In my hand I had Pharaoh's goblet; I plucked the grapes in Pharaoh's goblet and put the goblet into Pharaoh's hand." Joseph said to him, "This is the meaning of your dream: The three branches are three days; in three days' time Pharaoh shall set you free and restore you to your post. Remember me when that day comes and be good to me. Tell Pharaoh about me, so that he sets me free as well. For, in truth, I was carried off from the land of the Hebrews and have done nothing here to deserve being put in this dungeon."

The chief baker saw that it had been a favourable interpretation, and he said to Joseph, "This is my dream: There were three baskets of white bread on my head. In the top basket there was every kind of food which the baker prepares for the Pharaoh, but the birds ate it out from the basket on my head." Joseph answered him, "This is what it means: The three baskets are three days. In three day's time Pharaoh will behead you and hang you up on a tree, and the birds of the air will eat your flesh." Thus, on the third day, which was the day of Pharaoh's birthday, he gave a feast for all his servants, he remembered his chief butler and his chief baker.

He restored the chief butler to his post of putting the goblet into Pharaoh's hand, whereas he hanged the chief baker as Joseph had said. But the chief butler forgot about Joseph.

Pharaoh's dreams[1]. Two years later, it happened that Pharaoh had a dream: he was standing by the Nile, and from the Nile there came up seven cows, sleek and fat, which grazed on the reeds. But after them seven other cows came up from the river, gaunt and lean, and stood on the river-bank beside the first cows. The cows that were gaunt and lean devoured the cows that were sleek and fat. Then Pharaoh woke up. He fell asleep again and had a second dream: he saw seven ears of corn, full and ripe, growing on one stalk. Growing up after them were seven other ears, thin and shrivelled by the east wind. The thin ears swallowed up the ears that were full and ripe. Then Pharaoh woke up and saw that it was a dream.

---

1. God arranged things to prove that Joseph was innocent.

Next morning Pharaoh was troubled in mind. He summoned all the magicians and sages of Egypt, but there was no one who could interpret his dreams[1]. Then the chief butler said to Pharaoh, "Now I remember my fault. Pharaoh was angry with their servants and imprisoned myself and the chief baker in the house of the captain of the guard. On that same night we had a dream with a different interpretation. There, with us, was a young Hebrew man, a slave of the captain of the guard. We told him our dreams and he interpreted them for us. And it happened as he told us: I was restored to my position, and the other was hanged."

Thereupon Pharaoh sent for Joseph. They brought him out of the prison hurriedly. He was shaved and his clothes were changed, and came in to Pharaoh. And Pharaoh said to Joseph, "I have had a dream, and nobody has been able to interpret it. But I have heard it said that you can interpret dreams." Joseph replied, "I am nothing, but God will answer for Pharaoh's welfare[2]." "The dream of Pharao is one dream: God has showed Pharaoh what he is going to do. The seven good cows are seven years, seven leant and gaunt cows that came up after them are seven years, and the empty ears of corn blighted by the east wind will be seven years of famine. It is as I have said to Pharaoh: God has let Pharaoh see what he is going to do. There are to be seven years of great plenty throughout the land. After them will come seven years of famine; all the years of plenty in Egypt will be forgotten, and the famine will ruin the country. The good years will not be remembered in the land because of the famine that follows; for it will be very severe. The doubling of Pharaoh's dream means that God is already resolved to do this, and he will very soon put it into effect. Pharaoh should now look for a shrewd and intelligent man, and put him in charge of the country. Appoint controllers over the land, and take one fifth of the produce of Egypt during the seven years of

---

1.   Egipt was a land of magicians and sages, but its science is surpassed by the
     science which God gives its people.
2.   The interpretation of the future is a gift of God. Dreams are nothing in
     themselves, they fade away.

plenty. They should collect all this food produced in the good years that are coming and put the corn under Pharaoh's control in store in the cities, and keep it under guard. This food will be a reserve for the country against the seven years of famine which will come upon Egypt. Thus the country will not be devastated by the famine."

Joseph's elevation. Pharaoh and his courtiers were pleased by the plan, and Pharaoh said to them, "Can we find a man like this man, one who has the spirit of God?" Then Pharaoh said to Joseph, "Since God has let you know all these things there is no man more shrewd and intelligent than you." And he added: "I appoint you ruler over the land of Egypt." Pharaoh took off his signet-ring and put it in Joseph's finger[1], he had him dressed in fine linen and put a gold chain round his neck. He mounted him in the second of his chariots and gave the order that men cried "Abrek" before him.

Thus he was made ruler over the whole land of Egypt. Pharaoh said to Joseph, "I am the Pharaoh, but without your consent no man shall lift hand or foot in the land of Egypt." Pharaoh named Joseph Zaphenathpaneah, and he gave him as a wife Asenath the daughter of Potiphera priest of On[2]. Joseph was thirty years old when he came to Pharaoh, king of Egyp, left his presence and made a tour of inspection of Egypt. During the seven years of plenty the land produced abundant harvests. Joseph collected all the food of the seven years in which there was abundance in the land of Egypt, and he stored it in the cities, putting in each the food from the surrounding country. And he stored the grain like the sand of the sea, in such huge quantities that he could not count it.

When the seven years of abundance in Egypt came to an end, there came seven years of famine, as Joseph had foretold. There was hunger everywhere, but in Egypt there was bread. So when the famine spread throughout Egypt, the people appealed to Pharaoh for bread, and he said to all the Egyptians: "Go to

---

1. The royal signet-ring was like his signature, it authorised the decrees.

2. He was made viceroy of Egypt, his vizier. He presented him before the people with his investiture and gown.

Joseph and do as he says." Joseph, seeing that there was famine in the whole country, opened the stores, and he sold to the Egyptians, for the famine was severe in Egypt. The whole world came to Egypt to buy corn from Joseph, so severe was the famine everywhere.

Joseph's brothers come down to Egypt. When Jacob saw that there was corn in Egypt, he said to his sons, "Why do you stand staring at each other? I have heard that in Egypt there is corn for sale. Go there, then, and buy some for us so that we can live and not starve." Ten of Joseph's brothers went down to Egypt to buy corn. But Jacob did not let Joseph's brother Benjamin go with them. "He might come to harm", he said.

So the sons of Israel went down to buy corn with other travellers, for there was famine in the land of Canaan[1]. Josep was governor of all Egypt and sold corn to everybody. When the brother of Joseph came to him, they bowed low to him. Joseph recognized them as soon as he saw them, but he pretended not to know them, and treated them harshly. He said to them, "Where do you come from?" And they answered, "We come from the land of Canaan to buy corn."

Joseph had recognized his brothers, but they did not recognize him. Then he remembered the dreams that he had had about them, and said to them, "You are spies[2], you have come to spy out the weak points in our defences." They answered, "No, sir, your servants have come to buy corn. We are all sons of the same father, we are honest men." But he said to them, "No, you have come to spy out the weak points in our defences." And they replied, "Your humble servants are twelve brothers, all of them sons of the same father in the land of Canaan. The youngest is still with our father, and one is dead." Joseph said, "It is as I have told. You are spies. You shall be put to proof: unless your younger brother comes here, by the life of Pharaoh, you shall not leave this place. Send one of you to fetch your brother, and the rest shall be my prisoners. Thus you shall

---

1. Very soon God's wisdom was obvious, for he had given Joseph wisdom to administer his kingdom and save his people from the famine.

2. At that time in Egypt ruled the Hiksos, Semites.

be tested, and we shall see whether you are telling the truth or not. If not then, by the life of the Pharaoh, you are spies!" And he kept them in prison for three days.

On the third say Joseph said to them, "If you want to remain alive, do as I tell you, for I am a God-fearing man: If you are telling the truth, one of you must remain in prison, and the rest can leave and buy the corn for your hungry households. But you must bring me your youngest brother. Thus you shall be tested, and your lives will be spared." They did as he had told them. And they said to one another, "We deserve to be punished because of our brother, whose suffering we saw; for when he pleaded with us we refused to listen. That is why these sufferings have come upon us." But Reuben said, "Did I not tell you not to do the boy a wrong? But you would not listen, and now his blood is on our heads."

They did not know that Joseph could understand them, because there was an interpreter between them. Then Joseph turned back and cried. He came back and talked to him. He took Simeon and, before them, jailed him[1].

Return to Canaan. Joseph ordered that their bags were filled with grain and that they were given silver and supplies for the journey. All this was done. They loaded the corn on their asses and left. But when they encamped in the night, one of the opened his bag to give something to eat to his ass and saw that his silver was at the top of the pack; he said to his brohters, "They have given me my money back; it is here, in my bag." They were bewildered and trembling, and they said to each other, "What is this that the Lord has made to us[2]?"

When they came before their father Jacob in the land of Canaan they told him the whole story. When they emptied the bags they saw that the bundles of silver were in the bags. When they saw them there were afraid. Then Jacob their father said to them, "You have robbed me of my children: Joseph disappeared, Simeon too, and now you want to take Benjamin away?' Everything is against me!' Reuben said to his father,

---

1. Joseph wanted to test his brothers before revealing himself before them.
2. God wanted to make them expiate their cruelty towards their brother.

"Kill my two children if I do not come back with Benjamin."
But Jacob replied, "My son shall not come down with you; his
brother has died and he is the only left. If he comes to any harm
of the journey, you will bring down my grey hairs in sorrow to
the grave."

New journey towards Egypt with Benjamin. Meanwhile
the famine was more and more severe in the country. When
they had used up the corn they had brought from Egypt, their
father told them: "Come back to Egypt and buy some more
food." Judah said to him, "That man warned us plainly that we
should not go into his presence without our younger brother. If
you let him go with us we shall come down and buy food, but if
not, we will not go. That man questioned about ourselves and
our family, he asked, 'Is your father still alive? Do you have
more brothers?' And we answered it. How could we know that
he would say 'Bring me your brother'?" Then Israel, his father,
said to them, "If it must be so, then do this; take with your
baggage, as a gift for the man, some of the produce for which
our country is famous: a little balsam, a little honey, gum
tragacanth, myrrh, pistachio nuts, and almonds. Take double the
amount of silver that was returned to you in your packs. Perhaps
it was a mistake. Take your brother with you. Stand up and go
to see that man. May God Almighty make him kindly disposed
to you, and may he sent back the one whom you left behind,
and Benjamin too. As for me, if I am bereaved, then I am
bereaved."

Meeting with Joseph. So our men took the gifts, double
quantity of silver and Benjamin, and they set out for
Egypt. When they came there they presented themselves to
Joseph[1].

When Joseph saw Benjamin with them, he said to his
steward: "Show these men in, kill a beast and prepare the
dinner, for they shall eat with me at noon."

When Joseph came in they offered him their gifts and bowed
low to him. He asked them how they were and asked them, "Is
your father well, the old man of whom you spoke? Is he still

---

1.   There was no other choice: either go to Egypt or starve.

alive?[1]" And they answered, "Yes, your servant, our father, is well and still alive." And they bowed to the ground before him. When he looked up he saw his brother Benjamin, his mother's son, and asked, "Is this your younger brother of whom you spoke?" And to Benjamin he said, "God is gracious to you, my son." Then he was overcome; his feelings for his brother mastered him, and he was near to tears. So he went into the inner room and wept. Then he washed his face and came out; and, holding back his feelings, he ordered, "Serve the meal." Joseph was served separatedly, and the brothers by themselves[2], and the Egyptians separatedly. He sent them each a portion from what was before him, but Benjamin's was five times larger than any of the other portions[3]. Thus they drank with him and all grew merry.

Joseph's goblet in Benjamin's pack. Afterwards Joseph gave his steward the following order: "Fill the men's packs with as much food as they can carry and put each man's silver at the top of his pack. And put my silver goblet at the top of the youngest brother's pack, with the silver for the corn." He did as Joseph had commanded him.

In the morning the brothers left with their asses. They had not gone very far from the city when Joseph said to his steward, "Stand up, follow those men, and when you catch up with them say, 'Why have you repaid good with evil? Is that not the goblet which my master uses for drinking and divination?[4] You have done a very wicked thing'." When he caught up with them, he repeated all this to them, but they replied, "How can you say such things, my lord? No, sir, far from our minds to do any such thing! You remember the silver we found at the top of our packs? We brought it back to you from Canaan. Why should we steal silver or gold from your master's house? If any one of us is found with the goblet, he shall die, and, what is more, we will

---

1. Joseph cared specially for his father, whom he loved very much, and his brother Benjamin, who was innocent.
2. The Egyptians did never eat with foreigners, and even less with poor people, lest they could be contaminated.
3. To see if his brothers were jealous of Benjamin.
4. The Egyptians were supersticious.

all become your slaves." The steward said, "Very well; let it be as you say: the man in whose possession it is found shall become my slave, and the others may go free." They unloaded their packs quickly, and every one opened his. He searched them, beginning with the elders and finishing with the youngest, and the goblet was found in Benjamin's pack. All of them tore their clothes, loaded their asses and returned to the city.

Joseph was still in his house when Judah and his brothers came in. They bowed to the ground before him. Joseph asked them: "What have you done[1]. You might have known that a man like me could practise divination?" And Judah answered, "What can we say to you, how can we prove our innocence? It is God who has found out our sin. We are ready to be made your slaves, we ourselves as the one who was found with the goblet." But Joseph said, "God forbid that I should do such a thing! Only the man who has been found with the goblet shall become my slave, you can come back in peace to your father." Then Judah went up to him and said, "Please, listen, sir. Let me say a word to your lordship, I beg you. Do not be angry with me, because you are as great as Pharaoh. My lord asked his servants, 'Do you still have father or brothers?' and we answered to our lord, 'We have a father who is very old, and a brother who was born when our father was at a very old age. One of his brothers is dead, so he is the only one left from his mother, and his father loves him dearly.' Then you said to your servants, 'Bring him to my presence so that I may see him.' We replied, 'The youngest son cannot leave his father; if he leaves him, he will die.' And you insisted, 'If your youngest brother does not come with you you shall not enter my presence again.' Thus, when we came back to your servant, my father, we told him our lord's words. And when our father said, 'Come back to buy some food to us' we answered, 'We cannot come back unless our youngest brother comes with us, because we cannot

---

1. His brothers were not thieves, for they brought the money back, but they could not explain what had happened with the goblet. They were expiating their guilt. He wanted to find out if they were jealous of Benjamin by putting the blame on him.

enter his presence if our youngest brother does not come with us.' Then your servant, our father, said to us, 'You know that my wife has only given me two children. One left me when he was with me and was probably torn to pieces, for I have never seen him again. If you should take this away from me, and he should come to any harm, then you will bring down my grey hairs in trouble to the grave.' So that if I come back to your servant, whose spirit is bound up with the boy's, and he sees that the boy does not come back with us, he will die, and your servants will make his grey hairs come down in trouble to the grave. It was I who went surety for the boy to my father. Therefore, I pray you, let me remain as your servant instead of the boy, and let him come back with my brothers. How can I return to my father without the boy? I could not bear to see the misery which my father would suffer[1].

Joseph makes himself known to his brothers. Joseph could no longer control his feelings in front of the people and said, "Let everyone leave my presence." So that he was alone when he made himself known to his brothers, but so loudly did he weep that the Egyptians and Pharaoh's household heard him.

Joseph said to his brothers, "I am Joseph. Is my father still alive?" His brothers could not answer him, dumbfounded as they were. Then he said, "I am Joseph, your brother, the one you sold into Egypt. But do not be distressed for having sold me here, for God sent me ahead of you to save men's lives. Therefore it has been God who sent me here, not you. He has made me father of Pharaoh and lord over his household, ruler of all Egypt. Make haste and go back to my father, and give him this message: 'These are the words of your son Joseph: God has made me lord over Egypt. Come down to me without delay. You shall live in the land of Goshen, and you shall be near me, you and your sons and the sons of your sons, your herds and flocks, and everything you possess. I will take care of you there, so that you and your family and everything you posses do not

---

1. Judah spoke on behalf of his brothers because he made himself resonsible for the fate of Benjamin before his father. They had tricked their father and felt remorse for his sin.

starve, because there are still five years of famine to come.' You
and my brother Benjamin can see for yourselves, that it is
Joseph who is speaking. Tell my father of all the honour which
I enjoy in Egypt, tell him all you have seen, and make haste to
bring him down here. Then he threw his arms round his brother
Benjamin and cried, and Benjamin cried too embracing him.
Then he kissed all his brothers, and he cried when he embraced
them. Afterwards his brothers talked to him.

Pharaoh's invitation. When the news that the brothers of
Joseph had came to the Pharaoh's household, Pharaoh and all
his courtiers were pleased. Pharaoh said to Joseph, "You have
authority to order: 'Do as I say: take wagons from the land of
Egypt for your children and women, take your father and come
here. Do not be sad because you leave your households, because
the very best of the land of Egypt is yours'."

Return to Canaan. The sons of Israel did as they were told.
Joseph provided them with wagons and food for the journey,as
Pharaoh had commanded. They were also given clothes, but to
Benjamin he gave three hundred pieces of silves and five
changes of clothing[1]. For his father he sent ten asses carrying
the best that there was in Egypt, and ten asses loaded with corn,
bread and food for the journey. So he dismissed his brothers,
and said to them, "Do not quarrel on the way."

Thus they went up from Egypt and came to the land of
Canaan, where Jacob his father lived, and they told him the
news, saying, "Joseph is still alive and is the ruler of all Egypt."
But he was not moved, for he could not believe it, but when
they told him Joseph's words, and when he saw the wagons
which Joseph had sent him to take him to Egypt, he was moved.
Then Israel said, "Yes, Joseph, my son, is still alive. I will come
down to him and see him before I die."

Jacob moves to Egypt with all his family. Jacob set out
from Beersheba. Israel's sons conveyed their father Jacob, their
dependants, and their wives in the wagons which Pharaoh had

---

1. Joseph made a distinction with Benjamin as his father had done with him, for
    he was the best. He gave him a sleeved robe, as his father had done before he
    was sold to the merchants.

sent to carry them. They took their herds and flocks and everything they possessed in the land of Canaan with them, and moved to the land of Egypt, Jacob and all his descendants.

Jacob's meeting with Joseph. Israel sent Judah ahead so that he might appear before Joseph in Goshen. Meanwhile they came to the land of Goshen. Joseph had his chariot made ready and went up to meet his father Israel in Goshen. When he saw him he threw his arms round him and wept. Israel said to Joseph, "Now I can die, I have seen your face and you are still alive." Joseph said to his brothers, "I am going to say to Pharaoh, 'My brothers and my father's family who were in Canaan have come to me'."

Audience with Pharaoh. So Joseph came to Pharaoh and said to him, "My father and my brothers have come from the land of Canaan with their flocks and herds and everything they possess, and they are already in Goshen." Then Pharaoh said to Joseph, "Your father and your brothers have come to you, the land of Egypt is before you; settle them in the best part of it. Let them live in Goshen,and if you know of any capable men among them, make them chief herdsmen over my cattle."

In the land of Goshen[1]. Then Joseph brought his father in and presented him to Pharaoh, and Jacob gave Pharaoh his blessing. Pharaoh asked him, "How old are you?" And Jacob answered, "The years of my earthly sojourn are one hundred and thirty; hard years they have been, and few, and I shall not equal the years that my fathers lived in their time." Jacob blessed Pharaoh again and went out from his presence. So Joseph settled his father and brothers, and gave them possessions in the land of Egypt, in the best part of the country, in the distric of Rameses, as Pharaoh had commanded[2] Joseph provided his father and brothers and all his father's family with food, according to the number of families.

Jacob asks to be buried in Hebron. The Israelites settled in Egypt, in the land of Goshen. They took possession of it and

1. The land of Goshen is precisely in the delta of the Nile; it is the region with the richest prairies for herds.

2. The Hebrews were welcomed, for they were Semites like the Hiksos.

increased largely in number. Jacob lived in Egypt for seventeen years and, in total, he lived one hundred and forly seven. The day of his death was drawing near, and he sent for Joseph and said to him: "If I may now claim this favour from you, put your hand under my tight[1] and swear by the Lord that you will deal loyally and truly with me and not bury me in Egypt. When I die like my forefathers, you shall carry me from Egypt and bury me in their grave." Joseph answerd, "I will do as you say." Jacob added, "Swear it." So Joseph swore the oath, and Israel sank down over the end of the bed.

Jacob blesses his sons. Afterwards Jacob called his sons and said to them: "Come near, I want to tell you what will happen to you in the days to come." To Judah he said,

"Judah, your brothers shall praise you,
your hand on the neck of your enemies.
The sons of your father will bow down to you.
Judah is a lion's whelp,
you have returned from the kill, my son,
and crouch and stretch like a lion;
like a lioness, who dares to rouse you?
The sceptre shall not pass from Judah,
nor the staff from his feet,
until the One to whom it belongs comes
the One whom the peoples shall obey."

Death of Jacob. Then Jacob gave them their last charge, and said, "I shall soon be gathered to my father's kin; bury me with my fathers in the cave on the plot of land which belonged to Ephron the Hittite, that is, the cave on the plot of land at Machpelah east of Mamre in Canaan, the field which Abraham bought from Ephron the Hittite for a burial-place. There Abraham was buried with his wife Sarah; there Isaac and Rebecca were buried too, and there I have buried Lea. The field and the cave were bought by Abraham to the sons of the Jet." When he had finished giving his last charge to his sons, he drew

---

1. Ritual of oath-swearings in those primitive times.

his feet up on to the bed, breathed his last, and was gathered to his fathers.

Jacob's burial in Hebron[1]. Then Joseph threw himself upon his father, weeping and kissing his face. Then he ordered the physicians in his charge to embalm his father. Joseph went to bury his father, and with him went all the Pharaoh's courtiers, the elders of his court, the elders of Egypt, all the family of Joseph, his brothers and his father's family. Only the children,

1. Old city south of Palestine. There is the grave of the Patriarchs: Abraham, Isaac and now Jacob. There David was crowned, and later on the crusaders built a church.

flocks and herds were left in the land of Goshen. Joseph, after burying his father, came back to Egypt with his brothers and all those who had come to him to bury his father.

Joseph's last years. When their father was dead Joseph's brothers were afraid and said, "What if Joseph should bear a grudge against us and pay us out for all the harm that we did to him?" They therefore sent for Joseph and said this to him, "Your father, before dying, gave us a message for you: 'I ask you to forgive your brother's crime and their sin; I know they did you harm; forgive, then, now, the crime of the servants of the God of your father'." And Joseph cried while they were said this to him. Later his brothers went to him and prostrated themselves before him, and said, "You see, we are your slaves." But Joseph said to them, "Do not be afraid, am I in the place of God? You meant to do me harm; but God meant to bring good out of it by preserving the lives of a great people, as we see today. Therefore, do not be afraid; I will provide for you and your children." Then Joseph said to his brothers, "I will die, but God will not fail to come to your aid and take you from here to the land which he promised on oath to Abraham, Isaac and Jacob." He made the Sons of Israel swear an oath, saying, "When God thus comes to your aid, you must take my bones with you from here." So Joseph died at the age of a hundred and then. He was embalmed and laid in a coffin in Egypt.

EXODUS

PART ONE

PREPARATION OF THE EXODUS

1. OPPRESSION OF THE PEOPLE

Oppression of the Israelites. These are the names of the sons of Israel, who came down to Egypt with Jacob, each one of them with his family: Reuben, Simeon, Levi, Judah, Isaachar, Zebulun and Benjamin, Dan and Naphtali, Gad and Asher. Jacob had seventy sons. Joseph was already in Egypt[1].

Joseph died, he and all his brothers and his whole generation. The sons of Israel, fruitful as they were, multiplied extraordinarily and increased progressively until they came to be so numerous that they overrun the whole country. Meanwhile a new king ascended the throne of Egypt[2], who knew nothing about Joseph, and said to his people: "These people of the sons of Israel are more numerous and powerful than us. We must see that they do not increase any more, or we shall find that, in case of war, they would join the enemy and

---

1. Joseph is the figure of Jesus. He was handed in by his brothers, and died to save them. He was resurrected and glorified, and now he is universal king.
2. Seti I, who expelled the Hiksos. Rameses II after him.

fight against us and leave the country[1]." And so they set above them officers that made them work hard, in the building of Pithom and Rameses[2], store-cities of the Pharaoh. But the more oppressed they were, the more they multiplied and increased, until the Egyptians came to loathe the sons of Israel. They were reduced to the condition of slaves, were ill-treated and their life was made bitter for them with rough work; they made clay and bricks, and they worked the land. They were used as slaves in every sort of hard labour. Then the Pharaoh of Egypt spoke to his people: "Throw to the river every male that is born, but let the females live."

2. MOSES' VOCATION

Birth of Moses. A man of the house of Levi took as a wife the daughter of another Levite woman. The wife had a child, and as he was bery beautiful she had him hidden for three months. But as she could conceal him no longer, she got a rush basket for him, made it watertight with clay and tar and put the baby inside. Then she left the basket among the reeds along the banks of the Nile.

The sister of the child remained near him to see what happened. The daughter of the Pharaoh came down to the river to bathe while her ladies-in-waiting were walking along the river. As she saw the basket among the reeds, she sent one of her ladies-in-waiting to fetch it. She opened it and saw the child, who was crying; she was filled with pity for him and said, "This is a child of the Hebrews." Then the sister of the child said to Pharaoh's daughter, "Shall I go and fetch you one of the Hebrew women as a nurse to suckle the child for you?", "Do", said the daughter of the Pharaoh, and the girl went to fetch the mother of the child. The daughter of the Pharaoh said to her "Take this child and suckle him for me, I will give you fair

---

1. God promised to Abraham that he would be father of a numerous people, and he did so.
2. Pithom and Rameses (Real House), residence of Rameses II. They were in the old capital of the Hiksos, later Tamis.

reward." The woman took the child and suckled him. When he grew up she took him to the Pharaoh's daughter, who adopted him and called him Moses, "Because", she said, "I drew him out of the water[1]."

Moses escapes to Midian. In the days when Moses was grown up he came to his brothers. He saw their heavy labour, and watched as an Egyptian stroke one of his fellow-Hebrews. He look to either side and did not see anybody, so he killed the Egyptian and buried his body in the sand. He went out next day, and saw two Hebrews quarrelling, and asked the man in the wrong, "Why are you striking him?" He answered, "Who set you up as prince and judge over us? Do you intend to kill me as you did with the Egyptian?" Pharaoh had already heard of it, and was trying to murder Moses.

So Moses escaped from Pharaoh, and settled in the land of Midian[2].

Meanwhile, and after a long time, the king of Egypt died. The sons of Israel still groaned under their slavery. They cried out, and their appeal for rescue from their slavery rose up to God. God heard them and remembered his covenant with Abraham, Isaac and Jacob. God saw the plight of Israel, and he took heed of it.

Moses' Vocation. Moses was minding the flock of Jethro, his father-in-law, priest of Midian. When he was driving the flock beyond the desert, he came to the mountain of God, the Horeb[3]. There the Lord appeared to him in form of a flame which was burning in a bush, and he saw that the bush was not being burned up. Moses said to himself, "I will come near to see this wonderful sight, for the bush is not burning away." As the Lord saw that Moses came near to have a look, he called him out of the bush, and said, "Moses, Moses", and he replied, "Here I am". God said to him[4], "Come no nearer. Take your

---

1. Moses grew up in the court of Pharaoh
2. The Midianites were nomadic tribes of the desert, descendants of Midian, son of Abraham.
3. The Sinai.
4. From the burning bush.

sandals off your feet, for the place in which you are standing is holy ground." And he added, "I am the God of your father, the God of Abraham, the God of Isaac and the God of Jacob." Moses hid his face, for he was afraid of gazing to God. The Lord went on, "I have seen the misery of my people in Egypt, I have heard their plight against their oppression and I know their sufferings. I have come[1] to set them free from the Egyptians, to take them out of this land to a fine and wide land, a land flowing with mild and honey, to the home of the Canaanites, the Hittites, the Amorites, the Perizzites, the Hivites, the Jebusites. I have heard the outcry of the sons of Israel. I have also seen the oppression in which they live under the Egyptians. Go, then, I send you to the Pharaoh to bring my people, the Hebrews, out of Egypt." Moses said to the Lord, "Who am I to ask Pharaoh to bring the Hebrews out of Egypt?", and God said to him, "I shall be with you, and this shall be the proof that it is I who has sent you. When you have brought the people out of Egypt, you shall all worship God on this mountain[2]."

Moses said to God, "I will meet the sons of Israel and say to them 'The God of your fathers has sent me to you', but what if they ask me for your name, what shall I tell them?". And God said to Moses, "I am, that is who I am. This shall you answer them; 'I am' has sent me to you. This is my name for ever, and this is my title for every generation[3]."

"Go, then, and assemble the elders of Israel and say to them, 'The Lord, the God of your fathers, the God of Abraham, of Isaac and of Jacob has appeared to me and has said, 'I have certainly visited you, and I have seen what is being done to you in Egypt. I have decided to take you out of the misery of Egypt to the land of Canaan, a land which is flowing milk and honey'. They will listen to you. Then the elders of Israel and you must go to the king of Egypt and tell him, 'The Lord, God of the

---

1. Antrophomorphic expression.
2. Sinai, Horeb.
3. Jehovah. I am, that is who I am: the Being from whom all living beings receive their being. Creator of all, that has always existed and will always exist.

Hebrews, has appeared to us. So now give us leave to a three-day journey across the desert to offer a sacrifice to the Lord, our God.' I know very well that the king of Eypt will not allow you to leave unless he is compelled to do so. But I shall stretch out my powerful hand and punish the Egyptians with all the miracles I shall work among them; after that he will allow you to leave."

The magic staff. Moises answered, "They will not believe or listen to me, they will say that the Lord has not appeared to me." The Lord said to him, "What have you got in your hand?", and he replied, "A staff." The Lord said, "Throw it on the ground." He did so and the staff turned into a snake. When Moses saw the snake, he ran away from it. But the Lord said to Moses, "Put out your hand and seize it by the tail." He put out his hand, seized it by its tail and it turned back into a staff in his hand. "In this way they shall be convinced that the Lord has appeared to you, the God of your fathers, God of Abraham, of Isaac and Jacob."

Moses said to the Lord, "But Lord, I am not a man of ready speech and I never was one, not even now that You have spoken to your servant. I am rather slow and hesitant of speech." The Lord was very angry with Moses and said to him, "Have you not a brother, Aaron, the Levite? I know that he is a man of easy speech. Look, he will come to meet you and when he sees you his heart will be happy. You will speak to him and put the words in his mouth; I will be in your mouth and in his and tell you what you have to do. He will talk to the people for you, and you will be the god he speaks for. Take, then, this staff, for with it you are to make the signs[1]."

Moses comes back to Egypt. The Lord had spoken to Moses in Midian: "Go, and come back to Egypt because those who wished to kill you are dead." Moses took his wife and children and headed for Egypt, with the staff of God in his hand. God said to him, "When you are in Egypt remember to make all the portents I have given you power to do,

---

1. Miracles.

However, I will make him obstinate, and he will not let the people go[1]."

The Lord said to Aaron: "Go and meet Moses in the desert". Aaron went there and when he met his brother in the mountain of God, he kissed him. Moses told Aaron the words that the Lord had said to him and the portents that he had commanded him to perform. Moses and Aaron left and assembled all the elders of the sons of Israel. Aaron told them everything that the Lord had said to Moses and performed some portents before them. The people believed him, and as they understood that the Lord had shown his concern for the sons of Israel and had seen his misery, they bowed down and worshipped him.

Moses and Aaron before Pharaoh. After this, Moses and Aaron came to Pharaoh and said to him, "These are the words of the Lord, God of Israel: Let my people go so that they can keep a feast in the desert." "Who is the Lord", said the Pharaoh, "that I should obey his words and let Israel go? I do not know any Lord and I will not let the Israelites go." They replied, "The God of the Hebrews has appeared to us. Let us go then to the desert, on a three-day journey, to offer our sacrifice to the Lord, our God, so that he does not come to us with pestilence or sword." But the king of Egypt answered, "Moses and Aaron, why do you distract the people from their duty? Back to your labour." And he added, "Now that your people in the earth outnumber the Egyptians, would you have them stop working?"

The Oppression of the People increases. In this way the overseers and inspectors went to see the people and said to them, "These are the words of Pharaoh: 'From now on I shall not provide you with straw. Go and get it for yourselves wherever you may find it, but your task shall not be reduced[2]'." The people, then, scattered all over Egypt to find straw. The overseers urged them and said, "Do your work, according to your daily tasks, as when you were given the straw."

The overseers of the people of Israel were concerned about them because they had been told: "Your daily tally of bricks

---

1. Before the last plague.
2. This was the commandment they had got from Pharaoh.

shall not be reduced[1]." When they left the house of Pharaoh they came across Moses and Aaron, who were waiting for them, and said to them "May this bring the judgement of the Lord upon you; you have made us bad to the eyes of the Pharaoh and of the servants; you have put a sword in their hands to kill us." Then Moses appealed to the Lord and said, "Oh Lord, why do you bring misfortune to this people? Why have you sent me to them? Why, since I came to the Pharaoh to talk to him about them, has he treated them so bad, and you make nothing to rescue them?"

And the Lord said to Moses, "Today you shall see what will I do to the Pharaoh. For he will let them go with strong hand, nay, will drive them from his country with strong hand."

Moses and Aaron did everything exactly as the Lord had told them. When they talked to Pharaoh Moses was eighty years old, and Aaron was eighty-three.

Afterwards, the Lord spoke to Moses and Aaron in the following way, "When Pharaoh says to you, 'Do, as a test, some portent', you must say to Aaron, 'Take your staff and throw it beforer Pharaoh.' The staff will turn into a snake." When Moses and Aaron came to Pharaoh they did as the Lord had told them. Aaron threw the staff before Pharaoh and his servants and it turned into a snake. But Pharaoh summomed his wise men and sorcerers, and the magicians of Egypt did the same with their spells. Every one of them threw his staff before the Pharaoh, and they turned into snakes, but he staff of Aaron swallowed up theirs. The heart of the Pharaoh grew hard, and as the Lord had foretold, he would not listen to them.

3. THE PLAGUES

First Plague: water turns into blood. The Lord said to Moses, "Pharaoh is obstinate and refuses to let the people go. Meet him tomorrow morning when he is bathing, wait to meet

---

1. The principal men of the Hebrews complained to Pharaoh, and they put the blame on Moses and Aaron for their bad negociation.

him on the bank of the river with the staff turned into a serpent in your hand. Say this to him: "The Lord, God of the Hebrews, has sent me to say this to you: 'Let this people go so that they can worship me in the desert', and so far you have not listened to his words. So now the Lord has said, "Now you shall know that I am the Lord; I shall strike the waters of the river with the staff, and they will turn into blood."

So did Moses and Aaron, as the Lord had commanded them. Aaron, then, lifted up his staff, stroke the waters of the river in the sight of the Pharaoh and his servants, and the waters of the river turned into blood[1]. The fish in the river died and the river stank, the Egyptians could not drink its waters and there was blood throughout the whole earth of Egypt. But Pharaoh remained obstinate, and he did not listen to them, as the Lord had foretold. Pharaoh turned away and went into his house dismissing the matter. The Egyptians dug under the banks of the river for drinking, for they could not drink from the river. And so seven days went on from the time when the Lord struck the Nile.

Second Plague: the Frogs. The Lord said to Moses, "Go to Pharao's presence and say to him, 'The Lord has said, 'Let my people go so that they can worship me. And if you refuse to let them go, I will plague the whole of your land with frogs. The river shall swarm with them, and they shall come up into your house, into your bed, into the house of your servants and of your people, into your ovens and kneading-troughs. They shall clamber over you, your people and your servants'."

The Lord said to Moses, "Say to Aaron, 'Take your staff in your hand[2] and stretch it out over the rivers, streams and pools, and you shall bring up frogs over the land of Egypt'." Aaron stretched out his hand over the waters of Egypt, and the frogs came up and covered all the land of Egypt.

Then Pharaoh summoned Moses and Aaron and said to them, "Pray to the Lord to take the frogs away from me and my people, and I shall let your people go to worship the Lord."

---

1. A sign of the authority of the Lord.
2. The Lord uses natural things to make his miracles.

Moses said to the Pharaoh, "Appoint me a time when shall I intercede for you, your servants and all your people so that you and your houses may be rid of the frogs, and none be left except in the river." He replied, "Tomorrow", and Moses added, "It shall be as you say, so that you may know that there is no one like the Lord, our God." Moses and Aaron left Pharaoh, and Moses prayed to the Lord according to the promise he had made to Pharaoh regarding the frogs. And the Lord did as Moses bid him: the frogs died and disappeared from the houses and country. They heaped them in piles and the land stank. But Pharaoh, feeling a great relief, became obdurate again and did not listen to them, as the Lord had foretold.

Third Plague: the Maggots[1]. The Lord then said to Moses: "Say to Aaron: 'Stretch out your staff and strike the dust on the earth so that the whole earth of Egypt turns into maggots'." They did so. Aaron stretched out his hand with his staff, stroke the dust on the earth, and swarms of maggots covered men and beasts; all the dust on the earth turned into maggots over the whole Egypt. But Pharaoh remained obstinate and did not listen to them, as the Lord had foretold.

Fourth Plague: the Flies. The Lord said to Moses, "Rise up early tomorrow, and go to meet Pharaoh as he bathes and say to him: 'The Lord has said, 'Let my people go so that they may worship me. If you do not let them go, I will send swarms of flies upon you and your servants, upon your people and houses, and they will fill the houses of the Egyptians and the ground which they tread. I shall make a distiction between your people and mine. Tomorrow this sign shall appear'."

The Lord did as he had told, and dense swarms of flies invaded the house of the Pharaoh and his servants; throughout Egypt the land was threatened with ruins by the flies. The Pharaoh called Moses and Aaron and said to them, "Go and worship your God in this country." But Moses said, "We cannot do that, because what we sacrifice to the Lord is an abomination to the Egyptians. If we offer a sacrifice which they loathe, will they not stone us to death? We must go through the desert on a

---

1. Others translate mosquitoes or flies.

three-day journey to offer sacrifices to the Lord, our God, as he commands us." The Pharaoh said, "I will let you go to the desert to offer sacrifices to your God, only do not go too far[1]. Pray for me." Moses said, "As soon as I leave I will intercede with the Lord. Only let not Pharaoh trifle any more with the people by preventing them from going to offer sacrifice to the Lord." Moses left Pharaoh and interceded with the Lord. The Lord did as Moses told him, he removed the swarms of flies from Pharaoh, the servants and the people. Not one was left. But Pharaoh was obstinate again, and he did not let the people go.

Fifth Plague: the Pestilence. The Lord said to Moses: "Go into Pharaoh's presence and say to him: These are the words of the Lord, God of the Hebrews: 'Let my people go so that they can worship me. If you refuse to do so and keep your hold on them, the Lord will strike your grazing herds. A terrible pestilence shall fall over your horses, asses, camels, cattle and sheep'." The Lord fixed a deadline and said: "Tomorrow everything will be done." The next day the Lord carried it away: the cattle of the Egyptians died, but not even one beast of the cattle of the Israelited did. The Pharaoh was still obturate, and he did not let the people go.

Sixth Plague: the Boils. Then the Lord said to Moses and Aaron, "Take a handful of soot from a kiln. Moses shall throw it up into the air in Pharaoh's sight. It will turn into a fine dust over the whole earth of Egypt, and it will cause festering boils on man and beast throughout Egypt." They took soot from a kiln and, in Pharaoh's sight, Moses tossed it into the air and it caused festering boils on man and beast. But the Lord made Pharaoh obstinate, and he did not let the people go, as the Lord had foretold.

Seventh Plague: the Hailstorm. The Lord said to Moses: "Tomorrow you shall rise early in the morning, go into the Pharaoh's presence and say to him: These are the words of the Lord, God of the Hebrews: 'Let my people go so that they can worship me. This time I intend to strike with all my plagues against you, your servants and your people, so that you may

---

1. Pharaoh was shrewd enough to take them in.

know that there is nobody like me in the whole earth. For if I had stretched out my hand to strike you with the pestilence, you would have vanished from the earth. But I have kept you alive so that my power may shine on you, and to spread my fame on the land. Do you dare to rise against my people? Since you do not let them go, tomorrow at this time I shall send a violent hailstorm, such as has never been seen in Egypt since the day it was founded until now. Every man or beast that is in the open and is not brought in shall die, for the hail will fall on it'."

The Lord said to Moses, "Stretch out your hand towards the sky to bring down hail over the land, over man and beast, and over the grass of the fields." Moses stretched out his staff towards the sky and the Lord sent thunder and hailstorm, and fire flashing down to the ground. And so it rained down hail on the land of Egypt, mixed with fire, as heavily as it had never rained before in Egypt since its beginnings. The hail destroyed everything in the fields, man and beast. It struck every growing thing in the fields, plants and trees. Only the land of Goshen, where the sons of Israel lived, had no hail.

Then Pharaoh summoned Moses and Aaron and said to them: "This time I have sinned. The Lord is fair, and I and my people are in the wrong. Intercede with the Lord, stop the thunder and hail; I will let you go, you shall stay here no longer." Moses replied, "As soon as I leave this city, I will spread out my hands towards the Lord, and the thunder and the hail shall cease, and in this way you shall know that the earth belongs to the Lord." Moses left Pharaoh and the city, and he spread out his hands towards the Lord. The thunder and hailstorm ceased, and there was no more rain on the earth. When the Pharaoh saw that rain and the hail had ceased, he sinned again, he and his servants. He remained obstinate and did not let the sons of Israel go, as the Lord had foretold through Moses.

Eight Plague: the Locusts. Then the Lord said to Moses: "Go into Pharaoh's presence, for I have made him and his servants obdurate to show my signs through them, so that you may tell them to your children and grandchildren how did I treat the Egyptians and what marvellous things did I perform among them, and for you to know that I am the Lord, God of the Hebrews: How long will you refuse to humiliate yourself before me? Let my people go to worship me. For if you refuse to let them go tomorrow I shall bring locusts over your country, and they will cover the surface of the earth[1], and they shall swallow what survived the hail. They will swallow every tree that grows in the fields. They will invade your house, the houses of your servants and the Egyptians, who never saw your fathers or grandfathers since they were on the earth until now." Moses withdrew and left the house of the Pharaoh.

Then the Lord said to Moses: "Stretch out your hand over the land of Egypt so that the locusts come, crawl upon the land of Egypt and swallow what survived the hail." Moses stretched out his staff over the land of Egypt and the Lord sent a wind roaring in from the east all that day and night. At dawn, the wind of the east had brought the locusts, which crawled over the earth of Egypt and settled over its territory in enormous swarms. Nothing like that had ever been seen before, and nothing would be seen afterwards. They covered the whole land of Egypt till it was black with them. They devoured all vegetation and all the fruits of the trees that the hail had spared. There was no green left on the trees, on the country, or on the land of Egypt, which was black with locusts. Then the Pharaoh summoned urgently Moses and Aaron and said to them: "I have sinned against the Lord, your God, and against you. I pray you to forgive my sin, just once. Intercede with the Lord, your God, so that He removes this death from me." Moses left the house of the Pharaoh, and he prayed to the Lord, and the Lord changed the wind into a westerly gale, which carried the locusts away and trew them into the Red Sea. Not even one of them was left in the land of Egypt. But the Lord made the Pharaoh obstinate, and he did not let the sons of Israel go.

Ninth Plague: the Darkness. Then the Lord said to Moses: "Stretch out your hand towards the sky so that there is darkness over the land of Egypt, darkness that can be felt." Moses

---

1. The plague of locusts was already known in Egypt, but Moses announced it for the next day for the whole of the country.

stretched his hand towards the sky and there was pitch darkness for three days and three nights throughout the land of Egypt. They could not see each other; for three days nobody left his home. But there was light wherever the sons of Israel lived. Pharaoh summoned Moses and said to him: "Go and worship the Lord, but your cattle and sheep must be left here; you can take your children with you[1]." Moses answered: "You must yourself supply us with animals to offer as sacrifices and whole-offerings to the Lord, our God. We must also take our cattle, not a beast shall be left, for we need our cattle to offer them to the Lord, our God." But the Lord made Pharaoh obstinate, and they did not let them go. Pharaoh said, "Get out of here! See that you do not come into my presence again, for the day in which you see my face again you shall die." And Moses said, "You are right, I shall never come into your presence again[2]."

News of the Last Plague. Later on, the Lord said to Moses: "I shall bring upon Pharaoh and Egypt one last plague; after that he will let you go, or rather, he will send you packing. Tell the people that each one of them, man or woman, should ask their neighbours for jewellery of silver and gold." And the Lord made the Egyptians well-disposed towards the people; even Moses himself was well considered by the servants of Pharaoh and the Egyptians.

Then Moses said: "These are the words of the Lord: 'At midnight I will go among the Egyptians, and every first-born baby in the land of Egypt shall die: the first-born of Pharaoh, who sits on the throne of Egypt, the first-born of the slave, who works on the handmill, and the every first-born of the cattle. A great outcry will be heard throughout Egypt, a cry the like of which has never been heard before, nor ever will be again'."

Institution of the Passover. Moses summoned all the elders of Israel and said to them: "Go, take a lamb for every family, and slaughter the Passover. Then take a bunch of marjoram, dip

---

1. Pharaoh thought that in this way they would die from thirst.
2. The punishments of God are good: he sent the plagues so that Pharaoh would repent his obstination of not letting the people go.

it in the blood in the basin and smear some blood from the basin on the lintel and the two door-posts. Nobody may go out of his house till tomorrow morning. The Lord shall come to punish the Egyptians, and when he sees the blood on the lintel and the two door-posts he shall pass over that door, he will not allow the destroyer to come into your houses to hurt you. This shall be kept as an everlasting rule for you and your children. Once you have entered the land that the Lord is going to give you, you shall observe this rite. And when your children ask you, What is the meaning of this rite?, you shall answer, "It is the Lord's Passover, who passed over the houses of the sons of Israel in Egypt when he stroke the Egyptians, sparing their houses." The people bowed low and worshipped him. And the sons of Israel did as the Lord had told Moses and Aaron.

Death of the Egyptian first-borns. And so it happened that around midnight the Lord killed every first-born in Egypt: from the first-born of the Pharaoh in his trhone till the first-born of the slave, jailed, and every first-born animal of the cattle.

On the night the Pharaoh rose, with all his servants and the whole Egypt, and there was a great cry of anguish, for not a house in Egypt was without its dead. The Pharaoh summoned Moses and Aaron, while it was still night, and said to them: "Hurry up, take leave from us, you and the sons of Israel, go to worship your God as you said. Take your cattle and sheep, as you said, and go; ask God's blessing on me as well."

PART TWO

EXODUS OF THE ISRAELITES FROM EGYPT

1. EXODUS AND CROSSING OF THE RED SEA

Exodus of the People. The Egyptians urged the people and hurried them out of the country, for they said, "We are all going to die." The people picked up their dough before it was leavened, wrapped their kneading-thoughs in their cloaks and slung them on their soulders. The sons of Israel had done as Moses had told them, and they had asked the Egyptians for clothing and jewellery of silver and gold. The Lord had made the Egyptians well-disposed towards them, so they plundered the Egyptians.

The sons of Israel left Rameses[1] on the way to Succoth, about six thousand men on food, as well as children. With them went also a great number of people, flocks and herds in abundance.

The sons of Israel had been settled in Egypt for four hundred and thirty years. It was a night of vigil while the Lord brought them out of Egypt. And on that night all the sons of Israel keep their vigil generation after generation.

Towards the Red Sea. When Pharaoh let the people go God did not led them through the land of the Philistines,

---

1. Residence of Pharaoh; there gathered all the Hebrews of the delta.

although it was the shortest, for he said to himself, "The people may change their minds when they see war before them, and they may want to come back to Egypt." So the Lord made them go round through the desert towards the Red Sea[1].

Moses took with him the bones of Joseph, for he had exacted an oath from the sons of Israel: "God shall certainly visit you; you shall then take my bones with you."

Once they had left Succoth they encamped at Etham, on the edge of the desert. By day the Lord guided them in form of a pillar of cloud to show them the way, by night in form of a pillar of fire to give them light; in this way they could travel night and day. The pillar of cloud did never leave the people by day, nor the pillar of fire by night.

Through the Red Sea. They told the king of Egypt about the exodus of the people, and the Pharaoh and his servants turned against them, and said, "What have we done? We have let Israel go, and now they shall be no longer our slaves?" So Pharaoh put horses to his chariot and took his troops with him. The Lord had made Pharaoh obstinate, and he pursued the sons of Israel with high hand. The Egyptians, the horses and chariots of Pharaoh pursued them and overtook them where they were encamped beside the sea by Pi-hahiroth, in front of Baal-zephon.

As Pharaoh approached to them the sons of Israel looked up and saw the Egyptians coming after them. Full of terror they clamoured to the Lord. Then they said to Moses, "Were there no graves in Egypt, that you have brought us here to die in the desert? Why have you brought us out of Egypt? Did not we say to you 'Leave us alone, we want to be slaves to the Egyptians'?" Moses said to the people: "Do not be afraid and stand firm, because the Lord shall give you the victory on this day. The Egyptians you see now, you shall never see them again. The Lord will fight for you, so hold your peace."

And the Lord said to Moses, "Why do they claim against me? Tell them to move. As for you, rise you staff, stretch out

---

1. The Lord wanted to lead them to the Sinai, Horeb, to be worshipped by them and to establish his covenant with them.

your hand over the sea and cleave it in two, so that the sons of Israel may pass through the sea on dry ground. I will make the Egyptians obstinate and they shall follow you behind; thus I will win glory at the expense of the Pharaoh and his army, of the chariots and his cavalry. And they will know that I am the Lord when I win glory at the expense of Pharaoh, of his chariots and his cavalry."

The Angel of God, who went before the sons of Israel, moved away to the rear. The pillar of cloud moved as well to the rear, and so came between the Egyptians and the Israelites. There was shadow and darkness, and so in the night they could not come near the Israelites. Moses stretched out his hand over the sea[1] and the Lord drew the sea away all night along with a strong east wind, and turned the sea-bed into dry land. The sons of Israel went through the sea on dry ground as the waters made a wall for them to right and left. The Egyptians pursued them, all the army of Pharaoh, his chariots and cavalry went far into the sea. In the morning the Lord looked at the army of the Egyptians from the pillar of cloud and fire and He threw them into a panic. He clogged their chariot wheels and made them lumber along heavily. Then the Egyptians said to themselves, "Let us flee, for it is the Lord that is fighting for them agains the Egyptians." And the Lord said to Moses, "Stretch out your hand over the sea so that the waters flows back over the Egyptians, over their chariots and cavalry." Moses stretched out his hand over the sea and at dawn the sea returned to its place, but the Egyptians were in flight as it advanced.

In this way the Lord swept them out into the sea. The waters, as they flowed back, covered chariots and cavalry and the whole army of Pharaoh that had pursued the sons of Israel. No man was left alive[2]. But the sons of Israel had passed along the dry ground as the sea made for them a wall on either side. Thus saved the Lord on that day Israel from the Egyptians, and Israel

---

1. The crossing of the Red Sea took place, it is believed, through the Bitter Seas (Salted. The sea stretched out until there, 15 m depth, walled on each side.)

2. It is not recorded that the Pharaoh of the Plagues, Merenplah, died in the Red Sea. His mummy was shown at the Museum of The Cairo some years ago.

saw the dead Egyptians on the sea-shore. Israel saw the power which the Lord had put forth against Egypt, and they feared the Lord. They put faith in the Lord and in Moses, his servant.

Song of Moses. Then Moses and the sons of Israel sang a song to the Lord:

"I will sing to the Lord that has risen up in triumph, horse and
        rider he has hurled into the sea.
My strength and my song is the Lord.

As the horses of Pharaoh, with chariots and cavalry came into the sea, the Lord threw the waters of the sea over them, while the sons of Israel passed on foot on dry land through the sea."

Miriam the profetess, sister of Aaron, took up her tambourine; all the women followed her, singing to the sound of the tambourines. And Miriam answered to them:

"Sing to the Lord, for he has risen up in triumph:
Horse and rider he has hurled into the sea!"

2. JOURNEY THROUGH THE DESERT

The Manna and the Quails. The whole community of the sons of Israel set out from Elim and arrived in the desert of Sin, between Elim and Sinai. This was on the fifteenth of the second month after they had left Egypt. The whole community of the sons of Israel complained to Moses and Aaron in the desert[1]. They said to them, "If only we had died at the Lord's hand in Egypt, when we sat up beside the fleshpots and had plenty to eat! But you have brought us to this desert to starve all this people to death."

The Lord said to Moses, "Look, it will rain bread from heaven for you. The people shall come out every day to collet their daily supply, so that I can put them to the test and see whether they follow my instructions or not. But on the sixth day

---

1. Very soon.

they must take twice as much as they collect every day." Then Moses and Aaron said to the people of Israel, "In the evening you shall know that the Lord has brought you out of the land of Egypt, and in the morning you shall see the glory of the Lord, for He has heard your complaints against the Lord. It is not against us that you have complained; we are nothing." And he added, "This evening the Lord will give you meat to eat, and in the morning he will give you plenty of bread, for he has heard your complaints against him. But we are nothing, your complaints are not against us, but against the Lord." Then Moses said to Aaron, "Tell the community of the sons of Israel: come to the Lord, for he has heard your complaints."

While Aaron was talking, they looked up to the desert, and the glory of the Lord appeared in the cloud.

In the evening a flock of quails flew in and settled all over the camp[1], and in the morning there was a lay of dew around it. When the dew was gone, over the surface of the desert appeared some fine flakes, fine as a hoar-frost on the ground. When the sons of Israel saw it, they said, "Man-hu? = What is that?", because they did not know what it was. Moses said to them, "This is the bread that the Lord gives you to eat. This is what the Lord has sent to you. Gather as much as you can eat, an omer a head for every person in a tent." The sons of Israel did so, gathering some more, some less, but when they measured it by the omer, those who had gathered more had not too much, and those who had gathered less had not too little. Each had just what he could need. They gathered it every morning, every one according to his need. When the sun drew hot, it melted away.

Moses said, "This is the command which the Lord has given: 'Take a full omer of it to be kept for future generations, so that they may see how I fed you in the desert when I brought you out of the land of Egypt'." Then Moses said to Aaron, "Take a jar and fill it with an omer of it, and put it in the presence of the Lord, in order to keep it for our future generations." Aaron did as the Lord had commanded, he put the jar before the

---

1. The Lord made a flock of quails fall over the camp, so that they had plenty to eat, as He had announced.

Testimony for safe keeping. The sons of Israel ate the manna[1] for forty years, until they came to an inhabited land. They ate it until they reached the borders of the land of Canaan. An omer is one tenth of an ephah.

The Rock in Horeb. The whole community of the sons of Israel set out from the deset of Sin and travelled by stages as the Lord had told them. They encamped at Rephidim, where there was no water for the people. They complained against Moses and said, "Give us water to drink." And Moses replied, "Why do you dispute with me? Why do you challenge the Lord?" But the people, thirsty as they were, complained against Moses and said, "Why have you brought us out of Egypt to let us die of thirst, our children and our herds?" Moses cried to the Lord, "What shall I do with them? In a moment they will be stoning me." And the Lord said to Moses, "Go ahead of the people, take some of the elders of Israel with you and your staff with which you stroke the Nile and leave. I will be in front of you, there, by a rock in Horeb. You shall strike the rock; water will pour out of it, and the people will drink." Moses did so before the elders of Israel. And he named that place Massah and Meribah, because the Israelites had disputed with him, and because they had challenged the Lord with their question, "Is the Lord amongst us or not?"

---

1. The manna was a miraculous food, unknown, that fell every day like dew over the camp. Later on the beduines of the desert called manna to a resin of the tamarisk. The Mana is the symbol of the Eucharist, bread fallen of heaven.

PART THREE

THE COVENANT OF THE SINAI

1. THE COVENANT AND THE COMMANDMENTS

Arrival at Sinai. In the third month after the sons of Israel had left Egypt, they came to the desert of Sinai. They set out from Rephidim and came to the desert of Sinai, where they encamped, opposite the mountains.

Moses came up to God, and the Lord called him from the mountain and said, "Speak thus to the house of Jacob and tell this to the sons of Israel: You have seen how I have treated the Egyptians and how I have carried you on eagle's wings and brought you to Me. If only you will listen to my words carefully and keep my covenant, then you shall be my special posession among all the peoples, for the whole earth is mine; you shall be a kingdom of priests, a holy nation[1]. These words you shall speak to the Israelites." Then Moses summoned the elders of the people and told them what the Lord had commanded him. And all the people answered together, "We shall do as the Lord has said." Moses said to the Lord what the people had said. And the Lord said to Moses, "I shall come to you as a thick cloud so that the people may listen when I speak to you, and thus their faith in you shall never fail." And Moses told the Lord the words of the people.

---

1. God announces his covenant. If you follow the commandments that I shall give you, you shall be my people, and I shall be your God.

Then the Lord said to Moses, "Go to the people and hallow them today and tomorrow[1], and make them wash their clothes. They must be ready by the third day, because on the third day the Lord will descend upon Mount Sinai in the sight of the people. You must mark barriers around the mountain and say, "Keep from going up the mountain or even touching the edge of it. Any man that touches the mountain shall die." Moses went down the mountain, hallowed the people and they washed they clothes. And he said to the people, "Be ready for the third day."

Divine Apparition in the Mountain. On the third day, at dawn, there were peals of thunder and lightning, a thick cloud over the mountain and a loud trumpet blast; and all the people in the camp were terrified. Moses made the people left the camp to meet God, standing at the foot of the mountain. The Mount Sinai was all smoke because the Lord had come down upon it on fire. The smoke rose like the smoke of a kiln, and the mountain trembled. At the same time the blast of the trumpet grew louder and louder. Moses spoke to him, and God answered to him in a peal of thunder.

The Commandments. God spoke, and these were his words: "I am the Lord, your God, who brought you out of Egypt, out of the land of slavery.

You shall have no other god to set against me. You shall not make an image for yourself nor the likeness of anything in the heaven above, or on the earth below, or in the waters under the earth. You shall not bow down or worship them, for I, the Lord, your God, am a jealous god, and I punish those who loathe me. But I keep faith with thousands, with those who love me and keep my commandments.

You shall not make wrong use of the name of the Lord your God; the Lord will not leave unpunished the man who misuses his name.

Remember to keep the sabbath day holy. You shall labour six days and do all your work. But the seventh day is a sabbath of the Lord. On that day you shall not do any work, you, your

---

1. The Israelites purified themselves by continence, washing of the body and dressing.

son, your daughter, your slave or slave-girl, your herds or the foreigner that lives with you; for in six days the Lord made heaven and earth, the sea and everything that is in them, and on the seventh day he rested. Therefore the Lord blessed the sabbath day and declared it holy.

Honour your father and your mother so that your days are long in the land which the Lord your God is giving you.

You shall not commit murder.

You shall not commit adultery.

You shall not steal.

You shall not give false evidence against your neighbour.

You shall not covet your neighbour's house; nor his wife, slave or slave-girl, his ox, his ass, or anything that belongs to him."

All the people saw the thunder and lightning, the trumpet sound and the mountain smoking. And when they saw this, they trembled and stood at a distance. They said to Moses, "Speak to us yourself, and we will listen to your words. But if God speaks to us we will die[1]." Moses said to the people, "Do not be afraid; the Lord has come only to test you, so that the fear of him may remain within you and keep you from sin." The people, then, stood at a distance, while Moses approached the cloud where the Lord was.

2. THE COVENANT

Ratification of the Covenant. The Lord had said to Moses, "Come up to the Lord, you and Aaron, Nadab and Abihu, and seventy elders of Israel. You shall worship from a distance. Only Moses must approach the Lord by himself. The people may not go up with him." Moses came and told the people the words of the Lord, and all his laws regarding justice. And the people answered with one voice, "We shall do all that the Lord has told us."

---

1. The people did not only see the miracles of the mountain, they did also heard the voice of God that gave the law.

Moses wrote the words of the Lord. He rose up early, built an altar at the foot of the mountain, and put up twelve sacred pillars[1], one for each of the twelve tribes of Israel. Then he sent some young men of the sons of Israel to offer sacrifices, and they sacrificed bulls as whole-offerings and shared-offerings. Then Moses took one half of the blood and put it in jars, and the other half he flung it upon the altar. He took the book of the Covenant and read it in front of the people, and the people said, "We shall do as the Lord has said". Then Moses took the blood and flung it over the people, and said, "This is the blood of the Covenant that the Lord has made with you with these words."

Moses receives the Tablets of the Law. The Lord said to Moses: "Come up the mountain and stay there. I will give you the tablets of stone, the law and the commandment, which I have written down so that you may teach them." Then Moses rose with Josuah, his assistant, and as they were to come up the mountain, he said to the elder: "Wait for me here until we come back. Aaron and Hur are with you: if anyone has a dispute, let him go to them." Moses went up the mountain and the cloud covered it for six days. On the seventh day the Lord called to Moses from within the cloud. The glory of the Lord looked to the sons of Israel like a devouring fire over the top of the mountain. Moses entered the cloud and went up the mountain in which he remained for forty days and forty nights.

---

1. Monolites of stone as testimony and remembrance. The blood was the seal of the Old Covenant, as the blood of Christ is the seal of the New. Its value is infinitely superior.

PART FOUR

LAWS REGARDING WORSHIP

1. APOSTASY AND RECONCILIATION

The golden Bull-calf. The people, seeing that Moses was so long in coming down from the mountain, gathered around Aaron and said to him: "Come, make us gods to go ahead of us, for of that Moses, who brought us out of Egypt, we have no news." Aaron said to them, "Strip the gold rings from the ears of your wives, sons and daughters, and bring them to me." Then all the people stripped themselves of the gold earrings and brought them to Aaron. He took them in his hands, cast the metal in a mould, and made them into a bull-calf. Then they said, "This is your God[1], Israel, the one that brought you out of the land of Egypt!" As Aaron saw this, he built an altar in front of the calf[2] and said, "Tomorrow there is to be a feast to the Lord." Next day they rose up early and offered whole-offerings and shared-offerings peacefully. The people sat down to eat and drink, and later they gave themselves up to revelry.

But the Lord said to Moses, "Go down the mountain, for your people, the people you brought out of Egypt, have done a disgraceful thing. They have turned away from the way I have commanded them very early; they have made an image of a bull-calf and have postrated them to it; they have made

---

1. Later the people degenerated into the idolatry of Egypt.
2. Similar to the Egyptian bull Apis.

whole-offerings and have said, 'This is your God, Israel, the one that brought you out of the land of Egypt'." And the Lord added, "I see that your people is a stubborn people. Now, let me vent my anger upon them, so that I may put an end to them." Then Moses prayed to his Lord and said to him, "But Lord, why should you vent your anger upon your people, whom you brought out of Egypt with great power and strong hand? Why let the Egyptians say, 'He meant evil when he let them go out of the land of Egypt, to kill them in the mountains and wipe them off the surface of the earth?' Turn from your anger, and forget the evil you intend on your people. Remember Abraham, Isaac and Jacob, your servants, to whom you swore and said, 'I will make your descendancy countless as the stars in heaven, and I will give the land that I have promised you to your descendants to posses it for ever'." And the Lord relented and spared the people the evil that he intended.

Moses came down the mountain with the two tablets of the Tokens in his hands, written on both sides, on the front and on the back. The tablets were the handiwork of the Lord, and the writing was the writing of the Lord, engraved on the tablets. Joshua heard the uproar of the people and said to Moses, "There is fighting in the camp!" Moses replied, "This is not the clamour of a victory, nor the clamour of defeated people, but the sound of singing." As they approached the camp, Moses saw the bull-calf and the dancing. Then, angry as he was, he threw the tablets to the ground and shattered them to pieces at the foot of the mountain. He took the bull-calf that they had made, burnt it and ground it to powder, and sprinkled it on water, and this water he made the sons of Israel drink. Moses said to Aaron, "What did these people to you that you have brought to them such a great guilt?" Aaron answered, "Do not be angry, sir. You know that these people tend to wrong-doing. They said to me, 'Make us a god that goes ahead of us, because of Moses, who has brought us out of the land of Israel, we have no news.' And I have said to them, 'Those of you who have any gold, strip it off.' They gave it to me, I threw it in the fire, and out came this bull-calf."

The Punishment. Moses, as he saw that the people were out of control because of Aaron until they were laid open to the malice of their enemies, stood at the gate of the camp and said: "Those of you who are on the Lord's side, come to me." All the sons of Levi[1] gathered around him. He told them, "Arm yourselves with your sword. Go through the camp from gate to gate and back again, and kill your brother, your friend, your relative." The Levites did as Moses had told them, and that day died about three thousand men of the people. Then Moses said, "Today you have consecrated yourselves to the Lord, because you have brought each against his own son and his own brother, and so today He gives you his blessing[2]."

Moses intercedes for the people. The next day Moses said to the people, "You have committed a great sin. However, I will go up to the Lord; maybe he can forgive you." Thus Moses went back to the Lord and said, "Oh, Lord, these people had committed a great sin. They have made a golden god. Will you forgive them anyway? But if not, blot out my name from the book that you have written." The Lord said to Moses, "I will blot out from my book the man who has sinned against me. Now go and led your people to the place I have commanded you. My angel shall go ahead of you, but a day will come in that I will punish them for their sin." And the Lord punished the people for having made the bull-calf.

The Tent outside the camp. Moses took his tent and pitched it at a distance outside the camp, and he called it "The Tent of the Presence[3]". Everyone that sought the Lord went out to the Tent of the Presence, placed outside the camp. Whenever Moses went to the Tent, all the people stood up, at the gate of his tent, and followed him with their eyes until he came in the Tent. And when Moses went inside it happened that the pillar of cloud came down, and stayed at the entrance to the tent, and the Lord spoke to Moses[4]. As the people saw the pillar of cloud at

---

1. Most of them had refrained from idolatry.
2. And they destined them to divine cult.
3. Like the model of Solomon's Temple.
4. The pillar of cloud was the sign of the presence of the Lord. The oracle of God.

the entrance of the gate, they stood up and prostrated themselves, every man at the entrance of his tent. And the Lord spoke to Moses face to face, as friends do. Then Moses came back to the camp, but Joshua, his assistant, son of Nun, never moved from the Tent.

Renovation of the Covenant. Nine Tablets of Stone. The Lord said to Moses, "Cut two tablets of stone, as the first ones that you broke, and I shall write upon them the words which were on the first tablets. Be ready by tomorrow morning, come up the Mount Sinai by early morning, and wait for me there. Come up all alone, no man shall be seen on the whole mountain, not even grazing flocks or herds." Moses cut two tablets similar to the first ones, he rose up early in the morning and came up the Mount Sinai, as the Lord had told him, having the two tablets of stone[1] with him.

The Lord came down in the cloud, stood up in front of him and Moses called the name Jehova. When He passed by Moses he said, "Oh Jehova, my Lord, a God compassionate and gracious, long-suffering, ever constant and true, ; if I have won your favour, my Lord, then may the Lord go in our company. However stubborn a people they are, forgive our iniquity and our sin and take us as your own possession." The Lord answered, "Here and now I shall make a covenant; in full view of your people I will do such miracles as never have been performed in the whole earth or in any nation. All the people among whom you are shall be the work of the Lord.

I will drive out the people in front of you, and I shall widen your borders, and nobody will disturb you when you go to the presence of your Lord three times a year."

Then the Lord said to Moses, "Write these words down, because the covenant I make with you and with Israel is in those words." And Moses was there with the Lord for forty days and forty nights, and he neither ate nor drank. And the Lord wrote on the tablets the ten words, the ten words of the covenant.

---

1. Also Tablets of the Covenant.

2. BUILDING OF THE SANCTUARY

Moses does the Commandment of the Lord. Moses did everything as the Lord had told him. On the first month of the second year, on the first day of the month, the Tabernacle was set up. Moses set up the Tabernacle. He put the sockets in place, inserted the planks, fixed the crossbars and set up the posts.

Then he spread the tent over the Tabernacle and fixed the covering of the tent above it, as the Lord had commanded him. He took the Tokens and put them in the Ark, inserted the poles in the Ark and put the cover over the top of the Ark. He brought the Ark into the Tabernacle, set up the Veil of the screen and so screened the Ark of the Tokens, as the Lord had commanded him. He put the table in the Tent of the Presence on the north side of the Tabernacle outside the Veil and arranged bread on it before the Lord, as the Lord had commanded him. He set the lamp-stand in the Tent of the Presence opposite the table at the south side of the Tabernacle and mounted the lamps as the Lord had commanded him. He set up the gold altar in the Tent of the Presence in front of the Veil and burnt fragrant incense on it, as the Lord had commanded him. He set up the screen at the entrance of the Tabernacle, fixed the altar of whole-offerings at the entrance of the Tabernacle, the Tent of the Presence, and offered on it whole-offerings and grain-offerings, as the Lord had commanded him. He set up the basin between the Tent of the Presence and the altar and put water there for washing, and Moses and Aaron and his sons used to wash their hands and feet when they entered the Tent of the Presence or approached the altar, as the Lord had commanded Moses. He set up the court all around the Tabernacle and the altar, and put a screen at the gateway of the court. Thus Moses completed the work[2].

---

1. Where the oracle of the Lord was. In it there was the Ark of the Testament with the Tablets; in front of them, separated by a screen, were the Altar, the Table and the Lamp-hold. In the gateway, the altar of whole-offerings and the washing basin.

2. Everything was walled by pillars and screens; the Sanctuary, with the Santa and the Santa Santorum within the great Tent of the Presence.

The glory of the Lord and the cloud. Then the cloud covered the Tent of the Presence and the glory of the Lord filled the Tabernacle. Moses could not enter the Tent of the Presence, because the cloud had settled on it, and the glory of the Lord filled the Tabernacle. As the cloud lifted form the Tabernacle, the sons of Israel left by stages. And if the cloud did not lift, they did not break camp until it lifted. For the cloud of the Lord hovered over the Tabernacle by day and, in the night, it shone like fire, so that the Israelites could see it at every stage of their journey[1].

---

1. The cloud went on guiding them.

LEVITICUS

PART ONE

LAWS CONCERNING SACRIFICES

Whole-offerings. The Lord summoned Moses and spoke to him from the Tent of the Presence in these words: "Say this to the sons of Israel: Whenever any of you presents an animal as an offering to the Lord, it may be either from the herd or from the flock.

If his offering is a whole-offering from cattle, he shall present a male without blemish, he shall present it at the entrance to the Tent of the Presence so that it is accepted by the Lord[1].

Grain-offerings. Whenever any man wants to present an offering as a grain-offering, it shall be a flour-offering. He shall pour oil on it and frankincense to it.

If your offering to the Lord is a grain-offering of first-ripe grain, you must present fresh corn roasted, crushed meal from fully ripened corn. You shall add oil to it and put frankincense upon it. This is a grain-offering. The priest shall burn as its

---

1. In the old days the whole-offerings were thanksgiving acts, but in the Leviticus they were expiatory. Blood was life, and it was forbidden to eat meat with blood.

token some of the crushed meal, some of the oil, and all the frankincense as a food-offering to the Lord.

Shared-offerings[1]. If a man's offering is a shared-offering from the cattle, male or female, he shall present it without blemish before the Lord. He shall lay his hand on the head of the victim and slaughter it at the entrance to the Tent of the Presence. The sons of Aaron, the priests, shall fling the blood against the altar all round. One of them shall present part of the shared-offering as a food-offering to the Lord. The sons of Aaron shall burn it on the altar on top of the whole-offering which is upon the wood on the fire, a food-offering of soothing odour to the Lord.

If a man's offering is a shared-offering to the Lord from the flock, male or female, he shall present it without blemish. If the offering is a ram, he shall present it before the Lord, lay his hand on the head of the victim and slaughter it in front of the Tent of the Presence, and the sons of Aaron shall fling the blood against the altar all round. It shall be burnt at the altar, and offered to the Lord as a food-offering.

Sin-offerings. The Lord spoke to Moses and said, "Speak to the sons of Israel and say to them: If any of you inadvertently transgresses any of the commandments of the Lord and does anything prohibited by them:

a) The Anointed Priest. If the anointed priest sins so as to bring guilt on the people, he shall present to the Lord a young bull without blemish as a sin-offering.

b) The Community of Israel. If the whole community of Israel has sinned inadvertently and the matter is not known to the assembly, and they do what is forbidden in any commandment of the Lord, then, when the sin they have commited is notified to them, the assembly shall offer a young bull as a sin-offering. It will be led to the Tent of the Presence; the elders of the community shall lay their hands over the head of the young bull

---

1. The Communion Sacrifice is a sacred banquet. Part of it is eaten by the people present, and the other is offered to the Lord. It is an expression of community of God and men.

before the Lord, and, before the Lord shall the young bull be slaughtered."

PART TWO

LAWS OF LEGAL PURIFICATION

Clean and unclean Animals. The Lord spoke to Moses and Aaron and said to them: "Speak to the sons of Israel and say to them: 'These are the animals you may eat among all the animals on land. You may eat any animal which has a parted food or a cloven hoof and also chew the cud; those which have only a cloven hoof or only chew the cud you may not eat. You shall regard as unclean, subsequently, the camel, the rabbit, the hare and the pig. You shall not eat their flesh or even touch their dead bodies. You shall regard them as unclean.

Of the creatures that live in water you may eat those that have fins and scales, whether in salt water or fresh.

Of the birds, you shall regard as vermin and for this reason not eat them, the eagle, the vulture of any kind, the crow of any kind and so on.

Of the animals that teem on the ground you shall regard as unclean the weasel, the rat, the lizard, the mole-rat, and so on.

Anything that teems on the ground you shall regard as unclean and not eat it. As I am the Lord, your God, you shall keep yourselves holy, and be holy, for I am holy'."

Cleansing of a Man suffering from a malignant Skin-disease. The Lord spoke to Moses and said to him: "This shall be the law regarding the men suffering from malingnant skin-diseases on the day of their cleansing: 'He will be taken to the priest; the latter shall come to meet him outside the camp to examine him; if the man is healed from his disease, he shall order two clean small birds to be brought alive for the man who is cleansed[1]."

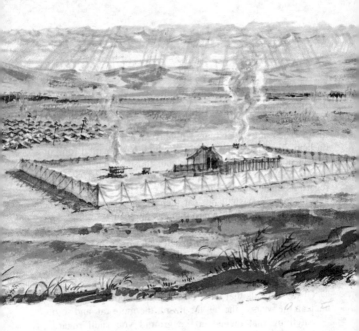

---

1. It is a social legal law.

PART THREE

THE LAW OF HOLINESS

Laws regarding Holiness, Charity and Justice. The Lord spoke to Moses and said to him: "Speak to the whole community of the sons of Israel and say to them: 'You shall be holy, because I, the Lord, your God, am holy. You shall revere you father and your mother, and keep my sabbaths: I am the Lord your God. Do not follow idols and do not make gods of cast metal for yourselves. I am the Lord your God.

When you reap the harvest of your land, you shall not reap right into the edges of your field; neither shall you glean the loose ears of your crop; you shall not completely strip your vineyard nor glean the fallen grapes. You shall leave them for the poor and the alien. I am the Lord your God.

You shall not steal; you shall not cheat or deceive each other. You shall not swear in my name in order to deceive and thus profane the name of your God. I am the Lord. Do not oppress your neighbour, nor rob him; you shall not keep back a hired man's wages till next morning. You shall not treat the deaf with contempt, nor put an obstruction in the way of the blind. You shall fear your God. I am the Lord. No shall not pervert justice, either by favouring the poor or by subvervience to the great. You shall judge your fellowmen with justice. You shall not go about spreading slander among your relatives nor take sides against your neighbour on a capital charge. I am the Lord. You shall not nurse hatred against your brother, but rather reprove yourself so that you do not have a new guilt. You shall not seek revenge, or cherish anger towards your kinsfolk. You shall love your neighbour as a man like yourself. I am the Lord. You shall keep my sabbaths and revere my Sanctuary: I am the Lord. You shall not resort to fortune-tellers nor necromancers, nor make yourselves unclean by consulting them: I am the Lord, your God'."

Faults agains the Family. When any man reviles his father and his mother, he shall be put to death. He has reviled his father and his mother, and his blood shall be on his own head. If a man commits adultery with his neighbour's wife, both adulterer and adulteress shall be put to death.

Conclusion. Be holy, because I am holy, the Lord, who has separated you from the people so that you are mine.

Appointed Seasons in the Religious Year. The Lord spoke to Moses and said to him: "Speak to the sons of Israel and say to them: 'These are the appointed seasons of the Lord, namely, the sacred assemblies to which you shall proclaim to the sons of Israel:

The Sabbath. On six days you will work, but the seventh is the sabbath of sacred rest, a day of sacred assembly, on which you shall do no work. Wherever you may live, it is the Lord's sabbath.

Passover and Unleavened Bread. These are the appointed seasons of the Lord, the sacred assemblies to which you shall proclaim in their appointed order. In the first month on the fourteenth day between dusk and dark is the Lord's Passover, and on the fifteenth of the same month is the feast of Unleavened Bread of the Lord: for seven days you shall eat Unleavened Bread."

First Sheaves. The Lord spoke to Moses and said to him: "Speak to the sons of Israel and say to them: 'When you have entered the land that I give you and you reap its harvest, you shall bring the first sheaf of your harvestto the priest. He will present it to the Lord so as to gain acceptance for yourselves'."

Day of Atonement. The Lord spoke to Moses in this way: "On the tenth of the same seventh month is the Day of Atonement. On that day you shall have a sacred assembly and you shall mortify yourselves. On that day you shall do no work, for it is the Day of Atonement, to make expiation for you before the Lord your God."

Pilgrim-feast of Tabernacles. The Lord spoke to Moses and said: "Speak to the sons of Israel and say to them: 'On the fifteenth day of this seventh month begins the pilgrim-feast of the Tabernacles, and it shall last for seven days, in honour of the Lord.

On the day fifteenth of the seventh month, once the harvest has been gathered, you shall keep the Lord's pilgrim-feast for seven days; the first and the seventh day are days of rest. On the first day you shall take beautiful fruits, falm fronds and leafy branches, and willows from the river-side, and you shall rejoice before the Lord your God for seven days. You shall keep this pilgrim-feast on the seventh-months. During the seven days you shall live in tents."

The Bread of the Proposal. The Lord spoke to Moses and said: "You shall take flour and bake it into twelve loaves, two tenths of an ephah to each. You shall arrange them in two rows, six to a row on the table, ritually clean, before the Lord. You shall sprinkle pure frankincense on the rows, and this shall be a token of the bread, offered to the Lord as a food-offering. Sabbath after sabbath he shall arrange it regularly before the Lord as a gift from the sons of Israel.

This is a covenant for ever; it is the privilege of Aaron and his sons, and they shall eat the bread in a holy place, because it is the holiest of the holy gifts. It is his due out of the food-offerings of the Lord; this is an ever-lasting law.

Blasphemy and Tallionic law. Whoever utters the Name of the Lord shall be put to death: all the community shall stone him; alien or native, if he utters the Name, he shall be put to death.

When one man kills another, he shall be put to death. Whoever kills a beast shall make restitution, animal for animal. When one maninjures his fellow-countrymen, it shall be done to him as he has done; fracture for fracture, eye for eye and tooth for tooth, namely, the injury that he has inflicted upon another shall be inflicted upon him. Whoever kills a beast shall pay for it, and whoever kills a man shall die."

NUMBERS

PART ONE

IN THE MOUNT SINAI

List of people per tribes. This is the number of people as recorded by Moses, Aaron and the twelve princes of Israel, one per tribe. According to this number, listed by families, all the sons of Israel over twenty, apt to war, were 603,550 men. The Levites were not included in the lists with their fellow-Israelites.

The cloud guides the people of Israel. On the day in which they set up the Tabernacle, the cloud covered it, namely, the Tent of the Tokens, and from the evening till morning it was over the Tabernacle in form of fire. In this way the cloud covered it night and day. Whenever the cloud lifted from the Tent the sons of Israel would leave, and where the cloud had hovered encamped the sons of Israel. The sons of Israel left and encamped as the Lord commanded them, and they continued in camp as long as the cloud hovered over the Tent. When the cloud stayed long over the Tent, the sons of Israel worshipped the Lord and did not move on; but if the cloud stayed only a few days, then they encamped and left as the Lord commanded them. When the cloud stopped from evening to morning, and then lifted, they left. If the cloud hovered for one day and one night, and then it lifted, they left. Whether it was for a day or two, a month or a year, while the cloud hovered over the Tent, the sons of Israel remained encamped and did not move; but when it lifted, they left. At the Lord's command they encamped, and at the Lord's command they would leave. And they worshipped the Lord as the Lord had commanded Moses.

PART TWO

JOURNEY THROUGH
THE DESERT

Command to leave. On the second year, on the second month, on the twentieth day of the month, the cloud abandoned the Tent of the Tokens, and the sons of Israel moved by stages from the desert of Sinai towards the desert of Paran, where the cloud came to rest. This was the first time that they broke camp at the Lord's commandment, given through Moses.

Moving off. They moved off from the mountain of the Lord and journeyed for three days. The Ark of the Covenant of the Lord went ahead the three days, looking for a place to rest. The cloud of the Lord hung over them by them since they had moved camp. Whenever the Ark began to move, Moses would say,

"Up, Lord, and be your enemies scattered,
    let that hate you flee before you."

And when it halted he would say,

"Rest, Lord, among the thousands of Israel."

Exploration of the Promised Land. The Lord spoke to moses, and said: "Send some men to explore the land of Canaan which I am giving to the sons of Israel; you shall send one of each tribe, taken from their princes." Moses did as he was told and sent them from the desert of

Paran[1]; according to the Lord's commandment, they were all princes among the sons of Israel. Moses called the son of Nun Joshua, not Hoshea.

Moses sent them to explore the land of Canaan, and said to them: "Make up your way by the Negeb; and to on into the hill-country. See what the land is like, and whether the people that inhabit it are strong or weak, few or many. See whether it is a good or bad land, what its cities are like, opened or walled; what the land is like, fertile or barren, and does it grow trees or not? Be brave and bring some of its fruits." It was the season when the first grapes were ripe.

The explorers went up and explored the country from the desert of Sin until the Rehob by Lebo-hamath. They went up the Negeb and came to Hebron, where Ahiman, Sheshai and Talmai, the descendants of Anak, were living (Hebron was ounded seven years before Zoan in Egypt). They came to the valley of Eshcol, and there they cut a branch and a single bunch of grapes, and they carried it on a pole two at a time, together with pomegranates and figs. This place was named the valley of the bunch of grapes, for there the sons of Israel had cut the bunch of grapes.

After forty days they returned from exploring the land. They went before Moses, Aaron and the whole community of the sons of Israel in the desert of Paran, at Kadesh[2], and they made their report to them and showed them the fruits of the land.

Dark Story of the Explorers. This is their report: "We went to the land to which you sent us. It is certainly a land flowing with milk and honey; see its fruits. But the people that inhabits is sturdy, and its cities are strong and great; we have even seen descendants of Anak[3]. The Amalekites occupy the region of the Negeb; Hittites, Jebusites and Amorites live in the hill-country; the Canaanites live by the sea and on the banks of the Jordan."

---

1. Starting and ending point of the explorers. David's refuge as he was prosecuted by Saul.
2. Spring with many wells and pounds. Great oasis.
3. Anak, known as a giant.

Calleb called the people for silence, for they were rising up against Moses, and said: "We shall go up and conquer it, we are well able to do so." But those who went up with him said: "We cannot attack these people, they are stronger than us." And they made their report discouraging the people, and said, "The land that we have explored is a land that swallows up its inhabitants. All the men that we have seen are great in size. We have seen even giants, sons of Anak; before them we looked like grass-hoopers, and thus we looked to them as well."

Revolt of the People. Then the whole community cried out in dismay; they cried all night long, and the sons of Israel complained against Moses and Aaron. The whole community said: "If only we had died in Egypt! Why should we not die in this desert? Why does the Lord led us to that land to be killed under their swords and to give our wives and children as a loot? Would it be not better to back to Egypt?" And they said to each other, "Let us choose a leader and go back to Egypt."

Moses and Aaron postrated themselves on the ground before the assembled community of the sons of Israel. And Joshua, son of Nun and Caleb, son of Jephunneh, rent their clothes and addressed the sons of Israel, and they said, "The land that we have explored is a good land, even better, it is a very good land. If the Lord is pleased with us, he will make us enter the land, and he will give it to us. It is a land flowing with milk and honey. Do not rebel against the Lord, nor be afraid of the people in that land, for we shall swallow them as a piece of bread. They have been left without defence, and the Lord is with us. Do not be afraid of them."

Anger of the Lord; Moses intercedes. The whole community threatened to stone them when the glory of the Lord appeared to them all in the Tent of the Presence. And the Lord said to Moses, "How longer will this people treat me with contempt? How longer will they refuse to trust me in spite of all the signs I have shown among them? I will strike them with pestilence, I will destroy them. You and your descendants I will make into a nation greater and more numerous than they." But Moses replied to the Lord, "But the Egyptians shall hear of it, for it was you who brought them out of Egypt, and they will let it be known among the inhabitants of this land. They know that you, oh, Lord, are among your people, that you appear in a pillar of cloud and in a pillar of fire by night. If you put them all to death at one blow, those nations that have heard about you shall say, 'The Lord has not been able to introduce this people into the land which he promised them by oath, and so he destroyed them in the desert.' Now, my Lord, let your might be shown, as you said.

Forgive, then, the sin of this people, by your great love, as you have done from Egypt until now."

Pardon and Punishment. The Lord said, "I will forgive them as you say, but as I live in very truth the glory of the Lord shall fill the earth. Not one of those who have seen my glory and the signs which I brought in Egypt and in the desert and that have tested me ten times without listening to my voice shall see the earth which I promised to their fathers by oath. None of those who despise me shall see it. But my servant Caleb, who showed a different spirit and obeyed me faithfully, I will bring into the land in which he has already been, and his descendants shall possess it. Come back tomorrow and set out for the desert by way of the Red Sea."

The Lord spoke to Moses and Aaron, and said: "Say to them: 'As I live, word of the Lord, that I shall treat you according to the words that I have heard you utter. In this desert your bones shall lie, every one of you that registers more than twenty years old and has complained against me. I swear that you shall not enter the land, in which, lifting my hand, I had sworn should be your home, except Caleb, sons of Jephunneh and Joshua son of Nun. However, your sons shall enter, those sons who you said would become the spoils of war; they will know the land that you have rejected. You shall not know it, your bones shall lie in this desert. Your sons shall wander in the desert for forty years. For forty years you shall pay the penalty of your iniquities[1]."

---

1. The Lord make them retreat to the Red Sea, and they wandered in the desert for forty years.

Rebellion of Korah[1], Dathan and Abiram. Korah, son of Isar, son of Kohath, son of Levi; Dathan and Abiram sons of Eliab and On, son of Peleth, descendants of Reuben, challenged the authority of Moses, together with 250 sons of Israel, all of them men of rank, princes and members of the assembly. They gathered around Moses and Aaron and said to them, "You should be equal to all the rest. Every member of the community is holy and the Lord is among them all. Why do you set yourselves up above the community of the Lord?" When Moses heard these words, he protrated himself on the ground.

The Punishment. Moses said to Korah, "You and your company should go tomorrow before the presence of the Lord, and Aaron as well. Take your censers and place incense on them, and see the Lord with your 250 censers. You and Aaron too." Each man took his censer, put fire in it and put incense on it, and they stood at the entrance to the Tent of the Presence. Together with Moses and Aaron the whole community was at the entrance to the Tent of the Presence, and then the glory of the Lord appeared to the whole community.

The Lord spoke to Moses and Aaron, and said to them, "Stand apart from this people, so that I may put an end to them in a single instant."

Hardly had Moses spoken when the ground beneath them split; the earth opened its mouth and swallowed them and their homes up, and also all the men of Korah and all their goods. They went down alive into the seplucro, they and all their goods. The earth closed over them, and they disappeared among the assembly. When they heart their cries all the Israelites that were around fled, in case the earth would swallow them up too.

Fire had come out from the Lord and burnt the 250 men who offered the incense.

Death of Aaron. They set out from Kadesh, and the whole community of the sons of Israel came to Mount Hor. The Lord spoke to Moses and Aaron at Mount Hor, near the frontier of the land of Edom, and said, "Aaron must go and be gathered to

---

1. Korah, Moses and Aaron's cousin, and his Levite followers were jealous of his being priest and rebelled against him.

his people, for he cannot come into the land that I have given to the sons of Israel, because you challenged my authority over the waters of Meribah. Take Aaron and his son Eleazar, and go up Mount Hor. Strip Aaron of his robes and dress Eleazar his son with them. Aaron died on the top of the mountain. Moises and Eleazar went down the mountain. The whole community saw that Aaron had died, and all Israel mourned him for thirty days.

The bronze Serpent. They set out from Mount Hor by way of the Red Sea, to go round the land of Edom. On the way the people grew impatient and spoke against the Lord and Moses, and said, "Why did you make us leave Egypt to die in this desert? There is no bread nor water, and we are sick of this miserable fare."

Then the Lord sent snakes of fire that bit and killed many people in Israel. The people came to Moses and said, "We sinned when we spoke against the Lord and you. Please, plead the Lord to rid us of the snakes." Moses pleaded with the Lord for the people. The Lord said to Moses, "Make a serpent of bronze and erect it as a standard, and anyone that has been bitten can look at it and recover." Moses made a bronze serpent and erected it as a standard, so that when a man had been bitten by a serpent, he could look at the bronze serpent and recover[1].

Towards the East Bank. The sons of Israel set out and encamped at Oboth. They moved on from Oboth and encamped at Iye-abarim, in the desert on the eastern frontier of Moab. They moved on from there and encamped at Zared valley. They left and encamped on the other side of the Arnon...

This valley extended from the wilderness into Amorite territory, for the Arnon was the Moabite frontier, namely, between Moab and the Amorites.

---

1. That stubborn people rebelled again against the Lord and Moses, and the Lord sent them poisonous snakes. The bronze snake was figure of Christ, who said, "when I am risen high, I shall atrack them all to me." The Cross is a source of salvation.

PART THREE

IN THE PLAINS OF MOAB

1. BALAK AND BALAAM

Balak, king of Moab[1], calls Balaam[2]. The sons of Israel set out and encamped in the Plains of Moab, on the other side of the Jordan, at Jericho. At that time Balak was king of Moab, son of Zippor, who sent a deputation to Beor, by the river, on the land of the sons of Ammau to summon Balaam, son of Beor, and said, "A people that covers the whole earth has left Egypt, and they are settling at my door. Come and lay a curse on these people, for they are far more numerous than me, so that I may be able to defeat them and drive them from the country. I know that those whom you bless are blessed, and those whom you curse are cursed."

In this way the elders of Moab and the elders of Midian set out, and took the fees for augury with them. They came to Balaam and told him what Balak had said. He said to them, "Stay overnight and I will tell you whatever answer the Lord gives to me." The princes of Moab stayed over with Balaam. God came to Balaam in the night and said to him "These people have come to fetch you. Rise up and go with them, but do only what I tell you to do."

---

1. To the East of the Dead Sea. The waters of the Arnon go to the Dead Sea. His bead is the border of Moab.
2. Prophet of the country of Aram. God can speak through anybody.

Balaam and Balak's Meeting. Balak knew that Balaam was coming, and he went to meet him at Ar of Moab, over the frontier of the Arnon, on the edge of the frontier. Balaam said to Balak, "I am here with you. What power have I to say anything? Whatever God puts into my mouth, that is what I will say."

Balaam's Oracles. Balaam said to Balak, "Erect seven altars here[1] and prepare for me seven bulls and seven rams." Balak did as Balaam had said, and they both offered a bull and a ram on each altar. Balam said to Balak, "Stay here with your sacrifice and let me go off by myself. The Lord might come to meet me; what he says to me, I will tell you."

First Oracle. Balaam uttered his oracle[2]:

"Balak king of Moab has brough me from the mountains of
      Quedem:
Come, lay a curse on Jacob, come, execrate Israel.
How could I curse if God does not curse?
How could I execrate if God does not execrate?

From the rocky heights I see them, I watch them from the top of the hills. It is a people that dwells alone, that has not made itself one with the nations. Who could count the dust of Jacob[3]? Who could number the sands of Israel. Let me die as the righteous men do! Grant that my end may be as theirs!

Balak said to Balaam, "What have you done to me? I sent you to curse my enemies, and you have blessed them." Balaam said, "Must I not utter the words that the Lord puts in my mouth?"

Second Oracle. Balaam uttered this oracle:

"Come up, Balak, and listen:
I have received command to bless; I shall bless, and I cannot
      gainsay it.
I see no iniquity in Jacob, nor perversity in Israel.

---

1. Where his idol Chamos was worshipped. He intends to worship his gods, but they are not valid. He will do as the Lord says.
2. Balaam spoke only what God said to him, although in his poetic language, as he used to do.
3. Jacob was the people of Israel.

The Lord, his God, is with him, aclaimed as king among them.
The god that brought them from Egypt is as the curving horns
      are to the wild ox.
For there is no divination against Jacob, or augury against
      Israel[1].
See a people rearing up like a lioness,
      rampant like a lion,
        that does not couch till he devours the prey
        and drinks the blood of the slain."

Balak said to Balaam, "If you cannot curse them, at least do not bless them." Balaam replied to Balak, "Had I not told you, 'I will do as the Lord[2] says to me?'"

Third Oracle. Balaam saw that the Lord wished to bless Israel, and he did not resort to divination as before. He turned towards the desert, and, when he looked up, he saw Israel encamped by tribes. The spirit of God came over him and he uttered his oracle:

"Oracle of Balaam, son of Beor,
      oracle of the man whose sight is clear.
How beautiful are your tents, Jacob,
      and your dwelling-places, Israel!
As vallies stretching out,
      like gardens by the banks of a river,
      like lign-aloes planted by the Lord,
      like cedars beside the water!
A heroe is growing among his descendants,
      who rules over powerful peoples.
      His kingdom shall be over Agag,
      where his kingship is exalted.
Blessed be the one who blesses him,
      and cursed the one that curses him!"

---

1. His powers are not valid.
2. Balaam did not speak like a magician or a sorcerer of the gods, but inspired by the truly God, constrained by Him, and he did not let himself be blinded by the gold that Balak promised him.

Balak was very angry with Balaam and, beating his hands together, he said to him, "I sent you to curse my enemies and you have blessed them three times already. Go home. I intended to confer great honour upon you, but the Lord has kept them from you." Balaam answered Balak, "But I told your own messengers whom you sent, 'Even if Balak gives me all the silver and gold in his house, I could not disobey the command of the Lord, or do anything of my own will, good or bad. What the Lord speaks, that is what I will say faithfully' Now I shall leave with my people; see what this people will do to yours in the days to come."

Fourth Oracle. And he uttered his oracle:

"Oracle of Balaam, son of Beor,
  oracle of the man whose sight is clear,
oracle of the one who hears the words of God, who shares the
  knowledge of the Most High.
  I see what Sadai makes him see,
  he falls and his eyes are open.
I see him, but not now[1],
  I behold him, but not near:
  a star comes forth out of Jacob,
  a comet arise from Israel.
  It smashes the heads of Moab,
  and the skulls of the sons of Set.
Edom shall be his,
  and Seir will be his possession.
  Israel shall do valiant deeds.
Jacob will rule over his enemies,
  and destroy the last survivors from Ar.

Balaam arose and returned home, and Balak also went his way.

---

1. Prediction of future. Messianic announcement. A powerful king under the image of a star and a sceptre, the promised Messiah. It has been understood in this way by Jews and Christians.

2. NEW DISPOSITIONS

New List of the People. After the plague, the Lord spoke to Moses and Eleazar, son of Aaron, priest, and said to them: "Number the whole community of the sons of Israel who are over twenty fit for military service by fathers." Moses and Eleazar the priest spoke to them on the Plains of Moab, by the Jordan near Jericho. The total number of sons of Israel was 601,730[1].

Josuah is elected Moses' successor. The Lord said to Moses, "Go up this mountain, Mount Abarim, and look over the land which I am going to give to the sons of Israel.

When you have looked over it, you shall be gathered to your relatives, like Aaron, your brother, for you were rebels in the desert of Zin when the community disputed with me as I told you to uphold my holiness before them at the waters." (These are the waters of Meribah[2]-by-Kadesh, in the desert of Zin.)

The Lord replied to Moses, "Take Josuah, son of Nun, a man endowed with spirit, and put your hand over him. Set him before Eleazar, the priest, and the whole community, and in their presence your shall give him commandments and delegate him part of your authority, so that the whole community of the sons of Israel obeys him. He shall go before Eleazar, the priest, who will obtain for him the decision of the Urim[3] before the Lord. At his word they shall go out, both Josuah and the whole community of the sons of Israel."

Moses did as the Lord had commanded him. He took Josuah, presented him to Eleazar the priest and, before the whole community put his hands on him and gave him his commission, as the Lord had told him.

---

1. It was the second time that Moses made a list of the Israelites. At the beginning and at the end of their pilgrimage across the desert.
2. It means rebellion. The people rebelled because they lacked water at Massa, a place in the desert.
3. Oracle of the Lord.

DEUTERONOMY

PART ONE

MOSES' PRIMARY CHARGE

Introduction. On the first day of the eleventh month of the fortieth year, Moses spoke to the sons of Israel as the Lord had commanded him.

Josuah is elected Moses' successor. Then I pleaded with the Lord and said to him, "Oh, Lord, You have begun to show to your servant the greatness and the power of your arm, for is there any god in heaven or earth that can match your works and deeds? Allow me to cross over and see that rich land that lies beyond the Jordan, that fine country and the Lebanon." But the Lord was angry with me because of you and did not listen to me. He said, "Enough!, say no more about this! Go to the top of Pisgah[1] and look west, north, south and east, and look well at what you see, for you shall not cross the Jordan. Give instructions to Josuah, encourage him and strenghten him, for it is him who will lead this people across, and who will put them

---

1. Pisgah, mountain of the Nebo range, from which Moses watched the Promised Land.

in possession of the land you see before you." And so we stayed in the valley, very near Beth-peor[1].

Exhortation to the Observance of the Law. Now, then Israel, listen to the statutes and laws that I will teach you, and put them into practice so that you have life and occupy the land which the Lord gives you, the God of your fathers.

Keep them and carry them out, and they shall make you wise and understanding before the peoples. When they hear about these statures they will say, "What a wise and understanding people is this great nation!. True, what nation is so great that its gods are close at hand as the Lord our God is close to us whenever we call to him? What great nation is there that whose statutes and laws are just, as is all this Law that I am setting before you today? Be careful, and do not forget what you have seen with your eyes so that it never leaves your heart, but teach them to your sons, and to the sons of your sons. Remember the day in which you were before the Lord, your God, at Hobreb, when the Lord said to me, "Gather your people around me so that I can let them hear my words and may learn to fear me all their lives on earth and they may teach their children to do so." You came near and stood at the food of the mountain, while it was ablaze with fire that reached the heart of the sky; darkness, cloud and thick mist. Then the Lord spoke to us from the middle of the fire. You heard the voice speaking, but did not see any figure; you only heard the voice. The Lord announced his covenant to you, and commanded you to put it into practice; on two tablets of stone he wrote the Ten Commandments. At the same time he charged me to teach you the statutes and laws that you should observe in the land in which you are about to occupy.

Condemnation of Idolatry. Be careful! On the day in which the Lord spoke to you from the middle of the fire in the Horeb you saw no figure of any kind, so take care not to fall into the degradation of making carved figures of any kind, in the form of a man or woman, of an animal that lives on the

---

1. Place or village at the foot of the mountain where Moses was buried, by the Jordan.

ground or bird that flies in the air, of reptile that teems on the ground or fish that lives under the waters. Nor must you raise your eyes to the sky and, seeing the sun, the moon, the stars and all the host of heaven, let you to bow down to them to worship them.

Only One God. Search into the days gone by, long before your time, beginning at the day in which God created man on the earth, from one end of heaven to the other, has any thing or deed so great ever been heard or seen? Or has any people heard the voice of their God speaking out of the fire as you have done, and remain alive? Or did ever a god attempt to take a nation for himself away from another nation, with a challenge, and with signs, portents, and wars, with a strong hand and an outstretched arm, and with great deeds of terror, as the Lord your God did for you in Egypt in the sight of you all? You have seen all this so that you know that the Lord is the true God, and that there is no other. Observe his laws and commandments which I give you today so that you may be happy, and your sons after you, and that you may live long in the land that the Lord, your God, gives you."

PART TWO

MOSES' SECONDARY CHARGE

The Ten Commandments. Moses summoned all Israel and said to them, "Listen, oh, Israel, to the laws and commandments that today I proclaim in your hearing. Learn them and be careful to observe them. The Lord our God[1] made a Covenant with us at Horeb. The Lord did not make this Covenant with our fathers, he made it with us, that live here today. The Lord spoke to us face to face on the mountain out of the fire. I was by them between the Lord and you to report the words of the Lord, because you did not go up the mountain for fear of the fire. He said, 'I am the Lord, you God, who has brought you out of the land of Egypt, the land of slavery. I shall be your only God'."

Moses reports the people the words of the Lord. Listen carefully and do as the Lord says. Do not turn from it to

right or to left. Follow the way that the Lord, your God, has shown to you; in this way you shall live and be happy, and you will live long in the land which you are to possess.

Call to the Love of God. Listen, oh, Israel: The Lord, our God, is the one Lord. Love the Lord, your God, with all your heart, with all your soul and all your strength. Keep in your heart the words that I say to you today. Teach them to your sons, and repeat those words to them when you are abroad, when you lie down and when you rise. Bind them as a sign on

---

1. The Lord set his Laws to be worshipped. The Commandments received at Mount Sinai were the terms of the Covenant, signed with his people.

the hand and wear them as a phylactery on the forehead; write them up on the doorposts and on the gates of your houses[1].

When the Lord, your God, has led you to the land which he swore to your forefathers Abram, Isaac and Jacob, and has given you as a possession the great and rich cities which you did not built, the houses full of good things which you did not provide, the cisterns that you did not hew, do not forget the Lord, who brought you out of the land of Egypt, land of slavery. Fear the Lord, your God, serve him alone and take your oaths in his name.

The Trials of the Desert. Your clothes did not wear out, nor did your feet swell all these forty years. You shall learn, thus, that the Lord, your God, disciplines you as a father disciplines his son. Keep the commandments of the Lord, your God, follow his path and fear him. The Lord, your God, will bring you to a rich land, a land of streams, of springs and underground waters gushing out in hill and valley, a land of wheat and barley, of vines, fig-trees, and pomegranates, a land of olives, oil, and honey. It is a land where you will never live in poverty nor want for anything, a land whose stones are iron-ore and whose hills you will dig copper. You will have plenty to eat and will bless the Lord your God for the rich land that he has given you.

The Victory is thanks to the Lord, not to the deeds of the people. Listen, Israel, you are about to cross the Jordan to occupy the territory of nations greater and more powerful than you, and great cities with walls towering the sky. It is a numerous people, of tall people, descendants of the Anakim, of whom you know already and of whom you have heard, "Who can withstand the sons of Anak?" Know from today that it is the Lord, your God, who goes ahead of you as a devouring fire that shall destroy them. He will subdue them and you shall drive them out and overwhelm them, as the Lord promised you. When the Lord, your God, has driven them out before you, do not say to yourselves, "Because I am a fair man the Lord has given to me the possession of this land", while because of their

---

1. Some Jews took them seriously: some of the important ones would stich them to their clothes and stack texts from the Law on their foreheads.

iniquity he is driving those peoples out far from you. It is not because of your merit or your integrity that you are entering their land to occupy it; it is because of the wickedness of these nations[1] that the Lord your God is driving them out before you; and also to fulfil the promise which he made to your fathers, Abram, Isaac and Jacob. Know then that it is not because of any merit of yours that the Lord your God is giving you this rich land to occupy; indeed, you are a stubborn people.

You have been rebels to the Lord since the very day he knew you. When your fathers came down to Egypt there were 70 of you, and now, the Lord, your God, has made you countless as the stars in the sky.

---

1. They worshipped false gods, were idolaters, of wicked habits; they even had human sacrifices, sacred prostitution and bestiality.

GOD'S LAWS DELIVERED
TO MOSES

The Prophets. When you enter the land which the Lord, your God, is giving you, do not imitate the abominable customs of those peoples which inhabit it now.

I will raise up for them a prophet[1] like you, one of their own race, and I will put my words into his mouth, and he shall say as I command him. If anyone does not listen to the words he shall say in my name, I will require satisfaction to him. But the prophet who presumes to utter in my name what I have not commanded him or who speaks in the name of other gods: that prophet shall die.

If you ask yourselves, How can I know the word that the Lord has not uttered?, this is the answer: When the word spoken by the prophet in the name of the Lord is not fulfilled and does not come true, it is not a word spoken by the Lord. The prophet has spoken presumptuously, do not fear him.

Protection of the Israelite. You shall not charge interest on anything you lend to a fellow-countryman, money or food or anything else on which interest can be charged. You may charge interest on a loan to a foreigner but not on a loan to a

---

1. The Law of the 10 Commandments. Supreme Law, superior to all human laws. It is based on the natural law in everyone's heart. The Mosaic law was intended for the Jews.

fellow-countryman, for then the Lord your God will bless you in all you undertake in the land which you are entering to occupy.

When you go into another man's vineyard, you may eat as many grapes as you wish to satisfy your hunger, but you may not put any into your basket. When you go into another man's standing corn, you may pluck ears to rub in your hands, but you may not put a sickle to his standing corn.

Humanity and Moderation. You shall not keep back the wages of a man who is poor and needy, whether a fellow-countryman or an alien living in your country in one of your settlements. Pay him his wages on the same day before sunset, for he is poor and his heart is set on them: he may appeal to the Lord against you, and you will be guilty of sin.

Justice and Moderation. When two men go to law and present themselves for judgement, the judges shall try the case; they shall acquit the innocent and condemn the guilty. If the guilty man is sentenced to be flogged, the judge shall cause him to lie down and be beaten in his presence; the number of strokes shall correspond to the gravity of the offence. They may give him forty strokes, but no more; otherwise, if they go further and exceed this number, your fellow-countryman will have been publicly degraded.

You shall not muzzle an ox while it is treading out the corn.

Levi's Law. When two brothers live together and one of them dies without leaving a son, his widow shall not marry outside the family. Her husband's brother shall have intercourse with her; he shall take her in marriage and do his duty by her as her husband's brother. The first son she bears shall perpetuate the dead brother's name, so that it may not be blotted out from Israel.

PART FOUR

THIRD CHARGE
AND END OF MOSES

Israel before Life and Death. Look, today I put before you life and hapiness, death and misery. If you observe the commandments of the Lord, your God, that I give you today, if you love the Lord, your God, if you follow his way, observe his commandments, laws and statutes, you shall live and multiply, and the Lord, your God, shall bless you in the land in which you are to enter to possess it. But if your heart turns astray, if you do not obbey and let yourself be led to bow down and worship other gods, I tell you this day that you will perish; you will not live long in the land which you will enter to occupy after crossing the Jordan. I summon heaven and earth to witness against you today. I offer you the choice of life or death, blessing or curse. Choose life and then you and your descendants will live; love the Lord your God, obey him and hold fast to him: that is life for you and length of days in the land which the Lord swore to give to your fathers, Abram, Isaac and Jacob.

Josuah's Mission. Moses still said this words to the people of Israel: "I am one hundred and twenty years old, I cannot not longer move about as I please. Besides, the Lord has said to me. "You shall not cross the Jordan." It is the Lord, your God, who shall cross it before you; it is him who will destroy these nations before you. From now on it is Josuah who shall lead you across, as the Lord has said. The Lord will do to them as he did to Sihon with Og, kings of the Amorites, and to their land; he will destroy them. He will deliver them into your hands, and you will do to them as I have commanded you. Be strong, be resolute; do not dread them or be afraid, for the Lord, your God, is with you. He will not leave or fail you." Then Moses called Josuah[1] and said to him before the whole Israel, "Be strong, be resolute, for you must lead this people into the land which the Lord swore to give their fathers; it is you who are to bring them into possession of it. The Lord shall go at your head, He will be with you, he will not leave you or fail you; do not be abraid or discouraged."

Instructions regarding Josuah and the Song of Moses. Then the Lord said to Moses, "The day of your death is drawing near. Call Josuah and come to the Tent of the Presence so that I may give him his comission." Moses and Josuah took their stand in the Tent of the Presence, and the Lord appeared in the Tent in a pillar of clour that stood at the entrance to the Tent.

The Lord said to Moses, "You are here to sleep[2] with your fathers. This people is going to go wantonly after foreign gods, those gods of the peoples which inhabit the land now. They will abandon me and break the Covenant which I have made with them. But then my anger will be roused, and I will abandon them and hide my face from them. Terrible disasters will come upon them. Then they shall say, "If these disasters have come it is probably because our God is not among us." Yes, I shall hide my face from them, because of all the evil they have done in turning to other gods.

When I have introduced them into the land which I swore to their fathers, a land flowing milk and honey, when they have had plenty to eat and have grown fat, then shall turn to other gods, which they will worship, and they will spurn me and break my Covenant. Yes, I know which way their thoughts incline already, before I have introduced them into the land which I swore them."

---

1. Josuah will be his successor, God will be with him.

2. The sleep of death

And the Lord gave Joshua, son of Nun, his commission, and said to him, "Be strong, be resolute, for it is you who shall bring the sons of Israel into the land which I swore them; I shall be with you."

Death of Moses. Moses went up from the Plains of Moab to mount Nebo, to the top of Pishgah, opposite Jericho. And the Lord showed him the whole land: Gilead as far as Dan, the whole of Naphtali, the land of Ephraim and Manasseh, the whole land of Judah as far as the Western Sea, the Negeb and the valley of Jericho, the Vale of Palm Trees, as far as Zoar.

And he said to Moses, "This is the land which I swore to Abram, Isaac and Jacob in these words: 'I shall give this land to your descendancy. You can see it with your eyes, but you will not cross over into it'." Moses, servant of God, died there, in the Plains of Moab, as the Lord had commanded. The Lord buried him in the valley, in the land of Moab, opposite Beth-peor, and so far nobody knows his burial-place. When he died Moses was one hundred and twenty years old. His sight had not dimmed nor had his vigour failed. The sons of Israel mourned him for thirty days in the Plains of Moab, then the time of mourning for Moses was ended. Joshua, son of Nun, was filled with the spirit of wisdom, because Moses had laid his hands on him. The sons of Israel obeyed him as the Lord had commanded.

JOSHUA

PART ONE

CONQUEST OF THE PROMISED LAND

Preparation for the conquest. Fidelity to the Law. After the death of Moses, servant of the Lord, the Lord spoke to Joshua, son of Nun and assistant of Moses, and said to him, "Moses, my servant, has died. Now it is for you to cross the Jordan, which you can see now, you and you people, towards the land which I give to the sons of Israel. Every place where you set foot is yours, as I said to Moses. From the desert and the Lebanon to the Great River, the river Euphrates, and the Great Sea, towards the west, shall be your country. No one will ever be able to stand against you all your life; I shall be with you as I was with Moses, I shall not leave you nor fail you. Be strong, be resolute, for you shall give this people the possession of the land which I swore I would give to their fathers. Only be strong and resolute, and observe faithfully the laws and commandments which Moses, my servant, has given you; do not turn from it to right or left, and you will prosper wherever you go. The book of this Law shall always be on your lips; think over it day and night to fulfil exactly everything that is written on it. In this way you shall be successful in all that you do. Have I not commanded you, 'Be strong, because the Lord, your God, is with you wherever you go[1].'"

Invitation to the tribes on the other side of the Jordan. Then Joshua told the officers to pass through the people the following order, "Go throught the camp and pass the following order, Get food ready, for in the next three days you shall cross the Jordan to occupy the land which the Lord, your God, gives you to possess."

The seekers of Jericho. Then Joshua, son of Nun, sent two spies out from Shittim[2] secretly with the following order, "Go and explore the land of Jericho." They left and came into the house[3] of a prostitute named Rahab, and spent the night there. The king of Jericho was reported the news in the following way, "Some Israelites have arrived tonight to explore the country." Then the king sent to Rahab and said, "Bring out the men that came to your house because they have come to explore the whole country." But the woman took the two men, hid them and said, "It is true, they came to me, but I did not know where they came from; at nightfall, when it was time to shut the gate of the city, they left and I do not know where they went. Hurry up and you will catch them up!" But she had taken them up onto the roof and had hidden them among the stalks of flax which she had laid out there in rows. The messengers of the king went in pursuit down the Rod to the Jordan, towards the fords, and the gate was closed as soon as they had gone out.

Deal between Rahab and the seekers. They had not yet gone to bed when she took them on to the roof and said to them, "I know that the Lord has given this land to you, that the fear of your name has descended upon you, and that every inhabitant of the earth is panic-stricken. For we have heard how the Lord dried up the waters of the Red Sea before you when you came out of Egypt and how have you treated the two Amorite kings beyond

---

1. Good hopes and promises if he observes the law.
2. Last post of the Israelites before crossing the Jordan, opposite Jericho.
3. According to other sources, an inn. It was probably the first one they came across.

the Jordan, Sion and Og, to whom you have handed in the anathema[1]. When we heard this our strength has failed, and there is no spirit left in any of us, because the Lord, our God, is God in heaven above and in earth below. However, I beg you to swear by the Lord that as I have treated you well, that you spare the house of my father, and that you five me a sign; promise that you will spare the lives of my father and my mother, my brothers and sisters and their relatives, and that you will save us from death." The men replied, "We would die in your place so that you would not tell anybody about this deal; when the Lord gives us this land, we will deal honestly with you and faithfully."

The seekers come back. Then she let them down with a rope through the window, for her home was attached to the wall, and she herself lived over the wall. And she said to them, "Go to the mountain so that those who pursue you do not find you; remain there for three days until the seekers come back and then go your way." The men replied, "We shall be free from the oath we have taken if you not do so: when we enter this land, you shall fasten this strand of scarlet cord, in the opening through which you have lowered us, and you shall gather with you, at home, your father, your mother, your brothers and sisters and all your family. If anybody goes out of doors in the street, his blood shall be on his own head, and we will be innocent; but those of you who are with you indoors, his blood will blood over our head if somebody touches him. But if you betray our business, we shall quit of the oath which you have made us take." She answered, "Let it be as you say." Then she sent them away. They went off, and she fastened the strand of scarled cord to the window.

The men left, came to the mountain and remained there for three days until their pursuers returned, who searched everywhere and did not find them. Then the two spies returned as well. They came down the mountain, crossed the river and returned to Joshua son of Nun. They told him all that had

---

1. Anathema (the herem. hebr. = exclude). The part separated by God, absolute lord of everything. Something like his loot in the disaster.

happened to them. And they said to Joshua, "The Lord has given all this land to us, for all its peoples are panic-stricken at our approach."

Preparation to cross the Jordan. Joshua rose up early in the morning and set out from Shittim with all the sons of Israel. They came to the Jordan; there they stayed overnight before crossing it. Joshua said to the people, "Hallow yourselves[1], because tomorrow the Lord shall make a great miracle among you." And to the priests he said, "Take the Ark of the Covenant and go ahead of the people." They took the Ark of the Covenant and went ahead of the people.

Last dispositions. Then the Lord said to Joshua, "Today I shall make you great before the eyes of Israel, so that they know that I am with you as I was with Moses. You shall give this order to the priests that carry the Ark: when you come to the edge of the waters of the Jordan, they are to take their stand in the river."

Crossing of the Jordan. When the people set out from their tents to cross the Jordan, they came to the Jordan, and the feet of the priests that were carrying the Ark touched the edge of the water —the Jordan is in full flood in all its reaches throughout the time of harvest—, the waters that came downstream were brought to a standstill, and piled up like a bank for a long way back, as far as Adam[2], to the city which is near Zarethan, and those which came down to the Sea of the Arabah, the Dead Sea[3] Those priests who carried the Ark of the Covenant stood firm on the dry bed in the middle of the Jordan, while the whole Israel crossed over on dry ground until the whole people had crossed the Jordan.

The Ark, in the middle of the Jordan. The priests who were carrying the Ark of the Covenant stood firm on dry bed inthe middle of the Jordan until all the promises of the Lord to

---

1. Purify yourselves.
2. Adam, city two kilometers from the Jordan, on the west.
3. Dead Sea: It is called as such because it has no life, animal or plants. It has 85x15 km in its surface, 401 m deep and it is 390 m under the Mediterranean Sea.

Joshua were fulfilled. The people hurried to cross over. Once the people had passed over, the Ark of the Lord passed, and the priests stood ahead of the people.

The Lord said to Joshua, "Tell the priests who carry the Ark of the Covenant to come out of the Jordan." Joshua told the priests, "Come out of the Jordan". And it happened that, once the priests who carried the Ark of the Covenant were out of the river, the waters came back to their place and filled up all their reaches as before.

Conquest of Jericho. Jericho was bolted and barred against the sons of Israel; no one went out, no one came in. Then the Lord said to Joshua, "Look, I have delivered Jericho and her king into your hands. You shall march round the city with all your fighting men, making the circuit of it once, for six days running. Seven priests shall go in front of the Ark carrying seven trumpets. At the blast of the ram's horns, whe whole army shall raise a great shout. Then the wall of the city will collapse and the people shall advance, every man straight ahead.

Joshua had said to the people, "Do not shout, raise your voice or utter a word till the day when you are told, 'Shout!' comes, then you shall shout."

Pilgrimage around Jericho. The Ark of the Lord went around the city once; then they all went back to the camp, where they spent the night. Joshua rose early in the morning and the priests took the Ark of the Lord. The seven priests who carried the seven trumpets of ram's horns marched in front of the Ark of the Lord, blowing his trumpets as they went; the drafted men were in front of them, and the rearguard following the Ark of the Lord, the trumpets sounding as they marched. On the second day they went around the city as well, and then they came back to the camp. They did this for six days. On the seventh day they rose at dawn, and went around the city in the same way, that was the only day on which they marched round seven times. The seventh time the priests blew their trumpets and Joshua said to the people, "Shout!, for the Lord has given you the city."

Jericho under the ban. "This city shall be under solemn ban: everything in it belongs to the Lord. No one is to be spared except the prostitute Rahab and everyone who is with her in the house, because she hid the men whom we sent. And you must beware of coveting anything that is forbidden under the ban; you must take none of it for yourselves; this would put the Israelite camp itself under the ban and bring trouble on it. All the silver and gold, all the vessels of copper and iron, shall be holy; they belong to the Lord and they must go into the Lord's treasury." So they blew the trumpets, and the people raised a great shout, and down fell the walls. The people advanced on the city, every man straight ahead, and they took the city. And the put under the ban everything in the city.

Rahab and her family's salvation. Joshua said to the two spies who had explored the land, "Go into the prostitute's house and bring out her and her relatives, as you swore to do." The young spies went into her house and brought her out, her father, her mother and her brothers and sisters with all their belongings.

Joshua spared the lives of Rahab, the prostitute and his family with all their belongings.

The Lord went with Joshua, and his fame spread throughout the country.

The expedition against Ai fails. About three thousand men of the people went up to Ai, but they turned tail before the men of Ai. The men of Ai killed thirty-six men, and they pursued them from the door to Shebarim, and killed them on the pass. The courage of the people melted and flowed away like water.

Ambush against Ai. Joshua prepared his army to attack Ai. He roused early in the morning, mustered the army and marched against Ai, he himself and the elders of Israel at the head of the people. All the armed forces who were with him marched on until they came within sight of the city. They encamped north of Ai. Between him and Ai there was a valley. Joshua took five thousand men and set them in ambush between Bethel and Ai, west of the city. The people encamped north of the city; the ambush was west of the city. Joshua spent the night in the camp.

When the king of Ai saw the situation, he hurried to do battle against Israel, he himself and all his people, in the hill before the Arabah, but he did not know that there was an ambush set for him behind the city. Joshua and all Israel made as if they were routed by them and fled towards the desert. Then all the people in the city pursued them, and were drawn away from the city. There was nobody left in Ai, they had all gone in pursuit of the Israelites, and in their pursuit they had left the city undefended.

Conquest of Ai. Then the Lord said to Joshua, "Point towards Ai with the dagger you are holding, for I will deliver the city into your hands." So Joshua pointed the dagger he was holding towards the city. When he stretched out his hand, the men in ambush rose quickly from their places and, entering the city at a run, took it and promptly set fire to it.

When the people of Ai looked back they were powerless to escape in any direction, because the people that fled towards the desert turned on their pursuers. Those who had come out to meet the Israelites were now hemmed in with the Israelites on both sides of them, and the Israelites cut them down until there was not a single survivor, nor had any escaped.

Conquest of Southern Palestine. When the news of these happenings reached all the kings west of the Jordan, in the hill-country, the Shephelah, and all the coast of the Great Sea running up to the Lebanon, the kings of the Hittites, Amorites, Canaanites, Perizzites, Hivites, and Jebusites agreed to join forces and fight against Joshua and Israel.

Alliance of five Southern kings against Gibeon. When Adoni-zedeck king of Jerusalem heard that Joshua had captured Ai and destroyed it, dealing with Ai and her king as he had dealt with Jericho and her king, and that the inhabitants of Gibeon had made their peace with Israel and were living among them, he was greatly alarmed; for Gibeon[1] was a large place, like a royal city, it was larger than Ai, and all his men were brave. So Adoni-zedeck king of Jerusalem sent to Hoham king of Hebron, Piram king of Jarmuth, Japhia king of Lachiish, and Debir king of Eglon, and said, "Come up and help me, and we will attack the Gibeonites, because they have made their peace with Joshua and the Israelites." So the five Amorite kings joined forces and

---

1. The Gibeonites had come to Joshua as if they had come from foreign lands and had signed an agreement with the Israelites, that is why they lived near them. Gibeon was near.

advanced to take up their positions for the attack on Gibeon. They encamped near the city and attacked it.

Joshua helps the Gibeonites. The people of Gibeon sent this message to Joshua to the camp at Gilgal, "Do not abandon us, your servants. Come quickly to our relief, for the Amorite kings that live in the hill-country have joined their forces against us." Joshua went up to Gilgal with his army, his best fighting men. The Lord said to Joshua, "Do not fear them, for I have delivered them into your hands, none of them will be able to stand against you." Joshua came upon them suddenly, after marching all night from Gilgal.

The Lord threw them into confusion before the Israelites, and Joshua defeated them utterly in Gibeon; he pursued them down the pass of Beth-horon and kept up the slaughter as far as Azekah and Makkedah[1]. As they were fleeing from Israel down the pass of Beth-horon[2], the Lord hurled great hailstones at them out of the sky all the way to Azekah, and many of them died. More died from the hailstones than the Israelites slew by the sword. Then Joshua spoke to the Lord on the day in which the Lord delivered the Amorites into the hands of Israel, and he said,

"Oh sun, stand still over Gibeon,
       and you, moon, over the Vale of Aijalon."

And the sun stood still and the sun halted until the people had taken vengeance on its enemies[3].

Conquest of the Southern cities. On that same day Joshua captured Makkedah; he did to the king of Makkedah what he had done to the king of Jericho. Then Joshua, and all Israel with him, moved from Makkedah to Libnah and attacked it. The Lord delivered the two, the city and his king, into the hands of

---

1. Place of refuge of the five kings.
2. From the top to the plain.
3. Miraculous intervention of the Author of the sun and the moon. It could have been limited to the battlefield, in the same way as the sun showed at Fatima and to the Pope Pius XII.

Israel, that put his people to the sword. And they dealt with his king as they had dealt with the king of Jericho.

Then Joshua with all Israel marched on from Libnah to Lachish. They took their positions and attacked it. The Lord delivered Lachish into the hands of Israel, and they captured it on the second day, as they had done with Libnah. Then the king of Gezer, Horam, advanced to help Lachish, but Joshua struck them and his people down until no survivor was left. Then Joshuah and all Israel moved on from Lachish to Eglon, took up their positions and attacked it. They took it on that very day, and put his inhabitants to the sword, as he had done with Lachish. From Eglon Joshua and all Israel marched on Hebron and attacked it. He captured it and put its inhabitants to the sword, as he had done with Eglon.

Then Joshua, and all Israel with him, went round towards Debir and attacked it. He captured it with its king and all its villages. He dealt with Dabir and his king as he had dealt with Hebron, Libnah and their king. Joshua conquered all the region: the mountain, the Negeb, the Shephelah, the watersheds and all their kings. Joshua carried the slaughter from Kadesh-barnea to Gaza, over the whole land of Goshen as far as Gibeon.

Joshua captured all these kings and their territories at the same time, for the Lord, God of Israel, fought for Israel. Then Joshua and all Israel came back to the camp at Gilgal[1].

Conquest of Northern Palestine. Alliance of the kings of the North. When Jabin king of Hazor heard of all this, he sent to Jobab king of Madon, to the kings of Shimron and Akshaph, and to the northern kings in the hill-country and in the plains of Kinnereth, and in the district of Dor on the west. They took the field with all their forces, countless as the grains of sand on the sea-shore, among them a great number of horses and chariots.

Victory over the waters of Merom[2]. All these kings made common cause, and encamped together at the waters of Merom to fight against Israel. And the Lord said to Moses, "Do not fear

1. With this expedition the conquest of Southern Palestine was completed. Gilgal was the main camp.

2. Small lake of the Jordan, between his wells and Tiberiades.

them, for tomorrow, at this time, I shall deliver them dead
before Israel; you shall hamstring their horses and burn their
chariots." Joshua and his army surprised them by the waters of
Merom and fell upon them. The Lord delivered them into the
hands of Israel, they struck them down and pursued them as far
as Greater Sidon, Misrephoth on the west, and the Vale of
Mizpah on the east. They struck them down until not a man was
left alive. Joshua dealt with them as the Lord had told him: he
hamstrung their horses and burnt their chariots.

In this way Joshua took the whole country: the hill country,
all the Negeb, all the land of Goshen, the Shephelah, the
Arabah, and the Israelite hill-country with the adjoining
lowlands from the mountain that leads up to Seir as far as
Baal-gad in the Vale of Lebanon under Mount Hermon. He took
all their kings, struck them down and put them to death. Joshue
fought a long was against all these kings.

PART TWO

THE DIVISION OF THE LAND AMONG THE TRIBES

Joshua became very old. Then the Lord said to him, "You are now a very old man, and there is a lot of land that remains to be occupied."

Division of the East Bank[1]. The moment has come to divide this land among the nine tribes and half the tribe of Manasseh. For half the tribe of the Reubenites and the Gadites had each taken their patrimony which Moses gave them east of the Jordan, as Moses the servant of the Lord had ordained. Only the tribe of Levi received no patrimony: the Lord the God of Israel is their patrimony, as He promised them.

Division of West Bank[2]. This is what the sons of Israel inherited in Canaan, allotted by Eleazar, priest, Joshua, son of Nun, and the heads of the families of the tribes of Israel. The division was made by lot, as the Lord had commanded Moses, among the nine and a half tribes, because Moses had already given the other two their inheritance beyond the Jordan. The sons of Joseph formed two tribes: Manasseh and Efraim.

---

1. The western part of the Jordan was for the tribes of Reuben and Gad, given by Moses and Manasseh, except that of Levi.
2. The Eastern part was divided among the nine and a half tribes of Manasseh that were left.

PART THREE

JOSHUA'S LAST DISPOSITIONS

The great Assembly of Shechem[1]. Joshua assembled all the tribes of Israel, their heads, judges and officers at Shechem, and they presented themselves before God. Joshua said to the people, "This is the word of the Lord, God of Israel: 'I have given you a land on which you have not laboured, cities which you have not built and in which you dwell; you eat the fruits of the vineyards and the olive-groves which you have not planted.'

Now hold the Lord in awe, and worship him loyally and truthfully. Banish the gods whom your fathers worshipped beyond the river and in Egypt and worship the Lord. If it does not please you to worship the Lord, choose here and now whom you want to worship, either the gods whom your fathers worshipped beyond the river or the gods of the Amorires, in whose land you dwell. I and my family shall worship the Lord."

Israel swears to worship the Lord. The people answered, "God forbid that we sould forsake the Lord to worship other Gods, for the Lord is our God."

Joshua said to the people, "You cannot worship the Lord, for he is a holy god, a jealous god, and he will not forgive your rebellion and your sins. But if you forsake the Lord to worship

---

1. Historical place among the mountains. Hebal and Garitzin, in the middle of the country. There built Abram an altar; Jacob opened a well and pinched his tents.

foreign gods, he will turn against you and, although he brought you so much prosperity, he will make an end of you."

The people answered to Joshua, "No! We want to worship the Lord." Then Joshua said to the people, "You are witnesses against yourselves that you have chosen to worship the Lord." And they replied, "We are witnesses." "Then banish the foreign god that are among you, and turn your heard to the Lord, God of Israel." The peole answered to Joshua, "We shall worship the Lord, our Lord, and we shall obey his voice."

Covenant of Shechem[1]. On that day Joshua made a covenant with the people; he drew up an statute and an ordinance for them in Shechem and wrote its terms in the book of the law of God. Then he took a great stone and set it up there under the terebinth in the Sanctuary of the Lord. And Joshua said to all the people, "This stone shall be the witness against ourselves, because it has heard every word which the Lord has spoken to us. It shall be a witness against you if you renounce your God. Then Joshua dismissed the people, each man to his patrimony.

Death of Joseph. After these facts, Joshua son of Nun, servant of the Lord, died at the age of one hundred and ten years. He was buried in his patrimony, in Timnah-serah in the hill country of Efraim to the north of Mount Gaash.

Israel served the Lord during the lifetime of Joshua and during the lifetime of the elders who outlived him and who well knew all that the Lord had made for Israel.

The bones of Joshua, brought from Egypt by the sons of Israel, were buried in Sechem, in the plot of land which Jacob had bought from the sons of Hamor father of Shechem for a hundred silver coins, and they passed into the patrimony of the sons of Jacob.

Eleazar son of Aaron died, and he was buried in Geba, city of his son Phineas, to whom it had been given in the hill-country of Ephraim.

---

1. Before dying he wanted to renew the Covenant of the Sinai. All promised fidelity. The covenant of Shechem seals the unity of the tribes in a theocratic regime.

JUDGES

PART ONE

THE TRIBES OF ISRAEL
IN CANAAN

Southern tribes. After the death of Joshua the Israelites asked the Lord, "Which tribe should attack the Canaanites first?". And the Lord answered, "Judah shall go first, I have delivered the country into his hands." Then Judah said to Simeon, his brother: "Come with me to the land that has been allotted to me to do battle with the Canaanites. Then I shall go with you into your territory." And Simeon went with him. So Judah advanced, and the Lord delivered the Canaanites and the Perizzites into their hands.

Then Judah went with Simeon, his brother. They defeated the Canaanites who lived in Zephath and they destroyed them. That is why that city was named Hormah. They followed the commandments of Moses; Hebron was given to Caleb, who drove out the three sons of Anak. However, the Jebusites[1], who lived in Jerusalem, were not driven out by the sons of Benjamin,

---

1. The Jebusites held the city of Jerusalem until they were driven out of it by king David.

and the Jebusites have lived on in Jerusalem with the Benjamites till the present day.

Behaviour of Israel during the period of the Judges. Death of Joshua. The people served the Lord during all the life of Joshua and the elders who outlived him and who had seen all the great works that the Lord had done in favour of Israel. Then another generation followed which did not know the Lord nor what he had done for Israel.

Infidelity and punishment of the future generations. Then the sons of Israel did what was wrong in the eyes of the Lord, and worshipped the Baalim. They forsook the Lord, God of their fathers, who had brought them out of the land of Egypt, and they went after other Gods, gods of the peoples among whom they lived, and they worshipped them, provoking the Lord to anger. They forsook the Lord to worship the Baal and the Ashtaroth[1]. So the Lord got angry with the Israelites; he made them the prey of bands of raiders and plunderers and sold them to their enemies all around them, and they could no longer made a stand.

Mission of the Judges. Then the Lord set Judges over them to rescue them from the power of their oppressors. But they did not obey their Judges, either. They turned wantonly to worship other gods and bowed low before them. They abandoned the path of obedience to the commandments of the Lordwhich their fathers had followed. They did not obey the Lord, so the Lord set Judges over them. The Lord was with the Judge and set them free from their enemies while the Judge was alive, for the Lord felt pity for them when he heard them groaning under oppression and ill-treatment. But as soon as the Judge was dead, they would relapse into deeper corruption than their forefathers; they did not abandon their evil practices and the wilful ways of their fathers.

Peoples which were left in the middle of Israel. These are the nations which the Lord left to test Israel through them. The five princes of the Philistines, all the Canaanites, the Sidonians and the Hivites who lived in Mount Lebanon, from the Mount

---

1. Baal and Ashtaroth were the main Canaanite gods.

Baal-hermon, as far as Lebo-hamat. They served as a means to test Israel, to see if the people observed the commandments which the Lord had given to their fathers through Moses[1].

---

1. When the people of Israel abandoned God, He sent some of their enemies to punish them, and when they felt penitent he sent them a chief.

HISTORY OF THE JUDGES[1]

Othoniel[2]. The sons of Israel did what was wrong in the eyes of the Lord. They forsook the Lord, their God, to worship the Baalim and the Asheroth. Then the Lord was angry with them, and he sold them to Cushan-rishathaim, King of Aram. The sons of Israel were kept by them in subjection for eight years, and the Lord sent them a a man to deliver them: Othoniel, son of Kenaz, the younger brother of Caleb. The spirit of the Lord came upon him and he set out to attack their enemies. The Lord delivered Cushan-rishathaim into his hands, king of Aram, and he defeated Cushan-rishathaim. Thus the land was at peace for forty years.

Aod[3]. After the death of Othoniel, son of Kenaz, the sons of Israel did what was wrong in the eyes of the Lord again, and the Lord gave power to Eglon, king of Moab, over Israel, for they had done what was wrong in the eyes of the Lord. Eglon mustered the Ammonites and the Amalekites, and advanced to attack Israel. He defeated them and took possession of Palm City. The sons of Israel were subject to Eglon king of Moab for eighteen years.

---

1. The Judges were providential men sent by the Lord to save His people from its enemies.
2. The first Judge, one of the so called Minor Judges.
3. Or Ehud, Benjamite.

The sons of Israel appealed to the Lord and the Lord sent them a man: Aod, son of Gera the Benjamite, who was left-handed. The sons of Israel sent him to pay their tribute to Eglon, king of Moab. Aod made himself a two-edged sword, only fifteen inches long, which he fastened on his right side under his clothes, and brought the tribute to Eglon king of Moab, a very fat man. Then Aod, with his left hand, drew his sowrd from his right side and drove it into his belly.

Aod went away, passed by the "Carved Stones" and escaped to Seirah. As soon as he came to the land of Israel, he blew the trumpet in the Mountains of Ephraim and the sons of Israel came down from the hills with him at their head. He said to them, "Follow me, for the Lord has delivered your enemy, in Moab, into your hands." They followed him, and seized the fords of the Jordan, allowing no man to cross. On that day Moab became subject to Israel, and the land was at peace for eighty years.

Debora-Barah. After the death of Aod, the sons of Israel did what was wrong in the eyes of the Lord again, and the lord delivered them into the hands of Jabin the Canaanite king, who ruled in Hazor, and whose commander of forces was Sisera, who lived in Harosheth-of-the-Gentiles.

The sons of Israel cried up to the Lord for help, because Jabin had nine hundred chariots of iron and had oppresed the sons of Israel harshly for twenty years.

At that time Israel was judged by Debora[1], prophetess, wife of Lappidoth. She sat under the palm tree of Debora, between Ramah and Bethel in the hill-country of Ephraim, and the sons of Israel wnet up to her for justice. She sent for Barak[2], son of Abinoam from Kedesh in Naphtali and said to him, "These are the commandments of the Lord, God of Israel: 'Go to Mount Tabor, and take ten thousand men of the tribe of Naphtali and Zebulum with you. There I shall bring you Sisera, Jabin's

---

1. Debora (Mother in Israel) made Barak fight Sisara on behalf of God. She sings beautifully. Barak was at that time Judge of Israel.
2. Barak (in Hebrew, lightning). Sisara. Commander of the Canaanite forces, whose king was Jabin.

commander, to the Torrent of Kishon with his chariots and all his rabble, and there I will deliver them into your hands'." Barak answered, "If you come with me I will go, but if not, I will not, for I do not know when the Angel of the Lord will be favourable to me." Debora replied, "Certainly I shall go with you, but this venture will bring you no glory, because the Lord will leave Sisera to fall into the hands of a woman." Then Debora set out and, with Barak, headed for Kedesh. Barak gathered Zebulum and Naphtali at Kedesh; ten thousand men were following him, and Debora accompanied him.

Flight and death of Sisara. Meanwhile Sisara was told that Barak, son of Abinoam, had gone up Mount Tabor. Sisara gathered all his chariots, nine hundred chariots of iron, and his troops, from Harosheth-of-the-Gentiles to the Torrent fo Kishon. Then Debora said to Barak, "Up! This day the Lord shall deliver Sisera into your hands. Is not the Lord before you?" And Barak came charging down Mount Tabor with his ten thousand men. The Lord put Sisera to rout with all his chariots and his army before Barak's[1] onslaught; but Sisera himself dismounted from his chariot and fled on foot. Barak pursued the chariots and the army as far as Harosheth, and the whole army was put to the sword and perished, not a man was left alive.

Sisara fled on foot towards the tent of Jel, wife of Heber the Kenite. Jael came out to meet Sisara and said to him, "Come, sir, come in; do not be afraid." He came into the tent and she covered him with a rug. He said to her, "Give me some water to drink; I am thirsty." She opened a skin full of milk, gave him a drink and covered him up again. Sisara said to her, "Stand at the tent door, and if anybody comes and asks if someone is here, say no." But Jael, wife of Heber, took a tent-peg, picked up a hammer, crept up to him, and drove the peg into his skull as he lay sound asleep, Meanwhile Barak was coming in pursuit of Sisera. Jael came to meet him and said to him, "Come and I shall show you the man that you are looking for." She entered with him. Sisara laid? there with the tent-peg in his skull. That

---

1. God swallowed up their chariots and confused their enemies.

they God humiliated Jabin, king of Canaan, before the sons of Israel. The hand of the sons of Israel pressed upon Jabin, the Canaanite king until he made an end of him, king of Canaan[1].

Gideon's vocation. The angel of the Lord came down and sat under the terebinth of Ophra, wich belonged to Joah of Abiezzar. Gideon, his son, was winnowing the corn in the threshing-floor to take it to Midian. The angel of the Lord appeared to him, and said, "The Lord be with you, brave warrior!" Gideon answered, "Please, my lord, if the Lord is with us, why does this happen to us? Where are all the miracles which our fathers tell us about, saying, 'The Lord has brought us out of Egypt, but now he has forsaken us and delivered us into the Midianite's hands'." The Lord turned to him and said, "Go with your strenght and you will save Israel from the power of Midian. It is not me who sends you?" Gideon replied, "Please, my Lord, how can I save Israel?" The Lord answered him, "I will be with you, and you shall defeat Midian as if it werw an only man." Gideon said to him, "If I have found your favour, give me a sign proving that it is you who is talking to me. Please, do not move until I come back. I will bring my offering to You." He said, "I will remain here until you come back."

Gideon left, prepared a calf and with a measure of flour he made unleavened bread; he put the meat into a basket and the broth in a pot, he took them to the terebinth and prostrated himself before the Lord. Then the angel of the Lord said to him, "Take the meat and the unleavened bread and put them on this stone, an then pour the broth over them." Gideon did as he was told. The angel of the Lord stretched out the end of his staff and touched the meat and the unleavened bread. The fire came up from the rock and burnt the meat and the unleavened bread, an the angel of the Lord disappeared before his eyes. Then Gideon realised that he was the angel of the Lord. Therefore

---

1. Sisara fell in the hands of a woman, as Deborah had foretold Barak. Jael thought he was doing as the Lord wanted when he killed the enemy of the people.

Gideon built an altar to the Lord and named it "Lord peace". This altar can still be found nowadays at Ophra of Abiezzar.

Invasion of the Midianites[1]. The whole region of Midian, Amalec[2] and the sons of the West had joined forces. They crossed the Jordan and encamped in the plains of Jezreel. Then the spirit of the Lord took possesion of Gideon, blew his trumpet and the Abiezriters followed him. They sent messengers all through Manasseh, and they too were called out. He sent messengers to Asher, Zebulum and Naphtali, and they came up to meet the others.

Defeat of the Gideon's army. Gideon and the people that were with him rose early, and they encamped at En-harod; the camp of Midian was in a valley to the north of theirs, north of the hill of Moreh. Then the Lord said to Gideon, "The people with you are more than I need to deliver Midian in your hands. Israel will claim the glory for themselves and say that it is their own stregth that has given them the victory. Now make a proclamation for all the people to hear, that anyone who is scared or frightened is to go back home." Twenty-two thousand of them went, ant ten thousand were left.

The Lord said to Gideon[3], "There are still too many. Bring them down to the water, and I will separate them for you there. When I say to you, 'This man shall go with you', he shall go; and if I say, 'This man shall not go with you?', he shall not go." So Gideon made all his troops descend to the water and the Lord said to him, "Every man who laps the water with his tongue like a dog stand on one side, and on the other every man who goes down on his knees and drinks." The number of those who lapped the water with his hands was three hundred. The rest of the people knelt down to drink. Then the Lord said to Gideon, "With the three hundred men who had lapped the water I will set you free and deliver the Midianites into your hands.

---

1. The Midianites were nomadic tribes of the Arabian desert. They lived by plundering and devastating.
2. Amalec was from the Southern Palestine as for as the Sinai.
3. Gideon (Hebrew, Giant). The angel sent him to fight against Baal and the Midianites.

All the rest may go home." The latter were sent every one to his tent, and he kept the three hundred[1]. The Midianite camp was below him, in the vale.

Surprise attack. Gideon divided his three hundred man into three companies. He gave them the trumpets and the empty jars and inside every jar he put a torch. Then he said to them: "Look at me and do as I so. When I come to the edge of the camps, do exactly as I do. When I and my men blow our trumpets, you too all round the camp will blow your trumpets, and shout, 'For the Lord and for Gideon'."

Gideon and those who were with him came to the edge of the camp at the beginning of the middle watch, the sentries had just been posted. They blew their trumpets and smashed their jars. With their left hand they took the torches and with their right hand they took the trumpets and shouted, "For the Lord and Gideon." Every man stood where he was, all round the camp, and the whole campt leapt up in a panic and fled. While the three hundred men were blowing their trumpets, the Lord set every man against his neighbour throughout the camp. All of them fled towards Beth-shittah, in Zererah, as far as the ridge of Abel-meholah by Tabbah[2].

MINOR JUDGES

Oppression of the Ammonites[3]. The sons of Israel did what was wrong in the eyes of the Lord again. They worshipped the Baalim and the Ashtaroth, the deities of Aram and of Sidon and of Moab, of the Ammonites and of the Philistines. They forsook the Lord and did not worship him. The Lord was angry with Israel and the sold them to the Philistines and the Ammonites, who for eighteen years harassed and oppressed the Israelites.

---

1. God reduced Gideon's army so that they could not claim the victory.
2. The panic spread throughout the camp and people fled. Gideon used more cunning than strength, and God gave him the triumph.
3. From Siria, whose capital was Damascus.

Jhephtah is elected Judge. Jhephtah the Gileadite was a strong and brave man.

Some time later, the sons of Ammon made war on Israel. And when the fighting began, the elders of Gilead sent for Jephteh to the land of Tob. And they said to him, "Come and be our commander so that we can fight the Ammonites[1]." Jhephtah answered them, "Did you not drive me from my father's house in hatred? Why do you come to me now that you are in trouble?" But the elders of Gilead replied, "It is because of that that we have come to you. Come with us to fight the sons of Ammon and you will be our lord, the lord of all the inhabitants of Gilead." Thus, Jhephtah set out with the elders of Gilead, and the people elected him lord and commander. And Jhephtah repeated his words before the Lord, at Mizpah.

The spirit of the Lord came upon Jephthah, who passed through Gilead and Manasseh, by Mizpeh of Gilead, and from Mizpeh over to the sons of Ammon. Jhephtah fighted the sons of Ammon, and the Lord delivered them into his hands.

He defeated them all the way from Aroer to Minnith, twenty cities, and to Abel-keramim. It was a great defeat, and the sons of Ammon were humiliated by the sons of Israel.

Death of Jhephtah. Jhephtah judged over Israel for six years. Then Jhephtah the Gileadite died, and he was buried in his own city in Gilead, in Mizpeh.

Announcement of the birth of Samson. The sons of Israel did again what was wrong in the eyes of the Lord, and the Lord sold them to the Philistines for forty years. There was a man from Zorahof the tribe of Dan whose name was Manoah and whose wife was barren and childless. The Angel of the Lord appeared to her and said to her, "You are barren and childless, but watch now; do not drink any wine or strong drink, and do not eat forbidden food, you will conceive and give birth to a child, and no razor shall touch his head, for the boy is to belong to the Lord from the day of his birth. He will strike the first blow to deliver Israel from the power of the Philistines."

---

1. The Ammonites worshipped Molok, the most bloodthirsty god of Canaan, to whom human sacrifices were offered.

The woman gave birth to a son, and she named him Samson[1]. The boy grew up, and the Lord blessed him. The spirit of the Lord began to drive him hard in the Camp of Dan, amon Sora and Estaol.

Samson marries a Philistine woman. Samson came down to Timnath and there he saw a woman among the daughters of the Philistines. His parents did not know that the Lord was at work in this, seeking an opportunity against the Philistines, who at that time were the masters of Israel[2].

Samson came down to Timnath and, as he came to the vines of Timnah a lion came at him growling. The spirit of the Lord suddenly seized him, and, having nothing in his hand, he tore the lion in pieces as if it were a young calf.

Samson burns the cornfields of the Philistines[3]. After a while, during the time of wheat harvest, Samson went to visit his wife. Samson went and caught three hundred jackals and got some torches; he tied the jackals tail to tail and fastened a torch between each pair of tails. Then he set the torches alight and turned the jackals loose in the cornfields of the Philistines. He burnt up corn and stooks as well, vineyards and olive groves.

The Philistines asked, "Who has done this?" They were told, "It was Samson." Then the Philistines went up and burnt his wife and his father's house. Samson said to them, "If you do things like this, I swear I will be revenged upon you before I have done." And he smote them hip and thigh with great slaughter; and after that he went down to live in a cave in the Rock of Etam.

The jawbone of the ass. The Philistines encamped in Judah, and they overran Lehi.

When Samson came to Lehi, the Philistines ran to meet him. Then the spirit of the Lord seized him, and as he saw the jawbone of an ass, all raw, he picked it up and slew a thousand men. And Samson said[4],

---

1. Samson was the last of the seven major Judges.
2. Samson was consecrated to the Lord since he was a child, hence his strength.
3. The Philistines came from the islands in the Aegean sea.
4. He had a tremendous strength. He fought the Philistines all alone.

"I have beaten them hard
with the jawbone of an ass,
with the jawbone of an ass
I have slain a thousand men."

Once he finished talking he threw away the jawbone; and he called that place Ramath-Lehi.

Samson runs away from Gaza. Samson then went to Gaza. The people of Gaza heard that Samson had come, "Samson is here", they said. They surrounded him and laid in wait for him all that night. During the night they were quiet, saying: "We shall wait until the break of the day, and then we shall kill him." Samson laid in bed till midnight; at midnight he rose, seized hold of the doors of the cigy gate and the two posts, pulled them out, bar and all, hoisted them on to his shoulders and carried them to the top of the hill east of Hebron[1].

Samson and Dalila. After this Samson fell in love with a woman from the valley of Sorek. Her name was Dalila[2]. The princes of the Philistines came to her and said, "Coax him and find out what gives him his great strength; and how we can bind him and hold him captive. Each of us will give you one thousand pieces of silver." Then Dalila said to Samson, "Please, tell me what gives you your great strength, and how could you be bound and held captive." Samson answered her, "If you bind me tightly with seven fresh bowstrings, not yet dry, I shall become as weak as any other man." The princes of the Philistines brought her seven fresh bowstrings, not yet dry, and she bound him with them. She had already people hidden in the inner room and, shouted, "Samson, the Philistines are upon you!" He snapped the ropes off his arms like pack-thread on fire; in this way his secret remained unknown.

Dalila said to him, "Do not say that you love me, because your heart is not with me! Tell me the secret of your great strength." She insisted every day until he was so tired that he

---

1. Samson's herculean strength was not natural, the spirit of the Lord had overtaken him, who was consecrated to the Lord.

2. She was a prostitute.

opened his heart to her, "The razor has never touched my head, because I am a Nazirite, consecrated to the Lord since I was born. If my head were shaved, I would lose all my strength and would be as weak as any other man." Then Dalila understood that this time he was sincere. And he called the Philistines, saying, "Come, for this time he has opened his heart to me." The princes of the Philistines came with the money. She lulled him to sleep on her knees, summoned a man and he shaved the seven locks of his hair for her. Then he began to feel weak and his strength abandoned him. She said, "Samson, the Philistines are upon you!" He woke from his sleep and said to himself, "I will go up as usual and defeat them." But he did not know that the Lord had abandoned him[1].

Samson in prison. The Philistines imprisoned him, gouged out his eyes and brought him down to Gaza. They bound him with fetters of bronze and he was set to grinding corn in the prison[2].

Meanwhile his hair began to grow as before it was shaved. The princes of the Philistines gathered to offer a great sacrifice to their god Dagon and to rejoice before him, and they said, "Our god had delivered Samson into our hands, our enemy."

As their heart was merry, they said, "Call Samson to enjoy ourselves." And they summoned Samson from the prison and he made sport before them. They stood him between the pillars. Then Samson said to the boy who held his hand, "Put me where I can feel the pillars which support the building, so that I can lean on them."

Samson's last revenge. The building was packed with people. The princes of the Philistines were all there, and on the roof there were around three thousand men and women watching Samson as he fought.

Then Samson called on the Lord and said, "Oh, Lord, remember me: give me strength just once more, and at one stroke I shall be avenged on the Philistines for my two eyes."

---

1. His infidelity towards his vote —he was a Nazirite, consecrated to God— caused his misery.

2. Although it may seem so, Samson has nothing to do with the Greek heroes.

Samson felt the two pillars in the middle, which supported the building, his right arm round one and his left round the other, and braced himself and said, "Let me die with the Philistines." Then Samson leaned forward with all his might, and the temple fell on the princes and on all the people who were in it. The dead whom he killed at his death were more than those he had killed in his life. His brothers and his father's family came down and took him with them.

THE BOOKS OF SAMUEL

FIRST BOOK OF SAMUEL

SAMUEL[1]

The parents of Samuel. There was a man from Ramthaim, a Zuphite from the hill-country of Ephraim, called Elkanah son of Jeroham, son of Elihu. Every year he came up from his city to worship and to offer sacrifice to the Lord of Hosts in Shiloh. There were the two sons of Eli, Hophni and Phinehas, as the priests of the Lord. One day Elkanah offered a sacrifice: he gave his share of food to Peninnah with all his sons and daughters, but although he loved Hannah, to her he gave one share, because the Lord had made her barren.

Plead and vow of Hannah. After eating and drinking at Shiloh, Hannah stood up and went before the Lord, while Eli the priest was sitting on his seat beside the door of the temple of the Lord. She was in deep distress, and prayed to the Lord, weeping bitterly. She made the following vow: "Oh, Lord of Hosts! if you will deign to take notice of my trouble and remember you servant and give me an offspring, I shall

---

1. Samuel is the first of the great Prophets, who mediated between God and his people. They passed on the Revelation. They spoke on behalf of God and predicted the future.

consecrate him to the Lord for his whole life, and no razor shall ever touch his head."

Birth of Samuel (around 1100 b.C.). They rose early in the morning, worshipped the Lord[1] and went back home at Ramah. Elkana had intercourse with his wife Hannah, and the Lord remembered her. Hannah conceived and gave birth to a son, whom she named Samuel, "Because", she said, "I asked the Lord for him."

Samuel is consecrated to the Lord in the temple. Once the child was weaned Hannah brought him into the house of the Lord at Shiloh. With him she took a bull three years old, an ephah of flour and a flagon of wine. The child went with her. They slaughtered the bull, and brought the boy to Eli. Hannah said to him, "The Lord has given me what I asked for. Now, I lend him to the Lord; for his whole life he is lent to the Lord. And she left him there before the Lord.

Evil behaviour of the sons of Eli. The sons of Eli were wicked men, they did not care for the Lord, nor for the rights of the priests before the people.

However, the young Samuel grew up in high and in the presence of the Lord and of men.

God summons Samuel. The young Samuel was at the Lord's service in the presence of Eli. In those days the word of the Lord was seldom heard, and no vision was granted. It happened that one day, while Eli was sleeping in his room, his eyes became so dim that he could not see. Before the lamp of God had gone oup, and Samuel was sleeping in the Lord's Temple where the Ark of the Lord was, the Lord called him, "Samuel, Samuel!" And he answered, "Here I am", he ran to Eli and said to him, "Here I am, for you have called me." Eli said, "I have not called you, go back to bed." And Samuel came back to bed. Again, the Lord said, "Samuel!" And Samuel stood up, came to Eli and said to him, "Here I am, for you have called me." Eli replied, "I have not called you, go to bed, my son." Samuel had never heard the Lord, and the Lord had never

---

1. Shiloh was the provisional capital of the tribes. There was kept the Testament's Ark and Eli, the last Judge, guarded her in his temple.

spoken to him. The Lord called him a third time, "Samuel!" He came to Eli and said, "Here I am, for you have called me" Then Eli understood that it was the Lord who called the young man, and he said to Samuel, "Go back to bed, and if somebody calls you, you shall say, 'Speak, of Lord, your servant is listening to you.'" And Samuel came back to bed.

The Lord came into the temple, and called again, "Samuel, Samuel!" And Samuel answered, "Speak, your servant is listening to you." Then the Lord said to Samuel, "Soon I shall do something in Israel which will ring in the ears of all who hear it. When that day comes I will make good every word I have spoken against Eli and his family from beginning to end. You are to tell him that my judgements on his house shall stand for ever because he knew of his son's blasphemies against God and did not rebuke them."

Samuel lay down till morning, and then he opened the gates of the temple of the Lord. Samuel was afraid of telling his vision to Eli, but the latter called him, and said, "Samuel, my son!" And he answered, "Here I am". Eli asked him, "What did the Lord tell you? Do not hide it from me. God forgive if you hide one word of all that He said to you." Then Samuel told him everything and hid nothing. Eli said, "He is the Lord, he shall do as he pleases[1]."

Samuel grew up, and the Lord was with him. None of his words was unfulfilled. All Israel knew, from Dan to Beersheba, that Samuel was confirmed as a prophet of the Lord. So the Lord continued to appear in Shiloh, because he had revealed himself there to Samuel. Eli was very old and his sons continued his wrongdoing before the Lord.

War against the Philistines and loose of the Ark. The Philistines mustered for battle against Israel. The Israelites came to meet them. The fighting was hard and Israel was defeated by the Philistines, and around four thousand men were killed. The people came back to the camp, and the elders wondered, "Why

---

1. God said to Samuel the punishments and miserys that would overtake the house of Eli and his sons. The Lord's words had not been a dream, for he was well awake.

has the Lord defeated us today before the Philistines? Let us go to Shiloh to fetch the Ark of the Covenant of the Lord so that it goes among us; in this way it shall deliver us from the hands of our enemies." The people went to Shiloh and from there they took the Ark of the Covenant of the Lord. As the Ark of the covenant of the Lord came to the camp all Israel greeted it with a great shout, and the earth rang with the shouting. The Philistines heard the noise and asked, "What is this shouting in the camp of the Hebrews?" And they knew that the Ark of the Lord had come to the camp. The Philistines were afraid and cried, "The Lord has come to the camp." The Philistines attacked and Israel was defeated, and every man fled to his tent. It was a great defeat. Thirty thousand Israelite foot-soldiers perished. The Ark of God was taken, and Eli's two sons, Hophni and Phinehas, were killed.

Death of Eli. A Benjamite ran from the battlefield and reached Shiloh on the same day, his clothes rent and dust on his head. When he arrived Eli was sitting on a seat by the road to Mizpah, for he was deeply troubled about the Ark of God. The man entered the city with his news, and the whole city cried out in horror. Eli heard the shouting and asked, "What does this uproar mean?" And the man hurried to Eli and told him the news. Eli was already ninety-eight years old, his eyes were sightless. The man said to Eli, "I come from the camp, I fled today from the battlefild." Eli asked him, "What is the news, my son?" The messenger answered, "The Israelites have fled from the Philistines; it has been a great defeat; your two sons, Hophni and Phineas, have been killed as well, and the Ark of God has been taken." When he mentioned the Ark of God Eli fell backwards from his seat by the gate and broke his neck, for he was old and heavy. Eli judged over Israel for forty years.

The Ark among the Philistines. After the Philistines had captured the Ark of God, they brought it from Eben-ezer to Ashdod[1]. The Philistines took the Ark of God, brought it into Dagon's temple and placed it beside Dagon himself. When the

---

1. One of the five Philistine cities on the coast. It was independent until Teglaphalasar III of Perse conquered it.

people from Ashdod rose in the morning they found that Dagon had fallen face downwards before the Ark of God, with his head and his two hands lying broken off beside its platform[1].

The Ark returns to Israel. The Philistines summoned their priests and soothsayers and asked them, "What shall we do with the Ark of God?" And they answered, "If you want to send the Ark of the God of Israel back, do not let it go without a gift, but send it back with a gift for him by way of indemnity. Take two milch-cows which have never been yoked; harness the cows to the wagon and let their calves back in their stalls. You shall take the Ark of the Lord and put it on the wagon." The people did as they were told; they took two milch-cows and harnessed them to the wagon leaving their calves in the stalls.

The Ark in Beth-shemesh. The cows went straight in the direction of Beth-shemesh, lowing as they went and turning neither right nor left. The princes of the Philistines followed them as far as the territory of Beth-shemesh.

Now the people of Beth-shemesh offered sacrifices and whole-offerings to the Lord. When the five princes of the Philistines saw this, they came back immidiately to Ekron. But the sons of Jeconiah did not rejoice with the rest of the men of Beth-shemesh when they welcomed the Ark of the Lord, and the Lord struck down seventy of them. The people mourned because the Lord had struck them so hard, and the people of Beth-shemesh said, "No one is safe in the presence of the Lord, this holy God. To whom can we send it, to be rid of him?" And they sent messengers to the people of Kiriath-jearim, saying, "The Philistines have returned the Ark of the Lord, come and take charge of it."

The Ark in Kiriath-jearim. The people of Kiriath-jearim came down and took the Ark of the Lord away; they brought it into the house of Abinadab on the hill and consecrated his son Eleazar as its custodian[2].

---

1. He was the god of the Philistines, god of gods.
2. God used the Ark of the Covenant to punish the Philistines, as a sign of his presence.

Samuel, Judge and liberator. So for a long while, twenty years, the Ark of the Lord was housed in Kiriath-jearim[1] and the whole house of Israel followed the Lord. Them Samuel[2] said to the whole people of Israel, "If your return to the Lord is whole-hearted, banish the foreign gods and the Ashtaroth from your shrines; turn to the Lord with heart and mind, and worship him alone, and he will deliver you from the Philistines." The sons of Israel then banished the Baalim and the Ashtaroth, and they worshipped the Lord alone. Then Samuel said, "Gather all Israel at Mizpah, and I will intercede with the Lord for you." They assembled there, drew water and poured it out before the Lord and fasted all day, saying, "We have sinned against the Lord." And Samuel judged the sons of Israel at Mizpah.

The Philistines heard that the sons of Israel had gathered at Mizpah, and the princes of the Philistines marched against them. The sons of Israel came to know this and grew afraid. Then the sons of Israel said to Samuel, "Do not cease to pray for us to the Lord our God to save us from the power of the Philistines." Samuel took a sucking lamb, offered it up complete as a whole-offering to the Lord, and he prayed aloud to the Lord on behalf of Israel, and the Lord listened to him. While Samuel was offering the sacrifice the Philitines advanced to battle with the Israelites. Then the Lord thundered loud and long over the Philistines and threw them into confusion. They fled in panic before the Israelites. The people of Israel, who set out from Mizpah, pursued the Philistines and defeated them till they reached a point below Beth-car.

Samuel Judge over Israel. The Philistines were subdued and no longer encroached on the territory of Israel; and the hand of the Lord was against them as long as Samuel lived. The cities they had captured were restored to Israel, and from Ekron to Gath the borderland was freed from the hands of the Philistines.

Samuel acted as Judge in Israel as long as he lived, and every year went on circuit to Bethel, Gilgal and Mizpah; he dispensed justice at all these places, returning always to Ramah.

---

1. City on the hill, 12 kms away from Jerusalem.
2. Already known as "the Prophet".

That was his home and the place from which he governed Israel, and there he built an altar to the Lord.

SAMUEL AND SAUL

The people ask for a king. When Samuel grew old he appointed his sons to be judges in Israel. So the elders of Israel met and came to Ramah to meet Samuel, and they told him, "You are old, and your sons do not follow your footsteps. Therefore appoint us a king to govern us, like other nations[1]." Their request for a king displeased Samuel, and he appealed to the Lord. But the Lord said to Samuel, "Listen to the people and all that they are saying, for they have not rejected you, it is I whom they have rejected to be their king. They are now doing to you what they have been doing to me since I brought them out of Egypt, forsaking me to worship foreing gods. Therefore do as they ask you; but warn them and tell them what sort of king will govern them."

Samuel told the people who asked him for a king what the Lord had said to him. And he said to them, "This will be the sort of king that will govern you: He will take your sons and make them serve in his chariots and with his cavalry, and will make them run before his chariot. Some he will appoint officers over units of a thousand and units of fifty. Others will plough his fields and reap his harvest; others again will make weapons of war and equipment for mounted troops. He will take your daughters for parfumers, cooks and confectioners, and will seize the best of your cornfields, vineyards, and olive-yards, and will give them to his lackeys. He will take a tenth of your grain and your vintage to give to his eunuchs and lackeys. Then you shall cry out against the king whom you have chosen; but it will be too late,and the Lord will not answer you." However, the people did not want to listen to Samuel, and they said, "No, we must have a king, like all the other nations. He will judge over us, lead us to war and fight our battles." Samuel listened to the

---

1. Religious and political centre of all tribes.

words of the people and told them to the Lord, and the Lord
said to them, "Do as they want and appoint them a king." Then
Samuel said to the people of Israel, Go everyone of you to his
city[1]."

Saul and his father's asses. There was a man from the tribe
of Benjamin, whose name was Kish son of Abiel, son of Zeror,
son of Bechorath, son of Aphia a Benjamite, he was a brave
man. He had a son called Saul, a young man in his prime. There
was no better man among the Israelites than he. He was a head
taller than all his fellows. When they came to the country of
Zpuh, Saul said to the servant with him, "Come, we ought to
turn back, or my father will stop thinking about the asses and
begin to worry about us." But the servant answered, "There is a
man of God in the city here, who has a great reputation, because
everything he says comes true. Let us go there, maybe he can
tell us which way we should follow." Saul agreed, and they
came up to the city. Just as they were going in the city, there
was Samuel coming towards them on his way up to the shrine.

However, the day before Saul came, the Lord had warned
Samuel, saying, "Tomorrow at this same time I shall send you a
man from the country of Benjamin. You shall anoint him prince
over my people Israel to save my people from the hands of the
Philistines, because I have seen the misery of my people and
their cry has reached my ears." When Samuel saw Saul, the
Lord said to him, "This is the man I talked to you about. This
man shall rule my people." Saul approached Samuel in the
gateway and said, "Would you tell me where the seer lives[2]?"
Samuel answered Saul and said, "I am the seer. Go on ahead of
the to the hill-shrine and you shall eat with me today; in the
morning I will set you on you way, after telling you what you
have on you mind. As for the asses lost three days ago, trouble
yourself no more about it, because they have already been
found." Samuel took Saul and his servant with him, and he

---

1.   Until David the monarchy was not consolidated.
2.   A seer was a prophet for the people, but actually it means "the man who
     speaks on behalf of God".

brought them in the dinning-room, and gave them a place at the head of the company, which numbered about thirty.

Saul is anointed king of Israel. At dawn Samuel called to Saul on the roof, "Get up, and I will set you on your way." Saul got up and they went together into the street. As they came to the end of the town, Samuel said to Saul, "Tell the boy to go on, but you stay here a moment so that I can tell you the word of God."

Then Samuel took a flask of oil, poured it over Saul and kissed his head, "Has the Lord not anoint you as king over Israel? You shall rule the people of the Lord and set them free from their enemies. You shall go down to Gilgal ahead of me, and I will come to you to sacrifice whole-offerings and shared-offerings. You shall wait for seven days until I come to you and tell you what you must do."

Return of Saul. As Saul turned to leave Samuel, God gave him a new heart.

Saul is elected king by lot (around 1050-1012 b.C.). Samuel gathered all the tribes of Israel, and Benjamin's was picked by lot. Then he presented the tribe of Benjamin, family by family, and the family of Matri was picked. Then he presented the family of Matri, man by man, and Saul son of Kish was picked. Samuel said to all the people, "Have you seen the elected of the Lord? There is none like him in the whole people." And the people shouted, "Long live the king[1]." Then Samuel explained to the people the nature of a king, and made a written record of it on a scroll which he deposited before the Lord. He then dismissed them to their homes. Saul went home too, to Gibeah, and with him went some fighting men whose hearts God had moved[2].

Samuel gives up his Judicature. Then Samuel said to Israel, "I have heard your voices and have anointed a king to rule over you. Now there you have the king who shall be your leader. I have grown old and my hair is white, and my children

---

1. God consecrated him and the people elected him by lot.
2. Saul's rule will not be very different from the rule of the Judges under the custody of Samuel.

are among you. I have been your leader since I was a child. Here I am, I want to judge you before the Lord and recite all the victories which he has won for you and for your fathers. When Jacob and his brothers came down to Egypt, the Egyptians subdued them and your fathers appealed to the Lord. The Lord sent Moses and Aaron to bring your fathers out of Egypt and bring them to this land. Now you have a king over you. If you are afraid of God and worship him, if you obey him and do not rebel against his commands, if you and your king follow the Lord you shall live, byt if you do not obey him and rebel against his commands, then he will set his face against you and your king, and you shall perish. Be afraid of the Lord and worship him sincerily with all your heart, taking into account what he has done for you. But if you persist in wickedness, you and your king shall perish."

The Israelites rise against the Philistines. Saul[1] picked three thousand men from Israel, two thousand to be with him in Michmash and the hill-country of Bethel[2], and a thousand to be with Jonathan in Gibeah of Benjamin; and he sent the rest of the people to their tent. When the Philistines knew that they were in Gibeah they said to themselves, "The Hebrews have rebelled." Meanwhile Saul sounded the trumpet all through the land, and the Isarelites all heard that Saul had killed a Philistine governor and that the name of Israel stank among the Philistines. All the people gathered around Saul at Gilgal. The Philistines assembled to fight against Israel with three thousand chariots, six thousand horse, with infantry as countless as sand on the sea-shore. They came up and camped at Michmash, to the east of Beth-aven. The people of Israel found themselves in sore straits, for the army was hard pressed, so they hid themselves in caves and holes, and among the rocks,in pits and cisterns. Some of them crossed the Jordan into the district of Gad and Gilead.

Breaking-off between Samuel and Saul. Saul was still in Gilgal, and the people who followed him were in alarm. He waited for seven days, as Samuel had told, but Samuel would

---

1. Saul (Hebrew = the Desired).
2. Old Canaanite temple; Abraham built an altar to the Lord.

not come to Gilgal[1], so the people began to drift away from Saul. He said therefore, "Bring me the whole-offering and the shared-offerings." And he offered the sacrifice. Saul had just finished the sacrifice when Samuel arrived, and he went out to greet him. Samuel said, "What have you done?" And Saul asnwered, "I saw that the people were drifting away, and you yourselves had not come as you had promised, and the Philistines were assembling at Michmash, and I said to myself, 'The Philistines will now move against me at Gilgal, and I have not placated the Lord', so I felt compelled to make the whole-offering myself." Samuel said to Saul, "You have behaved foolishly. You should have observed the command that the Lord, your God gave to you, the Lord would have established your dynasty over Israel for all time. But now your line will not endure[2]. The Lord will seek a man after his own heart, and will appoint him prince over his people, because you have not kept the Lord's command." Samuel stood up and left Gilgal without much ado, and went on his way. The rest of the people followed Saul, as he moved from Gilgal towards the enemy. At Gibeah of Benjamin he mustered the people who were with him; they were about six hundred men.

Preparations for the war. Saul and his son Jonathan and the people who were with them were in Gibeah of Benjamin. The Philistines were encamped in Michmash. Raiding parties went out the camp of the Philistines in three directions. One of them turned towards Ophrah in the district of Shual, another towards Beth-horon, and the third towards the range of hills overlooking the valley of Zeboim and the desert beyond[3].

No blacksmith was to be found in the whole country of Israel, because the Philistines had said, "the Hebrews shall not be able to make swords and spears." The Israelites had to go down to the Philistines for their ploughshares,mattocks, axes and sickles to be sharpened. So when war broke out none of the

---

1. Gilgal. Operation centre of Joshua, between Jerusalen and Samaria. Place of offerings.
2. The offering of sacrifices was Samuel's duty.
3. It was the first disobedience of Saul.

followers of Saul and Jonathan had neither sword nor spear;
only Saul and Jonathan carried arms. The Philistines had posted
a force in the pass of Michmash.

Defeat of the Philistines. Saul's guards, at Gibeah[1] of
Benjamin, saw that the camp surged to and fro in confusion.
Then Saul said to the people who were with him, "Call the roll
and find out who is missing." They called the roll and saw that
Jonathan and his servant were missing. Saul and all the people
who were with him gathered and made for the battlefield, and
they found the enemy fighting one another in complete disorder.
The Hebrews who up to now had been under the Philistines, and
had been with them in the camp, changed sides and joined the
Israelites under Saul and Jonathan. And all the men of Israel
who had hid in the hill-country of Ephraim heard that the
Philistines were in flight and pursued them. In this way the Lord
delivered the Israelites that day. The battle passed on beyond
Beth-aven[2].

Summary of the kingship of Saul. When Saul had made his
throne secure in Israel, he fought against his enemies around;
the Moabites, the Ammonites, the Edomites, the king of Zobah,
and the Philistines. And wherever he turned he was successful.
He displayed his strength by defeating the Amalekites and
freeing Israel from the hostile raids[3].

War against the Amalekites. Samuel said to Saul, "The
Lord has sent me to anoint you king over my people Israel.
Listen, then, the words of the Lord. These are the words of the
Lord of Hosts; he has resolved to punish what the Amalekites
did to Israel,when they attacked them on their way out of Egypt.
Go now and punish the Amalekites, and give in all their
possessions to the anathema[4]."

Saul defeated the Amalekites all the way from Havilah to
Shur on the borders of Egypt.

---

1. (Hebrew = hill). Southern border of Judah.
2. City on the slope of the mountain.It was a strategic site.
3. Saul's mission was to unify the country against its enemies, specially the
    Philistines.
4. Anathema, destruction.

Saul is rejected by God. The word of the Lord came to Samuel in this way, "I repent of having made Saul king, for he has turned his back on me and has not obeyed my commands." Samuel was angry, and he cried aloud to the Lord all night. When he rose in the morning Samuel came out to meet Saul. Samuel met him and Saul said to him, "The Lord's blessing upon you. I have obeyed the Lord's commands!" Then Samuel asked, "What is this bleating of sheep in my ears? Why do I hear the lowing of cattle?" And Saul answered, "They have been brought from Amalek, for the people had spared the best of the sheep and cattle to sacrifice to the Lord your God; the rest we have given in to the anathema[1].

Then Samuel said to Saul, "Shut up and let me tell you what the Lord has said to me today." He said, "Speak." And Samuel said, "Is it not true, that when you were a child became the leader of all the tribes of Israel? The Lord anointed you king of Israel. The Lord sent you with strict instructions to destroy that wicked nation, the Amalekites. Why have you disobeyed the command of the Lord? Why did you pounce upon the spoil and do what was wrong in the eyes of the Lord?" Saul answered to Samuel, "I have obeyed the Lord! I went where the Lord sent me, I brought back Agag king of the Amalekites and destroyed Amalek. Out of the spoil the people took sheep and oxen, the choicest of the animals laid under ban, to sacrifice to the Lord your God at Gilgal." Samuel answered, "Does the Lord desire offerings and sacrifices as he desires obedience? Because you have rejected the word of the Lord, the Lord has rejected you as a king[2]."

Saul implores forgiveness in vain. Then Saul said to Samuel, "I have sinned ignoring the Lord's command and his words, because I was afraid of the people and deferred to them. Now I implore you to forgive my sin, and come back with me, and I will make my submission before the Lord." Samuel answered to him, "I will not come back with you, because you have rejected the word of the Lord and therefore the Lord has

---

1. It was Saul's second disobedience to the Lord.
2. Saul disobeyed a second time.

rejected you as king over Israel." Samuel turned to go, but Saul caught the edge of his cloak and it tore. And Samuel said to him, "The Lord has torn the kingdom of Israel from your hand today and will give it to another, a better man than you. " Saul replied, "I have sinned, but honour me this once before the elders of my people and before Israel and come back with me, and I will make my submission to the Lord your God." Samuel came back to him and Saul worshipped the Lord[1].

Then Samuel went to Ramah, and Saul to his own home at Gibeah. He never saw Saul again to his dying day. Samuel mourned him, because the Lord had repented of having made Saul king of Israel.

SAMUEL AND DAVID

Samuel is consecrated king. The Lord said to Samuel, "How long will you mourn for Saul because I have rejected him as king over Israel? Fill your horn with oil. I send you to Jesse of Bethlehem[2]; for I have chosen myself a king among his sons." Samuel said, "How can I go? Saul will hear of it and kill me." The Lord replied, "Take a heifer with you. You shall say, 'I have come to offer a sacrifice to the Lord.' You shall invite Jeffer to the sacrifice, and I shall tell you what to do. You shall anoint for me the man whom I show you." Samuel did as the Lord had told him. When he came to Bethlehem, the elders of the city came out to meet him in haste, and said to him, "Is it all well?" And he answered, "All is well. I have come to offer a sacrifice to the Lord. Hallow yourselves and come with me to the sacrifice." He himself hallowed Jesse[3] and his sons and invited them to the sacrifice also.

When they came in and he saw Eliab[4] he thought, Here, before the Lord, is the anointed king. But the Lord said to

---

1. Saul was repentant, but it was too late. God chose another man who were more faithful. Before God the obedience is more important that our offerings.

2. Bethlehem, of Judah, 7 km away from Jerusalem.

3. Jesse or Isaiah.

4. Eliab was the eldest of seven brothers.

Samuel, "Take no account of him if he is handsome and tall; I have rejected him. The Lord does not see as man sees; men judge by appearances but the Lord judges by the heart." Then Jesse called Abinadab and made him pass before Samuel, who said, "This has not been chosen by the Lord, either." Jesse called Shammah, but Samuel said, "This has not been chosen by the Lord, either." Jesse made his seven sons pass before Samuel. Then Samuel said to him, "The Lord has not chosen any of these." And he asked him, "Are these all?" He answered, "No, the youngest is missing, he is looking after the sheep." Samuel said to him, "Send somebody to fetch him, for we will not sit down until he comes." Jesse sent and fetched him. He was fair-haired, good-looking and handsome. And the Lord said to Samuel, "Rise and anoint him, because this is the man[1]." Samuel took the horn with the oil and anoint him in the presence of his brothers. The spirit of the Lord came upon David[2] from that day onwards. Then Samuel left the house and came back to Ramah.

David enters the Court of Saul as a musician. The spirit of the Lord had abandoned Saul, and an evil spirit[3] coming from the Lord came upon him. Then the servant of Saul said to him, "An evil spirit, coming from the Lord, has come upon you. Why do you not command you servants here to go and find some man who can play the harp. When an evil spirit from God comes on you, he can play and you will recover." Saul answered to his servants, "Find, then, a man who can play well and bring him to me." Then a young man said, "I know a son of Jesse of Bethlehem who plays the harp very well. He is a brave man and a good fighter, wise in speech and handsome, and the Lord is with him."

Saul sent messengers to Jesse saying, "Sent me your son David[4], the one who is with the sheep." Jesse took five pieces of

---

1. It was David.
2. Only the kings and main priests were anointed and consecrated. The Annointed par excellence was Christ.
3. Melancholy, misery, desperation.
4. It means leader.

bread, a skin of wine and a kid, and he sent them to Saul through his son David. David came to Saul and entered his service. Saul loved him dearly, and he became his armour-bearer. Saul sent word to Jesse, "Let David stay in my service, for I am pleased with him." And whenever a spirit from God came upon Saul, David would take his harp and play on it, so that Saul found relief, he recovered and the evil spirit left him alone.

War against the Philistines. The Philistines collected their forces for war and massed at Socoh in Judah; they camped between Socoh and Azekah, at Ejphes-dammin. Saul and the men of Israel also massed, and camped in the vale of Elah. They drew up their lines facing the Philistines, the Philistines occupying a position on one hill and the Israelites on another; there was a valley between them. Then a champion came out from the Philistine camp, a man named Goliath[1], from Gath; he was over nine feet in height. He had a bronze helmet on his head, and he wore plate-armour of bronze, weighing five thousand shekels. On his feet he wore bronze greaves, and one of his weapons was a dagger of bronze, which he wore on his back. The shaft of his spear was like a weaver's beam, and its head, which was of iron, weighed six hundred shekels. His shield-bearer marched ahead of him.

He stood and shouted to the ranks of Israel, "Why do you come out to do battle? I am a Philistine, and you are Saul's slaves? Choose the man to meet me. If he can kill me in fair fight, we shall be your slaves and serve you; but if I prove too strong for him and kill him, you shall be our slaves and serve us." Then the Philistine said, "Today I defy the ranks of Israel. Give me a man and we will fight it out." When Saul and Israel heard the words of the Philistine, they were shaken and dismayed.

David comes to the camp. David was the son of an Ephrathite[2] of Bethlehem of Judah, called Kis[3], who had eight

1. A giant two or three meters high, descendant of Enac.
2. Bethlehem is also called Ephrata.
3. Kis, or Isaiah, or Jesse.

children. By Saul's time he had become a weak old man. The three eldest followed Saul. David used to go to Saul's camp and back to Bethlehem to mind his father's flocks. Morning and evening for forty days the Philistine came forward and took up his position[1].

Then Jesse said to his son David, "Take your brothers and an ephah of this parched grain and these ten loaves of bread, and run with them to the camp."

David rose early in the morning, left a shepherd in charge of the flock, took his packets and left, as Jesse had commanded him. He reached the lines just as the army was going out to take up position and was raising the war cry. The Israelites and the Philistines drew up their ranks opposite each other. David left his things in charge of the quartermaster, ran to the line and went up to his brothers to greet them. While he was talking to them the champion called Goliath, from Gath, came out of the ranks of the Philistines and repeated his words. David heard them.

David asked the men who were beside him, "What is to be done to the man who kills the Philistine and wipes out Israel's disgrace? Who is that uncircumcised Philistine who defies the army of the living God?" And the people answered, "Thus shall the man who kills him be treated." The people heard the words of David and told them to Saul, who sent for him.

David offers himself to fight against Goliath. David said to Saul, "Do not be discouraged, sir. I will go and fight the Philistine." Saul answered, "You cannot go and fight this Philistine, because you are young and he has been a fighting man all his life." But David said to Saul, "I am my father's shepherd; when a lion or bear comes and carries off a sheep from the flock, I go after it and attack it and rescue the victim from its jaws. Then if it turns on me, I seize it by the beard and batter it to death. Lions I have killed, and bears, and this uncircumcised Philistine will fare no better than they; he has defied the army of the living God." And David added, "The Lord, who has saved me from the lion and the bear will save me

---

1. Defying the Israelites and swearing about the Lord.

from this Philistine." Then Saul said to David, "Go, and the Lord will be with you."

David defeats and kills Goliath. David took his stick, chose five smooth stones from the brook and put them in a shepherd's bag and his sling, and walked out to meet the Philistine. The Philistine came on towards David, which his shield-bearer marching ahead. The Philistine looked at David and felt nothing but contempt, because he was young, fair-heared and handsome. He said to David, "Do you think I am a dog that you come out against me with sticks?" And he cursed David in the name of his god. Then the Philistine said to David, "Come to me, I shall give your flesh to the birds in the sky and the beasts in the earth." David answered the Philistine, "You come to me with your sword, your spear and dagger, but I come against you in the name of the Lord of Hosts[1], the God of the army of Israel which you have defied. Today the Lord will deliver you into my hands, I will cut your head off and leave your carcass and the carcasses of the Philistines to the birds in the sky and the wild beasts in the earth; and all the world shall know that there is a God in Israel."

When the Philistine moved towards him, David ran quickly out of the camp to meet the Philistine. He put his hand into his bag and took out a stone, which he slung. The stone stank into the Philistine's forehead, and he fell flat on his head on the ground. In this way David defeated the Philistine with his sling and stone; he struck Goliath down and gave him a mortal wound. There was no sword in David's hands. Then David ran towards him and stood over the Philistine, and grasping his sword, drew it out of the scabbard, dispatched him and cut off his head.

When the Philistines saw that his hero had been killed, they turned and ran away. Then the men of Israel raised their war-cry and pursued them all the way to Gath[2] and the gates of Ekron[3].

---

1. Prophetic expression = God of armies.
2. Old city of Canaan, of the Anakites. Later it became the capital of the Philistine Pentapolis.
3. Philistine city.

When the sons of Israel returned from pursuing the Philistines they plundered their camp. David took the Philistine's head and carried it to Jerusalem.

New presentation of David to Saul. When Saul saw that David came out to meet the Philistine, he asked Abner his commander-in-chief, "Whose son is that boy, Abner?" Abner answered, "By your life, I do not know." The king asked him, "Find out whose son he is."

When David came back from killing the Philistine, Abner took him to Saul with the Philistine's head in his hand. And Saul asked him, "Whose son are you, young man?", and David answered, "I am the son of your servant Jesse of Bethlehem."

Friendship of Jonathan with David. When David finished talking with Saul, he kept him and would not let him return any more to his father's house, for he saw that Jonathan[1] had given his heart to David and had grown to love him as himself. So Jonathan and David made a solemn compact because each one loved the other as dearly as himself. Jonathan stripped off the cloack he was wearing and his tunic, and gave them to David, together with his sword, his bow and his belt. David succeeded so well in every venture on which Saul sent him that he was given a command in the army, and his promotion pleased the ordinary people, and even Saul's officers.

When David returned from killing the Philistine, the women came out from all the cities of Israel, singing and dancing before the king of Saul with tambourines and harps. The women as they made merry sang to one another,

"Saul killed thousands,
and David killed tens of thousands."

Saul is jealous of David. Saul was furious, and the words rankled. He said, "They have given David tens of thousands, and me only thousands; what more can they do but make him king?" From that they forward Saul kept a jealous eye on David.

---

1. Son of Saul.

Next day an evil spirit from God seized upon Saul; he fell into a frenzy into the house, and David played the harp to him as he had before; Saul had a spear in his hand, and he hurled it at David, saying, "I will pin David to the wall", but David swerved aside twice. Saul was afraid of David, because the Lord was with him and had forsaken Saul.

Jonathan intercedes for David. Saul spoke to Jonathan his son and all his household about killing David. But Jonathan, son of Saul, was devoted to David and said to him, "Saul, my father, intends to kill you. Now, be on guard tomorrow morning, conceal youself and remain hidden. I will join my father in country where you are, and speak to him about you, and if I discover anything I will tell you."

Jonathan spoke up for David to his father Saul. And then he added, "Do not wrong your servant David, because he has not wronged you; his conduct towards you has been beyond reproach. He took his life in his hands when he killed the Philistine, and the Lord gave a great victory to all Israel. You saw this yourself, and you rejoiced. Why should you wrong an innocent man and put David to death without cause?" Saul listened to Jonathan's words and swore, "By the Lord, David shall not die." Jonathan called David and told him his father's words. Then he took him to Saul, and he was in attendance on the king as before.

Michal saves David. War broke out again, and David attacked the Philistines and dealt them such a blow that they ran before him. But an evil spririt from the Lord seized Saul; he was sitting in his house and had a spear in his hand. David was playing the harp. Saul tried to pin David to the wall with the spear, but David swerved and avoided Saul's blow, and the spear was driven into the wall. David escaped and got safely away.

Jonathan tries to save David. David made his escape from Naioth in Ramah and came to Jonathan, and said to him, "What have I done? What have I done wrong to your father that he intends to kill me?" He answered, "God forbid! You shall not die. My father does not do anything without telling me about it first. Why should he hide such a thing from me? I cannot

believe it!" David said, "Your father knows very well that you
love me dearly, and he thinks, 'Jonathan must not know it or he
will resent it.' But as the Lord and you live, there is only a step
between me and death." Jonathan replied, "What shall I do for
you?" David answered, "Look, it is new moon tomorrow[1], and I
ought to dine with the king. Let me go, and I shall conceal
myself in the fields until the afternoon comes. If your father
misses me, you shall tell him, 'David asked me for a leave to
pay a rapid visit to his city, Bethlehem, for it is the annual
sacrifice there for his family.' If he says, 'It is all right.' your
servant shall be safe, but if he gets angry, you shall know that
he is set in doing me wrong. My Lord, keep faith with me, for
you and I have entered into the Covenant of the Lord; and if I
am to blame, kill me yourself, Why let me fall into your father's
hands?" Jonathan said, "God forbid! If I know that my father is
set in doing you wrong, I will tell you about it myself?"

Jonathan pledged himself afresh to David for he loved him
dearly, as much as himself.

Jonathan defends David. So David hid in the fields. When
new moon came, the king sat down to eat. The king was sitting
in his place by the wall, as usual; Jonathan sat in fron of him,
Abner next to Saul, and David's place was empty." That day
Saul said nothing, because he thought, "It is empty by chance,
perhaps because he was ritually unclean." But on the second
day, the day after the new moon, the place of David was empty
again. And Saul asked Jonathan, his son, "Why has not the son
of Jesse come to dinner, either yesterday or today?" Jonathan
answered, "He asked me for a leave to go to Bethlehem. He
said, 'Allow me to go, for my family is holding a sacrifice in the
town, and my brothers have ordered me to be there. Now, if you
have any regard for me, let me slip away to see my brothers.'
That is why he has not come to dine with the king."

Then Saul got angry with Jonathan, and said to him, "You
son of a crooked and perverse mother! Did I not know that you
have made friends with the son of Jesse, to bring shame on

---

1. The Babilonians, as the Jews, counted the months and the years by the moons
   and the sun. Full moon was a holiday for the Jews.

yourself and dishonour on your mother? For while the Jesse's son remains alive on earth, you will not be safe, nor you kingdom. Now, sent for him and bring him into my presence, for he deserves death." But Jonathan[1] replied to Saul, his father, "Why does he deserve to die? What has he done?" Then Saul picked up his spear and threatened to kill him; and he knew that his father was bent on David's death. Jonathan left the table in a rage an ate nothing on the second day of the festival; for he was indignant on David's behalf because his father had humiliated him.

Jonathan tells David to escape. Next morning Jonathan went out into the fields, as he had agreed with David. Then David got up from behind the mount of stones and prostrated three times. Then they embraced and cried together for a long time. Jonathan said to David, "Go in peace; we have pledged each other in the name of the Lord, and the Lord shall always be between you and me, between your descendancy and mine."

David in the cave of Adullam[2]. David escaped and went to the cave of Adullam. His brothers and all the house of his fathers knew this and went there. Men in any kind of distress or in debt or with a grievance gathered round him, about four hundred in number, and he became their leader.

David in Ziph. Jonathan's visit. David remained in the desert, in the hill country of the desert of Ziph. Saul searched for him night and day, but God did not deliver him into his hands. David was afraid, for Saul wanted kill him. David was in the desert of Ziph, in Horesh.

David in the cave of En-gedi[3]. David went up and lived in the fastnesses of En-gedi. When Saul returned from pursuing the Philistines, he was told, "David is in the desert of En-gedi."

Then Saul took three thousand men with him, picked from the whole of Israel, and he went in search of David and his people as far as the Rocks of the Wild Goats. There beside the

---

1. Jonathan means Gift from God.
2. (Hebrew, closed place.) Old village. David hid in some of its caves.
3. Place and fastness of the desert of Judah, rich in palm trees in the old times, by the Dead Sea. It was called city of the Esenites.

rock were some sheepfolds, and nearby was a cave, which they entered to relieve his feet.

David spares Saul's life. David and his men were sitting concealed at the end of the cave, and the people of David said to him, "Look, today is the day that the Lord told you: I deliver your enemy into your hands; do with him as you please." David stood up and cut off a piece of Saul's cloak. And he said to his men, "God forbid that I should do such a thing to my lord; he is the Lord's anointed." David reproved his men severely and would not let them attack Saul[1].

Saul rose, left the cave and went on his way. Then David stood up, left the cave and called after Saul, "My lord the king!" When Saul looked round, David prostrated himself in obeisance and said to him, "Who told you that David is out to do you harm? Today you have seen that the Lord delivered you into my hands in the cave and I have not killed you. I have forgiven you saying, 'I cannot lift a finger against my master, he is the Lord's anointed.' Look, my dear lord, at this piece of your cloak in my hand. I cut it off, but I did not kill you; this will show you that I have no thought of violence or treachery against you, and that I have done you no wrong; yet you are resolved to take my life. May the Lord judge between us! but though he may take vengeance on you for my sake, I will never lift my hand against you."

Saul recognizes his guilt for a moment. When David had finished speaking with Saul, he said, "Is that your voice, my son, David?" And Saul wept. Then he said to David, "You are better than me, because you have treated me well, and I am doing you wrong. Today you have shown that you treat me well, for the Lord has delivered me into your hands and you have not killed me. May the Lord reward you well for what you have done with me. I know now for certain that you will become king, and that the kingdom of Israel will flourish under

---

1. He shows the greatness of his soul forgiving the man who is searching for him to kill him.

your hands." Then Saul went back to his home, while David and his men went up to their fastness[1].

Death of Samuel. Samuel died, and all Israel gathered to mourn him. They buried him in his house, in Ramah. Afterwards David went down to the desert of Mahon.

David spares Saul's life a second time. Men from Ziph came to Saul at Gibeah[2] to say to him, "Do you know that David is hidden in the hill of Hachilah overlooking Jeshimon, at the edge of the desert?" Saul went down at once to the desert of Ziph with three thousand men chosen of Israel to search for David in the desert of Ziph.

Saul encamped in the hill of Hachilah, at the edge of the desert, by the road. As soon as David knew that Saul had come to the wilderness in pursuit of him, he sent out scouts and found that Saul had reached such and such a place. Then David went towards the place where Saul had encamped, and he looked at the place where Saul and Abner, son of Ner, chief of his army, were sitting. David turned to Ahimelech the Hittite and Abishai son of Zeruiah, and asked them, "Who wants to go down to the camp of Saul with me?" Abishai answered, "I will go down with you." Therefore David and Abishai went there in the night, and Saul was lying asleep in the center of the camp, with his spear thrust into the ground by his head. Abner and the army were sleeping around him.

Abishai said to David, "Today the Lord has delivered your enemy into your hands. So now allow me to pin him to the ground with his own spear, with only one thurst." David said to Abishai, "Do not kill him! For, he has ever lifted a finger against the Lord's anointed and gone unpunished?[3]" And he added, "As the Lord lives the Lord will strike him down; either his time will come and he will die, or he will go down to battle and meet his end. God forbid that I should lift a finger against the anointed of the Lord." David took the spear and the

---

1. Saul had to recognize the loyalty and nobility of his servant, but David would not trust him and protected himself.
2. Northern city in the border.
3. The enemy's forgiveness is an evangelic command.

water-jar which were at his head and left. Nobody saw or noticed them, nobody even woke up, because the Lord had sent a heavy sleep upon them.

Then David crossed over to the other side and stood on the top of a hill; there was a great distance between them. Then David shouted to the army[1] and to Abner, son of Ner, saying, "Abner, answer me!" Abner answered, "Who calls me?" David said to Abner, "Do you call yourself a man? Is there anyone like you in Israel? Why, then, did you not keep watch over your lord the king, when someone came to harm your lord the king? This was not well done. As the Lord lives, you deserve to die, all of you, because you have not kept watch over your master the Lord's anointed. Look! Where are the king's spear and the water-jar what were by his head?" Then Saul recognized David's voice and said, "David, is that you, my son?" David answered, "Yes, sir, my king." And he added, "Why must your majesty pursue me? What have I done? What mischief I am plotting? Listen, my lord, to what I have to say. If it is the Lord who has set you against me, may an offering be acceptable to him; but if it is men, a curse on them in the Lord's name."

Saul repents for a moment. Then Saul said, "I have sinned. Come back to me, my son, David, I will not do you any harm again. I have behaved foolishly, and I have been sadly in the wrong." David answered, "Here is the king's spear. Let one of your men come across and fetch it. The Lord who rewards uprightness and loyalty will reward the man into whose power he put you today, when I refused to lift a finger against the Lord's anointed. As I held your life precious today, so may the Lord hold mine precious and deliver me from every distress." Saul said to David, "May the Lord bless you, David, my son. You shall be successful in everything you do, and your power shall be great." David went his way and Saul came back home.

Achish grants David the city of Ziklag. David thought, "One of these days I shall be killed by Saul. The best I can do is escape into Philistine territory. In this way Saul will cease from pursue me in the land of Israel and I will escape his clutches."

---

1. To Saul's mem.

So David and his six hundred men crossed the frontier forthwith to Achish son of Maoch king of Gath. David settled with his men beside Achish, in Gath, everyone of them with his family[1].

David said to Achish, "If I stand well in your opinion, grant me a place in one of your country towns where I may settle. Why should I remain in the royal city with your majesty?" On that very day Achish granted him the city of Ziklag. That is why nowadays Ziklag still belongs to the kings of Judah. David spent in the Philistine country one year and four months.

Defeat and death of Saul. The Philistines fought a battle against Israel, and the men of Israel were defeated, leaving their dead on Mount Gilboa. The Philistines hotly pursued Saul and his sons and killed the three of them, Jonathan, Abinadab and Malchishua. The battle went hard for Saul. The archers came upon him and he was wounded by them. Then Saul said to his armour-bearer, "Draw your sword and run me through, so that these uncircumcised brutes may not come and taunt me and make sport of me." But the armour-bearer was afraid, and he did not want to do it. Then Sau took his own sword and fell on it. When the armour-bearer saw that Saul was dead, he too fell on his sword and died with him. Thus they all died together, Saul, his three sons and his armour-bearer. When the Israelites who were on the other side of the valley by the Jordan saw that the sons of Israel had fled and that Saul and his three sons had died, they abandoned their cities and fled, and the Philistines went in and occupied them.

Next day, when the Philistines came to strip the slain, they found Saul and his three sons lying dead on Mount Gilboa[2]. They cut off their heads, stripped them of their weapons and sent messengers through the length and breadth of their land to take the good news to idols and people alike. They put their

---

1. David sook refure in the country of the Philistines, for he did not felt himself safe in the country of Saul. He did not want to fight him, but to protect his family and friends.

2. Between the Mediterranean Sea and the Jordan.

weapons in the temple of Ashtoreth and nailed his body on the wall of Beth-shan[1].

---

1. Still city of the Philistines. Afterwards it was of the tribe of Manasseh. In Pompey's times it was a free city and was named Escitopolis.

SECOND BOOK OF SAMUEL

David knows the death of Saul and Jonathan. After the death of Saul, David, who had fought the Amalekites again, was in Ziklag[1] for two days. On the third day a man came from Saul's army with his clothes rent and dust on his head. When he came to David he fell to the ground and prostrated himself before David. David asked him, "Where do you come from?" And he answered, "I have escaped from the camp of Israel." David asked, "What has happened? Tell me." He replied, "The people fled from the battle, and many have fallen in battle. Saul and his son Jonathan are dead too." David insisted, "How do you know that Saul and Jonathan are dead?" The man answered, "It happened that I was on Mount Gilboa by chance, and I saw Saul leaning on his spear with chariots and horsemen closing in upon him" He turned round and, seeing me, he called me. I answered, 'Here I am.' He asked, 'Who are you?', and I replied, 'I am an Amalekite.' Then he said, 'Come closer, please, and kill me, because altough I am still alive the throes of death have seized me.' So I stood over him and killed him, for I knew that, broken as he was, he could not live. Then I took the crown from his head and the bracelet from his arm and I have brought them to you, my lord." Then David took his clothes and rent them, and so did all the men with him.

---

1. Canaanite city allotted to David as his residence by the King Akis. It is located South of Negeb, between Beersheba and Hebron.

David's lament over Saul and Jonathan. David made a lament over Saul and his son Jonathan. It is written down in the Book of the Upright to be taught to the people of Judah. He said,

"Your glory, O Israel, has perished on your mounts.
　　　How are the men of war fallen?
Mounts of Gilboa!
　　　let no dew or rain fall on you,
　　　no showers on the fields,
　　　for there the shields of the heroes lay tarnished.
How did the heroes fall
　　　in the battlefield?
　　　Jonathan! your death has brought me misery,
How did the heroes fall,
　　　how died the weapons of fight[1]?"

HISTORY OF DAVID

David is anointed king at Hebron. After this, David inquired of the Lord, "Shall I go into one of the cities of Judah?" The Lord answered, "Go." David asked, "Where shall I go?" "The Lord answered, "To Hebron." David went to Hebron with the men who were with him, with their families, and they settled down in the cities of Hebron. The men of Judah came and David was anointed king over the house of Judah.

David rules in Hebron (around 1012-1004 b.C.). The war between the house of Saul and the house of David was long, but while David grew steadily stronger, the house of Saul became weaker and weaker.

David king of all Israel (1003-971 b.C.). Then all the tribes of Israel came to Hebron to see David, and they told him, "Look, we are bone from your bones and flesh from your flesh. In the past, while David was king over us, you led the forces of Israel, and the Lord has said to you, "You shall be the shepherd of my people Israel, and you shall be their chief." So all the

---

1. Lost piece of the "Book of the Upright".

elders of Israel came to Hebron, and King David made a covenant with them before the Lord, and David was anointed king of Israel.

David was thirty years old when he came to the throne, and he reigned for forty years. At Hebron he reigned over Judah for seven years and six months; at Jerusalem he reigned for thirty-three years over all Israel and Judah[1].

David conquers Jerusalem and makes it capital of the kingdom. The king and his men went to Jerusalem to attack the Jebusites, who inhabited the country[2].

David settled down in the stronghold and he called it "City of David". And around it he built a wall, starting at the Millo and working inwards. David grew steadily stronger, and the Lord, God of the armies, was with him.

Victories of David over the Philistines. When the Philistines knew that David had been anointed king over all Israel, they came up to seek him out. David heard about it and went down to the stronghold. The Philistines came and overrun the Vale of Rephaim. So David asked the Lord, "Shall I attack the Philistines? Will you deliver them into my hands?" And the Lord answered, "Attack them, for I will certainly deliver them into your hands." So David went to Baal-perazim and defeated them there. And David said, "The Lord has broken through my enemies' lines as a river breaks its banks." That is why that place was named Baal-perazim[3].

The Ark is taken to Jerusalem. David summoned again the picked men of Israel, thirty thousand men. David, with all the army that went with him, went to Baalath-judah to fetch the Ark of God which bears the name of the Lord of Hosts, who is enthroned upon the cherubim. They mounted the Ark of God on a new cart and conveyed it from the house of Abinadab on the hill, with Uzzah and Ahio, sons of Abinadab, guiding the cart. Uzzah was at one side of the Ark of God, and Ahio walked in

---

1. David's war with Israel finished with his anointment as king of all the other tribes.
2. They had walled the city.
3. David defeated the Philistines.

front. David and all the house of Israel were dancing before the Ark without restraint, singing to harps and lutes, tambourines and castanets and cymbals.

The Ark of the Lord was in the house of Obed-edom of Gath[1] for three months, and the Lord blessed Obed-edom and all his family. King David was told that the Lord had blessed Obed-edon and his family because of the Ark of God. Then David went there and brought up the Ark of God to the city of David with much rejoicing.

When the bearers of the Ark of the Lord had gone six steps he sacrificed an ox and a buffalo. David danced before the Lord without restraint, wearing a linen ephod. So David and all the house of Israel brought up the Ark of the Lord with shouting and blowing of trumpets.

Nathan's prophesy. When David was established in his house and the Lord had given him security from his enemies on all sides, the king said to the prophet Nathan, "Look, I am living in a house of cedar, while the Ark of the Lord is in your tent." And Nathan said to the king, "Do whatever you have in mind, because the Lord is with you[2]."

God promises David the eternal permanence of his kingdom. That night the word of the Lord came to Nathan, and he said, "Say to my servant David, 'This is the word of the Lord: Are you the man who is going to build me a house to dwell in? I have not dwelt in a house since I brought Israel out of Egypt; I made my journey in a tent and a tabernacle.

Now, then, speak to my servant David and say to him: This is the word of the Lord of Hosts: I took you from the pastures, and from following the sheep, to be prince over my people, Israel. I have been with you in your campaigns, I have defeated your enemies before you. I shall make your name great among the great ones of the earth.

---

1. When David achieved the national unity, he establishes Jerusalem as the political and religious capital of the People of Israel.
2. He brought the Ark of the Covenant to Jerusalem and thought of building a Temple to the Lord.

Besides, the Lord announces: I will build a house for you. When your days are over and you rest with your fathers, I will set up one of your family, one of your own children, to succeed you and I will establish his kingdom. He shall build a house in honour of my name, and I will establish his royal throne for ever. I will be a father for him, and he shall be a son for me. If he does wrong, I will punish them as any father would do. Your house and your kingdom will stand for all time in my sight, and your throne shall be established for ever." Nathan recounted these words to David.

David's thanksgiving. Then King David went into the presence of the Lord, and he said to him, "Who am I, my Lord, and what is my family, that you have brought me so far?" And even this is a small thing in your sight. My Lord, , and you have planned for your servant's house in days long past, for the whole duration of humanity. What else could I say to you? You know your servant, my Lord. You have made good your word, it was your purpose to spread your servant's fame and so you have raised me to this greatness. You are great indeed, O Lord, we have never heard of one like you; there is no god but you. Is there a people over the earth like your people Israel? Now, O Lord, perform what you have promised for your servant and his house, and for all time. Be your name in glory for ever."

David's wars. Afterwards, David defeated and subdued the Philistines. David took from them the control of their capital. He defeated the Moabites too. They were conquered by David and paid him tribute.

David surrounded Damascus' Syria, and the Aramaeans were conquered by him and paid him tribute. The Lord gave victory to David wherever he went.

David's double sin. Next year, when kings take field, David sent Joab, his officers and all the Israelite forces, and they ravaged Ammon and laid siege to Rabbah, while David remained in Jerusalem.

It happened that one evening, David got up from his coach and, as he walked about on the roof of the palace, he saw a woman bathing. This woman was very beautiful. David sent to inquire who she was, and they told him, "She is Bathsheba,

daughter of Eliam and wife of Uriah the Hittite." Then David
sent messengers to fetch her. The woman came to his house and
had intercourse with him. Then she came back to his house. She
bore a son and sent word to David saying, "I am pregnant."
Then David sent a messenger to Joab, "Fetch me Uriah the
Hittite." Joab sent him to David. When Uriah came to David, he
asked him how Joab was and how was the war.

Then David said to Uriah, "Go home and wash your feet."
Uriah left the palace and a present from the king followed him.
Uriah did not return to his house; he laid down by the palace
gate with the king's slaves[1].

David was told about this, saying, "Uriah has not gone
home." Then David asked him, "You have had a long journey,
why did you not go home?" Uriah answered, "The Ark, Israel
and Judah live in tents, why should I go home to eat and drink
and to sleep with my wife? By the Lord and your life, I cannot
do this!" Then David said to Uriah, "Stay here another night,
and tomorrow I will let you go." So Uriah stayed in Jerusalem
that night. The next day David invited him to eat and drink with
him and made him drunk; in the evening Uriah went out to lay
down in his blanket among the king's slaves, and he did not go
home.

The following morning David wrote a letter to Joab and sent
Uriah with him. He wrote, "Put Uriah opposite the enemy where
the fighting is fiercest and then fall back, and leave him to meet
his death." Joab, who was watching the city, put Uriah at a point
where he knew they would put up a stout fight. The men in the
city attacked Joab; many fighting men were killed, together with
servants of David and Uriah, the Hittite.

Joab sent David a dispatch with all the news. He said to the
messenger, "When you have finished your report to the king,
you shall say to him, 'Your servant Uriah the Hittite is dead
too'."

---

1. The Bible explains historic facts as they are, but it does not approve them; on
    the contrary, as in the case of David's double sin; he was ashamed of himself
    and God forgave him.

So the messenger left, and when he came to David, he did as he had been commanded by Joab.

Then David said to the messenger, "This is what you must say to Joab: 'Do not let this distress you; there is no knowing where the sword will strike'."

When Uriah's wife knew that her husband was dead, she mourned for him; and when the period of mourning was over, David sent for her and brought her into his house. She became his wife and bore him a son. But what David had done was wrong in the eyes of the Lord.

Parable of the rich mand and the poor man[1]. The Lord sent the prophet Nathan[2] to David. When he entered his presence he said, "In a city there were two men, one rich and the other poor. The rich man had large flocks and herds. The poor man had nothing except one little ewe lamb. He had reared it himself, and it grew up in his home with his sons. It was like a daughter to him. One day a traveller came to the rich man's house, and he, too mean to take something from his own flocks and herds to serve to his guest, took the poor man's lamb and served up that."

David was very angry, and burst out, "As the Lord lives, that man deserves death, and he shall pay four times for the lamb, because he has done this and shown no pity."

Then Nathan said to David, "You are that man! These are the words of the Lord, God of Israel: 'I anointed you as king of Israel and I set you free from Saul's hands. I have given you the hosue of Israel and Judah, and, besides, I would have added other favours as great. Why then have you flouted the word of the Lord by doing what is wrong in my eyes? You killed Uriah the Hittite[3] with the sword, and married his wife. You struck him down with the Ammonites' sword. So, since you have

---

1. This parable is a great work of delicacy and mastery.
2. The Prophets explained the messages they got from God by actions and parables (Hebrew = Gift of God).
3. The Hittites were a great empire of Minor Asia who expanded to Egypt. There were some of them left in Palestine.

despised me and taken the wife of Uriah the Hittite, your family
shall never again have rest from the sword."

David repents. David said to Nathan, "I have sinned against
the Lord." Then Nathan said to David, "The Lord has forgiven
your sin. You shall not die. But, because you have shown your
contempt for the Lord, the boy that will be born shall die."

Death of Bathsheba's son[1]. The Lord struck the boy whom
the wife of Uriah had given to David, and he was very sick.
David prayed for the boy; he fasted and went in and spend the
night laying on the ground. The elders of the house tried to get
him to rise from the ground, but he would not rise nor eat with
them. On the seventh day the boy died. David realised that the
servants were talking among them and he understood that the
boy had died. David asked them, "Is the boy dead?" And they
replied, "Yes, he is dead."

Then David rose from the ground, washed and anointed
himself. He put on fresh clothes and went to the house of the
Lord, where he prostrated himself.

Birth of Solomon. Afterwards David consoled Bathsheba,
his wife. He had intercourse with her and she conceived. He
named his son Solomon.

Murder of Ammon[2] **and rebellion of Absalom.**Some years
later, Absalom prepared a banquet as if it were the king's, and
he had commanded his servants, "When Ammon is merry with
wine and I said to you, 'Strike Ammon' do not be afraid,
because it is me who commands it. Be bold and resolute."
Absalom's servants did to Ammon what Absalom had
commanded them, whereupon all the king's sons mounted their
mules in haste and set off for home.

A young sentry looked up and saw a lot of people coming
down the hill from the direction of Horontaim, next to the
mountains. Then Jonadab said to the king, "The sons of the king
are coming, as your servant has said." He had hardly finished
talking when the king's sons arrived, and the broke into loud

1. Hebrew = the opulent woman.
2. Ammon was one of the king's sons.

lamentations. Also the king and his servants cried bitterly. Absalom escaped to Talmai son of Ammihur, king of Geshur.

Absalom's return. Then the king said to Joab[1], "You have my consent; go and fetch back the young man Absalom." Joab went at once to Geshur and brought Absalom to Jerusalem, but the king said, "Let him go to his own quarters; he shall not come into my presence." So Absalom went to his own quarters and did not enter the king's presence.

No man in all Israel was so greatly admired for his beauty as Absalom; he was without flaw from the crown of his head to the sole of his foot. He had three sons, and a daughter named Tamar, who was very beautiful.

Absalom remained in Jerusalem for two years without seeing the king. Then the king sent for him. He came into his presence and prostrated before him on the ground. And the king kissed Absalom.

Absalom's rebellion and other conflicts. After this, Absalom provided himself with a chariot and horses and a escort of fifty men. Absalom rose early and stood beside the road which runs through the city gate. He would hail every man that had a case to bring before the king for judgement and would ask him, "What city do you come from?" The man answered, "Your servant is from such and such a tribe of Israel." Then Absalom would say to him, "I can see that you have a very good case, but you will get no hearing from the king." And Absalom would add, "If only I were appointed judge in the land, it would be my business to see that everyone who brought a suit or a claim got justice from me." And whenever a man approached to prostrate himself, he gave him his hand and kissed him. In this way Absalom stole the affections of the Israelites who came to ask justice from the king.

Four years later, Absalom said to the king, "May I have leave now to go to Hebron to fulfil a vow there that I made to the Lord? When I was in Geshur[2], in Aram, I made this vow: If

---

1. Officer of the army. He interceded for Absalom before the king.
2. Guesur in the East Jordan, when he escaped from his father after having killed his brother Ammon.

the Lord makes me come back to Jerusalem, I shall offer him a sacrifice in Hebron." The king replied, "You may go." Then he rose and left for Hebron.

Absalom sent runners through all the tribes of Israel with this message, "As soon as you hear the sound of the trumpet you shall say, 'Absalom is king in Hebron.'" Two hundred men accompanied Absalom from Jerusalem; they were invited and went in all innocence, knowing nothing of the affair. The conspiracy gathered strength, and Absalom's supporters increased in number.

David fleds from Jerusalem. The news reached David, and he was told, "The heart of the people is leaving with Absalom" Then David said to his servants who were with him in Jerusalem, "Let us get away at once, otherwise there will be no escape from Absalom. Make haste, or he will soon be upon us and bring disaster on us, showing no mercy to anyone in the city." The king's servants said to him, "As your majesty thinks best; we are ready." The king and all his people departed, and he stopped in the last house. All his servants were with him. The Kerethite and Pelethite guards and Hittites, who had followed him from Gath[1], six hundred men under him marched past the king. The king remained standing by the gorge Kidron while all the people crossed the way which leads to the desert.

Absalom enters Jerusalem. Absalom entered Jerusalem with all the men of Israel. Ahithophel[2] was with him. In those days Ahithophel's advice was taken as an oracle of God himself. So were his advices, for David as for Absalom.

Husai's advice saves David. Ahithophel said to Absalom, "Let me choose twelve thousand men to pursue David tonight. I shall overtake him when he is tired and disispirited; I will cut him off from his people and they will all scatter; and I shall kill no one but the king." However, Absalom said, "Summon Husai[3] the Archite and let us hear what he has to say." Hushai came

---

1. The country of the Anakites, were David took refuge escaping from Saul's pursue.
2. Ahithophel was a counsellor of David who changed sides.
3. Husai, David's counsellor, had remained in Jerusalem to inform.

into Absalom's presence and said to him, "Ahithopel has said this, shall I do as he says? If not, say what you think." Husai said to Absalom, "For once the counsel that Ahithophel has given is not good. You know that your father and the men with him are hardened warriors and savage as a bear in the wilds robbed of her cubs. You father is an old campaigner and will not spend the night with the main body; even now he will be laying hidden in a pit or in some such place. Then if any of your men are killed at the outset, anyone who hears the news spread the rumour of disaster. The courage of the most resolute and lion-hearted will melt away, for all Israel knows that your father is a man of war and has determined men with him. My advice is this. Wait until the whole of Israel, from Dan to Beersheba, is gathered about you, countless as grains of sand on the sea-shore, and then you shall march with them in person. Then you shall come upon him somewhere, wherever he may be, and descend on him like dew falling on the ground, and not a man of his family or of his followers will be left alive." Then Absalom and the Israelites said, "The advice of Hushai the Archite is better than Ahithophel's."

Absalom pursues David across the East Jordan. David had come to Mahanaim[1] when Absalom crossed the Jordan with all the Israelites who were with him.

Defeat of Absalom and his followers. David mustered the people who were with him, and appointed officers over units of a thousand and a hundred.

Then David said to the army, "I will go with you to to the battle." The army answered, "No, you must not go. If we turn and run, no one will take any notice, nor will they, even if half of us are killed; but you are worth ten thousand of us, and it would be better now for you to remain in the city in support." The king said, "I will do as you think best." He stood beside the gate, and the army marched past in their unitts of a thousand and a hundred. The king gave orders to Joab, Abishai, and Ittai, "Deal gently with the young man Absalom for my sake." And

---

1. Walled city of the king of Israel where David lived after Saul's defeat, in the East Jordan.

everybody knew that the king had given this order on Absalom to all the officers.

The army took the field against the Israelites[1] and the battle was fought in the forest of Ephron. There the people of Israel were defeated by the followers of David, and that day the defeat was great: twenty thousand men were killed. The fighting spread over the whole countryside, and the forest took toll of more people that day than the sword.

Death of Absalom. Absalom met face to face the servants of David. He was riding a mule and, as it passed beneath a greak oak, his head was caught in its boughs; he found himself in mid air and the mule went on from under him. One of the men who saw it went and told Joab, "I saw Absalom hanging from an oak." While the man was telling him, Joab broke in, "You saw him? Why did you not strike him to the ground then and there? I would have given you ten pieces of silver and a belt." The man answered, "If you were to put in my hand a thousand pieces of silver, I would not lift a finger against the king's son; for we all heard the king giving orders to you and Abishai and Ittai that whoever finds himself near the young man Absalom must take great care of him. If I had dealt him a treacherous blow, the king would soon have known, and you would have kept well out of it." Joab answered, "I do not want to waste my time with you." He picked up three stout sticks and drove them against Absalom's chest while he was held fast in the tree and still alive. Then ten young men who were Joab's armour-bearers closed in on Absalom, struck at him and killed.

Absalom's burial. Then Joab sounded the trumpet and the army came back from the pursuit of Israel, because he had called off. They took Absalom's body and flung it into a great pit in the forest, and raised over it a huge pile of stones. The Israelites had all fled to their homes.

The pillar in the King's Vale had been set up by Absalom in his lifetime, for he said, "I have no son to carry on my name." He had named the pillar after himself; and to this day it is called Absalom's monument.

---

1. Absalom's followers.

David is told the news. David was sitting between the two gates. The sentry went up to the roof of the gatehouse, looked up and saw a man who ran towards them alone. The sentry called to the king and told the king about it. The king said, "If he is coming alone he has good news." As the man came nearer and nearer, the sentry saw another man running towards them, and he called to the king, "There is another man coming alone." And the king said, "This man has good news too." The sentry said, "I see by the way he runs that the first runner is Ahimaaz son of Zadok." The king answered, "He is a good man, and comes to bring good news."

Ahimaaz[1] came nearer and said to the king, "All is well", and he prostrated himself before the king, and added, "Blessed be the Lord, your God, who has delivered the men who rose their hand against you to you, the king." The king asked, "Is all well with the young man Absalom?" Ahimaaz answered, "I saw a great commotion, but I did not know what had happened." The king said, "Stand on one side and stood there." He turned aside and stood there.

Then the Cushite came in and said, "Good news, majesty. The Lord has avenged you this day on all those who rebelled against you." The king asked the Cushite, "Is all well with the young man Absalom?" He replied, "May all the king's enemies and all rebels who would do you harm be as that young man is."

David's mourning for Absalom. The king was deeply moved and went up to the roof-chamber over the gate and wept, crying out as he went "Oh my son, Absalom! My son, my son, Absalom! If only I had died instead of you! Oh Absalom, my son, my son!"

Joab was told that the king was weeping and mourning for Absalom. And that day victory was turned to mourning for the whole army, because they heard how the king grieved for his son. They stole into the city like men ashamed to show their faces after a defeat in battle. The king hid his face and cried aloud, "Absalom, my son, son! Absalom, my son, my son!"

---

1. Ahimaaz, with his brother Jonathan, mediated between David and his friend Husai, whom David had left in Jerusalem.

Preparations for the king's return. Then the men of Judah united themselves and sent a messenger to the king, and he said to him, "Come back, you and your servants."

So the king came back and reached the Jordan. Judah had come to Gilgal to meet the king.

David wants to count his people. The king said to Joab and the officers of his army, "Go round all the tribes of Israel, from Dan to Beersheba, and make a record of the people and report the number to me." Joab said to the king, "Even if the Lord your God should increase the people in a hundred and your majesty should live to see it, what pleasure would that give your majesty?" However, Joab and the officers of the army were overruled by the king, and they left his presence in order to count the people.

KINGS

FIRST BOOK OF KINGS

HISTORY OF SOLOMON[1]

Solomon is appointed king. Then Nathan said to Bathsheba, Solomon's mather, "Have you not heard that Adonijah[2] son of Haggith has become king, all unknown to our lord David? Now come, let me advise you what to do for your own safety and for the safety of your son Solomon. Go in and see King David and say to him, 'Did not your majesty swear to me, your servant, that my son Solomon should succeed you as king; that is was he who should sit on your throne? Why then has Adonijah become king?' Then while you are still speaking there with the king, I will step in and tell the whole story."

So Bathsheba entered the private chamber of the king. He was now very old, and Abishag the Shunammite was waiting on him. Bathsheba bowed before the king and prostrated herself. Then the king said, "What happens?" She answered, "My lord, you swore to me your servant, by the Lord your God, that my

---

1. Nathan named him Jedidja (favourite of God), but the name of Solomon prevailed (= Peace, welfare).
2. Adonijah (Hebrew = my Lord). With the King's consent and shouldered by the priest Abiathar and Joab, officer of the army, he tried to proclaim himself as king. He was the fourth son of the king.

son Solomon should succeed you as king, and that he should sit on your throne. But now, here is Adonijah become king, all unknown to your majesty. He has sacrificed great numbers of oxen, buffaloes, and sheep, and has invited to the feast all the king's sons, and Abiathar the priest, and Joab the commander-in-chief, but he has not invited your servant Solomon. And now, your majesty, all Israel is looking to you to announce who is to succeed you on the throne. Otherwise, when you, sir, rest with your forefathers, my son Solomon and I shall be treated as criminals."

She was still speaking to the king when Nathan the prophet arrived. The king was told that Nathan was there; he came into the king's presence and prostrated himself with his face to the ground. "My Lord" he said, "your majesty must, I suppose, have declared that Adonijah should succeed you and that he should sit on your throne. He has today gone down and sacrificed great numbers of oxen, buffaloes and sheep, and has invited to the feast all the king's sons, Joab the commander-in-chief, and Abiathar the priest; and at this very moment they are eating and drinking in his presence and shouting, 'Long live the King Adonijah.' but he has not invited me your servant, Zadok the priest[1], Benaiah son of Jehoiada[2], or your servant Solomon. Has this been done by your majesty's authority, while we your servants have not been told who should succeed you on the throne?"

Thereupon the king said, "Call Bathsheba", and she came into the king's presence and stood before him. Then the king swore and oath to her: "As the Lord lives, who has delivered me from all my troubles; I swear by the Lord the God of Israel that Solomon your son should succeed me and that he should sit on my throne, and this day I give effect to my oath." Bathsheba bowed low to the king and prostrated herself; and she said, "May my Lord, king David, live for ever!"

Then King David said, "Call Zadok the priest, Nathan the prophet, and Benaiah son of Jehoiada." They came into the

---

1. Distinguished priest who gave great services to David and Solomon.
2. Captain of David's personal guard.

king's presence and he gave them these orders: 'Take the officers of the household with you; mount my son Solomon on the king's mule and escort him down to Gihon[1]. There Zadok the priest and Nathan the prophet shall anoint him king over Israel. Sound the trumpet and shout, "Long live King Solomon!" Then escort him home again, and he shall come and sit on my throne and reign in my place; for he is the man that I have appointed prince over Israel and Judah. Benaiah son of Jehoiada answered the king, "It shall be done. And may the Lord, the God of my lord the king, confirm it! As the Lord has been with your majesty, so may he be with Solomon; may he make his throne even greater than the throne of my Lord King David."

So Zadok the priest, Nathan the prophet, and Benaiah son of Jehoiada, together with the Kerethite and Pelethite guards, went down and mounted Solomon on King David's mule, and escorted him to Gihon. Zadok the priest took the horn of oil from the Tent of the Lord and anointed Solomon; they sounded the trumpet and all the people shouted, "Long live King Solomon." Then all the people escorted him home in procession, with great rejoicing and playing of pipes, so that the very earth split with the noise[2].

David's last dispositions. When the time of David's death drew nearer, he gave this last charge to his son Solomon: "I am going the way of all the earth. Be strong and show yourself a man. Fulfil your duty to the Lord your God; conform to his ways, observe his statutes and his commandments, his judgements and his solemn precepts, as they are written in the law of Moses, so that you may prosper in whatever you do and whichever way you turn, and that the Lord may fulfil the promise that he made about me: 'If your descendants take care to walk faithfully in my sight with all their hearth and with all their soul, you shall never lack a successor on the throne of Israel."

---

1. A well outside the city that later was called well of Maria.
2. In that time kings were anointed by God and acclaimed by the people.

So David rested with his forefathers and was buried in the city of David[1], having reined over Israel for forty years, seven in Hebron and thirty-three in Jerusalem; and Solomon succeeded his father David as king and was firmly established on the throne.

Solomon's marriage. Solomon allied himself to Pharaoh king of Egypt by marrying his daughter. He brought her to the City of David, until he had finished building his own house and the house of the Lord and the wall round Jerusalem[2].

Vision at Gibeon: his prayer. He went to Gibeon[3] to offer a sacrifice, for that was the chief hill-shrine, and he used to offer a thousand whole-offerings on its altar. There that night the Lord God appeared to him in a dream and said, "What shall I give you? Tell me." And Solomon answered, "You showed great and constant love to your servant David my father, because he walked before you in loyalty, righteousness,and integrity of heart; and you have maintained this great and constant love towards him and have given him a son to succeed him on the throne. Now, O Lord my God, you have made your servant king in place of my father David, though I am a mere child, unskilled in leadership. And I am here in the midst of your people, the people of your choice, too many to be numbered or counted. Give your servant, therefore, a heart with skill to listen, so that he may govern your people justly and distinguish good from evil. For who is equal to the task of governing this great people of yours?"

The Lord was well pleased that Solomon had asked for this, and he said to him, "Because you have asked for this, and not for long life for yourself, or for wealth, or for the lives of your enemies, but have asked for discernment in administering justice, I gran your request[4]; I give you a heart so wise and so understanding that there has been none like you before your

---

1. The city of David was the old fortress kept by the Jebusites.
2. In this way he secured his borders from Egypt.
3. North of Jerusalem.
4. The Lord was pleased with Solomon's request, for he asked for wisdom instead of wealth and power. He granted him wisdom and wealth.

time nor will be after you. I give your furthermore those things for which you did not ask, such wealth and honour as no king of your time can match. And if you conform to my ways and observe my ordinances and commandments, as your father David did, I will give you long life." Then he awoke, came to Jerusalem and stood before the Ark of the Covenant of the Lord; there he sacrificed whole-offerings and brought shared-offerings, and gave a feast to all his household.

Solomon's Judgement[1]. Then two prostitute women came into the king's presence and one of them said, "My lord, this woman and I live in the same house, and I gave birth to a child when she was there with me. On the third day after my baby was born she too gave birth to a child. We were together and quite alone, no one else was there with us. Then one night this woman's child died because she overlaid it, and she got up in the middle of the night, took my child from my side while I was sleeping and laid it in her bosom, putting her dead child in mine. When I got up in the morning to feed my baby, I found him dead; but when I looked at him closely, I found that it was not the child that I had borne." The other woman broke in, "That is not true, my son is alive, and yours is dead." But the first woman said, "No, your son is dead, and the living child is mine." In this way they argued before the king.

Then the king spoke and said, "Bring me a sword." He was given a sword and then said, "Cut the living child in two and give half to one and half to the other." Then the mother of the living child, moved with love for her child, said to the king, "Oh, ser, let her have the baby; whatever you do, do not kill it." The other said, "Let neither of us have it, cut it in two."

Therefore the king spoke and gave judgement, "Let the first woman have the living baby and do not kill it. She is the mother." All Israel heard the judgement which the king had given, they all stood in awe of him, for they saw that he had the wisdom of God with him to administer justice.

---

1. His wisdom was soon being tested.

Solomon's wisdom and power. Solomon reigned over all Israel, from the river[1] to the land of the Philistines and the borders of Egypt. All of them payed him tribute and were subject to him all his life.

Solomon had forty thousand chariot-horses in his stables and twelve thousand cavalry horses[2]. The regional governors, each for a month in turn, supplied provisions for King Solomon and for all who came to his table; they never fell short in their deliveries. They provided also barley and straw, each according to his duty, for the horses and chariot-horses where it was required.

And God gave Solomon depth of wisdom and insight, and understanding as wide as the sand on the sea-shore, so that Solomon's wisdom surpassed that of all the men of the east and of all Egypt, and his fame spread among all the surrounding nations. He uttered three thousand proverbs, and his songs numbered a thousand and five. He discoursed of trees, from the cedar of Lebanon down to the marjoram that grows out of the wall, of beasts and birds, of reptiles and fishes. Men of all races came to listen to the wisdom of Solomon, and from all the kings of the earth who had heard of his wisdom he received gifts.

Embassy from Hiram: its contribution to the building of the temple. Hiram, king of Tyre[3], heard that Solomon had been anointed king instead of his father. He sent envoys to him, because he had always been a friend of David. Solomon sent this answer to Hiran, "You know that my father, David, could not build a house in honour of the name of the Lord his God, because he was surrounded by armed nations until the Lord made them subject to him. But now the Lord, God, has given me peace on every side; there is no one to oppose me, I fear no attack. So I intend to build a house in honour of the name of the Lord my God, following the promise given by the Lord to my

---

1. The river Euphrates was the borderline between Mesopotamia and Syria.
2. Solomon's famous stables have been found in Megido. His wisdom is well-known.
3. Phoenitian city isolated by the sea on a steep hill.

father David: 'You son whom I shall set on the throne in your place will build the house in honour of my name.' If therefore you wil now give orders that cedars be felled and brought from Lebanon[1], my men will work with yours, and I will pay you for your men whatever sum you fix; for, as you now, we have none so skilled at felling timber as your Sidonians."

Then Hiram said to Solomon, "I have received your message. In this matter of timber, both cedar and pine, I will do all you wish. My men shall bring down the logs from Lebanon to the sea and I will make them up into rafts to be floated to the place you appoint. You, on your part, will meet my wishes if you provide the food for my household." So Hiram kept Solomon supplied with all the cedar and pine that he wanted, and Solomon supplied Hiram with twenty thousand kor of wheat as food for his household and twenty kor of oil of pounded olives; Solomon gave this yearly to Hiram. The Lord had given Solomon wisdom as he had promised him, and there was peace between Hiram and Solomon and they concluded an alliance.

Building of the temple. In the four hundred and eightieth year after the Israelites had come out of Egypt, in the fourth year of Solomon's reign over Israel, in the second month of that year, the month of Ziv[2], Solomon began to build the house of the Lord. The Temple which King Solomon built for the Lord was sixty cubits[3] long by twenty cubits broad, and its height was thirty cubits. In the building of the house, only blocks of undressed stone direct from the quarry were used; no hammer or axe or any iron tool whatsoever was heard in the house while it was being built.

Then the Lord addressed Solomon and said, "As for this house which you are building, if you are obedient to my ordinances and conform to my precepts and loyaly observe all my commands, then I will fulfil my promise to you, the promise I gave to your father David, and I will dwell among the

---

1. Mountains with high cedars.
2. According to the Hebrew system of measuring time, around the year 960 b.C.
3. Cubit = 0,44 mm.

Israelites and never forsake my people Israel[1]." So Solomon finished the building of the Temple, lining the inner walls of the house with cedar boards, covering the interior from floor to rafters with wood; the floor he laid with boards of pine. All was cedar, no stone was left visible.

He prepared an inner Most Holy Place in the furthest recesses of the Temple to receive the Ark of the Covenant of the Lord. This inner Most Holy Place[2] was twenty cubits square and it stood twenty cubits hight; he overlaid it with red gold and made an altar of cedar before the Most Holy Place, which he overlaid with gold too. The whole Temple he overlaid with gold until it was all covered. In the Most Holy Place he made two cherubim of wild olive, each ten cubits high. He overlaid them with gold. Round all the walls of the house he carved figures of cherubim, palmtrees and open flowers, both in the inner chamber and in the outer. The floor of the Temple he overlaid with gold, both in the inner chamber and in the outer.

In the fourth year, in the month of Ziv[3], the foundation of the house of the Lord was laid; and in the eleventh year, in the month of Bul, that is, the eigth month, the Temple was completed in all its details. It was built in seven years.

Building of the palace. Then Solomon started to build a palace, and it took him thirteen years until it was finished. He built the palace "Forest of the Lebanon", a hundred cubits long, fifty broad, and thirty high, constructed of four rows extending over the beams, which rested on the columns.

Making of the objects of the Temple. He made the bronze Altar[4]: twenty cubits long, twenty cubits broad and ten high.

Then he made the Sea of cast metal[5]; it was round in shape, the diameter from rim to rim being ten cubits; it stood five

1. God keeps the promises that he made to David.
2. The Most Holy Place or the Sancta Sanctorum of the Sanctuary.
3. The name of this month can be found also in the Phoenitian language, and it is equivalent to the eigth Israelite month of the year.
4. Altar of the Offerings. In ancient times it was made of non-carved stones. It was situated in the middle of a central yard, with a horn at every corner, symbol of the divine power, and it was burning day and night.
5. For the washing.

cubits high, and it took a line thirty cubits long to go round it. All round the Sea on the outside under its rim, completely surrounding the thirty cubits of its circumference, were two rows of gourds[1], cast in one piece with the Sea itself. It was mounted on twelve oxen, three facing north, three west, three south, and three east, their hind quarters turned inwards; the Sea rested on top of them. Its thickness was a hand-breath; its rim was made like that of a cup, shaped like the calyx of a lily; it held two thousand bath[2] of water.

Solomon also did all the objects of the Temple of the Lord; the golden altar, the golden table upon which was set the Bread of the Presence; the lamp-stamps of red gold on the Most Holy Place, five on the right side and five on the left side; the flowers, lamps and tongs, of gold; the cups, snuffers, tossing-bowls, saucers, and firepans, of red gold; and the panels for the doors of the inner sanctuary, the Most Holy Place, and for the doors of the house, of gold.

When all the work which King Solomon did for the Temple of the Lord was completed, he brought in the sacred treasures of his father David, the silver, the gold, and the vessels, and deposited them in the storehouses of the Temple of the Lord.

The Ark is brought to the Temple. Then Solomon summoned the elders of Israel, all the heads of the tribes who were chiefs of families in Israel, to assemble in Jerusalem in order to bring up the Ark of the Covenant of the Lord from the City of David, which is called Zion. All the men of Israel assembled in King Solomon's presence at the pilgrim-feast in the mouth Ethanim, the seventh month. When the elders of Israel had all come, the priests took the Ark of the Lord and carried it up with the Tent of the Presence and all the sacred furnishings of the Tent; it was the priests and the Levites together who carried them up. Then the priests brought in the Ark of the Covenant of the Lord to its place, the inner shrine of the Temple, the Most Holy Place, beneath the wings of the cherubim. The cherubim spread their wings over the place of

1. Cucurbitatean leaves.

2. Of 45 litres.

the Ark; they formed a screen above the Ark and its poles. The poles projected, and their ends could be seen from the Holy Place. There was nothing inside the ark but the two tablets of stone which Moses had deposited there at Horeb, the tablets of the Covenant which the Lord made with the Israelites when they left Egypt.

Then the priests came out of the Holy Place, since the cloud was filling the Temple of the Lord, and they could not continue to minister because of it, for the glory of the Lord filled his Temple.

Words of Solomon. Then Solomon said, "The Lord has said that he will dwell in thick darkness.

I have built you a lofty house, a house for you to live in forever."

So the king turned round and blessed all the assembly of Israel as they stood waiting, and added, "Blessed be the Lord, God of Israel, who spoke directly to David, my father, and has himself fulfilled his promise."

The King's prayer. Then Solomon, standing in front of the altar of the Lord in the presence of the whole assembly of Israel, spread out his hands towards heaven and said, "Oh Lord, God of Israel, there is no God like you in heaven above or on earth beneath, keeping covenant with your servants and showing them constant love while they cointinue faithful to you in heart and soul. You have kept your promise to your servant David my father; by your deeds this day you have fulfilled what you said to me in words. Now therefore, O Lord God of Israel, keep this promise of yours to your servant David my father, 'You shall never want for a man appointed by me to sit on the throne of Israel, in only your sons look to their ways and walk before me as you have walked before me.' And now, O God of Israel, let the words which you spoke to your servant David my father be confirmed.

But can God indeed dwell on earth? Heaven itself, the highest heaven, cannot contain you. How much less this house that I have built! Yet attend to the prayer and the supplication of your servant, O Lord my God, listen to the cry and the prayer which your servant utters this day, that your eyes may ever be upon this house night and day, this place of which you said, 'My name shall be there'; so may you hear your servant when he prays towards this place. Hear the supplication of your servant and of your people Israel when they pray towards this place. Hear you in heaven your dwelling and, when you hear, forgive.

Listen to the supplications of your servant and your people Israel, and listen to their prayers, for you singled them out from all the peoples of the earth to be your possession; so you did promise through your servant Moses when you brought our forefathers from Egypt, O Lord God!"

Offering of sacrifices. Then the king, and all Israel with him, offered sacrifices to the Lord. Solomon offered as shared-offerings to the Lord twenty-two thousand oxen and a hundred and twenty thousand sheep; thus it was that the king and the Israelites dedicated the house of the Lord. On that day also the king consecrated the centre of the court which lay in front of the Temple of the Lord; there he offered the whole-offering, the grain-offering, and the fat portions of the shared-offerings, because the bronze altar which stood before the Lord our God for seven days. On the eight day he dismissed the people; and they blessed the king, and went home happy and glad at heart for all the prosperity granted by the Lord to his servant David and to his people Israel.

Solomon's second vision. When Solomon had finished the Temple of the Lord, the royal palace and all the plans for building on which he had set his heart, the Lord appeared to him a second time, as he had done at Gibon, and He said to him, "I have heard your supplication and prayer which you have offered me. I have consecrated this Temple which you have built, to receive my Name for all time, and my eyes and my heart shall be fixed on it forever. And if you, on your part, live in my sight as your father David lived, in integrity and uprightness, doing all I command you and observing my statutes and judgements, then I will establish your royal throne over Israel for ever, as I promised your father David when I said, 'You shall never want for a man upon the throne of Israel.' But if you or your sons turn back from following me and do not observe my commandments and my statutes which I have set before you, and if you go and serve other gods and prostrate yourself before them, then I will cut off Israel from the land which I gave them; I renounce this house which I have consecrated in honour of my name, and Israel shall become a byword and an object lesson among all peoples."

Solomon's fleet. Besides, King Solomon built a fleet of ships at Ezion-geber, near Eloth[1] on the shore of the Red Sea. Hiram sent men of his own to serve with the fleet, experienced seamen, to work with Solomon's men; and they went to Ophir[2] and brought back four hundred and twenty talents of gold, which they delivered to King Solomon.

Visit of the Queen of Sheba. The queen of Sheba[3] heard of Solomon's fame and of the Temple which he had built to the Name of the Lord, and she came to test him with hard questions. She arrived in Jerusalem with a very large retinue, camels ladden with spices, gold in great quantity, and precious stones. When she came into Solomon's presence, she told him everything that she had in her mind. Solomon answered all her questions; not one of them was too abtruse for the king to answer.

When the queen of Sheba saw all the wisdom of Solomon, the Temple which he had built, the food on his table, the courtiers sitting around him, and his attendants standing behind in their livery, his cupbearers, and the whole-offerings which he used to offer in the house of the Lord, there was no more spirit left in her. And she told the King, "What I had heard in my country about you and your wisdom is true. I did not believe it and came and saw for myself. Indeed, I was not told half of it; your wisdom and your prosperity go far beyond the report which I had of them. Happy are your people, happy are your courtiers who are always by your side and hear your wisdom! Blessed be the Lord your God who has delighted in you and has

---

1. In the Akaban Gulf, north of the Read Sea.
2. Unknown place: India? Sumatra? Eritrea? They brought gold, ivory and precious stones.
3. Sheba = Kush, Ethiopia.

set you on the throne of Israel! Because he loves Israel for ever, he has made you their king to maintain law and justice." Afterwards the gave the king a hundred and twenty talents of gold, spices in great abundance, and precious stones. Never again came such a quantity of spices as the queen of Sheba gave to King Solomon. And King Solomon gave the queen of Sheba all she desired, whatever she asked for, in addition to all that he gave her of his royal bounty. So she departed and returned with her retinue to her own land.

Solomon's wealth and luxe. Now the weight of gold which Solomon received yearly was six hundred and sixty-six talents[1], in addition to the tolls levied by the customs officers and profits on foreign trade, and the tribute of the kings of Arabia and the regional governors.

The king also made a great throne of ivory and overlaid it with fine gold. Six steps led up to the throne; at the back of the throne there was the head of a calf. There were arms on each side of the seat, with a lion standing beside each of them, and twelve lions stood on the six steps, one at either end of each step. Nothing like it had ever been made for any monarch. All Solomon's drinking vessels were of gold, and all the plate in the Palace "Forest of Lebanon" was of red gold; no silver was used, for it was reckoned of no value in the days of Solomon. The king had a fleet of merchantment at sea with Hiram's fleet at Tarsis[2]; once every three years this fleet came home, bringing gold and silver, ivory, apes, monkeys and turkeys.

Thus King Solomon outdid all the kings of the earth in wealth and wisdom, and all the world courted him, to hear the wisdom which God had put in his heart. Each brought him his gift, vessels of silver and gold, garnments, perfumes and spices, horses and mules, so much year by year. And Solomon got together many chariots and horses; he had fourteen hundred chariots and twelve thousand horses, and he stabled some in the chariot-towns and kept other at hand in Jerusalem[3].

---

1. Equivalent to 41.126 kilos.
2. Hispania.
3. Mainly in the famous stables at Megido, discovered in 1903 and 1925.

Solomon's sins. But King Solomon, apart from Pharaoh's daughter, married many foreign women, Moabite, Ammonite, Edomite, Sidonian and Hittite, from the nations with whom the Lord had forbidden the Israelites to intermarry, "because", he said, "they will entice you to serve their gods." But Solomon was devoted to them and loved them dearly. He had seven hundred wives, who were princesses, and three hundred concubines, and they turned his heart from the truth. When he grew old, his wives turned his heart to follow other gods, and he did not remain wholy loyal to the Lord his God as his father David had been. He followed Ashtoreth, goddess of the Sidonians, and Milcom, the loathsome god of the Ammonites. Thus Solomon did what was wrong in the eyes of the Lord, and was not loyal to the Lord as his father David. He built a hill-shrine for Kemosh[1], the loathsome god of Moab, on the height to the east of Jerusalem, and for Molech, the loathsome god of the Ammonites.

The Lord was angry with Solomon because his heart had turned away from the Lord the God of Israel, who had appeared to him twice and had strictly commanded him not to follow other gods; but he disobeyed the Lord's command. The Lord therefore said to Solomon, "Because you have done this and have not kept my covenant and my statutes as I commanded you, I will tear the kingdom from you and give it to your servant. Nevertheless, for the sake of your father David I will not do this in your day; I will tear it from your son's hand. Even so not the whole kingdom; I will leave him one tribe for the sake of my servant David and for the sake of Jerusalem, my chosen city."

Jeroboam's rebellion. Jeroboam son of Nebat, one of Solomon's courtiers, an Ephratite from Zeredah, whose widowed mother was named Zeruah, rebelled against the king. This is the story of his rebellion. Solomon had built the Millo and closed the breach in the wall of the city of his father David. Now this Jeroboam was a man of great energy; and Solomon,

---

1. Kemosh and Molech above all were offered human sacrifices. Kemosh was the god of the Ammonites. Women were King Solomon's ruin.

seeing how the young man worked, had put him in charge of all
the labour-gangs in the tribal district of Joseph. On one occasion
Jeroboam had left Jerusalem, and the prophet Ahijah[1], the
Shilonite[2] met him on the road. The prophed was wrapped in a
new cloak, and the two of them were alone in the open country.
Then Ahijah took hold of the new cloak he was wearing, tore it
into twelve pieces and said to Jeroboam, "Take ten pieces, for
this is the word of the Lord the God of Israel: 'I am going to
tear the kingdom from the hand of Solomon and give you ten
tribes. But one tribe will remain his, for the sake of my servant
David and for the sake of Jerusalem, the city I have chosen out
of all the tribes of Israel. I have done this because Solomon has
forsaken me; he has prostrated himself before Ashtoreth
goddess of the Sidonians, Kemosh god of Moab, and Milcom
god of the Ammonites, and has not conformed to my ways.'
After this Solomon sought to kill Jeroboam, but he fled to King
Shishak in Egypt and remained there till Solomon's death.

Death of Solomon. The other acts and events of Solomon's
reign, and all his wisdom, are recorded in the annals of
Solomon. The reign of King Solomon over the whole of Israel
lasted forty years. Then he rested with is forefathers and was
buried in the city of David his father, and he was succeeded by
his son Rehoboam.

DIVISION OF THE KINGDOM.
HISTORY OF JUDAH AND JERUSALEM

Rehoboam; the split of the ten tribes. Rehoboam went to
Sechem, for all Israel had gone there to make him king. When
Jeroboam son of Nebat, who was still in Egyp, heard of it, he
remained there, having taken refuge in order to escape King
Solomon. They now recalled him, and he and all the assembly
of Israel came to Rehoboam and said, "Your father laid a cruel

---

1. He foretold the division of the country and the misery of the house of
   Jeroboam under the rule of Basha.

2. From Shilo.

yoke upon us; but if you will now lighten the cruel slavery he imposed upon us and the heavy yoke he laid upon us, we will serve you." He answered, "Give me three days and come back again." So the people went away.

Then King Rehoboam consulted the elders who had been in attendance on his father Solomon while he lived. "What answer do you advise me to give to this people?" And they said, "If today you are willing to serve this people, show yourself their servant now and speak kindly to them, and they will be your servants ever after." But he rejected the advice which the elders gave him. He next consulted those who had grown up with him, the young men in attendance, and asked them, "What answer do you advise me to give to these people that have spoke to me in those terms?" The young men, who had grown up with him, replied, "Give this answer to these people: 'My little finger is thicker than my father's loins. My father laid a heavy yoke on you; I will make it heavier. My father used the whip on you; but I will use the lash'."

On the third day, as the king had commanded when he said, "Come into my presence in three days.", the people came before Rehoboam. But the king spoke to them harshly, and did not follow the advice that the elders had given him, speaking as the young men had said to him: "My father laid a heavy yoke on you; I will make it heavier. My father used the whip on you; but I will use the lash." When Israel saw that the king would not listen to them, they answered, "What share do we have in David? We have no lot in the son of Jesse. Back to your tents, Israel! Now watch your own house, David!"

And the Israelites went to their tents. Rehoboam ruled over those Israelites who lived in the cities of Judah. When the men of Israel heard that Jeroboam had returned, they sent and called him to the assembly and made him king over the whole set of Israel. The tribe of Judah alone followed the house of David[1].

---

1. From then on Solomon's kingdom is divided into two. Rehoboam followed the advice of the young men. Now the kindom of the North will be called Israel, and the kingdom of the South will be called Judah."

Once in Jerusalem, Rehoboam assembled all the house of Judah and the tribe of Benjamin, a hundred and eighty thousand chosen warriors to fight against the house of Israel and recover the kingdom of Rehoboam, son of Solomon. But God spoke to Shemaiah the man of God, "Say to Rehoboam and the rest of the people: 'This is the word of the Lord: You shall not go up to make war on your kinsmen the sons of Israel. Return to your homes, for this is my will." They listened to the word of the Lord and returned home, as the Lord had commanded.

Jeroboam I, king of Israel. The new worship. Jeroboam rebuilt Sechem in the hill-country of Ephraim and took up residence there. From there he went out and built Penuel. Then Jeroboam thought, "As things now stand, the kingdom will revert to the house of David. If this people go up to sacrifice in the Temple of the Lord in Jerusalem, it will revive their allegiance to their lord Rehoboam king of Judah, and they will kill me and return to King Rehoboam." So he made two calves of gold and said to the people, "It is too much trouble for you to go up to Jerusalem; here are your gods, Israel, that brought you out of Egypt." One he set up at Bethel and the other he put at Dan, and this thing became a sin in Israel, for the people went to Dan to worship one of them.

Profecy against the altar at Bethel. As Jeroboam stood by the altar to burn the sacrifice, a man of God[1] from Judah, moved by the word of the Lord, appeared at Bethel. He inveighted against the altar in the Lord's name, crying out, "O altar, altar! This is the named Josiah. He will sacrifice upon you the priest of the hill-shrines who make offerings upon you, and he will burn human bones upon you[2]." He gave a sign the same day, "This is the sign which the Lord has ordained: This altar will be rent in pieces and the ashes upon it will be split." When King Jeroboam heard the sentence which the man of God pronounced against the altar at Bethel, he pointed to him from the altar and said, "Seize that man." Immediately the hand which he had

---

1. Of the Nabim, minor Prophets.

2. Human bones on that altar. The prophecy would become true in King Josiah's times.

pointed at him became paralysed, so that he could not draw it back. The altar too was rent in pieces and the ashes were split, in fulfilment of the sign that the man of God had given at the Lord's command. The king appealed to the man of God: "Please, pacify the Lord my God and pray for me that my hand can be restored." The man of God did as he asked; his hand was restored and became as it had been before.

Rehoboam's reign. Rehoboam, son of Solomon, ruled over Judah. He was forty-one years old when he came to the throne, and he reigned for seventeen years in Jerusalem, the city which the Lord had chosen out of all the tribes of Israel to receive his Name. And Judah did what was wrong in the eyes of the Lord, rousing his jealous indignation by the sins they committed, beyond anything that their forefathers had done. They erected hill-shrines[1], Massebas[2] and Aseras[3] over any hill or under any spreading tree. All over the country there were male prostitutes attached to the shrines, and the people adopted abominable practices of the nations whom the Lord had dispossessed in favour of Israel.

In the fifth year of Rehoboam's reign Shishak king of Egypt attacked Jerusalem. He removed the treasures of the Temple of the Lord and of the royal palace, and seized everything, including all the shields of gold that Solomon had made[4].

There was continual fighting between Jeroboam and Rehoboam. The latter rested with his forefathers and was buried with them in the city of David. He was succeeded by his son Abiham.

Abijam king of Judah. In the eighteen year of the reign of Jeroboam son of Nebat, Abijam became king of Juda. He reigned in Jerusalem for three years. All the sins that his father had committed before him he committed too, nor was he faithful to the Lord his God as his ancestor David had been. But

---

1. Hills.
2. Massebas, pillars or poles, or sacred pillars.
3. Assera, Phoenitian godess. Ashterath, godess of Baal, god of the Canaanites.
4. Shishak, Jeroboam's protector, went up to Palestine, defeated Rehoboam, conquered 165 cities and broke into the Temple of Jerusalem. He founded the XIInd dinasty. He was from the Lebanon.

for David's sake the Lord his God gave him a flame to burn in Jerusalem, by establishing his dinasty, and making Jerusalem secure, because David had done what was right in the eyes of the Lord.

Asa king of Judah. In the twentieth year of Jeroboam king of Israel, Asa became king of Judah. He reigned in Jerusalem for forty-one years. Asa did what was right in the eyes of the Lord, like his ancestor David. He expelled from the land the male prostitutes attached to the shrines and did away with all the idols which his predecessors had made. Although the hill-shrines were allowed to remain, Asa himself remained faithful to the Lord all his life. He brought into the Temple of the Lord all his father's votive offerings and his own, gold and silver and sacred vessels. Asa was at war with Baasha king of Israel all through their reigns.

And Baasha, king of Israel, invaded Judah and fortified Ramah to cut off all access to Asa king of Judah. So Asa took all the gold and silver that remained in the treasuries of the Temple of the Lord and of the royal palace, and sent his servants with them to Ben-hadad son of Tabrimmon, son of Hezion, king of Aram[1], whose capital was Damascus, with instructions to say, "There is an alliance between us, as there was between our fathers. I now send you this present of silver and gold; break off your alliance with Baasha king of Israel, so that he may abandon his campaing against me." Ben-hadad listened willingly to King Asa; he ordered the commanders of his armies to move against the cities of Israel, and they attacked Iyyon, Dan, Abelbeth-maacah, and that part of Kinnereth which marches with the land of Naphtali. When Baasha heard of it, he stopped fortifying Ramah and fell back on Tirzah[2].

Nadab king of Israel. Nadab son of Jeroboam became king of Israel in the second year of Asa king of Judah, and he reigned for two years. He did what was wrong in the eyes of the Lord and followed in his father's footsteps, repeating the sin which

---

1. Aram, Syria.

2. It was residence of the kings after Sechem. Years later the king's residence was at Samaria, as the capital of the reign.

he had led Israel to commit. Baasha son of Ahijah, of the house of Assachar, conspired against him and attacked him at Gibbethon, a Philistine city, which Nadab was besieging with all his forces. And Baasha slew him and usurped the throne in the third year of Asa king of Judah. As soon as he became king, he struck down all the family of Jeroboam, destroying every living soul and leaving no survivors, as the Lord had said to Ahijah. It happened because of the sins of Jeroboam and the sins which he led Israel to commit, and because he had provoked the anger of the Lord the God of Israel[1].

Baasha king of Israel. In the third year of Asa king of Judah, Baasha son of Ahijah became king of all Israel in Tirzah and reigned twenty-five years. He did what was wrong in the eyes of the Lord, and followed in Jeroboam's steps, repeating the sin which he had led Israel to commit.

The Prophet Jehu against Baasha. Then the word of the Lord came to Jehu son of Hanani concerning Baasha: "I raised you from the dust and made you a prince over my people Israel, but you have followed in the footsteps of Jeroboam and have led my people Israel into sin, and have provoked me to anger with their sins. Therefore I will sweep away Baasha and his house and will deal with it as I dealt with the house of Jeroboam son of Nebat. Those of Baasha's family who die in the city shall be food for the dogs, and those who die in the country shall be food for the birds."

Elah king of Israel. Zimri's rebellion. In the twenty-six year of Asa king of Judah, Elah son of Baasha became king of Israel and he reigned in Tirzah two years. Zimri, who was in his service commanding half the chariotry, plotted against him. The king was in Tirzah drinking himself drunk in the house of Arza, controller of the household there, when Zimri broke in and attacked him, murdered him and made himself king. This took place in the twenty-seventh year of Asa king of Judah. As soon as he became king and was enthroned, he struck down all the family of Baasha and left not a single mother's son alive, kinsman or friend. He destroyed the whole family of Baasha,

---

1. Hill-shrines, wells and trees were sacred places.

and thus fulfilled the word of the Lord concerning Baasha, spoken through the prophet Jehu. This was what came of all sins which Baasha and his son Elah had committed and the sins into which they had led Israel, provoking the anger of the Lord the God of Israel with their worthless idols.

Short reign and death of Zimri. In the twenty-seventh year year of Asa king of Judah, Zimri reigned in Tirzah for seven days. At the time the army was investing the Philistine city of Gibbethon. When the Israelite troops in the field heard of Zimri's conspiracy and the murder of the king, there and then in the camp they made their commander Omri king of Israel by common consent. Then Omri and his whole force withdrew from Gibbethon and laid siege to Tirzah. Zimri, as soon as he saw that he city had fallen, retreated to keep the royal palace, set the whole of it on fire over his head and so perished. This was what came of the sin he had committed by doing what was wrong in the eyes of the Lord and following in the footsteps of Jeobam, repeating the sin into which he had led Israel.

Omri's reign. It was in the thirty-first year of Asa king of Judah that Omri became king of Israel and he reigned twelve years, six of them in Tirzah. He bought the hill of Samaria from Shamer for two talents of silver and built a city on it which he named Samaria[1] after Shemer, the owner of the hill. Omri did what was wrong in the eyes of the Lord; he outdid all his predecessors in wickedness. He followed in the footsteps of Jeroboam son of Nebat, repeating the sins which he had led Israel to commit, so that they provoked the anger of the Lord their God with their worthless idols.

Ahab king of Israel. Ahab son of Omri became king of Israel in the thirty-eight year of Asa king of Judah, and he reigned over Israel in Samaria for twenty-two years. Ahab did what was wrong in the eyes of the Lord; he outdid all his predecessors. As if it were not enough for him to follow the sinful ways of Jeroboam son of Nebat, he contracted a marriage with Jezebel daughter of Ethbaal king of Sidon, and went and

---

1. Since then Samaria was the capital of the kingdom of the North, Israel, until it was destroyed.

worshipped Baal[1]; he prostrated himself before him and erected
an altar to him in the temple of Baal which he built in Samaria.
He also set up a sacred pole; indeed he did more to provoke the
anger of the Lord the God of Israel than all the kings of Israel
before him.

Elijah the Prophet. Then Elijah the Tishbite, of Tishbe in
Gilead, said to Ahab, "I swear by the life of the Lord the god of
Israel, whose servant I am, that there shall be neither dew nor
rain these coming years unless I give the word."

Then the Lord spoke to him and said, "Leave this place and
turn eastwards; and go into hiding in the ravine of Kerith east of
the Jordan. You shall drink from the stream, and I have
commanded the ravens to feed you there." He did as he was
told; he went and stayed in the ravine of Kerith east of the
Jordan, and the ravens brought him bread in the morning and
meat in the evening, and he ate from the stream.

Shortage in the country. After a while the stream dried up,
for there had been no rain in the land. Then the Lord said, "Go
now to Zaraphath, a village of Sidon, and stay there; I have
commanded there a widow to feed you." So he went off to
Zarephath. When he reached the entrance to the village, he saw
a widow gathering sticks, and he called to her and said, "Please
bring me a little water in a pitcher to drink."

As she went to fetch it, he called after her, "Bring me,
please, a piece of bread to eat." Then she replied, "As the Lord
your God lives, I have no food to sustain me except a handful of
flour in a jar and a little oil in a flask. Here I am, gathering one
or two sticks to go and cook something for my son and myself
before we die." "Never fear", said Elijah, "go and do as you
say; but first make me a small cake from what your have and
bring it out to me; and after that make something for your son
and yourself. For this is the word of the Lord the God of Israel:
'The jar of flour shall not give out nor the flask of oil fail, until
the Lord sends rain on the land[2]'." So she went and did as Elijah
had said, and there was food for him and for her and her family

---

1. He introduced the worship of Ashtareth, godess of the Sidonians, Assera.

2. That land.

for a long time. The jar of flour did not give out nor did the flask of oil fail, as the word of the Lord foretold through Elijah.

Resurrection of the son of the widow. Afterwards it happened that the son of the mistress of the house fell ill and grew worse and worse, until at last his breathing ceased. Then she said to Elijah, "What made you interfere, man of God? You came here to bring my sins to light and kill my son." Elijah said, "Give me your son." He took the boy from her arms and carried him up to the roof-chamber where his lodging was, and laid him on his own bed. Then he called out to the Lord, "Oh Lord my God, is this your care for the widow with whom I lodge that you have been so cruel to her son?" Then he breathed deeply upon the child three times and called on the Lord, "O Lord my God, let the breath of life, I pray, return to the body of this child." The Lord listened to Elijah's prayer and the breath of life returned to the child's body, and he revived. Elijah lifted him up and took him down from the roof into the house, gave him to his mother and said, "Look, your son is alive." Then the woman said to Elijah, "Now I see that you are a man of God, and that the Lord is with you."

Challenge of Elijah to the prophets of Baal. Sacrifice at Mount Carmel. Time went by, and in the third year the word of the Lord came to Elijah: "Go and show yourself to Ahab, and I will send rain upon the land." So he went to show himself to Ahab.

As soon as Ahab saw Elijah, he said to him, "Is it you, you troubler of Israel?" "It is not I who have troubled Israel." he replied, "but you and your father's family, by forsaking the commandments of the lord and your father's family, by forsaking the commandments of the Lord and following Baal. But now, send and summon all Israel to meet me on Mount Carmel, and the four hundred and fifty prophets of Baal with them and the four hundred prophets of the goddess Asherah, who are Jezebel's pensioners." So Ahab sent out to all the Israelites and assembled the prophets on Mount Carmel.

Elijah stepped forward and said to the people, "How long will you sit on the fence? If the Lord is God, follow him; but if Baal, them follow him." Not a word did they answer. Then

Elijah said to the people, "I am the only prophet of the Lord still left, while there are four hundred and fifty prophets of Baal. Bring two bulls; let them choose one for themselves, cut it up and lay on the wood without setting fire to it. You shall invoke your god by name and I will invoke the Lord by name; and the god who answers by fire, he is God." And all the people shouted, "All right."

Then Elijah said to the prophets of Baal, "Choose one of the bulls and offer it first, for there are more of you; invoke your god by name, but do not set fire to the wood." So they took the bull provided for them and offered it, and they invoked Baal by name from morning until noon, crying, "O Baal, answer us" but there was no answer, no sound. They danced wildly around the altar they had set up. At midday Elijah mocked them: "Call louder, for he is a god; it may be that he is deep in thought, or engaged, or on a journey; or he may have gone to sleep and must be woken up." They cried still louder and, as was their custom, gashed themselves with swords and spears until the blood ran. All afternoon they raved and ranted till the hour of the regular service, but still there was no answer, no sound, no sign of attention.

Then Elijah said to all the people, "Come to me." They all came, and he repaired the altar of the Lord which had been torn down. He took twelve stones, one for each tribe of the sons of Jacob, the man named Israel by the word of the Lord. With these stones he built an altar in the name of the Lord; he dug a trench around it big enough to hold two measures of seed; he arranged the wood, cut up the bull and laid it on the wood. Then he said, "Fill four jars with water and pour it on the wood." They did so, and he said, "Do it again." They did it again, and he said, "And again." They did it a third time, and the water ran all around the altar and even filled the trench.

At the hour of the sacrifice the prophet Elijah came forward and said, "Lord God of Abraham, of Isaac, and of Israel, let it be known today that you are God in Israel and that I am your servant and have done all this things at your command. Answer me, O Lord, answer me and let this people know that you, Lord, are God and that it is you who have caused them to be backsliders." Then the fire of the Lord fell. It consumed the whole-offering, the wood, the stones, and the earth, and licked up the water in the trench. When all the people saw this, they prostrated and cried, "Tle Lord is God, the Lord is God." Then Elijah said to them, "Seize the prophets of Baal; let not one of them escape." They seized them, and Elijah took them down to the Kishon and slaughtered them there in the valley. Then Elijah said to Ahab, "Go back now, eat and drink, for I hear the sound of coming rain."

Elijah climbed to the crest of the Carmel. There he prostrated on the ground with his face between his knees. He said to his servant, "Go and look out to the west." He went and looked, "There is nothing to see," he said. Sevent times Elijah ordered him back, and seven times he went. The seventh time he said, "I see a cloud no bigger than a man's hand, coming up from the west." "Now go", said Elijah, "and tell Ahab to harness his chariot and be off, or the rain will stop him." Meanwhile the sky had grown black with clouds, the wind rose, and heavy rain began to fall[1]. Ahab mounted his chariot and headed for Jezreel.

Elijah's runaway across the desert. Ahab told Jezebel all that Elijah had done and hose he had put all the prophets of Baal to death with the sword. Then Jezebel sent a messenger to Elijah, saying, "The gods do the same to me and more, unless by this time tomorrow I have taken your life as you have taken theirs[2]."

Elijah finished and fled for his life. When he arrived in Beersheba in Judah, he left his servant there. Then he went into the desert, and came upon a broom-bush, and he sat down under it and prayed for death. He said, "O Lord, it is enough! Take my life, for I am not better than my forefathers." He lay down under the bush and fell asleep. But then an angel touched him and said, "Rise and eat." He looked around and saw at his head a cake baked on hot stones, and a pitcher of water. He ate and drank and laid down again. The Angel of the Lord came again

---

1. The power of the prayer.
2. To swear asking for bad things is of no use.

and, as he touched him, said, "Rise and eat, for the journey is too much for you." He rose and ate and drank, and, sustained by this food, he went on for forty days and forty nights to Horeb[1], the Mount of God.

Theophany at Horeb. When he arrived in Mount Horeb he entered a cave and stayed there. Then the Lord spoke to him and said, "What are you doing here, Elijah?" He answered, "Because of my great zeal for the Lord the God of Hosts", he said. "The people of Israel have forsaken your covenant, torn down your altars and put your prophets to death with the sword. I alone am left, and they seek to take my life."

And the Lord answered him, "Go back through the desert to Damascus, enter the city and anoint Hazael[2] to be king of Aram; anoint Jehu son of Nimshi to be king of Israel, and Elisha son of Shaphat of Abel-meholah to be prophet in your place."

Elisha's vocation. Elijah set off and found Elisha son of Shaphat ploughing; there were twelve pair of oxen ahead of him, and he himself was with the last of them. As Elijah passed, he threw his cloak over him, and Elisha, leaving his oxen, ran after Elijah and said, "Let me kiss my father and mother and then I shall follow you." Elijah answered, "Now go, what have I done to prevent you?" He followed him no further but went home, took his pair of oxen, slaughtered them and burnt the wooden gear to cook the flesh, which he gave to the people to eat. Then he followed Elijah and became his disciple.

Naboth's[3] vineyard. After this it happened that Naboth of Jezreel, who had a vineyard near the palace of Ahab king of Samaria, spoke Ahab to him in this way: "Give me your vineyard so that I can use it as a garden; I will give you a better vineyard in exchange for it or, if you prefer, its value in silver." But Naboth answered him, "The Lord forbid that I should give you the land which my family has always possessed!" So Ahab

---

1. Sinai. We need food for the soul, the holy Communion in our pilgrimage towards the Homeland.
2. Hazael as king of Syria, and Jehu for Samaria. The latter was commander of the Samarian army, which was besieging Ramot of Galaat in the war against Syria.
3. Hebrew = son.

went home sullen and angry because Naboth had said, "I shall not give you my ancestral land." He lay down on his bed, covered his face and refused to eat.

His wife Jezebel came to him and said, "Why are you so sullen and angry, and why do you not eat?" He answered, "Because I have spoken to Naboth of Jezreel and said to him, 'I want to buy your vineyard.' But he answered, 'I will not sell it to you'." Then Jezebel his wife said, "Are you not king of Israel? Stand up, eat and take heart. I will give you the vineyard of Naboth of Jezreel[1]."

Jezebel's crime. She wrote a letter in Ahab's name, sealed it with his seal and sent it to the elders and notables of Naboth's city, who sat in council with him. She wrote: "Proclaim a fast and give Naboth the seat of honour among the people. And see that two scoundrels are seated opposite him to charge him in this way: 'He has cursed God and the king, then take him out and stone him to death'." So the elders and notables of Naboth's city, who sat with him in council, carried out the instructions Jezebel had sent them in her letter: they proclaimed a fast and gave Naboth the seat of honour, and these two scoundrels came in, sat opposite him, and charged him publicly with cursing God and the king. Then they took him outside the city and stoned him, and sent word to Jezebel: "Naboth has been stoned to death."

As soon as she knew that Naboth had been stoned and was dead, she said to Ahab, "Get up and take possession of the vineyard which Naboth refused to sell you, for he is no longer alive; he is dead." When Ahab heard that Naboth was dead, he got up to go to the vineyard of Naboth of Jezreel to take possession.

Foretelling of the punishment. But then the word of the Lord came to Elijah the Tishbite; "Go down at once to meet Ahab, king of Israel, to Samaria. He is in Naboth's vineyard, where he has gone to take possession. You shall tell him: 'This is the word of the Lord: So after having committed murder you

---

1. A very fertile plain between Mount Carmel and Gilgal (Hebrew = God sows) where Acab built a palace for himself (Jezreel or Esdrel).

take possession as well!' And you shall add, 'This is the word of the Lord: In the same place in which the dogs have licked Neboth's blood, they will lick your blood too'."

Ahab said to Elijah, "Have you found me, my enemy?" "Yes, I have found you," answered, Elijah, "for you have done what is wrong in the eyes of the Lord. I will bring misery upon you; I will sweep you away and destroy every mother's son of the house of Ahab in Israel. As for Jezebel, the dogs shall eat her by the rampart of Jezreel. Of the house of Ahab, those who die in the city shall be food for the dogs, and those who die in the country shall be food for the birds."

Campaign against Ramoth-gilead[1]. For three years there was no war between Aram and Israel. In the third year Jehoshaphat king of Judah went down to visit the king of Israel. The king of Israel said to his courtiers, "As you know Ramoth-gilead belongs to us, and, however, we we do nothing to recover it from the king of Aram." And he said to Jehoshaphat, "Will you join me in attacking Ramoth-gilead?" Jehoshaphat answered the king of Israel, "What is mine is yours, myself, my people, and my horses."

Battle and death of Ahab. So the king of Israel and Jehoshaphat king of Judah marched on Ramoth-gilead, and the

---

1. City on the border between Samaria and Syria (Aram).

king of Israel said to Jehoshaphat, "I will disguise myself to go into battle, but you shall wear your royal robes." And so the king of Israel went into battle in disguise. But the king of Aram had given orders to the thirty-six chiefs of his chariots saying, "Do not engage all and sundry but the king of Israel alone." And it happened that when they saw Jehoshaphat they said, "That must be the king of Israel," and attacked him. Jehoshaphat shouted, and then they realised that he was not the king of Israel, and stopped pursuing him.

But one man drew his bow at random and hit the king of Israel where the breastplate joins the plates of the armour. Then the king said to his driver, "Wheel round and take me out of the line, I am wounded." When the day's fighting reached its height, the king was facing the Aramaeans propped up of the chariot, and in the evening he died. At sunset the herald went through the ranks, crying, "Every man to his city, every man to his country." Thus died the king. He was brought to Samaria and they buried him there. The chariot was swilled out at the pool of Samaria, and the dogs licked up the blood, and the prostitutes washed themselves in it, as the Lord had said.

Jehoshaphat king of Judah. Jehoshaphat son of Asha became king of Judah in the fourth year of Ahab king of Israel. He was thirty-five years old when he came to the throne, and he reigned in Jerusalem for twenty-five years. He followed in the footsteps of Asha his father and did not swerve from them; he did what was right in the eyes of the Lord. However, the hill-shrines did not disappear, and the people continued to slaughter and burn sacrifices there. Jehoshaphat remained at peace with the king of Israel.

Ahaziah king of Samaria. Ahaziah son of Ahab became king of Israel in Samaria in the seventeenth year of Jehoshaphat king of Judah, and reigned over Israel for two years. He did what was wrong in the eyes of the Lord and followed in the footsteps of his father and mother and in those of Jeroboam son of Nebat, who had led Israel into sin. He served Baal and worshipped him, and provoked the anger of the Lord the God of Israel exactly as his father had done.

SECOND BOOK OF KINGS

MORE HISTORY OF JUDAH AND ISRAEL

Illness and death of Ahaziah. After Ahab's death Moab[1] rebelled against Israel. Ahaziah fell through a latticed window in his roof-chamber in Samaria and injured himself; he sent messengers and said to them: "Ask Baalzebub[2] the god of Ekron whether I will recover from my illness or not."

Then the Angel of the Lord spoke to Elijah the Tishbite: "Go up to meet the messengers of the king of Samaria and say to them, 'Is there not a God in Israel that you go to inquire of Baal-zebub the god of Ekron? This is the word of the Lord: You shall not rise from the bed where you are lying; you will die'." And Elijah left.

So Ahaziah died as the Lord had foretold through Elijah, and because he had no son, his brother Jehoram succeeded him in the second year of Joram son of Jehoshaphat king of Judah.

Elijah is taken to heaven. The time came when the Lord would take Elijah up to heaven in a whirlwind. Elijah and Elisha left Gilgal, and Elijah said to Elisha, "Stay here, I pray you, for the Lord has sent me to Bethel." Elisha replied, "As the Lord lives, your life upon it, I will not leave you." Elijah said to Elisha, "Stay here, I pray you, for the Lord has sent me to

---

1. Country on the other side of the Jordan.
2. According to the Pharisees, Prince of the devils. Different form of Baal-Zebub.

Jericho." But he replied, "As the Lord lives, your life upon it, I will not leave you."

They arrived in Jericho. Then Elijah said, "Stay here, please, for the Lord has sent me to the Jordan." And he replied, "As the Lord lives, your life upon it, I will not leave you." So they set off together. Then Elijah took his cloak, rolled it up and struck the water with it. The water divided to right and left, and they both crossed over on dry ground.

Once they had crossed, Elijah said to Elisha, "Ask me what you want me to grant you before I am taken from you." And Elisha said, "Let me inherit a double share of your spirit." Elijah replied, "You have asked a hard thing. If you see me taken from you, your wish will be granted. If not, it shall not be granted." And it happened that as they went on, talking as they went, chariots and horses of fire appeared suddenly, which separated them one from the other, and Elijah was carried up in the whirlwind to heaven.

Elisha, Elijah's successor. Elisha saw him and shouted, "My father, my father, the chariots and the horsemen of Israel" and he saw him no more. Then he took his mantle and rent it in two, and he picked up the cloak which had fallen from Elijah and came back and stood on the bank of the Jordan. Then he struck the waters with Elijah's cloak and said, "Where is the Lord God of Elijah?" When he struck the water, it was again divided to right and left, and he crossed over.

Jehoram king of Israel. Jehoram son of Ahab became king of Samaria in the eighteenth year of Jehoshaphat king of Judah. He reigned for twelve years. He did what was wrong in the eyes of the Lord, although not as his father and his mother had done. He did remove the sacred pillar of the Baal which his father had made. However, he persisted in the sins into which Jeroboam son of Nebat had led Israel, and did not give them up.

Resurrection of the son of the Shunammite woman. Once Elisha went over to Shunem[1]. There was a great lady there who pressed him to accept her hospitality, and so, whenever he came that way, he stopped to take food there. That woman she said to

---

1. Place near Mount Carmel.

her husband, "I know that this man who comes here regularly is a holy man of God. Why not built up the wall to make him a little roof-chamber, and put in it a bed, a table, a seat, and a lamp, and let him stay there whenever he comes to us?"

One day Elisha arrived and went to this roof-chamber and lay down to rest. Then he said to Gehazi, his servant, "Call this Shunammite woman." He called her in and Elisha said, "You have taken all this trouble for us, what can I do for you? Shall I speak for you to the king or to the commander-in-chief?" She answered, "I live among my own people." But Elisha said, "What could we do for her?" Gehazi replied, "There is only this; she is childless and her husband is old." "Call her", he said. He called her in, and Elisha said, "Next year this time you shall have a son in your arms." She answered, "No, no, my lord, you are a man of God and would not lie to your servant." Next year in due season the woman conceived and had a son, as Elisha had foretold.

The boy grew up. One day he went out to the reapers where his father was. Suddenly he said to his father, "My head, my head!" His father told a servant to carry him home. He took him to his mother, and the boy sat on her lap till midday, and then he died. She went up and laid him on the bed of the man of God, shut the door and went out. She called her husband and said, "Send me one of your servants and a she-ass, I must go to the man of God as fast as I can, and come straight back."

When Elisha entered the house, the boy was dead, lying on the bed. He came in, shut the door on the two of them and prayed to the Lord. Then he got on to the bed, laid upon the child, put his mouth to the child's mouth, his eyes to his eyes and his hands to his hands, and, as he pressed upon him, the child's body grew warm. Elisha got up and walked once up and down the room; then, getting onto the bed again, he pressed upon him and breathed into him seven times; and the boy opened his eyes. The prophet summoment Gehazi and said, "Call this Shunammite woman." She answered his call and the prophet said, "Take your child." She came in and fell prostrate before him. Then she took up her son and went out.

Naaman's healing. Naaman, commander of the king of Aram's army, was a great man highly esteemed by his master, because by his means the Lord had given victory to Aram; but he was a leper. On one of their raids the Aramaeans brought back as a captive from the land of Israel a little girl, who became a servant to Naaman's wife. She said to her mistress, "If only my master could meet the prophet who lives in Samaria, he would rid him of his disease."

Naaman went in and reported to his master what the girl had said. And the king of Aram said, "Very well, go and I will send a letter to the king of Israel."

So he set off, taking with him ten talents of silver, six thousand shekels of gold, and ten changes of clothing. He delivered the letter to the king of Israel, which read thus: "I inform you that I am sending my servant Naaman to you, and I beg you to rid him of his disease." When the king of Israel read the letter, he rent his clothes and said, "Am I a god to kill and to give live that this fellow sends to me to cure a man of his disease? Surely you must see that he is picking a quarrel with me." When Elisha, the man of God, heard how the king of Israel had rent his clothes, he sent to him saying, "Why did you rent your clothes? Let the man come to me, and he will know that there is a prophet in Israel."

So Naaman came with his horses and chariots and stood at the entrance to Elisha's house. Elisha sent out a messenger to say to him, "If you go and wash seven times in the Jordan, your flesh shall be restored and you will be clean." Naaman was furious and went away, saying, "I thought he would at least have come out and stood, and invoked the Lord his God by name, waved his had over the place and so rid me of the disease. Are not Abana and Pharpar, rivers of Damascus, better than all the waters of Israel? Can I not wash in them and be clean?" So he turned and went off in a rage. But his servants came up to him and said, "If the prophet had bidden you do something difficult, would you not do it? How much more then, if he tells you to wash and be clean?"

So he went down and dipped himself in the Jordan seven times as the man of God had told him, and his flesh was restored as a little child's, and he was clean. Then he and his retinue went back to the man of God and stood before him; and he said, "Now I know that there is no god on the earth except in Israel. Will you accept a token of gratitude from your servant?" But Elisha replied, "As the Lord lives, whom I serve, I will accept nothing." He was pressed to accept, but he always refused. Elisha said, "Go in peace."

Joram, king of Judah. In the fifth year of Jehoram son of Ahab king of Israel, Joram son of Jehoshaphat king of Judah became king. He was thirty-two years old when he came to the throne, and he reigned in Jerusalem for eight years. He followed the practices of the kings of Israel as the house of Ahab had done, for he had married Ahab's daughter; and he did what was wrong in the eyes of the Lord. But for his servant David's sake the Lord was unwilling to destroy Judah, since he had promised to give him and his sons a flame, to burn for all time.

Ahaziah king of Judah. In the twelfth year of Jehoram son of Ahab king of Israel, Ahaziah son of Joram king of Judah became king. Ahaziah was twenty-two years old when he came to the throne, and he reigned in Jerusalem for one year; his mother was Athaliah granddaughter of Omri king of Israel. He followed the practices of the house of Ahab and did what was wrong in the eyes of the Lord like the house of Ahab, with which he was connected.

He allied hilself with Jehoram son of Ahab to fight against Hazael king of Aram at Ramoth-gilead; but King Jehoram was wounded by the Aramaeans, and returned to Jezreel to recover from the wounds which were inflicted on him at Ramoth in battle with Hazael king of Aram; and because of his illness Ahaziah son of Joram king of Judah went down to Jezreel to visit him.

Jehu is anointed and proclaimed king. Then Elisha the prophet summoned one of the sons of the prophets and said to him, "Hitch up your cloak, take this flask of oil with you and go to Ramoth-gilead. When you arrive, you will find Jehu son of Jehoshaphat, son of Nimshi; go in and call him aside from his fellow-officers, and lead him through to an inner room. Then take the flask and pour the oil on his head and say, 'This is the

word of the Lord; I anoint you king over Israel'; then just open
the door and flee for your life."

So the young prophet set off for Ramoth-gilead, and he got
there when the commanders of the army where gathered in
assembly. He said, "Sir, I have to talk with you." Jehu
answered, "With whom of us?" "With you, Sir." He answered.
Jehu stood up and came into the house. Then the prophet poured
the oil on his head and said, "This is the word of the Lord, God
of Israel: 'I anoint you king over Israel, the people of the Lord.
You shall strike down the house of Ahab your master, and I will
take vengeance on Jezebel for the blood of my servants the
prophets and for the blood of all the Lord's servants. All
the house of Ahab shall perish." Then he opened the door and
fled for his life.

Jehu's rebellion. Then Jehu son of Jehoshaphat, son of
Nimshi, laid his plans against Jehoram. He said, "If you are on
my side, see that no one escapes from the city to tell the news in
Jezreel." He mounted his chariot and drove to Jezreel, for
Jehoram was laid up there, and Ahaziah king of Juda had gone
down to visit him.

The watchman standing on the watch-tower in Jezreel saw
Jehu and his troop approaching and called out, "I see a troop of
men." Then Jehoram said, "Fetch a horseman and send to find
out if they come peacefully." So the horseman went to meet
them and said, "The king asks, 'Is it peace?'" Jehu said, "What
is peace to you? Fall in behind me."

Death of Joram, Ahaziah and Jezebel. Then Joram
commanded, "Harness my chariot!" They did so, and Joram,
king of Israel, and Ahaziah, king of Judah, came out to meet
Jehu, each one of them in his own chariot. They met him in the
plot of Naboth of Jezreel. When Joram saw that it was Jehu,
asked, "Is it peace, Jehu?" But he replied, "Do you call it peace
while your mother Jezebel keeps up her obscene image-worship
and monstrous sorceries?" Then Joram turned round and fled,
crying out to Ahaziah, "Treachery, Ahaziah." But Jehu had
already taken his bow and shot Joram between the shoulders, in
such a way that the arrow pierced his heart and he sank down in
his chariot. Jehu said to Bidkar, his lieutenant, "Pick him up and

throw him into the plot of land belonging to Naboth of Jezreel, remember how, when you and I were riding side by side behing Ahab his father, the Lord pronounced his sentence against him:

Have I not seen the blood of Naboth and his sons?
Oracle of the Lord.
In this plot I shall requite you.
Oracle of the Lord.

Therefore pick him up and throw him into it and thus fulfil the word of the Lord." When Ahaziah saw this, king of Judah, he fled towards Beth-haggan, but Jehu pursued him, saying, "Make sure of him too!" And he was wounded in his chariot on the road up to Gur, near Ibleam. He fled to Meggido[1] and died there. His servants took him to Jerusalem in a chariot and buried him in his shrine, with his fathers, in the city of David. Ahaziah became king over Judah in the eleventh year of Joram, son of Ahab.

Meanwhile Jehu came to Jezreel[2]. When Jezabel heard this, she painted her eyes and dressed her hair, and she stood looking down from a window. As Jehu entered the gate, she said, "Is it peace, you Zimri, you murderer of your master?" Jehu looked up at the window and said, "Who is with you?" Two or three eunuchs looked out, and he said, "Throw her down." They threw her down, and some of her blood splashed on to the wall and horses, which trampled her underfoot. Then he went in and ate and drank. "See to this accursed woman," he said, "and bury her; for she is a king's daughter." But when they went to bury her they found nothing of her but the skull, the feet,and the palms of the hands; and they went back and told him. Jehu said, "It is the word of the Lord which his servant Elijah the Tishbite spoke, when he said, 'In the plot of ground at Jezreel the dogs shall devour the flesh of Jezebel, and Jezebel's corpse shall be like dung upon the ground in the plot at Jezreel so that no one will be able to say: This is Jezebel'."

---

1. Camp-site of the stables and chariots of Solomon.
2. Where Ahab had built his palace beside Naboth's vineyard.

Extermination of Ahab's family. Jehu left the place and came across Jehonadab, son of Rechab[1], who had came to meet him. He greeted him and said, "Is your heart sincere towards me, as mine is towards you?" Jehonadab answered, "Yes." Then Jehu said, "If it is as you say, give me your hand." He gave him his hand and led him towards his chariot, saying, "Come with me and you shall see my zeal for the Lord." So he took him with him in his chariot. When he came to Samaria, he put to death all of Ahab's house who were left there and so blotted it out, in fulfilment of the word which the Lord had spoken to Elijah.

Abolition of the worship of Baal. Then Jehu summoned all the people and said to them, "Ahab worshipped Baal; Jehu will worship him much. Now, summon all the prophets of Baal, all his priests and worshippers. Not one must be left, for I am holding a great sacrifice to Baal. No one who is missing will live." Jehu outwitted the ministers of Baal in order to destroy them. And he commanded, "Make a feast for Baal." And it was announced. Jehu sent messengers throughout Israel, and all the worshippers of Baal were present, not one of them was missing, and they came into the temple of Baal, which was filled from end to end.

And when the sacrifice was over, Jehu ordered the guards and the lieutenants: "Come, kill them! Nobody must escape!" So they slew them without quarter in the temple of Baal. Then they took the Asera out of the temple of Baal and burnt it, and so they did with Baal's Masseba. They demolished the temple of Baal, and used it as a stable for mules up to nowadays. In this way Jeshu stamped out the worship of Baal in Israel.

Jehu's behaviour as king. However, Jehu did not abandon the sins of Jeroboam son of Nebat who led Israel into sin, but he maintained the worship of the golden calves of Bethel and Dan. The Lord said to Jehu, "You have done well what is right in my eyes and have done to the house of Ahab all what was in my mind to do. Therefore your sons to the fourth generation shall sit on the throne of Israel." But Jehu did not care to follow the

---

1. A Rechabite who was on Jehu's side, follower of the law.

law of the Lord, God of Israel, with all his heart, and he did not abandon the sins of Jeroboam, who led Israel into sin.

Athaliah queen of Judah. When Athaliah mother of Ahaziah saw that his son was dead, she set out to destroy all the royal line. But Jehosheba daugther of King Joram, sister of Ahaziah, took Ahaziah's son Joash and stole him away from among the princes who were being murdered. She put him and his nurse in a bedchamber where he was hidden from Athaliah[1]. In this way he was not murdered. And he was hidden with his nurse in the Temple of the Lord for six years, while Athaliah ruled the country.

In the seventh year, Jehoiada[2] sent for the captains of units of a hundred, both of the Carites and of the guards and he brought them into the Temple of the Lord. He made an agreement with them and put them on their oath in the Temple of the Lord, and showed them the king's son.

The captains carried out the orders of Jehoiada the priest to the letter. Each took his men, both those who came on duty on the sabbath and those who came off, and came to Jehoiada. The priest handed out to the captains King David's spears and shields, which were in the Temple of the Lord. Then the guards took up their stations, each man carrying his arms at the ready, from corner to corner of the house to north and south, surrounding the king. Then he brought out the king's son, put the crown on his head, handed him the warrant and anointed him king. The people clapped their hands and shouted, "Long live the king."

When Athalia heard the noise of the people and the guards she went to the Temple of the Lord, and she saw the king standing, as was the custom, on the days, among outbursts of son and fanfares of trumpets in his honour, and all the populace rejoicing and blowing trumpets. Athaliah rent her clothes and cried, "Treason, treason!"

---

1. Athaliah was the daughter of Jezebel and Ahab. She murdered all the royal line and became queen.
2. Jehoiada (Hebrew = God knows) hid the young king Joash and put him in Athaliah's throne.

But Jehoiada the priest order the captains of the army the following, "Take her out of the Temple." So they took her out, and as she entered the gates of the stables in the royal palace the guards killed her.

Then Jehoiada made a covenant between the Lord and the king and people that they should be the Lord's people. And all the people went into the temple of Baal and pulled it down; they smashed to pieces its altars and images, and they slew Mattan the priest of Baal before the altars. Then Jehoiada set a watch over the house of the Lord; he took captains of units of a hundred, the Carites and the guards and all the people, and they escorted the king form the house of the Lord through the Gate of the Guards to the royal palace, and seated him on the royal throne. The whole people rejoiced and the city was quiet. That is how Athaliah was put to the sword in the royal palace.

Joash king of Judah. Joash was seven years old when he came to the throne. In the seventh year of Jehu, Joash became king, and he reigned in Jerusalem for forty years. His mother was Zibiah of Beersheba. He did what was right in the eyes of the Lord all his days while Jehoiada was with him. However, the hill-shrines were not removed, the people still continued to sacrifice and make smoke-offerings there.

Defeat and death of Joash. Then Hazael king of Aram came up to attack Gath, and he conquered it. Then Hazael intended to attack Jerusalem, but Joash, king of Judah, took all the gold he could find in the Temple of the Lord and in the royal palace and sent it to Hazael, king of Aram, who did not attack the city. His servants revolted against him and struck him down in the house of Millo[1]. He was buried with his forefather in the city of David. He was succeeded by his son Amaziah.

Jehoahaz king of Israel. In the twenty-third year of Joash son of Ahaziah king of Judah, Jehoahaz son of Jehu became king over Israel in Samaria, and he reigned seventeen years. He did what was wrong in the eyes of the Lord and continued the sinful practices of Jeroboam, son of Nebat who led Israel into sin. Therefore, the anger of the Lord was roused against Israel

---

1. A tower situated north-west of the City of David.

and he made them subject to Hazael king of Aram all those years. Jehoahaz rested with his forefaters and was buried in Samaria. He was succeeded by Joash, his son.

Last prophecy and death of Elisha. Elisha was ill and lay on his deathbed, and Jehoash king of Israel went down to him and wept over him and said, "My father, my father! Chariot and chavalry of Israel!" Elisha said to him, "Take a bow and arrows." Joash took his bow and some arrows. And Elisha ordered the king of Israel, "Take your bow." He did so, and Elisha put his hand over the hands of the king and added, "Open the window toward the east"; he opened it, and Elisha said, "Shoot!" And she shot, and then Elisha cried, "An arrow for the victory of the Lord! Victory over Aram! You shall defeat Aram utterly at Aphek"; and he added, "Take your arrows." He did so. Then Elisah ordered the king of Israel, "Strike the ground with them." She struck it three times and stopped, then the man of God was furious with him and said, "You should have struck five or six times; then you would have defeated Aram utterly; as it is, you will strike Aram three times and no more." Elisha died and was buried.

Hazael king of Aram died and was succeeded by his son Ben-haddad. Then Joash son of Jehoahaz recaptured the cities which Ben-hadad had taken in war from Jehoahaz his father. Jehoash defeated him three times and recovered the cities of Israel.

Amaziah king of Judah. In the second year of Jehoash son of Jehoahaz king of Israel, Amaziah son of Joash king of Judah succeeded his father. He was twenty-five when he came to the throne, and he reigned in Jerusalem for twenty-nine years. He did what was right to the eyes of the Lord, but not like David, his father. He did as Joash his father had done. However, the hill-shrines did not disappear, therefore the people still offered sacrifices and burnt parfumes in them.

War against Israel and defeat of Amaziah. Then Amaziah sent messengers to Joash son of Jehoahaz son of Jehu king of Israel, to tell him, "Let us meet." But Joash replied to Amaziah, king of Judah, "As you have defeated utterly Edom it has gone to your head. Stay at home and enjoy your triumph. Why should you involve yourself in disaster and bring yourself to the ground, and Judah with you?" But Amaziah would not listen, and Joash, king of Israel came up and met Amaziah, king of Israel, at Beth-shemesh, which belonged to Judah. and Judah was defeated by Israel, they all fled to their tents. Joash king of Israel captured Amaziah king of Judah at Beth-shemesh. Then he came to Jerusalem and broke down the city wall from the Gate of Ephraim to the Corner Gate, a distance of four hundred cubits; he took all the gold and silver and all the vessels found in the Temple of the Lord, and all the treasuries in the royal palace. He took hostages and returned to Samaria.

Joash rested with his forefathers and was buried in Samaria, with the kings of Israel. He was succeeded by his son Jeroboam.

Amaziah son of Joash king of Judah still lived fifteen years after the death of Joash son of Jehoahaz, king of Israel.

Jeroboam II king of Israel. In the fifteen year of Amaziah son of Joash, king of Judah, Jeroboam, son of Joash, king of Israel came to the throne in Samaria, when he was forty-one years old. He did what was wrong in the eyes of the Lord and did not abandon the sins of Jeroboam son of Nebat. He re-established the frontiers of Israel from Lebo-hamath to the Sea of the Arabab, according to the word of the Lord, God of Israel, through his servant the prophet Jonah son of Amittai, of Gath-hepher.

Azariah king of Judah. In the twenty-seventh year of Jeroboam, king of Israel, Azariah son of Amaziah king of Judah came to the throne. He was sixteen when he came to the throne, and reigned in Jerusalem for fifty-two years. He did what was right in the eyes of the Lord, as his father Amaziah had done.

Zachariah and Shallum kings of Israel. In the thirty-eigth year of Azariah king of Judah, Zachariah son of Jeroboam reigned over Israel in Samaria for six months. He did what was wrong in the eyes of the Lord, as his forefathers had done, and did not abandon the sins of Jeroboam. But Shellum, son of Jabesh formed a conspiracy against him, attacked him in Ibleam, killed him and usurped the throne. The rest of the events of the life of Zachariah are recorded in the annals of the kings of Israel. Thus the word that the Lord had spoken to Jehu was fulfiled: "You sons to the fourth generation shall sit on the throne of Israel." And so it happened.

Menahem king of Israel. In the thirty-nineth year of Azariah king of Judah, Menahem, son of Gadi came to the throne of Israel, and he reigned in Samaria for ten years. He did what was wrong in the eyes of the Lord. In his time Pul[1] king of Assyria invaded the country, and Menahem gave Ful one thousand talents of silver so that he would help him to consolidate his royal power. Menahem laid a levy on all the men of wealth in Israel, and each had to give the king of Assyria fifty silver shekels. Then the king of Assyria withdrew without occupying the country.

Pekahiha and Pekah kings of Israel. In the fiftieth year of Azariah king of Judah Pekahiah son of Menahem came to the throne of Israel in Samaria. He reigned for two years. He did what was wrong in the eyes of the Lord. But Pekah son of Remaliah, his lieutenant, formed a conspiracy against him and killed him in Samaria, in the tower of the royal palace.

In the fifty-second year of Azariah, king of Judah, Pekah son of Remaliah came to the throne over Israel in Samaria, and he reigned for twenty years. He did what was wrong in the eyes of the Lord. In time of Pekah king of Israel, Tiglath-pileser king of Assyria came and seized Iyyon, Abel-beth-maacah, Janoah, Kedesh, Hazor, Gilead and Galilee, with all the land of Naphtali, and deported the people to Assyria[2].

Jotham king of Judah. In the second year of Pekah son of Remaliah king of Israel Jotham son of Uzziah king of Judah came to the throne. He was twenty-five when he came to the throne, and reigned in Jerusalem for sixteen years. He did what was right in the eyes of the Lord, as Uzziah, his father, had done.

Ahaz king of Juda[3]. In the seventeenth year of Pekah son of Remaliah Ahaz son of Jotham kinf of Judah came to the throne.

---

1. Teglat-piliser III. Conqueror of Babylon (729 b.C.).
2. Assyria. Nineveh. First deportation of Israel.
3. He was attacked by the Syrians and the Israelites together against the Assyrians, who had taken Damascus.

He was ten years old when he came to the throne, and he reigned in Jerusalem for sixteen years. He did not do what is right in the eyes of the Lord, his God, as his father David, but he followed in the footsteps of the kings of Israel, and he even passed his son through the fire, adopting the abominable practice of the nations whom the Lord had dispossessed in favour of the Israelites. He slaughtered and burnt sacrifices at the hill-shrines and on the hill-tops and under every spreading tree.

Ahaz rested with his forefathers and was buried with them in the city of David. He was succeeded by his son Hezekiah.

Hoshea last king of Israel. In the eighteenth year of Ahaz king of Judah, Hoshea, son of Elah became king over Israel in Samaria, and he reigned for nine years. He did what was wrong in the eyes of the Lord, but not so much as the kings of Israel who came before him. Shalmaneser king of Assyria made war upon him and Hoshea became tributary to him. But when the king of Assyria discovered that Hoshea was being disloyal to him, sending messengers to the king of Egypt at So, and withholding the tribute which he had been paying year by year, the king of Assyria arrested him and put him in prison. Then the invaded the whole country and, reaching Samaria, besieged it for three years. In the ninth year of Hoshea he captured Samaria and deported its people to Assyria and settled them in Halah[1] and on the Habor, the river of Gozan, and in the cities of Media.

Destruction of Samaria, punishment of the Lord. This happened because the sons of Israel had sinned against the Lord, his God. The people observed the laws and customs of the nations whom the Lord had dispossesssed before them, and those which the kings of Israel had introduced, worshipping idols, although the Lord had said, "Do not do such thing."

Forsaking every commandment of the Lord their God they made themselves images of cast metal, two calves, and also a sacred pole; they prostrated themselves to all the host of heaven

---

1. Halah, Assyrian city at Shinar. Residence of the Assyrian kings, founded by Nimrod, who filled it with palaces. It is by the river Tigris. There disappeared the Israelites from Samaria.

and worshipped the Baal, and they made their sons and daughters pass through the fire. They practised augury and divination; they sold themselves to do what was wrong in the Eyes of the Lord and so provoked his anger. And the Lord got angry against Israel and banished them from his presence; only the tribe of Judah was left[1].

And Israel was deported from his country to Assyria; and they are there to this day[2].

Repopulation of the Northern Kingdom with foreigners. Origins of the Samaritans. Then the king of Assyria brought people from Babylon, Cuthah, Avva, Hammath, and Sepharvaim, and settled them in the cities of Samria instead of the Israelies. They took possession of Samaria and settled down in its cities.

HISTORY OF THE KINGDOM OF JUDAH UNTIL THE EXILE

Hezekiah king of Judah. In the third year of Hoshea son of Elah king of Israel, Hezekiah son of Ahaz king of Judah became king. He was twenty-five years old when he came to the throne, and reigned in Jerusalem for twenty-nine years. He did what was right in the eyes of the Lord, as his father David had done. He suppressed the hill-shrines, smashed the Massebas and cut down the Asseras. He put his trust in the Lord the God of Israel; there was no one like him among the kings of Judah who succeeded him, or among those who had gone before him. He remained loyal to the Lord and did not fail in his allegiance to Him, and he kept the commandments which the Lord had given to Moses. The Lord was with him; he was successful in all his campaigns. He rebelled against the king of Assyria and was no longer subject to him.

---

1. Samaria was conquered by Zhargon II in the year 721 b.C.)
2. The 30,000 deported people were substituted by foreigners.

Sennacherib attacks Jerusalem. In the fourteenth year of the king Hezekiah, Sennacherib king of Assyria attacked the fortified cities of Judah and conquered them.

From Lachish the king of Assyria sent the commander-in-chief, the chief eunuch, and the chief officer with a strong force to King Hezekiah at Jerusalem, and they went up and came to Jerusalem and halted by the conduit of the Upper Pool on the causeway which leads to the Fuller's Field. The chief officer stood and shouted in Hebrew: "Hear the message of the Great King, the king of Assyria. These are his words: Do not listen to Hezekiah; he will only mislead you by telling you that the Lord will save you. Did the god of any of these nations save his land from the king of Assyria? Where are the gods of Hamath and Arpad? Where are the gods of Sepharvaim, Hena and Ivvah? Where are the gods of Samria? Did they save Samaria from me? Among all the gods of the nations is there one who has saved his land from me? And how is the Lord to save Jerusalem?"

But the people remained silent and answered not a word, for the king had given orders that no one was to answer him. Then Eliakim son of Hilkiah, controller of the household, Shebna the assistant-general and Joah son of Asaph, secretary of state, came to Hezekiah with their clothes rent and reported what the chief officer had said.

Isaiah comforts the king. When King Hezekiah heard this, he rent his clothes and wrapped himself in sackcloth, and went into the Temple of the Lord. The servants of the King came to Isaiah, and he answered, "Tell this to your lord: 'This is the word of the Lord: Do not be afraid by the words you have heard when the servants of the king of Assyria blasphemed me. I will put a spirit on him and he shall hear a rumour and withdraw to his own country; and there I will make him fall by the sword'."

Hezekiah's prayer and Isaiah's prophecy. Hezekiah took the letters from the hands of the messengers, and, once he read them, the went to the Temple, spread them out before the Lord and prayed, "O Lord, God of Israel, enthroned on the cherubim, you alone are God of all the kingdoms of the earth; you have made heaven and earth. Turn your ear to me, O Lord, and listen;

open your eyes, O Lord, and see; hear the message that Sennacherib has sent to taunt the living God. But now, O Lord our God, save us from his power, so that all the kingdoms of the earth may know that you, O Lord, alone are God."

Then Isaiah[1], son of Amosh, sent to Hezekiah and said, "This is the word of the Lord, God of Israel: 'I have heard your prayer to me concerning Sennacherib king of Assyria. This is the word that the Lord has spoken against him:

Whom have you taunted and blasphemed,
    against whom have you claimed?
    You have looked up to heaven
    against the Holy One of Israel.
As you have got angry against me,
    and I have heard your arrogance,
    I will put my ring in your nose
    and my hook in your lips,
    you shall go back by the road
    on which you have come.
Thus, this is the word of the Lord for the king of Assyria:
    He shall not enter this city,
    nor shoot an arrow there;
    no shield shall attack it,
    no siege-ramps shall be cast up against it.
He shall go back by the way on which he came,
    for he will not enter this city.
    This is the word of the Lord.

And it happened that that night the angel of the Lord went out and struck down a hundred and eighty-five thousand men in the Assyrian camp. And when they got up in the morning, the saw the corpses. Then Sennacherib king of Assyria broke camp, went back to Nineveh[2] and stayed there. and as he was

---

1. Of the royal family. He might have been the greatest of the prophets. He made prophesies in the times of Jothan, Ahaz and Hezekiah; he was a great help and protector of the latter. He went through martyrdom, probably by Manases.

2. Probably the Black Death spread across the camp at Lakish, on the south-east of Jerusalem. With the news of a rebellion in the capital he left in a rush.

worshipping in the temple of his god Nisroch, Adrammelech and Sharezer his sons murdered him and escaped to the land of Ararat. He was succeded by his son Esarhaddon[1].

Hezekiah rested with his forefathers and Manasseh succeeded him.

Manasseh's reign. Manasseh was twelve years old when he came to the throne, and he reigned in Jerusalem for fifty-five years. He did what was wrong in the eyes of the Lord, following the abominable practices of the nations which the Lord had disposed in favour of the Israelites. He built the hill-shrines again, those which his father had demolished, and built altars to Baal, made an Asherah, as Ahaz, king of Israel, had done, and worshipped all the host of heaven. He also built altars in the Temple of the Lord. He made his son pass throught the fire, he practised soothsaying and divination, and dealt with ghosts and spirits. He did much wrong in the eyes of the Lord and arose his anger.

Then the Lord spoke through his servants the prophets, "Because Manasseh king of Judah has done these abominable things, outdoing the Amorites before him in wickedness, and because he has led Judah into sin[2], this is the word of the Lord the God of Israel: I will bring disaster on Jerusalem and Judah, disaster which will ring in the ears of all who hear it. I will mark down every stone of Jerusalem with the plumbline of Samaria and the plommet of the house of Ahab; I will wipe away Jerusalem as when a man wipes his plate and turns it upside down, and I will cast off what is left of my people, my own possession, and hand them over to their enemies. They shall be plundered and fall a pray to all their enemies."

Besides, Manasseh shed so much innocent blood that he filled Jerusalem full to the brim, not to mention the sin into which he led Judah by doing what was wrong in the eyes of the Lord.

---

1. Herodotus II.141.
2. The kings thought that they were free from the noose of the Assyrians, but it was not so.

Manasseh rested with his forefathers and was buried in the garden of his palace, the garden of Uzza. He was succeeded by his son Amon.

Amon's reign. Amon was twenty-two years old when he came to the throne, and he reigned in Jerusalem for two years. He did what was wrong in the eyes of the Lord, as his father Manasseh had done. He followed in the footsteps of his father; he worshipped the idols whom his father had worshipped. He forsook the Lord, God of his fathers and did not follow the commandments of the Lord. His servants conspired against him and murdered him in his own house; but the people of the country murdered all those who had conspired against him, and they made his son Josiah king in his place.

He was buried in his grave in the garden of Uzza; he was succeeded by his son Josiah.

Josiah king of Juda. Josiah was eight years old when he came to the throne, and he reigned in Jerusalem for thirty-one years. He did what was right in the eyes of the Lord, and followed in the footsteps of David, his father, swerving neither right or left.

And it happened that in the eighteenth year of king Josiah the king sent Shaphan son of Azaliah to the Temple, and said to him, "Go to the high priest Hilkiah and tell him to melt down the silver that has been brought into the house of the Lord, which those on duty at the entrance have received from the people, and to hand it over to the foremen in the Temple of the Lord, so that they can hand it over to the workmen who are carrying out repairs in the Temple of the Lord."

Finding of the Book of the Law[1]. And Hilkiah, the high priest, said to Shapahn the secretary, "I have found the Book of the Law in the Temple of the Lord." And Hilkiah gave the book to Shapan. Then Shaphan told the news to the king, saying, "Hilkiah the priest has given me a book." And Shapan read it before the king.

---

1. With the works of repair in the Temple it was found the Book of the Law (Deuteronomy). Year 621 b.C.

When the king heard the words of the Book of the Law, he rent his clothes and ordered Hilkiah the priest, Ahikam son of Shaphan, Akbor son of Micaiah, Shaphan the adjutant-general, and Asaiah the king's attendant: "Go and seek guidance of the Lord for myself, for the people and for all Judah about the words of this book which we have found, for great is the Lord's wrath because our forefathers did not obey the commands in this book and do all that is laid upon us."

Religious reformation of Josiah[1]. Then the king gathered all the elders of Judah and Jerusalem. And he went to the Temple of the Lord with all the men of Judah and all the people living in Jerusalem, priests, prophets and the people, from the eldest to the youngest, and he read all the words of the book of the Covenant found in the Temple of the Lord. Then the king, standing on the days, made this covenant before the Lord: "I will obey you and keep your commandments, your testimonies and your statutes, with all my heart and soul, and so fulfil the terms of the covenant written in this book." And all the people pledged themselves to the covenant.

Destruction of idolatry[2]. Then he removed the idolatrous priests appointed by the kings of Judah who had burnt sacrifices in the hill-shrines, in the cities of Judah and in the neighbourhood of Jerusalem; he also suppressed those who had burnt parfumes to Baal, to the sun and the moon, the planets and all the host of Heaven.

He removed the symbol of Asherah from the Temple of the Lord to the gorge of the Kidron outside Jerusalem; he burnt it there and pounded it to dust. Besides he desecrated Topheth in the Valley of Ben-hinnom, so that no one might make his son or daughter pass throught the fire in honour of Molech. He destroyed the Asheras and filled its places with human bones.

Restoration of the Passover. Then the king ordered to the people, "Keep the Passover to the Lord your God, as it is written in the book of the Covenant." Actually, no such

---

1. The Covenant of the Lord was renewed.
2. That was Israel's great sin. Josiah intended to remove all signs of it, Baalim, Asheras and altars in wells, trees and all holy places.

Passover had been kept either when the judges were ruling Israel or during the times of the kings of Israel and Judah.

Death of Josiah. In his reign Pharaoh Necho king of Egypt set out for the river Euphrates to help the king of Assyria. King Josiah came to meet him, but Pharaoh slew him at Megiddo.

Jehoahaz's reign. Jehoahaz was twenty-three years old when he came to the throne, and he reigned in Jerusalem for three months. He did what was wrong in the eyes of the Lord, as his forefathers had done. But Pharaoh Necho removed him from the throne in Jerusalem, and imposed on the land a fine of a hundred talents of silver and one talent of gold. Pharaoh Necho made Josiah's son Eliakim king in place of his father and changed his name to Jehoakim. He took Jehoahaz and brought him to Egypt, where he died.

Jehoakim's reign. Jehoakim was twenty-five years old when he came to the throne, and he reigned in Jerusalem for five years. He did what was wrong in the eyes of the Lord, as his forefathers had done.

Nebuchadnezzar's first incursion[1]. In his time Nebuchadnezzar king of Babylon attacked him, and Jehoakim paid him tribute during three years. But then he rebelled against him.

Jehoiachin's reign. Jehoiachin was eighteen years old when he came to the throne, and he reigned in Jerusalem for three years. He did what was wrong in the eyes of the Lord, as his father had done.

At that time Nebuchadnezzar's troops, king of Babylon, attacked Jerusalem, and the city was besieged. Nebuchanezzar king of Babylon came while his troops were besieging it[2]. And the king of Babylon captured them in the eigth year of his reign. He took, as the Lord had foretold, all the treasuries of the Temple of the Lord and of the royal palace, and smashed all the pieces of gold which Solomon king of Israel had made for the Lord's Sanctuary. He carried the people of Jerusalem into

---

1. With the destruction of Nineveh Nebupolazzar founded the great Babylonic Empire, and his son Nebuchadnezzar made it greater.

2. In his campaign against Egypt, he passed by Jerusalem and burnt it.

exile, the officers and the fighting men, ten thousand in number, together with all the craftsmen and smiths; only the weakest class of people were left.

He deported Jehoiachin to Babylon; he also took into exile the mother of the king and his wives, his eunuchs and the foremost men of the land. And the king of Babylon, instead of Jehoiachin, made Mattaniah, his uncle, king, and changed his name to Zedekiah.

Zedekiah, last king of Judah. Zedekiah was twenty-one years old when he came to the throne, and he reigned in Jerusalem for eleven years. He did what was wrong in the eyes of the Lord, as Jehoiachin. Zedekiah rebelled against the king of Babylon.

Zedekiah's death. In the ninth year of his reign, on the tenth day of the tenth month, Nebuchadnezzar king of Babylon advanced with all his army against Jerusalem, besieged it, and built watch-towers against in on every side. The city was besieged until the eleventh year of King Zedekiah. On the ninth day of the fourth month, the shortage was so great that there was no bread for the people. Then the city was thrown open; all the army left the city and fled by night through the gate called Between the Two Walls, near the king's garden. Then they escaped towards the Arabah[1], although the Chaldaeans were surrounding the city. But the Chaldaean army pursued the king, and overtook him in the lowlands of Jericho; and all his company was dispersed. They seized the king and brought him before the king of Babylon at Riblah[2], where he pleaded his case before him. He slain his sons before his eyes; then his eyes were put out, and he was brought to Babylon in fetters of bronze.

Destruction of the Temple and deportation of Judah. On the seventh day of the fifth month —that was the nineteenth year of King Nebuchadnezzar, king of Babylon—, Nebuzadaran, captain of the king's bodyguard, came to

---

1. Dead Sea.
2. General headquarters of Pharaoh Necho and Nebuchadnezzar in their attack to Jerusalem. Riblah was situated in the right bank of the Oront (Asia Minor).

Jerusalen; he set fire to the Temple of the Lord and the royal palace, all the houses of the city, especially those belonging to important people. All the Chaldaean army with the captain of the guard pulled down the walls around Jerusalem, and Nebuzadarn, captain of the guard, deported the rest of the population of the city, those who had deserted to the king of Babylon and any remaining artisans. He left only the weakest class of people to be vine-dressers and labourers.

So Judah went into exile from their own land[1].

Gedaliah governor of Judah. As for the people who were left in Judah, the people whom Nebuchadnezzar king of Babylon had left, he appointed Gedaliah son of Ahikham, son of Shaphan governor. When the captains of the army and their men heard that the king of Babylon had appointed Gedaliah governor, they came into his presence at Mizpah[2]. Gedaliah gave them and their men this assurance: "Do not fear the Chaldaean officers. Settle down in the land and serve the king of Babylon; and then all will be well with you."

Gedaliah's murder[3]. But in the seventh month, Ishmael son of Nethaniah, son of Elishama, who was a member of the royal house, came with ten men and murdered Gedaliah and the Jews and the Chaldaeans who were with him at Mizpah. Then all the people, high and low, and the captains of the army fled to Egypt[4] for fear of the Chaldaeans.

---

1. To Babylon.
2. Mizpah (Hebrew = watchtower). Political and religious centre of the Tribes of Israel. Fortified city.
3. Favourable to and friend of Jeremiah.
4. Taking the prophet with them.

EZRA AND NEHEMIAH

EZRA

FIRST RETURN OF THE EXILES

Proclamation of Cyrus[1] **(559-529 b.C.).** In the first year of
Cyrus, king of Persia, so that the word of the Lord spoken
through Jeremiah might be fulfiled, the Lord stirred up the heart
of Cyrus king of Persia; and he issued a proclamation
throughout his kingdom, by word and in writting, to this effect:
"This is the word of Cyrus king of Persia: The Lord, God of
heaven, gave all the kingdoms on earth to me. And now he asks
me to build a Temple for him in Jerusalem, in Judah. To every
man of his people God be with him; let him go up to Jerusalem,
in Judah, to built the Temple of the Lord, God of Israel, the God
that lives in Jerusalem. And all the remaining Jews wherever
they live should be helped by the people by giving them silver,
gold, good, cattle and other voluntary offerings for the Temple
of the Lord in Jerusalem."

The heads of the families of Judah and Benjamin, the priests
and the Levites, all those whose spirit had been moved by the

---

1. The real founder of the Persian Empire. He defeated the Medes, Astages, the
   Lidian Cresus and he was lord over the whole Asia Minor. In the year 539 he
   took over Babylon.

Lord went up to rebuild the Temple of the Lord. And all their neighbours provided them with all kinds of things: silver, gold, goods, cattle, precious things and other voluntary offerings.

King Cyrus produced the vessels of the house of the Lord which Nebuchadnezzar had removed from Jerusalem to put them in the Temple of his God. Cyrus King of Persia handed them over into the charge of Mithredath the treasurer, who made an inventory of them for Sheshbazzar the ruler of Judah.

List of prisoners who came back in the year 538 with Zerubbabel[1]. The whole assembled people of the country numbered forty-two thousand three hundred and sixty, without their slaves, which numbered seven thousant three hundred and thirty-seven. They had two hundred singers.

The priests, the Levites and a part of the people settled down in Jerusalem.

Rebuilding of the altar and restoration of the worship (538 b.C.). In the seventh month, when the sons of Israel had already settled in their cities, the people gathered in Jerusalem. Then Jeshua son of Jozadak and his fellow-priests, and Zerubbabel, son of Shealtiel and his kinsmen set to work and built the altar of the God of Israel to offer sacrifices on it, as it is written in Moses's Law, man of God. So they put the altar in its place first, because they lived in fear of the people of the country, and they offered sacrifices to the Lord, morning and evening offerings. They also kept the pilgrim-feast of the Tabernacles as ordained, in the number prescribed for each day, and, in addition to these, the regular whole-offerings and the offerings for sabbaths, for new moons and for all the sacred seasons appointed by the Lord, and all voluntary offerings brought to the Lord.

First works in the Temple. In the second month of the second year of his arrival in the Temple of the Lord in Jerusalem, Zerubbabel son of Shealtiel and Jeshua son of Jozadak started to work, aided by the rest of their brothers,

---

1. From the house of David. Contemporary of the prophets Aheus and Zachariah. He was the governor of those who were sent home

priests and Levites, and all those who had come from their exile to Jerusalem.

When the builders had laid the foundation of the Temple of the Lord, the priests in their robes took their places with their trumpets, and so did the Levites sons of Asaph[1] with their cymbals, to praise the Lord, according to David's Law, king of Israel. They chanted praises and thanksgivings to the Lord, singing: "Because He is good, because his love towards Israel endures for ever." And all the people shouted in praise to the Lord.

The Samarians are against the building of the Temple. Then the people of the country[2] caused the Jews to lose heart and made them afraid to continuate the building; and in order to defeat their purpose they bribed officials at court to act against them. This went on throughout the reign of Cyrus king of Persia and into the reign of Darius king of Persia.

The governor stops the building of the Temple. This was the answer of the king: "To Rehum the high commissioner, Shimshai the secretary and all their colleagues living in Samaria and in the rest of the province beyond the Euphrates, greeting. The letter which you sent me has been carefully read in my presence. I have given orders and search has been made, and it has been found that the city in question has a great history of rebellions against the monarchy. Powerful kings have ruled in Jerusalem, exercicing authority over the whole province of beyond the Euphrates, and general levy, poll-tax and land-tax have been paid to them. Therefore, issue orders that these men must desist their work. This city will not be rebuilt until a decree is issued. See that you do not neglect your duty in this matter, lest more damage and harm be done to the monarchy."

When the text of the letter of King Artaxerxes was read before Rehum the high commissioner, Shimshai the secretary, and their colleagues, they hurried to Jerusalem and forcibly

---

1. Family of great singers already in the times of David and Solomon. The works of rebuilding had started.

2. The Samaritans, people of the country, betrayers and idolaters who came from other places like Mesopotamia took the place of the exiles.

compelled the Jews to stop working. They had to stop the work in the rebulding of the Temple of the Lord in Jerusalem until de second year of Darius's reign, king of Persia.

Continuation of the building of the Temple (520-515 b.C.). Then the prophets Haggai and Zechariah son of Iddo upbraided the Jews in Judah and Jerusalem, prophesying inthe name of the God of Israel. Then Zerubbabel son of Shealtiel and Jeshua son of Jozadak at once began to rebuild the Temple of the Lord in Jerusalem, supported by the two prophets of God who were by their side.

Tattenai, governor of the province beyond the Euphrates, Shethar-bozenai and their colleagues came to them and said, "Who issued a decree allowing you to rebuild this Temple and complete its wall?" And they added, "What are the names of the people who are building this Temple?" But the elders of the Jews were under God's watchful eye, and they were not prevented from continuing the work until a report reached Darius and a royal letter was sent in answer.

Favourable Edict from Darius I (520 b.C.). Then King Darius ordered that search should be made in Babylon, in the files, and in Ecbatana, in the royal residence in the province of Media, a scroll was found which read,

"Memorandum.

First year of king Cyrus. King Cyrus had decreeted as regards the Temple of the Lord in Jerusalem that it is rebuilt as a place to offer sacrifices and to bring fire-offerings.

Now, Tattenai, governor of the province beyond the Euphrates, Shethar-bozenai, and your colleagues, the inspectors in the province of beyond the Euphrates, keep away from Jerusalem; and let the governor of Judah and the elders of the Jews continue the works of the Temple of God. They must rebuilt the Temple of God on its original site. These are my orders regarding what you must do with the elders of the Jews and the rebuilding of the Temple of God."

End and dedication of the Temple (515 b.C.). Then Tattenay, governor of the province beyond the Euphrates, Shethar-bozenai and their colleagues carried out to the letter the instructions which King Darius had sent them. So the elders of the Jews continued the works successfuly, supported by the words of the prophets Haggai and Zecharia son of Iddo. And they finished the building successfully, according to the commandment of the God of Israel and the instructions of Cyrus and Darius. The Temple was finished in the sixth year of Darius's reign.

The Passover of the 515 b.C. On the fourteenth day of the first month the exiles who had returned kept the Passover. The Levites had purified themselves one and all. All of them were clean[1]; they killed the passover lamb for all the exiles who had returned, for his kinsmen, for the priests and for themselves. It was eaten by the sons of Israel who had come back from exile with all those who had separated themselves from the people of the land and their uncleanness and sought the Lord God of Israel.

EZRA'S RETURN AND REFORMATION[2]

Ezra comes back to Jerusalem with many Jews. After these events, in the reign of Artaxerxes king of Persia, Ezra son of Seraiah came back from Babylon. He was a scribe learned in the Law of Moses, given by the Lord, God of Israel, The king granted him everything he wanted, because the hand of the Lord, his God, was with him. In the seventh year of Artaxerxes also came with him to Jerusalem other Israelites: priests, Levites, singers, doorkeepers and Temple-servants. Ezra came to Jerusalem in the fifth month of the seventh year of the king. He had left Babylon on the first day of the first month, and on the first day of the fifth month he came to Jerusalem, because the gracious hand of his God was with him. For Ezra had devoted himself to study the Lay of the Lord, to put it into practice and to teaching Israel the statutes and ordinances.

Journey and arrival in Jerusalem. I assembled them by the river which flows toward Ahava; and we encamped there for

1. Legal purification.
2. Ezra (Hebrew = God helps).

three days. There I proclaimed a fast by the river so that we might mortify ourselves before our God and ask from him a safe journey for ourselves, our dependants, and all our possessions. For I was ashamed of asking the king for troops and chavalry to protect us from occasional enemies in our journey after having talked to him in this way: "Our God stretches out his hand to bless us, we and all those who search him. His power and his strength, however, is for those who forsake him." So we fasted and asked our God for a safe journey, and He listened to our prayer.

When they arrived in Jerusalem they rested there for three days. Those who came from captivity, the exiles, offered sacrifices to the God of Israel: twelve bulls all for all Israel, ninety-six rams and seventy-two lambs, with twelve he-goats as a sin-offering; all these were offered as a whole-offering to the Lord. And the king's commission was also delivered to the royal satraps and governors in the province beyond the Euphrates, and these supported the people and the Temple of God.

NEHEMIAH

NEHEMIAH'S MEMORIES

Nehemiah's grief over the situation of Jerusalem. These are the words of Nehemiah son of Hacaliah. In the month of Kislev[1] in the twentieth year of King Artaxerxes, while I was in the fortress of Susa[2], Hanani, one of my brothers, came with some men from Judah. I asked him about the Jews, the families who survived the captivity, and about Jerusalem. They told me, "Those who have survived captivity are facing great trouble and reproach; the wall of Jerusalem has been broken down, and the gates have been destroyed by fire."

When I heard these words I sat down and wept. I mourned for some days, fasting and praying before the God of heaven.

Nehemiah, authorised by Artaxerxes I, goes to Jerusalem in the year 445. In the month Nisan, in the twentieth year of King Artaxerxes, when I was the king's cupbearer, I took his cup and handed it to the king. I had never been sad before him. And the king said to me, "Why do you look so unhappy? You are not ill, it can be nothing but unhappiness." Then, feeling suddenly unhappy, I answered, "Long live the king. How can I feel happy if the city where the graves of my fathers are is destroyed and its gates have been burnt up?" The king replied,

---

1. Kislev. Assiran-Babilonic name common among the Jews after the exile. Month between November and December.
2. Persia's capital.

"What do you wish?" I, after having prayed to the God of heaven, asked the king, "If it is all right for you, and if I enjoy your favour, let me go to Judah, the city where the graves of my fathers are, to rebuild it." The king, with the queen sitting beside him, asked, "How long is your journey going to take, and when will you be back?" I told him the dates and he agreed, so he allowed me to go. Then I said to the king, "If it pleases your majesty, let letters be given to me for the governors in the province beyond the Euphrates with orders to grant me all help I need for my journey to Judah, and a letter for Asaph, the keeper of your royal forests, so that he supplies me with timber to make beams for the gates of the citadel which adjoins the city, for the walls of the city and for the house in which I will live." The king granted all this to me, for the graceful hand of God was on me.

Nehemiah exhorts to the building of the wall of Jerusalem. When I arrived in Jerusalem, I stayed there for three days. Then I got up at night, taking a few men with me, in secret, riding the only horse I had. So I left in the night, through the Dung Gate, inspecting the places where the walls of Jerusalem had been broken down and the gates burn up. Later I continued through the Fountain Gate and the King's Pool; but as there was no room for me to ride through, I went up again by the stream, inspecting the wall, till the Valley Gate. Then I told them, "You see our wretched plight. Jerusalem lies in ruins, its gates destroyed by fire. Come, let us rebuild the wall of Jerusalem and be rid of scorn." And I told them how the gracious hand of the Lord protected me, and the words that the king had told me. They shouted, "Let us get up and start the building!" So they set about this task vigorously.

The rebuilding continues, weapons at hand. When Sanballat the Horonite, Tobiah, the Arabs, the Ammonites and the Azzotites heard that the rebuilding of the wall of Jerusalem was going forth, they got angry and plotted to attack Jerusalem and do as much harm as they could. Then we prayed to our God and watched them day and night.

Every builder hold his spear while he worked. And the trumpeter was always beside me. For I had told the nobles, the magistrates and all the people, "This work is great and covers much ground, and we are isolated on the wall, each man at some distance from his neighbour. Whenever you hear the sound of the trumpet, run to meet your fellowmen, and our God shall fight for us." In this way, while half the men held the swords, the other half worked from dawn until the first stars could be seen.

The wall was finished on the twenty-five of the month of Elul[1], and its rebuilding lasted fifty-two days. And when our enemies heard about it, all the neighbouring nations got afraid and recognized that this word had been accomplished with the help of our God.

REFORM AND ORGANIZATION

Public penance and confession. On the twenty-fourth day of that same month, the Israelites, dressed in sackcloth and with earth on their heads, assembled for a fast. Those who were of Israelite descent separated themselves from the foreigners, and standing up the confessed their sins and the iniquities of their forefathers. They stood up and read in the book the Law of the Lord, their God, for one fourth of the day. For another fourth they confessed their sins and prostrated themselves before the Lord, their God.

Renovation of the Covenant with God. Subsequently, we accepted a serious compromise in writing. Our princes, our Levites and our priests witnessed the sealing.

Also the rest of the people compromised, when the oath was put to them, to walk according to the Law of God, given through Moses, God's servant, and to observe and put into practise all the commandments of the Lord our God, his statutes and his laws, not to give our daughters to the people of the country nor take their daughters for our sons.

---

1. Elul. According to the Babylonic calendar, the month of June.

TOBIT

TOBIT[1] AND SARAH ARE PUT TO THE TEST BY GRIEF

Marriage and captivity. When I came of age I married a woman of our family whose name was Anna, who bore me a son named Tobias. When I was captured by the Assyrians[2] I came to Nineveh. My brethen and kinsmen ate pagan food, but I did not eat them, for I remembered my God with all my heart. God the Most High granted me a presence which won me the favour of Shalmaneser[3]. I became his buyer of supplies. As long as he lived I bought for him, and this is the reason why I went to Media. I deposited bags of money to the value of ten talents of silver with my kinsman Gabael son of Gabri in Media. But when Shalmaneser died, who was succeeded by his son Sennacherib, the roads to Media were cut, and I could no longer make my journey.

Tobit's good works[4]. In the time of Shalmaneser I did many acts of charity for my fellow countrymen. I gave bread to those who were hungry and clothes to the naked; I buried the corpses of my dead fellowmen whom I saw behind the walls of

---

1. The pious Tobit, struck by his blindness, is comforted by his son's marriage, and he will be cured of his blindness because of his prayers and good deeds.
2. First deportation of Samarians to Assyria.
3. Son of Teglaphalazzer II; he besieged Samaria, and Sargon II conquered it.
4. Tobit lived in Nineveh.

Nineveh. I also buried all those killed by Sennacherib when he returned from Judah, when the King of heaven executed judgement on him for all his blasphemies. In his rage he killed many Israelites, and I, concealing myself, hid their corpses so that I could bury them later. Sennacherib searched for them, but he could not find them. One of the Ninevites informed the king that I was giving burial to his victims. When I knew that the king knew what I was doing and that he was looking for me to kill me, I took fright and ran away. All my property was seized and put into the royal treasury. I had nothing else than Anna, my wife, and Tobias.

In the reign of Esarhaddon I returned to my house, and I was given back my wife Anna and my son Tobias.

Tobit, blind. That night, after washing myself, I fell asleep by the wall of the yard, my face uncovered because of the warmth. I did not realise that there were sparrows on the wall, and, as my eyes were wide open, and their droppings fell, still warm, right into my eyes and produced white patches.

THE ARCHANGEL RAPHAEL IS SENT TO TOBIT AND SARAH

Then Tobit remembered the money he had deposited with Gabael[1] at Rages[2] in Media.

He sent for Tobias, his son, and when he came he said to him, "When I die give me decent burial. Show proper respect to your mother, and do not leave her in the lurch as long as she lives; do what pleases her, and never grieve her heart in any way. When she dies, bury her with me in the same grave. Do never forsake the Lord, my son, and do never sin or break his commandments.

And now, my son, let me tell you that I deposited ten talents of silver with Gabael son of Gabri at Rages, in Media."

---

1. Gabael was Tobit's relative.
2. Rages (Hebrew = Ragaun). Old capital of the Medes.

The archangel Raphael, walker and guide. Then Tobias answered his father, "I will do as you say, father, but how can I get the money if he does not know me and I do not know him? Can I give him a sign so that he knows that it is me and gives me the money? I do not know the road to Media, either." Tobit said to his son, "Gabael gave me his note of hand, and I gave him mine, which I divided into two. He took one and I gave him the money. I deposited the money twenty years ago. My son, find someone reliable to go with you."

Tobias set out to find someone who could accompany him to Media, and he found the angel Raphael, but he did not know that he was an angel of God. And he said to him, "Where do you come from, young man?" He answered, "I am one of the sons of Israel, your brethen, who has come to find a job." Tobias added, "Do you know how can I get to Media?" He answered, "Certainly. I have been there lots of times, and I know the road very well. I have been to Media and used to lodge with one of our brethen, Gabael, who lives at Rages in Media. It is two days' journey from Ecbatana[1] to Rages, among the mountains." Tobias replied, "Wait for me, young man, I want to tell this to my father, for I need you to come with me, and I will pay your wages." He answered, "I will wait, but do not be too long."

Tobit went home and told the news to his father, "I have found one of the sons of Israel, our brethen." His father answered, "Call him so that I know to which family and tribe does he belong and whether he is reliable or not." Tobias left and said to him, "Young man, my father is calling you." As soon as he entered Tobit greeted him, and the angel answered, "May all be well with you." But Tobit added, "How can anything be well with me now? I am a blind man; I cannot see the light of heaven; I lie in darkness like the dead who cannot see the light. Although I am alive, I am among the dead. I hear the voice of living people, but I cannot see them." The angel

---

1. Capital of the Medes, half-way to Rages, where Gabael lived. Rages was residence of the Persian kings. And in Ecbatana lived Ragel, father of the young Sarah.

replied, "Take heart, the Lord will cure you soon." Tobit said to him, "My son wants to go to Media, can you go with him and guide him?" The angel answered, "I am familiar with the routes, I have been there often, I have gone through the plains and mountains and I know all its roads."

"Tell me, my friend, which family and tribe do you belong to?" asked Tobit. "You do not need to know," he answered. "But I would like to know exactly who you are and what is your name," said Tobit. "I am," —he answered—, Azarias[1], son of the older Ananias[2], one of your brethen". Tobit said, "God keeps you safe and sound, my friend! Be welcome!" And he added, "I will pay you a drachma per day, and when you need it, like my son. So leave with him and if you come sound I will pay you more." He answered, "All right. I will go with him. Do not be afraid, we are leaving safe and sound and so shall we come back, for the way is safe." Tobit said to him, "Have a good journey, my friend." And to his son, "My son, prepare all the necessary things for the journey and leave with your friend. May God in heaven guide your journey and brings you back safe and sound. May his angel go with you and protect you on the way, my son." When everything was prepared and they were ready to leave, Tobias embraced his parents.

Setting off. The fish in the Tigris[3]. So the young man, the angel and the dog set out. They walked until the evening came. They spent the night by the river Tigris. The young man went down to the Tigris to bathe his feet in the river. A huge fish leapt out of the water and tried to swallow the boy's foot, and he shouted[4]. The angel said to him, "Catch the fish and do not let him go." The young man catched the fish and put it on the ground. "Split the fish open and take out its gall, heart and liver; keep them by you; but throw the guts away. The gall, heart and liver can be used as medicines." The young man split the fish

---

1. Azarias (Hebrew = "God's help").
2. Ananias (Hebrew = "The Lord is pious").
3. Great river which, together with the Euphrates, crosses the country of Mesopotamia. It comes from Armenia and dies in the Persian Gulf.
4. Could it be a calionimus, as Plinius writes in his books?

open and took out the heart and the liver. He cooked part of the fish and threw away the rest. They continued their journey until they came near Media. The young man questioned the angel, "My friend Azaries, what medicine is there in the heart, the liver and the gall of the fish?" The angel said, "The heart and the liver of a fish must be burnt before a man or woman attacked by the devil or an evil spirit, and then the attack will give no further trouble. The gall is used as an oinment for the white patches of the eyes; or for blowing on the white patches in the eyes; the eyes will recover."

Arrangement of his marriage to Sarah. As they came to Media and as they came near Ecbatana, Raphael said to the young man, "My friend Tobias." He answered, "What happens?" "Tonight," added Raphael, "we will spend the night at Ragel's. He is a relative of yours. He has a daughter called Sarah. He does not have any more children, Sarah is the only heiress. She is a very sensible, brave and very beautiful girl, beloved of his father. You have a right to have her. Listen, my friend: Tonight I will talk to her father so that he gives her to you as your wife, and later, when we come back from Rages[1] you will get married. I know that Ragel cannot deny her to you to marry her to another man, for he would incur the death penalty according to the Law of Moses. His daughter belongs to you by right more than to any other man. Listen to me, my friend, we will talk about her tonight and will betroth her to you; and when we come back from Rages, we will take her home with us." Tobit answered Raphael, "My friend Azarias, I have heard that the girl has already been given to seven husbands who died at the very moment they went into the bridal chamber with her. I have also heard that a devil killed them. Sincerely, I am afraid. He does no harm to her, because he loves her. But he does kill anyone who approaches her. I am the only son of my father and I fear that if I die my parents will die from grief, for they have no other child to give them a decent burial." The angel replied, "Do you not remember that your father advised you to marry a woman of your own family? My friend,

---

1. After getting the money which Gabael owed Tobit.

do not fear the devil and marry her. I can assure you that tonight she will be your wife. When you come into the bridal chamber, take some of the fish's liver and its heart, and put them on the smoking incense. The smell will spread, and when the devil smells it, he will ran away for ever. But before your meeting, you must pray to the Lord in heaven to have pity on you and to protect you. Do not be afraid, for she has always been designed to be yours; you shall save her. She will come with you and she will give you children who will be like brothers for you. So do not be afraid[1]."

When Tobias heard what Raphael said, and learnt that she was his kinswoman and of his father's house, he was filled with love for heart and set his heart on her.

Arrival in Sarah's house. When they came to Ectabana, Tobias said, "My friend Azarias, take me quickly to Ragel's house, our kinsman." He took him to Ragel's, who was in the yard. After greeting each other, he said to them, "Welcome, my friends." And he took them to his home. He said to Edna, his wife, "Do you not think that this young man looks after my brother Tobit?" Edna asked them, "Where do you come from, my friends?" They answered her, "We are the sons of Nephtali, captives at Nineveh." "Do you know," he added, "Tobit, our friend?" "He is alive and well." Tobias added, "He is my father." Then Ragel stood up and embraced him in tears. Then he said to him, "Blessed be, young man, son of so excellent a father. What a pity that such an honest and pious man has gone blind." He embraced Tobias and wept. Edna, his wife, and Sarah, his daughter were weeping too. Then he slaughtered a ram of the flock and made them a warm welcome.

Once they had washed themselves, they sit at the table. Tobias said to Raphael, "My friend Azarias, say to Ragel that he gives me his cousin Sarah for a wife." Ragel heard this and said to the young man, "Eat and drink, and enjoy yourself tonight, for my daughter Sarah belongs to you by right more than to anybody else." Besides, I cannot give her to anybody else than

---

1. With these words Tobias lost his fear.

you, for you are my closest relative[1]. Now I must tell you the truth. I have given her to seven men of our tribe and they all died in the bridal chamber. But do eat and drink, the Lord will take care of you."

Marriage of Tobias and Sarah. Tobias answered, "I shall not eat nor drink until you decide what to do." So Ragel said, "Well then, I give her to you as a wife according to the Law of Moses. Heaven has ordained that she shall be yours. The Lord of heaven prosper you both this night, my son, and grant you mercy and peace." Then Ragel called his daughter Sarah. When she came, he took her by the hand and gave her to Tobias, saying, "Take her to be your wedded wife in accordance with the law and and the ordinance written in the book of Moses, and take her to your father's house. May the God of heaven keep you safe." Sarah asked her mother to bring paper to write the marriage contract on it granting Sarah to Tobias as his wife, as the Law of Moses ordains. And she sealed it. Later they ate and drank.

Sarah's healing. After dinner they went to bed, and they accompanied the young man to the bridal chamber. Then Tobias remembered Raphael's words. He took the fish's liver and heart out of the bag in which he kept them, and put them on the smoking incense. The smell from the fish held the demon off, and he took flight. They were left alone and the door was shut. Then Tobias stood up and said to Sarah, "My cousin, stand up, let us pray and beseech our Lord to show us mercy and keep us safe." She stood up and they prayed and beseeched the Lord to keep them safe[2].

Tobias's prayer. Then Tobias said,

"Blessed be, O God of our forefathers,
    and blessed be your Name for ever.
    May heaven bless you
    and all what you have created.

---

1. It had to be so accordig to the Law of Moses.
2. As the Angel had said.

You made Adam, and you gave Eva to him, his wife,
>   as his helper and mate, and they were parents
>   of the human race.
>   You said: It is not good for the man to be alone,
>   let us make him a helper like him.
Now, my Lord, I take my cousin,
>   not out of lust but in true marriage.
>   Grant that she and I may find mercy, and that we grow
>   old together."

And they both said, "Amen, amen." And they slept all night long.

Ragel's worries. Ragel rose early and said to his wife, "Sent a servant to see if he is alive, for if he is dead we will bury him so that nobody may know." She sent a servant. The servant lighted a lamp, opened the door, came into the room and saw that they were soundly asleep. The servant came out and told them that he was alive, and that nothing evil had happened to them[1].

Then they blessed the Lord thus,

"Blessed be, O God, we praise you.
>   Blessed be all the saints and the creatures,
>   and all the angels for all centuries."

He told his wife to bake a great batch of bread; he went to the herd and brought two oxen and four rams and told his servants to slaughter them, and they started to prepare them.

Then he sent for Tobias and said to him, "For forty days you shall stay with me eating and drinking in my house and rejoicing my daughter, who has suffered so much. Then you shall have half my goods and leave happy for the house of your parents. The other half will be yours when my wife and I die. Take heart, my son, for I will always be your father and Edna your mother, as we are Sarah's father and mother."

---

1. Sarah's liberation of the devil and Tobit's healing of his blindness are deeds of God, who used the fish's gall, its heart and its liver.

The angel Raphael recovers the money. Tobias called Raphael and said to him, "My friend Azarias, take four servants and two camels and go to Rages. See Gabael, give him the bond and collect the money, and invite him to our wedding. You know that my father is counting the days and, if I am even one day late, it will distress him. You see what Ragel has sworn, and I cannot go against his oath." So Raphael left with four servants and two camels for Rages in Media, and they stayed at Gabael's. They gave him the bond and he told him that Tobias, son of Tobit was getting married, and that he had been invited to the wedding. Gabael counted out the bags to him with their seals intact, and they put them together. They all made an early start and came to the wedding. When they came into Ragel's house, they found Tobias at the feast. He stood up and greeted Gabael. With tears in his eyes Gabael blessed him so, "Good and upright man, son of an honest, upright and charitable man! May the Lord bless you with heavenly blessings, you, your wife and her parents. Blessed be the Lord, for I have seen Tobias so like my cousin.

Anguish of Tobias's parents. Day after day Tobit counted out the days which Tobias would take for his journey there and back. When the days had passed and his son had not returned, he thought, "Maybe he had been detained at Rages, or maybe Gabael has died and there is nobody who can give him the money." He started to worry. Anna, his wife, said, "My son is dead." And she cried and mourned saying, "O my child, light of my eyes, why did I let you go?" But Tobit replied, "Be quiet, woman, do not worry, he is safe and sound. Something has happened there to distract them. The man who goes with him is a reliable person, and he is one of our kinsmen. Do not be sad, woman, he will be back soon." When the fourteen days of wedding promised by Ragel in honour of his daughter were over, Tobias told him, "Let me go. I know that my parents think that I am dead. I pray you, then, to let me go to my father's house. I told you how I left him[1]."

---

1. Tobias's parents were upset because his son did not arrive on the date he should have been back.

The young couple heads for Nineveh. Then Ragel stood up, gave Sarah, his wife, to Tobias, and half his possessions; servants and maids, oxen and sheep, asses and camels, clothes, silver and vessels, and he let him go sound and safe, saying, "Goodbye, my son, have a good journey. May God in heaven grant you and Sarah, your wife, a safe journey, and may I live to see your children before I die."

When they came near Caserin close to Nineveh, Raphael said to Tobias, "You know how your father was when we left him. Now let us hurry on ahead of your wife to prepare the house before she arrives." They went ahead, and Raphael said, "Take some gall." The dog went with them, and it walked ahead of them. Anna meanwhile, was watching the road by which her son would return. She saw him coming and exclaimed to his father, "Look, your son is coming with the man which whom he left." Raphael had said to Tobit before his father drew near, "Certainly his eyes will be opened. Spread the fish-gall on his eyes, and the medicine will make the white patches shrink and peel off. Your father will get his sight back, and he shall see the light." Anna embraced her son, saying, "I can see you again, my son, now I can die." And she cried.

Tobit is healed from his blindness. Tobit stood up too and came stumbling out throught the courtyard. Tobias came to meet him having the gall of the fish in his hand. He blew onto his eyes and embraced him, saying, "Take heart, father." Then he put the medicine on and applied it, using both hands he peeled off the patches from the corners of his eyes. Tobit embraced his son and said in tears, "My son, I can see you now, light of my eyes." And he added,

"Praised be, O God, and blessed be your Name.
    Praised be your angels and all your saints for ever
    because you punished me, but now I can see my son."

Tobias came happily praying God aloud, and telling his father about his happy journey, how he had recovered the silver, how he had married Sarah, Ragel's daughter, who was already near the gates of Nineveh. Tobit, happy, blessed the Lord, and came to meet his daughter-in-law at the gate of Nineveh.

Sarah comes to Nineveh. Then he came to meet Sarah, Tobias's wife, and he blessed her so, "Be welcome, my daughter. Blessed be your parents, blessed be Tobias, my son, and blessings on you, my daughter. Come in to your home with blessings and joy; come in, my daughter." That was a day of joy for all the Jews of Nineveh. Ahikar and Nadab, Tobit's cousins, came to rejoice with him. The wedding lasted seven days, in which they received many gifts.

The angel makes himself known. Then the angel called father and son and told them secretly, "Bless the Lord and thank him; honour him and praise him before all living creatures, because he has been favourable to you.

I will tell you the truth now. When you and Sarah prayed, it was I who brought your prayers into the presence of the Lord. When you buried the dead men I was with you. When you left your meal to bury the dead, I was sent here to put you to the test. And God sent me to cure you and Sarah, your daughter-in-law. I am Raphael, one of the seven angels who stand in attendance of the Lord and enter his glorious presence."

Then they were shaken, and prostrated themselves in awe. But he said, "Do not be afraid, all is well. Praise God for ever. Now bless the Lord and be thankful to him; I am ascending to him who sent me. Write down what has happened to you." And he disappeared.

JUDITH

HOLOPHERNES'S CAMPAIGN[1]

Resistance of the Israelites[2]. Then the Israelites and the inhabitants of Judah knew what Holophernes, Nebuchadnezzar's commander-in-chief, king of Assyria, had done to the peoples, and how he had taken and destroyed their temples. They became afraid when he came to their gates, thinking of Jerusalem and its Temple.

Pleas to God. All the Israelites cried out to the Lord their God, and they fasted. Men and their wives, their children, even babies; their animals, foreigners, workers and slaves put spiked belts on their bodies. All the Israelites, men, women and children who lived in Jerusalem prostrated themselves before the temple, covered their heads with ashes and sackcloth before the Lord.

The Lord heard their plight and understood their suffering. The people fasted day after day in Judah and Jerusalem watching the Temple of God Almighty.

Bethulia is besieged by Holophernes. Next morning Holophernes ordered his army and troops which were with him to attack Bethulia[3], seize the passes into the hill-country and

---

1. Commander-in-chief of King Nebuchadnezzar of Babylon and Nineveh.
2. Nebuchadnezzar made war to all the western nations which did not help him in the war against Arphaxat of Media.
3. In Northern Samaria, near Dothan, before the plains of Jezreel (Hebrew = housemaid).

fight the Israelites. All his warriors set out that day, an army of a hundred and seventy thousand infantry and twelve thousand cavalry, not counting the baggage train of the infantry, and inmense host.

The people, desperate, decides to give in to the Assyrians. Desperate, the Israelites claimed to the Lord, their God, when they saw that they had been besieged by their enemies without any possibility of escape. The Assyrian army, infantry, chariots and cavalry besieged them for thirty-four days. The supplies of water came to an end in Bethulia. The cisterns too were running dry; drinking-water was so strictly rationed that there was not a day when their needs were satisfied. The children were lifeless, the women and young men faint with thirst. They collapsed in the streets and gateways from sheer exhaustion. Then all the people, young men, women and children, gathered round Ozias[1] and the magistrates of the town, shouting loudly.

Ozias quietens the people. Ozias said to them, "My friends, be calmed; let us resist still five days. In these days our God may show us mercy again, He will not forsake us. If after five days no help should come, I will do as you say." He sent the people to their posts: the walls and the towers of the city. He sent the women and the children to their homes. Throughout the town there was deep dejection.

JUDITH'S INTERVENTION[2]

Judith, the heroine, comes on stage. Then Judith heard all this, daughter of Merari. Judith became a widow three years and four months ago, and she did not leave her home. She had a shelter erected on the roof of her house; she put on sackcloth and a spike belt while she courned. She fasted every day except sabbath eve, the sabbath itself, the eve of the new moon, the new moon and the Israelite feasts and days of public rejoicing since she became a widow. She was very beautiful and

---

1. Bethulia's priest: Azarias?
2. Judith (Hebrew = Jew).

charming. Manasseh, her husband, had left her gold and silver, male and female slaves, livestock and land, and she lived on her estate. No one spoke ill of her, for she was a very devout woman.

Judith attacks the chiefs of the people. Judith had been told the harsh words of the people against the chiefs because of the lack of water. She also knew Azarias's answer, and how he had sworn to surrender the city to the Assyrians after five days. Then, through the maid who was in charge of all her possessions, she summoned Ozias, Chabris and Charmis, the elders of the town. When they arrived she told them, "Listen to me, magistrates of Bethulia. You had no right to speak as you did to the people today, and to bind yourselves by oath before God to surrender the town to our enemies if the Lord sends no relief within so many days. Who are you to test God at a time like this, and openly set yourselves above him? You are putting the Lord Almighty to the proof, when you will never understand."

Judith tells her plans. Then Judith said, "Listen. I am going to do a deed which will be remembered among our people for all generations. Tonight be at the gate of the city; I will get out with my maid and, before the day on which you have promised to surrender the town to our enemies, the Lord will deliver Israel by my hand. Do not try to know my deed; you shall not know it until it is done." Ozias and the chiefs said to her, "Go with our blessing, and may the Lord be with you to take vengeance on our enemies."

Judith's prayer. Then Judith prostrated herself on the ground, put ashes on her head and showed her spike belt[1]. She claimed to the Lord and said, "Oh Lord, my God! Listen to this widow! Yours is the past, the present and the future; you know what now exists and the future is in your hands. The Assyrians are assembled in their strength, proud of their horses and riders, boasting the power of their infantry, and putting their faith in shield and javelin, bow and sling. They do not know that you

---

1. Spike belt: belt with sharp spikes on the edges attached to the body used by penitents.

are the Lord who stampts out wars. Shatter their strength by your power and crush their might in your anger, for they intend to desecrate your Sanctuary, to pollute the Tabernacle. Mark their arrogance, put your wrath on their heads and give my hand of widow strength.

Punish with the charm of my words the slave and the lod, the chief and his servant. End his arrogance by my hand of woman. Give me charming words to harm and destroy those who have such evil plans against your Covenant, against your Sanctuary, the Mount of Zion and the house of your children. Give the whole nation and every tribe the knowledge that you alone are God Almighty, and that there is no other shield for Israel."

Beautiful and richly dressed, Judith leaves Bethulia. When she ended her prayer, Judith stood up, called her maid, went to the rooms where she spent her sabbaths and feasts, removed the spike belt and her widow clothes. She had a bath and anointed herself with perfume. She did her hair, put on a headband and dressed in her gayest clothes, which she used to wear when her husband Manasseh was alive. She put on sandals, bracelets and rings, her ear-rings and all her ornaments, and made herself very attractive. She gave her maid a skin of wine and a flask of oil; then she filled a bag with roasted grain, cakes of dried gids and the finest bread. She packed all up and gave it to her.

Then they headed for the gate of Bethulia and there they came across Ozias and the two elders of the people, Chabris and Charmis. When they saw her so transformed in appearance and clothes, they were filled with admiration, and said to her, "The God of our fathers grants you grace and fulfils your plans so that Israel may triumph and Jerusalem may be exalted!" She worshipped God and said to them, "Order the gate to be opened for me so that I can go out to do what you have said." The people in the city followed her with their eyes while she came down the mountain towards the valley. Then they saw her no more.

Judith is captured and taken to Holophernes. They both walked hurriedly accross the valley when they met Assyrian sentries. They stopped Judith and asked her, "Who are you,

where do you come from and where are you going?" She
answered, "I am a Hebrew, but I am running away from my
people, for they are about to be defeated by you. I am going to
see Holophernes, your commander-in-chief, to give him some
information. I will show him the way to have the whole
mountain without losing a man or a living creature." When they
heard these words, and as they were amazed at her beauty —her
beauty was great—, the soldiers said to her, "You have saved
your life coming to see our commander-in-chief. Go, then, to
his tent; we will escort you to him. Do not be afraid, say to him
what you have said to us, and he will be good with you."

Holophernes's personal guards and all his assitants came out
and showed her into the tent. Holophernes was having a rest on
his bed under a mosquito-net of purple interwoven with gold,
emeralds, and precious stones. When Judith was announced he
came out to the front part of the tent, with silver lamps carried
before him.

He and his attendants were all amazed at the beauty of her
face as she stood before them. She prostrated herself and did
obeisance to him; but his slaves raised her up.

Holophernes's welcoming attitude. Holophernes said
toher, "Woman, trust in me, do not be afraid. I have never
illtreated those who have decided to serve Nebuchadnezzar,
king of the whole earth. So tell me why have you fled and
joined us. You have done it to save your life. Take heart, you
are in no danger tonight or in the future. Nobody will do you
any harm. They will treat you well, as the servants of my lord
Nebuchadnezzar are treated."

Judith's great skill. Judith answered, "My lord, grant your
slave a hearing so that I can speak freely tonight, for I shall tell
you no lie.

We have heard of your wisdom and cleverness, and you are
known throughout the world as the man of ability unrivalled in
the whole empire, of powerful intelligence and amazing skill
in the art of war. They have resolved to use up the first-fruits of
the grain and the tithes of wine and oil, although these are
dedicated and reserved for the priests who stand in attendance
before our God in Jerusalem. So I, your servant, knowing all

this, have fled from them, and God has led me to do with you things that will be the wonder of the world.

For your servant is a religious woman, night and day I worship the God of heaven. I will stay by you, my lord, and your servant will go to the valley every night to pray to God so that he tells me when have they sinned. When they do I will tell it to you so that you can attack them with your army, and then nobody will oppose you. I will guide you across Judah untill you reach Jerusalem, and I will set up your throne in the heart of the city."

Holophernes and his assistants are impressed by Judith's wisdom. These words delighted Holophernes and all his assistants, who were amazed at her wisdom. They said, "There is no woman as beautiful and wise in the whole world." Holophernes said to her, "Thanks God for sending you out from your people, to bring strength to us and destruction to those who have insulted my lord. You are beautiful and wise. If you do as you have said, your God shall be my God, you will live in Nebuchadnezzar's palace and be renowned throughout the world."

The assistants took her to her tent, where she slept until midnight. She rose up early. She had asked Holophernes, "My lord, order that I am allowed to go out and pray." Holophernes had granted it. She remained in the camp three days, and every night she went to the Valley of Bethulia and bathed in the spring. While she went there, she prayed the God of Israel to prosper her undertaking to restore her people. She came back purified and stayed in her tent until evenig, when she had her meal.

Judith attends Holophernes's banquet. On the fourth day Holophernes gave a banquet for his personal servants only, none of his officers was invited. And he said to Bagoas, the eunuch in charge of his affaires, "Try to convince the Hebrew woman so that she comes and eats with us. It would be a disgrace if we let such a woman go without enjoying her company. If we do not win her favour she will laugh at us." Bagoas left his presence and went to Judith's tent, and said to her, "O beautiful woman, do not doubt to come with my lord to be honoured in his company, drink the wine of you with us and be like one of the Assyrian woman in attendance at Nebuchadnezzar's palace." Judith answered, "Who am I to oppose my lord's wishes? I am eager to do whatever pleases him; and it will be something to boast of till the day I die."

She proceeded to dress herself up and put on all her femenine finery. Her maid was ahead of her, and she spread on the floor, by Holophernes, the skins which Bagoas had given her for her daily use, to eat reclined on them. Judith came in and sat down. Holphernes shook with passion and was filled with an ardent longing to possess her; indeed he had been looking for an opportunity to seduce her since he had seen her for the first time. Holophernes said to her, "Drink and enjoy yourself with us." Judith replied, "With pleasure, my lord, this is the greatest day of my whole life." And she ate and drink before him out of what her maid had prepared for her. Holophernes was delighted with her, and he drank so much wine than he had ever drunk on any single day since he was born.

VICTORY OF THE JEWISH PEOPLE

Judith beheads Holophernes. When it grew late, Holophernes' servants withdrew. Bagoas closed the tent from outside, shutting out all the attendants form his master's presence, and they went to bed, tired of having drunk so much. Judith was left alone in the tent with Holophernes, who was spread on the bed, dead drunk. Judith, standing by his bed, said to herself, "O Lord, God Almighty, look now the deed of my hind for Jerusalem's exaltation. The moment has come to help your possession and carry out my plans for crushing the enemies who have risen up against us." She went to the bed-rail beside Holophernes' head and took his sword. She drew near his bed, took him by his hair and said, "O Lord, God of Israel, give me strength." She struck at his neck twice with all her might, and cut off his head. Then she rolled the body off the bed and took the mosquito-net from its posts. She went out quickly and gave her maid Holophernes' head, who put it in the bags of

food. Then they crossed the field, and round that valley, and up
the hill to Bethulia until they reached the gates.

Judith called the sentries from a distance, "Open the door!
God, our God, is with us showing his power in Israel and his
might with his enemies, as he has done today."

Judith is praised and blessed in Bethulia. As soon as the
men of the city heard her voice, they ran to meet her at the gate,
and they called the elders. They all ran, young and old, because
they did not expect her back. They opened the gate, welcomed
them, and lighted a light to know them. She shouted, "Praise
God, praise him! Praise God, who has been merciful to the
people of Israel. Tonight he has defeated our enemies through
me." She threw the head out of her bag and showed it to them,
saying, "This is Holophernes's head, commander-in-chief of the
Assyrian army. This is the net under which he was sleeping,
dead drunk. The Lord struck him down by the hand of a
woman. Long live the Lord, who has protected me on my way!
My face seduced him to destruction, he committed no sin with
me, and my honour is unblemished."

All the people, astounded, prostrated worshipping God and
shouted, "Praised be our Lord, who has humiliated the enemies
of your people today."

Holophernes's head on the wall. Judith said to them,
"Listen, my friends, let us take the head and put it on the wall[1]."

It was early in the morning, and Holophernes's head was
already on the wall. Every man took his weapons and left in
groups towards the mountains. The Assyrians saw the head and
told it to their officers, who told it to their generals and captains.
They came to Holophernes's tent, and said to his steward,
"Wake up our commander-in-chief, for the slaves have dared to
attack us for their total destruction." Bagoas entered and
knocked at the screen of the tent, supposing that he was sleeping
with Judith. As there was no reply, he drew the screen aside,
went into the sleeping-apartment and found the dead body
sprawled over a footstool, and the head gone. Then he gave a

---

1. Judith's behaviour is like that of her contemporaries.

great cry, wailing and groaning aloud, and tore his clothes. Then he entered Judith's tent and did not found her.

He ran to the people and said, "The slaves have played us false! The Hebrew woman has brought shame on Nebuchadnezzar's kingdom. Look, Holophernes is lying on the ground, and his head is gone!" When the chiefs of the Assyrian army heard these words, they tore their clothes and the camp rang with their shouts and cries.

The Israelites pursue the Assyrians, who fled. When those who were in the tents knew what had happened, they shouted and cried, and they scattered in terror and panic. They fled by every path across the plain and the hill-country. Those who were watching Bethulia fled too. Then the Israelites who were prepared for war attacked them. Ozias sent messengers to Bethomesthaim, Choba and the whole territory of Israel to let everybody know the facts, so that they would pursue and kill the enemies.

When the Israelites knew it, the attacked them and killed them to Choba. Those in Jerusalem and in the hill-country came too, for they already knew what had happened. Those in Gilead and Galilee defeated them beyond Damascus and the district round it.

The High Priest praises Judith. The High Priest Joakim and the senate of Israel came from Jerusalem and came to see the great things the Lord had done for his people, and to see Judith and praise her. When they saw her they blessed her saying,

"You are the glory of Jerusalem;
      you, the glory of Israel,
      you, the glory of our race."

And all the people answered, "Amen."

ESTHER

Ahasuerus' banquet[1]. The events here related happened in the days of Ahasuerus, the Ahasuerus who ruled from India to Ethiopia over one hundred and twenty-seven provinces. At that time he sat on his royal throne in the city of Susa. In the third year of his reign he gave a banquet for all the princes, governors and officers of the Persian and Mede armies, and for the nobles and governors of the provinces.

Vashti is desthroned. Queen Vashti gave also a banquet for the women at Ahasuerus' palace. On the seventh day, when the king was merry with wine he sent the seven eunuchs who served him, Mehuman, Biztha, Harbona, Bigtha, Abagtha, Zethar and Carcas, to bring Queen Vashti to his presence with the royal crown to show her beauty to the people, for she was very beautiful. But Queen Vashti refused to come, despite the royal command brought by the eunuchs. The king grew hot with anger, and he inquired the wise men, expert in law, for it was a custom to consult all who were versed in law and religion. "What should be done with Queen Vashti for disobeying the king's command, brought by the eunuchs?", asked the king.

Then Memucan, before the king and the princes, replied, "The Queen has done wrong, and not to the king alone, but also to all the officers and to all the peoples in all the provinces of King Ahasuerus. If it please your majesty, let a royal decree go

---

1. King Xerxes, son of Darius. He is famous for his frequent attacks to Egypt and Asia minor. He fought and was defeated by the Greeks in the Medic Wars.

out from you and let it be inscribed in the laws of the Persians and the Medes, never to be revoked, that Vashti shall never appear before King Ahasuerus; and let the king give her place to other woman who is more worthy of it than her. Thus when this royal edict is heard through the length and breadth of the kingdom, all women will give honour to their husbands, high and low alike."

This advice pleased both the king and the princes, and the king did as Memucan had said.

Queen Esther. After these events, when the anger of King Ahasuerus had died down, he recalled what he had done and what he had decreed against her. His servants told him, "Let beautiful young virgins be sought out for your majesty; and let your majesty appoint commissioners in all the provinces of your kingdom to bring all these beautiful young virgins into the women's quarters in Susa the capital city. Let them be committed to the care of Hegai, the king's eunuch in charge of the women, and let cosmetics be provided for them; and let the one who is most acceptable to the king become queen in place of Vashti." These words pleased the king, and it was done.

In the city of Susa there was a Jew named Mordecai son of Jair, son of Shimei, of the tribe of Benjamin, carried into exile from Jerusalem with the captives who were deported with Jeconiah king of Judah by King Nebuchadnezzar. He had a foster-child Hadassah, that is, Esther, daughter of an uncle of his, who had neither father nor mother. She was beautiful, and when her parents died Mordecai adopted her. After the edict of the king many girls were taken to the city of Suse and committed to the care of Hegai. Esther was chosen too, and taken to the royal palace, under the care of Hegai, the women's keeper. She attracted his notice and received his special favour; he readily provided her with her cosmetics and her allowance of food, and also with seven picked maids form the king's palace, and he gave her and her maids privileges in the woman's quarters. Everyday Mordecai walked across the courtyard to see Esther and to know what happened.

When the turn came for Esther, daughter of Abihail the uncle of Mordecai her adoptive father, she did not ask for nothing to take with her except what was advised by Hegai, eunuch of the king and keeper of the women. But Esther charmed all who saw her. She was taken to King Ahasuerus, to his royal palace, on the seventh month, the month of Tebeth, in the seventh year of his reign. And the king preferred her to the other women and treated her with greater favour and kindness than the rest of the virgins. He put the royal crown on her head and chose her as queen instead of Vashti. Then Ahasuerus gave a great banquet for all the princes and courtiers, the banquet of Esther. He also proclaimed a holiday throughout the provinces and distributed things worthy of a king.

Mordecai discovers a plot against the king. When she was in the second harem, with the young girls, Esther had not disclosed her family or race, as Mordecai had told her. She still observed his advices, as when he was his ward.

By then Mordecai was sitting by the royal gate, and Bigthan and Teresh, two of the king's eunuchs, enraged, were plotting the death of King Ahasuerus. This became known to Mordecai and told it to Queen Esther, who told it to the king on behalf of Mordecai. When the report was confirmed the two men were hanged on the gallows. All this was recorded in the royal chronicle in the presence of the king.

Haman[1], enemy of the Jews. Some time later King Ahasuerus promoted Haman, son of Hammedatha the Agagite, advancing him and giving him precedence above all his fellow-officers. All the servants of the king, who were in service at the palace gate, knelt down and prostrated when Haman passed by, as the king had decreed. So the servant of the king at the palace gate asked him, "Why do you flout this majesty's command?" Every day they asked him the same question, but he would not answer. Then they denounced him to Haman, to see if Mordecai's refusal would be tolerated, for he had told them that he was a Jew. Haman checked that Mordecai did not kneel down nor prostrated himself when he passed by, and he got angry. And as he had heard of Mordecai's race, he scorned

---

1.   Haman, Hebrew, main of the courtiers. He hated the Jews.

to lay hands on him alone, and looked for a way to destroy all the Jews in the whole kingdom of Ahasuerus.

Decree against the Jews. Hamman said to King Ahasuerus, "Among the uncontable peoples of your kingdom and throughout your provinces, there is a certain dispersed people who keep themselves apart. They have different laws and do not keep the laws of the king. It does not benefit your majesty to tolerate them. If it pleases you issue a decree to destroy them, and I will give your officers ten thousand talents of silver which shall be deposited in the royal treasury." Ahasuerus took out his ring and gave it to Haman, son of Hammedatha the Agagite, pursuer of the Jews, and said to him, "Keep your silver, and do as you please with that people."

On the thirteenth day of the first month, the month of Nisan[1], the secretaries of the king were summoned to get copies of the royal commands and to sent them to all the king's satraps, the governors of the province and to the chiefs of each people, according to the writing of each province and the language of each people. The copies were signed by King Ahasuerus and sealed with his royal seal. The couriers sent the letters to all the provinces of the kingdom, with the order to destroy, slash and exterminate all the Jews, both children and elder, babies and women, on the same day, that is, on the thirteenth day of the twelfth month, the month of Adar[2] and to plunder their possessions.

As soon as Mondecai[3] learnt all this, he put on sackcloth and ashes, and he went through the city crying loudly and bitterly. He came to the palace gate, for nobody could cross it clothed with sackcloth. In all the provinces and places where the edict of the king was published there was nothing else but mourning, fast, weeping and crying on the part of the Jews. The beds of many of them were made of sackcloth and ashes. Esther's handmaids and eunuchs came to her and told her the news. The queen was moved and sent clothes to Mondecai for him to take

---

1. Nisan = January.
2. Adar = December.
3. Mondecai. Hebrew = related to Marduk.

off the sackcloth and put her clothes on. But he did not want them.

Then Esther called Hathach, one of the eunuchs that the king had put to her service, and sent him to Mondecai to see why did he behave that way. Hathach left and went to Mondecai, in the square opposite the royal gate. Mondecai told him the news and told him the exact amount of money which Haman had offered the king if he acceded to the extermination of the Jews. He also gave him a copy of the edict of extermination, issued in Susa, to gave it to Esther.

Mondecai sent to Esther the message that she went before the king to ask for his mercy and intercede for her people. "Remember —he said— the days when you were not queen, when I fed you. Haman, the second most important man in the kingdom, has spoken against us asking for our destruction. Pray to the Lord, speak for us to the king and set us free from death."

Hathach came back and told Esther what Mondecai had told her. Esther told Hathach and gave him this answer for Mondecai, "All the servants of the king and the people in the provinces know that anybody, man or woman, who enters the inner yard without having been called, is condemned to the death penalty, unless the king stretches out to him the golden sceptre, then he is forgiven. It is now thirty days since I myself was called to go to the king." Hathach told these words to Mondecai, who answered, "Do not think that because you live among the people of the king you will save yourself among all the Jews. If you keep silent, the Jews will find help and will be saved from another quarter, but you and the house of your father shall perish. Who knows whether it is not for such a time as this that you have come to the royal throne?"

Esther sent him this answer, "Go and assemble all the Jews of Susa, and fast for me. Do not eat or drink for three days and three nights. I and my handmaids will fast too. Then I will come into the king's presence, against the law, though, and if I have to die, I will." Mondecai left and did as Esther had told him.

All Israel claimed to the Lord insistently, for they still feared death.

Esther's prayer. Queen Esther, afraid of the danger which was drawing near, also prayed to the Lord. She took off her royal clothes and put on clothes of mourning. And she prayed to the Lord, God of Israel,

"My Lord, our king, you are the Only One.
>   Help me in my loneliness,
>   for you are my only help,
>   and death is waiting for me.
Lord, do not forsake us and let you be seen on this day of our anguish.
>   Give me strength, king of gods, and Almighty God.

Put on my lips the proper words
>   when I am before the lion.

You know everything
>   and you also know that I hate the glory of the impious men,
>   that I hate the bed of those who are uncircumcised
>   as much as the bed of any foreigner.

You know the need I feel
>   and also that I hate the sign of my highness,
>   that binds my head on the days of exhibition.

Your servant has never been happy
>   from my election till today
>   but in your presence, O Lord, God of Abraham.

O God, more Mighty than any other!
>   Listen to the words of the hopeless,
>   set us free from the evil men
>   and set me free from my fears."

Esther comes into Ahasuerus' presence. On the third day, after her prayer, she took off her mourning clothes and dressed herself as the queen. Looking very beautiful she prayed to the Lord, the saviour, and took two handmaids. She leaned delicately on one of them; the other held her clothes. She looked fine, beautiful and attractive, but her heart was beating quickcly. After having passed through all the gates she came to the king. He was sitting on his throne, dressed with all the royal finery, with gold and precious stones. He had an impressive appearance. He looked up to her full of anger. The queen grew pale, felt sick and was leaning on her handmaid. Then God put some sweetness in the king's heart, who stood up hurriedly, took the queen in his arms until she felt better and with sweet words told her, "What is up with you, Esther? I am your brother, do not be afraid. You shall not die. This law is for the others. Come near." And as he stretched out the golden sceptre towards her, he kissed Esther and said to her, "Tell me." So Esther said to him, "Oh my lord, I saw you like an angel of God and my heart got afraid of your majesty. You are wonderful, my lord, and also charming." While she said these words she fainted again. The king was moved while his servants were helping her.

Esther's banquet. Three days afterwards, Esther, dressed as a queen, came to the inner courtyard, before the royal chamber. Ahasuerus was on the throne in the royal chamber, looking at the door. When he saw Queen Esther standing in the courtyard, he was taken by her charm and stretched out his golden sceptre towards her which he had in his hand. Esther touched the edge of the sceptre. The king asked her, "What is is, Queen Esther? What do you want?" "If it pleases the king, said Esther, attend today with Haman the banquet which I have prepared." "Let Hamman know about it so that Esther is pleased", said the king. During the banquet the king said to Esther, "Tell me what do you want and it shall be granted. Up to half my kingdom, it shall be given to you." Esther answered, "What I ask for is this: If I have won your majesty's favour, if it pleases you to grant me my wish, attend tomorrow the banquet which I will prepare again, and then I will do as your majesty has said."

A gallows for Mordecai. Haman went away that day in good spirits and well pleased with himself. But when he saw Mordecai sitting by the royal gate without standing up or moving to him, he was filled with rage, but he kept control of himself and went home. Then he sent for his friends and his wife Zeresh and held forth to them about the splendour of his wealth and his many sons, and how the king had promoted him and advanced him above the other officers and courtiers. "That is not all", he said, "Even queen Esther invited no one but myself to accompany the king to the banquet which she had prepared; and she has invited me again tomorrow with the king. Yet all this means nothing to me so long as I see that Jew Mordecai in attendance at court." Then his wife Zeresh and all his friends said to him, "Let a gallows seventy-five feet high be set up, and advise the king in the morning to have Mordecai hanged upon it. Then go with the king to the banquet in good spirits." Haman thought this an excellent plan, and he set up the gallows.

Haman's fall and Mordecai's promotion. But it happened that the king could not sleep that night, and he ordered the chronicle of daily events to be brought and read to him. There was recorded that Mordecai had given information about Bigthana and Teresh, the two royal eunuchs who plotted to kill the king. "What honour or dignity has been conferred on Mordecai for this?", asked the king, "None", answered his servants. Then the king asked, "Who is there in the courtyard?" At that moment had just entered the outer court of the palace to advise the king that Mordecai should be hanged on the gallows which he had prepared for him. The king's servants answered, "It is Haman standing there" The king bade him enter. He came in, and the king said to him, "What should be done for the man whom the king wishes to honour?" Haman said to himself, "Whom would the king wish to honour more than me?" And he said to the king, "For the man whom the king wishes to honour, let there be brought royal robes which the king himself wears, and a horse which the king rides, with a royal crown upon its head. And let the robes and the horse be delivered to one of the king's most honourable officers, and let him attire the man whom the king wishes to honour and lead him mounted on the horse through the city square, calling out as he goes, 'See what is done for the man whom the king wishes to honour'." Then the king said to Haman, "Fetch the robes and the horse at once, as you have said, and do all this for Mordecai the Jew who is in attendance at court. Leave nothing undone of all that you have said." So Haman took the robes and the horse, attired Mordecai and led him mounted throught he city square, calling out as he went, "See what is done for the man whom the king wishes to honour."

Then Mordecai came back to the royal gate, while Haman came back home sad and mourning. He told his wife Zeresh and all his friends everything that had happened to him. And then the king's eunuchs arrived and hurried him away to the banquet which Esther had prepared.

A gallows for Haman. The king and Haman came to Esther's banquet. This second day the king said again to Esther, "Tell me, Queen Esther, what do you want, and it shall be granted to you although it is half my kingdom." "If I have found grace with your majesty, oh king, grant me my life, this is my wish, and the life of my people. For me and my people are doomed to extermination, to be destroyed. At least if we would have been sold as slaves, I would have been quiet, but the enemy will not be able to compensate all the harm he has done to the king." King Ahasuerus break in to ask her, "Who is it who has planned such a barbaric deed?" "The oppresor, our enemy, is Haman", answered Esther. Then Haman was filled with terror before the king and the queen.

Ahasuerus got into a rage, stood up and left the banquet. He left for the inner yard; meanwhile Haman understood that his fate was determined and pleaded for his life to Esther. When the king came back from the garden to the banquet, he found Haman leaning on the couch on which Esther was reclined. Then the king exclaimed, "Will he even assault the queen here in my presence?" No sooner had the words been uttered than Haman hid his face in despair. Then Harbona, one of the king's eunuchs, said, "At Haman's house stands the gallows, seventy-five feet hight, which he himself has prepared for Mordecai, who once served the king well." "Hang Haman on it", said the king. So Haman was hanged on the gallows that he himself had prepared for Mordecai. After that the king's rage abated.

On that day King Ahasuerus gave to Esther the house of Haman, the enemy of the Jews, and Mordecai came into the king's presence, for Esther had revealed the king that he was his foster father. The king took off his signet-ring, which he had

taken back from Haman and put in into Mordecai's finger.
Esther put Mordecai in charge of the house of Haman[1].

1. On the 14th and the 15th of December the Jews celebrate the Feast of
    the Pruim, in remembrance of the liberation of the Jews from the hands of the
    cruel Haman in Persia.

BOOKS OF THE MACCABEES

THE FIRST BOOK OF THE MACCABEES[1]

THE GREEKS IN ISRAEL

Alexander the Great and his successors. After Alenxander of Macedon, son of Philip, marched from the land of Kittim, defeated Darius, king of Persia and Media, he came to the borders of the earth and captured many nations. And then the word lay quiet under his rule.

Alexander had reigned twelve years when he died. His generals took over the government, each in his own province. After his death, they were all crowned as kings, and his sons after them for many years, but they filled the earth with evil.

Antiochus Epiphanes IV. At that time there appeared in Israel a group of wicked men who seduced many men, saying, "Let us make a covenant with the neighbouring nations, for since we segregated ourselves from them disaster has overtaken

---

1. The Maccabees. The brothers of Judah Maccabee were called so (in Hebrew it means hammer, as it seems), third son of Mathatiah, hero in the war of the Jews against Syria.

us." The people thought this a good argument, and they ran to
meet the king, who authorised them to follow gentile rites. They
built a sportstadium in the gentile style in Jerusalem. They
repudiated the Holy Covenant to join the gentiles, and they
abandoned themselves to evil ways.

Prosecution of the Jews. When Egypt was defeated,
Antiochus[1] came back in the year 143 and attacked Israel and
Jerusalem with a numerous army. He entered the Temple
proudly, and took the golden altar and the lamp-stand with all
its equipment. When he had it all he came back to his country
after causing much bloodshed, and he gloated over all he had
done. There was great mourning in Israel.

Two years later, the king sent to the towns of Judah a high
revenue official, who came to Jerusalem with a huge army. He
uttered deceitful words of peace and the people trust him. But
suddenly he broke into the city and struck it, and he hill many
Israelites. He plundered the city and set it ablaze, destroying the
houses and the walls which surrounded it. Their peoples made
prisoners to women and children, and took their herds. They
fortified the city of David with an only and stout wall defended
by powerful towers, and turned it into a citadel. They brought in
wicked people who took the power of the citadel.

The king issued in the whole kingdom the order of their
peoples to become one people, abandoning their customs and
religion. All the nations accepted the command of the king.
Many Israelites accepted his worship, sacrificing to idols and
profaning the sabbath. The king even sent messengers to
Jerusalem and to the cities of Judaea with written orders for
them to accept the customs foreign to their country, to abolish
the whole-offerings, sacrifices and libations in the temple and to
profane the sabbath and the feasts; and to defile the temple and
its ministers. Altars, idols and sacred precincts were to be
established; swine and other unclean beasts to be offered in
sacrifice. Their sons must be left uncircumcised; they must

---

1. Antiochus Epiphanes IV, usurper of the throne, organized a violent
   prosecution against the Jews. He wanted to set up a Hellenic style in Palestine
   by sweeping away all religious signs.

make themselves in every way abominable, unclean, and profane, and so forget the law and change their statutes. Disobedience was punished with the death penalty. To this end the king wrote to all the kingdom appointing superintendents over all the people and ordered that all the cities of Judah offered sacrifices.

On the fifteenth day of the month Kislev[1], in the year 145, Antiochus erected the abominable idol of desolation on the altar[2], and he set up altars in all the neighbouring cities of Judah. Incense was offered at the doors of houses and in the streets. All the scrolls of the law which were found were torn up and burnt. Anyone discovered in possession of a Book of the Covenant, or conforming to the law, was put to death by the king's sentence. In spite of all this, many Israelites stood firm and resolved not to eat unclean beasts. They prefered the death to be contaminated by the food prohibited by the Holy Covenant, and they died because of it.

REVOLT OF THE JEWS

Mattathias[3] and his sons. In those days Mattathias, son of John, son of Symeon, priest of the family of Joarib, left Jerusalem and settled down at Modin. He had five sons: John called Gaddis, Simon called Thassis, Judas called Maccabaeus, Eleazar called Avaran, and Jonathan called Apphus.

Mattathias refuses the sacrifice. Meanwhile the messengers of the king came to Modin to enforce apostasy and sacrifice. Many Israelites followed them, but Mattathias and his sons stood aside. Then the messengers of the king spoke to Mattathias, "In this city you are a famous and powerful chief, with sons and brothers at your back. So come nearer and obey the king's command, as the inhabitants of Judah and those who

---

1. Kislev, between November and December.
2. The abominable idol on the altar of the offerings was a statue of the Olympic Jupiter, denounced by the prophets.
3. Mattathias (Hebrew = gift of God) stood firm before the orders of the king, beginning the political and religious war of the Maccabees.

have stayed in Jerusalem. You and your family will be honoured with the friendship of the king, and you shall be rewarded with silver, gold and other gifts." Mattathias, shouting, answered them, "Although all the nations which constitute the empire would follow the king, abandoning the religion of their fathers and obeying his orders, I, my sons and my family would follow the Covenant of our forefathers. God forbid that we abandon the Law and our traditions. We will not hear the king's commands and we shall not abandon our religion, nor will we deviate one step from our forms of worship."

Then Mattathias shouted, "Follow me those of you who are zealous for the law and strive to maintain the covenant." And he and his sons fled to the mountains, leaving their belongings in the city.

Mattathias prepares himself for war. Then a lot of followers of justice and the Law went to the desert, where they lived with their sons, daughters and herds, for their miseries where more than they could bear.

The Hasidaeans[1] join Mattathias in the Holy War. Then a group of Hasidaeans joined them, brave men of Israel and enthusiast defenders of the Law. All those who fled from their troubles joined them, adding to their strength. So they formed a powerful army which was able to punish in its anger the sinners and wicked men, who were searching for their salvation among the gentiles. Mattathias and his men attacked them and destroyed their altars.

Death of Mattathias. Then Mattathias blessed them and joined his forefathers. He died in the year 146. His sons buried him at Modin, in their forefather's grave, and all Israel mourned him.

---

1. The Hasidaeans were a kind of sect similar to that of the Hesenians of the Qum-Ram by the shore of the Dead Sea.

JUDAS MACCABEUS LEADER OF THE JEWS

Judas Maccabeus, national hero. Judas Maccabeus succeeded his father. His brothers and all those who had followed his father helped him to fight the battles of Israel.

Judas's victories. Apollonius collected a gentile force and a powerful army of Samaritans to fight against Israel. As soon as Judas knew about it he attacked him, defeated him and killed him. Many of them fell, and the rest fled. They took their corpses; Judas kept Apollonius' sword and used it for war when he needed it. Then Seron, commander-in-chief of the Syrian army, when he knew that Judas had gathered himself of a lot of followers, reliable and brave men, said to himself, "I will become famous and will win glory in the kingdom fighting Judah and his followers, who do not obey the king's command."

Seron marched to take vengeance upon the Israelites with an army of wicked men. When they came to the hill of Bethoron[1] Judas came out to meet him with his men, who, when they saw the army which was going to attack them, said to Judas, "How are we going to fight so numerous and powerful an army?"

Judas answered them, "It is easy for the army of many men to fall in the hands of those who are few, and for heaven it is the same to save many souls than to save only a few. For in war, victory does not depend on numbers, for our strength comes from heaven. They come against us full of arrogance and wickedness to take away our women and children, and to seize our possessions. We fight for our lives and our laws, and He will deliver them into our hands. Do not be afraid of them." As soon as he finished talking Judas attacked their enemies. Seron and his army were defeated. They pursued them down the hill of Bethoron until the plain. More than eight hundred men fell, and the rest fled to the country of the Philistines.

---

1. Hill on the hill-country until the plains of Jezreel, or Hesdralon, towards the sea.

Judas and his brothers began to be feared, and fear of them spread throughout the neighbouring nations. Their fame came to the king, and all peoples talked about their deeds.

Antiochus Epiphanes IV prepares to made war on the Jews. When these events were known, Antiochus got very angry and assembled all the forces of his kingdom to form an extremely powerful army. Then he paid to the soldiers the wages of a whole year from the royal treasury, saying to them that they should be prepared for any duty. But he realised that he did not have enough money and that the tributes of the provinces had lessened because of the disaffection and violence which he had caused when he abolished their old laws. He became very worried and decided to go to Persia to get the tributes from those provinces and thus collect some money.

He left Lysias, a nobleman member of the royal family, in charge of vicerroy of the territory from the Euphrates until the borders of Egypt, and also of the education of his son Antiochus until he came back.

The king, with the other half of the army, left Antioch, the capital of his kingdom in the year 147; he crossed the Euphrates and continued his way through the Northern regions.

Lysias sends troops against the Jews. Lysias chose Ptolemaeus son of Dorymenes, Nicanor and Gorgias, important noblemen, out of the friends of the king. He put them ahead of forty thousand infantry soldiers and seven thousand cavalry soldiers, so that they went to Judah to destroy it, according to the king's command. They left with their troops and encamped in the plain by Emmaus. The merchants of the country, when they knew about their coming, came to the camp with a lot of silver and gold, and chains to buy the Israelites as slaves.

Judas and his brothers saw that the situation was grewing worse, and that some troops were encamping in their territory. They also had news about the command of the king which said that the people should be destroyed, and they said to themselves, "Let us set our people free from misery, and let us fight for them and for the Temple." They made an assembly to fight Antiochus's troops, praying to God that he should grant them piety and forgiveness.

Assembly at Mizpah[1]. After these events Judas named chiefs of the people: officers over thousands, hundreds, fifties and tens. Then those who were building houses, or were about to marry, or sew vineyards, or were afraid were told to go back to their homes, as the law allowed. Later they encamped South of Emmaus. Judas spoke to his men, "Take your swords, be brave and be ready to attack those people who come against us to destroy us and our Temple tomorrow. It is better to die fighting than to see the abominations of our nation and our Temple. It will be as Heaven wills."

Gorgias is defeated at Emmaus. Gorgias took fifty thousand infantry soldiers, and one thousand cavalry horses with him, and he set off in the night to attack the Jews and defeat them unawares. The people in the citadel served them as guides. When Judas knew about this he set off too with the bravest men to attack the royal army, which was at Emmaus. Meanwhile, the royal army was still dispersed. Gorgias came to Judas's camp by night, but he found it empty, and he began to sought for them in the hills. He said, "They flew before us."

At dawn Judas appeared in the plain with three hundred men who did not have the shields or swords appropriated for them. Judas said to them, "Take heart. All the nations shall know that there are people who fight and defeat their enemies for the sake of Israel."

The foreigners looked up and as they saw that the Jews were coming towards them they left their camp to fight them. The men of Judas sounded their trumpets and began the fight. The gentiles, astonished, fled to the plain; but those at the rear were killed. They were pursued as far as Gazara[2], in the plains of Idumaea, Azotus and Jamnia. Around three thousand enemies fell.

---

1. Mizpah (Hebrew = watchtower). Centre of the rebellion of Antioch against Selucidas, Antiochus IV. It was considered one of the most important fortresses of Palestine.

2. Old city in the South of Palestine given by Pharaoh to Solomon as a marriage portion. Important place in the routes of caravans, in the plains of Idumaea.

Then Judas turned back to plunder the camp, and the soldiers took a lot of gold, silver, violet and purple stuffs, and great riches. When they came back to their camp they praised and blessed heaven, "because it is good, because its piety lasts for ever." On that day Israel saw a great deliverance.

The foreigners who escaped told Lysias what had happened. He was overwhelmed with disappointment, for things in Israel had not followed his plans nor the king's commands.

Judas defeats Lysias. In the following year Lysias gathered seven thousand chosen men and five thousand cavalry officers to fight the Jews. When they came to Idumaea they encamped near Bethsura. Judas attacked them with ten thousand men.

Five thousand men from the army of Lysias started the fighting. When Lysias saw how his men fled and the Jews' enthusiasm, who were willing to live or die like heroes, he went back to Antioch[1] to gather mercenaries and attack Judaea with more power than before.

Reestablisment of the worship. Then Judas and his brothers said, "As our enemies have been defeated, let us purify and consecrate the Temple again." They gathered all their army and went to Mount Zion[2] When they saw the Temple empty, its altar profaned, the gates burnt down, the grass growing in the yards as in the woods or the hills, and the rooms devastated, they tore their clothes and put ashes on their heads. They prostrated on the ground and, when they heard the trumpets, they shouted to heaven. Judas ordered his men to fight the people in the citadel while the purification of the Temple was taking place. And he chose priests without blemish, observers of the Law, who purified the Temple. And taking non-carved stones according to the Law they built a new altar similar to the old one. Once the sanctuary was repaired and the inner part of

---

1. Antioch. Capital of the Selucides. Syria.
2. Zion. Fortress of the Jebusites, conquered by David. Afterwards, it became City of David, and later the Mount of the Temple and all the city. Then, the Western hill, and nowadays it is the Eastern hill, the old City of David. The Hophel.

the Temple, they purified the yards, made new holy vessels, and took the lamp-stand, the altar of parfumes and the table.

Victory over Timotheus. They crossed the Jordan and came to the great plain of Bethshan. During their journey Judas cared for those at the rear and encouraged the people to go on till Judaea. With great rejoicing they came up Mount Zion and offered sacrifices because they had returned happily and without any loses.

Death of Antiochus Epiphanes IV. While King Antiochus went through the Northern provinces he knew that at Elymais, in Persia, was a famous city because of the abundance of gold and silver that could be found in it; that there was a rich Temple with gold shields, coats of mail and arms left by Alexander son of Philip, king of Macedon, first king of Greece. He went there and tried to conquer the city, but he could not do it because its inhabitants went out to defend it from him with arms. He fled sadly to go back to Babylon.

When he was still in Persia, the king was told about the defeats of his armies sent to Judaea. He was told that Lysias, although he had gone with a very powerful army, had had to fled from the Jews, who had made themselves stronger with the arms and loot of the defeated armies. And also that they had destroyed the abominable idol erected by him on the altar of Jerusalem, and that they had surrounded their Temple and Bethsura[1], one of their cities, as they were before. When he heard those news he was thrown into great dismay; he took to his bed, ill with grief at the miscarriage of his plans. He was ill for many days, his bitter grief breaking out again and again. He thought that he was going to die, so he summoned his friends and told them, "It is for the evil which I have done to Jerusalem that these misfortunes have come upon me, and so I must die of grief in a foreign land."

Antiochus Eupator V[2] in Judaea. The people in the citadel were to see the king and said to him, "When will you do justice and avenge our brothers? We accepted to serve your father,

---

1. Bethsura (Hebrew = City of rocks). Canaanite city fortified by Judas.

2. Eupator, his son.

obey his commands and his laws, and we have been hated for this by our own people. They have killed as many of us as they have been able to, and our properties have been seized. And not only us, they have also attacked the neighbouring countries. Now, besides, they have surrounded the citadel of Jerusalem to conquer it, and they have walled the Temple of Bethsura. If you do not act quickly, they will do even worse things, and you will not be able to stop them." When he heard these words the king got very angry and assembled his friends, the officers of the army and cavalry captains. Mercenary troops came from other kingdoms and from islands on the sea, and they gathered an army of one hundred thousand infantry soldiers, twenty thousand cavalry soldiers and thirty-two war-elephants. Then Judas withdrew from the citadel and encamped at Bethzacharia, opposite the camp of the king. The king rose early and ordered his army to attack quickly Bethzacharia, where his troops were drawn up for battle and the trumpets were sounded. The elephants were roused for battle with the juice of grapes and mulberries to make them aggresive in battle. They distributed the animals among the phalanxes. Beside each elephant one thousand men with coats of chain-mail and bronze helmets were placed, and also five hundred chosen cavalry soldiers. A part of the king's army was deployed over the heights, another part on the plains, and they all advanced firmly and orderly. They were afraid, for they heard the shouts of the marching multitude, so many people marching and fighting. Indeed, it was a numerous and powerful array. Judas came with his army and attacked, and six thousand men of the royal army fell.

But the Jews, as they saw the forces of the king and the bravery of his army, withdrew.

Jerusalem is besieged. Then the royal army pursued them as far as Jerusalem, and encamped in Judah, besieging Mount Zion.

For many days they were encamped before the Temple and there they put emplacement sand siege-engines, with flame-throwers, catapults, and barbed missiles and slings. Also the besieged people built engines to counter his engines, and they fought each other for a long time. But they lacked victuals in their stores, for it was the seventh year and the Israelites who came to Judah from gentile countries had eaten up all the remains of the provisions.

Meanwhile, Philip, whom King Antiochus had put in charge of the education of his child Antiochus when he was alive to prepare him for the rule of his kingdom, had returned from Persia and Media with the army which had accompanied the king, and he intended to take over the government. When Lysias heard about this, he wanted to leave, saying to the king, the commanders of the army and the soldiers, "Every day we are growing weaker, provisions are low, the place we are besieging is strongly defended and the affairs of the state are pressing. Let us offer our hand to these men by making a covenant with them and their nation." These words pleased the king and the commanders, and an offer of peace was sent to the Jews, who accepted it. The king and the commanders confirmed the treaty with an oath. Then he left hurriedly and came back to Antioch, where he found Philip as the ruler of the city. He fought him and the city was taken by storm.

Demetrius king of Asia. In the year 151 Demetrius son of Seleucus left Rome and landed with some men at a town on the coast, where he proclaimed himself king. As he advanced towards Antioch, royal residence of his parents, the army took Antiochus and Lysias as prisioner to hand them to them. When Demetrius knew about this, he said, "I do not want to see their faces." The soldiers killed them and Demetrius sat on his kingdom's throne.

Nicanor against Judas. The king sent Nicanor, a distinguished commander, and enemy of Israel, with orders to wipe them out.

Defeat and death of Nicanor. Nicanor encamped at Beth-horon, where he was joined by the Sirian army. On his part, Judas encamped at Adasa with three thousand men. On the thirteenth day of the month of Adar the two armies joined battle. Nicanor's army was defeated; he fell the first one in battle. When the army saw that Nicanor was dead, they threw their arms and fled. The Jews pursued them during a whole day from Adasa as far as Gazara, sounding trumpets after them. The

people went out of their villages of Judaea and surrounded their
flanks, forcing them back to their pursuers. In this way they all
fell to the sword; no even one was left.

Glorious death of Judas Maccabaeus. When Demetrius
knew about Nicanor's death and the defeat of his army, he
decided to sent Bacchides and Alcimus a second time to Judah
as commanders of the right flank of his army. Judas had his
camp at Alasa, with three thousand chosen men. But when
his men saw such great number of enemies, they grew afraid,
and many of them fled from the camp. Only eight hundred men
were left. When Judas saw that his army had melted away and
that the fight was about to begin, he felt miserable, for he had
no time to gather them all again. Anguished, he spoke to those
who were left, "Let us fight our enemies, we may even defeat
them. If our time has come, let us die bravely for our brothers
and leave not stain on our honour."

The other army let its camp and faced them with its cavalry
divided into two flanks. The earth shook at the din of the armies
as battle was joined in the morning and it lasted until well in the
evening. Judas realized that Bacchides and the strongest part of
the army were on the right side, and he joined his bravest man
to defeat the right side, and pursued its soldiers as far as the
Mount Azotus. Those on the left side, when they saw the defeat
of those on the left side, followed Judas and his men on their
heels. It was a very heavy fighting, and on both sides people
fell. Also Judas fell. The rest of them fled.

Jonathan and Simon took their brother and buried him in the
graves of his forefathers at Modim. All the people of Israel
mourned him and wept for him for a long time, saying,

"The hero has fallen,
Israel's saviour!"

JONATHAN SUCCEEDS JUDAS

Jonathan leader of Israel. Then the friends of Judas
assembled and said to Jonathan, "Since your brother Judas's
death there has been nobody like him, who is able to fight our

enemies, Bacchides and those who loathe our nation. We choose you to take his place as our leader and guide in our battle." Then he received the power and succeeded his brother Judas.

When Bacchides knew about this he tried to kill Jonathan. But as Jonathan, his brother Simon and those who went with them knew about it they fled to the desert of Tekoa.

Alcimus' death. Jonathan and Simon withdrew with their men to Bethbasi, in the desert they repaired its ruins and fortified it.

As Bacchides knew this, he gathered all his people and let his followers in Judah know about it. Then he encamped near Bethbasi, besieged it for several days and built war engines. Jonathan, leaving his brother Simon in the city, made an escape through the country with a handful of men. Simon and his men left the city and burnt up the engines. They attacked Bacchides and defeated him. He fell into a great depression, for neither his plans nor his attack had been successful. When Jonathan knew this he sent messengers to sign a treaty of peace with them and exchange prisoners. He accepted, promised fidelity to the oaths and swore not to harm him during his lifetime. After the restitution of the prisoners captured in Judah he came back to his country to never come back again.

Jonathan, Tryphon's prisoner[1]. Tryphon dreamed of reigning over Asia, take over the throne and kill king Antiochus. But he feared that Jonathan would not allow him to do so and declared war on him, he was searching for a way to kill him. He made his way as far as Bethsan. Jonathan came to meet him with forty thousand chosen men, and he came to Bethsan too. When Tryphon saw Jonathan's troops, he was afraid of attacking him. Therefore, he welcomed him, introduced him to all his friends, gave him gifts and ordered his friends and soldiers to obey Jonathan as they obeyed him. And then he said to Jonathan, "Why have you gathered this army, if

---

1. Greek = drunken. Alexander Balash's commander, tutor of his youngest son Antiochus VI, whom he killed. After fighting to usurp the throne, he committed suicide.

we are not fighting anyone? Send them away, keep some of them and come with me to Ptolemaida[1]. I will give you the city and other fortresses, as well as the rest of the troops and all the officers; then I shall return, for I have only come for this." Jonathan believed him and did as he had told him. He sent his troops away, and they returned to Judah. He was left with three thousand men: he left two thousand at Galilee, and only one thousand went with him. But as soon as Jonathan entered Ptolemaida its inhabitants shut its gates, took him and killed those who entered with him. Tryphon sent his army and cavalry to Galilee and to the great plain to kill those who were favourable to Jonathan. But when they knew that Jonathan had been imprisoned together with those who went with him, took heart and left willing to attack their enemies. When the pursuers saw them willing to fight for his life they came back. Thus, without being attacked, they entered Judah, mourned Jonathan and his men and grew afraid. All Israel mourned Jonathan. Then all the neighbouring nations intented to destroy them saying, "They lacked a leader and helper; let us fight them and wipe them out of the earth."

SIMON PRINCE OF THE JEWS

Simon succeeds Jonathan. Simon knew that Tryphon had gathered a powerful army to attack Judah and wipe it out. Then, as he saw that the people was afraid of him, he went to Jerusalem, assembled the people and said to them, "You know all that I, my brothers and my father's house have done for the Laws and the Temple, as well as the wars and fears which we have endured. All my brothers have died for Israel, I am the only one left. So I shall never try to save my life in times of oppression, for I am not better than my brothers. I shall defend my people, your sons and your wives now that all the nations which loathe us are plotting to wipe us out." When the people heard these words they took heart and shouted, "Be our leader

---

1. Ptolemaida = Achre.

instead of Judas and Jonathan, take over their place and we shall obey you in war."

Then Simon gathered all warmen and hurried to finish the walls of Jerusalem and fortified them.

Death of Jonathan. After these events, Tryphon advanced towards Judah with the aim of destroy it, surrounding Adora, but Simon and his army opposed them wherever he went. Near Bascama he put Jonathan to death and buried him there. Then he returned to his country. Simon sent for the body of Jonathan and buried him at Modim, the city of his forefathers. All Israel mourned him and wept for him for many days.

Israel's independence. In the year 170 Israel was set free from the gentile yoke, and the people began to write in the public events and in the contracts, "First year of Simon, high priest, general and leader of the upright."

THE SECOND BOOK OF THE MACCABEES

ANTIOCHUS' PROSECUTION

The prosecution's providential character. I beg to those who read this book that they are not amazed by the adversities, but that they believe that the events here related have not happened for our ruin, but for the improvement of our people.

Eleazar's martyrdom. Eleazar[1], one of the main scribes of great age and distinguished bearing, was forced to open his mouth and eat swine meat[2], but he preferred a glorious death to an unclean life.

Those who were in charge of the unclean banquet, seized by the friendship which they had with him, took him aside and encouraged him to ask for the food allowed by the king, prepared by himself in order to simulate that he had eaten from the food of the sacrifices[3], according to the edict of the king.

But he, elevating himself to the highest decisions, worthy of his years and dignity, and of the grey hairs he had attained to and of the clean life he had led from his childhood, and, above all, of the Holy Laws established by God, answered that he prefered being put to death "because, he said, it is not worthy of

---

1. Eleazar, scribe. As he did not abandon the Mosaic Law on the prohibited food, he was martyrized by Antiochus Epiphanes.
2. Prohibited by the Law.
3. Offered to the idols.

my age to deceive, for the young people could say that Eleazar, on his old age, has turned to the foreing customs. And they would be led astray because of my deceit, and only to avoid my present suffering. And it would bring shame on me on my old age, for although I could escape from the hands on men, I could not escape the hands of God Almighty[1] neither alive nor dead." Those who led him, when they heard this, hated him, for they thought that he was speaking senseless and obstinate words. When he was about to die because of his flogging he said to them in sighs, "The Lord of wisdom and holyness agreeds to my suffering instead of mine being released; but my soul suffers all this willingly because I am a man fearful of God." And so he died, leaving not only the young people but also the whole nation an example of nobility and a monument to virtue and strength.

Martyrdom of the seven brothers[2]. Seven brothers and their mother were imprisoned and forced to eat swine flesh. As they refused to eat them they were flogged with whips and thongs. One of them, speaking for all, said, "What do you expect from us? We are all willing to die rather than break the laws of our fathers." Enraged, the king ordered to put fire under the pans and cauldrons, and when they were heaten up he gave order to cut the spokeman's tongue, that he should be scalped and mutilated before the eyes of his brothers and his mother. So, mutilated as he was, he ordered that he was taken to the fire. The smoke from the cauldron streamed out and wide, and the mother and the brothers urged themselves to die generously saying, "God sees everything and will have compassion on us[3]."

When the first had died in this way, they drew the second nearer to torture him. His hair and skin were torn off, and they asked him, "Will you eat, before we tear you limb from limb?" He replied in his native tongue, "Never!" Therefore he

---

1. Great confession of faith to the Lord because of his power and provicence.
2. We do not known the name of these heroes; they are named Maccabees because of the book in which they were included.
3. We do not know what to admire more, if their bravery or the cruelty of their executioners.

underwent the same torture than his brother. Before dying, he said, "You, fiend, you set us free from this present life, but the king of the world will give everlasting life[1] to those who die for his Laws."

Afterwards the third brother underwent the same tortures, they asked him to show his tongue. He did so, and he stretched out his hand, and said courageously, "From heaven I have received these, and now his laws mean more for me than they, for I know that one day heaven will give them back to me." The king and those who were with him admired his courage.

When he died, they called the fourth brother and put him under the same tortures. When he was about to die, he said, "It is better to be killed by men and cherish God's promise to raise us again, but here will be no resurrection to life for you." They brought the fifth one and tortured him. Then he looked at the king and said, "You have authority over men, mortal as you are, and can do as you wish. But you do not think that our nation has been abandoned by God. Wait a little and you shall feel its great power upon you, and it shall punish you and your descendancy."

Then they brought the sixth brother, who, before dying, said, "Do not delude yourself. It is our own fault that we suffer these things, for we have sinned against our God. But do not think that you will escape the consequences of your acts[2]."

But the mother was the most remarkable of all, and deserves to be remembered with special honour. She watched her seven sons all die in the space of a single day, yet she bore it bravely because she put her trust in the Lord. Filled with noble resolution, she encouraged each in her native language, her woman's thought fired by a manly spirit she said to them, "I do not know how have you appeared in my womb, for it was not I who gave you the spirit of life, nor have I joined gracely your bodily frames. God Creator of the Universe and of the human

---

1. Beautiful confession on the resurrection and everlasting life.
2. The beautiful expressions of the mother and her small child are full of faith and courage.

race will give you back life and breath again in his mercy, since now you put his laws above all thought of the self."

Antiochus felt that he was being treated with contempt and suspected an insult in her words. But he encouraged the only brother who was still left, and promised him by oath to make him rich and the happiest men in the world, and, once he had abandoned his religion and the father laws, he would have him as a friend and would provide him with all the necessary things, besides giving him a post in the government. The child did not listen to him, therefore, the king called the mother and told her to give advice to her child to that he could save his life. As the king insisted, she acceded to convince her son. So floating the cruel tyrant, she said in her native language, "My son, take pity of me. I carried you nine months in the womb. I beg you, my son, that looking at the sky and the earth; see all that is in them and realize that God made them out of nothing, and that man comes into being in the same way. Do not be afraid of this butcher; accept death and prove yourself worthy of your brothers, so that by God's mercy I may receive you back again along with them."

She was still speaking when the child exclaimed, "What do you expect? I will not submit to the king's command; I obey the command of the Law given by Moses to our forefathers. But you shall suffer the punishment due to your arrogance. I, like my brothers, give in my body and my life for the father's laws, begging the Lord to take pity on me and his people soon, and to you that he obliges you with turments and punishments to confess that only He is God."

Thus the latter died too, without blemish, utterly faithful to God[1].

Afterwards, the mother died, and this must conclude our account of the outrages committed.

---

1. The martyrdom of the seven brothers and their mother is one of the most beautiful chapters of the Old Testament.

JOB

FOREWORD

Job's virtue and happiness. There lived in the land of Uz[1] a man named Job: a perfect man, upright, who feared God and set his face against evil[2].

He had seven sons and three daughters; he owned seven thousand sheep, three thousand camels, five hundred yokes of oxen, five hundred female asses, as well as many servants. Thus, this man was the greatest of all the Eastern men.

Satan puts Job to the test. One day on which the sons of God came into the Lord's presence, Satan was also among them.

And the Lord asked Satan, "Where do you come from?" Satan answered the Lord, "I come from ranging over the earth, from end to end." And the Lord said to Satan,

"Have you realised that there is no man in the earth like my servant Job, an upright man, who fears God and sets his face against evil?"

Satan answered the Lord,

---

1. Unknown region to the East of Palestine.
2. Job's thesis is this: Why does God punish the upright man? The answer can be found in the New Testament. Jesus Christ offered himself for the sins of the whole world, and he was as innocent.

"Does Job fear God without any reason? Stretch out your hand and touch his possessions, and you will see how he will curse you to your face."

And the Lord said to Satan,

"There he is. His whole property is on your hands. Only be careful not to put your hands on it[1]."

First misfortunes and resignation of Job. And it happened that one day on which his sons and daughters were eating and drinking at his elder brother's, a messenger came to Job and told him, "The oxen were plouging and the asses grazing beside them when the Sabaeans swooped down and took them away, after having killed your servants. Only I could escape to tell you the news."

He was still speaking when another servant came and said, "The fire of God fell from heaven, which burnt up sheep and shepherds, and ate them up. Only I could escape to tell you the news."

He was still speaking when another servant came and said, "While your sons and daughters were eating and drinking wine at your elder brother's, a whirlwind swept across from the desert and struck the four corners of the house, and it fell on the young people and killed them. Only I could escape to tell you the news."

Then Job stood up, tore up his clothes and shaved his head. Then he prostrated on the ground, worshipped and said,

"I was born naked from my mother's womb,/ and there I shall come back as naked./ The Lord had given, the Lord has removed:/ Blessed be the Name of the Lord."

Job did not sin, nor said him nothing offensive to the Lord.

The last proof. Another day on which the sons of God[2] went into the Lord's presence, Satan went with them again. And the Lord said to Satan, "Where do you come from?" Satan answered the Lord, "I come from ranging over the earth, from end to end."

---

1. God owns life and death. God does not always punish, some times he wants to test our virtue.
2. The angels.

And the Lord said to Satan, "Have you realised that there is no man in the earth like my servant Job, an upright man, who fears God and sets his face against evil? You incited me to ruin him without a cause, but his integrity remains unshaken."

Satan answered the Lord, "Skin for skin; there is nothing the man will grudge to save himself. But stretch out your hand and touch his bone and flesh and he shall curse you to your face."

And the Lord said to Satan, "He is in your hands. However, spare his life[1]."

Satan left the Lord and hurted Job with running sores[2] from head to foot, so that he took a piece of a broken pot to scratch him and sat over the ashes[3].

Then his wife said to him, "Are you still unshaken in your integrity? Curse God and die!"

But he answered, "You speak like a foolish woman; if we accept good from God, we must also accept evil." Throughout all this, Job did not sin in any way.

DIALOGUE: JOB AND HIS FRIENDS[4]

Job waits for more pity from Lord than from his friends. O, if my eyes have seen all this./ My ears have heard and understood it.

But listen to my complaints, please,/ listen to my defence.

Invitation to repentance. So make friends with him again and make peace./ So you shall recover your fortune.

Receive the lesson from his mouth./ Keep his words in your heart.

If you humiliate yourself before the Almighty./ If you keep iniquity away from your tent.

---

1. All dialogue of the Lord with Satan is an antropomorphism of the holy author to provide us with an example of the amazing patience of the Lord.
2. Leper elephantiasis.
3. Over the ashes of the burnt up ruins.
4. His three friends who want to comfort him they want to convince him that the Lord is punishing him because of his sins. God does not punish, but he is putting his patience, faith and fidelity to the test.

Job's soliloque: his former happy life. All of them listened carefully to me,/ silently, to listen to my advice.

To my sentence there was no complaint,/ and my words fell upon them.

They waited for me as a man waits for the rain,/ and they opened their mouth as a man would open his to the late water.

If I would smile them, they could not believe it,/ willingly they accepted the favour of my face.

Ahead of them I guide them,/ I sat among their troops like a king,/ like a comforter of miserables.

His current misfortunes. Violently has the Lord taken my coat from me,/ he has seized me as the neck of my coat.

He has thrown me in the mud,/ I am like the dust and ashes.

I claim to you and you give me no answer,/ I insist but you do not listen to me.

You have become cruel to me,/ you stretch out your hand towards me.

You leave me at the wind's will,/ you break me with your storms.

I know that you are leading me to death/ meeting point of all living men.

I have been brother of jackals,/ and friend of ostrichs.

My blakened skink can be torn off,/ my bones are burning with fever.

My harp has accompanied the sons of mourning,/ my flute the voice of those who lament!

Job undoes his words. I recognise, my Lord, your Might,/ no plan is impossible for you.

I had already heard of you,/ but now my eyes have seen you.

That is why I undo my words,/ and I do penance in dust and ashes[1].

---

1. Once the test is passed Job recognises his saviour, who has helped him, and affirms that some day he will see him with his own eyes in the end of times.

EPILOGUE

God recognises Job's innocence and restablishes him his past fortune. And the Lord restituted him to his past state, for he had interceded in favour of his friends. Besides, the Lord doubled all his properties.

All his brothers and sisters and friends and acquitances came to visit him; they gave a banquet at his home, and they had pity on him for all the troubles which the Lord had brought upon him. And every one of them gave him as a gift a piece of silver and a golden ring.

And the Lord bleesed Job more than ever.

After these events Job lived one hundred and forty years, and saw his sons and grandsons up to the fourth generation.

And so Job died at a very old age.

PSALMS

PSALM 1[1] [2]. Prologue to the psalter

Happy is the man who does not follow the advice of the
     wicked nor walks the road of the sinners.
He is like a tree planted beside a watercourse, which yields its
     fruit in season, and whose leaves never fall; in all he
     does he prospers.
Wicked men are not like this. They are like straw driven by
     the wind. They shall not be at the judgement, nor shall
     sinners stand in the assembly of the righteous. For the
     Lord knows the way of the righteous, but the way of
     the wicked fades away.

PSALM 2. Glory of the messianic king

Why are the nations, those plots of peoples, in turmoil?
The kings of the earth stand ready, and the princes plot
     against the Lord and his anointed king[3].
"Let us break their fetters, let us throw off their chains!"

---

1. Psalms, from the Greek psalmós. It means song accompanied by string
   instrument.
2. Psalms 1 and 2 are a prologue to the psalter and a summary of the moral
   doctrine of the Messiah.
3. The kings and the priest were anointed. Jesus Christ is the anointed one and
   the truly priest par exelence.

The one who dwells in heaven laughs, the Lord scorns them.
Then, he rebukes then in anger, he threatens then in his wrath:
"My king is already enthroned in Zion, my holy mountain".
I will announce the Lord's decree; he has said: "You are my
    son[1]. I have made you. Ask me for what you will, and I
    will give you the nations as your inheritance, the ends
    of the earth as your possesion.
Blessed be those who find refuge in Him.

PSALM 8. Glory of God and dignity of man

From David.

Oh God, our Lord, how great is your name in all the earth,
    your majesty is praised over heaven!
When I look up at your skies, the work of your hands, the
    moon and the stars that you set, what is man that you
    remember him, mortal man that you are for him?
You made him little less than a god, and crowned him with
    glory and splendour; you made him master over the
    work of your hands. You put every thing under his feet:
All sheep and oxen, and even the beasts in the wilderness,
and the birds in the air and the fish in the sea, and all that
    moves in the paths of the ocean.
Oh God, our Lord, how great is your name in all the earth!

PSALM 14. Mourning for general Loathsomeness

The impious fool says in his heart, "There is no God[2]."
    Men are vile, depraved and loathsome, not one does
    anything good.
The Lord looks down from heaven[3] to mankind, to see if any
    wise man seeks out God.

---

1. Messianic text.
2. Errors and evil deeds come from a heart perverted and blinded by vices.
3. Antropomorphic.

But they do not call upon the Lord, but they will tremble in fear when their hour comes. The Lord the righteous men are dear to him.

PSALM 21. Prayer of the dying righteous man

O God, my God, why has you forsaken me? My groans are far from saving me!

O my God, I cry in daytime but you do not answer, and it the night I get no answer!

And yet you are enthroned in the Santuary among the praises of Israel.

Our fathers put their trust in you; they waited and you rescued them; they cried and were delivered; they trusted and were not put to shame.

But I, a worm, not a man[1], abused by all men, scorned by the people; all who see me jeer at me, make months any wag their head:

"He trusted in the Lord, let the Lord deliver him, for he holds him dear."

Be not far from me, for trouble is near. Come close to me, for nobody helps me.

Countless bulls surround me; the beasts of Bashan have beset me; hungry they open their mouths wide against me, as roaning and ravening lions.

I drain my self away like water; all my bones are loose. My heart has turned to wax and melts within me. My mouth is dry as a potsherd, and my tongue sticks to my jaw[2]; I am laid low in the dust of death.

The huntsmen are all around me; a band of ruffians rings me down; they hack off my hands and my feet[3].

I can count my bones; they look on and gloat; they share out my clothes and cast lots for my robe.

---

1. Messianic text. Foretells the taunts of the Calvary, of Jesus on the Cross before his enemies.
2. Jesus' words, "I am thirsty". Nailed by hands and feet.
3. Division and casting of his clothes.

But O Lord, do not be far from me. O my strength, hasten to
    my aid.

Deliver my soul from the sword, from the paws of the dog;
    save me from the mouth of the lion, my poor body
    from the horns of the wild ox.

I will say your name to my brethen. I will praise you in the
    midst of the assembly.

The whole earth shall remember the Lord and turn their eyes
    towards him, and the families of the people shall
    worship Him[1].

For kingly power belongs to the Lord, and dominion over the
    nations is his.

Those buried in the earth shall bow down to him, those who
    come down to dust shall do him homage[2].

And I shall live for him, my descendants shall serve him.

They will tell about the lord to future generations, his doings
    shall be told to a people yet unborn: "This is what he
    did."

PSALM 23. Song to the holy shepherd

The Lord is my shepherd, I shall want nothing; he makes me
    lay down in green pastures; he leads me to the waters
    of peace, and renews my soul.

For his name's sake he guides me in the right path.

Although I walk through a dark valley, I fear no evil, for your
    staff and your crook are with me,and they are my
    comfort.

You lay a table for me before my enemies; and bathe my head
    with oil, and my cup rans over.

Goodness and love unfailing shall follow me all the days of
    my life; I shall dwell in the house of the Lord for
    many, many years.

---

1. "When I am risen, they will all come to me."
2. The dead will resuscite and bow down to him.

PSALM 24. Solemn entrance to the temple

The earth is the Lord's, and all that is in it; the world and
those who dwell therein; for it was Him who founded it
upon the seas and planted it firm upon the waters.
Who could go up the mountain of the Lord? Who may stand
in his holy place?
He who has clean hands and a pure heart, he who does not set
his mind on falsehood and has not committed perjury.
He shall be blessed by the Lord, and shall receive justice from
the Lord.
This is the fortune of those who search him, those who seek
the face of the God of Jacob.
You, gates, lift up your heads, lift yourselves up, eternal gates,
so that the king of glory may enter!
Who is the king of glory! The Lord is strong and mighty. The
Lord, mighty in battle.
O gates, lift up your heads, lift yourselves up, eternal gates, so
that the king of glory may enter!
Who is the king of glory? The Lord is the king of glory.

PSALM 25. Plead of the righteous in misery

To you, O Lord, I lift up my heart, O my God!
I trust in you: do not put me to shame, let not my enemies
exult over me.
Let no man who hopes in you be put to shame, only to those
who break faith without cause.
Show me your paths, O Lord, teach me your ways.
Lead me in truly and teach me, for you are my God, my
saviour.
I trust in you all day long, for your goodness, Lord.
Remember, Lord, your tender care and love unfailing which
last for ever.
Do not remember the offences of my youth, but remember me
in my unfailing love.

The Lord is good and upright; he teaches the way to those
    who sin.

He guides the humble man in doing right, and shows his ways
    to the humble.

All the ways of the Lord are loving and safe to those who
    keep his covenant and commandments.

For your name, O Lord, forgive my wickedness, great as it is.

Who fears the Lord? He shall show him the way to follow.

His son shall enjoy lasting prosperity, and his children shall
    inherit the land.

The purposes of the Lord is for those who trust in him, and
    his covenant is their to know.

My eyes are ever on the Lord; he can free my feet from the
    net.

Come back to me and show me your favour, for I am lonely
    and miserable.

Relieve the sorrows of my heart and bring me out of my
    distress.

Put an end to my misery and my trouble, and forgive all my
    sins.

PSALM 27. Trust in the test

The Lord is my light and my salvation, whom should I fear?
    The Lord is the courage of my life, of whom should I
    go in dread?

Although an army encamps against me, I shall feel no fear;
    even if a war breaks out against me, I shall be
    undismayed.

One thing I ask the Lord, only one thing I seek: that I be in
    the House of the Lord all the days of my life, to
    contemplate the beauty of the Lord in his temple.

For he will keep me safe beneath his roof in the day of
    misfortune; he will hide me in his tent, like on a high
    rock.

And now I raise my head high above the enemies about me,
and I will acclaim him with sacrifice before his tent; O!
I shall sing and praise the Lord!

Listen, O Lord, my claim, show me favour and answer me.

My heart speaks to you, and my face seeks you. It is your
face, Lord, that I am seeking.

Do not hide your face from me, do not turn away your servant
in anger; you are my help. Do not forsake me, or leave
me, O Lord my saviour.

If my father and my mother forsake me, the Lord will care for
me.

Show me your way, O Lord, and guide me through the right
path.

PSALM 31. Claim and thanksgiving of a miserable man

With you, O Lord, I seek shelter. Let me never be put to
shame! Deliver me in your righteousness, hear me,
come quickly to my rescue!

To me you shall be a rock of refuge and a stronghold that
saves me. You are my Rock[1]. Lead me and guide me
for your Name!

Set me free from the net men have hidden for me; for you are
my refuge; I commit my spirit into your keeping.

Be gracious to me, O Lord, for I am in distress! My eyes and
life are worn away with sorrow!

For my life is miserable, and I sight with age; my misery
defeats my strength, there is disease in my bones.

But I trust in you, Lord, and say, "You are my God."

My days are in your hands; set me free from enemies, from
those who persecute me; show your face to your
servant. Save him in your love!

---

1. Symbol of steadfastness and trust in God.

PSALM 33. Hymn to the mighty and providential God

Shout for joy before the Lord, you righteous men. To you comes praise; give thanks to the Lord on the harp; sing to him to the ten-stringed lute. Sing a new song. Give thanks on the harp among the claims.

For true is the word of the Lord, all his works are true.

He loves righteousness and justice; the land is filled with his grace.

Heaven was made by the word of the Lord, his army by a blow of his mouth.

He gathered the sea like water in a goat-skin, he laid up the deep in his store-chambers.

Let the whole world fear the Lord, and everything that lives in it stand in awe of him.

For he spoke, and it was done; he commanded, and it was done.

Happy is the people whose god is the Lord, the people he had chosen for his own possession!

The Lord looks up from heaven, and sees the sons of men; from his dwelling place he watches all the inhabitants of the earth;

He, who fashioned the hearts of all men, and discerns all what they do.

The king does not defeat because of a great army, nor the hero because of his bravery.

But the eyes of the Lord are those who fear Him, those who await His favour, to keep their soul safe from death, and to keep their life in happiness.

Our soul waits for the Lord. He is our help and our shield; our heart is joyful on His account, we trust in His holy name.

Let your goodness be with us, O Lord, as it is our hope.

PSALM 34. God protector of the upright

I shall bless the Lord continually; his praise shall be always
    on my lips.

In the Lord I will glory; the humble shall hear and be glad.

O glorify the Lord with me, and let us exalt his name together.

I sought the Lord's help and he answered me; he set me free
    from all my terrors.

Look towards him and shine with joy; no longer hang your
    heads in shame.

Here was a poor wretch who cried to the Lord; he heard him
    and saved him from all his troubles.

The Angel of the Lord is on guard round those who fear him,
    and rescues them.

Taste, then, and see that the Lord is good. Happy the man
    who finds refuge in him!

Fear the Lord, all you his holy people; for those who fear him
    lack nothing.

PSALM 37. Fortune of the good and the evil men

Do not strive to outdo the evildoers or emulate those who do
    wrong. For like grass the soon wither, and fade like the
    green of spring.

Trust in the Lord and do good; settle in the land and find safe
    pasture. Defend upon the Lord, and he will grant you
    your heart's desire.

Commit your life to the Lord; trust in him and he will act. He
    will make your righteousness shine clear as the day and
    the justice of your cause.

Wait quietly for the Lord, be patient till he comes; do not
    strive to outdo the successful nor envy him who gains
    his ends.

Be angry no more, have done with wrath; strive not to outdo
    in evildoing. For evildoers will be destroyed, but they
    who hope in the Lord shall possess the land.

A little while, and the wicked will be no more; look well, and
    you will find their place is empty. But the humble shall
    possess the land and enjoy untold peace.

The wicked mutter against the righteous man and grind their
    teeth at the sight of him; the Lord shall laugh at them,
    for he sees that their time is coming.

The wicked have drawn their swords and strung their bows to
    bring low the poor and needy and to slaughter honest
    men. Their swords shall pierce their own hearts and
    their bows be broken.

Better is the little which the righteous has than the great
    wealth of the wicked. For the strong hand of the wicked
    shall be broken, but the Lord upholds the righteous.

All whom the Lord has blessed shall possess the land, and all
    who are cursed by him shall be destroyed.

It is the Lord who directs a man's steps, he holds him firm
    and watches over his path. Though he may fall, he will
    not go headlong, for the Lord grasps him by the hand.

I have been young and am now grown old, and never have I
    seen a righteous man forsaken nor his descendancy
    begging. Day in, day out, he lends generously, and his
    children become a blessing.

Turn from evil and do good, and live at peace for ever; for the
    Lord is a lover of justice, and will not forsake his loyal
    servants.

The righteous man utters words of wisdom and justice is
    always on his lips. The law of God is in his heart, his
    steps do not falter.

The wicked watch for the righteous man and seek to take his
    life; but the Lord will not leave him in their power, nor
    let him be condemned before his judges.

Wait for the Lord and hold his way.

I have watched a wicked man at his word, rank as a spreading
    tree in its native soil. I passed by one day, and he was
    gone; I searched for him, but he could not be found.

Now look at the good man, watch him who is honest, for the
    man of peace leaves descendants; but transgressors are

wiped out one and all, and the descendants of the
wicked are destroyed.

Health for the righteous comes from the Lord, their refuge in
time of trouble. The Lord will help them and deliver
them; he will save them because they seek shelter with
him.

PSALM 40. Thankfulness. Zeal. Plight

I waited, waited for the Lord, he bent down to me and heard
my cry. He brought me up out of the muddy pit, out of
the mire and the clay.

On my lips he put a new song, a song of praise to the Lord.
Many when they see will be filled with awe, and will
learn to trust in the Lord.

Happy is the man who makes the Lord his trust, and does not
look to brutal and treacherous men.

You did not want sacrifices, but you listened to me. If you
had asked for whole-offering and sin-offering I would
have said, "Here I am. My desire is to do your will, O
Lord, and your law is my soul[1]."

In the great assembly I have proclaimed what is right, I do not
hold back my words, you know that, Lord.

I have not kept your goodness hidden in my heart; I have
proclaimed your faithfulness and saving power and not
concealed your unfailing love and truth from the great
assembly.

You, O Lord, do not withhold your tender care form me; your
unfailing love and truth for ever guard me.

Let all those who seek you be jubiland and rejoice in you, and
let those who long for your saving help ever cry, "All
glory to the Lord!"

---

1. Obedience is more valuable than sacrifices and offerings (1 Samuel 15-22). This
text has a messianic sense. In all the Scriptures the Messiah is talked about and
longed for.

PSALM 42-43. Longing for God and his Temple

As a hind longs for the running streams, so do I long for you,
     O God.

With my whole being I thirst for God, the living God. When
     shall I come to God and appear in his presence?

Day and night, tears are my bread; "Where is your God?" they
     ask me all they long.

As I pour out my soul in distress, I call to mind how I
     marched in the ranks of the great to the house of God,
     among exultant shouts of praise, the clamour of the
     pilgrims.

How deep I am sunk in misery, groaning in my distress. Yet I
     will wait for God; I will praise him continually, my
     deliverer, my God.

I am sunk in misery, therefore will I remember you, though
     from the Hermons and the springs of Jordan, and from
     the hill of Mizar.

Deep calls to deep in the roar of your cataracts, and all your
     waves, all your breakers pass over me.

The Lord makes his grace shine forth alike by day and night;
     his praise on my lips is a prayer, to the God of my life.

I will say to God my rock, "Why have your forgotten me?
     Why must I go like a mourner because my foes opress
     me?"

My enemies taunt me, jeering at my misfortunes; "Where is
     your God?", they ask me all day long.

How deep I am sunk in misery, groaning in my distress: yet I
     will wait for God; I will praise him continually, my
     deliverer, my God.

Plead my cause and give judgement against an impious race;
     save from malingnant men and liars, O God.

You, O God, are my refuge; why have your rejected me?

Send forth your life and your truth to be my guide and lead
     me to your holy hill, to your tabernacle.

Then shall I come to the altar of God, the God of my joy, and
     praise you on the harp, O God, you God of my delight.

How deep I am sunk in misery, groaning in my distress: yet I
    will wait for God; I will praise him continually, my
    deliverer, my God.

PSALM 45. Wedding poem to the Messianic king

My head is stirred by a noble theme, in a king's honour I utter
    the son I have made, and my tongue runs like the pen
    of an expert scribe.
You surpass all mankind in beauty, your lips are moulded in
    grace, so you are blessed by God for ever.
With your sword ready at your side, warrior king, your limbs
    resplendent in their royal armour, ride on to execute
    true sentence and just judgement.
Your right hand shall show you a scene of terror: your sharp
    arrows flying, nations beneath your feet, the courage of
    the king's foes melting away!
Your throne is like God's throne, eternal, your royal sceptre a
    sceptre of righteousness. You have loved right and
    hated wrong; so God, your God, has anointed you
    above your fellows with oil, the token of joy.
Your robes are all fragrant with myrrh and powder of aloes,
    and the music of strings greets you from a palace
    panelled with ivory.
A princess takes her place among the noblest of your women,
    a royal lady at your side in gold of Ophir.
Listen, my daughter, hear my words and consider them: forget
    your own people and your father's house; and, when
    the king desires your beauty, remember that he is your
    lord.
Do him obeisance, daughter of Tyre, and the richest in the
    land will court you with gifts.
In the palace honour awaits her; she is a king's daughter,
    arrayed in cloth-of-gold richly embroidered. Virgins
    shall follow her into the presence of the king; her
    companions shall be brought to her, escorted with the

noise of revels and rejoicing as they enter the king's
palace.
You shall have sons, O king, in place of your forefathers and
will make them rulers over the land.
I will declare your fame to all generations; therefore the
nations will praise you for ever and ever!

PSALM 47. Song to the victorous God

Clap your hands, all you nations; acclaim our God with shouts
of joy.
How fearful is the Lord Most High, great sovereign over all
the earth!
He lays the nations prostrate beneath us, he lays peoples under
your feet; he chose our patrimony for us, the pride of
Jacob whom he loved.
God has gone up with a fanfare of trumpets.
Praise God, praise him with psalms; praise our king, praise
him with psalms.
God is king of all the earth; sing psalms with all your art.
God reigns over the nations, God is seated on his holy throne.
The princess of the nations assemble with the families of
Abraham's line; for the mighty ones of the earth belong
to God, and he is raised above them all.

PSALM 50. The true worship of God

God, the Lord God, has spoken and summoned the world
from the rising to the setting sun.
God shines out from Zion, perfect in beauty.
Our God is coming and will not keep silence: consuming fire
runs before him and wreathes him closely round. He
summons heaven on high and earth to the judgement of
his people.
"Gather to me my loyal servants, all who by sacrifice have
made a covenant with me." The heavens proclaim his
justice, for God himself is the judge.

Listen, my people, and I will speak; I will bear witness against
you, O Israel: I am God, your God, shall not find fault
with your sacrifices, though your offerings are before
me always?

I need take no young bull from your house, no he-goat from
your folds.

For all the beasts of the forest are mine, and the cattle in
thousands on my hills. I know every bird on those hills,
the teeming life of the fields is my care.

If I were hungry, I would not tell you, for the world and all
that is in it are mine.

Shall I eat the flesh of your bulls or drink the blood of he-goats?

Offer to God the sacrifice of thanksgiving and pay your vows
to the Most High. If you call upon me in time of
trouble, I will come to your rescue, and you shall
honour me.

God's word to the wicked man is this: "What right have you
to recite my laws and make so free with the words of
my covenant, you who hate correction and turn your
back when I am speaking?"

You are for ever talking against your brother, stabbing your
own mother's son in the back. All this you have done,
and shall I keep silence? You thought that I was
another like yourself, but point by point I will rebuke
you to your face.

Think well on this: He who offers a sacrifice of thanksgiving
does me due honour, and to him who follows my way I
will show the salvation of God.

PSALM 51. Miserere[1]

Be gracious to me, O God, in your true love; in the fullness of
your mercy blot out my misdeeds. Wash away all my
guilt, and cleanse me from my sin!

---

1. Himn of penance of David because of his double sin. He asks for God's
forgiveness sincerely and will expiate his sin, example for everybody.

For well I know my misdeeds, and my sins confront me all
the day long.

Against you, only you, I have sinned and done what
displeases you, so that you may be proved right in your
charge and just in passing sentence.

In iniquity I was brought to birth and my mother conceived
me in sin.

Yet though you have hidden the truth in darkness, through its
mistery you teach me wisdom.

Take hyssop and sprinkle me, that I may be clean; wash me,
that I may become whiter than snow.

Let me hear the sounds of joy and gladness, let the bones
dance which you have broken.

Turn away your face from my sins and blot out all my guilt.

Create a pure heart in me, O God, and give a new and
steadfast spirit, do not drive me from your presence, or
take your holy spirit from me.

Revive in me the joy of your deliverance and grant me a
willing spirit to uphold me. I will teach transgressors
the ways that lead to you, and sinners shall return to
you again.

O Lord God my deliverer save me from bloodshed, and I will
sing the praises of your justice. Open my lips, O Lord,
that my mouth may proclaim your praise.

You have no delight in sacrifice; if I brought you an offering,
you would not accept it.

My sacrifice, O God, is a broken spirirt; a wounded heart, O
God, you will not despise.

Let it be your pleasure to do good to Zion, to build anew the
walls of Jerusalem.

Then only shall you delight in the appointed sacrifices
—whole offering and one whole consumed—, then
shall young bulls be offered in your altar.

PSALM 53. Against common depravation

The impious fool says in his heart, "There is no God!" How
vile men are, how depraved and loathsome, not one
does anything good[1]!

God looks down from heaven on all mankind to see if any act
wisely, if any seek out God.

But all are unfaithful, all are rotten to the core; not one does
anything good, no, not even one.

When God restores his people's fortunes, let Jacob rejoice, let
Israel be glad.

PSALM 57. Trust in prosecution

Be gracious to me, O God, be gracious; for I have made you
my refuge. I will take refuge in the shadow of your
wings until the storms are past.

I will call upon God Most High, on God who fulfils his
purpose, for me.

My heart is steadfast, O God, my heart is steadfast; I will sing
and raise a psalm.

Awake my spirit, awake, lute and harp, I will awake at dawn
of day!

I will confess you, O Lord, among the peoples, among the
nations I will raise a psalm to you. For your unfailing
love is wide as the heavens, and your truth reaches to
the skies.

Show yourself, O God, high above the heavens; let your glory
shine over all the earth!

PSALM 65. Solemn New Year's Eve thanksgiving

We owe your praise, O God, in Zion; you heard prayer, vows
shall be paid to you.

---

1. This is an antropomorphism.

All men shall lay their guilt before you; our sins are too heavy
for us; only you can blot them out.

Happy is the man of your choice, whom you bring to dwell in
your courts. Let us enjoy the blessing of your house,
your holy temple.

By deeds of terror answer us with victory, O God of our
deliverance, in whom men trust from the ends of the
earth and far-off seas.

You are girded with strength, and by you might fix the
mountains in their place, calm the rage of the seas and
their raging waves.

The dwellers at the ends of the earth hold your signs in awe;
you make morning and evenign sing aloud in triumph.

You visit the earth and give it abundance, as often as you
enrich it with the waters of heaven, brimming in their
channels, providing corn for men.

For this is your provision for it, wattering its furrows,
levelling its ridges, softening it with showers and
blessing its growth.

You crown the year with your good gifts and the palm-trees
drip with sweet juice.

The pastures in the wild are rich with blessing and the hills
wreathed in happiness, the meadows are clothed with
sheep, and the valleys mantled in corn, so that they
shout, they break into song.

PSALM 69. In mortal anguish

Save me, O God; for the waters have risen up to my neck. I
sink in muddy depths and have no foothold; I am swept
into deep water, and the flood carries me away.

I am wearied with crying out, my throat is sore, my eyes grow
dim as I wait for God to help me.

Those who hate me without reason are more than the hairs of
my head; they outnumber my hairs, those who accuse
me falsely.

But I lift up this prayer to you, O Lord: accept me now in
    your great love, answer me with your sure deliverance,
    O God. Rescue me from the mire, do not let me sink.

Answer me, O Lord, in the goodness of your unfailing love,
    turn towards me in your great affection. I am your
    servant, do not hide your face from me. Make haste to
    answer me, for I am in distress. Come near to me and
    redeem me; ransom me, for I have many enemies.

Reproach has broken my heart, my shame and my dishonour
    are past hope; I looked for consolation and received
    none. They put poison in my food and gave me vinegar
    when I was thirsty.

But by your saving power, O God, lift me high above my pain
    and my distress, then I will praise God's name in son,
    and glorify him with thanksgiving; that will please the
    Lord more than the offering of a bull, a young bull with
    horn and cloven hoof.

See and rejoice, you humble flok, take heart, you seekers after
    God; for the Lord listens to the poor and does not
    despise those bound to his service. Let sky and earth
    praise him, the seas and all that move in them!

PSALM 72. To the Messianic king

O God, endow the king with your own justice.

He shall live as long as the sun endures, long as the moon,
    age after age. He shall be like rain falling on early
    crops, like showers watering the earth. In this days
    righteousness shall flourish, prosperity abound until the
    moon is no more.

May he hold sway from sea to sea, form the River to the ends
    of the earth. His enemies shall crouch low before him;
    his enemies shall lick the dust. The kings of Tarshish
    and the islands shall bring gifts. The kings of Sheba
    and Seba shall present their tribute, and all kings shall
    pay him homage, all nations shall serve him.

May the king live long and receive gifts of gold from Arabia;
       prayer be made for him continually, blessings be his all
       the day long.
Long may the king's name endure, may it live for ever like
       the sun; so shall all the peoples pray to be blessed as he
       was, all the nations tell of his happiness.
Blessed be the Lord, God of Israel, who alone does
       marvellous things! Blessed be his glorious name for
       ever, and may his glory fill all the earth! Amen, Amen!

PSALM 73. The question of the impious's happiness

How good God is to the upright, to those who are pure in
       heart!
My feet had almost slipped, my foothold had all but given
       way, because of the boast of sinners rouse my envy
       when I saw how they prospered.
No pain, no suffering is theirs; they are sleek and sound in
       limb; they are not plunged in trouble as other men are,
       nor do they suffer the torments of mortal men.
       Therefore pride is their collar of jewels and violence
       the robe that wraps them round. Their talk is all sneers
       and malice; scornfully their spread their calumnies.
They slanders reach up to heaven, while their tongues ply to
       and fro on earth.
And so my people follow their lead[1] and find nothing to
       blame in them, even thought they say, "What does God
       know? The Most High neither knows nor cares." So
       wicked men talk, yet still they prosper, and rogues
       amass great wealth.
So it was all in vain that I kept my heart pure and washed my
       hands in innocence. For all day long I suffer torment
       and am punished every morning.

---

1. The material happiness which impious men have in this world is transitory and
often fictitious. God rewards his few works in this life, but he awaits them in
the next world. Upright men are treated the other way round, they will have
they reward in the next world, because the Lord is justice.

Yet had I let myself talk on in this fashion, I should have
      betrayed the family of God. So I set myself to think this
      out, but I found it too hard for me.

Until I went into God's sacred courts; there I saw clearly what
      their end would be. How often you set them on slippery
      ground and drive them headlong into ruin! Then in a
      moment how dreadful their end, cut off root and branch
      by death with all its terrors, like a dream when a man
      rouses himself, O Lord, like images in sleep which are
      dismissed on waking.

They who are far from you are certainly lost; you destroy all
      who wantonly forsake you. But my chief good is to be
      near you, O God; I have chosen you, Lord God, to be
      my refuge[1].

PSALM 80. Song to the devastated vine

You brought a vine out of Egypt; you drove out nations and
      planted; you cleared the ground before it, so that it
      made good roots and filled the land. The mountains
      were covered with its shade, and its branches were like
      those of mighty cedars. It put out boughs all the way to
      the Sea and its shoots as far as the River[3].

Why have you broken down the wall round it so that every
      passer-by can pluch its fruit? The wild boar from the
      thickets gnews it, and swarming insects from the fields
      feed on it. O God of Hosts, once more look down from
      heaven, take thought for this vine and tend it, this stock
      that your right hand has planted.

Let them that set fire to it or cut it down perish before your
      angry face. Let your hand rest upon the man at your
      right side, the man whom you have made strong for

---

1. The happiness of the upright, although they are sometimes put to the test, is
    truly and eternal.
2. The vine is the representation of the People of God.
3. The devastation is applied to the destroyed cities of Samaria and Jerusalem
    after their first plundering by Nebuchadnezzar.

your service. We have not turned back from you, so
grant us new life, and we will invoke you by name.

Lod God of Hosts, retore us; make your face shine upon us
that we may be saved!

PSALM 81. Himn for a solemn feast[1]

Sing out in praise of God our refuge, acclaim the God of
Jacob!

Take pipe and tabor, take tuneful harp and lute! Blow the horn
for the mew month, for the full moon on the day of our
pilgrim-feast.

This is a law for Israel, an ordinance of the God of Jacob, laid
as a solemn charge on Joseph when he came out of
Egypt.

When I lifted the load from his shoulders, his hands let go the
builder's basket. When you cried to me in distress, I
rescued you.

Unseen, I answered you in thunder. I tested you at the waters
of Meribah[2]. Listen, my people, while I give you a
solemn charge —but O do listen to me, O Israel!

You shall have no strange god nor bow down to any foreign
god; I am the Lord your God who brought you up from
Egypt; open your mouth and I will fill it.

But my people did not listen to my words and Israel would
have none of me; so I sent them off, stubborn as they
were, to follow their own devices. If my people would
but listen to me, if Israel would only conform to my
ways, I would soon bring their enemies to their knees
and lay a heavy hand upon their persecutors.

Let those who hate them come cringing to them, and meet
with everlasting troubles.

---

1. The first day of the moonly month was a holiday. The seventh month was
   considered for a long time the first of the year.
2. Name given by Moses to the place where he drew water out of a rock.

PSALM 84. Pilgrimage to the Temple

How dear is your dwelling-place, you Lord of Hosts!
I pine, I faint with longing for the courts of the Lord's temple;
    my whole being cries out with joy to the living God.

Even the sparrow finds a home, and the swallow has her nest,
    where she rears her brood beside your altars, O Lord of
    Hosts, my King and my God.

Happy are those who dwell in your house; they never cease
    from praise you.

Happy are the men whose refuge is in you, whose hearts are
    set on the pilgrim way.

As they pass through the thirsty valley they find water from a
    spring; and the Lord provides even men who lose their
    way with pools to quench their thirst.

So they pass on from outer wall to inner, and the God of gods
    shows himself in Zion.

O Lord, hear my prayer; listen, O God of Jacob. O God, look
    upon our lord the anointed king[1].

Better one day in your courts than a thousand days at home;
    better to linger by the threshold of God's house than to
    live in the dwellings of the wicked.

The Lord God is a battlement and a shield; grace and honour
    are his to give. The Lord will hold back no good thing
    from those whose life is blameless.

O Lord of Hosts, happy is the man who trusts in you.

PSALM 87. Himn to Zion, mother of the peoples

The Lord loves the gates of Zion[2] more than all the dwellings
    of Jacob; her foundations are laid upon holy hills, and
    he has made her his home.

---

1. King or monarch.
2. Primitively, City of David, Eastern; the Ophel. Then it was considered the
   Mount of the Temple, then all the city or high Western part, and today the
   Ophel.

I will count Egypt and Babylon among my friends; Philistine,
      Tyrian and Nubian shall be there;
And Zion shall be called a mother in whom men of every race
      are born.
The Lord shall write against each in the roll of nations: "This
      one was born in her."
Singers and dancers alike all chant your praises, proclaiming
      glorious things of you, O city of God.

PSALM 89. The glory of the house of David is clouded

I will sing the story of your love, O Lord, for ever; I will
      proclaim your faithfulness to all generations.
You announced in a vision and declared to your servants; "I
      have endowed a warrior with the crown, so that the
      youth I have chosen towerss over his people
I have discovered my servant David, I have anointed him with
      my holy oil. My hand shall be ready to help him, and
      my arm to give him strength.
No enemy shall strike at him and no rebel bring him low; I
      will shatter his foes before him and vanquish those who
      hate him.
My faithfulness and true love shall be with him and through
      my name he shall hold his head high. I will extend his
      rule over the Sea, and his dominion as far as the River.
He will say to me, 'You are my father, my God, my rock and
      my safe refuge.' And I will name him my first-born,
      highest among the kings of the earth."

PSALM 90. Pity for human fragility!

Lord, you have been our refuge from generation to generation.
Before the mountains were brought forth, on earth and world
      were born in traveil, from age to age everlasting you
      are God. You turn man into dust; "Turn back", you say,
      "you sons of men", for in your sight a thousand years

are as yesterday; a night-watch passes, and you have
cut them off; they are like a dream at daybreak, they
fade like grass which springs up with the morning but
when evening comes is parched and withered.

So we are brought to an end by your anger and silenced by
your wrath. You lay bare our iniquities before you and
our lusts in the full light of your presence. All our days
go by under the shadow of your wrath; our years die
away like a murmur.

Seventy years is the span of our life, eighty if our strength
holds; the hurrying years are labour and sorrow, so
quickly they pass and are forgotten. Who feels the
power of your anger, who feels your wrath like those
that fear you?

Teach us to order our days rightly, that we may enter the gate
of wisdom. How long, O Lord? Relent, and take pity on
your servants. Satisfy us with your love when morning
breaks, that we may sing for joy and be glad all our
days.

Repay us days of gladness for our days of suffering for the
years you have humbled us. Show your servants your
deeds and their children your majesty. May all
delightful things be ours, O Lord our God; establish
firmly all we do.

PSALM 92. To the fair and providential God

O Lord, it is good to give your thanks, to sing psalms to your
name, O Most High, to declare your love in the
morning, and your constancy every night, to the music
of a ten-stringed lute, to the sounding chords of the
harp.

Your acts, O Lord, fill me with exultation; I shout in triumph
at your mighty deeds. How great are your deeds, O
Lord! How fathomless your thoughs! He who does not
know this is a brute, a fool is he who does not
understand this: that though the wicked grow like grass

and every evildoer prospers, they will be destroyed
forever. While you, Lord, reigns on high eternally; your
foes will surely perish, all evildoers will be scattered.

The righteous will flourish like a palm-tree, they will grow tall
as a cedar on Lebanon,

Planted as they are in the house of the Lord, they flourish in
the courts of our God, vigorous in old age like trees full
of sap, luxuriant, wide-spreading, eager to declare that
the Lord is just, the Lord my rock, in whom there is no
up.

PSALM 94. Himn to God, judge of the earth

Rise up, judge of the earth; punish the arrogant as they
deserve.

How long shall the wicked, O Lord, how long shall the
wicked exult? Evildoers are full of bluster, boasting and
swaggering,

they beat down your people, O Lord, and oppress your chosen
nation; they murder the widow and the stranger, and do
the fatherless to death; they say, "The Lord does not
see, the God of Jacob pays no heed."

Pay heed yourselves, most brutish of the people; you fools,
when will you be wise? Does he that planted the ear
not hear, he that moulded the eye not see? Shall not he
that instructs the nations correct them? The teacher of
mankind, has he not a knowlegde?

The Lord knows the thoughts of man, that they are but a puff
of wind.

Happy the man who you instruct, O Lord, and teach out of
your law, giving him respite from adversity, until a pit
is dug for the wicked.

Shall sanctimonious calumny call you partner, or he that
contrives a mischief under cover of law? For they put
the righteous on trial for his life, and condemn to death
innocent men.

PSALM 95. Invitation to praise

Come! Let us raise a joyful song to the Lord, and shout of
    triumph to the Rock of our salvation. Let us come into
    his presence with thanksgiving, and sing him psalms of
    triumph.

For the Lord is a great God, a great king over all gods; the
    farthest places of the earth are in his hands, and the
    folds of the hills are his; the sea is his, he made it; the
    dry land fashioned by his hands is his.

Come! Let us throw themselves at his feet in homage, let us
    kneel before the Lord who made us; for he is our God,
    we are his people, we the flock he shepherds.

You shall know his power today if you will listen to his voice:
    Do not grow stubborn, as you were at Meribah[1], as the
    time of Massah in the desert, when your forefathers
    challenged me, tested me and saw for themselves all
    that I did.

For forty years I was indignant with that generation, and I
    said: There are a people whose hearts are astray, and
    they will not discern my ways. As I swore in my anger,
    "They shall never enter my rest."

PSALM 96. Himn to God, universal king

Sing a new song to the Lord[2]; sing to the Lord, all men on
    earth! Sing to the Lord and bless his name, proclaim his
    triumph day by day! Declare his glory among the
    nations, his marvellous deeds among all the peoples.

Great is the Lord and worthy of all praise; he is more to be
    feared than all gods. For the gods of the nations are
    idols every one; but the Lord made the heavens.

---

1. Meribah = dispute. Massah = temptation. This is the name that Moses gave to
    the place where there was the spring on the rock in the desert.

2. It is a scatological himn. It celebrates the divine highness and its coming as a
    Judge in the end of times.

Majesty and splendour attend him, might and beauty
are in his sanctuary.
Ascribe to the Lord, you families of nations, ascribe to the
Lord glory and might; ascribe to the Lord the glory due
to his name, bring a gift and come into his courts. Bow
down to the Lord in the splendour of holiness, and
dance in his honour, all men on earth. Declare among
the nations, "The Lord is king. He has fixed the earth
firm, immovable; he will judge the peoples justly."
Let the heavens rejoice and the earth exult, let the sea roar and
all the creatures in it, let the fields exult and all that is
in them; then let all the trees of the forest shout for joy
before the Lord when he comes to judge the earth. He
will judge the earth with righteousness and the peoples
in good faith.

PSALM 100. Song to the entrance to the Temple

Acclaim the Lord, all men on earth, worship the Lord in
gladness; enter his presence with songs of exultation[1].
Know that the Lord is God; he had made us and we are his
own, his people, the flock which he shepherds.
Enter his gates with thanksgiving and his courts with praise.
Give thanks to him and bless his name.
For the Lord is good and his love is everlasting, his constancy
endures to all generations.

PSALM 103. Song to the love of God

Bless the Lord, my soul; my innermost heart, bless his holy
name, bless the Lord, my soul, and forget none of his
benefits.
He pardons all my guilt and heals all my suffering. He rescues
me from the pit of death and surrounds me with
constant love, with tender affection; he contents me

---

1. Exhortation to the worship of the pilgrims as they entered Jerusalem.

with all good in the prime of life, and my youth is ever
new like an eagle's. The Lord is righteous in his acts;
he brings justice to all who have been wronged. He
taught Moses to know his way and showed the
Israelites what he could do. The Lord is compassionate
and gracious, long-suffering and for ever constant.

He will not always be the accuser or nurse his anger for all
time. He has not treated us as our sins deserve or
requited us for our misdeeds.

For as heaven stands high above the earth, so his strong lvoe
stands high over all who fear him. Far as east is from
west, so far has he put our offences away from us. As a
father has compassion of his children, so has the Lord
compassion on all who fear him. For he know how we
were made, he knows full well that we are dust.

Man's days are like the grass; he blossoms like the flowers of
the field: a wind passes over them, and they cease to
be, and their place knows them no more.

But the Lord's love never fails those who fear him; his
righteousness never fails their sons and their grandsons
who listen to his voice and keep his covenant, who
remember his commandments and obey them.

The Lord has established his throne in heaven, his kingly
power over the whole world. Bless the Lord, all his
angels, creatures of might who do his bidding.

Bless the Lord, all his hosts, his ministers who serve his will.
Bless the Lord, all created things, in every place where
he has dominion. Bless the Lord, my soul!

PSALM 104. The glory of God in the creation

Bless the Lord, my soul! O Lord my God, you are great
indeed! You are clothed in majesty and splendour, and
wrapped in a robe of light. You have spread out the
heavens like a tent and on their waters laid the beams
of your pavilion; who took the cloud for your chariot,

riding on the wings of the wind; who made the winds
your messengers and flames of fire your servants.

You fixed the earth on its foundation so that it can never be
shaken; the deep overspread it like a cloak, and the
waters lay above the mountains. At your rebuke they
ran, at the sound of the thunder they rushed away,
flowing over the hills, pouring down into the valleys to
the place appointed for them. You fixed a boundary
which they might not pass, they shall not return to
cover the earth.

You made the springs break out in the gullies so that their
water runs between the hills. The wild beasts all drink
for them, the wild asses quench their thirst; the birds of
the air nest on their banks and sing among the leaves.
From your high pavilion you water the hills, the earth is
enriched by your provision. You made grass grow for
the cattle and green things for those who toil for man,
bringing bread out of the earth and wine to gladden
men's hearts, oil to make their faces hine and bread to
sustain their strength. The trees of the Lord are green
and leafy, the cedars of the Lebanon which he planted;
the birds build their nests in them, the stork makes her
home in the tops. High hills are the haunt of the
mountain-goat, and boulders a refuge for the
rock-badger.

You have made the moon to measure the year and taught the
sun where to set. When you make darkness and it is
night, all the beast of the forest come forth; the young
lions roar for prey, seeking their food from God. When
you made the sun rise, they slink away and go to rest in
their lairs; but man comes out to his work and to his
labours until evening. Countless are the things which
you have made, O Lord. You have made all by your
wisdom; and the earth is full of your creatures, beasts
great and small. Here is the great immeasurable sea, in
which move creatures beyond number. Here ships sail
to and fro, here is Leviathan whom you have made
your plaything.

May the glory of the Lord stand for ever and may he rejoice
in his works! When he looks at the earth, it quakes;
when he touches the hills, they pour forth smoke. I will
sing to the Lord as long as I live, all my life I will sing
psalms to my God. May my meditation please the Lord,
as I show my joy in him! Away with all sinners from
the earth and may the wicked be no more!
Bless the Lord, my soul! Hallelujah!

PSALM 108. Morning prayer, and plea for the people

My heart is steadfast, O God, my heart is steadfast. I will sing
and raise a psalm; awake, my spirit, awake, lute and
harp, I will awake at dawn of day!
I will confess you, O Lord, among the peoples, among the
nations I will raise a psalm to you; for your unfailing
love is wider than the heavens, and your truth reaches
to the skies.

PSALM 110. The Messiah king and priest

The Lord said to my lord, "You shall set at my right hand
when I make your enemies the footstool under your
feet."
When the Lord from Zion hands you the sceptre, the symbol
of your power; "March forth through the ranks of your
enemies."
At birth you were endowed with princely gifts and resplendent
in holiness. You have shone with the dew of youth
since your mother bore you.
The Lord has sworn and will not change his purpose: "You
are a priest for ever, in the succesion of Melchizedeck."

PSALM 113. To the superior and good God

Hallelujah! Praise the Lord, you that are his servants, praise
the name of the Lord. Blessed be the name of the Lord

now and evermore! From the rising of the sun to its
setting may the Lord's name be praised!

High is the Lord above all nations; his glory above the
heavens. Who is there is like the Lord our God in
heaven or on earth, who sets his throne so high but
deigns to look down so low?

He lifts the weak out of the dust and raises the poor from the
dunghill, giving them a place among princes, among
the princes of his people; who makes the woman in a
childless house a happy mother of children.

PSALM 114. The miracles of the Exodus

Hallelujah! When Israel came out of Egypt, Jacob from a
people of outlandish speech, Judah became his
sanctuary, Israel his dominion.

The sea looked and ran away; Jordan turned back. The
mountains skipped like rams, the hills like young sheep.

What was it, sea? Why did you run? Jordan, why did you turn
back? Why, mountains, did you skip like rams, and
you, hills, like young sheep?

Dance, O earth, at the presence of the Lord, at the presence of
the God of Jacob, who turned the rock into a pool of
water.

PSALM 115. Greatness and goodness of the true God

Not to us, O Lord, not to us, but to your name ascribe the
glory, for your true love and for your constancy. Why
do the nations ask, "Where is then their God?" Our
God is in high heaven, he does whatever pleases him!

The house of Israel trusts in the Lord; he is the helper and
their shield. The house of Aaron trusts in the Lord; he
is their helper and their shield. The Lord remembers
us, and he will bless us.

PSALM 117. Thanksgiving

Hallelujah! Praise the Lord, all nations, exult him, all you
      peoples; for his love protecting us is strong, the Lord's
      constancy is everlasting!

PSALM 118. Himn for the feast of the Tabernacles

Hallelujah[1]! Give thanks to the Lord, for his love endures for
      ever! My stregth and my power are the Lord, He was
      my deliverer!
Shouts of joy and health under the tents of the upright: The
      Lord would drive them away, the Lord rose me, the
      Lord drove them away! O no, I shall not die, I shall live
      to announce the deeds of the Lord; he punished me, the
      Lord punished me, he did not gave me in to death.
Open the gates of justice, I shall enter and thank the Lord.
      This is the gate of the Lord, upright men shall go
      through it. I thank you, because you have listened to
      me, you have been my saviour. The stones which the
      builders rejected have become the chief corner-stone.
      This is the day on which the Lord has acted: let us
      exult and rejoice in it.

PSALM 121. God keeper of his people

I lift up my eyes to the hill, where shall I find help? Help
      comes only from the Lord, maker of heaven and earth.

PSALM 122. Greeting of the pilgrim to Jerusalem

I rejoiced when they said to me[3], "Let us go to the house of
      the Lord." Now we stand within your gates,

---

1. Hallelujah! (Hebrew = praise the Lord).
2. Jerusalem (Hebrew = City of peace). Salom = peace.
3. Greeting of the pilgrims.

O Jerusalem! Jerusalem that is built to be a city where
people come together in unity.

There come the tribes, the tribes of the Lord, to give thanks to
the Lord himself, the bounden duty of Israel. For in her
are set the thrones of justice, the thrones of the house of
David.

Pray for the peace of Jerusalem, "May those who love you
prosper, peace be within your ramparts and prosperity
in your palaces." For the sake of the house of the Lord
our God I will pray for your good.

PSALM 126. For the total restoration

When the Lord recovered the captives of Zion, we were like
dreamers[1]. Our mouths were full of laughter and our
tongues sang aloud for joy.

The word went round among the nations, "The Lord has done
great things for them." Great things indeed the Lord
then did for us, and we rejoiced! Turn once again our
fortune, O Lord, as streams return in the Negeb[2]! Those
who sow in tears shall reap with songs of joy.

A man go out weeping, carrying his bag of seed; but he will
come back with songs of joy, carrying home his
sheaves.

PSALM 127. Only God the saviour

Unless the Lord builds the house, its builders will have toiled
in vain. Unless the Lord keeps watch over a city, in
vain the watchman stands on guard.

In vain you rise up early[3], and go late to rest, toiling for the
bread you eat; he supplies the need of those he loves[4].

---

1. The return from the exile from Babylon foresees the messianic coming.
2. The streams in the Negeb are dry in the summer and fertile in the winter. God
   fertilizes the sowing.
3. The work of man is of no value if it is not blessed by the Lord.
4. During the sleep God makes the seeds grow.

Sons are a gift from the Lord, and children a reward
from him[1]. Like arrows in the hand of a fighting man
are the sons of a man's youth.

Happy is the man who has his quiver full of them; such men
shall not be put to shame when they confront their
enemies at court.

PSALM 128. Prosperity of the upright

Happy are all who fear the Lord, who live according to his
will.

You shall eat the fruit of your own labours, you shall be
happy and you shall prosper.

You wife shall be like a fruitful vine in the heart of your
house; your sons shall be like olive-shoots round about
your table.

This is the blessing in store for the man who fears the Lord.

May the Lord bless you from Zion; may you share the
prosperity of Jerusalem all the days of your life, and
live to see your children's children!

Peace be in Israel!

PSALM 130. Penance and hope

Out of the depths have I called to you, O Lord, Lord, hear my
cry! Let your ears be attentive to my plea for mercy! If
you, Lord, shoud keep account of sins, who, O Lord,
could hold up his head? But in you there is forgiveness,
and therefore you are revered.

I wait for the Lord with all my soul, I hope for the fulfilment
of his word.

Like men who watch for the morning, O Israel, look for the
Lord, for in the Lord is love unfailing, and great is his
power to set men free. He alone will set Israel free
from all their sins.

---

1. Sons are a gift of God.

PSALM 132. The throne of David is forever

O Lord, remember David, in the time of his adversity, how he
    swore to the Lord and made a vow to the Mighty One
    of Jacob:
The Lord swore to David[1] an oath which he will not break:
    "A prince of your line will I set upon your throne. If
    your sons keep my covenant and heed the teaching that
    I give them, their sons in turn for all time shall sit upon
    your throne." For the Lord has chosen Zion and desired
    it for his home:
"This is my resting place for ever; here will I make my home,
    for such is my desire. I will richly bless her destitute
    and satisfy her needy with bread. With salvation will I
    clothe her priests; her loyal servants shall shout for joy."

PSALM 133. Brotherly friendship

How good it is and how pleasant for brothers to live together!:
It is like the dew of Hermon[2] falling upon the hills of Zion[3].
       There the Lord bestows his blessing, life for evermore.

PSALM 137. Nostalgia for the exile

By the rivers of Babylon we sat down and wept when we
    remembered Zion. There on the poplars we hung up our
    harps.
There our captors called on us to be merry, "Sing us one of
    the songs of Zion."
How could could we sing the Lord's son in a foreign land? If
    I forget you, O Jerusalem, let my right hand wither
    away.

---

1. The Lord renews his promises with David and his covenant if his
    commandments are kept, and he will always be in his Temple.
2. Mount Hermon, north of Palestine, 2,700 metres high, always snowed.
3. Zion = for Tsion, people under the mount. Because of its distance the dew
    does not reach Zion.

Let my tongue cling to the roof of my mouth if I do not
remember you, if I do not set Jerusalem above my
highest joy.

Remember, O Lord, against the people of Edom the day of
Edom the day of Jerusalem's fall, when they said,
"Down with it, down with it, down to its very
foundation!"

O daughter of Babylon, destroyer, happy the man who repays
you, for all that you did to us! Happy is the man who
seizes you children and dashed them against the rock!

PSALM 139. God is everywhere

Lord, you have examined me and know me. You know all,
whether I sit down or rise up; you have discerned my
thoughts from afar.

For there is not a word on my tongue but you, Lord, know
them all. You have kept close guard before me and
behind and have spread your hand over me. Such
knowledge is beyond my understanding, so high that I
cannot reach it.

Where can I escape from your spirit, where can I flee from
your presence? If I climb up to heaven, you are there;
if I make my bed in Sheol, again I find You.

If I take my flight to the frontiers of the morning or dwell at
the limit of the western sea, even there your hand will
meet me and your hand will hold me fast.

If I say, "Surely darkness will steal over me, night will close
around me, darkness is no darkness for you, and night
is luminous as day.

For it was you who fashioned my inward parts; you knitted
me together in my mother's wob. I will praise you, for
your works are wonderful.

You knew me through and through, my body is no mystery to
you. How I was secretly kneaded into shape and
patterned in the depths of the earth.

You saw my limbs unformed in the womb, and in your book
      they are, and in your book they are all recorded; day by
      day they were fashioned, not one of them was late in
      growing.
How deep I find your thoughts, O God, how inexhaustible
      their themes! Can I count them? They outnumber the
      grains of sand; to finish the count, my years must equal
      yours.

PSALM 144. Prayer of the king for victory

Blessed is the Lord, my rock, who trains my hands for war,
      my fingers for battle; my help that never fails, my
      fortresss, my strong tower and my refuge, my shield in
      which I trust, he who puts nations under my feet.
O Lord, what is man that you care for him, what is mankind,
      why give a thought to them? Man is no more than a
      puff of wind, his days a passing shadow.
I will sing a new song to you, O God, psalms to the music of
      a ten-stringed lute. O God who gave victory to kings
      and deliverance to your servant David.
Happy are we whose sons in their early prime are like tall
      towers, our daughters like sculptured pillars at the
      corners of a palace. Our barns are full and furnish
      plentiful provision; our sheep bear lambs in thousands
      upon thousands; the oxen in our fields are fat and sleek;
      there is no miscarriage or untimely birth, no cries of
      distress in our public places. Happy are the people in
      such a case as ours! Happy the people who have the
      Lord for their God!

PSALM 146. Himn to the Almighty God

Hallelujah! Praise the Lord, my soul! As long as I live I will
      praise the Lord; I will sing psalms to my God all my
      life long.

Put no faith in princes, in any man, who has no power to save.
He breathes his last breath, he returns to the dust; and
inthat same hour all his thinking ends.
The Lord shall reign for ever, your God, O Zion, for all
generations! Hallelujah!

PSALM 147. To the saviour of Israel

O praise the Lord. How good it is to sing psalms to our God!
How pleasant to praise him!
The Lord is rebuilding Jerusalem; he gathers in the scattered
sons of Israel. It is he who heals the broken in spirit
and binds up their bounds.
He numbers the stars one by one and names them one and all.
Mighty is our Lord and great his power, and his
wisdom beyond all telling. The Lord gives new heart to
the humble and brings evildoers down to the dust.
To Jacob he makes his word known, his statutes and decrees
to Israel; he has not done this for any other nation, nor
taught them his decrees! Hallelujah!

PSALM 148. Universal prayer

Praise the Lord out of heaven, praise him in the heights, praise
him, all his angels, praise him, all his host!
Praise him, sun and moon; praise him, all you shining stars;
praise him, heaven of heavens, and you waters above
the heavens!
Let them all praise the name of the Lord, for he spoke the
word and they were created; he established them for
ever and ever by an ordinance which shall never pass
away!
Praise the Lord from the earth, you water-spouts and ocean
depths; fire and hail, snow and ice, gales of wind
obeying his voice; all mountains and hills; all fruit-trees
and cedars; wild beasts and cattle, creeping things and
winged birds; kings and all earthly rulers, princes and

judges over the whole earth, young men and maidens,
old men and young together!

Let all praise the name of the Lord, for his name is high above
all others, and his majesty above earth and heaven, he
has exalted his people in the pride of power and
crowned with praise his loyal servants, all Israel, the
people nearest him. Hallelujah!

PSALM 150. Final doxology

Hallelujah! O praise the Lord in his Sanctuary, praise him in
the vault of heaven, the vault of his power; praise him
for his mighty works, praise him for his immeasurable
greatness.

Praise him with fanfares of the trumpet, praise him upon lute
and harp; praise him with tambourines and dancing,
praise him with flute and strings; praise him with the
clash of cymbals, praise him with triumphant cymbals.
Let everything that has breath praise the Lord!
Hallelujah!

PROVERBS

TITLE AND THEME[1]

Proverbs of Solomon, son of David, king of Israel. The fear of the Lord[2] is the beginning of knowledge;/ the fools scorn wisdom and discipline.

REPROOF TO FOLLOW KNOWLEDGE

Do not go with bad men. Listen, my son, to your father's instruction/ and do not reject the teaching of your mother;

for they are a garland of grace on your head/ and a chain of honour round your neck.

My son, if bad men tempt you, do not fall.

Exhortation of wisdom. Wisdom cries aloud in the streets,/ it cries aloud in public places.

She calls at the top of the walls,/ she claims at the open gates of the city:

"How long, you fools, will you be content with simplicity,/ insolent men delight in their insolence, stupid men hate knowledge?

If you would respond to my reproof:/ I would spread my spirit upon you,/ and I would give you my counsel:

---

1. The title in the Hebrew, Greek and Latin Bibles is "Proverbs of Solomon", because the book contains many proverbs attributed to him.
2. The Fear of the Lord is religion. From its piety comes Wisdom.

But I have called and you have refused to listen,/ I have stretched out my hand and nobody cared,

because you have spurned all my advice,/ and would have nothing to do with my reproof;

and in my turn I will laugh at your doom,/ and I will take vengeange when terror overcomes you;

when terror overcomes you like the hurricane/ and your doom descends like a whirlwind,/ when misery and anguish overcome you.

Then they shall call me, and I shall not answer;/ they shall look for me, and they shall not find me.

For they hate knowledge[1],/ and have not chosen to fear the Lord,

they have not listened to his counsels,/ they have spurned all my reproof,

but whoever listens to me shall live without a care, undisturbed by his fear of evil."

Wisdom, remedy against bad men. For the Lord is the one who gives wisdom,/ and knowledge and intelligence come out of his mouth.

He keeps his help for the upright men,/ he is a shield for the upright.

How to get knowledge. May your good faith and loyalty never fail/ but bind them about your neck, write them in your heart, thus you will win favour and success in the sight of God and man.

Put all your trust in the Lord,/ and do not rely on your own understanding.

Think of Him in all your ways,/ and he shall smooth your paths.

Do not think yourself as wise,/ fear the Lord and turn from evil.

Excelences of wisdom. My son, do not spurn the Lord's correction[2],/ and do not be angry because of his reproof,

---

1. Of sciences: Virtue.
2. From correction and advise comes the knowledge of Virtue.

for the Lord reproves those whom he loves,/ as a father reproves his beloved son.

Wisdom is more precious than pearls,/ and all treasures you can wish cannot match her.

Happiness of the wise man. The Lord's curse is in the house of the wicked,/ but he blesses the house of the upright.

He scorns the insolents,/ and favours the upright.

Advantages of knowledge. Listen, my sons, to the instruction of a father,/ and consider how to gain understanding.

I was also a child for my father,/ tender and beloved in my mother's eyes.

He taught me and said to me, "Hold fast to my words,/ keep my commands and you shall live.

Acquiere wisdom, acquire understanding,/ do not foresake it,/ do not turn from the words of my mouth.

Do not forsake it, and it shall keep you/ love it, and she shall guard you.

Over your head it shall set a garland of grace,/ and bestow on you a crown of glory."

The right path. Listen, my son, and to my words,/ and your life shall be longer.

I show you the path of wisdom,/ I guide you through the ways of uprightness.

If you walk, you will not slip,/ and if you run, nothing will bring you down.

But cling to discipline[1], never let it go,/ keep it because it is your life.

Do not follow the path of the wicked[2]/ do not follow the way of evil men.

The path of the righteous[3] is like the light of day,/ growing brighter till it is broad day.

The way of the wicked is like darkness,/ they do not see their downfall.

Swerve neither right nor left,/ keep clear of every evil thing.

---

1. Instruction.
2. Wicked=non-pious.
3. The righteous=good men, those who follow the commandments of the Lord.

Be faithful to your wife. Drink from the waters of your own pit, the streams that come out of your well.

The ant and the sluggard. Go to see the ant, you sluggard!,/ Watch her ways and get wisdom.

She has no overseer, no governor nor ruler,

but in summer she prepares her store of food,/ and lies in her supplies at harvest./ Or go to see the bee,/ and see how industrious she is,/ and what works does she perform;/ kings and mortals use her products to restore their health;/ she is desired and respected by everybody;/ she is weak,/ but also very much esteemed, for she has honoured wisdom.

Seven abominations. There are six things which the Lord hates,/ and seven that his soul loathes:

a proud eye, a false tongue,/ hands that shed innocent blood,

a heart that forges thoughts of mischief,/ and feet that run swiftly to do evil,

a false witness telling lies,/ and one who stirs up quarrels between brothers.

Against adultery. Keep, my son, your father's commands,/ and do not reject the teaching of your mother.

For a command is a lamp,/ and a teaching a light;/ reproof and correction are the path of life.

to keep you away from the wife of another man,/ from the seductive tongue of the loose woman.

Do not desire her beauty in your heart,/ and do not let yourself be seduced by her glances.

Can man kindle fire in his bosom,/ without burning his clothes?

Can man walk on hot coals,/ without burning his feet?

So is he who sleeps with ihs neighbour's wife;/ no one can touch such a woman and go free.

But the man who rapes is a fool,/ he will ruin himself.

He will get blows and contumely,/ and will never live down the disgrace;

for jealousy will rise the husband's anger,/ and in the day of the vengeance he will show no mercy.

Seductions of the adulteress. She pressed him with seductive words,/ with the persuasiveness of her lips.

Like a simple fool he follows her,/ like an ox on its way to the slaughterhouse,/ like an antelope bounding into the noose,

until the arrow pierced his vitals;/ like a bird hurrying into the trap;/ he did not know that he was risking his life.

Praise of wisdom by itself. "I, Wisdom, live with Understanding,/ and have knowledge and prudence.

To fear the Lord is to loathe evil;/ arrogance and pride,/ bad manners and wicked mouth/ are loathed by me.

I have understanding, and also ability;/ force and power are mine.

Through me kings are sovereign/ and governors make just laws.

I love those who love me,/ and those who search for me find me.

Riches and glory are with me,/ together with boundless wealth and virtue.

My fruit is better than gold, than red gold;/ and my rewards are better than pure silver."

Wisdom, Creator. "The Lord created me the beginning of his works,/ before all else that he made.

I was fashioned back in eternity,/ at the beginning, before the origins of the earth.

When the abyss did not exist I was born,/ when there were no wells, full of water.

Before the mountains were created,/ before the hills, I was born,

when the earth and the fiels had not yet been created, nor the elements of dust of the world.

When He created heaven I was there,/ when he created the vault above the waters,

when he fixed the clouds in the sky,/ when he fixed the streams of the abyss,

when he prescribed its limit for the sea,/ and knit together earth's foundation;

I was by her side, as an architect,/ and every day I was his delight,/ playing in his presence, while my delight was in mankind."

New invitation of Wisdom. "And now, my sons, listen to my words,

Listen to my instructions, and be wise, do not reject them.

Happy are the men who follow my path.

Happy are the men who listen to me/ watching daily at my threshold/ with his eyes on the doorway.

For the man who finds me, finds life,/ and wins favour with the Lord;

but the man who finds me not, hurts himself,/ those who hate me, love death."

The banquet of wisdom. Wisdom has built her house,/ she built seven pillars,

sacrificed her offerings, prepared her wine,/ and spread her table.

She sent her servants/ to say from the highest parts of the city, "You, simpletons, come in."/ To the fool she says,

"Come, eat my bread,/ and drink the wine that I have prepared. Cease to be silly, and you will live,/ and follow the path of intelligence."

Advices. Correct an insolent man, and be sneered at for your pains;/ correct a bad man, and you will put youself in the wrong.

Do not correct the insolent or they will hate you; correct a wise man, and he will be your friend.

I you are wise, it is for your good;/ if you are an insolent, only you will suffer the consequences.

FIRST COLLECTION OF SOLOMON'S PROVERBS

Solomon's proverbs. The wise son is the joy of his father,/ a foolish son is his mother's bane.

Ill-gotten wealth brings no profit;/ uprightness is a safeguard against death.

The speech of the upright. Hate is always picking a quarrel/ but love turns a blind eye to every fault.

The man of understanding has wisdom on his lips;/ the wicked are choked by their own violence.

The happiness of the upright. The blessing of the Lord makes him rich.

The hope of the upright ends up with joy,/ but the hope of the wicked fades away.

Fruits of uprightness and wickedness. After arrogance comes ignominy,/ but the wisdom is with the honest man.

Charity and its fruits. The man who follows justice tends to life;/ those who do evil tend to death.

A virtuous woman is the crown of his husband,/ but a bad woman is like deathwatch beetle in his bones.

Industry. Life is in the path of uprightness,/ but the swerving path leads to death.

Poorness and wealth. Some think that they are rich and have nothing,/ some think that they are poor and they have great goods.

Quick wealth disappears,/ but the man that collects wealth slowly, increases it.

Obedience. Go with wise men, and you will be wise,/ those who go with foolish men will be like them.

Effects of Wisdom and Foolishness. The Wise woman builts her home,/ the Foolish woman destroys it with her hands.

The wisdom of the sensible man is to know his own way,/ the unsensibility of the foolish men is to deceive themselves.

A way can look right to a man,/ but, in the end, it may lead to death.

The wise man fears the Lord and keeps from evil,/ but the foolish man is insolent and believes himself safe.

The man who rejects his kinsmen sins;/ happy is the man who has mercy for the poor people.

All work is fruitful,/ but boasting only leads to poverty.

Religion and Government. The fear of the Lord is a safe shelter,/ and a refuge for his sons.

A numerous people is the glory of the king,/ few subdits is the ruin of the prince.

Impatience runs into folly;/ distinction comes from careful thought.

A quiet heart is life for the body,/ but jealousy is bad for the bones.

The man who oppresses the poor insults his Maker;/ he who is generous to the needy honours him.

Righteousness raises a people to honour;/ to do wrong is a disgrace to any nation.

Effects of mildness. A kind answer quiets anger,/ a sharp word makes tempers hot.

A wise man's tongue spreads knowledge;/ a stupid man talks nonsense.

A soothing word is a staff of life,/ but a mischievous tonge breaks the spirit.

Plans fail because of lack of thought,/ but they are carried out by counsellors.

Hateful and loved of God. A fool spurns his father's corrections,/ but to take a reproff to heart shows good sense.

Divine Providence. A man with an arrogant heart is an abomination to the Lord,/ and he shall not be unpunished.

The King. Oracles are on the lips of the king,/ and there is justice in his mouth.

Scales and balances are the Lord's concern;/ all the weights in the bag are his business.

Wickedness is abhorrent to the kings,/ for a throne rests firm on righteousness.

Honest speech is the desire of kings,/ they love a man who speaks the truth.

A king's anger is a messenger of death,/ and a wise man will appease it.

In the light of the king's countenance is life,/ his favour is like a rain-cloud in the spring.

Wisdom and modesty. It is better to gain wisdom than gold,/ and to gain intelligence than silver.

The way of the righteous is to avoid evil,/ the man who watches his way keeps his life.

Pride comes before disaster,/ and arrogance before a fall.

It is better to sit humbly with those in need/ than divide the spoil with the proud.

The words of the wise man and of the impious man. The wise man's mind guides his speech,/ and what his lips impart increases learning.

Kind words are like honey,/ sweetness for the spirit and health for the body.

A path may seem right for man,/ but, at the end, it may lead to death.

Grey hair is a crown of glory,/ and it is won by a virtuous life.

Goodness and fidelity with one's kinsmen. The melting-pot is for silver and the crucible for gold,/ but it is the Lord who assays the hearts of men.

A man who sneers at the poor insults his Maker,/ and he who gloats over another's ruin will answer for it.

Grandchildren are the crown of old age,/ and sons are proud of their fathers.

A reproof is felt by a man of discernment/ more than a hundred blows by a stupid man.

Better face a she-bear robbed of her cubs/ than a stupid man with his folly.

If a man repays evil for good,/ evil will never quit his house.

Justice. To acquit the wicked and condemn the righteous/ both are abominable in the Lord's sight.

A wicked heart does not attain happiness,/ and a deceitful tongue falls in misery.

A joyful heart is an excellent remedy,/ but low spirits sap a man's strength.

A wicked man accepts a bribe under his cloak,/ to pervert the course of justice.

A stupid son exasperates his father,/ and is a bitter sorrow to the mother who bore him.

Experience uses few words,/ discernment keeps a cool head.

Even a fool, if he holds his peace, is thought wise;/ keep your mouth shut and show your good sense.

Misery of the wicked and understanding of the righteous. To answer a question before you have heard it out,/ is both insulting and stupid for you.

A man's spirit may sustain him in sickness,/ but if the spirit is wounded, who can mend it?

Knowledge comes to the discerning mind;/ the wise ear listens to get knowledge.

Juries and trials. Some friends will bring misery to you,/ but some others are more than a brother.

The poor man and the rich man. It is better to be a poor and honest man,/ than a wicked rich man.

False witnesses shall not go unpunished,/ neither liars.

Many search for the favours of the generous man,/ everybody is a friend of the man who gives.

The understanding man and the foolish man. The sensible man is understanding,/ it is his glory to overlook faults.

The anger of the king is like the roar of a lion,/ but his favour is like dew upon grass.

A foolish son is a punishment for his parents,/ a nagging wife is like water dripping endlessly.

Fear of God. To keep the commandments keeps a man safe,/ but scorning the way of the Lord brings death.

He who is generous to the poor lends to the Lord;/ He will repay him in full measure.

A man's heart is full of schemes,/ but the Lord's purpose will prevail.

Righteousness. If a man leads a good and upright life,/ happy are his sons after him!

A double standard in weights and measures/ is an abomination to the Lord.

Fate of the wicked. The wicked are caught by their own violence,/ because they refuse to do what is just.

The criminal's conduct is tortuous;/ straight dealing is a sign of integrity.

Charity and justice. If a man shuts his ear to the cry of the helpless,/ he will cry for help himself and not be heard.

When justice is done, all good men rejoice,/ but it brings ruin to evildoers.

What is worth and what is bad. Rich and poor have this in common,/ the Lord has made them both.

The fruit of humility is the fear of God;/ riches, honour and life.

The crooked man's path is full of snares and pitfalls;/ the cautious man will steer clear of them.

Start a boy on the right road,/ and even in old age he will not leave it.

Oppression of the poor may bring gain to a man,/ but giving to the rich leads only to penury.

COLLECTION OF THE WORDS OF THE WISE

Words of the wise. Pay heed and listen to my words,/ open your mind to their knowledge.

Do not move the ancient boundary-stone/ which your forefathers set up.

Do you see a skilful man at his craft?/ He will serve kings,/ he will not serve common men.

Education of children. Do not withhold discipline from a boy;/ take the stick to him, and save him from death.

The drunkard. Whose is the misery? Whose the remorses?/ Whose are the quarrels and the anxiety? Who gets the bruises without knowing why?/ Whose eyes are bloodshot?

Those who linger late over their wine,/ those who are always trying some new spiced liquor.

Do not gulp down the wine, the strong red wine,/ when the droplets from on the side of the cup,/ it is so sweet!

Your eyes will see strange things,/ your wits and your speech will be confused.

You will become a man tossing out at sea,/ like one who clings to the top of the rigging.

When shall I wake up? I shall turn to it again.

New advices on wisdom. Wisdom builts the house,/ understanding makes it secure.

Wisdom prevails over strength,/ knowledge over brute force.

For the war is made with skilful strategy,/ and victory if the fruit of long planning.

A wise man falls seven times, but he rises up again,/ but the fool are ruined.

SECOND COLLECTION OF SOLOMON'S PROVERBS

Prudence. Rid silver of its impurities,/ then it may go to the silversmith.

Like the clouds and the wind that bring no rain/ is the man who boasts of gifts he never gives.

A prince may be persuaded by patience,/ and a soft tongue may break down solid bone.

Moderation. Be sparing in visits to your neighbour's house,/ if he sees too much of you, he will dislike you.

Like a city that has burst out of its confining walls/ is a man who cannot control his temper.

The fool. Do not answer a stupid man in the language of his folly,/ or you will grow like him.

Answer a stupid man as his folly deserves,/ or he will think himself a wise man.

Do you see that man who thinks himself so wise?/ More is to be expected from a fool than from him.

The quarrelsome. Like a dog caught by his ears/ is the quarrelsome man.

The false man. Glib speech that covers a spiteful heart/ is like glaze spread on earthenware.

With his lips an enemy may speak you fair,/ but inwardly he harbours deceit;

when his words are gracious, do not trust him,/ for seven abominations fill his heart.

If he digs a pit, he will fall into it;/ if he rolls a stone, it will roll back upon him.

Against vanity and jealousy. Do not flatter yourself about tomorrow,/ for you never know what a day will bring forth.

Let flattery come from a stranger, not from yourself,/ from the lips of an outsider and not from your own.

The blows a friend gives are well meant,/ but the kisses of an enemy are perfidious.

Oil and perfume bring joy to the heart,/ but cares torment a man's very soul.

Friends and neighbours. A neighbour at hand is better than a brother far away.

As iron sharpens iron,/ so one man sharpens the wits of another.

He who guards the fig-tree will eat its fruit,/ and he who watches his master's interest will come to honour.

Keeping of the Law. The wicked man runs away with no one in pursuit,/ but the righteous is like a young lion in repose.

A tyrant oppressing the poor/ is like driving rain which ruins the crop.

Those who forsake the law, follow the wicked,/ but those who keep the law are angry against him.

The wicked do not understand justice,/ but those who search for the Lord understand everything.

The man who keeps the law is an intelligent son,/ the man who goes ashtray is his father's shame.

The man who sows his fields will have bread,/ the dreamer will be hungry.

Against the greedy and the violent. The faithful man will be blessed,/ but the man who grows rich hurriedly will not be without blame.

To rob your father or mother and say you do not wrong/ is no better than wanton destruction.

Rules for a fair government. When the righteous are in power, the people rejoice,/ but they groan when the wicked hold office.

A man who flatters his neighbour/ is spreading a net for his feet.

The righteous man is concerned for the cause of the helpless,/ but the wicked understand no such concern.

A stupid man gives free rein to his anger;/ a wise man waits and lets it grow cold.

If a prince listens to falsehood,/ all his servants will be wicked.

Rules for education and virtue. Rod and reprimand impart wisdom,/ but a boy who runs wild brings shame on his mother.

When the wicked are in power, sin is in power,/ but the righteous will gloat over their downfall.

Correct your son, and he will be a comfort to you/ and bring you delights of every kind.

When there is no one in authority, the people break loose,/ but a guardian of the law keeps them on the straigh path.

Pride will bring a man low,/ a man lowly in spirit wins honour.

A man's fears will prove a snare to him,/ but he who trusts in the Lord has a high tower of refuge.

Many seek audience of a prince/ but in every case the Lord decides.

The righteous cannot abide an unjust man,/ nor the wicked a man whose conduct is upright.

WORDS OF AGUR[1]

Mediocrity. Two things I ask of you, do not withhold them from me before I die:

Put fraud and lying far from me; give me neither poverty nor wealth.

Provide me only with the food I need,

If I have too much,/ I shall deny you and say,/ "Who is the Lord"/ If I am reduced to poverty,/ I shall steal and blacken the name of my God.

POEM OF THE CAPABLE WIFE[2]

Who can find a capable wife?/ Her worth is far beyond coral.

Her husband's heart is with her,/ and children are not lacking.

---

1. Agur, born in Massah, was not an Israelite, but son of an Ishmaelite tribe.
2. Beautiful poem of the perfect housewife. The Church applies it in liturgy.

She repays him with good, not evil/ all her life long.

She chooses wool and flax/ and toils at her work.

She is like a ship laden with merchandise,/ she brings home food from far off,/ and work for her servants.

She wishes a field, and buys it,/ and plants a vineyard out of her earnings.

She sets about her duties with vigour/ and braces herself for the work.

She sees that her business goes well,/ and never puts out her lamp at night[1].

She holds the staff in her hand,/ and her fingers grasp the spindle.

She is open-handed to the wretched/ and generous to the poor.

She has no fear for her household when it snows,/ for they are wrapped in two cloacks.

She makes her own coverings,/ and clothing of fine linen and purple.

Her husband is well known in the city gate,/ when he takes his seat with the elders of the land[2].

She weaves linen and sells it,/ and supplies merchants with their shashes.

She is clothed in dignity and power,/ and can afford to laugh at tomorrow.

When she opens her mouth, it is to speak wisely,/ and loyalty is the theme of her teaching.

She keeps her eye on the doings of her household/ and does not eat the bread of idleness.

Her sons with one accord call her happy;/ her husband too, and he sings her praises:

"Many a woman shows how capable she is;/ but you excel them all."

Charm is a delusion and beauty fleeting;/ it is the God-fearing woman who is honoured.

---

1. A burning light at home is a sign of prosperity and life. It only consumes itself with misery and death.

2. It is the place of the assemblies and trials of the city.

Exult her for the fruit of all her toil,/ and let her labours bring her honour in the city gate.

ECCLESIASTES

Title and theme. These are the words of Cohelet[1], son of David, kin in Jerusalem. Vanity, vanity, says Cohelet. What does man gain from his toil under the sun?

PROLOGUE

All is vanity. A generation goes, and another comes, and the earth is still there. And the sun rises, and the sun goes down, and it returns to its place, from where it rises again. The winds blow south, the winds blowh north, round and round and return full circle. All the streams run into the sea.

BODY OF THE WORK[2]

Vanity of knowledge. I, Cohelet, have been king over Israel in Jerusalem. And I devoted myself to study and explore all that is done under heaven. This is a sorry business which the Lord has given to his children. I have seen everything that is done under the sun, and everything is vanity and chasing the wind.

---

1. The author of the Ecclesiastes calls himself Cohelet, son of David. The Jewish tradition attributes it to Solomon. It was written after the exile.

2. The thesis of the book is that everything is vanity except the love of God. For the Christian everything, except sin, can be used as a means to know him and love him. "Everything belongs to you, but you belong to Christ and Christ belongs to the Lord." (1 Cor. 3-23)

And I said to myself, "I have acquired knowledge, more than my predecessors in Jerusalem, and my heart is full of knowledge and wisdom." And I devoted myself to knowledge and wisdom, foolishness and stupidity, and I learnt that this is chasing the wind too.

Vanity of pleasures. And I said to myself, "I want you to feel pleasure, and enjoy myself." But also that was vanity. I called laughter "Madness", and of joy I wondered, "What is its good?" I decided to give some wine to my body, guiding my heart by wisdom. I undertook great works: I built myself palaces and planted vineyards; I made myself gardens and parks and planted all kinds of fruit-trees. I made myself pools of water to irrigate a fertile wood. I bought male and female servants, and their sons were born under my roof. I also had cattle, cows and sheep, more than all my predecessors in Jerusalem. I amassed silver and gold also, and treasures of kings and provinces; I acquired singers, men and women, and what is the delight of the sons of man, lots of princesses. And I continued growing more than all my predecessors in Jerusalem, but my knowledge was by my side. Whatever my eyes coveted, I refused them nothing, nor did I deny myself any pleasure. Yes indeed, I got pleasure from all my labour, and for all my labour this was my reward. Then I reviewed all my handiwork, all my labour and toil, and saw that everything is vanity.

Vanity of human toil. Man is dominated by events.

For everything its season, and for every activity under heaven
    its time,
A time to be born and a time to die; a time to plant and a time
    to uproot.
A time to kill and a time to heal; a time to destroy, and a time
    to build.
A time to weep, and a time to laugh; a time for mourning, and
    a time for dancing.
A time to throw stones, and a time to gather them; a time to
    embrace, and a time to refrain from embracing.
A time to search, and time to throw away; a time to keep, and
    a time to waste.

A time to tear and a time to mend; a time for silence, and a
time for speech.

A time to love, and a time to hate; a time for war, and a time
for peace.

Vanity of wealth. The man who loves money has never
enough, and who loves riches gains nothing from them. This is
vanity too.

Impotence of virtue to grant happiness. Those who keep
the commandments will not have miseries.

Youth and old age. Light is sweet, and the eyes like to see
the sun. And if man lives many years, let him enjoy them, and
let him bear in mind that there will also be many years of
darkness; everything is vanity.

Delight in your boyhood, young man, make the most of the
days of your youth; let your heart and your eyes show
you the way; but remember that for all these things God
will call you to account.

Remember your Creator in the days of your youth, before the
dark days come, and with them those years of which
you will say, "I find no pleasure in them."

Before the sun and the light, the moon and the stars grow dim,
and the clouds return after the rain.

Before the silver cord is snapped, and the golden bowl is
broken, before the pitcher is shattered at the spring and
the wheel broken at the well.

And let dust return to the earth, and the spirit return to the
Lord who has granted it.

Vanity of vanities, says Cohelet, and everything is vanity

EPILOGUE

Conclusion of the discourse. This is the end of the matter.
Fear God and obbey his commands, there is no more to man
than this. For God will bring everything we do to judgement,
every secret too, whether good or bad.

THE SONG OF SONGS[1]

FIRST MEETINGS BETWEEN THE BRIDEGROOM AND THE BRIDE

The bride comes in

The bride

I am dark, but lovely, daughters of Jerusalem,
    like the tents of Kedar,
    like the tent-curtains of Shalmah[2].
Do not take into account that I am dark,
    it is because I am scorched by the sun.

Wish to find the bridegroom

Tell me, my true love,
    where do you mind you flocks,
    where do you lead them at midday,
    so that I am not wandering
    as I sit among your companion's herds.

---

1. Superlative Hebrew form, as the Saint of Saints of the Sanctuary. It can be translated as The Song par excelence.

2. Shalmah = Solomon. The book is attributed to Solomon.

MUTUAL LOVE GROWS [1]

The bridegroom searches for the bride

The bride
A voice! My beloved[2]!
　　　He is coming
　　　bounding over the mountains,
　　　leaping over the hills.
He is like a gazelle,
　　　or a young wild goat:
　　　here he stands outside our wall,
　　　peeping in at the windonws,
　　　glancing through the lattice.
He speaks up and says,
　　　Stand up, my darling,
　　　my fairest, come away.
For look, the winter is past,
　　　the rains are over and gone.
Flowers appear in the countryside,
　　　Stand up, my darling,
　　　my fairest, come away!
My dove, that hides in the holes in the cliffs,
　　　or in crannies on the high ledges,
　　　let me see your face,
　　　let me hear your voice,
　　　for your voice is sweet,
　　　and your face is charming.

---

1. The plot is a bridal song between the bride and the bridegroom.
2. The Lord is the shepherd of Israel who comes to find the love of his people, bride, and call her.

THE LOVE OF THE BRIDE IS TESTED

Nightly visit of the bridegroom!1•

The bride

I was sleeping, but my heart was awake...
>   A voice! My beloved was calling,
>   "Open the door, my sister, my friend,
>   my dove, my perfect one:
>   for my head is drenched with dew,
>   my locks with the moisture of the night."

I woke up to open the door,
>   my hands dripped with myrrh;
>   the liquid myrrh from my fingers,
>   ran over the knobs of the bolt.

I opened the door,
>   but my beloved was gone.
>   My sould fled after him.
>   I searched for him but did not find him,
>   I called him but he would not answer.

The watchmen met me!2•,
>   those who watch the city;
>   they struck me, they hurt me.

I charge you, daughters of Jerusalem,
>   if you find my beloved,
>   what shall you tell him?
>   That I am faint with love.

Companions

What is your beloved more than any other,
>   o fairest of women?
>   What is your beloved more than any other,
>   that you give us this charge?

---

1. For some people the song has a mystical sense: union of God with his recovered people.

2. Foreign peoples ill-treated her.

Beauty of the bridegroom[1]

The bride

My beloved is fair and ruddy,
     a paragon among ten thousand.
His head is gold, finest gold;
     his locks are black as palm-fronds.
His eyes are like doves
       by the waters of the stream,
     splashed by milky water
     as they sit where it is drawn.
His cheeks are like bed of spices
     or beds full of perfumes
     His lips are lilies,
     and drop liquid myrrh.
His hands are golden rods
     set in stones from Tirzah;
     his chest, a plaque of ivory
     overlaid with zaphire.
His mouth is sweetness itself,
     wholy desirable.
     Such is my beloved, such is my friend,
     daughters of Jerusalem.

Companions

Where is your beloved gone[2],
     O fairest of women?
     Where did he go to,
     that we may help you to seek him?

The bride

He has gone down to his garden,
     to the beds where the balsam grows,
     to mind his flock in the gardens,
     to pick up lilies.

---

1. For others this collection of songs celebrates human love, the union of the couple. Right and religious love, for God has blessed the marriage.
2. The beloved has gone and she seeks him.

I belong to my beloved, and my beloved belongs to me.
  He minds his flock in the lilies.

BRIDAL SONG OF THE BRIDE

The bridegroom is found by the bride

The bridegroom
You are beautiful, my friend, like Tirzah[1],
    lovely as Jerusalem[2],
    like a charging army.
Turn your eyes away from me
    for they dazzle me.
Your teeth are like a flock of ewes
    come up fresh from the dipping.
Your cheeks like a pommegranade cut open,
    through your veil[3].
You are my only dove,
    my perfect dove:
    she, her mother's only child,
    devoted to the mother who bore her.
    The maids have seen her
    and praise her[4].
"Who is this that looks out like dawn,
    beautiful as the moon,
    bright as the sun,
    majestic as a charging army?"
I went down to a garden of nut-trees,
    to look at the rushes by the streams,
    to see if the vine had budded
    or the pommegranades were in flower...
Without realising, my desire led me
    to the chariots of my people, as a prince.

---

1. Tirzah was the capital of the Northern kingdom.
2. Jerusalem, capital of the South. Kingdom of Judah.
3. God has recovered his bride, and he courts her already in exile.
4. All the nations praise the bride in love.

THE TOTAL POSSESSION

Stability and vitality of love.

The bride

Wear me as a seal upon your heart![1],
    as a seal upon your arm;
    for love is strong
    as death.
Many waters cannot quench love,
    no floods could sweep it away.

---

1. Seal of eternal possession and of a love stronger than death.

THE BOOK OF WISDOM[1]

WISDOM AND DESTINY OF MAN

Dispositions for Wisdom: keep your heart pure and refrain from sin. Love justice, you rulers of the earth;/ set your mind upon the Lord,/ seek simplicity of heart.

God did not make death,/ nor is he satisfied with the death of the living creatures.

For God created man not to be corrupted,/ and made him in his image.

But for jealousy of the devil the death entered the world,/ and those who belong to her die.

Life and death of the righteous and the evildoer. The souls of the righteous are in the hands of the Lord,/ and no turment will come to them[2].

To the eyes of the fool their souls are dead,/ and their end was judged as miserable.

They left us in misery,/ but now they rest in peace.

In the eyes of men they have been punished,/ his hope is full of immortality.

For every small misery they will get great favours,/ for the Lord tested them,/ and they were worthy of Him.

---

1. It was attributed to Solomon, but its author was a Helenic Jew, probably from Alexandria, principal centre of the culture of the diaspora.

2. The righteous, after the trials of life, will get their reward.

He tested them like gold in the melting-pot,/ and they were offered to them.

When their reward comes they shall be happy,/ and they will run like fire in the woods.

They will judge over the nations and rule the peoples,/ and their Lord will rule for ever.

Virtue and vice. They will be afraid when they come to be judged for their faults,/ and their iniquities will accuse them[1].

Then the righteous[2] will feel himself secure,/ before those who have oppressed him,/ and those who scorned his toil.

They will tremble with fear when they see him,/ when they see that he is safe and hopeful.

They will say,/ in their deluded way,/ This is the man whom we scorned before,/ object of our laughter.

How foolish we were, who had him for a madman,/ and his end without honour.

He was included within the sons of God,/ and now he shares the luck of the Holy!

We did not choose the path of truth,/ the light of justice did not give light to us,/ neither did the sun rise.

For the hope of the evildoer is like the surf of the sea blown by the wind.

The righteous live for ever,/ and the Lord has their reward,/ the Most High cares for them.

Thus they shall get to the kingdom of glory,/ and they will have the most beautiful crown from the hands of the Lord.

THE TRUE WISDOM[3]

Excelencies of Wisdom. So I have prayed and I was granted understanding;/ I prayed and the spirit of wisdom came to me.

---

1. On the Day of the Final Judgement.
2. Justice = Virtue and holiness. A man is holy when he lives in the Grace of God.
3. In the biblical language, wisdom and understanding mean virtue, holiness = Grace or supernatural Life, in Christian language, acquired by the Christening.

I prefered the spirit to sceptres and thrones,/ and I did not value wealth.

I did not compared it to a precious stone,/ for all the gold is like a handful of sand before her,/ her brightness is for ever.

With her came all my goods,/ and an enormous wealth.

Nature of Wisdom. It is a part of the power of God/ which comes from the glory of the Almighty;/ therefore nothing blemished can come to her.

It is the brightness of the eternal light,/ immaculate mirror of God's activity,/ image of his love.

And although she is only one, she is mighty,/ and within herself she renews everything,/ she comes to holy spirits in all ages,/ maken them friends of God and the prophets.

Goods of Wisdom. If a man loves justice,/ his toils turn into virtues, for he shows prudence and understanding,/ justice and strength,/ and there is nothing more useful for men in their lives.

ECCLESIASTICUS[1]

WISDOM AND PRACTICAL LIFE

All wisdom comes from the Lord,/ wisdom is with Him for ever.

Who can count the sand of the sea, the drops of rain,/ and the past days?

Who can measure the height of the sky, the breadth of the earth,/ the depth of the abbys and wisdom?

Wisdom was first of all created things,/ intelligent purpose from the beginning.

Trust in God. My son, if you decide to worship God,/ prepare your soul for the test[2].

Set a straight course, be resolute,/ and to not lose your head in time of disaster.

Hold fast to him, never desert him,/ if you would end your days in prosperity.

Accept every hardship that is sent to you,/ be patient under humiliation.

For gold is assayed by the fire,/ and the Lord proves men in the furnace of humiliation.

Those who fear the Lord try to please him/ and those who love him keep to his Laws.

---

1. Its author is Ben-Sirach, an erudite and merciful rabbi. The book contains several sayings, like those of the Proverbs of Solomon.
2. God proves his worshippers in this world.

Modesty. The greater you are, the more you have to humiliate yourself,/ and the Lord will favour you.

For great is the power of the Lord,/ and he is honoured by the poor men.

Virtue and human respect. Do not be ashamed of confessing your sins,/ nor swim against the stream.

Fight to death for the truth,/ and the Lord God will fight for you.

Do not be a lion at home,/ nor arrogant with your servants.

Do not stretch out your hand to recive,/ and not to give.

Wealth and pride. Come back to the Lord without delay,/ do not put it off from one day to the next,/ or suddenly the Lord's wrath will be upon you,/ and you will perish at the time of reckoning.

Do not rely upon ill-gotten gains,/ for they will not avail in time of calamity.

Moderation of speech. Do not gain a name for being a gossip,/ or lay traps with your tongue.

There is shame in store for the thief,/ so there is harsh censure for duplicity.

Avoid the little faults of your heart,/ for they will tear you apart like a bull.

They would devour your leaves, will throw down your fruits,/ and you would be like a withered tree.

Violent passions lose those who feel them,/ and he becomes motive of laughter for his enemy.

True friendship. If you have a friend put him to the test,/ and do not trust him at first.

For some friends are loyal when it suits them,/ but desert you in time of trouble.

When you are prosperous, he will be your second self,/ and make free with your servants.

But if you are humiliated, he will turn against you,/ and you will not see him again.

Keep off you enemies,/ and watch your friends.

A faithful friend is a powerfuld shield,/ and the man who finds him has a treasure.

A faithful friend is beyond price,/ money cannot buy him.

Family life. Do not despise a good wife,/ for he is worth more than gold.

Do not ill-treat a slave who works honestly,/ or a hired servant whose heart is in his work.

Norms of prudence in social relationships. Do not fight the powerful,/ you could fall into his hands.

Do not quarrel with a rich man,/ for he will outbid you.

Do not rebuke a man who is already penitent;/ remember that we are all guilty.

Do not despise an old man,/ we will grow old as well.

Do not ignore the discourse of your elders,/ for they themselves learned from their fathers,/ they can teach you to understand,/ and to have an answer ready in time of need.

Do not kindle a sinner's coals,/ for fear of being burnt in the flames of his fire.

Do not let a man's insolence bring you to your feet,/ he will only sit waiting to trap you with your own words.

Do not lend to a man with more influence than yourself,/ or, if you do, write off the loan as a loss.

Do not stand surety beyond your means,/ and, when you do stand surety, be prepared to pay.

Do not be advised by a fool,/ for he will not keep your secret.

Do not say a secret to a foreigner,/ for you do not know what may come up.

Do not show your heart to everybody,/ he could take your happiness away

The deal with women. Do not be jealous of the women you love,/ and do not do her any harm.

Do not give your will to your wife,/ in case she rules you.

Many have been seduced by the beauty of a woman,/ which kindles passion like fire.

The deal with men. Do not desert an old friend,/ a new one is not worth as much./ A new friend is like new wine,/ you do not enjoy it until it has matured.

A craftsman is recognized by his skilful hand/ and a councillor by his words of wisdom.

OTHER MAXIMS

Do not rely on appearances. The bee is a small animal,/ but hers is the sweetest fruit.

Do not condemn before proving,/test the man, and then correct him.

Moderation. Do not answer before listening,/ and do not break in another man's discourse.

Mind your own business,/ and do not interfere in the quarrels of sinners.

Exalt his head,/ for everybody's praise.

Trust in God. Good and evil, life and death,/ poverty and wealth come from the Lord.

Knowledge, wisdom and knowledge of the Law/ come from the Lord. Love and good works come from Him.

The gift of the Lord remains with merciful men,/ their mercy will make them always prosperous.

Do not praise anybody before dying,/ for the man shall be recognized because of his end.

True and false friends. You can not know the friend in prosperity,/ nor can the enemy be hidden in adversity.

Join your kinsmen. The man who touches tar, is stained,/ and the man who goes with arrogant men becomes like them.

The rich man is unfair and boasts it,/ a poor man is unfairly treated and still he must apologize.

While you are useful to him, he will use you,/ but if you find yourself in need, he will forsake you.

If you own something he will live with you,/ but he will ruin you if he can.

Do not be anxious to be accepted,/ but do not walk too far so that you may be remembered.

Do not trust him or his words,/ for he will try you with his gossip,/ and he will make you speak with his smile.

He is a merciless man who keeps his word,/ and he will not spare you blows nor chains.

Watch out and keep yourself safe,/ for you are walking with your own misery.

Every living creature loves his equal,/ and all man his kinsmen.

True happiness. Son, remember that death is never late,/ and you do not know when she will come.

Freedom in sin. Do never say, "It is the Lord who moved me to sin",/ for you must not do what He hates.

Do not say, "He moved me to sin.",/ for he does not need a sinner.

He made man at the beginning,/ and let him do according to his own will.

If you want, you may keep the commandments,/ and it is up to you to remain faithful to him.

Life and death are before man/ and you will have whatever you want.

His hands look upon those who fear him,/ and knows all the works of men.

He has commanded no man to sin,/ and he has allowed nobody to do so.

God Creator. The Lord created man on earth,/ and he will return him to her.

He said a concrete date and time,/ and he gave him power over the living creatures on the earth.

Knowledge. Sensible use of speech. There are unlucky speeches,/ and silences which reveal a sensible man.

The man who says "I am to blame" is forgiven.

Some men lose their soul for human respect,/ and think themselves lost before a fool.

Some men promise a gift to a friend for human respect,/ and so they gain a new friend without any cause.

Keep off sin. My son, have you sinned? Do it no more,/ and ask pardon for your past wrongdoing.

Avoid wrong as you would a snake,/ for if you go near, it will bite you.

To built a house with borrowed money/ is like collecting stones for your own tomb.

The road of the sinners is smoothly paved,/ but it leads straight down to the grave.

The unfaithful wife. The same will happen to the wife who forsakes her husband,/ and bears another man's son.

For firstly she shall disobey the Law of the Most Hight,/ secondly, she will sin against her husband,/ and thirdly she was stained with adultery,/ bearing the children of another man.

Praise of wisdom. I am the word which was spoken by the Most High,/ and I covered the earth like a mist.

I lived in high heaven and my throne was a pillar of cloud.

Alone I made a circuit of the sky,/ and I walked the depth of the abyss.

The waves of the sea, the whole earth,/ every people and nation were under my way.

Among them I looked for a home,/ a place to settle down.

Then the Creator of the universe laid a command upon me,/ and my Creator decreed where I should dwell,/ and told me, "Pitch you tent in Jacob,/ and settle down in Israel."

He created me at the very beginning, before the centuries,/ and I will live for ever.

In the sacred tent I ministered in his presence,/ and so I came to be established in Zion.

He settled me in the city he loved,/ and I had authority in Jerusalem.

I took root among the people whom the Lord had honoured,/ by choosing them to be his special possession.

There I grew like the cedar in Lebanon,/ like a cypress on the slopes of Hermon.

I grew, like a palm-tree at Engedi,/ like a rose at Jericho;/ like an olive-tree in the plains,/like a plane-tree.

Like cassia or camel-thorn I was redolent of spices;/ I spread my fragrance like choice myrrh,/ like galban, aromatic sheel, and gum resin;/ I was like the smoke of incense in the Tabernacle.

I spread out my branches like a terebinth,/ branches of glory and wealth.

Come to me, those who search me,/ and eat from my fruits.

For my memory is sweeter than honey,/ and my possession sweeter than the comb.

Other maxims. Three sights warm my heart,/ beautiful in the eyes of the Lord and in the eyes of men;/ concord among brothers, friendship among neighbours/ and inseparable man and wife.

My soul loathes three kinds of people,/ and disgust me:/ a poor man who is arrogant, a rich man who lies,/ and an old fool who commits adultery.

Old men. If you have not gathered in your youth,/ what are you to find in your old age?

Sound judgement sits well on grey hairs,/ and ripe counsel in men of eminence!

Long experience is the old man's crown,/ and his glory is the fear of the Lord.

GOD'S MAJESTY

In nature. There is no thought unknown to Him,/ no word can remain hidden from Him.

He has disposed the wonders of his wisdom orderly,/ for he exists from eternity to eternity.

ISAIAH[1]

PART ONE

THREATS AND PUNISHMENTS

Isaiah's vocation. In the year of the death of king Uzziah's death, I saw the Lord sitting on a throne, high and exalted; the skirt of his robe filled the temple. Attendant seraphims were above Him; each one had six wings; two of them covered his face, other two his feet, and other two were spread in flight. And they called to one another,

"Holy, holy, holy is the Lord of Hosts,/ the whole earth is full of his glory."

The threshold shook at their calls, and the Temple was filled with smoke. I cried,

"Woe is me, I am lost,/ I am a man of unclean lips,/ and my eyes have seen the king, Lord of Hosts!"

Then one of the seraphim flew towards me with a glowing coal which he had taken from the altar with a pair of tongs. He touched my mouth with it and said,

---

1. Isaiah (Hebrew = The Lord's Salvation). He is the first of the prophets because of the importance of his prophecies, the vastness of his work and his elegant style.

"The coal has touched your lips,/ your iniquity has been removed,/ your sin is wiped away."

And I heard the voice of the Lord saying, "Who shall I send? Who shall go for us?" And I said, "Here I am, send me."

Severe threat of corruption to the people. Listen, O heavens, listen, O earth,/ for the Lord speaks;/ I have fed your sons,/ and they have risen against me.

The ox knows his master/ and the ass his master's stable./ However, Israel does not know,/ my people does not understand.

O nation of sin,/ criminal people,/ evildoers, wicked sons!/ They have forsaken the Lord,/ and despised the Holy One of Israel, / they have turned their back to him.

Why go on stricking you,/ if you still rebell?/ My head is aching,/ my heart is anguished.

Your country is a desert,/ your cities have been burnt up by fire,/ your soil, even to your eyes,/ is devoured by foreigners:/ desolation, like the ruins of Sodom.

Zion's daughter is now/ a hut in a vineyard,/ a hovel in a melon plot,/ like a besieged city.

If God/ had not left anything for us,/ this would be like Sodom,/ like Gomorrah.

Jerusalem is invited to do penance. Therefore come, let us count your faults,/ —says the Lord./ And if your sins are like the pommegrane,/ they will get white like snow;/ if they are purple red,/ they will turn white like wool.

If you are obedient and mild,/ you shall eat the fruits of the country.

But if you reject them and rebell,/ you shall be put to the sword./ These are the words of the Lord.

Jerusalem, centre of the messianic kingdom. Isaiah's vision, son of Amoz, about Judah and Jerusalem.

In the days to come it will happen/ that the mount of the Temple of the Lord/ shall settle on the top of the mountains,/ and it will raise above the cliffs./ Everybody will come to see it and they will say,/ "Let us go up the Mount of the Lord,/ to the house of the God of Jacob,/ so that He shows us his way/ and we may follow his paths./ For the Law will come from Zion,/ and the word of the Lord will come from Jerusalem."

He will rule the nations,/ and give his laws to numerous peoples,/ and they change their swords for ploughs/ and their spears for sickles./ They will not fight each other,/ and will not prepare themselves for war.

Come, house of Jacob,/ let us walk in the light of the Lord.

The rest of Jerusalem is honoured. On that day the people of the Lord shall be ornament and glory,/ and the fruit of the land/ shall be pride and splendour/ of those Israelites who have been saved.

The barren vineyard, a symbol for Israel. I want to sing for my friend/ a lovesong to his vineyard./ My friend had a vineyard/ on a steep slope.

He dug it, removed the stones,/ planted the best vines;/ in the middle he built a tower,/ and he put a winepress./ He expected the vines to produce grapes,/ but they only produced wild grapes.

Now, inhabitants of Jerusalem, men of Judah,/ judge me and my vineyard.

What else could be done to my vineyard/ that I have not already done?/ Why did it only produce wild grapes?

Therefore I shall tell you/ what I will do with my vineyard:/ I will cut the bush down and herds will graze on it;/ I will destroy the wall and it will be stepped upon.

I will turn it into a desert,/ it will never be pruned again;/ it will be full of bush and thistles,/ and I will order the clouds/ not to send rain again upon it.

Yes, the vineyard of the Lord/ is the people of Israel,/ and the men of Judah, his chosen seed./ He expected righteousness,/ and there has been bloodshed;/ he expected justice/ and there are only cries of distress.

Threats against the sinners. Shame on you! you who add house to house,/ and join field to field,/ until there is no more place/ and they are left to own the whole land!

In my hearing has sworn/ the word of the Lord:/ "Many houses shall go to ruin,/ great and beautiful, there will be no one to inhabit them.

Harp and lute, tabor and pipe, and wine in their feasts,/ but they do not see the work of the Lord,/ they do not see what he has done.

Therefore my people are dwindling away,/ because of its lack of wisdom;/ its nobles shall starve,/ and the common men shall die of thirst.

But the Lord sits high in his judgement,/ the holy God/ will show himself holy in his justice.

Shame on you who call evil good/ and good evil,/ who call darkness light,/ and light darkness,/ who give bitter for sweet,/ and sweet for bitter!

Shame on the wise men to their own eyes,/ and understanding in their own esteem.

Therefore, as the tongue of the plain devours the bush,/ and as the straw is burnt up by fire,/ so shall its roots get rotten,/ and their flowers turned to dust,/ for they rejected the law of the Lord,/ and despised the word of the Holy One of Israel.

BOOK OF IMMANUEL. MESSIANIC PROPHECIES

First warning of Isaiah to Ahaz. This happened in the time of Ahaz, son of Joatham son of Uzziah, king of Judah. "Within five and six years/ Ephraim shall be destroyed, it will cease to be a nation./ If you do not have faith, you will not survive."

Second warning: the virgin mother of Immanuel[1]. The Lord spoke to Ahaz and said, "Ask the Lord your God for a sign, from lowest Sheol or from highest heaven." Ahaz answered, "I will not ask for it, I do not want to tempt the Lord."

Then Isaiah added,

"Therefore listen, house of David;/ Are you not content with wearing out men's patience,/ that you must also wear out my God's?

---

1. Immanuel (Hebrew = God with us). The awaited Messiah. This has been the interpretation of the Jews and of the Christian tradition.

The Lord himself shall give you a sign./ Look: the pregnant virgin shall bear a child/ and he shall be named Immanuel[1].

Immanuel, saviour and scandal of Israel. Only the Lord is holy,/ fear Him alone, tremble before Him alone.

He will be a boulder and a rock/ for the two houses of Israel,/ a trap and a snare / to those who live in Jerusalem.

Many shall stumble over them,/ many shall fall and be broken,/ many shall be snared and caught[2].

Birth of the kingdom of Christ. The people which wandered in darkness/ saw a great light/ upon the inhabitants of the country of deathly darkness/ light has dawned.

You have increased their joy,/ have given them gladness,/ they rejoice before you/ as men rejoice in harvest,/ as they share out the spoil.

For you delivered them/ of the yoke that burdened them,/ the collar that lay heavy on their shoulders/ the driver's goat, as on the day of Midian.

A boy has been born for us,/ we have been given a son;/ the symbol of dominion is on his shoulders./ and his name will be:/Counsellor, powerful God,/ for ever Father, Prince of peace[3],

to expand his dominion,/ for a endless peace,/ in the line of David and his kingdom,/ to establish it and sustain it from now and for ever more./ The zeal of the Lord of Hosts shall do all this.

Punishment of Samaria and Israel. The Lord has sent his word against Jacob,/ and it will fall upon Israel.

All the people shall know it,/ Ephraim and Samaria's inhabitants,/ who say in their pride,/ in their heart's arrogance,

"The bricks have fallen down,/ we will build in hewn sotne;/ the sycomores are hacked down,/ but we will use cedars instead."

---

1. It is the miraculous birth of a Virgin mother who is Mary, Mother of God.
2. Many were scandalized by Jesus, stumbled and got lost, for they refused to acknowledge him as the Messiah.
3. The boy Jesus came from the line of David.

But the Lord raises their foes against him,/ he spurs on his enemies:

Syria from the west and the Philistines from the east,/ who swallow Israel,/ but his anger is not yet gone,/ his arm is still stretched out.

Yet the people did not come back,/ to the one who struck them,/ they have not searched for the Lord of Hosts.

Features of the Messiah and his kingdom. A remnant shall come from the line of Jesse,/ a remnant will come of his roots[1].

The spirit of the Lord shall rest upon him,/ spirit of wisdom and understanding,/ spirit of advice and strength,/ spirit of knowledge and fear of the Lord;

if he fears the Lord he shall be fruitful./ He will not judge by appearances/ he will not believe what he hears;/

he shall judge the weak rightly,/ and defend the humble in the land with equity;/ he will strike the tyrant with the staff of his mouth,/ he will slay the evildoer with this words.

Justice will be his belt,/ loyalty his girdle round his body[2].

The wolf shall live with the sheep,/ the leopard with the kid;/ the calf and his young lion shall graze together,/ a child shall lead them.

The cow and the bear shall graze together,/ their young shall rest together,/ and the lion shall eat grass like an ox.

The infant shall play/ next to the hole of the cobra,/ over the viper's nest,/ he shall put his hand within.

They shall not hurt or destroy/ in my holy mountains,/ for the country will be full/ of the knowledge of the Lord/ as the sea is full of water.

Return of the exiles. On that day the line of Jesse/ shall rise as the standard of the people;/ peoples shall search it/ and its dwelling place shall be glorious.

On that day the Lord will rise his hand again/ to recover the remnant of his peole,/ what is left from Assyria and Egypt,/

---

1. Jesse = Isaiah the Betlemite, David's father. Jesus was that remnant, from the line of David, Son of David.

2. Paradisiacal and symbolic description.

from Pathros, from Cush and Elam,/ from Shinar, Hamath and the islands[1].

Then he will raise a signal to the nations,/ and gather together the exiles of Israel,/ he shall recover Judah's scattered people,/ from the four corners of the earth.

Return from exile. The Lord has broken the staff of the wicked,/ the sceptre of the tyrants,

the one who struck the peoples,/ without delay,/ the one who crushed the nations in anger,/ without mercy.

And now the earth rests in peace,/ exultant with joy.

Even the cypress trees are glad for you,/ even the cedars of the Lebanon:/ "Since you are dead,/ nobody cuts us down[2]."

PUNISHMENT AND SALVATION OF ZION

Song of the vineyard. On that day they shall say,/ O the sweet vineyard,/ sing to it!

I am the Lord, its keeper,/ I water it day and night/ to keep its leaves alive,/ I keep it day and night.

I am not angry now./ As soon as it has briars and thorns,/ I shall fight them,/ and I will burn them all up,

unless they come under my refuge and make peace with me,/ yes,/ unless they make peace with me.

Future of the people of God. In the future Jacob will take root,/ Israel will flourish and give fruit,/ and it shall fill the earth with its fruits.

It has been scattered and punished with exile,/ removing her by a cruel blast/ when the east wind blows.

This then purges Jacob's iniquity,/ and this will be the price of his sin,/ that he grinds all altar stones/ to powder like chalk;/ no sacred poles and incense-altars are left standing.

For the fortified city is left solitary,/ abandoned dwelling,/ bare like a dessert;/ there the calf grazes,/ there lies down and crops every twig.

---

1. Only a remnant of the people will be saved.
2. The Babylonians cut down woods and fruit trees in the cities they besieged and conquered.

When the boughs grow dry,/ they snap off,/ and women come and burn them,/ for they are a people without intelligence,/ so their Creator has no mercy for them,/ he who formed them will show them no favour.

On that they the Lord will beat out the grain/ from the streams of the River to the Torrent of Egypt[1],/ and you shall be gleaned one by one,/ sons of Israel.

Kingdom of the Lord at Zion. Your eyes shall see the king in his beauty,/ they will see an immense country.

Watch Zion, the city of our feasts;/ your eyes will see Jerusalem/as a safe place,/ a tent that shall never be shifted;/ whose pegs shall never be pulled up,/ not one of its ropes cast loose.

The new Israel. Rejoice the desert and the wilderness,/ rejoice and flourish the bare land, filled with flowers like the narcissus,/ rejoice and be happy./ For the glory of the Lebanon has been granted to it,/ and the splendour of Mount Carmel and Sharon[2];/ and the glory of the Lord will be seen,/ the splendour of our God.

Strenghten the weak hands,/ and those trembling knees!

Say to the cowards,/ "Take heart, do not be afraid! Look, it is our God,/ vengeance is near, God's vengeance;/ He himself is coming to save you."

Then the eyes of the blind shall be opened,/ and so shall be the ears of the deaf.

The lame shall jump like a deer,/ the mute's tongue shall shout in joy,/ for there will flow streams of water in the desert,/ and in the wilderness;

the burning land will turn into a pond,/ and the thirsty soil into a pool full of water,/ and the place where the jackals laid/ will be green with reeds and rushes.

There there will be a plain path,/ which shall be called holy way;/ no wicked or foolish man/ shall step upon it.

---

1. The river par excelence for the Israelites was the Euphrates on the North and the Torrent of Egypt on the Southern border.
2. Sharon was the plain between Mount Carmel and Lebanon. It was a very fertile land.

There will be no lions there,/ nor wild beast to thread upon;/ only the redeemed people will walk along the holy way.

By the holy way shall return those saved by the Lord,/ they will come to Zion among cries of joy,/ a joy which is for ever shall overcome them,/ gladness and hapiness will come with them,/ their miseries and sufferings will flee from them.

Hezekiah's illness and prayer. At this time Hezekiah fell dangerously ill. Then the prophet Isaiah son of Amoz came to him and said, "This is the word of the Lord: Give your last instructions to the household, for you are going to die, you will not recover." Then Hezekiah turned to the wall and prayed to the Lord, "O Lord, remember, please, that I have walked before you faithfully with a loyal heart, doing what is right in your eyes." And he wept bitterly. Then the Lord said to Isaiah, "Go and say to Hezekiah: This is the word of the Lord, God of your father David: I have listened to your prayer, I have seen your tears, and I am going to heal you. In three days you will be able to go to the Temple of the Lord. I shall grant you fifteen years. I will deliver the king of Assyria into your hands and then I will protect this city."

"How shall I know that I must go up the Temple again?"

Isaiah answered, "This shall be your sign from the Lord that he will do what He has promised: I am going to bring the shadow of the sun on Ahaz backwards ten steps." And the sun went back ten steps on the stairway down which it had gone.

BOOK OF THE CONSOLATION

Announcement of the liberation. Comfort, comfort my people,/ says your God.

Speak to the heart of Jerusalem,/ and tell her this,/ that she has fulfilled her term of bondage,/ that her penalty is paid,/ she has received the Lord's hand,/ double penance for all her sins.

The forerunner. A voice shouts, "Prepare a road/ for the Lord in the desert,/ clear a highway across the wilderness/ for our God.

Every valley shall be lifted up/ every mountain and hill brought down,/ rugged places shall be made smooth,/ and mountain-ranges become valleys.

The glory of the Lord will be revealed,/ and all mankind shall see it,/ for the Lord has spoken."

A voice says, "Cry"/ and I say, "What shall I cry?"/ "Every mortal man is grass,/ all his glory like a flower in the countryside.

The grass withers, the flower fades,/ when the Lord blows upon them./ Yes, byt the people is the grass!

The grass withers, the flower fades,/ but the word of our God/ remains for ever."

Go up the mountain top,/ messenger of good news from Zion,/ lift up your voice / messenger of good news from Jerusalem,/ and shout fearlessly,/ say to the cities of Judah:/ "Here is your God!"

Here is the Lord coming in might;/ his arm rules everything./ He comes with the price of his victory/ and his rewards come before him.

He tends his flock like a shepherd,/ he takes the sheep with his arm./ He carries the lambs in his bosom/ and leads the ewes to water.

God's ommipotence and freedom. Who has gauged the waters in the palm of his hands,/ or with its span set limits to the heavens?/ Who has held all the soil of the earth in a bushel,/ or weighed the mountains on a balance/ and the hills on a pair of scales?

Who has guided the spirit of the Lord,/ and what counsellor has taught him?

Nations are like drops of water from a bucket,/ like a grain of sand on the scales;/ islands weigh as light as specks of dust.

The Lebanon does not yield wood enough for fuel,/ or beast for sacrifices.

God is our only hope. Jacob, why do you say, and you, Israel, state,/ "My fate is unknown to the Lord,/ God overlooks my rights?"

Do you not know? Have you not heard it?/ The Lord is the God for ever,/ Creator of the boundaries of the earth,/ he is never tired or weary,/ his intelligence is unmeasurable.

He gives vigour to the weary,/ and comforts the weak.

God will destroy all the enemies of his people. Yes, they shall be ashamed, confused,/ all those who rise against you,/ will be destroyed and will perish,/ those who fight you.

You shall search for them, and you will not find/ those who hate you;/ they will be destroyed, reduced to nothing/ those who fight you.

For I, the Lord, your God,/ will hold your right hand,/ and I will say to you, "Do not be afraid,/ I come to your aid."

Do not be afraid, little worm of Jacob,/ Israel's poor louse;/ It is I who helps you, says the Lord,/ your ransomer is the Holy One of Israel.

Look, I will turn you/ into a sharp threshing-sledge,/ you shall thresh the mountains and crush them,/ the hills shall be reduced to straw.

You shall win them now and the wind shall carry them away,/ the gale shall scatter them;/ but you shall rejoice in the Lord,/ and glory in the Holy One of Israel.

So that they may see and know,/ take into account and know/ that this has been done by the hand of the Lord,/ and has been created by the hand of the Holy One of Israel.

The servant of the Lord[1]. This is my servant, whom I protect,/ my chosen one, my spirit is glad with him./ To him I have given my spirit/ so that he brings the law to the nations.

He will not shout, nor lift up his voice,/ he will not speak in the streets.

He will not break a bruised reed,/ or snuff out a smouldering wick./ He will make justice faithfully.

He will not falter, nor break down,/ until his right has been planted on earth,/ while islands wait for his teaching.

This is the word of the Lord, God,/ who created the skies and stretched them out,/ who fashioned the earth and all that grows in it,/ who gives the breath of life to the people that inhabits it,/ and to the living creatures that live upon it.

I, the Lord, have called you with justice,/ I have taken you by the hand and taught you,/ I have set you as my Covenant with my people/ and light of the nations,

to open the eyes of the blind,/ to bring captives out of prison,/ out of the dark dungeons where they lie.

I am the Lord, this is my name,/ I will not give my glory to any other.

What I foretold in the ancient times has come true,/ and I announce new things,/ I let you know about them before they happen[2].

Song of victory. Sing to the Lord a new song,/ a praise from the ends of the earth;/ let the sea and all that it embraces exult him,/ the islans with all their inhabitants.

---

1. The Messiah will be a peaceful King, beloved by the Lord. The ruler will open his people's eyes and will be a light for the nations, who will obey his laws.

2. In the future His prophecies and promises made to his People came true. He will make a Covenant with God and will give his spirit to the new People of God.

I shall lead the blind through roads they do not know,/ through unknown paths I will guide them;/ I will turn for them darkness into light,/ and rugged plains into plains./ All this is what I am going to do,/ and I will accomplish all of it.

I am your saviour. But now, thus speaks the Lord,/ your Creator, Jacob,/ the one who made you, Israel:/ "Do not be afraid, for I have redeemed you;/ I have called you by your name, you belong to me.

For you are valuable for me,/ you are wonderful and I love you./ Therefore I change men for you,/ and peoples for your life.

Do not be afraid, for I am with you./ I will make your line come from the west/ and I will gather you all from the east."

Israel will still be the people of God. But now listen, Jacob, my servant,/ Israel whom I have chosen. Thus speaks the Lord, your maker,/ who formed you in the mother's womb and comes to your aid:/ "Do not be afraid, Jacob, my servant,/ Israel whom I have chosen."

God wants the absolute monotheism. Thus speaks the Lord, king of Israel,/ its saviour the Lord of Hosts:/ "I am the first and the last,/ there is no other god but me[1]."

The Lord promises the victory over Cyrus. I create light and darkness;/ I give you happiness and misery;/ it is me, the Lord, who does all this."

O heavens, deliver your dew, and let the clouds rain their victory!/ Let the earth burn,/ and heal;/ let justice flourish:/ I, the Lord, have created all this.

Absolute power of God. Woe the man who quarrels with his Creator,/ when he is only a flowerpot! Does the clay say to the potter, "What are you doing?"/ And does his work say to him, "Have you got hands?"

"It is me who created the earth,/ and I have created man on it;/ it is me who has stretched out the skies with my hands,/ and I give orders to its whole army.

---

1. Only God is absolute. Except for God, everything is unimportant and does not lead to him.

I have made him victorious,/ and I have made his roads flat;/ he will rebuilt my city,/ and will bring back my exiles,/ pricelessly and without blackmail," —says the Lord of Hosts.

Fall of Babylon. Come, sit on the dust,/ virgin, daughter of Babylon!/ Sit on the ground, down from your throne,/ daughter of the Chaldaeans,/ for you shall never be called again/ "sweet, delicate".

Sit silent, off into the shadows,/ daughter of the Chaldaeans,/ for you shall never be called again/ "Mistress of Kingdoms".

I am angry with my people,/ I dishonoured my own possession,/ I abandoned it in your hands,/ but you showed no mercy;/ you laid your heavy yoke/ on the aged.

You said, "I will always/ be the queen";/ but you did not consider this,/ nor its end.

But disaster will overcome you,/ and you will not know how to prevent it;/ evil shall come upon you,/ and you will not be able to master it;/ ruin will befall you/ unexpectedly.

So continue with your spells,/ and with your sorcery,/ which you have done since your youth./ You might get some profit,/ maybe even inspire awe!

They all will be like straw/ burned up by fire./ They will not save their lives/ from fire./This is no glowing coal to bake/ or warm them at home.

God chose Cyrus. Listen to me, Jacob,/ and you, Israel, because I have called you:/ It is me, the first one,/ and also the last one.

It was my hand that created the earth,/ and my right hand that stretched out the skies;/ I call them/ and they come.

Assemble yourselves and listen:/ "My friend shall carry out my wish/ against Babylon and the line of the Chaldaeans[1]."

It is me who speaks and calls,/ I have brought him here to carry out his orders.

Invitation to leave Babylon. Leave Babylon,/ flee from the Chaldaeans! Shout joyfully/ and let people know/ here and in

---

1. He treats Cyrus as a friend, although he is a pagan, for he obeys his will to destroy the wicked Babylon. The prophets speack about the future in the present tense.

the whole world!/ Say, "The Lord has redeemed/ his servant Jacob."

There is no peace for the wicked,/ —says the Lord.

The Messiah, servant of the Lord. Listen to me, islands,/ far away peoples:/ The Lord has called me to the womb of my mother,/ he has said my name inside her womb.

He turned my mouth into a sharpened sword/ and kept me by his hand./ He turned me into a sharpened arrow/ and hid me in his pit.

And He says, "To be my servant is not much/ to restablish the tribes of Jacob,/ and bring back Israel's exiles./ I have set you as the light of the peoples,/ to send my salvation/ to the ends of the earth[1]."

The Messiah, master and victim[2]. The Lord has given me/ the tongue of an expert/ so that I can give an answer to the weary./ Every morning my ear wakes me up/ so that I can listen to my master.

The Lord has opened my ears,/ and I have not refused/ I have accepted him.

I have given my back to those who struck me,/ my cheeks to those who touched my beard;/ I have not hid my face/ from insult and of the gobbet of spit.

The Lord comes to my aid/ but I cannot stand this ignominy;/ for I have made my face a flint, and I shall not be deceived.

Israel's salvation. Listen, you who seek justice,/ those who seek the Lord./ Look at the rock from which you were cut,/ the hole from which you were taken.

The Messiah to all the nations. Listen carefully, peoples,/ nations, listen,/ for the law comes from me,/ and my law shall be the light of the peoples[3].

---

1. Ecumenical, universal mission, the Messiah's. He will not only save his People but also all the nations of the world.

2. The Messiah suffered his Passion while he was insulted and tortured.

3. God wants all mankind to be saved and to attain the knowledge of truth. This is his mission.

I will make my justice come down suddenly,/ my salvation shall come up like the light./ My arm is going to judge the peoples./ The islands were waiting for me,/ they trust in my arm.

Look up to the sky,/ and down to the earth;/ the skies shall be scattered like smoke,/ the earth shall be worn up like a dress/ and its inhabitants will perish like mosquitoes;/ but my salvation will be for ever,/ and my justice shall know no end.

The waking of the Lord: "Do not be afraid". So the free men of the Lord shall come back,/ and they will come to Zion joyfully;/ an eternal joy will crown them;/ gladness and joy will come with them,/ sighs and miseries will go away.

A messenger from good announces the salvation to Zion. O, the feet of the messenger are beautiful,/ through the mountains,/ he who announces salvation/ and says to Zion: "Your God will rule over you[1]!"

Listen! Your sentries are shouting,/ shouting with joy,/ because they see the Lord face to face,/ they see the Lord coming back to Zion.

Shout with joy,/ ruins of Jerusalem,/ for the Lord has mercy for his people,/ and redeems Jerusalem.

The Lord stretches out his holy arm,/ to the eyes of all the peoples,/ and throughout the world they will see our God's salvation.

Do not flee,/ do not run away,/ for the Lord shall walk before you,/ and behind you shall walk the God of Israel.

Prophecy of the servant of the Lord. My servant will prosper,/ he will rise and grow highly.

If many people had been terrified at his sight,/ —so disfigured was his face/ that he did not look like a man—, now the kings will shut their mouths when they see him,/ for they will be seeing an event never told before,/ and they will be seeing something unbelievable.

Prophecy of the servant's passion. Who will believe what we are hearing,/ and the arm of the Lord,/ to whom has been shown?

---

1. Like a messenger of the Messiah who brings salvation.

He grew up before him like a child,/ like a root on dry ground./ He was not good-looking,/ his sight caused no delight.

Despised, rejected by mankind,/ man of pains, used to suffering,/ like one who hids his face,/ he was despised and insulted[1].

However, he was bearing our sufferings,/ our pains weighted upon him,/ while we thought he was being flogged,/ hurt and humiliated by God[2].

He has paid for our sins,/ ill-treated because of our iniquities;/ his punishment, the price of our peace/ and we have been healed because of his sores.

All of us, like sheep, walked aimlessly,/ each of us followed his own way./ And the Lord has brought upon him/ the iniquity of all mankind.

He was ill-treated but consented it,/ and he never complained;/ like a sheep taken to the slaughterhouse,/ like a mute calf taken to the shearer,/ without complaint.

He was imprisoned without mercy, who cares for him?/ He was killed,/ deathly wounded because of the sins of my people.

He was prepared a grave among the wicked,/ he was joined to evildoers[3]./ He was never unfair,/ and did never deceive anyone.

But the Lord wanted to kill him with suffering./ If he offers his life in expiation,/ he shall have children, he shall live longer/ and the people with be forgiven on his account.

After the sufferings of his soul,/ he will see the light and will be rewarded./ Because of his sufferings, many people shall be forgiven, for he was a fair man, and will carry on him their iniquities[4].

Therefore I will give him countless children,/ and lots of people as a loot,/ for he has given himself in to death/ and has

---

1. Isaiah describes in one of his visions the Passion of the Saviour. He was so disfigured because of torture that he hardly had human form.
2. He took the pains of mankind upon him to compensate our sins.
3. He was nailed to the cross between the two thieves.
4. He saved us with his death.

been taken for an evildoer;/ who, who was carrying everybody's burden,/ and asked for the evildoer's pardon.

Invitation to the next redemption. Listen and come to me,/ listen to me and your soul will live./ I will make an everlasting Covenant with you,/ as I promised David.

I have set him as a witness for the nations,/ ruler and master of the nations.

Look, you shall call peoples unknown to you,/ and they will come to you,/ because of the Lord, you God,/ and of the Holy One of Israel, who glorifies you.

Search for the Lord while he can be found,/ call Him while he is near.

Let the evildoer leave his ways,/ and the wicked his ideas;/ let them turn to the Lord, who shall be merciful to him,/ to our God, who is so full of mercy.

For my thoughts are not your thoughts,/ nor my ways your ways/ —says the Lord—.

As the sky rises upon the earth,/ so far are my ways from yours,/ and my thoughts from yours.

And as rain and snow fall from heaven,/ and do not come back without making the seeds grow,/ so that the sower may have bread,

so does the word that comes out of my mouth,/ it does not come back to me/ without doing what I wished/ and achieving its aim[1].

---

1. The word of the Lord is always successful. Only one word of His created the vault. Only one word of His healed and resuscitated the dead.

PART THREE

THE MESSIANIC KINGDOM

The universal kingdom. These are the words of the Lord,/ "Keep my commandments and be just/ for my salvation is about to come,/ and my justice is about to be revealed to you.

Against the bad shepherds. All our watchmen are blind,/ they do not understand anything;/ they are like mute dogs/ they cannot bark;/ they are always dreaming,/ they only want to sleep.

Hungry dogs;/ shepherds who do not understand,/ they only go their way,/ seeking their profit.

Promise of forgiveness. And people shall say,/ "Leave, leave the way,/ remove every stone from the road of my people!"

For these are the words of the Most Hight, the Only One,/ who lives in his eternal dwelling/ and whose name is holy,/ "I live in a sweet and holy dwelling,/ but I am with the repentant and with the humble man too,/ to give them strength."

The true religion. Shout up wihout fear,/ sing as the bugle./ Tell my people their iniquities, tell the house of Jacob about their sins.

Glory of the new Jerusalem. Arise, brighten the sky, for your light is coming/ and the glory of the Lord is rising behind you.

The nations shall walk in your light,/ and the kings shall follow the brightness of your dawn.

Look up and see,/ how they all gather and come to you,/ your sons come from far away lands,/ and your daughters are brought by the arm.

When you see this you shall be happy,/ you heart whall be filled with emotion,/ for the treasures of the sea will come to you/ with the wealth of the nations.

Thousands of camels shall come to you,/ dromedaries from Midian and Epha,/ they will all come from Sheba,/ bringing incense and gold,/ and praising the glory of the Lord.

Who are those who fly like a cloud/ like a dove to her dovecot?

Yes, the ships assemble for me,/ and before them the ships from Tarzi,/ to bring your sons to you,/ with their gold and silver,/ for the name of the Lord your God,/ for the Holy One of Israel, your splendour.

Announcement of the Year of Grace. The spirit of the Lord is within me,/ because the Lord has anointed me./ He has sent me to tell the good news to the poor,/ to heal the miserable hearts,/ to tell the captives about freedom;

to proclaim a year of grace of the Lord,/ a day of vengeance for our God./ To comfort the heartbroken[1].

Future glory. As the land grows its seeds,/ as a garden grows its plants,/ so does the Lord grow justice, and glory in all nations.

The true worship of the Lord. These are the words of the Lord,/ "Heaven is my throne,/ and the earth the low stool under my feet./ Where could you build me a house/ where I could rest?"

Conversion of the peoples. I will come to gather the peoples of all languages, and they shall come and see my glory.

For, as the new heaven/ and the new earth which I have created/ live on thanks to me —says the Lord—,/ so shall your line and name survive.

---

1. The Prophet Isaiah is the figure of Jesus Christ himself, whose mission was to announce the Good News to the poor, heal the sick, release the captives, etc. Gospel of Grace and Mercy.

JEREMIAH[1]

PROLOGUE

Jeremiah's vocation and mission. The word of the Lord came to me and said,

"Before I formed you in the womb I knew you;/ before you were born I consecrated you;/ I appointed you a prophet to the nations."

I said, "O Lord God, I cannot speak; I am a child!" But the Lord said to me,

"Do not say: 'I am a child!'/ For you shall go whatever people I send you to/ and say whatever I tell you to say./ Do not be afraid of them,/ for I will keep you safe./ Word of the Lord."

And the Lord stretched out his hand, touched my mouth and said,

"I will put my words in your mouth:/ Look, this day I give you authority over nations and over kingdoms,/ to pull down and uproot,/ to destroy and to demolish,/ to built and to plant."

---

1. Jeremiah (Hebrew = the Lord comforts) was born in Anathot in a family of priests. He was a prophet for forty years exclusively in Jerusalem before and after its destruction.

REPROVAL OF THE JEWS

Infidelity of the people towards the Lord. The word of the Lord came to me and said, "Go, make a proclamation in Jerusalem:

Listen to the words of the Lord,/ house of Jacob,/ and all the families of the house of Israel./ These are the words of the Lord,/ What fault did your forefathers find in me/ that they wandered far from me?/ They pursued vanity and/ they became empty beings.

I brought you to a true country,/ for you to enjoy its fruits and goods./ But you, as you entered, you defiled it,/ you made the home I gave you loathsome.

O heaven, are you not amazed?/ Tremble!/ says the Lord./ My people has committed double iniquity:/ he has abandoned me,/ the well of living water,/ to dig pits, cracked pits,/ which do not retain water.

Is Israel a slave[1],/ a slave born at home,/ that he has been despoiled?/ Lions have roared and growled at him./ Its land has been laid waste,/ its cities razed and abandoned./ Even the sons of Noph and Tahpanhes[2]/ have shaved your head./ Has all this not happened to you/ because you forsake the Lord your God/ when he showed you his way?

Degradation will be punished. Like a shameful thief when he is caught,/ thus shall be punished the men of the house of Israel,/ they, their kings and their masters./ Their priests and their prophets,/ who say to the log: "You bore me"./ They show me their backs and not their faces,/ but when they suffer they call out to me:/ "Come and save us!"/ Where are the Gods who made you?/ Let them come to see if they can save you/ when you are in affliction!/ For your gods, O Judah/ are so numerous as your cities.

The kingdoms of Israel and Judah rebel against the Lord. The Lord told me in king Josiah's time: "Have you seen

---

1. A man born free could recover his freedom, but the son of a slave was a slave for ever.
2. Noph was Memphis, and Tahpanhes a harbour in the delta.

what Israel the rebel is doing? He has gone up to the hills, and he has worshipped foreign gods under every tree. I thought: 'After doing all this, he shall come back to me.' But he did not. And Judah, his wicked sister, has witnessed it all. She has seen that I rejected Israel because of all his betrayals. But his sister Judah was not amazed; she has betrayed me too. She has violated the earth with the shame of her betrayal: she has betrayed me with the stone and the log[1].

And so Judah, his wicked sister, has not come back to me wholeheartedly, but with lies" —says the Lord.

"Come back, you, rebel Israel, says the Lord,/ I will not turn my face away from you,/ for I am merciful, says the Lord./ I will not be angry with you for ever./ Only recognize your iniquity;/ you have rebelled against the Lord, your God, you have worshipped foreign gods/ and have not listened to my words, says the Lord."

Judah and Israel, a unique kingdom in messianic times. Come back, you rebel sons —says the Lord—, for I am your master: I will choose one of every city and two of every family, and I will lead you to Zion. I will give you the shepherds whom my heart wants to grant you; they will look after you with patience and wisdom when you have children and multiply in the country in those days, —says the Lord.

Invitation to embrace the Lord. A shout is heard in the hills;/ the sons of Israel plea and cry,/ for they have lost their way,/ they have forsaken the Lord, their god./ Come back, rebel sons,/ I will heal your rebellious spirit,/ Here we are, we come to you,/ because you are the Lord, our god,/ O yes, hills are deceitful,/ as the mountains./ Actually only the Lord, our God,/ is Israel's salvation.

You can come back if you want. If you want to come back O Israel,/ —says the Lord—,/ you must come back to me,/ you must come back to me,/ if you want to stop being abominable in my sight, you shall not wander far from me./ If you swear an oath for the life of the Lord,/ truly, fairly and righteously,/ nations shall be happy with Him,/ and they will find glory in

---

1. Stone and wood pillars.

Him./ For this is the word of the Lord/ to the people of Judah and Jerusalem.

Sudden punishment: the invasion of the Chaldaeans[1]. Proclaim this in Judah,/ make in known in Jerusalem,/ blow the trumpets throughout the country,/ shout at the top of your voices and say:/ Come together and let us come into the walled cities!/ Rise a sign towards Zion,/ flee, do not stop!/ For I am going to bring misery upon the North,/ a great calamity./ The lion advances through the bushes,/ the destroyer of nations sets out./ He leaves his home/ to turn your country in to a desert./ Your cities shall be destroyed,/ their inhabitants will perish./

Vision of a wiped-off Palestine[2]. Yes, this is the word of the Lord:/ The whole country shall be wiped off,/ I will carry out a complete destruction./ And the earth shall mourn on his account,/ and heavens will darken./ For I have decided this, and I will not repent;/ I have not decided and shall not go back./ Against the shout of the cavalry and the arrows,/ all the cities flee./ People hide in the woods,/ they go up the rocks./ The city is completely empty; not a soul could be found./ And you, Palestine, wiped off as you are, what are you going to do?

Reasons for the punishments. Wander by the streets of Jerusalem,/ look, take notice,/ search its squares;/ you must find a man,/ only one, who is righteous,/ who is in search of truth:/ then I will forgive this city.

I will bring a faraway nation/ upon you,/ O house of Israel —says the Lord—;/ an unbeatable nation,/ an old nation,/ whose language you do not know,/ and whose speech you cannot understand./ Her pit is like an open grave:/ they are an army of heroes!/ She will devour your harvest and your bread;/ your sons and daughters,/ your calves and cows,/ your vineyards and figs./ She will wipe off your fortified cities,/ in which you trust so much.

---

1. The Assyrian armies, agents of the Lord's justice, continue their incursions into the Northern part of the country.
2. The prophecy will come true. Description of Judah and its devastation by the raiders.

However, —says the Lord—, even in those days I shall not destroy you completely. And when they ask, "Why the Lord our God has done all this to us?", he will answer, "As you have forsaken me to worship foreing gods in your own country, so shall you worship them in a foreign country."

Vision of the invader marching in. This is the word of the Lord,/ "Look, a people is coming from the Norh./ They have bows and swords,/ they are cruel, merciless./ Their shout is a great roar, like the sea,/ they ride horses./ They are prepared for battle/ against you, daughter of Zion./ We have heard the news,/ our arms have fallen down,/ we are afraid,/ like a woman when she gives birth./ Do not go into the open country,/ do not walk by the roads,/ for the sword of the enemy is there,/ terror everywhere./ Daughter of my people, put on your sackcloth,/ throw ashes upon your head,/ mourn your only child,/ cry bitterly./ For the invaders will fall upon us/ suddenly.

Frightening vision. Then —says the Lord—, the bones of the kings of Judah, her kings, her prophets and those of the inhabitants of Jerusalem shall be removed from their graves. They will be scattered under the son, the moon and all the hosts of heaven to whom they loved, serven and followed, and to those whom they consulted and worshipped. They will not be gathered nor buried, they will remain on the earth like dung. And death will be better than life for those who survive in this wicked race, everywhere whete I have put them —says the Lord of Hosts.

They all go for battle,/ as a horse flies where the battle is most fierce.

Do not trust in the Law if you do not follow its commandments. Even the stork in the sky/ knows the time to migrate,/ the dove and the swift and the wryneck/ know the season of return./ But my people do not know/ the Law of the Lord./ How can you say, "We are wise,/ we have the Law of the Lord?"/ They scribes with their lying pens/ have falsified it./ Wise men are put to shame,/ dismayed and have lost their wits./ They have dismissed the word of the Lord,/ what wisdom can they possess?/ Therefore I will give their wives to other men,/ their field to other owners./ For their are full of ill-gotten gain,/

all of them, high and low/ prophet and priest,/ they are frauds./ They heal my people's wound, but superficially, saying: Peace, peace!/ And there is no peace./ They should be ashamed/ of their abominable actions:/ but they are shameless now./ I will send them a people to destroy them.

Ruin without remedy. Why do we sit idle?/ Up, all of you together,/ let us go into the walled cities/ to die in them,/ for the Lord our God has struck us down,/ he gives us poisoned water[1],/ for we have sinned against him./ We expected peace, and no good has come;/ we expected a time of prosper, and terror came./The snorting of his horses is heard from Dan,/ at the neighing of the stallins/ the whole land trembles./ They came to devour land and goods,/ the city and its inhabitants./ I am overcome with sorrow,/ I am sick at heart./ The cry of the daughter of my people is heard throughout the country./ "Why is the Lord not in Zion?/ Her king is no more there?"/ Why have them provoked me with their images,/ with their foreign gods?/ Why have they not saved themselves before?/ O that somebody would turn my head into a well/ and my eyes into a stream of water,/ to weep day and night,/ for the dead of the daughter of my people!

Grief of the prophet for Judah's doom. O that I could find in the desert/ a shelter by the wayside!/ Then I would leave my people/ and depart/ for they are all adulterers,/ a mob of traitors./ The tongue is their weapon, a bow ready bent/ with lying, not with truth,/ which is the master in this land./ Yes, they go from one sin to another,/ and they do not know me, says the Lord./ They are sold, they cannot come back to me!/ They do not want to know me/ —says the Lord.

Therefore, this is the word of the Lord of Hosts,/ "I will assay them:/ What else can I do/ with the daughter of my people?/ Her tongue is like a poisonous arrow,/ she only utters lies./ She speaks amicably to another,/ while inwardly she plans a trap for him./ Shall I not punish them for this?/ —says the Lord—/ shall I not take vengeance/ on such a people"/ Over the mountains will I raise weeping and wailing,/ and elegy over

---

1. Enemies used to poison water.

the desert pastures,/ for they are scorched,/ and untrodden/ and the herds cannot be heard any more.

Birds and beasts/ have fled and are gone./ And I will make Jerusalem/ a heap of ruins,/ a haunt of wolves,/ and the cities of Judah an unpeopled waste./ Is there a wise man who can understand me?

Fidelity to the Covenant. The house of Israel and the house of Judah have broken the Covenant which I made with their forefathers. Therefore this is the word of the Lord, "I will send them a great crash, and they will not be able to flee; they will cry out to me, but I will not listen. Then the cities of Judah and the inhabitants of Israel can go and ask for help to the gods to whom they have burnt incense.

God's answer: do not intercede for this people. Those prophets who speak on my behalf without my consent and who think that in this country there will not be sword nor hunger, they will be put to the sword and starve[1].

And the people to which they make their prophecies shall be scattered into the streets of Jerusalem/ victims of hunger and sword/ and there will be no one to bury them, nor them nor their wives, sons and daughters./ I will let their own iniquity fall upon them.

You shall tell them this,/ "My eyes are full of tears/ night and day/ for the great crash which will destroy/ the virgin, the daughter of my people,/ because of her inmense wound.

When I go into the open field,/ I see nothing but dead;/ When I go into the city/ I see people starving./ Even prophets and priests/ wander throughout the country: they do not know it!"/ Have you dismissed Judah completely/ has your soul dismissed Zion?/ Why has you wounded us/ hopelessly?/ We expected peace, and nothing good is coming;/ we expected heal,/ and there is terror everywhere!"

---

1. The false prophets to deceive the people.

EXECUTION OF THE SENTENCE

Jeremiah's answer to Zedekiah's messengers. The word which came from the Lord to Jeremiah when King Zedekiah sent to him Pashhur son of Malchiah and Zephaniah the priest, son of Maaseiah, with this request: "Nebuchadnezzar king of Babylon is making war on us; inquire of the Lord on our behalf. Perhaps the Lord will perform a miracle as he has done in past times, so that our enemies flee." Jeremiah said to him, "You shall say this to Zedekiah, 'This is the word of the Lord, God of Israel: I will turn back upon you your own weapons with which you are fighting the king of Babylon and the Chaldaeans besieging you outside the wall, and I will bring them into the heart of this city. And I myself will fight against you in great fury, with an outstretched hand and a strong arm. I will strike down the inhabitants of this city, both men and beasts, with a great pestilence, and they shall perish. Then, says the Lord, I will take Zedekiah, king of Judah, his courtiers and the inhabitants of this city who have survived this pestilence and hand them over to Nebuchadnezzer without mercy, pity or compassion.' And you shall say to this people, 'This is the word of the Lord: Look, I offer you a choice between the way of life and the road of death. Those who remain in the city shall be put to the sword, starve or die by pestilence. Those who leave and surrender to the Chaldaeans besieging you shall survive'."

Against Israel's false prophets. Shame on the shephers who let the sheep of my flock scatter and be lost! Therefore, this is the word of the Lord, God of Israel, about the shepherds who guide my people: "You have scattered my flock, you have dispersed them. But now I will punish you —says the Lord— for your evildoings.

The future good shepherd[1]. I will gather the remnant of my sheep from all the lands to which I have dispersed them, and I will bring them back to their homes, where they shall be fruitful and increase. I will appoint shepherds to tend them; They shall

---

1. The good shepherd is the figure of Jesus Christ the Good Shepherd, who was of the line of David, Son of David.

never again know fear or dismay, and none of them shall ever be lost again —says the Lord.

The days are coming —says the Lord—/ in which I will make a righteous branch spring from David's line,/ and he shall rule as a true king, wisely,/ maintaing law and justice in the land./ Judah will be saved in his days,/ and Israel will live undisturbed./ And this man shall be called,/ The Lord is our Righteousness.

The days are coming —says the Lord— in which it shall not be said, "By the life of the Lord who brought Israel up from Egypt." But, "By the life of the Lord who brought the descendants of the Israelites back from a northern land and from all the lands to which he had dispersed them to live again on their own soil."

Announcement of the seventy years of exile. This is the word of the Lord to Jeremiah regarding the people of Judah, on the fourth year of Joachim, son of Josiah, king of Judah, that is, in the first year of Nebuchadnezzar, king of Babylon. The prophet Jeremiah made it known to all the people of Judah and to all the inhabitants of Jerusalem by saying, "All this country will be destroyed, and people shall live as slaves for seventy years. When they are over, I will visit the king of Babylon and that country —says the Lord— because of their iniquity, as I did with the Chaldaeans, and I will wipe them off for ever[1]. I will carry out against this country all that I have foretold, all that is written in this book.

Punishment of the nations. Prophecies of Jeremiah against all nations. For also they will be submitted by powerful nations and great kings, and I will punish them according to their deeds and actions.

Jeremiah's letter to the captives. This is the contents of the letter which prophet Jeremiah sent from Jerusalem to the elders in captivity, to the priests, prophets and to all the people who Nebuchadnezzar had deported from Jerusalem to Babylon after leaving Jerusalem. "This is the word of the Lord of Hosts, God

---

1. Its ruins were covered by the sand of the desert, and they remained undiscovered up to the last century.

of Israel, to all the captives, exiles from Jerusalem in Babylon:
Build houses and live in them, grow vegetables and eat them;
marry and have children; marry your children so that they can
be fruitful and multiply, so that you do not decrease in number.
Care for the nation to which I have deported you and pray for
her to the Lord, for her prosperity shall also be yours. Therefore
this is the word of the Lord of Hosts, God of Israel: Do not let
yourself be seduced by the prophets among you nor by your
soothsayers[1]; do not believe the dreams that they tell you, for
they do not speak on my behalf. I have not sent them" —says
the Lord.

This is the word of the Lord, "When a full seventy years has
passed over babylon, I will take up your cause and fulfil the
promise of good things I made to you, by bringing you back to
this place. I alone know my purpose for you, —says the Lord-,
prosperity and not misfortune, and a long line of children after
you. If you invoke me and pray to me, I will listen to you.

Promise of restoration. This is the word of the Lord to
Jeremiah: "This is the word of the Lord, God of Israel, Write in
a book all that I have said to you, for the time is coming —says
the Lord— when I will restore the fortunes of my people Israel
and Judah —says the Lord—; I will bring them back to the land
of their forefathers; and it shall be their possession." These are
the words of the Lord regarding Israel and Judah[2].

In that day —says the Lord of Hosts— I will break their
yoke off their necks and snap their cords. They will not be used
by foreigners any more, they will serve the Lord their God and
David, the king whom I will appoint for them.

Israel will come back to his land. Then —says the Lord—/
I will be the God of all families of Israel,/ and they shall be my
people./ This is the word of the Lord:/ In the desert they have
found grace/ the people has escaped from the sword./ Israel
goes to his rest./ The Lord has appeared to them in the distance./
I have always loved you,/ therefore you still have my favour.

---

1. The exiles fell into ignorance, and they were easily deceived by false prophets.
2. Jerusalem will be restored, but Nineveh and Babylon will disappear for ever.

I will built you again,/ O virgin of Israel,/ you will ornate yourself again with your tambourines,/ and you will dance again with joy./ You will plant vineyards/ in the hills of Samaria,/ people shall plant and harvest./ Yes, a day will come in which the sentries / will shout in the hill of Ephraim:/ "Come, let us go up to Zion,/ towards the Lord, our God!"/ This is the word of the Lord,/ "Shout with joy up for Jacob,/ for the first of the nations!"/ Say it to everybody, say,/ "the Lord has saved his people, the remnants of Israel[1]!"

And I bring them/ from the northern countries/ and I gather them from the edges of the earth./ They are all here; the lame and the blind,/ the pregnant wife and the woman giving birth;/ a great crowd coming back here./ They had left in tears,/ now I bring them back with mercy,/ by the streams,/ by a flat way,/ where they cannot fall./ For I am like a father for Israel,/ Ephraim is my first-born.

Then the maiden shall dance joyfully,/ young and old will live happily./ I will turn their mourning into joy,/ I will comfort them after their suffering./ I will give lots of grease to the priests,/ and my people shall be filled with my goods/ —says the Lord.

God's answer to Jeremiah. Then the word of the Lord came to Jeremiah, and He said to him, "Look, I am the Lord, the God of all mortal men: Is there anything impossible for me? Therefore this is the word of the Lord, I am going to hand this city over to the Chaldaeans and Nebuchadnezzar, king of Babylon, and he shall take it. The Chaldaeans who are besieging the city will burn it up, they will put its houses to the fire, on whose terraces sacrifices to Baal have been offered and they have worshipped foreign gods to make me angry. For the sons of Israel and Judah are evildoers from the beginning; yes, the sons of Israel have done no more than irritate me with their deeds —says the Lord—. Therefore this city is the target of my anger since the day of its foundation until nowadays, and I will come and wipe it off my sight, because of all the iniquities

---

1. Those who came back from captivity were the remnants which the Lord kept of the people of Judah to make up the new People of God.

which the sons of Israel and Judah have commited to arise my
anger, they and their kings, princes, priests, prophets, men of
Judah and inhabitants of Jerusalem[1]. They have shown me the
sword and not their faces, and while I tried to teach and educate
them insistingly they have refused to listen and to learn the
lesson. They have committed abominations even in my Temple
and have profaned it. They have built high places for Baal in the
valley of Ben-hinnon, to sacrifice their sons and daughters to
Moloc. I had never commanded such a thing, I had never
thought of such an abomination to make Judah sin. But now,
this is the word of the Lord, God of Israel, regarding this city, of
which you say, 'It has been handed over to the king of Babylon
by the sword, by hunger and by pestilence.' I will gather them
from all the countries where my anger has sent them. I will
bring them back to their place, where they will live in peace.
They will be my people and I will be their God, and I will give
them a new heart and a new way, so that they fear me for their
own good and their children's. And I will make an everlasting
covenant with them.

Everlasting kingdom and priesthood of the Messiah.
"The day is coming —says the Lord—, in which I will fulfil the
promise I made to the house of Israel and the house of Judah.

Then I will give David a son[2], a fair man who will be just
with the country. In those days Judah shall be saved, and
Jesuralem will live in peace; and this shall be his name: "The
Lord is our Justice."

Fall of Jerusalem and end of Zedekiah. In the ninth year
of Zedekiah, king of Judah, in the tenth month, Nebuchadnezzar
king of Babylon came with all his army against Jerusalem and
besieged it. In the eleventh year of Zedekiah, on the ninth day of
the fourth month, they broke into the city. And all the
commanders of the king of Babylon came in, and pinched

---

1. His People's abominations ended God's patience, and he will punish them.
   But in the end the Lord will have mercy on them.
2. The son whom God shall give David will be the Messiah, the long hoped-for
   of the nations after the destruction of Jerusalem. Meanwhile the prophecies
   were fulfiled.

their tents by the middle gate: Nergalsarezer of Simmagir, Nebusarseking the chief eunuch, Nergalsarezer the comander of the fromtiner troops and all the other officers of the king of Babylon. When Zedekiah king of Judah saw them and all the fighting men fled by night through the king's guard, through the gate called Between the Two Walls, taking the road to Arabah. But the troops of the Chaldaeans pursued them and overtook Zedekiah in the desert of Jericho. They took him as a prisoner before Nebuchadnezzar, king of Babylon at Riblah[1] in the land of Hamath, where he pleaded his case before him. The king of Babylon slew Zedekiah's sons before his eyes at Riblah; he also put to death the nobles of Judah. Then Zedekiah's eyes were put out, and he was bound in fetters of bronze to be brought to Babylon. The Chaldaeans burnt the royal palace and the house of the Lord and the houses of the people, and pulled down the walls of Jerusalem. Nebuzaradan captain of the bodyguard deported to Babylon the rest of the people left in the city, those who had deserted to him and any remaining artisans. He left behind the weakest class of the people, those who owned nothing at all, and made them vine-dressers and labourers.

Jeremiah is set free. As for Jeremiah, Nebuchadnezzar king of Babylon had given the following orders to Nebuzaradan captain of the guard, "Take him and care for him; do not do him any harm, but do for him whatever he says." Therefore Nebuzaradan chief of the guard, Nebushazban the chief eunuch, Nergalsarezer the commander of the chief troops and other officers of the king of Babylon fetched Jeremiah from the court of the guard-hosue and handing him over to Gedaliah[2] son of Ahikan, son of Shaphan, to take him out to the Residence. So he stayed with his own people.

They fled taking Jeremiah and Baruch with them. But Johanan son of Kareah, the captains of the armed bands and the people did not obey the commandment of the Lord of staying in

---

1. Riblah, Nebuchadnezzar's headquarters, by the river Oronteh, in Minor Asia.
2. The governor left by the Chaldaeans for the people who was left in Jerusalem. He was murdered two months later.

Judah[1]. So Johanan son of Charea and all the armed bands took all the remnants of Judah who had come back from the nations where they were scattered to live in their own land: men, women, children, princesses and all those who were left by Nebuzaradan chief of the guard with Gedoliah son of Ahikam son of Shaphan. They also took prophet Jeremiah and Baruch son of Neriah, and they came into the land of Egypt. Thus they disobeyed the word of the Lord and came to Taphnis[2].

---

1. Those who were left were afraid of the Chaldaean's vengeance and fled to Egypt.
2. On the delta, at that time Pharaoh's main city.

JEREMIAH'S LAMENTATIONS AND ELEGIES[1]

FIRST LAMENTATION

Jerusalem Desolate

How solitary lies the city, once so full of people!
>The great among the nations has become now a widow.
>The queen among provinces has been put to forced labour.

The roads to Zion mourn, for none attend her sacred feasts; all her gates are desolate, her priests sight, her maidens cry bitterly.

The oppresors have taken all their treasures; and she has seen the gentiles come into her Sanctuary, those to whom You had forbidden to enter your community.

All her people sight, looking for a loaf of bread; they give their jewelry for food to be alive. "Look, O Lord, and see how cheap I am accounted!"

---

1. They consist of five elegies about Jerusalem's destruction. In them Jeremiah tells about his sorrow and suffering. He asks the Almighty for mercy and asks for Penitence.

Those of you who pass by, look and see if there is any agony
lile mine, the agony with which the anger of the Lord
has struck me.

I weep every day, my tears run down my eyes, for the one
who will comfort me is far from me, the one who will
restore me. My children are desolate because the enemy
has defeated us.

But the Lord was in the right; for I was I who rebelled against
his laws. O listen, you peoples, and see my agony; my
maidens and young people have gone into captivity!

Look, O Lord, my angony! My stomach turns within me.

SECOND LAMENTATION

The Lord's wrath against Jerusalem

What darkness the Lord in his anger has brought upon the
daughter of Zion!

The Lord has despised his altar, he loathes his Sanctuary; he
had handed his palaces into the hands of his enemies,
shouts were heard in the Temple of the Lord, as on a
day of festival!

The Lord has decided to pull down the wall of the daughter of
Zion; he has mourned for the walls, and they perish
together.

Its gates lay on the ground; he broke their locks. Their king
and princes are among the people, There is no law!
Even their prophets have no visions from the Lord!

The inhabitants' bad conditions

They are sitting on the ground, and the elders of the daughter
of Zion are mute; the maidens of Jerusalem bow their
heads to the ground.

To whom shall I compare you? To whom shall you look like,
O daughter of Jerusalem? Who will save and comfort
you, O virgin daughter of Zion? Your ruin is wide as
the sea, who will heal you?

Your prophets had visions for you which were lies and
deceits. And they did not tell you your sin, to keep you
far from exile; they announced visions of lie, deceit and
wickedness.

All those who pass by snap their fingers at you; they hiss and
wag their heads at you, daughter of Jerusalem: "Is this
the city once called Perfect in beauty, Joy of the whole
earth?"

Lord, look and bear this in mind

O virgin daughter of Zion, shout up to the Lord, cry day and
night.

Up! Shout in the night; offer your heart to the Lord; stretch
out your arms to Him for your children who are
starving in the squares.

Children and elders laid on the ground; my maids and young
people were put to the sword; you sew death in the day
of your wrath, you have murdered without mercy!

THIRD LAMENTATION

Never ending disasters

I am the man who has known affliction, the road of the Lord's
wrath.

He has led me, he has made me wander in darkness, without
light.

He has barred my road with blocks of stone and tangled up
my way.

He lies in wait for me like a bear or a lion lurking in a covert.

He has struck his bow and made me the target for his arrows.

He has pierced my kidneys with shafts drawn from his quiver.

We were rebels and sinners

Let us examine our behaviour, and let us come back to the
Lord.

He has destroyed us before the other peoples.
All our enemies have opened their mouths against us.
Our fate has been terror and grave, murder and ruin.
Streams of tears flow from my eyes for the ruin of the
　　　daughter of my people.

You have heard my voice

They threw my life into a pit, and they threw stones upon me.
Waters covered my head, and I said, "I am lost!"
I called you name, O Lord, from the pit.
You heard my voice, "Do not shut your ears from my prayer."
The day in which I called you you came to me and said, "Do
　　　not be afraid."

FOURTH LAMENTATION

Hunger

How dulled is the gold, how tarnished the fine gold! The
　　　stones of the sanctuary lie strewn at every street corner!
The sons of Zion, once worth their weight in finest gold, now
　　　counted as pitchers of earthenware, made by any
　　　potter's hand!
Even jackals uncover the teat and suckle their young; but the
　　　daughters of my people are cruel as ostriches in the
　　　desert.
Those who once fed delicately are desolate in the streets.
The punishment of my people is worse than the penalty of
　　　Sodom, which was overthrown in a moment and no one
　　　wrung his hands.
The Lord gluttered his rage and poured forth his anger; he
　　　kindled a fire in Zion and it consumed its foundations.

Sins and punishments of the chiefs

The Lord showed no favour to priest, no pity for the elders.

Still we strain our eyes, looking in vain for help. We have
    watched and watched for a nation powerless to save us.

When we go out, we take to by-ways to avoid the public
    streets; our days are all but finished, our end has come.

Our pursuers have shown themselves swifter than vultures in
    the sky; they are hot on our trail over the hills, they
    lurk to catch us in the desert.

Rejoice and be glad, daughter of Edom, you who live in the
    land of Uz! The cup shall pass to you in your turn.

FIFTH LAMENTATION

Prophet Jeremiah's prayer

Remember, O Lord, what has befallen us, look and see how
    we are scorned.

Our patrimony is turned over to strangers and our homes to
    foreigners.

Slaves give orders to us, and nobody sets us free from them.

We bring in our food from the desert, risking our lives in the
    scorching heat.

Our skins are blackened as in a furnace by the ravages of
    starvation.

Women were raped in Zion, virgins raped in the cities of
    Judah.

Elders have left off their sessions in the gate, and young men
    no longer pluck the strings.

Joy has fled from our hearts, and our dances are turned to
    mourning.

The garlands have fallen from our heads; woe betide us,
    sinners that we are!

For this we are sick at heart, for all this our eyes grow dim:

for Mount Zion is desolate and over it the jackals run wild.

But you, O Lord, are enthroned for ever, from one generation
    to another.

O Lord, turn us back to yourself, and we will come back;
    renew our days as in times long past,

for if you have utterly rejected us, then great indeed has been
you anger against us!

THE BOOK OF BARUCH[1]

EXHORTATION AND PROMISES

God's wisdom, the only salvation

Listen O Israel, to the commandments of life, listen so that
     you may learn wisdom.
O Israel, why are you in the land of your enemies, you grow
     old in a foreign land, you have been contaminated by
     death, among those who go down to the Sheol.
Have you forsaken the well of wisdom? if you had followed
     the ways of God, you would have lived in peace
     eternally.
O Israel how great is the dwelling-place of God, how wide its
     properties!
It is great, and limitless, great and immense.
There were born the giants, the famous giants of the old times,
     high and experts in war[2].
But they were not chosen by God; he did not show them the
     way to wisdom, and so they perished.
The stars are bright in heaven with joy; He calls them and
     they answer: here we are, and they are bright for their
     Maker.

---

1. Baruch (Hebrew = blessed), Jeremiah's assistant and reader of his oracles
before the people and the gentiles.
2. The Anakites, inhabitants of Hebron who were expelled by the Israelites in the
conquest of Canaan.

She is the book of the commandments of God, the Law who
    remains for ever: all those who keep it will achieve life,
    but those who forsake it shall perish.
Jacob, come back and hold to it, follow its light.
Do not give your glory to another, nor your dignity to a
    foreign nation.
We are happy, Israel, for we have been told what is liked by
    the Lord.

Jerusalem exhorts and comforts her sons

Take heart, my people, memorial of Israel!
You have been sold to the nations, but not to be exterminated,
    but because you made God angry. That is why you
    have been delivered into your enemies' hands.
For you have irritated your Maker, offering sacrifices to the
    devil and not to God.
I had grown then up with joy, and I have seen them leave
    with suffering and sorrow[1].
Do not rejoice in me, because I am a widow, and have been
    abandoned by so many. I am alone because of my sons'
    sins, for they forsook the law of God. They did not
    obey its commandments, nor followed the paths of
    discipline according to its justice.
Come the neighbours of Zion! Remember how my children
    are captive, as the Eternal one commanded them.
For it was Him who brought a foreign nation upon them, a
    daring nation which had a strange speech, who did not
    spare the elders nor children, and took away the
    widow's first borns, and he left her desolate, without
    her daughters.

I wait for your salvation

And I, how can I help you[2]?

---

1. Leaving for the exile in Babylon.
2. Jerusalem, personified, is speaking to its neighbouring cities.

The one who brought misery upon you shall deliver you from
        you enemies.

Follow, my sons, your path! I will stay all alone.

Take heart, my sons, call to the Lord. He will set you free
        from the tyrant, he will deliver you from your enemies[1].

I have seen you leave with sorrow and mourning, but the Lord
        shall bring you back to me with joy and gladness for
        ever.

And as Zion's neighbours see you now captives, so they will
        soon see your salvation by God, who shall come with
        great glory and the splendour of the Eternal one.

My sons, bear with patience God's anger; you enemies have
        pursued you, but you shall soon see their fall.

My most cared-for children have had to walk by hard roads,
        they have been taken as a flock taken by the enemy.

Take heart, my sons, call to the Lord: for he who has
        punished you shall remember you; and if your only sin
        has been to forsake God come back to him now, and
        look for him ten times more eagerly.

For he who brought misery upon you shall bring you, together
        with salvation, joy for ever.

Comfort the the city's prophet

Take heart, Jerusalem, the One who gave you a name shall
        comfort you[2].

Woe betide those who ill-treated you, and who rejoiced in
        your fall!

Woe betide the cities to which your children served, woe
        betide those cities which received your children.

For as they rejoiced in your fall and celebrated your ruin they
        shall be sad for their devastation.

I will take them the joy of their numerous people, and their
        joy shall turn to mourning.

---

1. The message is announcing salvation.
2. Various messianic names.

Look West, Jerusalem[1], and see the joy that comes from God.

Look, your sons come back, those whom you saw leaving,
   they come back together from the west to the east, by
   the word of the Holy One, joyful at the glory of God.

Jerusalem, stop your mourning and sorrow and dress you up
   for the magnificence of the glory that comes to you
   from God.

Put on the cloak of justice of God, crown your head with the
   garland of glory of the Eternal One.

For God shall show his splendour to all the nations under
   heaven.

For the Lord will name you for ever, "Peace of Justice" and
   "Glory of mercy."

Up, Jerusalem, go up, look west[2].

---

1. They come back from the West, from Babylon.
2. From the West, on the Mount of the Olive-tree, she welcomes those who come
   back from exile.

EZEKIEL[1]

PART ONE

PROPHECIES UP TO
JERUSALEM'S FALL

PROLOGUE

Ezekiel's prophetic mission. The voice said to me, "Son of man, stand up for I am going to speak to you." He said to me, "Son of man, I send you to the sons of Israel, a people of rebels who have rebelled against me; they and their forefathers have always sinned against me up to this very day. Sons of bronze hace and hard heard are those to whom I send you. You shall tell them this: This is the word of the Lord God. Whether they listen or not —for they are a race of rebels—, they will know that there is a prophet among them.

And you, son of man, do not be afraid from them or fear their words. Do not be afraid, although you are among bushes and live among scorpions. Do not fear their words nor their

---

1. Ezekiel (Hebrew = God is strong) is one of the great prophets. He lived the disaster of Israel's destruction. He kept the faith and hope of the exiles.

gazes, for they are only a race of rebels. You shall tell them my words, whether they listen or not, for they are a race of rebells."

JUDGEMENT OF GOD AGAINST
THE CHOSEN PEOPLE

Ezekiel is given his mission. Then he said to me: "Son of man, go to the house of Israel and let them know my words."

You are my sentry. Seven days afterwards the Lord spoke to me and said, "Son of man, you will be the sentry of the house of Israel. When you heard a word from my mouth you shall preach to them on my behalf. When I say to a wicked man, You shall die!, if you do not preach to him and warn him that he will die if he does not abandon his behaviour, he will die because of his iniquity, but I will not blame you for his blood. But if you do preach to him and he does not abandon his behaviour he will die for his iniquity, but you will have saved yourself."

New covenant with the exiles. So make this announcement: "This is the word of the Lord: Yes, I have taken them to foreign nations, I have scattered them in strange lands; but I have also given them a sanctuary, in the short time they are going to spend in these countries. Therefore you must say, This is the word of the Lord: I will gather you from among the nations, I will assemble you from the countries among which you have been scattered, and I will give you the land of Israel. They will come and remove all the images and abominations. I will give them an only heart and a new spirit. I will remove their stone-heart and I will give them a flesh-heart, so that they keep my commandments and put them into practice.

They will be my people and I will be their God. But those whose heart follows the idols and their abominable practices I will punish severely," states the Lord God.

Exhortation to turn to God. Therefore, say to the House of Israel: This is the word of the Lord god: Turn to God, forget your images and your abominable practices.

Promise of the King Messiah. These are the words of the Lord God:

"I will also take a slip from the lofty crown of the cedar and
set it in the soil; I will pluck a tender shoot[1] from the
topmost branch and plant it myself on a lofty mountain
in Israel. It will put out branches, bear their fruit, and
become a noble cedar.

Winged birds of every kind will roost under it, they will roost
in the shelter of its sweeping boughs.

And all the trees of the country will know that I, the Lord,
bring low the tall tree, and raise the low tree high, and
dry up the green try and make the dry tree put forth
buds. I, the Lord, have spoken and will do it."

JUDGEMENTS OF GOD AGAINST THE NATIONS

Elegy to Tyre's destruction. The Lord spoke to me and
said, "Son of man, say an elegy to Tyre. You shall say to Tyre,

O, you were rich and powerful in the heart of the seas.

Your oarsmen brought you into many waters, but on the high
seas and east wind wrecked you.

You wealth, your staple wares, your imports, your sailors and
your helmsmen, your caulkers, your merchants, and
your warriors, all your ship's company were flung into
the sea on the day of your disaster.

The cries of your helmsmen will make the coast tremble.

Then all the rowers shall land from their ships. Sailors,
helmsmen, all together, shall go ashore.

And they will exclaim over your face, they will cry out
bitterly, they will throw ashes on their heads, and
sprinkle themselves with them.

They tear out their hair on your account and put on sackcloth;
they weep bitterly over you, bitterly wailing.

---

1. The tender shoot of a strange tree planted in Israel will take roots, and will
grow strong, giving the fruits that the great tree could not yield. A lesson of
humility for Israel.

In their lamentation they raise a dirge over you, and this is
    their dirge: "Who was like Tyre[1], which is now mute in
    the middle of the sea?"

When your wares were unloaded off the sea you met the
    needs of many nations, with your vast resources and
    your imports you enriched the kings of the earth.

But now you are broken by the sea in deep water; your wares
    and all your company are gone overboard.

All who dwell on the coasts and islands are aghast at your
    fate; horror is written on the faces of their kings and
    their hair stands on end.

Among the nations the merchants jeer in derision at you; you
    have come to a fearful end and shall be no more for
    ever.

Against Egypt[2]. In the tenth year, on the twelfth day of the
tenth month the word of the Lord came to me and said, "Son of
man, look towards Pharaoh king of Egypt and prophesy against
him and all Egypt. Say, these are the words of the Lord,

Here I am against you, Pharaoh, king of Egypt, giant
    crocodile, lurking in the streams of the Nile. You have
    said, "My Nile is my own, it was I who made it."

I will put hooks in your jaws, and make fish cling to your
    scales. I will hoist you out of its streams with all its fish
    clinging to your scales.

I will fling you into the desert, you and all the fish of your
    Nile. You will fall on the bare ground with none to pick
    you up and bury you. I will make you food for beasts
    and birds, so that all the people in Egypt know that I
    am the Lord.

For the support that you gave to Israel was no better than a
    reed, which splintered in the hand when they grasped

---

1.   Tyre, walled city upon a great isle by the coasts of Phoenicia. It was a great
commercial city in the Mediterranean sea.

2.   Egypt was the powerful empire which competed with Assyria to rule the tiny
kingdom of Palestine.

you, and tore their armpits; when they leaned upon you, you snapped, and their limbs gave way.

This is therefore the word of the Lord: Look, I will bring a sword upon you to destroy both man and beast."

Elegy to Pharaoh. In the eleventh year, on the first day of the twelfth month, the word of the Lord came to me and said, "Son of man, sing an elegy upon Pharaoh, king on Egypt. You shall say,

Young lion of the nations, you are undone! You were like a crocodile in the waters, scattering the water with its snout, churning the water with its feet and fouling the streams.

This is the word of the Lord God: I will throw my net upon you, a host of uncountable peoples; they will bring you to the shore with my net[1].

There I will abandon you, in the middle of the field. I will make you food for all the birs in the sky and all the beasts on the earth.

I will scatter your flesh on the hills and valleys.

I will water the earth with your kidneys, with your blood I will water up to the hilltops, until the streams flood.

When you are dead, I will cover the vault and darken the stars. The sun shall be covered by clouds, and the moon will not give any light.

I will darken all the hosts in the sky on your account, and I will fill your country with darkness, says the Lord.

I will make many people's heart grow sad when I take your captives through the nations, to lands unknown to you. I will terrify many nations on your account, and their kings shall tremble with fear when I take my sword before them. They will fear for their lives on the day of your fall."

This is the word of the Lord God: "The sword of the king of Babylon shall kill you.

---

1. Invasion of Nebuchadnezzar's army with fighting men from all nations.

I will defeat you innumerable people; the most fierce peoples
　　　shall put Egypt's pride to the sword, and its population
　　　will be exterminated.
I will kill all your herds by the waters. No human or animal
　　　shall ever make them dirty.
Then I will quieten your water, your streams shall run like oil,
　　　says the Lord God.
When I leave the land of Egypt empty and the country has
　　　been looted, when I wound all its inhabitants, they will
　　　know that I am the Lord."

　　This is the elegy which the daughters of the nations shall
sing. They will sing it over Egyp and all his people, says the
Lord God.

PART TWO

PROPHECIES OF THE RESTORATION[1]

PROLOGUE

Ezekiel, watchman of the people. The word of the Lord came to me and said, "Son of Man, say to your people, When I set armies in motion against a land, its people choose one of themselves to be a watchman. When he sees the enemy approaching and blows his trumpet to warn the people, then if anyone does not heed the warning and is overtaken by the enemy, he is responsible for his own fate.

Son of man, I have appointed you a watchman for the Israelites. You will take messages from me and carry my warnings to them. If when I say to a man 'You will die' you do not warn him to give up his ways, the guilt is his and because of his wickedness he will die, but I will hold you answerable for his death. On the contrary, if you warn him to give up his ways and he does not do so, he will die, and you will have saved your life.

God judges according to one's behaviour. Therefore say to them, As I live, says the Lord God, I do not rejoice the death of the wicked. I would rather that a wicked man should men his

---

1. These prophecies belong to the period among the siege of Jerusalem and the Restoration.

ways and live. Give up your evil ways, give them up. Why do you want to die, O house of Israel?

Son of man, say to the sons of your people: When a righteous man goes wrong, his righteousness shall not save him, When a wicked man mends his ways, his former wickedness shall not bring him down. When a righteous man sins, all his righteousness cannot save his life. If I say to the righteous man, 'You will die' but he, presuming on his righteousness, does wrong, none of his righteous acts shall be remembered. He will die because of his iniquity.

And if I say to the wicked man, 'You will die', and he gives up his evildoings and does what is right and just, that is, he restores the pledges he has taken, repays what he has stolen and follow the rules that ensure life and does not commit any more sins, he shall live, he shall not die. None of the sins that he has committed shall be taken into account. He has done what is right and just, therefore he will live.

But the sons of your people say, 'The ways of the Lord are not righteous', when it is their ways that are not righteous! If the righteous man leaves his justice and committs a sin, he shall die on its account. And if the wicked man gives up his behaviour and does what is right and just, he shall live. And you say, 'The ways of the Lord are not righteous', but I will judge you on your deeds, O house of Israel!"

"Jerusalem has been taken!" In the twelfth year of our captivity, on the fifth day of the tenth month a fugitive came to me from Jerusalem and said, "Jerusalem has been taken!" The hand of the Lord had come upon me that afternoon before the fugitive came. My speech was restored and I was no longer dumb.

The people's attitude towards Ezekiel[1]. "As for you, son of man, the people talk about you on the walls and at the doors of their homes, and they say to each other, 'Let us listen to the word of the Lord.' They come to you and sit before you. They

---

1. The people does not listen to him. They do not listen to his threats and warnings, they are proud about the future.

listen to your words, but they do not put them into practice, for in their mouths there is lie and they only pursue their benefit.

You are for them no more than a love song, finely sung accompanied by string instruments. They listen to your words but do not take them seriously. But when my prophecies are fulfiled —and it will be soon— they will know that there is a prophet among them."

THE FUTURE RESTORATION

The people's bad leaders. The word of the Lord came to me and said, "Son of man, prophesy against the shepherds of Israel and say: Shepherds, this is the word of the Lord: Woe betide the shepherds of Israel who only look after themselves! Is it not the flock which the shepherds must look after? You drink milk and are dressed with wool; you kill calves, but do not look after the sheep. You have not encouraged the weary, tended the sick, bandaged the hurt, recovered the straggler, or searched for the lost; and even the strong you have driven with ruthless severity. They are scattered, they have no shepherd, they have become the prey of wild beasts. The sheep of my flock are scattered over the whole country, with no one to ask after or search for them. Therefore listen, shepherds, to the word of the Lord: As I live, says the Lord God, that because my sheep are ravaged with wild beasts and have become their prey for lack of a shepherd, becasue my shepherds have not looked after them, looking after themselves instead.

Therefore, you shepherds, listen to the word of the Lord: This is the word of the Lord: Here I am, demanding my sheep from them. I will dismiss those shepherds; they shall care only for themselves no longer; I will rescue my sheep from their jaws, and they shall feed on them no more."

The faithful shepherd, figure of the Messiah. This is the word of the Lord God: I will care for my sheep myself and go in search of them. As a shepherd cares for his sheep when his flock is dispersed all around him, so I will go in search for my sheep and rescue them, no matter where they were scattered in dark and cloudy days. I will bring them out from every nation, gather them in from other lands, and lead them home to their own soil. I will graze them on the mountains of Israel, by her streams and in all her green fields. I will feed them on good grazing-ground, and their pasture shall be the high mountains of Israel. There they will rest, there in good pasture, and find rich grazing on the mountains of Israel. I myself will tend my flock, I myself pen them in their fold, says the God Lord. I will search for the lost, recover the straggler, bandage the hurt, strengthen the sick, leave the healthy and strong to play, and give them their proper food.

As for you, my flock, this is the word of the Lord: I will judge between one sheep and another. You rams and he-goats! Are you not satisfied with grazing on good herbage, that you must trample down the rest with your feet? Or with drinking clear water, that you must churn up the rest with your feet? Therefore, these are the words of the Lord: Now I myself will judge between the fat sheep and the lean. You hustle the weary with flank shoulder, you butt them with your horns until you have driven them away and scattered them abroad. Therefore I will save my flock, and they shall be ravaged no more; I will judge between one sheep and another.

An only shepherd, the Messiah, new David. "I will set over them a shepherd to take care of them, my servant David; he shall care for them and be their shepherd. I, the Lord, will become their God, and my servant David shall be a prince among them. I, the Lord, have spoken. I will make a covenant with them to ensure prosperity; I will rid the land of wild beasts, and men shall live in peace of mind on the open pastures and send them rain in due season, blessed rain. Trees in the countryside shall bear their fruit, the land shall yield its produce, and men shall live in peace of mind on their own soil. They shall know that I am the Lord when I break the bars of their yokes and rescue them from those who have enslaved them. They shall never be ravaged by the nations again nor shall wild beasts devour them; they shall live in peace of mind, with no one to alarm them. You are my flock, my people, the flock I feed, and I am your God," says the Lord God.

Vision of the withered bones, figure of the resurrection.
The hand of the Lord came upon me, and he carried me out by
his spirit and put me down in a plain full of bones. He made me
go to and fro across them until I had been round them all; they
covered the plain, countless numbers of them, and they were
very dry. And he said to me, "Son of man, can these bones live
again?" I answered, "Only you know that." And he said,
"Prophesy over these bones and say to them, O dry bones, hear
the word of the Lord. This is the word of the Lord God, I will
put breath into you, and you shall live. I will fasten sinews on
you, bring flesh upon you, overlay you with skin, and put breath
in you, and you shall live; and you shall know that I am the
Lord."

I began to prophesy as he had told me, and as I prophesied
there was a rustling sound and the bones fitted themselves
together. As I looked, sinews appeared upon them, flesh
covered them, and they were overlaid with skin, but there was
no breath in them. Then he said to me, "Prophesy to the wind,
prophesy, son of man, and say to it, these are the words of the
Lord God: Come, O wind, come from every quarter and breathe
into these slain, that they may come to life."

I did as he had told me; breath came into them; they came to
life and rose to their feet, a mighty host[1].

Explanation of the vision. And he said to me, "Son of man,
all these bones are the house of Israel. They say, Our bones are
dry, our hope is gone, we are lost for ever! Therefore, prophesy
and say, This is the word of the Lord: Listen, I shall open up
your graves, I will take you out of them, my people, and I will
bring you back to the land of Israel. And when I open up your
graves and take you out of them you will know that I am the
Lord, my people. I will breath my spirit into your bodies, and
you will come to life; I will set you on your soil and you will
know that I, the Lord, fulfil my promises", says the Lord.

Judah and Israel come together. Messianic promises. The
word of the Lord came to me and he said, "This is the word of

---

1. It was the prophesy of the resurrection of the people of Israel and of all the
peoples in the world at the end of times.

the Lord God: I will gather the sons of Israel from the nations to which they fled together to take them to their land. I will make our of them an only people on the earth, in the mountains of Israel, they will have only one king, and they shall no longer be two divided nations, two divided kingdoms. They will not be sinful with their images, abominations and iniquities any more. I will save them of their iniquities and I will also purify them. They will be my people and I will be their God. My servant David shall rule over them. They will have only one shepherd, and they will walk by the way of my commandments, they will observe my laws and put them into practice. They will people the earth which I gave to my servant Jacob, the land of your forefathers. They will live there, their sons and the sons of their sons for ever: David, my servant, shall be their ruler for ever. I will make an everlasting covenant of peace with them; I will set them there and make them fruitful, and I will set up my Sanctuary among them for ever. I will set up my dwelling-place among them; I will be their God and they will be my people. And the people shall know that I, the Lord, make Israel holy when my Sanctuary is among them for ever."

DANIEL[1]

PART ONE

MANIFESTATION OF
GOD'S POWER

PROLOGUE

Daniel and the three young men at Nebuchadnezzar's court. In the third year of the reign of Jehoiakim king of Judah, Nebuchadnezzar king of Babylon came to Jerusalem and besieged it. The Lord delivered Jehoiakim king of Judah and a part of the vessels of the Temple of God into his hands. He brought them over to the land of Shinar and put them into the treasure of his gods.

Then the king ordered Ashpenaz, his chief eunuch, to choose among the sons of Israel some young men of royal blood and of noble family: they had to be faultless, be goodlooking, at home in all branches of knowledge, well-informed, intelligent, and fit for service in the royal court. He also ordered that they would be instructed in the writing and the language of the Chaldaeans.

---

1. Daniel (Hebrew = God is my judge) came from a noble family in Judah. He was taken to Babylon in the first deportation. He was granted supernatural gifts because of his faith.

The king assigned them a daily allowance of food and wine from the royal table. Their training was to last for three years, and at the end of that time they would enter the royal service. Among them there were certain young men form Judah called Daniel, Hananiah, Mishael and Azariah; but the master of the eunuchs gave them new names: Daniel he called Belteshazzar, Hananiah Shadrach, Mishael Meshach and Azariah Abed-Nego.

Daniel determined not to contaminate himself by touching the food and wine assigned to him by the king, and he begged the master of the eunuchs not to make him do so. God made the master show kindness and goodwill to Daniel, and he said to him, "I am afraid of my lord the king: he has assigned you your food and drink, and if he sees you looking dejected, unlike the other men of your own age, it will cost me my head." Then Daniel said to the guard whom the master of the eunuchs had put in charge of Daniel, Hananiah, Mishael, and Azariah, "Submit us to this test for then days. Give us only vegetables to eat and water to drink; then compare our looks with those of the young men who have lived on the food assigned by the king, and be guided in your treatment of us by what you see." He accepted their proposal and tested them for ten days. At the end of ten days they looked healthier and better nourished than all the young men who had lived on the food assigned them by the king. So the guard took away the assignment of food and the wine they were to drink, and gave them only the vegetables. To all four of these young men God had given knowledge and understanding of books and learning of every kind, while Daniel had a gift for interpreting visions and dreams of every kind[1]. The time came which the king had fixed for introducing the young men to court, and the master of the eunuchs brought them into the presence of Nebuchadnezzar. The king talked with them and found none of them to compare with Daniel, Hananiah, Mishael and Azariah; so they entered the king's service.

Daniel was there till the first year of King Cyrus.

---

1. Supernatural dreams were a way for God to get in touch with men, and at the same time they gave a special charm to those who had them.

FIVE HISTORICAL EVENTS

Nebuchadnezzar's dream. In the second year of his reign Nebuchadnezzar had so troubled a dream that he could not sleep. The king summoned his magicians, exorcists, sorcerers and astrologers[1] and he commanded them to tell him about his dream. So they came and stood in the royal presence. And the king said to them, "I have had a dream, and my spirit demands an explanation." The Chaldaeans, speaking in Aramaic, said, "Long live the king! Tell your dream to your servants and we will give you an explanation to it." The king answered, "This is my declared intention. If you do not tell me both dream and interpretation, you shall be torn in peaces and your houses will be forfeit. But if you can tell me the dream and the interpretation you shall be richly rewarded and loaded with honours. Tell me, therefore, the dream and its interpretation."

The Chaldaeans replied, "There is no man on earth who can say what the king demands. In the same way there has never been a king, ruler or chief who asked for what the king asks to any magician, sorcerer or astrologer. What the king demands is difficult and nobody can give you the answer, but the gods, and they dwell remote from mortal men." Then the king lost his temper and in a great rage ordered the death of all the wise men of Babylon. A decree was issued that the wise men were to be executed, and accordingly men were sent to fetch Daniel and his companions for execution.

Daniel interprets the dream. Then Daniel came to Arioch, the captain of the king's bodyguard, who was setting out to execute the wise men of Babylon, and said to him, "Why has his majesty issued such a peremptory decree?"

Arioch explained everything; so Daniel went in to the king's presence and begged for a certain time by which he would give the king the interpretation. Then Daniel went home and told the whole story to his companions, Hananiah, Mishael and Azariah. They should ask the God of heaven in his mercy, he said, to

---

1. The Sorcerers came from Midia and were the first in the science of the time. They were astrologers and believed in the influence of stars.

disclose this secret, so that they and he with the rest of the wise men of Babylon should not be put to death.

Then in a vision by night the secret was revealed to Daniel, and he blessed the Lord in heaven.

Daniel therefore went to Arioch who had been charged by the king to put to death the wise men of Babylon and said to him, "Do not put the wise men of Babylon to death. Take me into the king's presence, and I will now tell him the interpretation of his dream." Arioch in great trepidation brought Daniel before the king and said to him, "I have found among the Jewish exiles a man who will make known to your majesty the interpretation of your dream." Thereupon the king said to Daniel, to whom he called Belteshazzar, "Can you tell me what I saw in my dream and interpret it?" Daniel answered in the king's presence, "The secret about which your majesty inquires no wise man, exorcist, magician or diviner can disclose to you. But there is in heaven a god who reveals secrets, and he has told King Nebuchadnezzar what is to be at the end of this age. This is the dream and these the visions that came into your head; the thoughts that came to you as you laid on your bed.

As you watched, O king, you saw a great image. This image, huge and dazzling, towered before you, fearful to behold. The head of the image was of fine gold, its breast and arms of silver, its belly and thighs of bronze, its legs of iron, its feet part iron and part clay. While you looked, a stone was hewn from a mountain, not by human hands; it struck the image on its feet of iron and clay and shattered them. Then the iron, the clay, the bronze, the silver and the gold were all shattered to fragments and were swept away like chaff before the wind from a threshing-floor in summer, until not trace of them remained. But the stone which struck the image grew into a great mountain filling the whole earth. That was the dream. We shall now tell your majesty the interpretation.

You, O king, king of kings, to whom the God of heaven has given the kingdom with all its power, authority, and honour; in whose hands he has placed men and beasts and birds of the air, wherever they dwell, granting you sovereignity over them all —you are that head of gold. After you there shall rise another kingdom inferior to yours, and yet a third kingdom, of bronze, which shall have sovereignty over the whole world. And there shall be a fourth kingdom strong as iron; as iron shatters and destroys all things, it shall break and shatter the whole earth. As, in your vision, the feet and toes were part potter's clay and part iron, it shall be a divided kingdom. Its core shall be partly of iron just as you saw iron mixed with the common clay; as the toes were part iron and part clay, the kingdom shall be partly strong and partly brittle. In the period of those kings the God of heaven will establish a kingdom which shall never be destroyed.

That kingdom shall never pass to other people; it shall shatter and make an end of all these kingdoms, while it shall itself endure for ever. This is the meaning of your vision of the stone being hewn from a mountain, not by human hands, and then shattering the iron,the bronze, the clay, the silver and the gold. The mighty God has made known to your majesty what is to be thereafter. The dream is sure and the interpretation is to be trusted."

Daniel, leader of the wise men of Babylon. Then king Nebuchadnezzar prostrated himelf and worshipped Daniel, and gave orders that sacrifices and soothing offerings should be made to him. "Truly," he said, "your God is indeed God of gods and Lord over kings, a revealer of secrets, since you have been able to reveal this secret." Then the king promoted Daniel, bestowed on him many rich gifts, and made him regent over the whole province of Babylon and chief prefect over all the wise men of Babylon. Moreover, at Daniel's request, the king put Shadrah, Meshach and Abed-nego in charge of the administration of the province of Babylon. Daniel himself remained at court.

Nebuchadnezzar makes an image of gold. King Nebuchadnezzar made an image of gold, ninety feet high and nine feet broad. He had it set up in the plain of Dura in the province of Babylon. Then he sent out a summons to assemble the satraps, prefects, viceroys, counsellors, treasurers, judges, chief constables, and all governors of provinces to attend the dedication of the image which he had set up. So they assembled for the dedication of the image erected by King Nebuchadnezzar. And the herarld exclaimed loudly, "O peoples and nations of every language, you are commanded, when you hear the sound of horn, pipe, zither, triangle, dulcimer, music, and singing of every kind, to prostrate yourselves and worship the golden image which King Nebuchadnezzar has set up. Whoever does not prostrate himself and worship shall forhwith be thrown into a blazing furnace." Accordingly, no sooner did all the peoples hear the sound of horn, pipe, zither, triangle, dulcimer, music and singing of every kind, than all the peoples and nations of every language prostrated themselves and worshipped King Nebuchadnezzar's golden image.

The three young men refuse to worship the image. However some Chaldaeans came to bring a charge against the Jews. They said to King Nebuchadnezzar, "O King, may you live for centuries. O king, you have issued an order that every man who hears the sound of horn, pipe, zither, triangle, dulcimer, music, and singing of very kind shall fall down and worship the golden image, and whoever does not do so shall be thrown into a blazing furnace. There are certain Jews, Shadrach, Meshach and Abed-nego, whom you have put in charge of the administration of the province of Babylon. These men, your majesty, have taken no notice of your command; they do not serve your god, nor do they woship the golden image which you have set up." Then in rage and fury Nebuchadnezzar ordered Shadrach, Meshach and Abed-nego to be fetched, and they were brought into the king's presence. Nebuchadnezzar said to them, "Is it true, Shadrach, Meshach and Abed-nego,that you do not serve my god or worship the golden image which I have set up? Are you ready to prostrate yourselves at once when you hear the sound of horn, pipe, zither, triangle, dulcimer, music, and singing of every king, and to worship the image which I have set up, well and good? If you do not do so, you shall be thrown into the blazing furnace, and what god is there that can save you from my hands?" Shadrach, Meshach and Abed-nego said to King Nebuchadnezzar, "We have no need to answer you on this matter. If there is a god who is able to save us from the blazing furnace, it is our God whom we serve, and we will save us from your hands, O king. But if not, it will be known to your majesty that we will neither serve your god nor worship the golden image that you have set up."

The three young men in the furnace. Then Nebuchadnezzar flew into a rage with Shadrach, Meshach and Abed-nego and his face was distorted with anger. He gave orders that the furnace should be heated up to seven times his usual heat, and commanded some of the strongest men in his army to bind Shadrach,Meshach and Abed-nego and throw them into the blazing furnace. They were bound and thrown into the furnace. Because the king's order was urgent and the furnace exceedingly hot, the men who were carrying Shadrach, Meshach and Abed-nego were killed by the flames that leapt out; and those three man, Shadrach, Meshach and Abed-nego, fell bound into the blazing furnace.

God's angel in the furnace. The servants of the king who had thrown them into the fire did not cease from poking the fire with naphts, tar, tow and sine shoots. The flames raised over the furnace up to forty-nine cubits, and it killed the Chaldaeans who were near the fire. But an angel of God came down into the furnace by Hananiah and his friends, push the flames outside and in the middle of the furnace he make the wind blow a slight breeze of dew, and they were not touched by fire, unharmed by the flames.

Song of the three young men. Then the three young men sang to the glory and blessing of God inside the furnace. They sang,

"Blessed be the Lord, God of our forefathers, praised and
    exalted for centuries. Blessed, glorious and exalted be
    your holy Name for centuries.
Blessed you be in the Temple of your holy Glory, praised and
    exalted for centuries.
Blessed you be in the throne of your kingdom, praised and
    exalted for centuries.
Blesseed you be on earth and heaven, praised and exalted for
    centuries.

Angels of the Lord, bless the Lord, praise him and exalt him
for centuries.

Heavens, bless the Lord, praise him and exalt him for
centuries.

Sun and moon, bless the Lord, praise him and exalt him for
centuries.

Hosts of heaven, bless the Lord, praise him and exalt him for
centuries.

Rain and dew, bless the Lord, praise him and exalt him for
centuries.

All winds, bless the Lord, praise him and exalt him for
centuries.

Fire and heat, bless the Lord, praise him and exalt him for
centuries.

Snow and ice, bless the Lord, praise him and exalt him for
centuries.

Cold and ice, bless the Lord, praise him and exalt him for
centuries.

Night and day, bless the Lord, praise him and exalt him for
centuries.

Light and darkness, bless the Lord, praise him and exalt him
for centuries.

Earth, bless the Lord, praise him and exalt him for centuries.

Mountains and hills, bless the Lord, praise him and exalt him
for centuries.

All those things who grown on the earth, bless the Lord,
praise him and exalt him for centuries.

Wells, bless the Lord, praise him and exalt him for centuries.

Seas and rivers, bless the Lord, praise him and exalt him for
centuries.

Fish and those who live in the sea, bless the Lord, praise him
and exalt him for centuries.

All birds in the sky, bless the Lord, praise him and exalt him
for centuries.

Wild beasts, bless the Lord, praise him and exalt him for
centuries.

Sons of men, bless the Lord, praise him and exalt him for
centuries.

Israel, bless the Lord, praise him and exalt him for centuries.

Priests, bless the Lord, praise him and exalt him for centuries.

Servants of him, bless the Lord, praise him and exalt him for
    centuries.

Souls of the righteous, bless the Lord, praise him exalt him for
    centuries.

Holy men and noble hearts, bless the Lord, praise him and
    exalt him for centuries.

Hananiah, Azariah and Mishael, bless the Lord, praise him
    and exalt him for centuries, for he has spared us hell,
    he has set us free form death, free from the furnace of
    the blazing flame. He saved us from the fire.

Bless the Lord, for he is good, and merciful."

Nebuchadnezzar recognizes and glorifies God. Then King Nebuchadnezzar drew near them and was amazed. Then he stood up and said to his courtiers, "Have we not thrown these three men bound into the fire?" And they answered, "Certainly, O King." The king added, "However, I see four men walking about in the fire free and unharmed; and the fourth looks like a god." Then Nebuchadnezzar approached the door of the blazing furnace and said to the men, "Shadrach, Meshach and Abed-nego, servants of the Most High God, come out, come here!"

Shadrach, Meshach and Abed-nego came out from the fire. And the satraps, prefects, viceroys, and the king's courtiers gathered round and saw how the fire had had no power to harm the bodies of these men; the hair of their heads had not been singed, their trousers were untouched, and no smell of fire lingered about them. Nebuchadnezzar spoke out, "Blessed is the God of Shadrach, Meshach and Abed-nego. He has sent his angel to save his servants who put their trust in him, who disobeyed the royal command and were willing to yield themselves to the fire rather than to serve or worship any god other than their own God!

Another dream of Nebuchadnezzar: the Tree. "King Nebuchadnezzar to all the peoples and nations of every language living in the whole world: May all properity be yours!

It is my pleasure to recount the signs and marvels which the Most High God has roked for me.

Great are his signs, overwhelming his marvels; his kingdom is
an everlasting kingdom, his sovereignity stands to all
generations!

Daniel interprets the dream of the tree to Nebuchadnezzar. I Nebuchadnezzar, was peacefully at home, living happily in my palace, when I had a dream which terrified me, and fantasies and visions which came into my head dismayed me. So I issued an order that all the wise men of Babylon should come into my presence to interpret my dream. Therefore, magicians, sorcerers, Chaldaeans and astrologers came to me, and I told them my dream, but they could not interpret it.

Eventually Danuel came into my presence, also called Belteshazzar after the name of my god[1], the man within whom the spirit of the Holy God is, and I told him my dream: Belteshazzar, chief of the magicians, I know that the spirit of the Holy God dwells within you and that there are no secrets for you; this is my vision, please, give me its interpretation.

This was the vision of my spirit, on my bed. I was looking; I
saw a tree of great heigh at the centre of the earth.
The tree grew and became strong; its top reached to the sky,
its leaves the earth's farthest bounds.
Its foliage was lovely, its fruit abundant; there was in it fruit
for everybody; the beasts found shelter beneath it, the
birds lodged in its branches, and all living creatures fed
from it.

I was watching the visions of my brains on my bed. Suddenly, a Watcher[2], a Holy One, who cried aloud:

---

1. The biblical god Beland Babel is Marduk, the Babylonian king of the times of Hammurabi, who was the master of heaven and earth. In the famous tower of his temple took place the marriages with goddess Sarpanitu, and the poem of the creation was read aloud.

2. An angel or archangel. They are also the watchers of the guard.

Hew down the tree, cut down its branches, strip away the
      foliage, scatter the fruit; let the wild beasts flee from its
      shelter, and the birds from its branches!
But leave the sumpt with its roots in the ground; tethered with
      an iron ring. Let him eat his fill of the lush grass; let
      him be drenched with the dew of heaven, and share the
      lot of the beasts in their pasture.
His heart will cease to be a man's heart, he will be given a
      beast's heart, and seven years shall pass over him.
This issue has been determined by the Watchers, and the
      sentence pronounced by the Holy Ones, so that the
      living creatures may know that it is God Most Hight
      who rules over the kingdom of men.

   This was my dream, King Nebuchadnezzar's. And you,
Belteshazzar, tell me his interpretation, for the wise men of my
kingdom were not able to give me one, but you are, for the spirit
of the Holy God dwells within you."
   Then Daniel, who was called Belteshazzar, was
dumbfounded for a moment, dismayed by his thoughts; but the
king said, "Do not let the dream and its interpretation dismay
you." Belteshazzar answered, "My lord, if only the dream were
for those who hate you and its interpretation for your enemies!
The tree which you saw grow and become strong, reaching with
its top to the sky and visible to earth's farthest bounds, its
foliage lovely and its fruit abundant, a tree which yielded food
for all, beneath which the wild beast dwelt and in whose
branches the birds lodged, that tree, O king, is you. You have
grown and become strong. You power has grown and reaches
the sky, your sovereignity stretches to the ends of the earth.
   The king saw a Watcher, a Holy One, coming down from
heaven and saying, "Hew down the tree and destroy it, but leave
its stump with its roots in the ground. So tethered with an iron
ring, let him eat his fill of the lush grass; let him be drenched
with the dew of heaven and share the lot of the beasts until
seven times pass over him." This is the interpretation, O King,
it is a drecree of the Most High which touches my lord the king.
You will be banished from the society of men; you will have to

live with the wild beasts; you will feed on grass like oxen and you will be drenched with the dew of heaven. Seven times will pass over you until you have learnt that the Most High is sovereign over the kingdom of men and gives it to whom he will.

The command was given to leave the stump of the tree with its roots. By this you may know that from the time you acknowledge the sovereignity of heaven your rule will endure. Be advised by me, O king: redeem your sins by charity and your iniquities by generosity to the wretched. So may you enjoy long peace of mind."

The dream comes true: Nebuchadnezzar's madness. All this befall king Nebuchadnezzar. Twelve months afterwards, while he was walking around his palace in Babylon, he wondered, "Is this not the great Babylon that I have built for my royal residence with my great power and for my majesty's glory[1]?" He was still speaking when a voice was heard from heaven, "I talk to you, Nebuchadnezzar; your kingdom has been taken from you; you will be banished from society, and you will go to live with the wild beasts."

At that very moment the judgement came upon Nebuchadnezzar; he was banished from society and started to eat grass like the oxen, at his body was drenched by the dew of heaven, until his hair grew long like goats' hair and his nails like eagle's talons.

Nebuchadnezzar humiliates himself and God returns him to his senses. "After those events, I, Nebuchadnezzar, looked up to heaven and returned to my right mind. Then I blessed God Most Hight, praised and exalted the one who lives for ever.

At that time I returned to my right mind, and my majesty and splendour was given back to me for the glory of my kingdom. My courtiers and noblemen came to fetch me: I was again on the throne, and my power was even greater. Therefore now, I,

---

1. Babylon was one of the most famous cities of the past. Its hanging gardens, the temple of Marduk and Meodak with its seven-storey tower of Bel are well-known.

King Nebuchadnezzar, praise, exalt and glorify the king of heaven, for all his works are true, all his ways are just, and because he brings low those whose conduct is arrogant."

Belshazzar's feast[1] and the strange words. King Belshazzar gave a banquet for a thousand of his nobles and was drinking wine in the presence of the thousand. Warmed by the wine, he gave orders to fetch the vessels of gold and silver which his father Nebuchadnezzar had taken from the Temple in Jerusalem, that he and his nobles, his concubines and his courtier might drink from them. So the vessels of gold and silver from the sanctuary in the house of God at Jerusalem were brought in, and the king and his nobles, his concubines and his courtesans, drank from them. They drank wine and praised their gods.

Suddenly there appeared the fingers of a human hand writing on the plaster of the palace wall opposite the lamp, and the king could see the back of the hand as it wrote. At this the king's mind was filled with dismay and he turned pale, he became limp in every limb and his knees knocked together. He called loudly for the exorcists, Chaldaeans, and viciners[2] to be brought in; then, addressing the wise men of Babylon, he said, "Whoever can read this writing and interprets it for me shall be dressed in purple, a golden necklace shall be put round his neck and will be the third man in the rule of the kingdom." All the wise men of the king drew near, but they could not read what was written, nor give an interpretation to it. Then King Belshazzar got angry and the colour of his face changed. His nobles were amazed too.

The queen, when she knew what was happening, entered the banquet's room and said, "Long live the king! Do not be afraid of your thought. There is in your kingdom a man within whom the spirit of the Holy God dwells. In your father's times he proved already to be intelligent and wise like gods, so that king Nebuchadnezzar, your father, appointed him chief of the

---

1. Belshazza. Babylonic = Bellar-Usur (Hebrew = Bel looks after the king). The last Babylonian king.
2. Astrology was the science of the Chaldaean and Babylonian astrologers who believed in the horoscope and were guided by the stars.

magicians, sorcerers, Chaldaeans and astrologers. Therefore summon Daniel, and he will give you the interpretation."

Daniel interprets the strange words. Daniel was summoned immediately into the king's presence, and he said to Daniel, "So you are Daniel, one of the Jewish exiles whom the king my father brought from Judah? I have heard that you possess the spirit of the holy gods, and great intelligence and wisdom. Right now they had brough magicians and wise men into my presence so that they could read what is written on the wall and interpret it, but they have been unable to do so. I have heard that you can do it. Therefore, if you read the writing and interpret in for me, you shall be robed in purple, a golden necklace shall be put round your neck and you shall be the third man in the rule of the kingdom."

Then Daniel answered and said to the king, "Keep your gifts or give them to another; I will read the writing for you anyway, and I will interpret it. O king, God Most High gave to your father Nebuchadnezzar the kingdom, the power, the majesty and the glory; and because he gave him this power, he was feared by all the peoples and nations of all languages. He killed whoever he liked, left alive whoever he wanted, exalted whoever he chose and humiliated whoever he pleased. But as soon as his heart grew hard and his spirit became insolent, he was deposed of his royal throne and his glory was taken from him. He was banished from the society of men, his mind became like that of a beast. But you, his son Belshazzar, did not humble your heart, although you knew all this. You have set up yourself against the Lord of heaven. The vessels of his temple have been brought to your table, and you, your nobles and his concubines have drunk from them. It was Him who sent the hand which wrote those words. This is what they mean: Mene, tekel and u-pharsin. Mene: God has numbered the days of your kingdom and brought it to an end. Tekel: you have been weighed in the balance and found wanting. U-pharsin: your kingdom has been divided and handed over to the Medes and the Persians."

Then Belshazzar gave Daniel a purple robe, a golden necklace and he was appointed the third in the rule of the country. That very night Belshazzar king of the Chaldaeans was murdered[1].

Darius the Mede took the kingdom. He was already sixty-two years old.

Thus Daniel lived with great honour in Darius's reign, and also in the reign of Cyrus the Persian.

---

1. By Gobriah, his officer who had gone to the Persians. Babylon's area was of 30,000 square kilometers. It seems that the Persians came in by the river (539 b.C.).

PART TWO

PROPHETIC VISIONS

Prophecy of Jeremiah's seventy weeks. In the first year of Darius, son of Artaxerxes, of the line of the Medes, who had been appointed king over the kindom of the Chaldaeans, in the first year of his reign, I, Daniel, started to study the scriptures and to calculate the number of years that, according to the word of the Lord to prophet Jeremiah, had to pass over the ruins of Jerusalem, that is, seventy weeks[1].

The archangel Gabriel interprets the prophecy. While I was still speaking and praying, confessing my own sins and my people Israel's sin, and presenting my supplication before the Lord my God on behalf of his holy hill. While I was praying, the man Gabriel, whom I had already seen in my vision, came close to me at the hour of the evening sacrifice, flying swiftly. He spoke clearly to me and said, "Here I am, Daniel. I have come to enlighten your understanding. As you were beginning your supplications a word went forth; this I have come to pass on to you, for you are a man greatly beloved. Consider well the word, consider the vision:

---

1. Jeremiah's seventy weeks turned into seventy weeks of sabbatical year until the coming of the Messiah, anointed by the H.S. Christ. This prophecy is divided into four groups: First, captivity, Second, until the death of the anointed, the priest Hoziah (Period of Restoration), Third, divided into two: Up to the prophanation of the temple (Period of prosecution, Maccabees), and finally, the longed-for Messiah.

Seventy weeks are fixed on your people and your holy city to
  bring their sin to an end, to expiate their iniquity, to set
  up an everlasting justice, so that vision and prophecy
  may be sealed and the Most Holy place anointed.

Know then and understand; since this order was given: "Let
  us rebuilt Jerusalem" until a Prince Messiah comes up,
  there will be seven weeks, and in seventy-two weeks
  the fortress and its walls shall be rebuilt, among the
  distress of times.

After the seventy-two weeks a Messiah shall be murdered[1],
  and no one shall defend him. The city and the sanctuary
  will be destroyed by a prince to come[2]. Its end shall be
  a deluge, and in the end there will be a war with all its
  horrors.

He shall make a covenant with the mighty for a week. In the
  middle of it sacrifice and offerings shall cease, and in
  the Temple will be the author of desolation[3], until what
  has been decreed concerning desolation will be poured
  out."

Resurrection and reward[4]. At that moment Michael
shall appear, the great prince, who watches over your
fellow-countrymen. There will be a time of distress such as has
never been since they became a nation until that day. Then they
will be saved, among your people, those whose name is written
in the book[5]. Many of those who sleep in the dust of the earth
will wake; some to everlasting life, some to the reproach of
eternal abhorrence. The wise men[6] shall shine like the
bright vault of heaven, and also those who guided the people.
But you, Daniel, keep these words secret and seal the book till

---

1. Honiah the chief priest.
2. Antiochus IV.
3. Jupiter's statue, which was set up on the altar of the sacrifices.
4. In the context of Antiochus's prosecution the prophecy of the end of the world
  is typical.
5. The Book of Life.
6. In the final resurrection, the righteous will be turned into glorious bodies.

the time of the end[1]. Many of them shall be lost, and iniquity will increase.

HISTORIAL APENDIX

Susanna and the two old men. There was a Hebrew, called Johachim, who lived in Babylon. He married a woman called Susanna, daughter of Helziah, very beautiful and afraid of God. Her parents were righteous and had educated their daughter according to the Mosaic Law. Johachim was a very rich man and had a garden by his house; the Jews used to go to his house, for he was a man highly esteemed[2].

On that year two judges were elected by the people. Two judges of whom the Lord says, "Iniquity has come to the Babylon of the old man and of the judges who made themselves leaders of the people." They came often to Johachim's house, and to them went all those who had some dispute. At midday, when everybody left, Susana used to walk in her husband's garden. The two old men saw her every day, and they started to desire her. They distied their minds and looked only towards her, they forsook their judgements. They were mad about her, but they did not say this to one another, for fear of discovering their passion and their wishes to lay with her. And everyday they did their best to see her. One day the said to each ohter, "Let us go home, it is time to have lunch." When they left, they parted company, but as soon as they turned round they met each other in the same place. They asked each other about the reason and they discovered their passion. Then they agreed on looking for a moment in which they could find her alone. Once, while they were waiting for the occasion, she left as the day before with two maids, and wanted to bathe in the garden, so warm it was. There was nobody there, except the two old men. So she

---

1. The last anouncement is the great apostasy of the end of times. "Whoever stands firm until the end shall be saved."

2. The Jewish community had a certain independence in Babylon. Nebuchadnezzar respected their laws and customs. They even used the capital punishment. This historical story is a beautiful example of conjugal fidelity.

said to the maids, "Bring me oil and soap, and then shut the doors so that I may bathe." They did as Susanna told them; they shut the gates of the garden and entered the house to bring her what she had ordered. They did not know that the old men were there.

As soon as the maids left the two old men stood up, ran towards her and said to her, "Look, the gates are shut and nobody can see us. We want to lay with you. Therefore, give yourself to us, otherwise we will bear a witness against you that you were with a young man and for that reason you sent the maids away." Susanna sighed and said, "What a sad situation! If I allow them to do as they want, death awaits me, but if I do not, I will not escape from your hands. But I prefer to fall in your hands than to give in to that which is a sin against God." And she shouted out, but the two old men shouted against her too. One of them opened the gates of the garden. Then the maidens entered to see what happened. When the two old men told their story, they were ashamed, for nobody had never said anything like that about Susanna.

On the next day, when the people gathered in his husband Johachim's house, the two wicked old men came too, decided to condemm her to death. And they said before the people, "Fetch Susanna, Helziah's daughter, wife of Johachim." And they sent somebody to fetch her. She came with her parents, her children and all her relatives. Susanna was delicate and very beautiful. Those wicked men ordered her to unveil her face —for she was wearing a veil— to be able at least to see her beauty, while her relatives and all those who saw her wept. The two old men, standing among the people, put their hands on Susanna's head. She, crying, looked up, for she trusted in the Lord. The two old men started speaking, "As we were walking in the garden, she entered with two maids, shut the gates and send the maids away. Then a young man who was hiding in the garden came to her and laid with her. We, who were in a corner, when we saw the iniquity, run towards them. We saw them together, but we could not get him, for he was stronger than us, he opened the gate and escaped. Then he took her and asked her about the young man, but he would not say his name. We were witnesses." The assembly believed them because they were elders and judges of the people, and condemned her to death. Susanna cried out, "O everlasting God, who know all secret things and know the things before they happen. You know that they have born false witness against me; I am going to die without having made anything of what they say." And the Lord listened to her words.

Daniel saves Susanna from death[1]. When she was being taken to die, God moved the Holy spirit of a boy called Daniel[2], who shouted out, "I am innocent of this woman's blood." All the people present turned to him and asked, "What do you mean?" He, standing among them, said, "Sons of Israel, do you not see? You have condemned a daughter of Israel without a clear knowledge of facts! Come back to the place of judgement, for the witness of these men against her is false!"

Then all the people turned back. And the two old men said to Daniel, "Sit down between us, and say what do you think, for the Lord has granted you the knowledge of age." But Daniel said, "Keep them far from each other and I will examine them." When they were apart, he took one of them and said, "O, wicked old man, now you will pay for the iniquities which you have made in the past, for you condemned the innocent and forgave those who were to blame, when the Lord has said, 'You shall not kill the innocent and righteous.' Therefore, if you saw this woman, say, under what tree?" He answered, "Under a beech." Daniel replied, "Your lie is obvious; an Angel of God has already received orders of cutting you in two." Then he summoned the other and said, "Race of Canaan, not of Judah, beauty has seduced you and passion has driven your heart mad. You could do that with the daughters of Israel, and they consented to your wishes because they were afraid, but a daughter of Judah did not bear your iniquity. So now say, under what tree did you saw them?" He answered, "Under an oak." Daniel said, "Your lie is obvious; the Angel of God is waiting for you with his sword, to cut you in two and destroy you."

---

1. The sin of adultery was punished among the Jews with death.
2. This event took place in the three first years of captivity.

Then all the people present rejoiced and blessed the Lord, who saves those who trust in Him. And they stood against the two old men, to whom Daniel had accused of false witness; and they did with them the same that they had done with their fellowmen. They were killed as the Mosaic Law dictates, and on that day innocent blood was spared. Helziah and his wife thanked the Lord for his daughter Susanna, as did Johachim, her husband, and all her relatives, for she had been found innocent[1].

And Daniel became highly esteemed by the people from that day on.

Daniel unmasks Bel's priests. King Astiages[2] joined his forefathers and was succeeded by Cyrus the Persian king. The people of Babylon had an image called Bel[3], in whose honour they spent every day more than six hundred litres of flour, forty sheep and more than two hundred litres of wine. But Daniel worshipped his God. One they the king said to him, "Why do you not worship Bel?" And he answered, "I do not worship those images made by men, but the living God, maker of heaven and earth and lord of every living creature." The king said, "Do you think that Bel is not a living god? Do you not see what he eats and drinks every day?" Daniel answered laughing, "Do not let yourself be deceived, king; this Bel is clay on the inside and bronze on the outside, and he has never eaten anything." Then the king in anger called the priests of the image and said to them, "If you do not tell me who is eating these offerings you shall die; but if you prove that it is Bel who has eaten them, then Daniel shall die, for he has sinned against Bel." Daniel said to the king: "Be it as you say." There were forty priests of Bel, not counting wives and children. The king and Daniel headed for the temple of Bel, and Bel's priests said, "Look, we will not move from here, and you, O king, serve the food and the wine; then shut the door and seal it with your signet. If tomorrow

---

1. God is providential and does not abandon the people who trust in him.
2. The last king of the Middle Kindgom. He was defeated and captured by Cyrus king of Persia, by then his subdit.
3. Bel = Baal. He was worshipped in hill-shrines, in wells and trees, which were holy places. He was worshipped in Mesopotamia an Assyria, as well as in Canaan.

morning, when you come to the temple, you do not see that everything has been eaten by Bel we shall die; but if the contrary happens then Daniel shall die, because he is lying." They had no fear, for they had opened a hole under the table by which they entered regularly and ate the food. When they were outside, the king made his servants bring the food before Bel, but Daniel ordered his servant to bring ashes and sprinkle them throughout the temple before the king; then they left, shut the door, sealed it with the king's signet and left. During the night the priests entered, as they used to do, with their wives and children and ate and drunk everything. On the next day, early in the morning, the king went to the temple with Daniel. And the king said, "Are the seals untouched, Daniel?" And he said, "O yes, my king." When the door opened, the king looked at the table and shouted, "You are great, Bel, and you are not a lie." But Daniel laughed, and prevented the king from coming in. Then he said, "Look at the floor, and see whose prints are these." The king said, "I see men's, women's and children's prints." And in a rage he made all the priests, their women and children prisoners, and they showed them the secret door through which they entered to eath what was on the table. Then the king ordered that they should be killed, and handed Bel over to Daniel, who destroyed him and his temple.

Daniel kills the drake[1]. the Babylonians worshipped also a great drake. And the king said to Daniel, "I hope that you are not going to say that this is also made of bronze; look, he is alive, eats and drinks, you cannot deny that he is a living god. Therefore worship him." But Daniel said, "I worship the Lord God because he is a living God. And you, O king, allow me to kill this drake without sword or spear and I will." The king said, "You are allowed to do so[2]."

Then Daniel took tar, grease and a lock of hairs, and he boiled them together. Then he did some balls with it and put them into the drake's mouth. And when the drake swallowed

---

1. This wonderful monster has a very important role in the Babylonic, Syrian and Phoenician mythology and cosmogony. He represented the god of evil.

2. The drake of Babylon was a great snake.

them up he broke out. And Daniel said, "This is what you worshipped." When the Babylonians heard about this they became angry and came against the king, saying, "The king has turned himself a Jew; he has allowed Bel, the drake and the priests to be murdered." They came into the king's presence and said, "Deliver Daniel into our hands; otherwise we shall kill you and all your relatives." As he was in danger the king delivered Daniel into their hands.

Daniel in the pit of the lions. They threw him in the pit of the lions, where he stayed for six days. In that pit there were seven lions to whom two human bodies and two sheep were given every day. But on that day they were given nothing at all so that they would devour Daniel. At that time in Judah lived the prophet Habakkuk[1]. He, after preparing a broth and some bread on a plate, headed for the field to bring it to the harvesters. But the angel of the Lord said to Habakkuk. "Take this food to Babylon for Daniel, who is in the pit of the lions." Habakkuk said, "My Lord, I have never been to Babylon, and I do not know where the pit is." But the angel of the Lord took him by his hair and put him in Babylon, in the pit of the lions as fast as the wind. Habakkuk shouted, "Daniel, Daniel, take the food which the Lord sends you." And Daniel exclaimed, "O God, you have remembered me, you do not forsake those who love you!" Then he stood up and ate, while the angel of the Lord took Habakkuk back to where he was.

The king recognizes Daniel's God. On the seventh day the king came to mourn Daniel. He looked at the pit and he saw Daniel sitting there. Then he exclaimed joyfully, "O God, you are great, God of Daniel, and there is no other God but you." And he ordered that Daniel should be taken out of the pit, and that those who had wanted him dead should be thrown into it. And they were devoured by the lions immediately before his eyes.

---

1. Habakkuk (Hebrew = basil or mint).

MINOR PROPHETS[1]

HOSEA[2]

THREATS AND PROMISES

Futility of the covenants with foreigners

Ephraim has seen that he was sick, and Judah its sores.
> Ephraim has gone to Assyria, and Judah to the great
> king, but they will not be able to heal you or your sores.
For I am like a lion for Ephraim, like a little lion for the house
> of Judah. I maul my preys and leave, I take and
> nobody can take them from me.
Yes, I shall go to my place until they have expiated their sin
> and look for my face. In their distress they shall search
> for me.

Apparent return to God

And he will come to us like the winter rain, like the spring
> rain which makes the land fruitful.

---

1. They are called Minor Prophets because their writings are short.
2. Hosea (Hebrew = God helps), born in the northern kingdom. He was a prophet
   in Samaria and Judah.

How shall I treat you, Ephraim? How shall I treat you, Judah?
Your love is like a morning cloud, like the dew which
disappears quickly.

For this reason I tore you in peaces through the prophets, I
have killed you with the words of my mouth.

For I do not want your love, nor sacrifices, knowledge of God
or offerings.

But they, like Adam, have broken the covenant and have been
unfaithful to me.

Evil covenants

Israel's arrogance shall bear a witness against him; but they
do not turn to the Lord their God; even so, they do not
search for him.

Ephraim is like an innocent dove laking intelligence: they call
to Egypt, they call to Assyria.

While they go away, I will tend my nets upon them, and I will
make them fall like birds of the sky, and I will punish
them for their wickedness.

Woe betide them, who have forsaken me! They will be
punished, for they have rebelled against me. Whenever
I wanted to save them, they told me lies.

And they do not call me in their hearts when they suffer in
their beds; they care for flour and wine, and rebel
against me.

I tought and strenghteen their arm but they plt against me.

They have turned to Baal, they have made a deceitful bow.
Their princes shall be put to the sword because of their
words, and Egypt will scorn them.

Punishment

Blow the trumpets! There is an eagle over the house of the
Lord, for they have broken my covenant, they have
trespassed my law.

They shout, "O God, the Israelites know you!"

But Israel has rejected the good things, and now the enemy
    pursues him.

They have appointed kings without asking me; they have
    appointed rulers without my consent. They have built
    images with their gold and silver which will bring ruin
    to them.

I reject your calf, Samaria, my anger is against them. Until
    when will they continue with blemish?

There are more altars at Ephraim, who have not been used for
    other aim than to sin.

Israel is taken to exile

The days of the punishment have come, the days of
    retribution. Israel is going to know the prophet. They
    say he is a fool, a madman. Yes, because your iniquity
    is great, and your rebellion is uncontrollable.

Ephraim, people of God, spies the prophet, tends him tricks
    on his ways, pursues him even in the house of God.

Ephraim is like a bird, his glory flies away; there are no births
    or pregnancies.

Even if they would have children, I will take them from them
    before they become men. Who betide those whom I
    forsake!"

Also the idols will disappear

Israel is like a rank vine ripening its fruit; his fruit grew more
    and more, and more and more his altars; the fairer his
    land becomes, the fairer he makes his sacred pillars.

His heart is divided: but now they shall pay for it. He will
    wipe out their altars.

The inhabitants of Samaria tremble for the calf-gold of
    Beth-aven[1]; the people mourn over it and its priests
    howl, for his glory has disappeared.

---

1. The image of the calf-gold of Beth-aven (Hebrew = pointless house) will be
taken to exile as a trophy.

He will also be taken to Assyria, as a present for the great
king. Disgrace shall overtake Ephraim, and Israel shall
feel the shame of their disobedience.

Samaria has disappeared!

I am going to come and punish them. The peoples will gather
against them when I punish them for their double sin.

Ephraim is like a heifer broken in, which loves to thresh corn,
across whose fair neck I have laid a yoke; I have
harnessed Ephraim to the pole that he may plough,
Jacob may harrow his land.

Sow for themselves in justice, and you will reap what loyalty
deserves. Break up your fallow, for it is time to seek
the Lord, seeking him till he comes and gives you just
measure of justice.

You have ploughed wickedness into your soil, and the crop is
mischeaf; you have eaten the fruit of treachery. Because
you have trusted in your chariots, in the number of your
warriors, the tumult of war shall arise against your
people, and all your fortresses shall be razed.

God will destroy the kingdom of Israel

When Israel was a child, I loved him, and I called my son
from Egypt.

The more I called him, the farther he got from me. They
offered sacrifices to the Baalim, and they brought
incense-offerings to the idols.

I taught Ephraim to walk, I hold it in my arms, but they have
not learnt that I looked after them.

I brought them to me with love, with understanding, and I was
for him like a man who holds a child on his neck and I
had bent down to feed him.

They will go back to Egypt, but they king shall be Assyrian,
for they have refused to turn to me.

The sword shall be swung over their cities, their children shall
be slain and devoured for their wicked actions.

My people tends to unfaithfulness; they call Baal, but none of
them shall sustain them.

How shall I abandon you, Ephraim, you shall I give you up,
Israel?

I will not let loose my fury, I will not destroy Ephraim again,
for I am God, not a man, among them I am the Holy
One, and I do not like to destroy.

They will follow the Lord, and He will roar like a lion; when
he roars, his western sons shall come immediately.

They will come from Egypt, like a bird, like a dove from the
country of Assyria, and I will make them dwell in their
homes —says the Lord.

Ruin of the idolatrous Ephraim

So then, I will be like a lion for them, like a leopard growling
by the wayside.

I will meet them like a she-bear robbed of her cubs and tear
their ribs apart, like a lioness I will devour them on the
spot, I will rip them up like a wild beast.

Israel will return to God

Samaria shall be punished because she has rebelled against
her God. Her children shall be put to the sword, they
shall be killed.

Israel, come back to your God the Lord, for of your fall only
you are to blame.

I will heal your infidelity, I will love you, for my anger has
gone away from them.

I will be like dew for Israel; and he will blossom like the iris,
and he will take roots like the Lebanon.

Its branches shall stretch out far away, it will blossom like an
olive-tree, and its fragrance like that of the Lebanon.

They will sit under my shadow; they will grow wheat, and
work in the vineyards. He shall be well known as the
wine from the Lebanon.

Efraim... does it have something in common with the images?
I will care for him and look after him. I am like a

cypress-tree always green, and you shall bear your fruit on my account.

Conclusion

Let the wise consider these things and let the man of understanding take note! For the ways of the Lord are straight; the righteous shall walk in them, while sinners stumble.

JOEL[1]

PUNISHMENT AND EXHORTATIONS

The invasion of the locusts[2]

Word of the Lord which came to Joel son of Pethuel.

Listen, you elders, listen, inhabitants of this country. Has
  something similar to this happened in your days or in
  the days of your fathers?

Tell it to your sons, and your sons to their sons, and their sons
  to the next generation.

For a people is attacking my country, a people numerous and
  powerful. Their teeth are a lion's teeth, they have the
  fangs of a lioness.

They have ruined my vines, and destroyed my fig-trees:
  everything has been plucked bare, and the branches
  have been left white.

Wail like a virgin wife in sackcloth, wailing over the
  bridegroom of her youht!

---

1. Joel (Hebrew = The Lord is God). He preached mainly in Judah and
   Jerusalem.
2. The devastation of the country by the Chaldaeans is like a plague of locusts,
   nothing is left.

The drink-offering and the grain-offering are lost to the house
    of the Lord[1]. The priests, ministers of the Lord are
    mourning.

The fields are ruined, the parched earth mourns, for the corn
    is ruined, the new wine is desperate, the oil has failed.

Despair, you husbandmen, you vinedressers, lament because
    the wheat and the barley, the harvest of the field, is lost.

The vintage is desperate, and the fig-tree has failed;
    pomegranate, palm and apple, all the trees of the
    country-side are parched, and none make merry over
    harvest!

Invitation to fasting

Priests, put on sackcloth and mourn, lament, you ministers of
    the altar; come, lie in sackcloth all night long, you
    ministers of my God, for the House of your God is now
    without grain-offering and drink-offering.

Proclaim a fast. You elders, summon all the people in the
    country in the House of the Lord, your God, and cry to
    the Lord.

Alas, what a day, the day of the Lord is near!

The soil is parched, the dykes are dry, the granaries are
    deserted, the barns ruinous; for the rains have failed.

The cattle are exhausted, the herds of oxen distressed because
    they have no pasture; the flocks of sheep wasted away.

I cry to you, O Lord; for fire has devoured the open pastures
    and the flames have burnt up all the trees of the
    country-side.

The very cattle in the field look up to you; for the
    water-channels are dried up, and fire has devoured the
    open pastures.

---

1. The daily grain and drink-offering consisted of fruits of the land, flour, wine
and oil.

The day of the Lord and the present devastation

Blow the trumpet in Zion, sound the alarm upon my holy hill;
   let all that live in the land tremble, for the day of the
   Lord has come.

Their vanguard a devouring fire, their rearguard leaping
       flame; before them the land is a garden of Eden, behind
       them a wasted wilderness; nothing survives their wrath.

They look like horses, they run like horsemen.

They bound over the peaks, they advance with the rattle of
       chariots, like flames of fire burning up the stubble, like
       a countless host in battle array.

Before them nations tremble, every face turns pale.

Like warriors they charge, they mount the walls like men at
       arms. They burst into the city, leap on the wall, climb
       into the houses like thieves.

Before them the earth shakes, the heavens shudder, sun and
       moon are darkened, and the stars forbear to shine.

The Lord thunders before his host; his is a mighty army,
       countless are those who do his bidding. Great is the day
       of the Lord and terrible, who can endure it?

Invitation to penitence

Blow the trumpet in Zion, proclaim a solemn fast, gather
       everybody, the people, the community. Summon the
       elders, the children and infants! Bid the bridegroom
       leave his chamber and the bride her bower.

Let the priests, the ministers of the Lord stand weeping
       between the porch and the altar and say, "Spare your
       people, O Lord, your own people, expose them not to
       reproach, lest other nations make them a byword and
       everywhere men ask, 'Where is their God'?"

THE DAY OF THE LORD

The Lord's pardon

The Lord's love burned with zeal for his land, and he was
　　　moved with compassion for his people.
He answered, "I will remove the northern peril from you, and
　　　banish them into a land parched and waste. Their
　　　vanguard into the eastern sea and their rear into the
　　　western.

Return of prosperity

O land, do not be afraid, rejoice and be glad, for the Lord has
　　　made great things.
O beasts of the fields, do not be afraid, for the pastures shall
　　　be green, the trees shall bear fruit, the vine and the
　　　fig-tree yield their harvest.

Outpouring of the spirit of the Lord

After this I will pour out my spirit on your flesh. Your sons
　　　and daughters shall prophesy, your elders shall have
　　　dreams, and your young people visions.
And in those days I will pour out my spirit even on male and
　　　female servants.

Judgement in the Valley of Josaphat

Let all the nations hear and go to the Valley of Josaphat.
　　　There I shall sit down to judge all the neighbouring
　　　peoples.
Ply the sickle, for the harvest is ripe; come, tread the grapes,
　　　for the press is full and the vats overflow, so great is
　　　the wickedness of the nations!
Multitudes, multitudes in the Vale of Decision! For the day of
　　　the Lord is near in the Vale of Decision.
The sun and the moon darken, the stars are not so bright.

The Lord roars from Zion, and thunders from Jerusalem, and
heaven and earth shudder. But the Lord shall be a
refuge for his people, a defence for the sons of Israel.
And then you shall know that I, the Lord, am your God.

AMOS[1]

REPROACHES AND THREATS TO ISRAEL

Israel's sin. Listen to the word which the Lord brings to you, sons of Israel, to all the family which I brought out from Egypt. Here it is:

For you alone I have cared among all the peoples in the earth; therefore I will punish you for all your iniquities. Do two men walk together unless they have agreed? Does the lion roar in his den if he has caught nothing? Does the bird fall into a trap on the ground if the striker is not set for it? Does a trap spring from the ground and take nothing? If the people sound the trumpet are not the people scared? If disaster falls on a city, has not the Lord been at work? For the Lord does nothing that he does not tell the prophets about. The lion roars, who will not prophesy? Let it be known in the palaces in Ashod/ and in the palaces in Egypt, and say, "Assemble on the hills of Samaria, and look at the tumult seething among her people and the oppression in her midst. They cannot do things honestly, says the Lord. They are ruled by violence and oppression.

Himn of praise. For this is the name of the one who created the mountains and the wind, and of the one who tells his thoughts to man, the maker of dawn and dusk, the one who

---

1. Amos (Hebrew = the Lord holds) from Tepoa. He had herds, and grew fig-trees. His job was not being prophet, a Nabbi. He fought the abominations and corruptions of the country.

walks on the top of the mountains; he is the Lord, the God of Hosts[1].

Invitation to conversion. Therefore this is the word of the Lord to the house of Israel: Search for me and you shall live. Search for the Lord and you shall live, lest fire shall burn the house of Joseph and devours Bethel[2] and nobody can put it out.

Himn of praise. It is Himn who made the Pleiades and Orion[3], who turned darkness into morning and day and night. It is Him who summoned the waters of the sea and poured them over the earth; his name is the Lord. It is Him who smiles destruction on the strong, and destruction comes on the fortified city.

Sacrifices without spirit. I hate and loathe your feasts, and do not like your celebrations. If you do your whole-offerings and shared-offerings I shall not accept them, and I will not watch the sacrifice of your fatted calves.

Those who live at ease and the wealthy. Woe betide those who live at ease in Zion and the untroubled on the hill of Samaria, men of mark in the first of nations, you to whom the people of Israel resort. Those of you who are thinking of keeping off the evil are hurrying the coming of violence. You who loll on beds inlaid with ivory and sprawl over your coaches, feasting on lambs from the flock and fatted calves, you who pluck the strings of the lute and invent musical instruments like David. You who drink wine by the bowful and lard yourselves with the richest of oild, but are not grieved at Joseph's ruin. Therefore now you shall head the column of exiles; that will be the end of sprawling and revelry.

The Lord God has sworn by himself; this is the word of the Lord, the God of Hosts: I loathe the arrogance of Jacob, and his palaces. I will abandon the city and all that is in it.

Injustice. Do horses run on rocks, or do oxen plough the sea? Thus you have turned your rights into poison and the fruit of justice into wormwood.

---

1. Hosts (Hebrew = God of the armies).
2. Old Canaanite Sanctuary where the golden calf was praised.
3. Pleiades and Orion, a group of stars which formed the Taurus constellation.

SYMBOLIC VISIONS

Prevention from the word of God. This is the word of the Lord: The days are coming on which I will bring famine on the country; not hunger for bread or thirst for water, but for hearing the word of the Lord. Men shall stagger from north to south, they shall range from east to west, seeking the word of the Lord, but they shall not find it. On that day fair maidens and young men shall faint from thirst; all who take their oath by Ashimah, goddess of Samaria, all who swear, "By the life of your god, O Dan!"

Final Himn. The Lord, the Lord of Hosts, the one who touches the earth and melts it, and all its inhabitants grow sad; the earth surges like the Nile and subsides like the river of Egypt. He who builts his stair up to the heavens and arches his ceiling over the earth[1]; he who calls the waters of the sea and pours them over the land; his name is the Lord.

Promise of salvation. On that day I will restore David's fallen house; I will repair its gaping walls to the ground. I will rebuild it as it was long ago, that they may possess what is left of Edom and all the nations who were once named mine. This is the very word of the Lord, who will do all this. A time is coming —says the Lord— when the ploughman shall follow hard on the reaper, and the vintager after him who sows the seed. The mountains shall run with fresh wine, and every hill shall wave with corn. I will restore the fortunes of my people Israel; they shall rebuild deserted cities and live in them, they shall plant vineyards and drink their wine, make gardens and eat the fruit. Once more I will plant them on their own soil, and they shall never again be uprooted from the soil I have given them. This is the very word of the Lord your God.

---

1. Peoples from the East and the Jews believed that the ceiling was a solid vault.

OBADIAH[1]

The new Israel

But on Mount Zion there will be those who escape, and it
    shall become a holy place; and the house of Jacob will
    recover all its possessions.

The house of Jacob shall be made of fire; the house of Joseph
    a flame, and the house of Esau shall be chaff, blazed
    and consumed: the house of Esau shall have no
    survivor, for the Lord has spoken.

Those in the Negeb will possess Mount Esau; those in the
    plains and in the Philistine country will possess the land
    of Ephraim and Samaria, and Benjamin will possess
    Gilead.

The exiles of this army, the sons of Israel, will possess
    Canaan as far as Zarephtah, and the exiles of Jerusalem
    who are now in Sepharad shall possess the southern
    cities.

And they shall go up Mount Zion safely, to judge over the
    Mount of Esau, and the kingdom shall belong to the
    Lord.

---

1. Obadiah (Hebrew = servant of the Lord), one of the Minor Prophets.

JONAH[1]

The Prophet's disobedience. The word of the Lord came to Jonah, son of Amittai: "Go to the great city Nineveh and say that I know about their wickedness." Jonah set out for Tarshish[2] to escape from the Lord. So Jonah went down to Joppa, where he found a ship bound for Tarshish. He paid his fare and went on board, meaning to travel by it to Tarshish out of reach of the Lord. But the Lord let loose a hurricane, and the sea ran so high in the storm that the ship threatened to break up. The sailors were afraid and cried out to their god for help. Then they threw things overboard to lighten the ship. Jonah had gone down into a corner of the ship and was lying sound asleep when the captain came upon him, "What, sound asleep? Stand up and pray to your god: He might think of us and save us from death." Then the seamen said, "Come and let us cast lots to find out who is to blame for this bad luck[3]." And the lot fell on Jonah.

Jonah is thrown overboard. Then they said to them, "Now then, let us know the reason for this bad luck. What is your business? Where do you come from? What is your country? What is your people?" He answered, "I am a Hebrew and I worship the Lord, God of heaven, who made the sea and the earth." Those men, even more afraid then, said to him, "What shall I do with you so that the sea goes down?" The storm grew

---

1. Jonah (Hebrew = dove), one of the Minor Prophets. He should not be mistaken with the main character of the book.
2. Hispania, that is, Spain, was the end of the world.
3. Ancient people thought that a guilty man was a danger for the rest of men.

worse and worse. He answered them, "Take me and throw me overboard, and the sea shall go down, for I know very well that I am to blame for this storm."

The crew rowed hard to put back to land but in vain, for the sea ran higher and higher. Then they called on the Lord and said, "O Lord, do not let us perish at the price of this man's life; not not charge us with the death of an innocent man. O Lord, all this is your set purpose[1]." Then they threw him overboard, and the sea went down. Then those men grew afraid of God, and offered sacrifice and made vows to him.

Jonah, in the fish's belly, prays to the Lord. The Lord made a great fish[2] to swallow up Jonah and Jonah was inside the fish's belly for three days and three nights[3]. Inside the fish's belly Jonah prayed to the Lord.

And the Lord commanded the fish to spew Jonah out on to the dry land[4].

Nineveh converts because of Jonah's preaching. Again the word of the Lord came to Jonah and he said to him, "Stand up, go to Nineveh[5], the great city, to preach what I will say to you." Jonah set out and headed for Nineveh as the Lord had commanded. Nineveh was a extraordinarily great city, it took three days to get there. Jonah was entering the city, walked around for a whole day and preached so: "Within forty days Nineveh will be destroyed."

The people of Nineveh trusted in God and ordered a fast. They put on sackcloth from the highest to the lowest[6]. When the news reached the king of Nineveh, he put on sackcloth and sat on ashes. He even announced that he and his noblemen were

---

1. They recognised who was to blame and were afraid of God.

2. A cetacean.

3. Jesus Christ recognised the miracle. "In the same way as Jonah was inside the fish for three days, so shall I be on the earth for three days and on the third day I will resuscitate."

4. In the Book of Jonah everything is miraculous. Everything is possible for the Lord, everything is normal.

5. It was the great sinner city for the Jews. Its area was of 664 hectares.

6. The attitude of the people of Nineveh contrasts with the Jew's infidelity and Jonah's egotism, who was displeased with their pardon; God's will makes people holy.

going to leave the city: "No man or beast, herd or flock, is to taste food, to graze or to drink water. They are to clothe themselves in sackcloth and call on God with all their might. Let every man abandon his wicked ways and his habitual violence. It may be that God will repent and turn away from his anger; and so we shall not perish." When God saw what they did and how they abandoned their wicked ways, he repented and did not bring upon them the disaster with which he had threatened.

God justifies his mercy. But Jonah was greatly displeased with this and got angry, and he prayed to the Lord and said, "O Lord, this is what I feared when I was in my own country, and that is why I went to Tarshish. I knew that You are a compassionate, long-suffering and ever constant god, and always willing to repent of the disaster. Therefore, Lord, I beg you to take my life, for I prefer dying to going on living." The Lord said to him, "Do you think you have a reason to be angry? You are sorry for the gourd, though you did not have the trouble of growing it, a plant which came up in a night and withered in a night. And should I not be sorry for the great city of Nineveh, with its hundred and twenty thousand people?"

MICAH[1]

FIRST SPEECH

Against Israel and Judah. This is the word of the Lord which came to Micah of Moresheth during the reigns of Jotham, Ahaz, and Hezekiah, kings of Judah. Visions concerning Samaria and Jerusalem.

Listen you all, peoples, listen, you earth, and all who are in it.
> The Lord is going to bear witness against you, the Lord
> from his Holy Temple.
For look, the Lord is leaving his dwelling-place, and comes
> and walks on the heights of the earth.
The mountains melt under his feet, the valleys are torn open,
> like wax before the fire, as torrents pouring down the
> hill-side.
All for the crime of Jacob and for the sins of the house of
> Israel. What is Jacob's infidelity? Is it not Jerusalem?
So I will make Samaria a heap of ruins in open country, a
> place for planting vines. I will pour her stones down
> into the valley and lay her foundations bare.
All her images shall be torn down. She ammassed them out of
> fees for harlotry and they shall be burnt up, I shall
> destroy all their images.

---

1. Micah (Hebrew = abridged form of Is there somebody like the Lord?).

Promises of Restoration

O Jacob, I will gather all your people, I will assemble the
　　　remnants of Israel; I will herd them like sheep in a fold,
　　　like a grazing flock with stampedes at the sight of a
　　　man, and they shall be sure, free of terror.

SECOND SPEECH

False Prophets

Listen, O leaders of Jacob, rulers of Israel, should you not
　　　know what is right?
But you hate good and love evil.
This is the word of the Lord on the prophets who seduce my
　　　people.
Therefore in the night you shall have darkness instead of
　　　visions, shadows instead of divination. The sun will go
　　　down over these prophet, the day will be dark for them.
Those prophets shall get ashamed in confusion, and they will
　　　speak no more for they will lack answers from God.

Restoration and peace after the exile

And in the future the mount of the Temple of the Lord shall
　　　sit on the top of the mountains, and it shall rise over the
　　　hills.
The peoples and nations will come to it, and they shall say,
　　　"Come, let us go up the mountain of the Lord, to the
　　　Temple of Jacob's God. He will show us his ways and
　　　we shall follow them." For the Law will come from
　　　Zion, and the word of the Lord from Jerusalem.
He will judge between may peoples, and arbiters among
　　　mighty nations afar; they shall bet their swords into
　　　mattocks, and their spears into prunning-knives. Nation
　　　shall not lift sword against nation, nor ever again be
　　　trained for war.

They shall sit under their vine, on the shadow of their fig-tree, and nobody will disturb us. This is the word of the Lord.

For every people walk in the name of their god; so we will walk in the name of the Lord our God for ever more.

But they do not know the ways of the Lord, they do not understand his commands. He has gathered them like sheaves to the threshing-floor.

Wake up and thresh, daughter of Zion. I will make your horns of iron, your hooves, your hooves I will make of bronze. You shall devote their ill-gotten gain to the Lord, their wealth to the Lord of all the earth.

And now, besieged city, gather strenth. The siege is pressed home against you; Israel's ruler shall be sturck on the cheek with a rod.

Profecy of the birth of the Christ of Bethlehem

And you, Bethlehem-Ephrata[1], you are small among the thousands of Judah, but The One who shall reign over Israel will come out of your people[2]. He has ancient origins, from the old days.

Therefore the Lord will abandon them until he gives birth to what he will give birth. Then the rest of his brothers will come back to the sons of Israel.

He will raise and graze the flock with the Lord's strong hand, with the majesty of the name of the Lord his God. They will live in peace, for then his power shall be with them over the whole earth.

And He shall be peace.

---

1. Bethlehem-Ephrata (Hebrew = Bet-lehem: house of bread), seven kilometers south of Jerusalem, city of the line of David. It is called Ephrata because its inhabitants came from the family Ephrat.
2. The awaited Messiah had to be born in Bethlehem. Christ, the Saviour of the world, worshipped by shepherds and kings. Constantin built him a huge temple.

THIRD SPEECH

Now listen to the words of the Lord,

"Up, state your case to the mountains, let the hills hear your
      plea!
My people, what have I done to you? In what have I bothered
      you? Answer me.
I brought you out of the land of Egypt, out of slavery, and I
      sent Moses and Aaron and Miriam to lead you.

Israel's hope in God their saviour

But I look at the Lord, I hope that he saves me, my God will
      listen to my plea.
Do not be glad for my luck, my foe[1]; I have fallen, but I shall
      rise; I am in darkness, but the Lord shall be my light.
I will bear the Lord's wrath, for I have sinned against Him,
      until he judges my case and sets my right. He will give
      me light, and I will watch his justice.
Then my foe shall come, she who said, "Where is your God
      the Lord?" My eyes shall be filled with her when she is
      trampled like the mud in the streets.
The day is coming in which your walls shall be rebuilt; on
      that day your possessions shall be greater.

---

1. Babel or Edom.

NAHUM[1]

Crimes are the cause of Nineveh's ruin

Woe betide you, bloody city, full of lie and violence, and of
    never ending looting!
Listen to the crack of the wip, the rattle of wheels and
    stamping of horses, bounding chariots, charters rearing,
    swords gleaming, flash of spears: corpses innumerable,
    men stumbling over corpses.
All for a wanton's monstrous wantonness, fair-seeming, a
    mistress of sorcery, who beguiled nations and tribes by
    her wantonness and her sorceries:
"Here I am against you" —says the Lord of Hosts.

---

1. Nahum (Hebrew = the Lord comforts), born in Elgoh. According to some
   people he was born in Galilee, and according to others he was born near
   Capernaun. In a village called Nahum near Capernaun?

HABAKKUK[1]

Why do wicked men have luck?

An oracle which the prophet Habakkuk received in a vision.

How long, O Lord, have I cried to you, unanswered, I cry
    "Violence!" and you do not come to my help.
Why do you let my see such iniquity, and you just watch
    oppression? Only at my looting and injustice there is
    trouble and quarrel.
Therefore the law dies, and justice is nowhere to be seen, for
    the wicked man besieges the good man, and justice is
    perverted.

The Chaldaeans, God's wip

For see that I set the Chaldaeans against you, that cruel and
    rapid people who runs throughout the earth to take
    possession of other people's dwelling-places.
Their are fearful and terrible; their strength and justice is their
    greatness: their horses are faster than leopards, keener
    than wolves in the evening; their cavalry wait ready,
    they spring forward, they come flying from afar like
    vultures swooping to devour the pray.

---

1. Habakkuk. Some people believe that he was the singer of the temple, a Levite.
He should not be taken for Judah's prophet (Daniel 14, 33-39).

Their whole army advances, violence in their hearts; a sea of
    faces rolls on; they bring in captives countless as the
    sand.

Kings they hold in derision, rulers they despise; they despise
    every fortress, they raise siege-works and capture it.

Then they pass on like the wind and are gone; and dismayed
    are all those whose strength was their god.!

Are you not from old, my Lord, my God, the Holy, the
    immortal! You have appointed them to execute
    judgement, as a rock to chastise us.

Your eyes are to pure to watch wickedness, you cannot look
    at the wicked men, and you remain silent when the
    wicked man devours another man righter than him?

God's answer to the prophet

I will stand at my post, I will take up my position on the
    watch-tower, I will watch to learn what he will say
    through me, what reply does he give to my plea.

And the Lord answered, "Write down your vision, inscribe it
    on talbets so that it can be easily read; for there is still a
    vision for the appointed time, but its time is coming in
    haste, and it will not fail. If it delays, wait for it, for it
    shall come."

The reckless will be unsure of himself, while the righteous
    man will live by being faithful.

Woe betide you who heap up wealth that is not yours and
    enrich youself with goods taken in pledge!

Will our your creditor suddenly start up, will not all awake
    who would shake you till you are emply, and will you
    not fall a victim to them?

Because you yourself have plundered mighty nations, all the
    rest of the world will plunder you, because of
    bloodshed and violence done in the land to the city and
    all its inhabitants.

Who betide you who seek unjust gain for your house, to built
    your nest on a height, to save yourself form the grasp

of wicked men! The very stones will cry out from the wall, and from the timbers a beam will answer them. Woe betide you who have built a town with bloodshed and founded a city on fraud!

ZEPHANIAH[1]

The day of the Lord

In that time I will search Jerusalem with a light and punish
those men who sit on its iniquities and say in their
hearts, "The Lord does neither good nor evil."

Their wealth shall be stolen, their houses destroyed; if they
built houses they shall not live in them, if they planted
vineyards they shall not drink their wine.

The day of the Lord is near, and it will come soon. His roar
can already be heard, and even the brave men will cry
with fear!

Neither their gold nor their silver will save them.

Exhortation to penitence

Assemble and gather yourselves, O wicked people, before the
decree is fulfiled and burns like straw.

Search for the Lord, you all, honest man on earth who have
followed his commandments; search for justice, search
for humility; so that you can be safe on the day of the
Lord.

---

1. Zephaniah (Hebrew = the Lord is a shield). Great-greatson of king Ezekiah.
   He lived in the same time than pophet Nahum. He preached in Jerusalem.

God's judgement against Jerusalem

Woe betide the rebel and contaminated city, the oppressive
     city! She has not listened to my words, she has not
     done what is right in my eyes. She has not trusted in
     the Lord, she has not come close to her God.

Her leaders are, among her, like roaring lions, her judges like
     nightly wolves who leave nothing for tomorrow.

Her prophets are arrogant and treacherous men, her priests
     desecrate the holy houses and trespass the law.

And I said, "At least you shall be afraid of me, you will
     accept my righteousness; you cannot forget my frequent
     visits to you." But they have done their best to go on
     with their veil deeds.

Therefore, wait for me —says the Lord— wait for the day
     when I stand up to accuse you!

Messianic promises: conversion of the pagans

Then I will give the peoples pure lips for them to invoke the
     Lord by name, and serve him by one consent.

From beyond the rivers of Cush my suppliants of the
     dispersion shall bring me tribute.

On that day you shall not be put to shame for all your deeds
     by which you have rebelled against me; for then I will
     rid you of your proud and arrogant citizens, and never
     again shall you flaunt your pride on my holy hill.

I will leave you in a people afflicted and poor who shall wait
     on the Lord's behalf.

The survivors in Israel shall find refuge in the name of the
     Lord; they shall no longer do wrong or speak lies, nor
     words of deceit shall pass their lips; for they shall feed
     and lie down with no one to terrify them.

Zion, cry out for joy, raise the shout of triumph, Israel; be
     glad, rejoice with all your heart, daughter of Jerusalem!

Return of the exiles

On that day this shall be the message to Jerusalem: Do not be
afraid, Zion, let not your hands fall slack.

The Lord is among you, a powerful saviour! He shall rejoice
over you and be glad, he shall show you his love once
more, he will dance for you with joy, as in feasts. I will
rid you of your oppressors, I will rid the ignominy
which is upon you.

Look; in that time I will deal with all your oppressors.

In that time I will bring you all back, I will assemble you.
And I will give you glory and fame among all the
peoples in the world when I bring back your prosperity,
and so you shall see it —says the Lord.

HAGGAI [1]

The reconstruction of the temple. In the second year of King Darius, on the first day of the sixth month the word of the Lord came to prophet Haggai to Zerubbabel son of Shealtiel, governor of Judah and to Joshua son of Jehozadak the high priest; This is the word of the Lord of Hosts: "This nation says to itself, The time to built the Temple of the Lord has not yet come!" And the word of the Lord came to prophet Ageo, Is it a time for you to live in your own well-roofed houses, while this house lies in ruins? Therefore this is the word of the Lord, "Consider your way of life. You sown much but reaped little; you eat but never as much as you wish, you drink but never more than you need, you are clothed but never warm, and the labourer puts his wages into a purse with a hole in it. Therefore go up into the hills, fetch timber, and build a house acceptable to me, where I can show my Glory, says the Lord."

And Haggai, sent by the Lord, spoke thus to the people, as the Lord had said, "I am with you, this is the word of the Lord." And the Lord moved Zerubbabel's spirit[2], son of Shealtiel, ruler of Judah, the spirit of Joshua, son of Jehozadak, high priest, and the spirit of the rest of the people, so that they came and started to built the Temple of the Lord of Host, their God, on the twenty-fourth day of the six month.

---

1. Haggai (Hebrew = born in feast). He encouraged the exiles together with Zachariah to rebuild that temple more glorious than the first one.

2. He inspired...

ZECHARIAH[1]

THE MESSIANIC KING AND HIS VIRTUES

The Messiah[2]. Rejoice, daughter of Zion,/ rejoice, daughter of Jerusalem./ Your king is coming to you:/ he is fair and victorious,/ humble and mounting an ass,/ young son of a she-ass./ And he will make/ that the war-chariots of Ephraim disappear;/ and the bow of war will disappear too./ He will announce peace to the nations/ and he will rule from sea to sea,/ and from the River to the edge of the earth[3].

---

1. Zechariah (Hebrew = the Lord remembered). This prophet lived in Haggai's times, head of a priestly family. He appeared in the second year of Darius the Perse.
2. This beautiful messianic prophecy refers to Jesus's entrance in the day of Palm Sunday in Jerusalem (Matthew, 21, 1-6).
3. The Messiah is the prince of peace. He will destroy weapons and bring peace over the whole world.

MALACHI[1]

PROLOGUE

The Lord's love for Israel. The word of the Lord came to Israel through Malachi.

THE NEW SACRIFICE

Against those who desecrate God's service. No, I am not pleased with you, and I am not pleased with the sacrifices that you offer me —says the Lord of Hosts—.

The sacrifice of the New Law[2]. My name is great from the East to the West, and everywhere incense offerings are done on my account, as a pure offering. For my Name is great among the peoples —says the Lord of Hosts—; while you desecrate it.

The announcing angel. And then I will send my messenger to prepare the road before Me, and then the Lord whom you are looking for shall come to his Temple, the one for whom you sight so much[3].

---

1. Malachi (Hebrew = My messenger).
2. God did not like the sacrifices and offerings of that people. From then on there will not be more than a victim, an only Sacrifice, a pure host, a victim whom shall offer himself for the East and the West (Jesus Christ).
3. Saint Mark applies this to John the forerunner.

RETREATS AND PROMISES

Days of the Lord and victory of the righteous. "You have used hard words against me —says the Lord—; but you say, 'What have we done against you?' You have said, 'It is pointless to serve God; what do we gain from keeping his commandments or behaving with deference to the Lord of Hosts? Therefore we call the proud men happy, because, although they do what is wrong in the eyes of the Lord they are fruitful, although they put God to the proof they come to no harm'." So spoke among them those who are afraid of God. But the Lord was listening and overheard what they said, and before Him a memorial book was written in favour of those who fear him and respect His Name. "They will become —says the Lord of Hosts— my property on the day which I am preparing; Yes, I will forgive them as a man forgives his son who serves him. Then you will see the difference between the righteous and the wicked again, between those who serve the Lord and those who do not.

Now that day is to come, burning like a turnace. Then all proud men and the evildoers shall be like chaff. On that day they shall be set ablaze —says the Lord of Hosts— it shall leave them neither root nor branch. For you, on the contrary, for those who fear my Name, the sun of justice will shine with salvation on its beams[1], and you will come out and you shall break loose like calves released from the stall. You shall trample down the wicked, for they will be ashes under the soles of your feet on the day which I am preparing" —says the Lord of Hosts.

EPILOGUE[2]

The preceeding prophet. "Remember the law of Moses my servant, the rules and precepts which I bade him deliver to all Israel at Horeb. Look, I will send you the prophet

---

1. Sun of justice which comes from Heaven; it is Jesus Christ.
2. The Kingdom of God is near: the time of the messianic prophecies is up.

Elijah[1] before the great and terrible day of the Lord comes. He
will reconcile fathers to sons and sons to fathers, lest I come and
put the land under a ban to destroy it."

---

1. Taken from heaven, he will come back. Jesus Christ said that he had already
   come in the person of John (Matthew, 17, 1-13).

NEW TESTAMENT

UNIFIED GOSPELS[1]

The Word[2]: John 1, 1-18

In the beginning was the Word, and the Word was with God
    and the Word was God.

He Himself was already with God at the beginning.

Everything came into existence through Him, and nothing
    which exists came to be except through Him.

Life was in Him, and life was the light of men.

The light shines in the darkness, but the darkness did not let it
    enter.

A man appeared, sent by God, his name was John[3].

He came as a witness to testify on behalf of the light, so that
    through it everybody would believe.

He was not the light, but a witness summoned to declare on
    behalf of the light.

The Word was the true light which, on arriving in this world,
    illuminates all men.

He was in the world, and the world started to exist through
    Him, but the world did not know it.

---

1. The New Testament is the fullness of the Revelation, the fulfillment of the
   Promises of the Old Testament and of the Alliance, of the Word of God
   delivered by the Prophets to His people. In the New Testament it is the same
   Son of God incarnate who talks to all mankind. His word is a message of
   salvation. "The Word of God was made flesh" to save the world from sin and
   death. It is he who has revealed to us the mysteries of the Kingdom of God.

2. The Word is the Son of God Himself, the second person of the Holy Trinity.

3. John the Forerunner.

He came to His home[1], but He was not welcomed.

However, He granted those who did receive Him, those who
    do believe in Him[2], the dignity of the children of God:

Who originate, not from blood, nor from carnal instinct, nor
    from man's free will, but from God[3].

And the Word was made man and lived amongst us and we
    have admired His glory, a glory which He receives
    from the Father as His Only son, full of grace and truth.

John declares on His behalf and exclaims: "this is He of
    whom I said: He who will come after me has
    preference over me, because he existed before me".

Because we have all received from his fullness, grace after
    grace:

Since, if the Law was given through Moses, grace and truth
    arrived through Christ[4].

Nobody has ever seen God; it is the Only Begotten Son, who
    is in the bosom of the Father, who has revealed Him.

John the Baptist: Luke 1, 5-25

In the time of Herod, the king of Judea, there was a priest
called Zacharias, from the turn of Abia, who was married to a
woman called Elizabeth, a descendant of Aaron. They were
both righteous in the eyes of God, and unreproachably observed
all the Lord's commandments and dispositions. And they had
no children, because Elizabeth[5] was barren and both were
advanced in years.

When he was practising his priestly ministry before God,
according to the turn that fell to him[6] by good fortune his lot
was to enter the Lord's sanctuary to offer incense, in accordance
with the liturgical ceremony. And all the assembled throng
remained outside, in prayer, during the oblation of the incense.

---

1. To His Chosen People, to prepare the way for the Saviour.
2. The Apostles and the Church.
3. Divine filiation witnessed by John.
4. The Grace of God.
5. The Hebrews considered children to be the blessing of a marriage.
6. The priests were divided into 24 families which were divided into 24 groups,
    which took turns in weeks.

And an angel of the Lord appeared to him, standing at the right of the incense altar.

When he saw him, Zacharias was alarmed and overwhelmed by fear. But the angel said to him: "Be calm, Zacharias, since your prayer has been heeded; and your wife Elizabeth will give you a son, whom you will give the name of John; and he will be your delight and your joy, and his birth will give everybody a reason for rejoicing. Because he will be great in the eyes of the Lord, and will not drink any wine or liquor, and will already be full of the Holy Spirit in his mother's womb, and he will convert many of the Sons of Israel to the Lord, their God; and he will walk before Him clothed in the spirit and power of Elias, to establish harmony between parents and children (Mal 4, 5-6) and instil prudence in the wayward, thus preparing a people duly amenable to the Lord." Zacharias said to the angel: "How can I be sure of this? Because I am old and my wife is advanced in years." The angel replied to him: "I am Gabriel, I am in the presence of God and I have been sent to speak to you and give you this welcome news. So then, you will remain in silence and unable to speak until the day when these things come about, because you had no faith in my words, which will be fulfilled in their due time."

The people were waiting for Zacharias and were surprised that he was taking such a long time in the sanctuary. And when he came out he could not talk to them, and because of this they understood that he had had a vision in the sanctuary. And he spoke to them with signs, since he had become dumb[1]. When the period for his ministry was over, he went home. Days later his wife Elizabeth conceived, and was in retreat for five months, and she said to herself: "The Lord has favoured me in this way by deigning to put turn His eyes on me in order to take away that which was a reason for disgrace among men[2]."

---

1. Because of his paltry faith.
2. Sterility was considered disgraceful by the Jews.

Gabriel's annunciation: Luke 1, 26-38

When Elizabeth was already in the sixth month, the angel Gabriel was sent by God to a city in Galilee called Nazareth[1] to a virgin, newly-married to a man called Joseph, from the house of David, and the name of the virgin[2] was Mary. And going up to where she was, he greeted her like this: "May God save you, full of grace[3], the Lord is with you." When she heard these words she was alarmed and started to wonder about the meaning of this greeting. The angel said to her: "Stay calm, Mary, since you have found grace in the eyes of God. Because of this you will conceive and give birth to a son, whom you will call Jesus. He will be great and the son of the Most High, and the Lord God will give Him the throne of David, His father[4], and He will reign over the house of Jacob for eternity and His reign will have no end." Mary said to the angel: "How will this come about, since I have not known a man[5]?" The angel answered her: "The Holy Spirit will come down upon you and the power of the Most High will wrap you in its shadow, and because of this the son born from you will be holy and the son of God[6]. Look, there you have your cousin Elizabeth who has also conceived a son in her old age, and she who was considered barren is now in her sixth month, because nothing is impossible for God." Mary replied: "Behold the Lord's slave". And the angel disappeared from her presence.

Visit to Elizabeth: Luke 1, 39-45

And in those days Mary took to the road, hurriedly heading for the mountain, to a city of Juda. And she entered the house of Zacharias and greeted Elizabeth. When Elizabeth heard Mary's greeting, the child jumped up and down with delight in her

---

1. An unknown village, it had the honour to play host to the Word Incarnate.
2. The mother of the Messiah had to be a virgin according to the prediction of the prophet Isaiah.
3. Sanctifying grace, exempt of all sin, even the Original.
4. The Son of the Most High as God, and of the lineage of David as a man.
5. Saint Joseph took no part in the birth of Jesus.
6. With Mary's yes, the sublime act of divine Maternity was carried out.

womb, and Elizabeth was filled with the Holy Spirit, and loudly exclaimed: "Blessed are you amongst women and blessed is the fruit of your womb. Who am I that my Lord's mother[1] should come to my house? Because, just imagine, when he became aware of your greeting, the child jumped for joy in my womb. She who believed that what was announced on the Lord's behalf will be fulfilled, is fortunate."

Magnificat: Luke 1, 46-55

Then Mary exclaimed: "My soul magnifies the Lord, and my spirit rejoices in God, my Saviour; because He turned his eyes on to the insignificance of his slave. So then: from now on all generations shall call me fortunate; because great things have been carried out in me by the Allmighty, whose name is Holy; whose mercy is passed on from generation to generation to those who worship Him. He has deployed the power of His arm and has thwarted the plans of the vain; He has toppled potentates from their thrones and elevated the humble; He has heaped riches on to the destitute and dismissed the wealthy with empty hands. He has taken His servant Israel under His protection, on behalf of Abraham and his descendants for ever and always, in accordance with His merciful intentions, as had been prophesied to our forefathers[2]."

Birth of John: Luke 1, 56-66

Mary stayed with her for three months[3] and then returned home. Meanwhile, the time for delivery arrived and she gave birth to a son. Her neighbours and relatives heard about the great favour which had been bestowed on her by the Lord and were pleased with her. After eight days, when they went to circumcise the child, they wanted to give him the name of his father, Zacharias. But his mother intervened, saying: "No, for he must be called John." They replied to her: "There's nobody in

---

1. For the Jews, God was the "Lord".
2. The Hymn of Mary's Magnificat is the hymn of gratitude and praise, because it elevates the humble and humiliates the arrogant.
3. Mary's presence filled Elizabeth's house with wealth.

your family that holds that name." Using signs they asked his father what he wanted him to be called. He requested a tablet and wrote: "His name is John". And everybody was astonished. He immediately recovered the use of his lips and tongue, and, praising God, he started to speak. These things were discussed all over the mountain of Judea. Whoever heard about it stopped to think about it and wondered: "What will this child turn out to be?" Because, truly, a special benevolence was reflected in him.

Canticle of Zacharias - "Benedictus": Luke 1, 67-80

And Zacharius, his father, was filled with the Holy Spirit, and, under its inspiration, he spoke in this way: "Blessed be the Lord, God of Israel, because He has intervened on behalf of His people, undertaking their rescue and giving rise to a powerful Saviour for us in the house of David, his servant, in compliance with what had been foretold in days of old through the mouths of the holy prophets: A saviour who delivers us from our enemies and from the power of all those who hate us; in this way He has granted mercy to our ancestors and has remembered his holy alliance, the oath that He swore to our father Abraham, that granted that we should serve Him without fear, free from the power of our enemies, in holiness and justice for the whole of our lives. And you, oh child, will be a prophet of the Most High, since you will go before the Lord to prepare His ways: To communicate to His people the knowledge of salvation through the remission of sins; the work of the loving mercy of our God, through which a rising sun from on high will visit us, to cast light on those who lie in the darkness and shadow of death, to guide our steps along the path of peace[1]." And the child grew up and became spiritually strong and lived in isolated places, until the day he devoted himself to knowing Israel[2].

---

1. When he recovered his speech, he intoned a hymn of praise.
2. Surely with the Essenes of Qum Ram.

Joseph, Mary's Husband: Mat 1, 18-25

The birth of Jesus took place in this way: His mother, Mary, had recently married Joseph; and before living together[1], she found herself pregnant by the Holy Spirit. Joseph, her husband, who was righteous and did not want to denounce her, was thinking of secretly disowning her. When he was absorbed in these thoughts, the angel of the Lord appeared to him in his dreams and said to him: "Joseph, son of David, do not continue having fear of welcoming Mary, your wife, into your house, since what has been conceived in her comes from the Holy Spirit. She will give birth to a son and you will give Him the name of Jesus, since He will save His people from their sins." With this was fulfilled the word of the Lord, through the prophet, which says: "Behold the Virgin will conceive and give birth to a son and they will give Him the name of Emmanuel, which means God with us." When he awoke from his dream, he did what the angel of the Lord commanded him[2] and welcomed his wife into his house. And, without having known him, she gave birth to a son, and she gave Him the name of Jesus.

Birth of Jesus: Luke 2, 1-7

At that time Caesar Augustus issued a decree that the census[3] should be carried out in the entire empire. This first census was undertaken when Cyrenius was governor of Syria. And everybody went to register, each in their own city. Joseph also went to register, along with his wife Mary, who was pregnant, from the city of Nazareth, in Galilee, to the city of David in Judea, which is Bethlehem, as it was the seat of the family of David. And when the time for delivery came she was there and she gave birth to her Only Begotten Son, and she

1. Joseph and Mary had celebrated the betrothal when they were living in their own houses, before the wedding, and were legally married.
2. In this way the mystery of the Incarnation was revealed.
3. Palestine was a kingdom associated with Rome, governed by Herod the Great, the usurper.

wrapped Him in swaddling clothes and laid Him down in a manger[1], since there was no room for them in the inn.

Angels and shepherds: Luke 2, 8-14

There were some shepherds in the same area who were passing the night in vigil and kept watch in turns to guard their flock, and an angel of the Lord appeared before them, and the glory of the Lord enveloped them in its light, and they trembled with fright. The angel[2] said to them: "be calm, for know that I am bringing you good news which will cause great joy for you and all the people: today, in the city of David, a Saviour who is the Messiah, the Lord, has been born to you. And this is the sign which will serve you to identify Him: you will find the child wrapped in swaddling clothes and laying in a manger." And suddenly a great crowd from the heavenly world joined the angel and they gave praise to God, saying:

"Glory to God on high, and on earth peace to those men with whom God is pleased."

---

1. A cave nearby.
2. Probably Gabriel, who appeared to Zacharias and Mary.

Adoration of the shepherds: Luke 2, 15-20

The angels had barely retired towards the heavens when the shepherds began to say to each other: "Let's go, then, to Bethlehem to see this event about which the Lord has notified us." They went at full speed and found Mary and Joseph, and the child laying in the manger[1]. And when they saw Him they started to reveal what they had been told about this child[2]. And everybody that heard them admired these things and meditated on them in the depth of their hearts. The shepherds returned glorifying and praising God for everything they had seen and heard, in accordance with what had been announced to them.

Circumcision: Luke 2, 21

When the eighth day came, on which He had to be circumcised, they gave Him the name of Jesus, as He had been called by the angel before His conception.

Presentation: Luke 2, 22-32

And when the time came that they had to be purified under Mosaic law, they took Him to Jerusalem to present Him to the Lord, as is ordained in God's Law: "Every first-born male will be consecrated to the Lord (Ex 13,2) and, following the commands of the Lord's Law, a pair of turtledoves or two pigeons shall be offered in sacrifice (Lv 12,8)."

Light of the people: Luke 2, 25-32

At that time there was a man in Jerusalem called Simeon. And this man was upright and pious and awaited the messianic restoration of Israel; and the Holy Spirit dwelled in him; and the Holy Spirit had revealed to him that he would not die before seeing the Lord's Anointed. He came to the temple, driven by the Spirit. And when the parents entered with the infant Jesus to

---

1. The Birth of Jesus is described with this sublime simplicity.
2. The shepherds went to Bethlehem to announce to everybody the occurence which they had contemplated with their own eyes.

fulfill in Him that prescribed in the Law, he took Him in his arms and praised God in this way[1]:

"Now, Lord, you can let Your servant go in peace, according to Your word;
because my eyes have contemplated He who brings salvation,
which You have made visible to all peoples:
a light to illuminate the Gentiles[2] and the glory of your people Israel."

Simeon and Anna: Luke 2, 33-38

His father and His mother where astonished at the things which were said about Him. Simeon blessed them and said to His mother Mary: "Bear in mind that this child is set for the fall and resurgence of many from Israel and as a signal of contradiction[3], and a sword will pierce your own soul, in order that the thoughts at the bottom of many hearts may come out."

The old prophetess Anna, the daughter of Phanuel, of the tribe of Aser, was also there. Having lived for seven years with her husband after her marriage, she was now a widow aged eighty-four. She did not use to leave the Temple, and served God night and day, given over to fasting and prayer. And when she arrived at that very moment, she started to praise God and talk about the child to all those who were awaiting the salvation of Jerusalem.

Nazareth: Luke 2, 39-40

Once all the commands of the Lord's Law had been satisfied, they returned to Galilee, to their city of Nazareth. The Child grew and became strong and full of wisdom, and God's benevolence was made apparent in Him.

---

1. Simeon was not a priest and received a grace with the characteristics of the Spirit and the gift of prophecy.
2. Universal Saviour.
3. Signal of contradiction: for unbelievers, damnation, and for believers, salvation.

Adoration of the Magi: Mat 2, 1-12

When Jesus was born in Bethlehem in Judah in the time of King Herod, some magi arrived from the East asking: "Where is the newly born King of the Jews? Because we saw His star[1] and we have come to adore Him." When King Herod knew about this, he and all of Jerusalem lost their calm. And he gathered together all the chief priests and the people's scribes and asked them where Christ was due to be born. They answered him: "In Bethlehem in Judah, since the prophet wrote thus:

«And you, Bethlehèm, in the land of Judah, you are in no way the smallest of the principal cities of Judah; because the prince who will be the shepherd of my people of Israel will emerge from you» (Mic 5,2)."

Then Herod, calling the Magi aside, diligently requested information about the time when the star appeared and, when they were setting off for Bethlehem, said to them: "Go and thoroughly investigate everything concerning the child; and, when you have found him, let me know, so that I too can go and adore him[2]". Once they had received the King's instructions, they left. And the star, which they had seen in the East, went ahead of them before stopping when it reached the place where the baby was. When they saw the star, they were extraordinarily happy. They went into the house and saw the child with Mary, His mother, and, falling to the ground, they adored Him; afterwards they opened up their coffers and offered Him presents of gold, incense and myrrh. And, having been warned by God in dreams not to go back to Herod, they returned home by another route.

The Holy Innocents: Mat 2, 16-18

Then Herod, seeing that he had been deceived by the Magi, rose up in fury and ordered the death of all children aged two or

---

1. The magi from the East must have known about the prophecy of the star of Jacob from exiled Jews.
2. The cunning King was hypocritically thinking of killing Him.

under in Bethlehem and its outskirts, following the timescale he had diligently informed himself about from the Magi[1].

Flight to Egypt: Mat 2, 13-15

After their departure, an angel of the Lord appeared to Joseph in his dreams and said to him: "Get up, take the child and His mother and flee to Egypt and stay there until you receive a new command; because Herod is going to search for the child in order to kill Him." Then he got up, took the child[2] and His mother and, still at night, set off for Egypt. And they were there until the death of Herod.

Return: Mat 2, 19-23

Once Herod was dead, an angel of the Lord appeared to Joseph in Egypt, in his dreams, and said to him: "Get up, take the child and His mother and go back to the land of Israel; because those who were making an attempt on the child's life are dead." He got up, took the child and His mother and entered into the land of Israel. But when he knew that Archelaus was reigning in Judea, as a successor to his father Herod, he was afraid to go there. And, having been advised by God in dreams, he went to the region of Galilee and set up home in a city called Nazareth.

In the Temple: Luke 2, 41-50

His parents went to Jerusalem every year for the Passover festival. And when He was now twelve years old they went as usual to this festival; when the days of their stay were over and they returned, the Child Jesus stayed in Jerusalem without letting His parents know. And they travelled for a day, thinking that He had come with the caravan; but then they went to look for Him amongst their relatives and acquaintances; and, not finding Him, they returned to Jerusalem to search for Him. After three days they found Him in the temple, seated in the

---

1. But God was keeping watch over the Child and gave Joseph orders.
2. There was a journey of nine days through the desert from Bethlehem to Egypt.

midst of the masters, listening to them and asking them questions; and everybody who heard him was amazed by His intelligence and His replies[1]. His parents were moved when they saw Him; and His mother said to Him: "Son, why have You done this to us[2]? Your father and I have been walking around looking for You, filled with anguish." He said to them: "Why did you bother to look for Me? Didn't you know that I must have been in my Father's house?" But they did not understand His words.

Hidden life: Luke 2, 51-52

Then He accompanied them to Nazareth, and lived in perfect submission to them. His mother preserved all these things in her heart. And Jesus continued to grow in wisdom, in years and in the gratification of God and men.

John's mission: Luke 3, 1-6

In the fifteenth year of the empire of Tiberius Caesar, when Pontius Pilate was the governor in Judea; Herod the tetrarch of Galilee and Philip, his brother, the tetrarch of Iturea and Trachonitis, and Lysanias the tetrarch of Abilene, under the high priesthood of Annas and Caiphas, the word of God came to John, the son of Zacharias, in the desert[3]. And he devoted himself to travelling around the Jordan region preaching a baptism of penance to pardon sins, in accordance with what was written in the book of the prophet Isaiah: "The voice which cries out in the desert: «Prepare the way of the Lord, trace His paths in a straight line; every valley will be filled, every hill and mountain shall be brought down; and the twisted will be straightened and the escarpments will be flattened; and thus all men will be able to see the salvation sent by God[4]» (Is 40, 3-5)."

---

1. Listening and asking in the inner courtyards of the temples, in accordance with the didactic system of the synagogues.
2. This was not a reproach, but the relief of her grieving heart.
3. To fulfill his mission.
4. John's baptism did not wipe away sins, but prepared for penitence.

Penitence: Mark 1, 5-6

And all the inhabitants from the Jerusalem and Judea area went out to meet him; confessing their sins, they were baptized by him in the river Jordan. John wore camelskin clothes with a leather sash round his waist and he lived on grasshoppers and wild honey.

Fruits of repentance: Luke 3, 7-9

And he said to the throngs who came to be baptized by him: "Who has taught you to avoid the wrath of God which is coming down upon you? Make, then, fruits of sincere repentance. And don't start to say inside: We have Abraham as a father. Because I say to you that God can make the sons of Abraham spring forth from these stones: Moreover, the axe is already in position at the root of the trees. Every tree, then, which does not give good fruit is cut down and flung on to the fire[1]."

Charity and justice: Luke 3, 10-14

People used to ask him: "What, then, must we do?" He answered them: "He who has two tunics, give one of them to somebody who doesn't have any; and he who has provisions, do the same." Some publicans also came to be baptized and they said to him: "Master, what must we do?" And he said to them: "Do not ask for more than the rate that has been set for you." Some soldiers also asked him: "And us, what must we do?" And he replied to them: "Don't practice any extortion or make any false denunciations."

Testimony: Luke 3, 15-18 (Mat 3, 11-12; Mark 1, 7-8)

As all the people were intrigued as regards John and everybody was wondering if he was perhaps the Messiah, John started to say to them: "I baptize you with water; but somebody

---

1. He upbraided arrogance, hypocrisy and the injustices which impeded the Saviour's arrival. The austerity of his life was all a sermon.

is coming now who is more powerful than me, 'behind me', of whom I shall not be worthy of prostrating myself to untie the straps of His sandals; He will baptize you with the fire of the Holy Spirit: In His hand He holds the rake to weed His plot of land and gather the wheat in His granary; but he will burn the straw with a fire that will never go out. In this way, with these and many other exhortations, he announced the good news to the people[1]."

Jesus's baptism: Mat 3, 14-17 (Mark 1, 9-11; Luke 3, 21-33)

«After all the people had been baptized» «Jesus came from Nazareth in Galilee and was baptized by John in the Jordan[2]». John tried to dissuade Him, saying: "It is I who need to be baptized by You and You come to me?" Jesus answered him: "Let me do it now, because it is fitting that in this way we satisfy all righteousness." Then John let Him do it: Once He had been baptized Jesus came out of the water. «Being in prayer». Suddenly the skies opened; and He saw the Spirit of God come down like a dove and come on to Him. And a voice, which came from the sky, said: "This is My much-loved Son in whom I am pleased[3]." «When Jesus began, He was around thirty».

Fasting and temptations: Mat 4, 1-11 (Mark 1, 12-13; Luke 4, 1-13)

Then Jesus was taken by the Spirit to the desert to be tempted by the Devil, «living with the wild animals». And, having fasted for forty days and forty nights, He was finally hungry. The tempter approached Him and said to Him: "If you are the Son of God, order these stones to turn into bread[4]." He replied: "It is written: «Man does not live off bread alone, but of

---

1. There was a great expectation about the arrival of the Messiah. The 70 weeks of the years of Daniel had been completed.
2. The humility of Jesus was matched by that of John.
3. The Father, Son and Holy Spirit were present at the Baptism of Jesus by the Forerunner. The Most Holy Trinity.
4. Jesus begins His mission with a rigorous fast.

every word emanating from God's mouth» (Deut 8,3)." Then the
Devil took Him to the holy city (Luke) «of Jerusalem», put Him
on the pinnacle of the temple and said to Him: "If you are the
son of God, throw yourself down; because it is written: «He will
give orders to the angels around you and they will take you in
their hands so that your foot does not stumble against any
stones» (Ps 90, 10-11)." Jesus replied to him: "It is also written:
«You will not tempt the Lord, your God[1]» (Dt 6,10)." The Devil
again took Him to the top of a very high mountain, made Him
look at all the kingdoms of the world in their magnificence[2], and
said to Him: "I will give you all these things if you fall at my
feet to worship me." Then Jesus answered him: "Go away,
Satan; because it is written: «You will adore the Lord, your
God, and you will only worship Him» (Dt 6,13)." Then He left
the Devil and the angels approached to serve Him.

John the Baptist: John 1, 19-28

John's declaration, when the Jews sent priests and Levites
from Jerusalem to interrogate him: "Who are you?" He freely
confessed the truth and openly declared: "I am not the
Messiah." "Who, then?", they asked him. "Are you Elias?" And
he answered: "I am not." "Are you the Prophet?" And he
replied: "No." But they badgered him insistently: "Who are
you?, so that we may give a reply to those who have sent us.
What do you say about yourself?" He answered: "According to
the prophet Isaiah (40, 3), «I am the voice that cries out in the
desert; track the path of the Lord in a straight line»." The
envoys were Pharisees, and they continued their questioning:
"Why, then, do you baptize if you are neither the Messiah, nor
Elias, nor the Prophet?" John answered them: "I baptize with
water; there is amongst you He whom you do not know, He
who has to come after me, and I am not worthy of undoing the
strap of His sandal[3]." This took place in Bethany, on the other
side of the Jordan, where John used to baptize.

---

1. The three great temptations of humanity are: pleasures, honours and riches.
2. The world of idolatry are his kingdoms.
3. John defined himself as Forerunner and Baptist.

Lamb of God[1]: John 1,29-34

The following day he saw Jesus walking towards him, and exclaimed: "This is the Lamb of God, who wipes away the sin of the world. This is He of whom I said: Behind me is arriving one who has been placed ahead of me, because He existed before me. And I did not know Him; but I have come to baptize with water to reveal Him to Israel." John made this declaration: "I have seen the Spirit come down from the sky like a dove and rest on Him. I did not know Him, but He who sent me to baptize with water said to me: 'He on whom you see the Spirit descend and remain is He who must baptize with the Holy Spirit[2].' I have seen Him and I declare that He is the Son of God."

John, Andrew and Peter: John 1, 35-42

The next day John remained there with two of his disciples, and, seeing Jesus pass by, said: "Look at the Lamb of God." When they heard this two of his disciples went in pursuit of Jesus. Jesus turned round and, seeing that they were following Him, said to them: "What are you looking for?" They answered Him: "Rabbi (which means Master), where do You live?" He replied to them: "Come and you will see"; so they went and saw where He lived and spent that day in His house; it was more or less four or five o' clock in the afternoon. One[3] of the two who had heard John and followed Jesus was Andrew, Simon Peter's brother. The first person he met was his brother Simon, to whom he reported: "We have found the Messiah (which means Christ)." He took him to Jesus. Turning His gaze on him, Jesus said: "You are Simon, the son of John; you will be called Cephas (which means Peter)."

---

1. The Prophets called the Messiah Lamb of God, the victim of our sins. John reveals and introduces Him.
2. The day of Pentecost.
3. The other was the apostle John, the evangelist.

Philip and Nathaniel: John 1, 43-51

The next day Jesus decided to leave for Galilee, and, meeting Philip, said to him: "Follow me." Philip came from Bethsaida, the town of Andrew and Peter[1]. Philip met Nathaniel[2] and said to him: "we have found He who is written about by Moses in the Law, and by the Prophets, Jesus, the Son of Joseph of Nazareth." "Something good can come out of Nazareth?", Nathaniel answered him. Philip insisted: "Come and you will see Him". When Jesus saw Nathaniel coming towards Him, He exclaimed: "Here is a true Israelite arriving, in whom there is no deceit." Nathaniel asked him: "Where do You know me from?" "Before Philip called you, I saw you when you were under the fig tree," Jesus replied to him. Nathaniel answered: "Rabbi, You are the Son of God, You are the King of Israel." Jesus replied to him: "Have you believed because I have told you that I saw you under the fig tree? You will see greater things." And He added: "I say to you with certainty: You will see the sky open and the angels of God rising up and coming down on the Son of man."

The wedding at Canaan: John 2, 1-11

Three days later, a wedding was celebrated in Canaan in Galilee. Jesus' Mother was among the guests. Jesus and His disciples were also invited to the wedding. When there was no wine, His Mother said to Jesus: "They have no wine." "Woman, Jesus answered her, why are you meddling in my plans? My time has still not come[3]." The mother advised the waiters: "do what He tells you." There were six stone jars, for the purifications of the Jews, the capacity of which varied from eighty to one hundred and twenty liters. Jesus commanded the waiters: "Fill the jars with water." And they filled them to the brim. Then He added: "Now pour some out and take it to the steward." This they did. The steward had barely tasted the water

---

1. Beside the lake. They were fishermen.
2. In Hebrew = Gift of God, or rather: Bartholomew, from Canaan, more important than Nazareth.
3. Mary, with her intercession, brought it forward. She knew Jesus very well.

turned into wine, not knowing what it was (although he knew that the waiters had poured out the water), when he called the groom to say to him: "Everybody serves the best wine first; and when the guests have already drunk well, they serve the weakest wine. You have kept the best wine until now." This was Jesus's first miracle. He performed it in Canaan in Galilee; in this way He demonstrated his glory and His disciples believed in Him.

Capernaum: John 2, 12

Later He went down to Capernaum with His mother, relatives and disciples.

Expulsion of the hawkers: John 2, 13-25

When the Passover[1] of the Jews was approaching, Jesus went up to Jerusalem. He found hawkers of oxen, sheep and doves in the temple, and also money changers sitting behind their tables. And, making a whip from some cords, He threw them out of the temple, along with the sheep; He scattered the changers' money and turned over their tables. And He said to those who were selling doves: "Take that away from here; you are not turning my Father's house into a market." His disciples remembered the sentence from the Scriptures: «The zeal of your temple will consume me[2]. "My Father's house is a house of prayer".» (Ps 68, 9). The Jews confronted Him and asked Him: "What sign can you show us to justify what you're doing?" Jesus answered them: "Destroy this temple and I will rebuild it in three days." "It took forty-six days to build this temple, replied the Jews, and you are going to build it in three days?" But He was refering to the temple of His body. When He came back from the dead, the disciples came to understand what He had said, and they believed in the Scriptures and the word of Jesus. During His stay in Jerusalem for the Passover festival, many believed in Him when they saw the miracles which He performed.

---

1. One of the three big feasts that the Jews had to celebrate in Jerusalem.
2. He was indignant when He saw the profanation of the Temple.

Nicodemus: John 3, 1-13

A Pharisee, an aristocrat amongst the Jews, called Nicodemus, approached Jesus at night to say to Him: "Master, we know that You come as a doctor on God's behalf, since nobody could work the prodigies which You work if God was not with Him." Jesus answered Him: "I say to you frankly: Whoever is not born again cannot see the Kingdom of God." Nicodemus replied to Him: "How can a man who is already old be born? Will he perhaps be able to reenter his mother's womb to be born?" "I guarantee that whoever is not born of water and the Spirit cannot enter into the Kingdom of God[1]. That which is born of flesh is flesh; that which is born of the Spirit is spirit. Do not be surprised at what I have told you: You must be born again. The wind blows where it wants to and you hear its noise, but you don't know where it is coming from or where it's going to. The same thing occurs with everyone born of the Spirit." "How can this come about?" replied Nicodemus. Jesus answered him: "You are a doctor in Israel and you don't understand these things? Sincerely I say to you: We speak about what we know, and we bear witness to what we have seen and you still don't believe our testimony. If you don't believe when I speak to you of earthly things, how are you going to believe if I speak to you of heavenly things? However, nobody has gone up to heaven without Him who has come down from heaven, the Son of man[2]."

Light and darkness: John 3, 14-21

In the same way that Moses took up the snake in the wilderness, likewise the Son of man must be taken up[3]; so that everybody who believes in Him may have eternal life. Since God loved the world in such a way that He gave it His Only Begotten Son, so that everybody who believes in Him does not perish, but has eternal life. Because God did not send His son to

---

1. In Baptism sin is wiped away and birth into the Supernatural Life of Grace occurs.
2. Jesus Christ has come from the other world, from Heaven, to teach us.
3. Taken up on the cross.

the world to condemn the world, but so that through Him the world should be saved. Whoever believes in Him is not condemned, because he believed in the Only Begotten Son of God.

Final testimony: John 3, 22-35

Later, Jesus marched with his disciples to the territory of Judea, where He stayed with them and baptized[1]. John was also baptizing in Aenon, near Salim, where there was plenty of water and people came to be baptized. Since John still hadn't been put into prison. An argument about baptism arose between the disciples of John and a Jew. And when they came to John, they said to him: "Master, He who was with you on the other side of the Jordan, on whose behalf you declared, look how he is baptizing[2] and everybody is running to Him." "Nobody can receive anything unless it has been given to him from heaven", replied John. "You yourselves are witnesses to what I have said: I am not the Christ, only His herald. It is the husband who possesses the wife; the godfather who is there to listen to the voice of the husband is intensely happy when he hears his voice. That is my happiness; now it has been fulfilled. It is fitting that He grows and I get smaller."

John in prison: Luke 3, 19-20

But the tetrarch Herod[3], who had been reprimanded by him because of Herodias, his brother's wife, and because of all the foul deeds he had committed, added another to the rest of these foul deeds: that of locking John up in the prison.

Samaritan: John 4, 5-26

Then he arrived at a city in Samaria[4], called Sychar, near the plot of land that Jacob had passed on to his son Joseph; Jacob's

---

1. This was a rite that still was not Baptism.
2. They were probably his disciples. He was like that of John.
3. Herod Antipa.
4. Capital of the ancient kingdom of Israel.

well was there. Jesus, tired from travelling, sat down next to the
well. It was more or less midday. A woman from Samaria came
to draw water. Jesus said to her: "Give me something to drink."
His disciples had gone to the city to buy food. The Samaritan
woman answered Him: "How can you, a Jew, ask for a drink
from me, a Samaritan?" (It should be pointed out that the Jews
had no contact with the Samaritans.) Jesus answered her: "If
you knew the gift of God and who it is that is saying to you:
Give me something to drink, you would certainly ask Him and
He would give you living water." "Sir, the woman said to him,
you don't have anything to draw it with and the well is deep[1]; so
from where are you going to draw living water? Perhaps you're
greater than our father Jacob, who left us the well from where
he, his sons and his livestock drunk?" Jesus replied: "Whoever
drinks this water will be thirsty again. But whoever drinks the
water which I give him shall never be thirsty, for the water that
I give him will become a fountain within him which will jump
up to eternal life[2]." "Sir, the woman said to Him, give me this
water, so that I am not thirsty and needn't come here to draw
it." Jesus answered her: "Go, call your husband and come back
here." The woman replied: "I have no husband." Jesus said to
her: "You are right in saying that you have no husband. Because
you have had five and the current one is not your husband. In
this you are telling the truth." "Sir, replied the woman, I see that
you are a prophet. Our ancestors worshipped on this mountain;
but you say we have to worship in Jerusalem." Jesus said to her:
"Believe Me, woman, because the time has come when you will
adore the Father neither on this mountain[3] nor in Jerusalem.
You worship what you don't know; we worship what we know,
since salvation comes from the Jews. But the time is coming,
and it is now, when true worshippers must worship Him with
spirit and sincerity. For these are the worshippers whom God

---

1. The well is one kilometre from Sychar and two from Naplus. The well is thirty
   metres deep.
2. He was talking about Sanctifying Grace.
3. The Samaritans had their temple on mount Garitzin, and the Jews theirs in
   Jerusalem.

loves. God is spirit and His worshippers must worship Him with spirit and sincerity." The woman replied to Him: "I know that the Messiah (called Christ) is going to come; when He comes He will reveal us everything." "It is I, who is talking to you", Jesus said to her.

At that moment His disciples arrived and were amazed that He was speaking with a woman[1]. However, nobody said to Him: "What are You asking or what are You talking about with her?" Then the woman left her pitcher and went to the city to say to her neighbours: "Come and see a man who has told me all that I have done. Perhaps He will be the Christ?" They left the city and walked towards Him. Meanwhile, the disciples pressed Him, saying: "Master, eat." He answered them: "I have meat to eat which you don't know about." The disciples were saying to each other: "Somebody has brought Him food?" "My food, Jesus said to them, consists in doing the will of He who has sent me and in finishing His work." Many Samaritans from that city believed in Him, on the basis of the woman's word, who stated: "He disclosed everything I have done." Because of this, when the Samaritans introduced themselves to Jesus, they requested Him to stay with them. And He stayed there for two days. And they believed a great deal more when they heard Him himself. And they said to the woman: "now we don't believe because of your word. We ourselves have heard Him, and we know that He is truly the Saviour of the world[2]."

The official's son: John 4, 46-54

He returned to Canaan in Galilee, where He had turned the water into wine. A functionary of the Court was there who had a sick child in Capernaum[3]. Hearing that Jesus had come from Judea to Galilee, he went to meet Him and begged Him to come down and cure his son, who was dying. Jesus said to Him: "If you don't see miracles and prodigies you don't

---

1. The Jews did not usually speak to any woman in public, even their wives.
2. Splendid confession of ecumenical faith, and even more so coming from Samaritans.
3. Commercial city beside the lake.

believe[1]." The Court functionary answered Him: "Lord, be good enough to come down before my son dies." Jesus replied to him: "Go, your son is well." The man believed in Jesus's word and went away. While he was on the way, his servants came out to meet him and say to him: "Your son is well." He asked them the time at which he had started to feel better; "yesterday, at about one o'clock in the afternoon", they replied. The father was checking if this was the same time when Jesus had said to him: "Your son is well." And he and his entire family believed in Him. This was the second miracle performed by Jesus after returning from Judea to Galilee.

Unsuccessful preaching: Luke 4, 16-30

He arrived in Nazareth, where he had grown up, and one Saturday he entered the synagogue, as is the custom, and got up to read[2]. They handed Him the book of the prophet Isaiah, and when he unrolled it He found the passage where it is written: «The Spirit of the Lord on me, because He has consecrated me; He has sent me to preach the good news to the poor, to announce liberation for the captives and the gift of sight for the blind; to set the oppressed free; to promulgate a year of grace to the Lord» (Is 61, 1; 63, 6). And, having rolled up the book, He handed it to the minister and sat down. And the eyes of all those present in the synagogue were turned on Him. He started to say to them: "Today this scripture has been fulfilled in your presence." Everybody praised Him fulsomely and admired the words full of grace which sprung from his lips, and they said: "Is this not the son of Joseph the carpenter, the son of Mary and brother of James, Joseph, Judas and Simon? And do His sisters not live amongst us? (Mark 6,3 "Relatives") Do here, in your homeland, all that we have heard that you have done in Capernaum." And He added: "Bear in mind that no prophet succeeds in his own country. I confidently say to you: There were many widows in Israel in the time of Elias, when the sky

---

1. He reproached their paltry faith: they needed miracles to believe, like the functionary.
2. As He had learned from the Rabbi.

remained without rain for a period of three years and six months, giving rise to great hunger all over the country; however, he was not sent to anybody, only excepting a widow who lived in Sarepta, in the territory of Sidon. And there were many lepers in Israel in the time of the prophet Eliseus, and only Naaman the Syrian was cured[1]." When they heard this, everybody who was in the synagogue was filled with rage. They rose up and expelled Him from the city and took Him to the top of the mountain on which the city was built, with the intention of hurling Him down. But He went on His way, passing between them.

"Convert": Mat 4, 13-17

And, leaving Nazareth, he set up home in Caparnaum, next to the sea, on the borders of Zabulon and Nepthalium, so that the prophet Isaiah's oracle should be fulfilled: Land of Zabulon and Nepthalium, by the sea road, beyond Jordan, Galilee of the Gentiles. «The people who lie in darkness have seen a great light, and a light has arisen on those who were sitting in the shadowy region of death» (Is 9,1). From then on Jesus started to preach. He said: "Convert; because the Kingdom of Heaven is near."

Miraculous fishing: Luke 5, 1-11 (Mat 4, 18-22; Mark 1, 16-22)

When He was moving along the sea of Galilee He saw Simon and Andrew, Simon's brother, who had their nets thrown into the sea, since they were fishermen.» When one time Jesus found himself on the shores of lake Gennesaret[2] the crowd squeezed round Him to hear the word of God. And He saw two boats on the shore of the lake; the fishermen, who had disembarked, were washing their nets. Getting into one of the boats, that of Simon, He requested that it should be moved a

---

1. Admiration turned to anger when He did not want to perform any miracles on account of their lack of faith, and He deemed them less worthy than the pagans.

2. Lake Galilee, also called Gennesaret or Tiberiades, is 21 kilometres long by 10 wide and is situated 200 metres below the Mediterranean.

little from the land and, sitting down, He taught the crowd from the boat. When He had finished speaking, He said to Simon: "Sail seaward, and cast your fishing nets." Simon answered Him: "We have worked hard all night[1] and we haven't caught anything, but, trusting in your word, I will cast the nets." Once this was done, they caught such a quantity of fishes that the nets were on the point of breaking. And they indicated to their companions in the other boat that they should come to their aid. They came to help and in this way they filled the two boats, which almost capsized. When Simon Peter saw this he threw himself at Jesus' feet, saying: "Stay away from me, Lord, because I am a sinner!" The fact is that astonishment had overcome him and all his companions, because of the quantity of fish they had attained, in the same way as James and John, sons of Zebedee, who were partners with Simon. And Jesus said to Simon: "Calm down: from now on you will be a fisher of men." And, after steering the boats to the land, they forsook everything and followed Him.

Possessed: Mark 1, 21-28 (Luke 4, 31-37)

They entered Capernaum; and when Saturday arrived He went to teach in the synagogue and admiration for His teachings grew, since He instructed them as somebody who possesses authority and not in the manner of the scribes[2]. There was then in His synagogue a man possessed by an impure spirit[3], who shouted: "What have You got to do with us, Jesus Nazarene? You have come to wipe us out. I know who You are, God's Saint." Jesus commanded him, saying: "Don't say anything and come out from him." And the impure spirit left him, tormenting him and yelling uproariously, «without causing him any harm». Everybody was astounded, to the point that they were wondering to each other: "What is this? A new teaching, full of authority!; for He commands the impure spirits and they obey Him." Soon

---

1. Fishing is done at night and Peter knew the fishing-grounds well.
2. The scribes monotonously recited the texts of the Scriptures.
3. Some epileptics were considered as possessed, but in this and other cases they really were. Only in the body.

His fame reached everywhere in the regions surrounding Galilee.

Jesus' prayer: Luke 4, 42-44 (Mat 4, 23-25; Mark 1, 35-39)

When it was day, but still dark, Jesus got up, left and went off to a solitary spot, where He proceeded to pray[1]. Simon and his companions went behind Him, and when they found Him they said: "Everybody has gone to look for You." He answered them: "Let's set off to other places, to the towns nearby, so that I can preach there as well; for I have gone out for this reason". And when they found Him they tried to keep Him at their side. But He said to them: "I must also announce the good news of God's kingdom to the other cities, since I have been sent to do that." And so he went preaching in the synagogues of Judea, throughout Galilee, preaching the good news of the kingdom and curing all kinds of illnesses and afflictions in the people, and also exorcising demons. His fame spread over the whole of Syria; and they brought to Him everybody who felt sick with any kind of illness and suffering from any pain, the possessed, the lunatics and paralytics, and He cured them. And a great throng followed Him from Galilee, from the Decapolis[2], from Jerusalem and from beyond the Jordan.

Leper: Mark 1, 40-45 (Mat 8, 1-4; Luke 5, 12-16)

A leper approached Him, imploring Him and saying, on his knees, «falling face down on to the ground»: "If You want to, You can clean me." And moved, He held out His hand and touched him, saying: "I do want to, be cleansed." And at that moment the leprosy left him and he remained clean. Then He sent him away, warning him with these words: "Look, don't tell anybody; but go, present yourself to the priest and, for your purification, offer what Moses commanded, to serve as proof of the deed[3]." But when he went off he started to make everything

---

1. Jesus did not pray for himself, but for us, whom he had come to save.
2. Region of ten cities in Transjordania.
3. Lepers had to live outside the city, in caves. If they were cured, a priest had to verify it.

public and divulge the event, so that Jesus could not enter publicly into any city; and so He stayed away in solitary places; but they came to Him from all over. «And a great number of people came to hear Him and obtain remedies for their illnesses. But He withdrew into solitary places and devoted Himself to prayer».

Paralytic: Mat 9, 1-8 (Mark 2, 1-12; Luke 5, 17-26)

He boarded a boat, crossed the lake and went to His city[1]. There they brought to Him a paralytic, lying in a bed. «And so many assembled that they didn't fit into the courtyard. And He addressed them. Then they brought Him a paralytic, carried by four people. And when they couldn't present themselves to Him because of the crowd, they found the roof where He was and, having made a hole, lowered the bed on which the paralytic was lying. When Jesus saw these peoples' faith, He said to the paralytic: "My son, your sins are pardoned." But some scribes were sitting there who took to arguing inwardly»: "This man blasphemes[2]!" Jesus, knowing their thoughts, said: "Why do you think evil in your hearts? What is easier, to say: Your sins are pardoned, or to say: Get up and walk? Well then, so that you know that the Son of man has the power to pardon on earth, get up, He said then to the paralytic, take your bed and go home[3]." And he got up and went home. When they saw this, the crowds were overcome with fear and glorified God for having given men such power.

Matthew's vocation: Mat 9, 9-13 (Mark 3, 13-17; Luke 5, 27-32)

When He left there, Jesus saw a man, «a publican[4].», «Levi, son of Alpheus», called Matthew, sitting at the table for collecting tributes, and He said to Him: "Follow me." He

---

1. Caparnaum.
2. Only God could pardon sins.
3. Jesus cured the paralyzed man as a proof of His divinity, since only God performs miracles.
4. Publican or tax collector. They were considered "public sinners".

immediately got up and followed Him, «abandoning everything, and Levi offered Him a great banquet in his house». Jesus was sitting at the table in his house, and many publicans and sinners also came and sat down at the table with Him and His disciples. When the Pharisees[1] saw this, they asked His disciples: "Why does your Master eat with publicans and sinners?" Jesus heard this and replied: "The healthy do not need a doctor, only the sick. Go and learn what this means: «I prefer mercy to sacrifice» (Os 6,6). Because I have not come to call the righteous, but the sinners."

Fasting: Mat 9, 14-17 (Mark 2, 18-22; Luke 5, 33-39)

Then, He was approached by the disciples of John «and of the Pharisees who were keeping fast» and they asked Him: "Why do we and the disciples of the Pharisees fast, and your disciples don't fast?" Jesus answered them: "The guests at a wedding can hardly be sad when the bridegroom is with them. The days will come when the bridegroom shall be taken away from them; then they will fast. Nobody puts a patch of unworn material on old clothes, because the piece will pull away from the clothes and the tear will be bigger. Neither does anybody put new wine[2] into old wineskins. On the contrary, the wineskins break, the wine is spilt and the wineskins are thrown away as lost. New wine is put into new wineskins and in this way they are both preserved." «No taster of old wine wants the new, because he says: The old is better».

The paralytic: John 5, 1-13

After this, Jesus went up to Jerusalem to celebrate the Jews' feast[3]. Next to the sheep market in Jerusalem there is a pool, called Bethesda in Hebrew[4], with five porches. Many sick people lay on these porches: the blind, the lame, the paralytic, waiting for the movement of the water. For an angel of the Lord

---

1. They were fanatics and hypocrites.
2. Jewish antiritualist evangelical doctrine.
3. The Jewish Passover.
4. Nourished by a spring of intermittent thermal water.

descended from time to time on to the pool and stirred up the water, and one sufferer was cured of illness. There was a man there who had been sick for thirty-eight years. Jesus, seeing him lying there and realizing how long he had been like that, said to him: "Do you want to be cured[1]?" The sick man answered Him: "Lord, I don't have anybody to throw me into the pool when the water is stirred up; when I try to go, somebody has already got in." Jesus said to him: "Get up, take your bed and go." This man was immediately cured, and he took up his bed and walked away. That day was the Sabbath. Because of this the Jews said to the newly cured man: "As it is the Sabbath you are not allowed to carry your bed." "He who has cured me, he answered them, He himself said to me: 'Take your bed and go'." They asked him: "Who is it that said to you: 'Take your bed and go'?". But the newly cured man did not know who He was, because Jesus had slipped into the refuge of the crowd that was in that place.

Jesus declares Himself God: John 5, 14-18

Later on Jesus met him in the temple and said to him: "Now you see that you've been cured; do not sin any more, since something worse could happen to you[2]." The man went away and told the Jews it was Jesus who had cured him. Because of this the Jews pursued Jesus, because he did these things on the Sabbath. But He answered them: "My Father is still working up until now, and so I work too." But this served for the Jews to try and kill Him with greater fervour: Because not only did He break the Sabbath, but because He called God His Father, equating Himself with God[3].

Jesus's apology: John 5, 19-30

"Because the Father loves the Son and reveals to Him everything that He does; and He will communicate to Him even

---

1. Only Jesus could ask such a question.
2. There are illnesses caused by sins themselves.
3. Because He was equal with God.

greater works than these, to amaze you[1]. Truthfully I say to you: Whoever listens to my word and believes in He who has sent Me, has eternal life and is not submitted to judgement, since he has already passed from death to life. I say to you confidently: The time is going to come, and we are in it now, when the dead will hear the voice of the Son of God and those who listen to it will live. Do not wonder at this, since the time will come when all those who are in the sepulchres will hear His voice. And those who did good will leave for the resurrection of life; those who committed evil for the resurrection of the condemnation."

"You examine the Scriptures[2], because you think of finding eternal life there; well, then, they declare on My behalf. And you don't want to come to me to obtain life. I do not claim the glory of men; moreover, I observe that there is no love of God in you. Do not think that I am going to accuse you before the Father. Moses, in whom you trust, accuses you. Because if you believed Moses, you would also believe me, since he wrote about Me. But if you don't believe his writings, how are you going to believe my words?"

Sabbath: Mat 12, 1-8 (Mark 2, 23-28; Luke 6, 1-5)

On one occasion, on the Sabbath, Jesus was passing through sown fields. His disciples, who were hungry, picked ears of corn and ate them as they went. When the Pharisees saw this, they said to Him: "Look, your disciples are doing something which is not permitted on the Sabbath[3]." He answered them: "And if you had understood the meaning of: «I prefer mercy to sacrifice» (Os 6, 6) you would not have condemned the innocent.

---

1. For this reason the Sabbath was not compulsory for Him. His works vouched for Him. He dominated the elements, cured all illnesses and even revived the dead.

2. But they interpreted them badly, and distorted them. They combed the letter without the spirit of the Law in relation to their Messiah, the earthly king, and were thus excluded from the Kingdom of God.

3. The law is for Man and not vice versa. The casuistry of the Pharisees was boundless, they had reduced the Sabbath to ridiculous trivia. They impeded good actions towards fellow-men.

Because the Son of Man is the master of the Sabbath."
«The Sabbath was instituted for Man and not Man for the
Sabbath.»

Cripple: Mat 12, 9-14 (Mark 3, 1-6; Luke 6, 6-11)

Leaving there He went into their «other Sabbath»
synagogue. There was a man there who had one withered hand.
«The scribes and Pharisees were on the alert to see if He would
undertake a cure on the Sabbath, in order to have a basis for
their accusation». Then they asked Him the following question:
"Is it lawful to cure on the Sabbath?" «But He, knowing their
thoughts, said to the man with the withered hand: "Get up and
go into the center"; and he got up and remained standing.

Jesus said to them: I ask you: What is preferable on the
Sabbath, to do good or evil?, To save a life or allow it to be
lost?» He answered them: "Is there anybody amongst you that,
if the only sheep he owns falls into a well on the Sabbath,
doesn't go to take it out? Well, how much more valuable is a
man than a sheep! Therefore, it is lawful to do good, on the
Sabbath as well." Then He said to that man: "Hold out your
hand." He held it out and it was as healthy as the other one.
«And they, in the delirium of insensitivity, changed their
feelings about what should be done with Jesus». Then the
Pharisees had a meeting devoted to Him, and the way to get rid
of Him.

Cures: Mat 12, 15-21 (Mark 3, 7-12)

When Jesus knew about this, He went away from there.
«Jesus withdrew to the sea accompanied by His disciples. A
great crowd accompanied Him from Galilee, whilst an enormous
crowd of people came to Him, from Judea, Jerusalem, Idumea,
from the other side of the Jordan and the regions neighbouring
on Tyre and Sidon, when they heard what He did.

Then He signalled to His disciples that a boat be made
available so that He should not be impeded by the pushing of
the crowds. Because He had cured many people, and many
others, bearing the mark of some illness, rushed towards Him in

order to touch Him[1]. And the impure spirits fell at His feet when they saw Him, crying: "You are the son of God".» But He warned them not to reveal Him: so that the oracle of the prophet Isaiah should be fulfilled: «"Look, this is My Servant, whom I have chosen, My Beloved, in whom my soul is pleased. I will put My spirit on Him, and He will announce the justice of nations. He will not quarrel or shout. His voice will not be heard in the market places. He shall not break the split reed, nor will he extinguish the smoking flax until He finally brings about the triumph of Justice. The Gentiles will put their faith in His name".» (Is 42, 1-4).

Calling of the Apostles: Luke 6, 12-16 (Mat 10, 1-4; Mark 3, 13-19)

In those days He went to the mountain to pray, and spent the night saying prayers to God[2]. When day broke He called His disciples and chose twelve of them, whom He named Apostles. «He called those who seemed to Him to be good and they came to Jesus. He chose twelve to stay with Him and to send out to preach, with the power to cast out demons»: Simon, whom He gave the surname Peter, and Andrew, his brother; James «son of Zebedee, and John, brother of James, whom He called Boanerges, which means Sons of Thunder»; Matthew, «the publican», and Thomas; James, son of Alphaeus, and Simon, «the Caananite», called Zelotes; Judas «Thaddeus, brother of James, and Judas Iscariot, who would be the traitor[3]».

Beatitudes: Mat 5, 1-12 (Luke 6, 17-26)

When Jesus saw the throng, He went up the mountain and sat down. His disciples approached him. And, taking the word, He instructed them, saying:

---

1. Jesus was neither a doctor nor a healer. If He cured the sick it was to win over their hearts and souls, the purpose for which He had come to the world.
2. For all men.
3. He formed the Apostolic College, and revealed His program to them. The Magna Carta of the Gospel: the poor, the meek and afflicted, the merciful and those who weep, the clean of heart and the persecuted.

"Blessed are the poor in spirit, because the Kingdom of
      Heaven is theirs.
Blessed are the meek, because they will possess the earth.
Blessed are the afflicted, because they will be consoled.
Blessed are those who are hungry and thirsty for justice,
      because they will be satiated.
Blessed are the merciful, because they will obtain mercy.
Blessed are the clean of heart, because they will see God.
Blessed are the pacifiers, because they will be called sons of
      God.
Blessed are those who suffer persecution for the cause of
      justice[1], because the Kingdom of Heaven is theirs.
Blessed you will be when they insult you, persecute you and
      produce all kinds of slanders against you, for my cause.
Be happy and rejoice, because your reward will be great in
      heaven; for the prophets, who were your ancestors,
      were persecuted in this way."

Curses: Luke 6, 24-26

"But, woe on you, the rich, because you have already received
      your consolation!
Woe on you who are full now, because you will be hungry!
Woe to those who laugh now, because you will weep and
      mourn!
Woe to all those men who speak well of you; because their
      ancestors did likewise with the false prophets!"

Ministers: Mat 5, 13-16 (Luke 11, 33-34)

"You are the salt of the earth[2], but if salt becomes tasteless,
how can it become salty again? It's not worth anything, only to
be thrown out and be trod on by men. You are the light of the
world. A city situated on a mountain cannot be hidden; neither

---

1. Special mention for those persecuted because of justice, religious reasons,
    virtue or holiness, martyrs, etc.
2. Just as salt seasons and preserves, so your example will preserve good
    customs; like light.

is a candle lit in order to put it under the bushel, but on the candlestick; in this way it casts light on everybody in the house. Let your light shine in the same way on men, so that, when they see your good deeds, they may glorify your Father who is in heaven."

Contemplating the Law: Mat 5, 1-19

"Do not go on thinking that I have come to abrogate the Law or the Prophets: I have not come to abrogate, but to perfect[1]. Because truly I say to you: Whilst the earth and sky exist, not one single point or stroke of the Law will pass without it having been fulfilled. Consequently, anybody who breaks one of these commandments, even the most insignificant ones, and teaches others to do the same, will be the pettiest in the Kingdom of Heaven."

Formalism: Mat 5, 20-26

"Because I assure you that if your virtue does not exceed that of the scribes and Pharisees[2], you will not enter the Kingdom of Heaven. You have heard what was told to the ancients: «You will not kill: anybody who kills will be submitted to judgement» (Ex 20, 13; 21, 12). But I say to you: Anybody who gets enraged against his brother will be submitted to the Sannedrin; whoever calls him «impious» will fall into Hell. Therefore, if you are going to present your offering on the altar and there you remember that your brother has something against you, leave your offering there, in front of the altar, and first go and make peace with your brother. Then come and offer your gift. Settle things amicably with your enemy whilst you are on the road with him, lest the enemy hands you over to the judge, and the judge hands you over to the guard and they put you in prison. Truly I say to you: Don't leave there until you have paid the last cent."

---

1. The Mosaic Law was abolished, but the Law of God, the Commandments, rule for ever and for all men, since they are based on human nature.

2. Without charity.

The sixth: Mat 5, 27-30

"You have heard what was said: «You will not commit adultery» (Ex 20, 14). But I say to you: Anybody who looks at a woman and desires her has already committed adultery with her in his heart. Therefore, if your right eye occasions sin for you, take it out and throw it far away from you; because it is better that one of your limbs perish than your entire body be cast into Hell. And if your right hand occasions sin for you, cut it off and throw it far away from you; because it is better that one of your limbs perish than your entire body be cast into Hell[1]."

Marriage: Mat 5, 31-32

"It was also said: «Whoever spurns his wife, let him give her the certificate of separation» (Dt 24, 1). But I say to you: Everybody who spurns his wife, except in the case of concubinage, causes her to be led into adultery; and whoever marries a spurned woman commits adultery."

Oathtaking: Mat 5, 33-37

"You have likewise heard what was said to the Ancients: «You will not commit perjury, but you will comply with what you have sworn to the Lord» (Ex 20, 7; Num 30, 2). But I say to you: Do not swear any kind of oath; neither by heaven, because it is God's throne; nor by the earth, because it His footstool; nor by Jerusalem because it is the city of the great King. Neither will you swear by your head; because you are incapable of turning a single hair white or black. Be, then, your word: yes, when it is yes; no, when it is no. Anything exceeding this comes from the spirit of evil."

Talionic law[2] : Mat 5, 38-42 (Luke 6, 2-36)

"You have heard what was said: «An eye for an eye and a tooth for a tooth» (Lev 34, 20). But I say to you: Do not take

---

1. Hyperbolical expressions against passive scandal, occasions and dangers. If it is with full awareness and consent it is already a sin.

2. It is a patently anti-Christian law.

vengeance against he who treats you badly; rather if somebody strikes your right cheek, offer him the other. And if somebody wants to sue you to take away your tunic, give him your cloak as well. And if someone requires you to accompany him for one and a half kilometers, go with him for three kilometers. Give to whoever asks you and do not turn your back on anybody who asks you for a loan, and do not reclaim anything from anybody who has taken his goods from you."

Good and wicked: Mat 5, 43-48 (Luke 6, 27-28; 31-36)

"You have heard what was said: «You will love your neighbour (Lev 19, 18) and you will hate your enemy[1]». But I say to you: Love your enemies and pray for those who persecute you. In this way you will be sons of your heavenly Father, because He makes His sun come out on the good and the wicked and causes rain to fall on the righteous and the sinners. Because if you love those who love you, what reward do you deserve? Don't even the publicans themselves do this[2]? And if you only greet your brothers, what else do you do? Don't even the pagans also do this? Be perfect, then, just as your Father is perfect."

a) Alms: Mat 6, 1-4

"Refrain from doing good deeds in front of men so that they see you: on the contrary, you will lose any reward from your Father who is in heaven. Therefore, when you give alms, don't let them blow the trumpet in front of you. This is what the hypocrites do in the synagogues and on the road so as to be praised by men. Truly I say to you: They have received their reward. Whenever you give alms, don't let your left hand know what your right hand is doing, so that your alms are secret; and your Father, who sees what is hidden, will reward you."

---

1. Hate is anti-Christian. We must love each other without any distinction because we are brothers and sons of God. Loving for the love of God is called charity.

2. Praying is conversing with God.

b) Prayer: Mat 6, 5-8

"When you pray, don't imitate the hypocrites: they prefer to pray standing up: in the synagagoues and in the corners of markets, to be seen by men. Truly I say to you: They have received their reward. You, when you want to pray, withdraw to your room, close the door and pray to your Father who is there, in secret; and your Father, who sees what is hidden, will reward you. When you say prayers, do not vainly multiply the words like the pagans, since they believe they will be heeded because of their charlatanism. Do not be like them, since your Father knows your needs before you ask Him."

"Our Father[1]": Mat 6, 9-15

"Pray, then, like this: Our Father, who art in heaven, blessed be thy name, Thy Kingdom come, Thy will be done on earth as it is in heaven. Give us our daily bread. Forgive us our sins as we forgive those who sin against us, and keep us from temptation and deliver us from evil. Because if you forgive men their sin, your heavenly Father will also forgive you; but if you don't forgive others, neither will your Father forgive your sins."

Penitence: Mat 6, 16-18

"When you fast, don't put on a gloomy face as the hypocrites do: they disfigure their appearance to make other people see that they're fasting. I say to you confidently: They have received their reward. When you fast, perfume your head and wash your face, so as not to let men see that you're fasting, only God who is there, in secret, and your Father, who sees what is hidden, will reward you."

Earthly riches: Mat 6, 19-23

"Don't pile up treasures on earth, where moths and rust destroy them; and thieves bore through walls to rob

---

1. This is the divine prayer. It contains 3 petitions for the Father, and 4 for ourselves: we request freedom from all danger and we condition our pardon to the rest.

them[1]. Better to accumulate treasures in heaven; for there neither moths nor rust destroy them, nor do thieves bore through walls to rob them. Because wherever your treasure is, there will be your heart. The light of the body is the eye; therefore, if your eye is healthy, all your body will be lit up. But if your eye is sick, all your body will be in darkness. If, then, the light that is in you is in darkness, what will darkness itself be like[2]!"

Providence: Mat 6, 24-33

"Nobody can serve two masters[3]: because you will either hate one and love the other or be loyal to one and despise the other. You cannot serve God and riches. Therefore I say to you: Do not worry anxiously about your lives, thinking about what you will eat or drink; nor about your body, with what you're going to wear. Isn't life worth more than food and the body more than clothing? Observe the birds in the sky. They don't sow, they don't reap, don't store in granaries, and yet your heavenly Father feeds them: aren't you worth more than them? Which of you is capable, through the effort of thinking, of prolonging his life by a single moment? And, on the subject of clothes, why do you worry with such anxiety? Look how the lilies of the field grow: they don't work, nor do they weave. And yet I assure you that not even Solomon in all his glory was dressed like one of them. So then, if God clothes in this way the grass which is in the field today and tomorrow is cast on to the fire, how much better will He clothe you, men of little faith? Therefore, do not be troubled, saying :'What are we going to eat, what are we going to drink, what are we going to wear!' The pagans anxiously search for these things. First, then, search for the Kingdom of God and His justice, and these things will be given to you in addition[4]."

---

1. Good works.
2. Bad intentions pervert good deeds. And good intentions save bad ones.
3. God and the world are incompatible.
4. Preoccupations of life must not distance us from God.

Faith: Mat 6, 34

"Do not worry, then, about tomorrow, because tomorrow has its own worries. Each day has enough of its own work[1]."

Judgements: Luke 6, 36-42 (Mat 7, 1-6)

"Be merciful, as your Father is merciful. Do not judge and you will not be judged; «the same judgement with which you judge will judge you»; do not condemn and you will not be condemned[2]; pardon and you will obtain pardon. Give and it will be given to you; good measure, pressed down, shaken, overflowing, will be poured into your lap; because other people will use the same measure with you that you use with them".

He also put forward a comparison. "Can a blind man lead a blind man? Won't they both fall into the hole? The disciple is not greater than the master; but the most advanced disciple will be like his master. Why do you focus on the splinter in your brother's eye and not notice the beam that is in your own? Oh, how do you dare say to your brother: 'Brother, let me take out the splinter which you have in your eye,' you who don't see the beam in your own? You clown, take the beam out of your own eye, and then you will see to take out the splinter in your brother's eye[3].

Don't give holy things to dogs or throw pearls to swine, in case they tread on them and turn against you and bite you[4]."

Persevering prayer: Mat 7, 7-11

"Ask and it will be given to you; search and you will find; knock and the door will be opened. Because he who asks, receives; he who searches, finds; and the door opens to he who knocks. Is there anybody who gives his son a stone when he asks for bread[5]? And if he asks you for a fish, will you give him

---

1. Providence aids our work.
2. Only God can know and judge intentions.
3. We see the splinter, other peoples' faults, more easily than our own.
4. Sacraments to the unworthy.
5. Our prayer to the Father is trusted.

a serpent. So if you wicked people know how to give good things to your sons, How many more good things will your heavenly Father give to those who ask Him!"

Narrow door: Mat 7, 12-14

"Do, therefore, to others everything which you would like them to do to you. These are the contents of the Law and the Prophets. Enter by the narrow door[1]; because the wide door and the broad road lead to damnation, and there are many who walk over them. How narrow is the door and how hard the road which leads to life, and how few are those who find it!"

False prophets: Mat 7, 15-21

"Beware of false prophets, who come to you disguised as sheep, but who are rapacious wolves within[2]. You will know them by their fruits. A good tree does not produce bad fruit, nor does a bad tree produce good ones. The tree which does not produce good fruit will be cut down and thrown on the fire. You will know them, then, by their fruit. Not everybody who says to Me:'Lord, Lord!' will enter into the Kingdom of heaven, only he who carries out the will of My Father who is in Heaven[3]."

Lord, Lord: Mat 7, 22-23 (Luke 6, 43-46)

"Many will say to me that day: 'Lord, Lord, haven't we prophesied in Your Name?, haven't we exorcised demons in Your Name?, haven't we performed miracles in Your Name?' Then I shall say to them: I have never known you. Get away from me, workers of iniquity." «The good man extracts good things from the treasure in his heart; and the wicked man, wicked to the core, extracts bad things; because his mouth speaks of that which fills his heart.»

---

1. The Father's house has a hidden, narrow door. Virtue demands constant effort.
2. False prophets and sects lead astray.
3. God looks at deeds for entering into Heaven.

On rock: Mat 7, 24-29 (Luke 6, 47-49)

"Therefore, whoever listens to these words I have just spoken and puts them into effect, can be compared to a wise man who has built his house on rock. The rain fell, the floods came, the winds blew and unleashed themselves against this house, but it did not sink; because it was founded on rock. But whoever listens to these words which I have just said and does not put them into effect, can be compared to a man who has built his house on sand, «without foundations». The rain fell, the floods came, the winds blew and were unleashed against that house and it collapsed, and was extensively ruined[1]." When Jesus finished this sermon, the crowds were astonished by His doctrine.

The centurion[2]: Mat 8, 1-13 (Luke 7, 1-10)

When Jesus came down from the mountain, a great throng of people followed Him. When He entered Capernaum, a centurion approached Him and pleaded with Him in these terms: "Lord, my servant is lying down at home, paralytic, and is suffering greatly." Jesus said to him: "I shall go and cure him." "Lord, replied the centurion, I am not worthy of You entering my house; only say a word and my servant will be cured. Because although I am a subaltern, I have soldiers under my command, and I say to one: go, and he goes; to another: Come, and he comes; and to my servant: Do this, and he does it." When Jesus heard this He was astonished and said to those who were following Him: "I confidently say to you: I have not found such great faith in Israel. And I assure you that many will come from East and West and will sit at the table with Abraham and Jacob, in the Kingdom of Heaven; whilst the sons of the Kingdom will be cast out into darkness. There will be weeping and grinding of teeth there." And at that very moment the servant was cured.

---

1. There are many religions in the world, but only one is true, that which Christ founded on the rock of Peter, the Catholic. The rest are human.

2. He had 100 soldiers under his command.

Widow of Nain: Luke 7, 11-17

Then Jesus set off towards a city called Nain[1], accompanied by His disciples and a large number of people. When He arrived near the city's gate, they brought out a dead body to bury[2], the only son of a widow, who was accompanied by many people from the city. When the Lord saw her, He felt compassion towards her and said to her: "Don't weep[3]." And He approached the casket, touched it —and those that bore it stopped— and He said: Boy, I say to you, get up." And the body sat up and started to speak. And he delivered him to his mother. Fear overcame them all, and they began to praise God, saying: "A great prophet has risen up in our midst; and God has come in aid of His people."

The forerunner: Mat 11, 2-10 (Luke 7, 18-23)

John, learning in prison of Christ's deeds, sent His disciples to ask Him: "Are You the one who was to come, or must we wait for another?" Jesus answered them: "Go and tell John what you are seeing and hearing: The blind recover their sight, the lame walk, lepers are cleansed, the deaf hear, the dead come to life and the poor are evangelized[4]. And blessed is He who does not find in Me the occasion for damnation." When the envoys left, Jesus set to speaking about John to the crowd: "What did you go to see in the desert? A reed shaken by the wind? Then, what did you go to see? A luxuriously dressed man? Those who wear luxurious clothes live in the palaces of kings. Then, what did you go for? To see a prophet. Yes, I assure you, and more than a prophet. Because this is he of whom it is written: «Look, I am sending a messenger before You, who must prepare the way for You»." (Mal 3, 1).

---

1. (Hebrew = The beautiful) Near Nazareth, and 28 kilometres from Capernaum.
2. The corpse, transported in a barrow, was wrapped in a sheet.
3. Jesus's heart was moved by the misfortune of that poor mother
4. John already knew that He was the Messiah, but not his disciples. Jesus replied with the Messianic miracles announced by Isaiah.

Jesus's testimony: Mat 11, 11-15 (Luke 7, 24-30)

«At that moment he cured many illnesses and physical infirmities and evil spirits, and he restored the sight of many blind people.»

Complaints: Mat 11, 16-19 (Luke 7, 31-35)

"I say to you confidently: Amongst those born of woman there has never been anybody greater than John the Baptist; but the least significant in the Kingdom of Heaven is greater than him[1]. Since the days of John the Baptist, the Kingdom of Heaven has been subject to violence and the violent have taken hold of it. All the prophets and the Law, up to John, have prophesied. And if you want to admit it, he is that Elias who is to come. Whoever listens, understands."

The sinner: Luke 7, 36-50

A Pharisee invited Jesus to eat with him[2]. So He went into the Pharisee's house and sat down at the table. A woman who was known in the city as a sinner immediately introduced herself[3]; and she, on learning that He was eating in the Pharisee's house, brought an alabaster jar full of perfume; and, from His rear, next to His feet[4], she, weeping, started to wash His feet and wiped them with her hair; she kissed them affectionately and anointed them with perfume. Seeing this, the Pharisee who had invited Him wondered to himself: "If this man were a prophet, He would know who and what kind of woman this is who is touching him, for she's a sinner." Jesus said to Him: "Simon, I have something to say to you." "Say it, Master", he replied. "A money-lender had two debtors: One owed him five hundred dinars; the other, fifty. As they didn't have anything with which to pay, he pardoned them both.

---

1. The righteous of the Old Testament still had not received Grace.
2. Out of curiosity, not friendliness.
3. This was neither Mary from Bethany, nor the Magdalene from Magdala, a coastal city, from whom Jesus had cast out 7 demons.
4. The Jews ate lying down

Which of the two, then, will love him the most?" Simon replied: "I think the one he pardoned the most." Jesus answered: "You have judged well." And, turning to the woman, He said to Simon: "Do you see that woman? I've entered your house and you haven't offered Me water for My feet; but she has washed them with her tears and wiped them with her hair. You have not given Me the kiss of peace; but she has not stopped kissing My feet since I've come in. You have not anointed my head with oil; but she has anointed my feet with perfume. Therefore, I say to you: She has loved greatly because many sins have been pardoned her. But whoever has had a little pardoned, loves little." And He said to the woman: "Your sins are pardoned." And the fellow guests started to say to themselves: "Who is this who even pardons sins?" Finally, He said to the woman: "Your faith has saved you; go in peace."

Holy women: Luke 8, 1-3; Mark 3, 20-21

After this Jesus went from city to city and from village to village, preaching the good news of the kingdom of God, and the twelve went with Him, and some women[1] who had been delivered from evil spirits and illnesses: Mary, called Magdalene, from whom seven demons had left. Joanna, the wife of Chuza, Herod's administrator. Susanna and many others, who supported them with their wealth. When Jesus went into a house, the crowd reassembled so that Jesus and His followers couldn't start eating.

Possessed: Luke 11, 14-26; Mat 12, 22-27 (Mark 3, 22-30)

He was casting out a dumb «and blind» demon, and, hardly had the demon come out when the dumb man spoke; and the people were amazed. However, some of those present said: "He casts out devils by using the power of Beelzebub, the chief of the devils[2]." Others, wanting to test Him, required of Him a

---

1. Grateful for His cures, they helped Him with their alms.
2. This was the greatest insult which could be made against Him, as He had come precisely to destroy his empire.

miracle coming from heaven. Knowing their thoughts, He said to them: "Every kingdom fighting against itself will come to ruin and will fall, one house after another. And if Satan is fighting against himself, how will his kingdom remain? Because you say that I cast out demons using the power of Beelzebub. And if I cast out demons using the power of Beelzebub, by what power do your children cast them out? Therefore, they themselves will clarify the question. But if I cast out demons with the power of God, it means that the kingdom of God has already come to you.

Against the Holy Spirit: Mat 12, 31-37 (Mark 3, 28-30)

"For this reason, I say to you: All sins and blasphemies will be pardoned men, but blasphemy against the Spirit[1] will not be pardoned. How can you say good things, when you are wicked?; because the mouth speaks from the abundance of the heart. The good man takes good things from his good heart, and the wicked man takes bad things from his bad heart. And I say to you that men will have to account for all the useless words on Judgement day. Because by your words you will be recognised and by your words you will be condemned."

Sign of Jonah: Mat 12, 38-42 (Luke 11, 29-32)

Then some scribes and Pharisees answered Him: "Master, we want to see a miracle done by You." But He answered them: "this wicked, adulterous race demands a miracle[2]; but no others will be given it, apart from that of the prophet Jonah. Because, just as Jonah was in the belly of the whale for three days and three nights, so the Son of man will be three days and three nights in the hollow of the earth[3]. The Ninevites will be revived on judgement day at the same time as this race, and they will condemn it; because they were converted through the preaching of Jonah; and here there is somebody greater than Jonas. The

---

1. The sin against the Holy Spirit was attributing to the Devil the exorcism of the Devil carried out by Jesus.
2. They needed miracles to believe.
3. Prophecy of His Resurrection.

queen of Midday will be revived on the day of judgement at the same time as this race, and she will condemn it; because she came from the remotest corners of the earth to listen to the wisdom of Solomon; and here there is somebody greater than Solomon."

Light of the body: Luke 11, 33-36 (Mark 6, 22-24)

"Nobody who lights a candle puts it in a hideaway or underneath a bushel, but on the candlestick, so those who come in can see its glow. The lamp of the body is your eye. If your eye is healthy, so also is your body bathed in light; but when it is sick, all your body is also sunk into darkness[1]. Ensure that the light within you is not darkness. But if all your body is lit up, without any dark parts, it will all shine, as when a lamp throws light on you with its radiance."

Jesus's relatives: Mat 12, 46-50 (Mark 3, 31-35; Luke 8, 19-21)

He was still talking to the crowds when His mother and relatives arrived, and, staying outside, wished to talk to Him, (Luke) «and couldn't reach Him because of the throng». (Mark) «The crowd had installed itself around Him.» Somebody said to Him: "Look, Your Mother and Your brothers are outside and want to talk to you[2]." He replied to the person who had announced this to Him: "Who is My Mother and who are My relatives?" And stretching out His hand to His disciples «and looking at the people forming a circle around Him», He said: "These are My Mother and My relatives. Because My Mother and My relatives are those who do the will of My Father, who is in heaven[3]."

---

1. If your eye is clean, you will see everything clean. If it is dirty, you will see everything dirty.
2. This is a Hebraism. The Jews called cousins or nephews, brothers. The so-called brothers were cousins.
3. Nobody carried out the will of the Father like Mary with her "yes" to the Incarnation.

Sower: Luke 8, 4-8 (Mat 13, 1-19; Mark 4, 1-9)

People who had come to Him from all the cities gathered together, and He spoke to them in parables: "A sower went out to sow his seed. And while he was sowing one part fell beside the road, where it was trodden on and the birds of the sky ate it. Another one, on rocky ground, and, barely having sprouted, it dried up due to the climate. Another part fell amongst thorns, which grew at the same time and suffocated it. Another part fell on to good earth and, once grown, produced a hundred for one". Having said this, He exclaimed: "Whoever has ears to hear, let him hear[1]."

Explanation of the parable: Luke 8, 9-15 (Mat 13, 10-23; Mark)

His disciples asked Him what the parable meant. He answered: "The knowledge of the mysteries of the kingdom of God has been conceded to you; but the rest are spoken to in parables, so that, seeing, they don't see and, hearing, they don't understand." This is the meaning of the parable: The seed is the word of God. The grains that fell by the road are those who hear, but then along comes the Devil and he snatches the word from his heart so that they do not believe and are not saved. The grains which fell on to rocky ground are those which embrace the word with pleasure when they hear it, but do not have roots; they grow for a while, but when the test comes, they succumb. The grain that fell between brambles represents those who listen, but, as time goes by, are asphyxiated by worries, riches and the pleasures of life, and do not end up by giving good fruit. The grain that fell on good earth indicates those who, having listened to the word with a noble and virtuous heart, conserve it and produce fruit through their constancy.

---

1. The fruit depends on each person's disposition.

Maxims: Luke 8, 16-18 (Mark 4, 21-25)

"Nobody lights a candle in order to cover it with a container or put it under the bed, but to put it on the candlestick[1], because there is nothing hidden which doesn't finish up being revealed, nor is there anything secret which does not end up being known and out in the open. Consider, then, the way in which you listen."

The grain which grows: Mark 4, 26-29

He also said: "The Kingdom of God is rather as if a man scattered seed on the ground[2] He can sleep or be up night and day. The seed germinates and develops in a way of which he is ignorant. The earth gives its fruits spontaneously: Firstly grass, then ears, finally grain filling the ear. And the fruit permits it, the scythe is brought out, since harvesting time has arrived."

Wheat and tares: Mat 13, 24-30

He put another parable to them: "The Kingdom of Heaven is like a man who had sowed good seed in his field. Whilst his people were asleep, his enemy came and sowed tares[3] in the middle of the wheat and went away. When the wheat grew and the ears appeared, the tares also then appeared there. The servants of the master of the house came to tell him. 'Sir, didn't you sow good seed in your field? How is it, then, that it has tares?' He answered them: 'Some enemy of mine has done this.' The servants asked him: 'Do you want us to pull them out?' 'No, he answered them, unless when you pull out the tares, you pull the wheat out with them. Let them both grow together until the harvest, and at harvest time, I shall say to the reapers: Firstly collect the tares and tie them into sheaves to be burnt; as for the wheat, store it in my granary[4]." Then He left the crowds and

---

1. So that it gives light.
2. It is sown, but it is God who makes it grow. The Church is likewise, it goes on growing.
3. Good and bad, we are mixed up in this world; at the end we shall be separated.
4. The Devil has his agents, sowers of tares. God has patience until the end of the world, when everybody will receive their deserts.

went back home. The disciples surrounded Him and said to Him: "Explain to us the parable of the tares in the field." He, taking up the word, said: "He who sows the good seed is the Son of man; the field is the world; the good seed are the children of the Kingdom; the tares, the children of evil; the enemy who sows them is the devil; the harvest is the end of the world and the harvesters the angels. So, in the same way that the tares are collected and burnt in the fire, so will it be at the end of the world. The Son of man will send his angels who will cast out of the Kingdom all scandals and workers of iniquity, and will throw them into the burning oven: There will be weeping and gnashing of teeth there. Then the righteous will shine like the sun, in the Kingdom of His Father. He who hears, understands."

Mustard and ferment: Mat 13, 31-35 (Mark 4, 30-34; Luke 13, 18-21)

He put another parable to them: "The Kingdom of God is like a grain of mustard which a man takes and sows in his field. It is the smallest of all the seeds; but, once it has developed, it is the biggest of all vegetables. And it ends up as a bush, so that the birds of the sky come to perch in its branches." He told them another parable: "The Kingdom of Heaven is like a little ferment which a woman takes and mixes with three measures of flour until it has all fermented[1]." Jesus said all these things in His parables to the crowds.

Treasure: Mat 13, 44-46

"The Kingdom of Heaven is like a treasure hidden in the field. The man who finds it hides it again, and, in his joy, sells everything he's got and buys that field. The Kingdom of God is also like a merchant who goes looking for precious pearls. When he finds one of great value, he goes and sells all his possessions and buys it[2]."

---

1. Christians must be ferment and yeast with the example of their lives.
2. To get hold of the Kingdom of Heaven it is necessary to free oneself of everything, even life itself. It is priceless.

Net: Mat 13, 47-52

"The Kingdom of Heaven is like a net which, when thrown into the sea, catches all types of fish. When it is full, the fishermen take it to the bank, sit down, gather the good ones in baskets and throw away the bad. The same thing will happen at the end of the world[1]. The angels will come and take out the wicked from the righteous, and will throw them into the burning oven. There will be weeping and gnashing of teeth there. Have you understood all this?" "Yes", they answered Him.

Tempest: Mat 8, 23-27 (Mark 4, 35-40; Luke 8, 22-25)

When He boarded the boat, His disciples followed Him. And it came about that a great tempest was unleashed on the sea, to such an extent that the waves were covering the boat. «Jesus was in the stern, sleeping on a cushion.» Then they approached Him and woke Him up, saying: "Lord, save us, we're perishing!" And He said to them: "Why are you so afraid, men of little faith?" He got up, gave orders to the winds and the sea, and a great calm was formed. The men were astonished and said to themselves. "Who is this whom even the wind and sea also obey[2]?"

Jairus and the hemophiliac: Mat 9, 18-26 (Mark 5, 21-43; Luke 8, 40-46)

Whilst he was saying these things, one of the chiefs of the synagogue, «called Jairus», came up to Him and prostrated Himself at His feet, saying: "My daughter has just died; but come, put Your hand on her and she will live." Jesus set off and His disciples followed Him. Meanwhile, a woman who had suffered from loss of blood for twelve years went up to Him from behind and touched the hem of his robe[3]; because she said

---

1.   It will be the end and final destiny for each person.
2.   The sea of life has its tempests. Jesus pretends to sleep, but in the end He saves us. He dominates all the natural elements. Miracles are something normal for Him.
3.   The distraught woman did not want to show herself to Jesus, it was a legal impurity, but she had faith and was cured.

to herself: "Merely by touching His robe I will be cured." When Jesus arrived at the house of the chief of the synagogue and saw the flute players and the noisy crowd, He said: "Withdraw, because the girl is not dead, but sleeping[1]." And they mocked Him. When the crowd was thrown out, He went in, took the girl's hand and she got up. This news spread throughout all that region.

Blind and possessed men: Mat 9, 27-34

When Jesus left there, two blind men followed Him shouting: "Son of David, have pity on us." When He went into the house, the two blind men came up to Him. Jesus asked them: "Do you think I can do this?" "Yes, Lord", they answered Him. Then He touched their eyes, saying. "Let it be done according to your faith." And His eyes opened. Then, Jesus warned them severely: "Make sure that nobody knows about this." But they had barely left when they let it be known throughout all that region.

Sick people: Mat 9, 35-38

Jesus toured the cities and villages, teaching in their synagogues, preaching the good news of the Kingdom and curing all kinds of illnesses and afflictions[2]. And when he saw the crowds He was moved to compassion by them, because they were tired and dejected, like sheep without a shepherd. Then He said to His disciples: "The harvest is large, but the workers are few. Ask, then, the Lord of the harvest to send workers to his harvest[3]."

The Apostles' mission: Mat 10, 1 (Mark 6, 6-7; Luke 9, 1-2)

Calling His twelve disciples to Him, He gave them the power to exorcise unworldly spirits, «above all demons», and

---

1. The girl was dead and He revived her. Life is a dream and death an awakening.
2. Jesus cured illnesses of the body to cure the illnesses and wounds of the soul.
3. He needs collaborators.

cure all kind of illness and affliction. «And He sent them in pairs to preach the Kingdom of God[1].»

Instruction of the Apostles: Mat 10, 5-10 (Mark 6, 7-11)

Jesus despatched these twelve after having given them the following instructions: "Do not go to the Gentiles and do not enter the cities of the Samaritans. Go first to the lost sheep in the house of Israel. Go and preach, saying: 'The Kingdom of Heaven is near'. Cure the sick, bring the dead back to life, cleanse lepers, exorcise demons. You have received this without payment; give it without payment. Carry neither gold, nor silver, nor copper on your belt; nor a travelling bag, «nor bread», nor two tunics, nor sandals, nor a stick, because the worker has a right to sustenance."

Envoys: Mat 10, 11-15 (Luke 9, 3-5)

"When you arrive at a city or town, find out if there is a worthy person and stay there until you leave. When you go into the house, invoke peace on it[2]. If the house is worthy, bring your peace down upon it; if it is not worthy, may your peace return to you. And if they don't welcome you or listen to your words, shake the dust from your feet when you leave that house or city, «as a sign of protest against them».

With certainty I say to you: On the day of judgement, Sodom and Gomorrah will have a more tolerable fate than that city."

Persecution: Mat 10, 16-23

"Look how I am sending you like lambs among wolves; be then as wise as serpents and as simple as doves. Take care with men: They will take you before the tribunals of the Sannedrin and they will beat you in their synagogues. You will be taken before governors and kings for my cause, to give testimony

---

1. When He sent them to preach He gave them charismatic powers for all kinds of miracles in His name. Firstly on the people of Israel.

2. He meant all kinds of riches.

before them and the Gentiles[1]. And when they have handed you over, do not worry by thinking about how to speak or what to say: because at that moment what you have to say will be given you. Because it is not you who are speaking then, but the spirit of your Father who speaks in you[2]. Brother will deliver brother to death; the father his son; and the sons will rise up against the fathers and put them to death. You will be hated by everybody because of My name, but he who has persevered until the end will be saved."

Disciples: Mat 10, 24-27

"The disciple is not superior to the master[3], nor is the servant superior to the employer. It is enough for the disciple to be like his master, and the servant like his employer: if they have called the head of the household Beelzebub, how much more will they do so to the members of his family! Consequently, do not be afraid; because there is nothing hidden which does not end up being revealed, and there is nothing secret which will not end up being known. What I'm saying to you in darkness, say it in broad daylight; and what is told you in your ear, preach it on the rooftops."

Do not fear: Mat 10, 28-33

"Do not fear those who kill your body, for they can't kill the soul; rather have fear of He who can make the body and soul perish in Hell. Aren't two birds sold for a few cents? And, however, not a single one falls to the ground without your Father's permission. As for you, even the hairs on your head will all be counted. Therefore, do not fear: aren't you worth a great deal more than the birds? He who defends Me in front of men[4], I will also defend in front of My Father, who is in heaven.

---

1. The millions of martyrs are a proof of this.
2. Christians must not fear persecutions, God is with them.
3. Nobody is superior to the Master Jesus.
4. Many are victims of lack of consideration for others. Jesus does not want cowards, but brave people.

He who denies Me in front of men, I will also deny in front of My Father, who is in heaven."

Denial: Mat 10, 34-39

"Do not think that I have come to bring peace to the earth; I have not come to bring peace, but war. I have come to separate the son from his father, the daughter from her mother, the daughter-in-law from her mother-in-law; in such a way that a man's enemies will be the people in his own house. He who loves his father or mother more than Me, is not worthy of Me; and he who loves his son or his daughter more than Me is not worthy of Me[1]. He who does not take up his cross and follow Me is not worthy of Me. He who tries to preserve his life for himself will lose it; and he who loses it for my cause, will find it."

Reward: Mat 10, 40-42

"He who welcomes you, welcomes Me; and he who welcomes Me, welcomes Him who has sent Me. He who welcomes a prophet, will have the reward of a prophet; he who welcomes a righteous man, because he is righteous, will have the reward of the righteous. And he who gives a glass of cold water to one of these little ones, because he is My disciple, I assure you he shall not be unrewarded."

Preaching: Mark 6, 12-13 (Mat 11, 1; Luke 9, 6)

And they left and preached in order to convert the people. And they cast out many demons «Everywhere», and they cured many sick people by anointing them with oil[2].

Herod[3]: Mark 6, 14-16 (Mat 14, 1-2; Luke 9, 7-9)

News about Jesus reached King Herod, since his name had become famous. People were saying: "John the Baptist has

---

1. God must be loved more than all things and more even than our own life.
2. The Church has seen in these anointings of the Apostles the symbolic origin of the sacrament of Extreme Unction.
3. Herod Antipa.

come back to life, and because of this such marvels are being performed in him." Others were saying, on the contrary: "He is Elias". And others: "He is a prophet like the other prophets". But Herod, having heard this, said: "It is John himself, whom I had beheaded, who has come back to life."

John's martyrdom: Mark 6, 17-29 (Mat 14, 3-12)

For this same Herod had indeed had John arrested and chained up in prison, on account of Herodias, his brother Philip's wife, whom he had married. Because John said to Herod: "It is not lawful to have your brother's wife." Because of this Herodias bore malice against him and wanted to kill him, although she couldn't since Herod held John in respect, for he considered him a righteous and holy man, and tried to protect him. And when he heard him, he was full of perplexity, although he listened to him with pleasure. When a propitious day had come, when Herod, on the occasion of his birthday, gave a banquet for his lords, for the tribunals and principals of Galilee, the daughter of the above-mentioned Herodias entered and pleased Herod and his fellow diners with her dancing. And then the King said to the young woman: "Ask whatever you want of me and I will give it to you." And he swore to her[1]: "I will give you what you ask of me, even if it is half my kingdom." She left and said to her mother: "What shall I ask for?" The latter replied: "The head of John the Baptist." And returning to the King at full speed, she made her demand: "I want you to give me straight away the head of John the Baptist on a tray." The King was saddened, but he did not want to deny her what she was asking, because of the oath and the presence of the guests. The King then sent for the executioner and ordered him to bring John's head. The executioner went and decapitated him in the prison, and brought his head on a tray and gave it to the girl, who in her turn gave it to her mother. And John's disciples, having found out about this, went and

---

1. The oath was invalid because it was something wicked.

took his body and put it in a sepulchre. «Afterwards they went to tell Jesus about it[1].»

First multiplication of the loaves: John 6, 1-15 (Mat 14, 13-23; Mark 6, 30-46; Luke 9, 10-17)

After Jesus went to the other side of the sea of Galilee and of Tiberias. A big crowd followed Him, because they had seen the miracles performed on the sick, «and they ran to that place on foot from all the cities». Jesus went up the mountain and there He sat down in the company of His disciples. The Passover, the festival of the Jews, was now approaching. Jesus raised up His eyes and, seeing that a great throng was coming towards Him, «He had pity on them, since they walked like sheep without a shepherd, and started to instruct them in many things», He said to Philip: "Where can we buy bread so that these people may eat?" He said this to test him, since He already knew what He had to do. Philip answered Him: "Two hundred dinars is not sufficient for every one to have a little". One of His disciples, Andrew, Simon Peter's brother, said to Him: "There's a boy here who has five barley loaves and two fishes, but what's that for so many people?" Jesus replied: "Tell the men to sit down." There was a lot of green grass in that place. The men then sat down, five thousand in number[2]. «They formed groups of a hundred and of fifty». Then Jesus took the loaves and, after giving thanks, shared them out amongst those who were stretched out; He did the same with the fishes, sharing out as many as required. When they were now satisfied, He said to his disciples: "Gather up the pieces left over so that nothing is wasted." So they gathered them up and filled twelve baskets with the pieces of the barley loaves left over from what they had eaten «and of the fishes which were left over, until they filled twelve baskets. There were some five thousand men who ate of the loaves». When the men saw the miracle He had performed

---

1. John sealed the truth he was preaching with his blood. He was the last of the Prophets.

2. They came from all over to see His miracles and teaching, and because of the imminence of the Passover.

they said: "This is really the Prophet who was to come to the world. But Jesus, knowing that they would come to take Him by force to proclaim Him king, again retreated alone to the mountain «to pray» «in private[1]».

On the waters: Mark 6, 47-52 (Mat 24-34; John 6, 16-21)

At nightfall, the boat was in the middle of the sea and He alone remained on the shore. And, seeing them row with enormous force because they were against the wind, He arrived there at about four in the morning, walking on the sea[2] and as if wanting to pass them by. When they saw Him walking on the sea, they thought that He was a ghost and started to shout, then they all recognised Him and were terror-stricken. But He spoke to them immediately, saying: "Do not be discouraged; it is I; do not be afraid." «Peter answered Him: "Lord, if it is You, order me to go to You over the waters", and he arrived close to Jesus. But, confronted by the violence of the wind, fear entered into him. Then he started to drown and cried out: "Lord, save me[3]". And Jesus immediately held out His hand, took hold of him and said to him: "Man of little faith, why have you doubted?"» And He got on board the boat by their side and the wind calmed down; in such a way that their stupefaction reached its limits, since they had not been completely overcome by what had happened with the loaves, as if their hearts were dulled. «And those who were in the boat prostrated themselves before Him, saying: "You are truly the Son of God[4]".»

You ate bread: John 6, 22-26

The next day the crowd, which had remained on the opposite shore, realised that there had only been one boat and Jesus had not boarded it with His disciples, but that His disciples had set off on their own. Some boats arrived from Tiberias, from next

---

1. This spectacular miracle would seem enough to give Him credit as the Messiah, and so because of this they would want to proclaim Him king.
2. He reached them by walking on the sea.
3. Only in the middle of the sea did he doubt.
4. When they emerged from their fright they worshipped Him.

to the place where they had eaten bread after giving thanks to the Lord. When the people saw that neither Jesus nor His disciples were there, they boarded the boats and headed for Capernaum in search of Jesus[1]; and when they found Him on the other shore, they said to Him: "Master, when did you arrive here[2]?" Jesus answered them: "I say to you with certainty: You have come looking for me not because you have seen prodigies, but because you ate bread until you were full."

Spiritual bread: John 6, 27-33

"Strive to attain not perishable food, but the food which remains until eternal life[3], which will be given to you by the Son of man, whom the Father, who is God, has endorsed with His seal." Then they asked Him: "What do we have to do to carry out God's works?" Jesus answered them: "This is the work of God, that you believe in Him whom He has sent." They answered Him: "And what prodigies do you perform for us to believe You when we see them? What do You do? Our forefathers ate manna in the desert, according to the Scriptures: «He gave them bread from Heaven to eat» (Ps 78, 24)." Jesus answered them: "I say to you with utter truthfulness: Moses did not give you bread from heaven, since it is my Father who gives you the true bread from heaven. Because the bread of God is that which comes down from the sky and gives life to the world[4]."

I am the bread of life: John 6, 34-39

"Lord, they begged, give us this bread always." Jesus answered them: "I am the bread of life; whoever comes to Me, will no longer be hungry, and whoever believes in Me will no longer be thirsty. However, you, as I have told you, had seen

---

1. The people followed Him everywhere, by land and sea.
2. They were astonished to find Him on the other shore.
3. The Eucharistic Bread.
4. When He remembered the multiplication He said to them: "Your fathers ate manna and died. I am the Bread come down from the Sky. Whoever eats of this Bread will never die.

Me and had not believed: All those the Father has given me will come to Me and I will not reject anybody who may come to Me, because I have come down from heaven, not to do my will, but to fulfill the will of He who has sent me. The will of He who sent Me is this, that I don't lose anything of what He has given Me, but that I bring it back to life on the last day."

Rumours: Luke 6, 40-47

"My Father's will is that anybody who sees the Son and believes in Him has eternal life and that I bring him back to life on the last day." Rumours about Him arose amongst the Jews, because He had said: "I am the bread which has come down from heaven", and they commented: "Is this not Jesus, the son of Joseph, whose parents we know well? How does he now say: I have come down from heaven?" Jesus answered them: "Don't whisper among yourselves. Nobody can come to Me if the Father, who has sent Me, does not drive him to it, and I will bring him back to life on the final day. It is written in the Prophets: «Everybody will be God's disciples» (Is 54, 13). Everybody who hears the Father and welcomes My teaching comes to Me. It is not that somebody has seen the Father, but Him who has come on behalf of God. He has seen the Father. In all confidence I say to you: Whoever believes has eternal life[1]."

Eucharist: John 6, 48-55

"I am the bread of life. Your ancestors ate mannah in the desert and died. This is the bread which comes down from the sky, in order that whoever eats it does not die. I am the living bread, which comes down from heaven; whoever eats of this bread lives forever, and the bread which I shall give is my flesh, on behalf of the world[2]." The Jews argued amongst themselves and wondered: "How can this man give us his flesh to eat?" Jesus insisted to them: "I say with confidence that if you don't

1. Jesus prepares them for the ministry of Eucharist with faith.
2. This heavenly Bread is His Body and Blood to feed souls. The Jews understood it as antrophagy.

eat the flesh of the Son of man and do not drink His blood, you will not have life within you. Whoever eats my flesh and drinks my blood has eternal life and I shall bring him back to life on the last day. Because my flesh is true food and my blood true drink."

Whoever eats my flesh: John 6, 56-59

"Whoever eats My flesh and drinks My blood remains in Me and I in him. In the same way that the Father who sent Me possesses life and I live through the Father, likewise whoever eats Me will live through Me. This is the bread that has come down from heaven, not like that which our forefathers ate before dying. Whoever eats this bread, will live forever." This is what He taught in the synagogue of Capernaum.

Reactions: John 6, 60-71

When they heard this, many of His disciples said: "These words are very strong! Who can accept them!" Jesus, knowing that His disciples were commenting on this, upbraided them: "This shocks you? What if you were to see the Son of man rise up to where He was before. The spirit is what gives life, the flesh is useless[1]; the words which I have said to you are the spirit of life. But there are amongst you some who don't believe" (Jesus already knew from the beginning who were those who did not believe and who was the one who was going to betray Him). And He added: "For this reason I have said to you that nobody can come to Me if it has not been conceded him by the Father." From this moment many of His disciples withdrew and did not now accompany Him. Jesus confronted the twelve: "Do you also want to leave?" Simon Peter answered Him: "Lord!, to whom shall we go[2]? You have the words of eternal life. And we have believed and known that You are God's Saint." Jesus answered them: "Did I not choose you

---

1. They understood Him in the literal sense, and for this reason many began to leave Him.
2. Peter's confession must have greatly consoled Jesus despite the attitude of Judas.

twelve? And yet one of you is a devil." He was talking about Judas, the son of Simon Iscariot, because He, who was one of the twelve, would betray Him.

Traditions: Mat 15, 1-9 (Mark 7, 1-13; John 7,1)

Then some scribes and Pharisees who had come from Jerusalem approached Him and asked Him: "Why don't Your disciples preserve the tradion of the Ancients, since they don't wash their hands before eating." «For the Pharisees and all the Jews do not eat without washing their hands with the utmost care, in accordance with the tradition of the Ancients; and they don't eat what comes from the market without purifying it first; and there are many other things which tradition taught them to observe; the washing of cups, containers and copper receptacles.» He answered them: "Why don't you observe what has been commanded by God by following your traditions? In this way you have annulled the word of God by your tradition: Hypocrites, Isaiah prophesied well of you, when he said[1]:

«This people honours me with its lips but its heart is far from me.

It tries in vain to honour Me, teaching doctrines which are human precepts.» (Is 29,13)

«By abandoning God's commandment, you will anchor yourselves to the tradition of men»."

Purity: Mat 15, 10-20 (Mark 7, 14-22)

Calling the people to Him, He said to them: "Listen and comprehend; it is not what enters the mouth which contaminates man, but what comes out of it; that is what contaminates man. Because out of the heart come wicked thoughts, homicides, adulteries, fornications, robberies, «ambitions, perversities, deceit, libertinage, envy, blasphemy, arrogance, insensitivity»,

---

1. The hypocritical Pharisees only looked after the external by scrubbing dishes and clothes which had touched something from the innumerable impurities and ridiculous precepts which they had multiplied.

false testimonies, blasphemies. These are the things which stain man; but eating without washing one's hands does not stain man."

Woman from Canaan: Mat 15, 21-28 (Mark 7, 24-30)

Leaving there, Jesus withdrew to the region of Tyre and Sidon[1]. There a woman from Canaan, «a pagan, a Syrophoenician by birth», who came from nearby, started to shout: "Have pity on me, Lord, son of David; my daughter is cruelly tormented by a demon." But He did not give any reply. Then His disciples approached Him and made Him this entreaty: "Bid her farewell, because she comes shouting behind us." He replied: "I have not been sent only to the lost sheep of Israel[2]." But she approached Him, «prostrating herself at His feet, she venerated Him, saying: "Lord, help me".» He replied: "It is not good to take bread from children to throw it to dogs[3]." "That's certain, she answered, but dogs also eat the scraps which fall from their masters' table." Then Jesus answered her: "Woman, your faith is great. Let it do what you want." And at very moment her daughter was cured. «And when she arrived at her home she found the girl lying on the bed, and the demons had gone out of her.»

Deaf mute: Mark 7, 31-37

He again left the confines of Tyre, set off for Sidon to the sea of Galilee, crossing the territory of Decapolis. And then one deaf mute man with a speech impediment was introduced to Him, and they requested that He put His hand on him. And taking him aside, away from the throng, He introduced His fingers into His ears and touched his tongue with His saliva, and, looking at the sky, He gave a sigh and said to him: "Efaza", which means open. And at that moment his ears were opened, his tongue was freed and He spoke correctly. He charged them not to tell

---

1. Maritime cities in Phoenicia, the Lebanon; they did not belong to the People of Israel.
2. Jesus wanted to test their faith and constancy.
3. The Jews called foreigners dogs.

anybody: And they were completely amazed, saying: "He has done everything good; he makes the deaf hear and the dumb speak."

Cures: Mat 15, 29-31

Jesus left there and arrived at the shore of the sea of Galilee. He went up the mountain and sat down there. And many people came to Him, bringing with them the lame and disabled, the blind and deaf and many others. They put them at His feet and He cured them. The crowds were amazed when they saw the dumb talk, the disabled healthy, the lame walk and the blind see. And they glorified the God of Israel.

Second multiplication of the loaves: Mark 8, 1-10 (Mat 15, 32-38; Mark 8, 1-9)

In those days, a great crowd was again to be found with Jesus without anything to eat, and He called His disciples to say to them: "These people sadden Me, since they have now been three days at My side and they don't have anything to eat. And if I send them home without eating, they will exhaust themselves on the way, for some of them have come a long way." His disciples answered Him: "Where are we going to get loaves from to fill these people, here in the wilderness?" But He asked them: "How many loaves have you got?" And the disciples replied: "Seven." He told the crowd to settle down on the ground; and, taking the seven loaves, he broke them, after reciting the blessing, and gave them to His disciples so that they would share them out amongst the crowd. And this they did. They also had some little fishes. He blessed them and ordered them to serve them out in the same way. They ate until they were full and gathered up seven baskets of leftover pieces. There were some four thousand in number, «without counting the women and children[1]».

---

1. How good and compassionate is the heart of Jesus! THe people looked for him everywhere like sheep without a shepherd. "Look for the Kingdom of God and the rest will be given to you as well".

Sign from Heaven: Mat 15, 39; 16, 1-4 (Mark 8, 10-13)

And, after taking leave of the throng, he left by boat «with His disciples» and came to the region of Magdala[1]. The Pharisees and the Sadducees approached Him and, in order to test Him, asked Him to make visible a sign from the sky. He answered them: "When the evening comes, you say: Good weather, because the sky is a burning red; and in the morning: Bad weather, because the sky is dark red. You know, then, how to distinguish the features of the sky, and you don't know how to distinguish the signs of the weather? This wicked, adulterous race asks for a sign; but no sign will be given, unless it is that of Jonah." And He left them, «embarked again and went away[2]».

Pharisees: Mat 16, 5-12 (Mark 8, 14-21)

When they went to the other bank, the disciples forgot to acquire bread, «so that they didn't even have one loaf with them in the boat». Jesus said to them: "Take care and preserve yourself from the fermenting of the Pharisees and Sadducees." Then they commented among themselves: "We haven't got any bread." Jesus realized and said to them: "What are you commenting about among yourselves, men of little faith, that you have no bread? You still don't understand? Don't you remember the five loaves for the five thousand men? How many baskets did you collect? Nor the seven loaves for the four thousand men? How many baskets did you collect? How did you not understand that I was not talking to you about bread? «Are your hearts hardened[3]? Don't you see with your eyes nor hear with your ears?» Preserve yourself from the fermenting of the Pharisees and Sadducees." Then they understood that He had not said that that they should preserve themselves from the fermenting of bread, but from the doctrine of the Pharisees and Sadducees.

---

1. Magdala was a city on the shore.
2. The Sadducees and Pharisees were acting with bad faith. They did not want to be converted or believe, but they spied on Him and schemed against Him to accuse Him and discredit Him.
3. The Apostles were coarse.

Primacy of Peter: Mat 16, 13-20 (Mark 8, 27-30; Luke 9, 18-21)

Then Jesus arrived in the region of Caesarea Philippi[1] and asked His disciples: "Who do the people say is the Son of man?" They replied: "Some say that it is John the Baptist, others Jeremiah or one of the prophets" "And you, He said to them, Who do you say that I am?" Simon Peter replied: "You are the Christ, the living Son of God." Jesus answered Him: "Blessed are you, Simon, son of Jonah[2], because men have not revealed this to you, but My Father who is in the heavens. And I say to you that you are Peter and on this stone I shall build my Church, and the gates[3] of Hell will not prevail against It. I shall give you the keys to the Kingdom of the Heavens[4] and everything which you achieve on earth will be achieved in heaven; and everything which you undo on earth will be undone in heaven." And He ordered His disciples not to say to anybody that He was Christ.

Passion and Resurrection: Mark 8, 31-33 (Mat 16, 2-23; Luke 9, 22)

And He took to teaching them how it was necessary for the Son of man to suffer many things, to be rejected by men of high standing, by the chief priests and by the scribes, to be delivered to death, and three days later, come back to life. And He laid things out with total clarity. Peter called Him aside and started to rebuke Him: «God does not want this, Lord; this will not befall You[5].» But, returning in view of His disciples, He reproached Peter with these words: "Get away from Me, Satan; "you are a seducer for me", since you don't take into account the things of God, only those of men."

---

1. Old Roman colony, restored by the tetrarch Philip, on the North of the lake.
2. By divine revelation.
3. The powers.
4. Vicar of Christ on earth.
5. Impulsive reply by Peter.

Abnegation: Mark 8, 34-39 (Mat 16, 24-28; Luke 9, 23-27)

And when He had made the people come, along with His diisciples, He said to them: "If anybody wants to follow Me, let him deny himself, take up his cross and follow me[1]. Because whoever wants to save his life, will lose it; but whoever loses his life because of Me and the Gospel, will save it[2]. For, what does man benefit by gaining the whole world and losing his soul? Thus, then, if somebody is ashamed of Me and My teachings before this sinful, adulterous race, the Son of man will also be ashamed of man, when He comes in glory from His father with the holy angels. «And then He will reward each person according to his deeds[3]»."

Transfiguration: Mat 17, 1-9 (Luke 9, 28-36)

Six days later Jesus took Peter, James and John with Him and took them aside to a high mountain «to pray, and whilst they were praying» He was transfigured before them. His face shone like the sun; and his clothes were as white as light. Then Moses and Elias appeared to them and started talking to Him, «who appeared dressed in glory, were concerned with the passing away which Jesus was going to do in Jerusalem. Peter and his companions were crushed by sleepiness, but, reviving themselves, they saw the glory of Jesus and the two men who were with Him». Peter, taking up the word, said to Jesus: "Lord: How good we are here! If you wish, I will put up three tents here; one for You, one for Moses and the other for Elias." «Without doubt he didn't know what he was saying, for they were frightened.» He was still speaking when a luminous cloud covered them with its shadow, «and they were terror-struck on finding themselves wrapped up in it», and this voice emerged from the cloud: "This is My beloved Son in whom I am pleased. You must listen to Him[4]." When they heard this, the disciples

---

1. Heaven is attained with the cross on the back.
2. The martyrs are an example.
3. Being ashamed of God is treason.
4. The Heavenly Father presents His Son and commends Him to all humanity. He has the word of Eternal Life.

fell face down on the ground and were very frightened. But Jesus approached them, touched them and said: "Get up and don't be afraid." And when they raised their eyes, «when they looked around», they didn't see anybody apart from Jesus. When He came down from the mountain, Jesus made this prohibition: "Don't tell anybody about this vision, until the Son of man has come back from the dead[1]."

Elias and John: Mat 17, 10-13 (Mark 9, 10-12)

His disciples put this question to Him. "Why do the scribes say that Elias must come first?" He answered them: "Yes, Elias will come and reestablish everything. However, I say to you that Elias has already come and they did not recognise him, but rather treated him however they wanted. In the same way, the Son of man must also suffer on their behalf." «But, don't you know that it is written of the Son of man that he will suffer greatly and will be despised?» Then His disciples realised that He had been speaking to them about John the Baptist.

Tribute from the Temple: Mat 17, 24-27

When they arrived at Capernaum, the collectors of the annual tribute for the temple approached Peter and asked him: "Doesn't your Master pay the annual tribute for the temple[2]?" "Yes", he replied. Afterwards, when He went into the house, Jesus barred his way, and asked him: "How does it seem to you, Simon? From whom do the earthly kings receive tributes or taxes, from their own children or from strangers?" And when he replied: "From strangers", Jesus continued: "Therefore the children are exempt. However, so as not to cause a scandal, go to the sea, cast your bait, take the first fish which bites, open its mouth and you will find a coin, the equivalent of double the annual tax of the temple, take it and give it to them for Me and for you[3]."

---

1. Jesus again predicts His Passion. They did not understand.
2. The tax was of a half sicle. The changers in the Temple changed Roman and Greek coins for those of the country.
3. They call the fishes of the lake Saint Peter.

Like children...: Mat 18, 1-4 (Mark 9, 32-35; Luke 9, 46-48)

At that moment the disciples approached Jesus and asked Him: "Who, then, is the greatest in the Kingdom of Heaven?" But Jesus, knowing the thought in their heart, asked them: "What were you debating on the way?" But they kept silent; because they had discussed with one another on the way who was the greatest. He, taking a seat, called the twelve and said to them: "If somebody wants to be the first he must be the last of all and serve all the rest". Jesus called a child, put him in their midst and said to them: "I say to you with certainty: If you don't change and become like children, you will not enter the Kingdom of Heaven. Therefore whoever makes himself small, like this child, will be the greatest in the Kingdom of Heaven[1]."

Abuse: Mat 18, 5-9 (Mark 9, 36-45)

"And whoever welcomes a child like this in my Name, welcomes Me. And whoever welcomes Me, does not welcome Me, but He who has sent Me. But whoever abuses one of these little ones, who believe in Me, it would be better for Him to have a millstone tied round his neck and be submerged in the depths of the sea[2]. Woe to the world for abuses! It is inevitable that there are abuses; but woe to him through whom the abuse comes[3]! If your hand or your foot occasion sin in you, cut them off and throw them far away: It is better for you to enter life maimed or lame than have two hands or two feet and be thrown into the eternal fire. And if your eye occasions sin in you, pull it out and throw it far away from you: It is better for you to enter life with only one eye than have two eyes and be thrown on to the fire of Hell, where their worm does not die and the fire is not extinguished[4]."

---

1. Through their innocence.
2. Abuse of children is a very serious sin
3. These expressions indicate their seriousness.
4. Passive abuse, giving oneself the opportunity and danger, is already a sin.

Tolerance: Mark 9, 38-41 (Luke 9, 49-50)

John said to Him: "Master, we saw somebody who does not accompany us casting out devils in Your name, and because of this we harassed him." But Jesus said: "Don't harass him; since there is nobody performing a miracle in my Name that is capable of then speaking ill of Me. Because whoever is not against us is for us. And whoever gives you a glass of water to drink in view of you coming from Christ[1], I assure you that he will not lose his reward."

Fraternal correction: Mat 18, 15-17

"If your brother has sinned, go and correct him on your own. If he takes notice of you, you will have won back your brother. If he takes no notice of you, still take with you one or two people, so that the question may be decided by the word of two or three witnesses. If he doesn't take any notice of them either, tell the Church about it; and if he doesn't take any notice of the Church, consider him to be like a pagan or a publican[2]."

Pardon: Mat 18, 21-22

Then Peter approached Him and asked Him: "Lord, if my brother offends me, how many times must I pardon him? Up to seven times[3]?" Jesus answered him: "I don't say to you up to seven times, rather up to seventy times seven."

You will be pardoned: Mat 18, 23-35

"Because of this, the Kingdom of God can be compared to a king who wanted to settle accounts with his servants. And, when he began to settle the accounts, one who owed ten thousand talents[4] was introduced to him. He didn't have anything to pay him with. Then the lord ordered that he, his

---

1. Given through the love of God.
2. This is the order of fraternal correction.
3. Seven is an undefined number in the Bible, Jesus's response is: always.
4. The silver talent weighed 34.272 grammes, 10,000 talents was a fantastic amount.

wife and children and everything he owned be sold to pay the debt. But the servant fell on his knees and begged him: 'Lord, have patience with me, and I shall pay you it all.' Moved to compassion, the lord of that servant, left him in liberty, and forgave him the whole debt."

Bad servant: Mat 18, 28-35

"But when that servant went out, he met one of his colleagues, who owed him one hundred dinars[1]. He grabbed him by the neck and was about to strangle him, shouting at the same time: 'Pay what you owe me.' His companion, falling to the ground, begged him in these terms: 'Have patience with me and I'll pay you it all.' But he didn't want to, rather he went and made them put him in jail until the debt was paid. When they saw this, his companions were very saddened; and they went to tell their lord what had happened. Then the lord called for him and said to him: 'Wicked servant!, I have pardoned all the debt because you pleaded with me. Mustn't you, then, have compassion for your companion, as I had for you?' And, full of rage, his lord handed him over to the torturers until all the debt was paid. My heavenly Father will treat you in the same way, if one of you does not forgive his brother with all your heart."

Conditions for following Jesus: Luke 9, 57-62 (Mat 8, 19-22)

And whilst they were on the road, one of them said to Him: "I shall follow You wherever You go[2]." Jesus answered him: "Vixen have their burrows, and birds of the sky, nests; but the Son of man does not have anywhere to lay down His head." And He said to the other man; "Follow me." but he replied: "Lord, allow me to first go and bury my father[3]." And Jesus: "Let the dead bury their dead; go and announce the kingdom of God." The other also said: "I shall follow you, Lord, but first

---

1. 100 dinars is a minute amount. If we want God to pardon us, we must pardon others.
2. Perhaps he wanted to profit from His miracles, He did not like his conduct.
3. Jesus, who was passing by, wanted a reply without delay.

allow me to say goodbye to the people in my house[1]." Jesus replied to him: "Nobody who looks back whilst he has the plough in his hand is fit for the kingdom of heaven."

The 72 disciples: Luke 10, 1-12, 16

After this, the Lord designated another seventy-two and sent them ahead of Him in pairs to every city and place where He was due to go. And He said to them: "The harvest is large but the workers are few. Request the Lord of the harvest to send workers for his harvests[2]. Go; look, I am sending you like lambs into the middle of wolves. Whoever hears you hears Me; and whoever rejects you, rejects Me; but whoever rejects Me, rejects Him who has sent Me[3]."

Unbelieving cities: Luke 10, 13-15 (Mat 11, 20-24)

"Woe to you, Chorazin! Woe to you, Bethsaida! Because if the prodigies done in you had been done in Tyre and Sidon, they would have made penance a long time ago, sitting on the ground covered in sackcloth and ashes. Because of this, Tyre and Sidon will be more benignly treated at the judgement than you. And you, Capernaum, do you think you will be towering into the sky? For you will be flung down into Hell[4]."

Return of the disciples: Luke 10, 17-20

The seventy-two returned very happy, saying. "Lord, even the demons submit to us[5] in your name!" He said to them: "I have seen Satan falling from Heaven like lightning into the abyss[6]. See how He has given you the power to walk over serpents and scorpions, and dominion over over all the enemy's power, and nothing will be able to harm you; but do not be glad

1. The family. He who has been called and turns back is not fit for the Kingdom of Heaven. Jesus demands fidelity to the vocation.
2. The request has to be made against the lack of apostles and missionaries.
3. Listening to the envoys is listening to Jesus sent from the Father.
4. Not even the ruins of the two cities remain.
5. The gift of miracles is a gift received from God.
6. A serious lesson of humility against pride.

because the spirits submit to you, but be glad because your names are written in heaven."

Christ our consoler: Mat 11, 25-30 (Luke 10, 21-22)

At that time, «He trembled with joy through the action of the Holy Spirit» and said: "I praise You and I give You thanks, Father, Lord of Heaven and earth, because You have hidden these things from the wide and prudent and have revealed them to the little ones. Yes, Father, because You have wanted it that way. All things have been given Me by My Father, and nobody knows the Son, only the Father; nobody knows the Father, only the Son and whoever the Son wants to reveal Him to. All of you who are tired and exhausted, come to Me and I shall relieve you. Take My yoke upon you and learn from Me, who is meek and humble of heart. You will thus find relief for your souls; because My yoke is smooth and my load light[1].

Great commandment: Luke 10, 23-28

And addressing the disciples in particular, He said to them: "Lucky the eyes which see what you see. Because I say to you that many prophets and kings wished to see what you see and they did not see it, and hear what you hear and they did not hear it."

A doctor of Law got up, intending to test Him, and asked Him: "Master, what must I do to come into possession of eternal life?" He said to him: "What is written in the Law? What do you read?" He replied: «You will love the Lord, your God, with all your heart, with all your soul, with all your strength, and your neighbour as yourself (Dt 6, 5; Lv 19,18).» "You have replied well, answered Jesus. Do that and you will live[2]" (Lv 18, 5).

---

1. God reveals Himself to the humble and helps them to carry the cross.

2. In order to enter the Eternal Life of Heaven it is necessary to comply with the Commandments. It is not enough to call oneself a Catholic.

Samaritan: Luke 10, 29-37

But he, wanting to justify the question proposed, said to Jesus: "And who is my neighbour[1]?" Jesus began to expound: "A man was going down from Jerusalem to Jericho and fell into the hands of some bandits, who stripped him of everything and, after beating him up, went off, leaving him half-dead. By chance a priest was going down the same road and, having seen him, went on by. A Levite, passing by in the same way, saw him and went on by. But a Samaritan, who was travelling, reached him, and his heart was touched when he saw him, and, approaching him, he bandaged his wounds, and poured oil and wine on them as well; and putting him on his own donkey, he took him to an inn and cared for him. And the following day, taking out two dinars, he gave them to the inn-keeper and said to him: Look after him and, if it costs more, I'll pay you when I return. Which of those three seems to have been a neighbour to the man who fell into the hands of bandits?" He answered Him: "The one who had mercy on him." Jesus replied to him: "Go and do the same."

Bethany: Luke 10, 38-42

While they were on the road, He entered a certain village[2]; and a woman called Martha gave Him the hospitality of her house. She had a sister called Mary, who, seated at the Lord's feet, listened to His Word. But Martha was very pressed by the many chores of hospitality. And, coming into Jesus' presence, she said to Him: "Lord, does it not bother You that my sister has left me alone with all the work? Tell her to help me." Jesus answered her: "Martha, Martha, you worry and fret over many things when only one is necessary[3]; Mary has rightly chosen the best part, which shall not be taken away from her."

---

1. The Jews understood as neighbours those of their race.
2. Bethany.
3. The only thing absolutely necessary in this world is to serve and love God and save the soul.

Divine origin: John 7, 25-31

Some neighbours from Jerusalem asked: "Isn't this the one they tried to kill? For He speaks freely without them saying anything to Him. Perhaps the authorities have really convinced themselves that He is the Christ? All said and done, we know where He comes from; but when Christ comes, nobody will know from where He comes from." Jesus, teaching in the temple, said in a loud voice: "You know Me and you know where I come from, and, all said and done, I have not come here on my own account, but He who has authority, whom you don't know, has sent Me. I do know Him, because I come from Him and He has sent Me[1]." They wanted to arrest Him, but nobody dared lay their hands on Him, because His time still hadn't come. Many people from the town believed in Him, and said: "Will the Messiah, when He comes, do more prodigies than Him?"

They try to detain Him: John 7, 32-36

The Pharisees found out about these rumours about Him which circulated among the people, and they and the chief priests sent police to arrest Him. Jesus started to say: "I am going to be with you for a short while, since I shall go to to Him who has sent Me. You will look for Me, but you will not find Me, and, wherever I am, you will not be able to come[2]." The Jews were saying amongst themselves: "Where will He go that we won't be able to find Him? Maybe he's going to the Diaspora of the Greeks to teach them? What does that mean, what he's just said: You will look for Me, but you will not find me; and, wherever I am, you will not be able to come?"

Promise: John 7, 37-39

On the last day, the most solemn one of the festival, Jesus, standing up, said in a loud voice. "Whoever is thirsty, come to

---

1. God loved the world so much that He sent His only Son to save it.
2. At the end of His life He prophesizes His imminent departure in order to return to the Father.

Me and drink[1]. He who believes in Me, as the Scripture says:«Torrents of living water streamed from His bosom» (Luke 44, 3...) With this He was refering to the Spirit which was going to receive whoever believed in Him. The spirit still had not been communicated, because Jesus still had not been glorified.

Opinions: John 7, 40-53

Those who had heard these words from the people said: "This is really the Prophet." Others stated: "This is the Christ." But others argued. "No, because the Christ's hardly going to come from Galilee. Doesn't the Scripture say that Christ comes from the seed of David, and from Bethlehem, David's town?" There was a diversity of opinions about Him among the people. Some of them wanted to arrest Him, but nobody put a finger on Him. Then the police went back to the chief priests and Pharisees; the latter reprimanded them: "Why have you not brought him?" The police replied: "No man has ever spoken like this one[2]." The Pharisees answered: "You also have allowed yourselves to be deceived? Maybe some man of standing or some Pharisee has believed in him? As for these people, who don't know the Law, they deserve contempt." One of them, Nicodemus[3], the same one who had interviewed Him earlier, said to them: "Is it the case that our Law condemns somebody without having first listened to Him and verified what He has done? Investigate and you will see that no prophet has come from Galilee[4]." And they all went home.

Adulterous woman: John 8, 1-11

Jesus went to the mount of Olives. But, at daybreak He presented Himself again in the temple and all the people came to Him. He sat down and instructed them. The scribes and Pharisees brought a women surprised in adultery, and putting her in their midst, they said to Him: "Master, this woman has

---

1. From the water of Grace.
2. Because His doctrine is not human, but divine.
3. He was a hidden disciple.
4. Jonah and Nahum were from there.

been surprised in flagrant adultery. Moses orders us in the Law to stone women like this. What's Your opinion[1]?" They said this to compromise him, in order to have something to accuse Him with. Jesus started to write on the ground with His finger. But as they insisted, He got up and said: "Let he who is without sin throw the first stone", and, squatting again, continued writing on the ground. When they heard this, they started to leave, one after another, beginning with the oldest; and he was left alone with the woman, who remained there in silence. Jesus got up and asked her: "Woman, where are your accusers? Has anybody condemned you?" "Nobody, Lord", she replied. "Well, I'm not condemning you either, added Jesus. Go, and from now on don't sin any more[2]."

Light of the world: John 8, 12-20

Jesus spoke to them again: "I am the light of the world. Whoever follows Me will not walk in darkness[3], but will possess the light of the world." The Pharisees objected: "You are declaring on your own behalf; your declaration is not worthy of faith." Jesus answered them: "Even though I declare on my own behalf, my declaration is worthy of faith, because I know where I have come from and where I'm going. You, on the other hand, don't know where I come from and where I'm going. You judge according to appearances, I don't judge anybody. If I judge, my judgement deserves respect, because I am not alone, since the Father who has sent Me is with Me. And in your Law it is written that the declaration of two persons is worthy of faith. I am He who declares on My behalf, but the Father who has sent Me also declares on My behalf." "Where is your Father?", they replied to Him. Jesus answers: "You know neither Me nor My Father. If you knew Me, you would know my Father."

---

1. They wanted to accuse Him either of prevarication over the Law or of intransigence if He ordered her to be stoned.
2. Merciful with the sinner but not with the sin.
3. Light of the world, darkness of death.

Where I go: John 8, 21-30

He said to them again: "I am going and you will look for Me, but you will die in your sin. Where I am going, you cannot come." The Jews said: "Maybe he's going to commit suicide, when he says: Where I am going, you cannot come?" But Jesus said to them: "You are from below, I from above. You are from this world, I am not of this world[1] For this reason I have said that you will die in your sins. If you don't believe what I am, you will die in your sins." They asked Him: "Who are You?" Jesus answered them: "I have been repeating it to you since the beginning[2]. I have many things to say and judge with respect to you; but He who has sent Me is truthful and I speak to the world of what I have heard from Him." They didn't understand what He was telling them about the Father. Then Jesus said: "When you have raised the Son of man on high[3], then you will know what I am and that I don't do anything on My own account, only what corresponds to what the Father has taught me, thus do I speak. And He who has sent Me is with Me; He has never left Me alone, for I always do what pleases Him." When He said these things, many believed in Him.

Divinity: John 8, 46-59

"Which of you can attribute a sin to me[4] And I tell you the truth, why don't you believe Me? Whoever belongs to God listens to God's words." The Jews replied: "Rather we say that you are a Samaritan and you are possessed[5]." Jesus replied: "I am not possessed, but I honour My Father and you abuse Me. I am not seeking applause in itself. Your father Abraham trembled with joy when he thought of seeing My day; He contemplated it and rejoiced[6]." The Jews answered Him:

---

1. Visible and temporal, but from Heaven.
2. That He was the Son of God.
3. On high on the cross.
4. We are all sinners, only Jesus is innocent.
5. The Jews only knew how to respond with insults.
6. Perhaps he knew about the Incarnation of the Messiah through a special revelation.

"You're not even fifty, and you've seen Abraham?" Jesus answered them. "With all certainty I say to you: Before Abraham was born, I already existed[1]." They grabbed stones to throw at Him. But Jesus slipped away and left the temple.

Blind at birth: John 9, 1-23

He saw a man who was blind at birth pass by. And His disciples asked Him: "Master, was he born blind for having sinned, he or his parents[2]?" Jesus replied: "Neither for having sinned, nor his parents, but so that the works of God may be revealed in him. Whilst it is daytime we must carry out the work of He who has sent Me. The night is going to come, when nobody can work. Whilst I am in the world, I am the light of the world." Having said this, He spat on the ground and made mud with His saliva and applied to his eyes, and said to him: "Go and wash in the pool of Siloam (this word means envoys)." He went, then, and bathed and returned with sight. The neighbours and those who had seen him earlier, since he was a beggar, asked themselves: "Isn't he the one who used to sit and beg for alms?" Some said to themselves: "It is." Others replied: "No, only one who looks like him." He said: "It's me." And they asked him: "How have your eyes opened?" He answered: "The man they call Jesus made mud and applied it to my eyes and said to me: Go to Siloam (the pool) and wash yourself. So I went, I washed myself and I recovered my sight." "Where is this man?", they asked him. They took the man who until then had been blind before the Pharisees. The day when Jesus had made mud and opened his eyes was the Sabbath. He answered them: "He put mud on my eyes, I washed and I can see[3]." Some Pharisees exclaimed: "This man isn't sent by God, since He doesn't observe the Sabbath." But others replied: "How can a sinner work such marvels?" And they were divided amongst themselves. They asked the blind man again: "What do you think of the man who has opened your eyes?" He replied: "He

---

1. Jesus, being God, has existed for all eternity.

2. The Jews believed that illnesses were punishments from God for sins.

3. Bodily light, and that of the soul, of Faith.

is a Prophet." But the Jews did not want to believe that this man had been blind and had recovered his sight[1] until they called his parents. And they asked them: "Is this your son, who you say was born blind? How, then, does he see now?" "We know that this is our son and that he was born blind. What we don't know is how he now sees and who has opened his eyes. Ask him, he's old enough; he himself can tell you." The parents said this because they were afraid of the Jews, since the latter had decided to expel from the synagogue anybody who recognised Him as the Messiah. Because of this his parents said: "He's old enough, ask him."

Now I can see: John 9, 24-41

They called the man who had been blind for a second time and said to him: "Give glory to God[2]. We know that this man is a sinner." He replied: "I don't know if he is a sinner, what I do know is that I was blind and now I can see." Then they asked him: "Who did this to you? How did he open your eyes?" He answered them: "I have already told you and you haven't taken any notice of me. Why do you want to hear it again? Perhaps you want to become His disciples[3]?" They abused him and said to him: "You will be his disciple; we are disciples of Moses, but as for this man, we don't know where he comes from." The man answered them: "That is what's wonderful, that you don't know where he comes from and, nevertheless, He opened my eyes. We know that God does not listen to sinners, but He does listen to to him who honours Him and does His will. It is unheard of that somebody has opened the eyes of a man who was born blind. If this man doesn't come from God, he couldn't do anything." They answered him: "You were born swathed in sins and you dare to give us lessons?" And they threw him out[4].

---

1. The Pharisees did not want to believe it.
2. It was hypocrisy.
3. Their indignation reached its limits when they heard these words; they showered him with insults.
4. Their obstinate attitude proves their blindness.

I believe, Lord: John 9, 35-41

Jesus heard that they had expelled him; and, when He met him, He said to him: "Do you believe in the Son of God?" He replied: "Who is He, Lord, that I may believe in Him?" Jesus answered him: "He who you see, and who is talking with you, that is Him." Then he exclaimed: "I believe, Lord" and prostrated himself before Him[1]. Jesus said: "I have come to this world for a discriminatory judgement; so that those who don't see, see, and those who see, turn blind." Some Pharisees who were with Him heard this and said to Him: "Are we also blind?" Jesus answered them: "If you were blind, you would be blameless. But now you say: We see, and for this reason your sin endures[2]."

I am the gate: John 10, 1-10

"With all certainty I assure you: Whoever does not enter through the gate of the sheep-pen, but climb over the top in another place, is a thief and a bandit[3]. He who enters through the gate is the sheeps' shepherd. The watchman opens the door for him, and the sheep hear his voice, and he calls the sheep by their name and leads them out. And when he has let all his sheep out, he walks in front of them and the sheep follow him, because they know his voice. However, they will not follow a stranger, but will run away from him, because they do not know strangers' voices." Jesus put this comparison to them, but they did not understand what he meant. And so Jesus insisted again: "Truly I say to you: I am the gate for the sheep. All those who have come before Me are thieves and bandits; but the sheep haven't listened to them. I am the gate; whoever enters through Me will be satisfied; he will come in and go out and will find the shepherd. The thief only comes to steal and butcher and exterminate. And I have come so that you may have a life, an exuberant life."

---

1. This confession of the divinity of Jesus is one of the most beautiful in the Gospel.
2. There is no worse blind man than the one who closes his eyes to the truth.
3. Jesus sheep-pen is the Church.

I am the shepherd: John 10, 11-16

"I am the good shepherd. The good shepherd gives his life for his sheep[1]. The hired worker, who is neither shepherd nor owner of the sheep, leaves the sheep and runs away when he sees the wolf coming, and the wolf snatches them and disperses them; because he is a hired worker and he doesn't care about the sheep. I am the good shepherd and I know My sheep, and My sheep know Me and I know the Father. I give up My life for My sheep. I have other sheep which are not from this fold[2], and I need to guide them. And they will hear my voice, and there will be one sole flock and one sole shepherd."

I give up My life: John 10, 17-21

"For this reason My Father loves Me, because I give up My life to take it back again. Nobody takes it away from Me, but I give it up voluntarily[3]. I am free to give it and free to take it back. This is the precept which I have received from the Father." Once again opinions among the Jews were divided because of these words.

Ask[4]: Mat 7, 5-13

He also said to them: "If one of you goes to a friend's house at midnight and says to him. 'Friend, I need three loaves, because a friend of mine who is on a journey has arrived and I have nothing to give him'; and if the other replies from inside: 'Don't bother me, the door is already closed, and my children are in bed with me; I can't get up to give it to you?; I assure you that if he doesn't get up and give them to him out of friendship, at least for his impertinence, he will get up and give him whatever he needs[5]. So I say to you: Ask and it will be given; seek and you will find; knock and it will be opened to you.

---

1. Jesus offered Himself on the cross to save us.
2. The Church. He wants them all to enter and form one sole flock under the crook of one sole Shepherd.
3. He feeds with His doctrine and His Sacraments.
4. Prayer has to be humble and persevering.
5. Stubborn.

Because everybody who asks receives, and whoever seeks finds, and whoever knocks will have the door opened to him."

Pharisees: Luke 12, 1-3

Meanwhile, the people having congregated in their thousands, to the point of stepping on each other, He started to say, firstly to His disciples: "Take care with the yeast of the Pharisees, that is, with hypocrisy. There is nothing covered over which does not end up being uncovered, nor is there anything hidden which does not end up being known. Because of this, whatever you have said in the dark will be listened to in the light, and what you have spoken in private rooms will be preached on the rooftops."

Avarice: Luke 12, 13-21

Somebody from amongst the crowd said to Him: "Master, tell my brother to share the inheritance with me." He said to him: "My friend, who has appointed Me your judge or executor?" And He said to them: "Preserve yourselves carefully from all covetousness; because, however much you may be swimming in richness, life does not consist of an abundance of wealth." And He put to them a parable: "There was a rich man whose fields gave copious fruits. And he was debating with himself: How will I arrange them, since I have nowhere to store my fruits? And he said to himself: I know what I must do: I shall knock down my granaries to make other bigger ones, and I shall guard all my grain and riches there; and I shall say to myself: My soul, you have many riches in reserve for many years; rest, eat, drink, have a good time. But God said to him: Fool, this very night they are going to demand of you your soul; and for whom will you have stored so much? This is what happens to anybody who piles up treasure for himself instead of enriching himself in the eyes of God[1]."

---

1. And so, no matter how much we have in this world, we can't take anything with us to the other. Only our deeds.

"Do not fear": Luke 12, 22-34

And He addressed his disciples thus: "Therefore I say to you: Do not fret about life, the people of the world are those who live worried by these things; as for you, your Father already knows that you have need of them[1]. Therefore, look for the kingdom of God and these things will be given to you as gratification. Do not fear, my little flock, because it has appeared good to your Father to give you the kingdom. Sell your goods and give alms; make yourselves bags which do not deteriorate, treasures which do not run out in heaven, where the thief does not come and the moth does not wreck. Because wherever your treasure is, there also will be your heart."

Vigilance: Luke 12, 35-40

"Let your loins be girdled and your lamps lit. Be like men who await the return of their master from the wedding, to open up as soon as he arrives and calls. Lucky are those servants whom the master finds vigilant; I say to you with confidence: He will put on his workclothes, he will make them comfortable and will proceed to serve them. They are lucky if he finds them like that, be it at midnight, be it at cockcrow. Consider that if the master of the house knew at what time the thief was coming, he would keep watch and would not let a breach be opened in his house. You also, be on the alert, since the Son of man can come when you least expect it[2]."

Administrators: Luke 12, 41-48

Peter said: "Lord, in this parable are you alluding to us alone or to the rest as well?" "Imagine, then, a faithful and prudent servant whom the master puts over the household to distribute the wheat ration when it is due. The servant whom his master, on arriving, finds working in this way is lucky. I say to you with confidence: He will consider him above all his wealth. But if

---

1. The treasures of the other world are our good deeds.
2. We know neither the day nor the hour when God will call us. We only know that it will come when we least expect it.

this servant says to himself: 'My master will take a long time in arriving', and starts to mistreat the servants, to eat and drink and get drunk, the master of that servant will come on the least supposed day and when he was least expected and he will subject him to torture, and he will provide him with the same fortune as the infidels. That servant who, knowing his master's will, has nothing prepared and has not acted according to his will, will receive many lashes[1]. He will demand a great deal of anybody he has given a lot to, and he will ask the most of whoever he has given the most[2].

Barren fig tree: Luke 13, 1-9

.On the very same occasion some people were presented who commented to Him on the case of the Galileeans whose blood Pilate had mixed with those of the sacrifices. He answered them: "Do you think that these Galileeans were greater sinners than all the rest of the Galileeans because they suffered this misfortune? No, I assure you; but if you don't do penance, you will all perish in the same way. Do you think that those eighteen people, on whom the tower of Siloam came crashing down and killed, were more guilty than all the other inhabitants of Jerusalem? No, I assure you; but if you don't do penance you will all perish in the same way." And He put this parable to them: "A man has a fig tree planted in his vineyard. He came in search of fruit, but did not find it. And he said to the vine-grower. 'For three years now I've been coming to this fig tree in search of fruit asnd I haven't found any. Cut it down: why, morever, is it necessary to degrade the earth?' But the vine-grower begged him:'Lord, leave it still for this year, and meanwhile I shall dig around it and I will throw in manure; perhaps it will bear fruit next year; if not, you will order it to be cut down[3]."

---

1. Therefore, let us be prepared, in order to give Him the account of our life.
2. He who has received more gifts, qualities, riches and material goods, etc., will be asked for more.
3. God patiently awaits the fruit of our good works. Let us practice Christian virtues.

The mystery of the Chosen People: Luke 13, 23-30

Somebody asked him: "Lord, are those who are saved a few?" He said to them: "Make an effort to enter by the narrow gate, because I assure you that many will try to enter and will not succeed[1]. Once the master of the house gets up and closes the door, if you are left outside, however much you bang on the door, saying: 'Lord, open for us', he will answer you: 'I don't know where you come from.' Then you will begin to say: 'We have eaten and drunk with you, and you have shown us our places.' And he will answer you: 'I repeat to you that I don't know where you come from; stay away from me all you who have committed evil[2].' There will be weeping and grinding of teeth there, when you see Abraham, Isaac and Jacob and all the prophets in the kingdom of God, whilst you are cast out. And they will come from East and West, from North and South, and they will sit down at the table in the kingdom of God. Bear in mind that there are the last[3] who will be the first and there are the first who will be the last."

I have told you: John 10, 22-30

At that time the feast of the Dedication was being celebrated; it was winter. Jesus went into the temple through the porch of Solomon. The Jews surrounded Him and they said to Him: "For how long are you going to keep us impatient? If You are the Christ, say it to us clearly." Jesus answered Him: "I have already told you: The works which I do in the name of My Father, they declare on My behalf. But you do not believe, because you do not come from My sheep. My sheep listen to My voice, and I know them and they follow Me. I give them eternal life and they will never perish, nor will anybody snatch them out of My hands. My Father, who has given them to Me, is the greatest of all, and nobody can snatch anything out of

---

1. Jesus tells us that it is not easy to enter the Father's house, even though we may have done some good works.
2. It is necessary to follow the way of the cross, with Christian asceticism.
3. Those called the last are the Gentiles, the first the Jews.

My Father's hands. The Father and I are one and the same thing[1]."

They picked up stones: John 10, 31-41

The Jews again picked up stones to stone Him. Jesus said to Him: "I have revealed many good works to you on behalf of My Father. For which of these works are you intending to stone Me?" The Jews answered Him: "No, we don't want to stone you for any good work, but for blasphemy, since you, a man, try to pass yourself off as God[2]."

He again passed over to the other side of the Jordan, to the same place where John had baptized for the first time, and He stayed there. And many came to Him and said: "It is certain that John performed no prodigies, but everything he said about this man was true; and many believed in Him in that very place."

Great feast[3]: Luke 14, 16-24

He said to them: "A man gave a great banquet and invited many people. At dinner-time he gave orders to his servant who said to the guests: 'Come, for now it is ready.' And all of them, down to the last one, started to make excuses. The first one said to him: 'I've bought a field and need to go and see it; I beseech you to excuse me,' Another one said: 'I've bought five yoke of oxen and I'm going to try them out; I beseech you not to take it badly'; and another exclaimed: 'I've just got married and I can't come because of that.' When he went back, the servant informed his master about this. Then the master angrily said to his servant: 'Go quickly to the squares and streets of the city, and bring me here the poor, the maimed, the blind and the lame.' The servant said: 'Sir, we have done what you have

---

1. This is the most diaphanous declaration of Christ's divinity: identity with the Father.
2. There was not a shadow of doubt in their words; they wanted to stone Him because he claimed Himself as God.
3. Jesus compares the Kingdom of Heaven to a banquet, and those of the Orientals sometimes lasted for whole months. The first guests were the Jews, the last the Gentiles.

ordered and there is still some room. The master replied to the servant: Go out to the highways and byways and force the people to come in so that my house is full. Because I say to you that none of those who had been invited will partake of my banquet'."

Conditions for following Jesus: Luke 14, 25-35

An enormous mass of people walked with Him and, going towards them, He said to them: "If somebody wants to come to Me and does not abandon his father and mother, his wife and children, his brothers and sisters, and even his own life, cannot be My disciple[1]. Whoever has ears to hear, let him hear."

Lost sheep[2]: Luke 15, 1-10

All the publicans went up to Him to listen to Him. And the Pharisees and the scribes were murmuring, saying: "This man welcomes sinners and eats with them." And He put to them this parable: "If one of you has a hundred sheep and loses one of them, is it not the case that you leave the ninety-nine in the desert and go in search of the lost one until you find him? And when you find him, you throw him on your shoulders and, arriving home, you gather together friends and neighbours and says to them: 'Celebrate with me, because I've found the sheep which was lost to me.' I say to you that in the same way there will be more rejoicing in heaven for a repentant sinner than for ninety-nine righteous men who do not need penitence. If a woman who has ten drachmas loses one, is it not the case that she lights a lamp, sweeps the house and searches with all her might until she finds it? And, having found it, she calls her friends and neighbours and says to them: 'Celebrate with me, because I have found the drachma which I had lost.' I say to you that in the same way there is rejoicing amongst God's angels for a sinner who repents."

---

1. Jesus wants to be the first in our love, before our most intimate relatives and our very own selves.

2. The image of the Good Shepherd is the first of the catacombs.

Prodigal son[1]: Luke 15, 11-33

And He added: "A man had two sons. And the younger of these said to his father: 'Father, give me the part of the inheritance which corresponds to me.' He divided the inheritance between them. After a few days, the younger son, having gathered everything together, set off for distant lands and there he squandered his estate by living licentiously. But when he had spent it all, a great hunger befell those lands, and he started to experience want. He put himself at the disposition of one of the natives of that region, who sent him to his fields to look after pigs. He would happily have filled his stomach with the carobs which the pigs ate, but nobody gave them to him. He said introspectively: 'How many of my father's day laborers have bread in abundance whilst I'm here dying of hunger. I'll go back to my father and I'll say to him: Father, I've sinned against heaven and against you; I don't deserve to be your son; treat me like one of your day laborers.' So he set off to see his father. He was still a long way off when his father saw him and was moved, and, running towards him, threw himself round his neck and covered him with kisses. The son said to him: 'Father, I have sinned against heaven and against you; I don't deserve to be your son.' The Father ordered his servants: 'Quick!, get out the best clothes and put them on him, put a ring on his finger and sandals on his feet; bring the fattest calf, kill it and let's eat and make merry; because this son of mine was dead and has come back to life; he was lost and has been found.' And they started the feast. His eldest son was in the field; when he came back, he heard music and dancing as he approached the house; and, calling one of the servants, he asked what it was. He told him: 'Your brother has come back, and your father has ordered the fattened calf to be killed, because he has welcomed him safe and sound.' He became angry and did not want to go in, and because of this his father had to go out and request him to enter. He said to his father: 'All the years that I've served you, without

---

1. The sinner who abandons the paternal home is marvellously expressed in this parable. God receives the repentant sinner in His arms and everybody rejoices.

ever having transgressed any of your commands, and you have never given me a kid-goat to celebrate with my friends; but, this son of yours, who has spent all his riches on evil women, has barely walked into the house before you have killed the fattened calf for him.' He answered him: 'My son, you are always with me, and all my things are yours; but it was necessary to have a party and rejoice, because this brother of yours was dead and has come back to life, he was lost and has been found[1].

Unfaithful steward: Luke 16, 1-9

He also said to His disciples: "There was a man who had a steward who was accused before him of squandering his goods[2]. He called for him and said to him. 'What is this they are telling me about you? Give me an account of your administration, because from now on you will not be able to continue as steward.' The steward said to himself: 'What am I going to do, since my master is going to take the administration away from me? Dig? I can't. Beg? I'd be ashamed. Now I know what to do to be welcomed in their houses when I am stripped of the administration.' And calling his master's debtors one by one, he said to the first one: 'How much do you owe my master?' He replied: 'One hundred barrels of oil.' He answered: 'Take your invoice, sit right down and put down fifty.' Then he said to the other one: 'And how much do you owe?' He said: 'One hundred measures of wheat.' He answered: 'Take your invoice and note down eighty.' The master praised the unfaithful servant for having acted astutely, for the children of this century are more astute[3] than the children of the light in these things."

Epulon and Lazarus[4]: Luke 16, 19-31

There was a rich man who wore purple and fine linen and ate sumptuously every day. On the other hand, a poor man

---

1. God's mercy is infinite. Distrust offends him.
2. God is the master of everything we have and are: we have to give account to God of goods, qualities, health, life- everything.
3. The master praised the astuteness of his bad administrator, not his badness.
4. This is the image of the wicked rich man and the poor man.

called Lazarus used to lay next to his door, covered in ulcers, hoping to eat his fill from what fell from the rich man's table[1]; and even the dogs came to lick his ulcers. Then the poor man died and he was taken by the angels to the bosom of Abraham[2]. The rich man also died and was buried. He was in Hell, in the midst of torments, and raised up his eyes and saw Abraham in the distance and Lazarus in his bosom. And he shouted: "Father Abraham, have pity on me and tell Lazarus to moisten his fingertip in water and refresh my tongue, because I'm roasting in these flames." Abraham said: "Son, remember that you received your good things whilst you were alive, and Lazarus, on the contrary, the bad ones; now, however, he is consoled here and you are in torment. And, moreover, an unbridgeable abyss has been placed between you and us, with the result that those who want to pass from here to you, or from there to us, cannot." "My father, I beg you to send word to my father, for I have five brothers, so that they are warned not to come to this place of torments." Abraham replied: "They already have Moses and the Prophets. Let them listen to them!" He answered: "No, father Abraham, if somebody from the land of the dead went to them, they would do penance." He answered him: "If they take no notice of Moses and the Prophets, neither will they do so with somebody brought back from the dead[3]."

Journey to Jerusalem: John 11, 1-16; Lazarus : John 11, 1-16

There was a sick man called Lazarus in Bethany[4], the hometown of Mary and her sister Martha. And the sick man, Lazarus, was their brother. The sisters then sent for Him to say: "Lord, your friend is sick[5]." When He heard this, Jesus said:

---

1. In our present society it is said that some die with their stomach full and others of hunger.
2. Jewish expression = Heaven, as opposed to Hell.
3. A dead person who is resuscitated.
4. Three kms from Jerusalem, on the road to Jericho.
5. Jesus used to lodge in the three siblings' house. The message was delicate and pressing. It appeals to His friendship.

"This illness is not mortal, but serves the glory of God, so that the Son will be glorified through it." Jesus loved Martha, her sister and Lazarus. Although He had heard about his illness, He remained there another two days more. Then He said to His disciples: "Let's go to Judea once more." They answered Him: "Master, a short while ago the Jews wanted to stone You, and You're going there again?" "Our friend Lazarus is sleeping, but I'm going to wake Him up[1]." His disciples replied: "Lord, if he's sleeping, he'll get better." But Jesus was refering to his death whilst His disciples thought He was speaking of ordinary sleep. Jesus then clearly said to them: "Lazarus has died[2]. And I'm glad for you that you weren't there, so that you believe. But let's go to his house." Then Thomas, whose surname was Didymus, said to his co-disciples: "Let us also go and die with Him."

I am the life: John 11, 17-27

When Jesus arrived He found that he had already been in the sepulchre for four days. Bethany was some three kilometers from Jerusalem. Therefore, many Jews were coming to Martha and Mary to convey their condolences for their brother[3]. When Martha heard that Jesus was coming, she went out to meet Him. But Mary stayed in the house. Martha said to Jesus: "Lord, if You had been here, my brother would not have died. But I already know that God will grant You whatever You ask Him[4]." Jesus said to her: "Your brother will come back to life." Martha answered Him: "I know that He will come back to life at the resurrection of the last day. Whoever believes in Me will live, even though he may die; and whoever lives and believes in Me, will never die. Do you believe this?" "Yes, Lord", she replied. "I have believed that You are the Christ, the Son of God, He who was due to come to the world[5]."

---

1. The sleep of death.
2. It appears that he died on the same day as the notification.
3. It was a distinguished family.
4. She considers Him not as God but as a prophet
5. Jesus illuminated her moderate faith.

Jesus's weeping: John 11, 28-37

And having said this, she went and called her sister Mary, whispering to her: "The Master is here and He's calling you." Hardly had she heard these words when she got up quickly and went towards Him. Jesus still hadn't arrived in the town, but was in the place where Martha had met him. When the Jews who were with Mary in the house, comforting her, saw her get up and leave so quickly, they followed her, thinking that she was going to the sepulchre to weep there. When Mary reached Jesus, she fell at His feet on seeing Him and said to Him: "Lord, if You had been here, my brother would not have died." Jesus, seeing her weep and seeing the Jews accompanying her weep, was moved and touched within[1]; and He asked: "Where have you put him?" They answered Him: "Lord, come and You'll see." Jesus started to weep. The Jews said to themselves: "This man, who opened the blind man's eyes, could He not have prevented this man dying[2]?"

Resurrection of Lazarus: John 11, 38-44

Jesus, once again visibly moved, reached the sepulchre. It was a cave covered by a stone[3]. Jesus said: "Remove the stone." Martha, the dead man's sister, answered Him: "Lord, he already smells bad, since he's been there for four days." "Haven't I told you, replied Jesus, that if you believe you will see the glory of God?" So they removed the stone and Jesus, raising His eyes to heaven, said: "Father, I give You thanks, because You have heard Me. I already knew that You always hear Me; but I have said it because of the crowd standing round, to convince them that You have sent Me." And, having said this, He shouted loudly: "Lazarus, come out!" And he came out, he who had been dead, with his feet tied and his hands in bandages and his face wrapped in a shroud. "Unwrap him and let him walk," Jesus ordered them.

---

1. Jesus was human, He had a very tender heart.
2. The man who had been blind from birth. All Jerusalem knew about this event.
3. Even today the sepulchre and the meeting-place with Jesus can be seen.

They decree Jesus's death: John 11, 45-57

Many Jews amongst those who were accompanying Mary believed in Him when they saw what He had done. But some of them went to the Pharisees, to report to them what Jesus had done. The high priests and the Pharisees had a meeting and they said to each other: "What are we to do? This man is performing many prodigies. If we leave him like this, all the people will believe in him, and the Romans will come and destroy our Temple and our nation." But one of them, Caiphas, who was the high priest that year, said to them: "You know nothing. Don't you realize that it is in our interests that one single man dies for the people and not that the whole nation perishes." He did not say this on his own account, but, being the high priest that year, he prophesied that Jesus was going to die for the nation; and not only for the nation, but to unite the scattered children of God. From that day onwards they were committed to killing Him[1].

For this reason Jesus did not now appear before the Jews in public, but withdrew to the region near the desert, to the city called Ephraim, and stayed there with His disciples[2]. The Jewish Passover was approaching and many people went up to Jerusalem to purify themselves before the Passover. They were looking for Jesus and said to each other in the Temple: "What does it seem to you? Won't He come to the Festival?" The high priests and Pharisees had ordered that anybody who knew where He was should denounce Him, to have Him arrested.

Lepers: Luke 17, 11-19

On the road to Jerusalem he crossed the frontiers of Samaria and Galilee. When He entered one particular village ten lepers came out to meet Him, who, keeping themselves at a distance, said loudly: "Jesus, Master, have compassion for us." When He saw them, He said to them: "Go and present yourselves to the priests." And while they were on the road, they were cleansed.

---

1. The resurrection of Lazarus had a double effect: some believed and others, the Pharisees, stubbornly persisted in their mortal hatred for Jesus.

2. His time had still not come.

When one of them realized he was cured, he turned back and praised God in a loud voice, and threw himself at Jesus's feet, face down in the ground, giving Him thanks. He was a Samaritan[1]. Taking the word, Jesus said: "Were not all ten cleansed? And the other nine, where are they? Hasn't anybody come back to give glory to God, apart from this foreigner?" And He said to Him: "Get up and go, your faith has saved you[2]."

Second coming: Luke 17, 20-37

Asked by the Pharisees: "When is the Kingdom of God going to come?" He replied: "The Kingdom of God does not have to come in an ostentatious way, nor will they say: 'Here it is, there it is'; don't go or walk behind them. Because, just as lightning strikes and crosses the entire sky with its splendour, from one end to the other, thus will be the coming of the Son of man on its day[3]. But it is necessary for Him to suffer greatly beforehand and be rejected by this race. And the same thing that befell in the times of Noah will likewise take place in the days of the Son of man: they ate and drank; men and woman got married, until the day in which Noah entered the ark and the flood came, destroying everything. The same happened in the time of Lot: they ate and drank; they bought and sold; they planted and built; but the day when Lot left Sodom, fire and sulphur rained down from heaven, destroying everything. The very same thing will occur when the Son of man appears."

Always pray: Luke 18, 1-8

He put to them a parable on the obligation of always praying and never getting tired. He started like this: "There was a judge in one city who neither feared God nor respected men. There was also a widow in that city who used to go to him and say : 'Do justice for me against my enemy.' For some time he did not

1. The Evangelist emphasizes his nationality: he was a Samaritan, the other nine were Jews.

2. Jesus was hurt by their ingratitude.

3. He will come in a spectacular but unexpected way.

worry about it. But one good day He said to himself: 'The truth is that I neither fear God nor respect anybody. As this widow importunes me so much, I will do justice for her, so that she doesn't give me any more headaches'." And the Lord concluded: "Listen to what the iniquitous judge says. Won't God give justice to His chosen ones who beseech Him night and day? Will He be slack in the defence of their cause? I say to you that He shall perform justice for them without delay[1] But do you believe that the Son of man, when he comes, will find faith on earth[2]?"

Pharisee and publican: Luke 18, 9-14

He proposed this parable for those who considered themselves righteous and looked down on the rest: "Two men went up to the temple to pray: one a Pharisee and the other a publican. The Pharisee, standing up, prayed within in this way: 'Oh God! I give you thanks, because I am not like other men: thieves, unrighteous, adulterers, nor like this publican either; I fast twice a week, I pay the tithe on everything I own.' But the publican, staying at a distance, did not dare even raise his eyes to heaven; he gave himself blows on the chest, saying: 'Oh God, have pity on me, I who am a sinner[3]. I say to you that the latter —as opposed to the formee— returned home justified; because everything that exalts itself will be humbled, and whoever humbles himself will be exalted."

Marriage and virginity: Mat 19, 1-2 (Mark 10, 1-12)

When Jesus finished these sermons, He left Galilee and came to the territory of Judea: A great crowd followed Him. «And as usual, He started to instruct them again» and He cured them there. Some Pharisees went up to Him and put Him this question in order to test Him: "Is it lawful for a man to

---

1. The prayer must be trusting and persevering. Communication with God ought to be habitual in a Christian.
2. Jesus passes through all nations.
3. The Pharisee went to praise himself, whilst the publican went to ask forgiveness.

repudiate his wife for any reason?" He replied: "What did Moses propose to you?" And they said: "Moses permitted the opening of an expedient for separation, and repudiation of the wife."»

But Jesus said to them: "Have you not read that «God made them male and female from the beginning of Creation», and that He said: «Because of this, man will leave his father and his mother to join up with his wife, and the two will be one single flesh?» (Gen 2,24); so they are thus not two, but one single flesh. Consequently, man cannot separate what God has brought together[1]."

They continued: "Why, then, did Moses order a petition for divorce to be delivered to a wife in order to repudiate her?" (Dt 24, 1). Jesus answered them: "Moses permitted you to repudiate your wives because of the hardness of your hearts; but in the beginning it was not like that. And I say to you: Whoever repudiates his wife, except in the case of concubinage, and marries another woman, commits adultery[2]."

«When they were home the disciples once again asked Him to explain the matter. And He said to them: "Whoever repudiates his wife and marries another, commits adultery with respect to the first one. And if a women marries another man after repudiating her husband, she commits adultery." Then the disciples said to Him: "If these are the conditions for relationships between man and woman, it is better not to get married." He answered them: "Not everybody understands this doctrine, but only those to whom it is conceded. Because there are men who, from their mother's womb, are impotent for marriage; there are others who make themselves impotent for the Kingdom of Heaven. Let He who is capable of understanding, understand."

---

1. According to the Mosaic law.
2. But not according to the Law of God, which prohibits it. Adultery is a serious sin. Separation is not divorce. For the kingdom of Heaven God virginity is superior to marriage.

Like children: Luke 18, 15-17 (Mat 19, 13-15; Mark 10, 13-16)

They also wanted to present the children to Him to touch; «so that he may put His hands on them and pray»; but when the disciples saw them, they scolded them. But Jesus «reprimanded them»; getting them to come to His side, He said: "Let the children come to Me, and don't impede them, because the Kingdom of Heaven is for those who are like them. I say to you with confidence: Whoever does not welcome the Kingdom of God like a child will not enter into it." «And squeezing them in His arms and putting His hands on them He blessed them[1].»

Poverty and perfection: Mat 19, 16-22

Then a young man approached Him and asked Him: "Master, what good must I do to to attain eternal life?" Jesus answered Him: "Why do you ask Me about what is good? There is only one Good. But if you want to enter the life, keep the commandments[2]." "Which ones?", he asked Him. And Jesus answered him: "You will not kill, you will not commit adultery, you will not steal, you will not bear false witness, you will honour your father and your mother and you will love your neighbor as you love yourself." The youth replied to Him: "I've already observed all that; What am I missing?" Jesus, «fixing His gaze on Him, felt affection for him and said to him: "You are missing only one thing.» If you want to be perfect, Jesus replied, go, sell what you own and give it to the poor and you will have a treasure in heaven. Then, come and follow Me." When he heard these words, the young man walked away in sadness, because he was very rich.

---

1. Jesus loved children: He defended them and put them forward as models because of their simplicity and innocence.
2. It is necessary to keep the Commandments to enter the Kingdom of Heaven.

Danger of riches: Mat 19, 23-30 (Mark 10, 23-31; Luke 18, 24-30)

And Jesus said to His disciples: "Truly I say to you: A rich man will enter into the Kingdom of Heaven with difficulty. And I repeat to you: It is easier for a camel to pass through the eye of a needle than for a rich man to enter the Kingdom of Heaven." When they heard this, the disciples were amazed and said: "Who, then, will be able to save himself?" Jesus looked at them fixedly and said to them: "This is impossible for men, but for God everything is possible[1]." «Those who possess riches will enter the Kingdom of God with difficulty.» Then Peter, taking the word, said to Him: "We have left everything and we have followed you, so what will there be for us?" Jesus answered Him: "I give you My word that, when the Son of man is seated on the throne of His glory at the resurrection, you who have followed Me will also sit on twelve thrones to judge the twelve tribes of Israel. And anybody who leaves their home, brothers or sisters, father or mother, sons or lands, for My Name, «and that of the Gospel,» «for the Kingdom of God», will receive a hundred times more and will attain eternal life[2] And many of the first will end up being the last; and the last, first[3]."

Vine-growers: Mat 20, 1-16

The Kingdom of Heaven is like a father of a family who left earlier in the morning to contract workers for his vineyard. And, having agreed on one dinar per day with the workers, he sent them to his vineyard. He also went out at nine o'clock and saw some others who were in the market square doing nothing, and he said to them: "Why are you here all day relaxing?" They answered him: "Because nobody has contracted us." "Go to the vineyard as well", he said to them. When it got dark, the owner

---

1. Riches are a great obstacle to entering into heaven, if it is not a miracle like that of the camel.
2. Above all Eternal Life.
3. Many of the first will be the last.

of the vineyard said to his steward: "Call the workers and pay them for the day, starting with the last ones and ending with the first." Those from five in the afternoon presented themselves and each one received a dinar[1]. When it was the turn of the first ones, they thought that they would get paid more; but they also received one dinar. And when they received this, they grumbled about the owner, saying: "These ones, the last ones, haven't worked for more than an hour and you treat them the same as us, who have borne the burden of the day and the heat." Then he answered one of them: "Friend, I'm not treating you unjustly; didn't you sign up with me for one dinar? Take what is yours and go. I want to give to this last one the same as you. Or aren't you allowing me to do what I like with what's mine? Or is that you're envious because I'm good?" Similarly, the last will be the first and the first the last.

New Proclamation of the Passion: Mat 20, 17-19 (Mark 10, 32-34; Luke 18, 31-34)

When He had to go up to Jerusalem, Jesus took the twelve aside and said to them by the road: "Look, we're going up to Jerusalem, and the Son of man is going to be handed over to the chief priests and to the scribes, who will condemn Him to death, and they will hand Him over to the pagans to mock, whip, «spit on» and crucify; but on the third day He will come back to life[2]." «But they did not understand anything of this; this was unintelligible language for them, and they did not know what He was saying to them.»

Blind man from Jericho: Luke 18, 35-43

When He approached Jericho, a blind man was sitting by the roadside, asking for alms. And when he became aware of the crowd passing by, he asked what it was. And they replied to him that Jesus of Nazareth was passing by. And he started to

---

1. Silver coin. It was what was agreed. The Christians, like converted pagans, will receive the same payment.

2. He knew very well what had to happen.

shout: "Son of David[1], have compassion for me." And those who were in front of the procession reprimanded him so that he'd keep quiet. But he shouted even louder: "Son of David, have compassion for me[2]." Jesus stopped and told them to bring him to Him. And when he had come closer, He asked him: "What do you want me to do for you?" He answered: "Lord, make me recover my sight." And Jesus said to him: "Recover your sight, your faith has saved you." And at that very moment he recovered it, and followed Him blessing God. And all the people started to praise God when they saw it.

Sons of Zebedee: Mat 20, 20-28 (Mark 10, 35-45)

Then the mother of the sons of Zebedee approached Him with her children, and prostrated herself before Him as if to ask Him for something. He asked her: "What do you want?" She replied: "Make it possible for these two sons of mine to sit in Your Kingdom, one on Your right and the other on Your left." «James and John, the sons of Zebedee, approached Him to say to Him: "Grant us seats in Your glory, one on Your right and the other on Your left".» "You don't know what you're asking for", replied Jesus. "Can you drink the chalice which I have to drink? «Or be baptized with what I'm going to be baptized[3]»" "We can", they answered. He said to them: "Yes, you will drink My chalice; but it is not for Me to grant you seats on My right or left; they are for those for whom My Father has prepared them."

The other ten were indignant with the two brothers when they heard about this[4]. And Jesus, calling them to Him, said to them: "You know that the chiefs of nations rule in them and that great men exercise their power over them. Don't be like that amongst yourselves: but whoever wants to be great among you, let him be your servant. In the same way as the Son of man,

---

1. This is what He was called.
2. Humble and fervent prayer.
3. Passion and martyrdom like Jesus.
4. Their ambition unleashed the anger and envy of the others.

who did not come to be served, but to serve and give His life as a ransom for many (for everybody)[1]."

Zacchaeus: Luke 19, 1-10

Jesus entered Jericho and started to cross the city. A man called Zacchaeus, who was the chief of the publicans[2] and had a lot of money, tried to see what Jesus was like and did not succeed because of the mass of people, and because he was small in stature. He began to run until he found his way to a place in front and climbed a sycamore[3] to see Him, since He was due to pass by there. When Jesus arrived at that spot, He looked up and said to him: "Zacchaeus, come down quickly, because today I must lodge in your house." He came down at full speed and wecomed Him with pleasure. When they saw this, everybody murmured, saying: "He went to lodge in the house of a sinner." Zacchaeus, standing up, said to the Lord: "Look, Lord, I'm going to give half my wealth to the poor, and, in the event that I have defrauded anybody, I will return four times the amount[4]." Jesus answered him: "Today salvation has arrived in this house, because this is also the son of Abraham, since the Son of man has come to look for and save what was lost[5]."

He cures two blind men: Mat 20, 29-34

Many people followed Him when He left Jericho. And then two blind men sitting by the side of the road started to shout, when they heard that Jesus was passing by: "Lord, son of David, have pity on us." The people abused them so that they'd be quiet; but they yelled even louder: "Lord, son of David, have pity on us[6]!" Jesus stopped, called them and asked them: "What

---

1. Sublime level of humility confirmed with His example.
2. Chief of the zone of Jericho, a commercial city.
3. Egyptian fig tree with horizontal branches.
4. This penalty was only imposed on thieves.
5. To bring temporal and eternal peace.
6. People abused them, because they did not want their progress to be delayed. The blind men's insistence was rewarded.

do you want Me to do?" They replied: "Lord, let our eyes be opened." And Jesus, moved to compassion, touched their eyes, and they immediately recovered their sight and followed Him.

In Bethany: John 12, 1-11 (Mat 26, 6-13; Mark 14, 3-11)

Six days before the Passover He arrived at Bethany; Lazarus, whom He had brought back from the dead, was there. There they offered Him a dinner. Martha served, and Lazarus was just one more diner. Mary, for her part, took a pound of perfume of authentic nard, of great value, and anointed Jesus's feet and wiped them with her hair; «breaking the alabaster jar, she poured the perfume over Jesus's head,» and the whole house was impregnated with the aroma of nard[1]. Judas Iscariot, one of His disciples, who was going to betray Him, said: "Why wasn't this perfume sold for three hundred dinars to give to the poor[2]?" He said this not because he cared about the poor, but because he was a thief and, being in charge of the purse, stole from what was put in there. "What's the purpose of this squandering of perfume? For this perfume could have been sold for more than three hundred dinars to give to the poor." And they showed their indignation against her.» But Jesus replied: "Leave her alone; she has kept this for the day of My burial. The poor are always with you «and you can do good to them whenever you feel like it,» but I'm not always going to be with you. «She did what was at hand, and approached Me to anoint My body for the tomb.» «I give you My word that wherever this good news is preached, anywhere in the world, what she has done will be recorded in its remembrance»." Soon the big throng of Jews found out that Jesus was there, and came not only to see Jesus, but also Lazarus, whom He had brought back from the dead.

---

1. This delicacy captivated Jesus.
2. This is the argument of those who criticize the crowns of the Virgin offered by the people.

He enters Jerusalem: Mat 21, 1-9 (Mark 11, 1-10; Luke 19, 29-38; John 12, 12-16)

When they were approaching Jerusalem and had reached Bethphage[1], next to the Mount of Olives. Jesus sent off two disciples with this mission: "Go to the town that is ahead of you and you will immediately find a female donkey tied up, with a male ass at her side; «tied up, and still unmounted by any man»; let them go and bring them to me. If anybody says anything to you, «why are you untying it?,» answer them: The Lord needs them; He will bring them back later." All this took place so that the oracle of the prophet could be fulfilled: «Say to the daughter of Zion: Look, your King is coming to you, full of meekness and mounted on an ass, the son of the she-donkey» (Zac 9, 9). «Now His disciples didn't understand this, but when Jesus was glorified, then they realized that all this had been written about Him.» The disciples went and did what Jesus had told them. «The envoys went and found everything as He had told them. And whilst they were untying the ass, his owners said to them: "Why are you untying the ass?" They answered: "Because the Lord needs him?" «And they let them.» They took the donkey and the ass, put their cloaks on them and He sat on them. A lot of people put their cloaks on the road; others scattered branches from the trees and scattered them on the way. The crowd which preceded Jesus and followed Him shouted. "Hosannah[2] to the Son of David[3], Blessed is He who comes in the name of the Lord, Hosannah in the most high of heavens." «The following day, the large crowd which had arrived at the festival, hearing that Jesus was coming to Jerusalem, took palm branches and went out to meet Him, shouting: "Hosannah! Blessed is He who comes in the name of the Lord, the King of Israel!"»

---

1. A hamlet near Bethany, 1 kilometer from Jerusalem. The popular triumph of the foretold Messiah, it deals very well with Jesus and the messianic Kingdom (Isaiah 62, 2).

2. Hosannah in Hebrew = "Save, then", converted into an acclamation.

3. Recognised as Son of David, a messianic title, and acclaimed as a King sent by God.

The stones will cry out: John 12, 17-19 (Luke 19, 39-40)

The crowd which was with Him acclaimed Him when He called Lazarus out of the sepulchre and brought him back from the dead. For this reason the people also went out to meet Him, because they heard that He had performed this miracle: But the Pharisees were saying to each other: "Look how you're not achieving anything! Look how the people follow Him." «And some Pharisees, who were among the people, said to Him: "Master, reprimand your disciples." He replied: "I tell you that if they keep quiet, the stones will speak".»

Hawkers in the temple: Luke 19, 41-47 (Mark 11, 15-19)

And when He was close and could see the city, He wept for it[1], exclaiming: "If only you also were to know on this day what peace brings! But now it has been hidden from your eyes: But days will come for you in which your enemies will surround you with parapets, besiege you and harass you on all sides, and they will devastate you with your children inside, and will not leave one of your stones standing on another because of not having known the time of the visit which was being made to you." And, having entered the temple, He started to expel the hawkers, «also knocking over the money-changers' tables and the seats from which they sold doves. And He didn't let anybody bring any object through into the temple. He instructed them», telling them: It is written: «My house will be a house of prayer» (Is 57, 7) but you have converted it into a den of thieves (Jr 7, 11). He taught in the temple every day; and the high priests and scribes, along with the town's influential men, searched for a way of finishing Him off.

Cursed fig tree: Mark 11, 12-14 (Mat 21, 18-19)

When they set off from Bethany early the following morning, Jesus felt hungry, and, seeing from afar a fig tree with foliage, He went up to see if He could find anything on it. And when He reached it He found only leaves, because it was not the

---

1. He weeps for the ingratitude of Israel.

season for figs. And He upbraided it, exclaiming: "Never ever will anybody eat fruit from you", «and the fig tree immediately dried up.» His disciples were listening to Him[1].

Prayer: Mark 11, 20-26 (Mat 21, 20-22)

When they passed by in the early hours of the morning, they saw that the fig tree had dried up to the root, and Peter, remembering, said to Him: "Master, look how the fig tree which you cursed has dried up." Jesus answered him: "Have faith in God[2]. I assure you, «if you had faith without any kind of hesitation, not only would you do that with the fig tree, but» if somebody says to this mountain: Get up and throw yourself in the sea, without any hesitation in his heart, but believing that what he said would happen, he would achieve it. Therefore I say to you: Everything that you ask for in your prayer, believe that you will receive it and you will achieve it."

Jesus's powers: Mark 11, 27-33 (Mat 21, 23-27; Luke 20, 1-8)

They again came to Jerusalem and, when He was walking through the temple, the high priests, scribes and men of standing approached Him, «whilst He was teaching,» and they said to Him: "With what authority do you do these things or who gives you that authority to do them?" Jesus said to them: "I'm going to ask you a question. Answer Me and then I shall say with what authority I do these things. Did John's baptism come from heaven or from men? Answer me." They set to arguing like this: "If we say from heaven, he'll reply: Why, then, didn't you believe him? On the other hand, what shall we say about men?" They were afraid of the people, since they all considered that John was a true prophet. And they said to Jesus in reply: "We don't know." Then Jesus answered

---

1. The cursed fig tree was the symbol of the people of Israel reproached by God, which will no longer produce any more fruit.

2. Israel had neither recognized nor accepted its Saviour

them: "Neither will I tell you with what authority I do these things[1]."

Sent to the vineyard: Mat 21, 28-32

"What do you think? A man had two sons. He addressed the first one and said: 'My son, go and work in the vineyard today.' He replied: 'Sir, I'm going'; but he didn't go. Afterwards he went to the second son and said the same thing to him. He answered: 'I don't want to', but later he repented and went. Which of the two sons did his father's will?" "The last one", they replied. Jesus said to them: "I give you My word that the publicans and prostitutes will go before you in the Kingdom of Heaven. Because John came to you and taught you the path of righteousness and you didn't believe him. The publicans and prostitutes believed him. And you have not repented to believe him even after having seen this[2]."

Homicidal vine-growers: Mat 21, 33-45 (Luke 20, 9-10; Mark 12, 1-12)

"Listen to another parable[3]: A householder planted a vineyard, fenced it in, dug a winepress in it and built a tower. He rented it out to some tenant farmers and went a long way away. When the time for the harvest approached, he sent his servants to the farmer to pick his fruit. But the tenant farmers grabbed hold of the servants, struck one, killed another one and stoned a third. He again sent some other servants, more than the first group, and the farmers did the same thing to them. Finally he sent his own son, saying to himself: 'They will respect my son.' But when the farmers saw the son, they said amongst themselves: 'This is the heir. Let's get rid of him and we shall

---

1. Because John also preached to them about the Messiah and they didn't believe him either. Their incredulity was complete.
2. Again He foretells that the Gentiles will precede them in the Kingdom of Heaven.
3. This is the most incisive parable against the people's ruling priests, scribes and Pharisees. The vine is the People of Israel. The envoys are the prophet. The son and heir is the Son of God, whom they killed outside the walls.

possess his inheritance.' They seized him, took him out of the vineyard and killed him. When the owner of the vineyard comes, what will he do to those tenant farmers?" They answered Him: "He will make those wicked men perish miserably and will rent out his vineyard to other farmers, who will give him his fruit at its due time." Jesus said to them: "Have you never read in the Scriptures: The stone which the builders have rejected has been converted into the cornerstone. This is the work of the Lord, and in our eyes it is wonderful. (Sl 117, 22-23). Therefore I say to you: The Kingdom of Heaven will be taken away from you and will be given to a people who produce its fruit. And whoever falls on to this stone[1] will crash; anything on which it falls will be flattened." When they heard His parables, the chief priests and Pharisees understood that He was talking about them, and wanted to arrest Him, but they were afraid of the people, because they held Him as a prophet.

Royal wedding: Mat 22, 1-14

Jesus took up the word again and spoke to them in parables: "The Kingdom of Heaven is like a king who prepared a banquet for his son's wedding. He told his servants to call the guests to the wedding, but they didn't want to come: He again sent some other servants with this assignment: 'Say to the guests: My banquet is already prepared; the bulls and fattened animals have already been sacrificed. Everything is prepared; come, then, to the wedding.' But they took no notice of it and went away, be it to their field or their business; and the others, seizing his servants, abused them and killed them. Then the king flew into a rage, sent his armies, killed those murderers and burnt their city. Later he said to his servants: 'The wedding banquet is prepared, but the guests are not worthy. Go, then, to the crossroads and invite whoever you meet to the wedding.' These servants went on to the roads, gathered together whoever they met, good and bad, and the wedding hall was filled with diners[2]

---

1. The key stone, Christ; without Him, everything will tumble down.
2. The Gentiles will be the new People of God who will sit down at the King's table.

When the king came in to see the diners, he saw there a man who was not wearing a wedding suit, and he asked him: 'Friend, how have you come in here without having a wedding suit.' He was dumbstruck. The king then called his servants: 'Tie his hands and feet and throw him out into the darkness; there will be weeping and gnashing of teeth there.' Because many are called, but few are chosen[1]."

To Caesar what is Caesar's: Mat 22, 15-22 (Mark 12, 13-17; Luke 20, 20-26)

Then the Pharisees withdrew to deliberate on the way to surprise Him in some statement. So they sent their disciples, along with some Herodians, «they despatched spies who pretended to be righteous men, with the aim of surprising Him in some statement and thus be able to hand Him over to the jurisdiction and authority of the court,» to put this question to Him: "Master, we know that you are truthful and teach us the way of God with sincerity, without caring out about anybody, because you do not pay attention to men's social status. So give us your opinion on this: Is it lawful to pay the tribute to Caesar or not?" Jesus, knowing their malice, answered them: "Why are you testing Me, you hypocrites? Show me the coin for the tribute." And they gave Him a dinar. "Whose image is this and whose inscription does it bear?", He asked them. "Caesar", they replied. Then He said to them: "Then, give to Caesar what is Caesar's and to God what is God's." They were amazed at this response and, leaving Him, went on their way.

Casuistry of the Sadducees: Mat 22, 23-33 (Mark 12, 18-27; Luke 20, 27-40)

That very same day the Sadducees, who denied the resurrection, approached Him and put this question to Him: "Master, Moses said: 'If a man dies without having children, his brother will marry his wife to give his brother posterity.' Well

---

1. In the Eucharist Banquet, the guest without nuptial dress —Grace— will be rejected.

then, there were seven brothers amongst us. The first got married, died without leaving descendants and left his wife to his brother. The same happened with the second, and the third, down to the seventh, «without leaving any succession.» After they had all died, the woman also died. At the resurrection, whose wife will she be, because they all had her?" Jesus answered them: "You are mistaken. You understand neither the Scriptures nor the power of God. Because at the resurrection, men neither take wives nor women husbands; but they will live like God's angels in heaven. And as for the resurrection of the dead, haven't you read God's oracle which tells you, «in the book of Moses, in the passage about the bramble: I am the God of Abraham, the God of Isaac and the God of Jacob?» (Ex 3,6). He is not, then, God of the dead[1], but of the living." And when the crowds heard Him, they were amazed at His doctrine.

Greatest commandment: Mat 22, 34-36 (Mark 12, 28-37; Luke 20, 41-44)

The Pharisees met when they knew that He had silenced the Sadducees. One of them, a doctor of Law, asked Him as a test: "Master, what is the greatest commandment in the Law?" Jesus answered him: «You will love the Lord, your God, with all your heart, with all your soul, with all your mind» (Dt 4) «and with all your strength.» This is the first and greatest commandment. The second is similar to the first: «You will love your neighbor as you love yourself». The Law and the Prophets are reduced to these two commandments[2]. The Pharisees being gathered together, Jesus asked them. "What do you think about the Messiah? Whose son is He?" "David's", they answered Him. Jesus went on to ask them: "How, then, does David, an inspired man, call Him Lord when he says: «The Lord has said to my Lord: Sit at my right hand until I put your enemies under your feet?» (Sl 99, 1). If, then, David calls Him Lord, how is he His

---

1. God is not God of the deceased, but of souls which do not die and one day will be united with their resuscitated bodies and glorified so as to never die again.

2. The key to the Commandments of the Law of God is the Love of God and of the Neighbor.

son[1]?" And nobody knew a single word of response. And from that day on, nobody dared ask Him anything else.

Scribes and Pharisees: Mat 23, 1-12 (Mark 12, 38-39; Luke 20, 45-46)

Then Jesus spoke to the people of the town and to His disciples: "The scribes and Pharisees are sitting in the pulpit of Moses. So do and observe what they say to you, but don't imitate their deeds, because they say and don't do[2]. They prepare heavy and cumbersome weights and put them on peoples' backs; their deeds to be seen by men; because of this they lengthen their phylacteries and widen the trimming on their cloaks. They like to occupy the prime positions at banquets and the first seats in the synagogues. They look out for greetings in the market places and being called "rabbi" (master) by the people. You don't want to be called "rabbi" because somebody is your Master. You are all brothers. And don't give anybody the title of father on earth because you have only Father, who is in heaven. Don't call yourselves doctors, either, because you have only one Doctor: Christ. The greatest among you will be your servant. Whoever exalts himself will be humiliated, and whoever humbles himself will be exalted."

Anathemas: Mat 23, 13-36 (Mark 12, 40; Luke 20, 47)

"Woe to you, hypocritical scribes and Pharisees! Because you are closing the door to the Kingdom of Heaven for others: neither do you enter, nor do you allow those who wish to enter to do so[3]. Woe to you, hypocritical scribes and Pharisees, who devour widows' houses «with the pretext of offering long prayers»! Woe to you, hypocritical scribes and Pharisees! Why do you scour land and sea to make one single proselyte and, when you have attained him, you make him two times worthier of Hell than yourselves. Because you pay the

---

1. The son is not the Lord, but the Father.
2. They have set themselves up as masters and doctors.
3. The ministry of the Word of God is a service to God and men; if it is not accompanied by a good example, it drags others to damnation.

tithes of mint, aniseed and cumin and neglect the most important things of the Law: justice, mercy, faithfulness[1]. It is necessary to do these things, but without omitting to do the others. Blind guides, who strain a mosquito and swallow a camel. Woe to you, hypocritical scribes and pharisees. Because you clean the outside of the glass and plate, and the insides are full of theft and avarice. Blind Pharisee, first clean the inside of the glass, so that the outside becomes clean as well. Woe to you, hypocritical scribes and Pharisees! Because you are like whited sepulchres. You seem beautiful on the outside; but inside they are full of dead people's bones and all kinds of filth. So also are you: outside you seem righteous to men, but on the inside you are full of hypocrisy and iniquity. So fill your fathers' measure to overflowing! Serpents, race of vipers, how will you be able to escape the condemnation of Hell[2]? Because I shall send you prophets, wise men and scribes; you will kill and crucify some, you will whip others in your synagogues and you will persecute them from city to city. In this way all the innocent blood spilt on earth will fall on you[3], from Zacharias, son of Barachias, whom you killed between the temple and the altar. I assure you that all these things will fall on this race."

Jerusalem, Jerusalem!: Mat 23, 37-39

"Jerusalem, Jerusalem, you who kill prophets and stone those who are sent you! How many times have I wanted to gather together your children just as the hen shelters her chicks under her wings, and you did not want it! Your house will remain uninhabited. I give you My word that from now on you will not see Me any more, until you say: 'Blessed is He who comes in the name of the Lord[4]' (Sl 97, 26)."

---

1. Their sins were pride, hypocrisy and contempt for others.
2. The religious authorities of the People of Israel were blind with envy and hatred until their evil nature was satisfied.
3. The condemnation also falls on the people.
4. Until the second Coming of Christ.

The widow's offering: Mark 12, 41-44 (Luke 21, 1-4)

And He sat down in front of the almsbox and observed how the people tossed money into it. Many rich men threw in large amounts. And a poor, solitary widow arrived and threw in two coins which were worth one cent. Then He called His disciples to say to them: "I say to you surely that this poor widow threw into the almsbox more than all the others[1]. Because everybody has thrown in what they didn't need, whilst she, in her poverty, gave whatever she had, everything that was her livelihood."

End of the teaching: John 12, 20-36

There were some Greeks among those who had gone up to worship at the festival. They introduced themselves to Philip, the one from Bethsaida in Galilee, and they asked him: "Sir, we want to see Jesus." Philip went to tell Andrew about this, and they both went to inform Jesus. And Jesus said to them: "The time has come for the Son of man to be glorified. I say to you with certainty: If the grain of wheat which falls to the ground does not die, it remains alone; but if it dies, it produces a lot of fruit[2]. Whoever loves his life, loses it; whoever despises his life in this world, he will keep it for eternity. If someone decides to serve Me, let him serve Me, and, wherever I am, he will also be there. My Father will honour whoever serves Me. Now My soul is troubled; but, how could I say: Father, deliver Me from this hour? If I have come precisely for this at this hour! Father, glorify Your name!" Then a voice came from the sky: "I have glorified it and I will glorify it again." The crowd which was there heard and said: "A thunderbolt has been produced." Others said: "An angel has spoken to Him." Jesus replied: "And, when I'm raised up on the earth, I will attract everybody to Me." With this He was alluding to the kind of death that He was going to undergo.

---

1. The widow's alms are more pleasing to God than those of the rich, because they go with sacrifice. What the rich don't need must be used to help the poor, according to charity.

2. The grain of wheat is the symbol of resurrection.

Incredulity of the Jews: John 12, 37-50

Despite having performed so many prodigies in their presence, they did not believe in Him. In this way Isaiah's saying was fulfilled: «Lord, who has believed our word and the power of God, to whom was it revealed?» (Is 53, 1). All said and done, many, even the men of position, finally believed in Him, but they did not show it out of fear of the Pharisees, so as not to be excluded from the synagogue. For they put the glory of men before the glory of God[1]. However, Jesus said loudly: "Whoever believes in Me, does not believe in Me, but in He who has sent Me, and whoever sees Me, sees Him who has sent me. I, the Light, have come to the world so that whoever believes in Me will not remain in darkness. I don't condemn anybody who hears My words and does not put them into practice; since I have not come to condemn the world, but to save it[2]. Anybody who rejects Me and does not welcome My words, already has somebody who will judge him; the words which I have spoken will judge him on the last day."

End of the world: Mat 24, 1-14 (Mark 13, 1-13; Luke 21, 5-19

Jesus left the temple, and when He was on the road, His disciples went up to Him to point out the construction of the temple. Jesus said to them: "Do you see all this? I guarantee you that not one stone will remain on top of another; everything will be overturned." He was seated on the Mount of Olives and the disciples approached Him and «Peter, John, James and Andrew» asked Him in secret: "Tell us when these things will occur, and what will be the signal of your coming and of the end of the world." Jesus answered them: "Be careful that nobody deceives you. Because many will come in My name and say: 'I am the Christ'; and they will seduce many people. You will hear talk of wars and rumours of wars. Be on the alert; don't be alarmed! Because this has to come; but still it is not the

---

1. Victims of human respect.
2. The first Coming was to save the world and the second will be to judge it.

end. One people will rise up against another, and one kingdom against another. There will be hunger, plague and earthquakes in several places; «dreadful phenomena and extraordinary signs in the sky;» but all that will be no more than the beginning of the afflictions. «They will hand you over to the tribunals and they will lash you in the synagogues, and they will make you appear before governors and kings for my cause, to declare before them. But before that the Gospel must be announced to all peoples[1]. And when they take you away to hand you over, don't then begin to worry about what you have to say; because it is not you who is speaking, but the Holy Spirit.» «So I shall give you such words and ideas that all your adversaries will not be able to resist or contradict.» Then, they will deliver you to tortures and death. You will be hated by everybody because of My Name. And then many will succumb to faith, they will denounce one another and mutually hate each other. Many false prophets will emerge and they will seduce many people. However, whoever perseveres until the end, will be saved. This good news of the Kingdom will be preached to all peoples, all over the world, as proof of the truth. Then the end will come."

Destruction of Jerusalem: Mat 24, 15-22 (Mark 13, 14; Luke 21, 29)

"So, then, when you see the extraordinary abomination in the Temple predicted by the prophet Daniel (whoever reads, let him understand) installed in the temple, then, those who are in Judea, let them flee to the mountains; whoever is on the terrace, let him not go down to take the things out of his house; and whoever is in the field, let him not turn round to take his cloak. Because then there will be tribulation of a magnitude that has not been seen since the beginning of the world until now; nor will it be seen. And if those days were not brief, nobody would be saved; but those days will be brief for the chosen ones."

---

1. The Gospel having been announced to all peoples does not mean that all peoples are Christian. For some it has already been and gone.

Coming of Christ[1]: Mat 24, 23-25

"Then, if they say to you: 'Christ is here, or there', don't believe it. Because just as lightning comes from the East and flashes towards the West, thus will be the coming of the Son of man. The vultures will assemble wherever the corpse is. Immediately after the tribulation of those days the sun will get dark and the moon will not give its life; the stars will fall from the sky and the galaxy will be shaken. Then the sign of the Son of man will appear in the sky[2], and all the peoples of the earth will beat their breasts; and they will see the Son of man come on the clouds of the sky with great power and glory. And He will send His angels with a powerful trumpet blast to gather together his chosen ones from the four cardinal points, from one end of the heavens to the other.

So keep watch, since you don't know when the master of the house will come, whether in the evening, at midnight, at cockcrow or at daybreak, so that, in this way, if he comes suddenly, he does not find you asleep. What I say to you, I say to everybody: Keep watch[3]."

The ten virgins: Mat 25, 1-13

"Then what will take place in the Kingdom of Heaven will be like ten young women who, taking their lamps, went out to meet the bridegroom. Five of them were foolish and five wise. The foolish ones did not avail themselves of oil when they took their lamps. The wise ones also took pots containing oil along with their lamps. When the bridegroom took a long time coming, they started to get dozy and fell asleep. At midnight a voice was heard: 'The bridegroom's coming now! Go out and

---

1. The destruction of Jerusalem is a symbol of the end of the world. The prophecy was fulfilled in the year 70. According to Flavio Josefo, a million Jews died, there were not enough crosses and 97,000 survivors were sold as slaves.
2. At the end of the world Christ will appear with the Cross.
3. So, keep watch! This parable, and the following ones, are an exhortation to vigilance. The maidens represent the souls when they meet Christ in our mortal passage.

meet him!' Then all those young women woke up and prepared their lamps. The foolish ones said to the wise ones: 'Give us your oil, because our lights are going out.' But the wise ones replied: 'No, there wouldn't be enough for us and you. It's better that you go to the traders and buy some yourselves.' But while they went to buy it, the bridegroom came. Those who were ready, went in with him to the wedding banquet and the door was closed. Later on the other young women arrived and said. 'Sir, sir, open up for us!' But he replied: 'I assure you that I don't know you.' So, keep watch, because you know neither the day nor the hour."

The talents: Mat 25, 14-30

"It will occur like a man who was going on a long journey. He called his servants and entrusted them with his goods: He entrusted one of them with five talents; another with two, and another with one; each according to his own capability; and he set off. The one who had received five talents immediately started to do business with them and earned himself five more. The one who had received two likewise earned himself two more. But the one who had received one made a hole in the ground and hid his lord's money. A long time afterwards, the master of those servants returned and began to settle his accounts with them. The one who had received five talents arrived[1] and presented five more, saying: 'Sir, you entrusted me with five talents; look, I've earned five more.' His master said to him: 'Well done, good and faithful servant; you have been faithful in things of little importance, I will give you power over more important things. Come in and participate in your master's feast.' The one who had received two talents also arrived, and said: 'Sir, you entrusted me with two talents; look, I've earned another two.' His master said to him: 'Well done, good and faithful servant; you have been faithful in things of little importance, I will give you power over more important things. Come in and participate in your master's feast.' Finally the one

---

1. One talent = 34.272 grammes of silver.

who had received one talent arrived and said: 'Sir, I knew that you were a hard man, who reaps where you have not planted and picks where you have not scattered seed. I was afraid and I hid your talent in the ground. Look, here it is.' His master answered him: 'Bad and slothful servant! You knew that I reap where I have not planted and pick where I have not scattered seed? You ought, then, to have handed my money over to the bankers, and when I came back I would have taken it out with interest[1]. Take out your talent, then, and give it to the one who has ten. Because whoever has will be given to and will have in excess; but whoever does not have, even if he does have, will have it taken away from him. And throw out the useless servant, into the darkness.' There will be weeping and gnashing of teeth there."

Final judgement: Mat 25, 31-46

"When the Son of man comes in His glory, accompanied by all His angels, He will sit down on the throne of His glory. Every nation will be gathered together in His presence; and He will separate, one from the other, just as the shepherd separates the sheep from the goats; He will put the sheep on His right and the goats on His left. Then, the King will say to those who are on His right: 'Come, blessed ones of my Father, take possession of the kingdom which has been prepared for you since the beginning of the world[2]. Because I was hungry and you gave Me something to eat; I was thirsty and you gave Me something to drink; I was a pilgrim and you gave Me lodging; I was naked and you clothed me; I was sick and you visited Me; I was in prison and you came to Me.' The righteous will ask: 'Lord, when did we see You hungry and give You something to eat, or thirsty and we gave You something to drink? When did we see You a pilgrim and give You lodging, or naked and we clothed You? When did we see You sick or in jail and visit You?' And the King will answer them: 'I say to you with certainty:

1. This servant was condemned as a sloth and a predator on his master.

2. We will be judged at the end for the love of our brothers.

Whatever you have done to the tiniest of My brothers, you have done to Me[1].' Then, He will also say to those on His left: 'Get away from me, accursed, to the eternal fire which has been prepared for the Devil and his angels. Because I was hungry and you did not give Me anything to eat; I was thirsty and you did not give Me anything to drink; I was a pilgrim and you did not lodge Me; I was naked and you did not clothe Me; sick and imprisoned, and you did not visit Me.' Then they will also ask Him: 'Lord, when did we see You hungry or thirsty, a pilgrim or naked, sick or in prison, and did not come to Your assistance?' He will answer them: 'Truly I say to you that anything you did not do to any one of these little ones, you omitted to do to me.' And they will go to the eternal torment; and the righteous to eternal life[2]."

The numbered days: Luke 21, 37-38

During the night He taught in the temple and then He withdrew to spend the night on the Mount of Olives. And everybody went to the temple to listen to Him.

Decree of death: Mat 26, 1-16 (Luke 22, 1-6; Mark 14, 1-11)

When Jesus finished all these sermons, He said to His disciples: "You know that in two day's time it will be the Passover, and the Son of man will be handed over to be crucified." Then, the high priests, «and the scribes,» and the men of position in the town, assembled in the palace of the Chief Priest, called Caiphas, and had a meeting about deceitfully detaining Jesus and killing Him. But they said: "Not during the festival, so that there are no disturbances among the people." «And Satan[3] entered into Judas, called Iscariot, who was one of the twelve; and he went to discuss with the high priests and police officials the way in which he would deliver

---

1. Jesus identifies with and represents the poorest and most needy.
2. Our destinies will be eternal.
3. The Devil entered his soul through mortal sin.

Him to them.» And he said to them: "How much will you give me to hand Him over?" They settled on thirty silver coins[1]. He agreed and set about looking for an opportunity to hand Him over out of view of the crowd[2].

Prepare the banquet: Mark 14, 12-16 (Mat 26, 17-19; Luke 22, 7-13)

And on the first day of the Unleavened Bread, when they sacrifice the Passover, His disciples said to Him: "Where do you want us to go to prepare to eat the Passover?" He sent two of His disciples, «Peter and John,» saying to them: "Go to the city; a man with a pitcher of water will come out to meet you; follow him; and say to the owner of the house where he enters: 'The Master asks for your guest room, where He is due to eat the Passover with His disciples.' And He will show you a big furnished hall, already available, on the upper floor. Prepare the things for us there." «The disciples did what Jesus had told them.» The disciples left and went to the city, and found everything just as He had said; «the disciples did this» and prepared the Passover.

The Last Supper[3]: Luke 22, 14-18-21-30 (Mat 26, 20; Mark 14, 17)

When it was time, He took His place at the table in the company of the Apostles. And He said to them: "I have ardently wished to celebrate this Passover[4] with you before suffering. Because I assure you that I will not celebrate any more until I find total fulfillment in the Kingdom of God[5]." Taking a cup[6], giving thanks, He said: "Take it and distribute it amongst you. Because I say to you that from this moment on you will not

---

1. Thirty silver coins was the price of a slave.
2. Avarice made him lose his faith in the Master and he betrayed Him.
3. The Cenacle was the house of John Mark the evangelist.
4. He chose the Passover, which was the principal feast of the Jews, to take His leave of the Apostles.
5. They ate at the table, reclining on divans or carpets.
6. Or a chalice.

drink any more fruit of the vine until the Kingdom of God has come. However, I am in the midst of you as the one who serves; you are the ones who have persevered with Me in My trials. For this reason I put the Kingdom at your disposition, as the Father has put it at Mine, so that you may eat and drink at My table in My Kingdom, and may sit on thrones to judge the twelve tribes of Israel."

Washing of the feet: John 13, 1-17

In the supper and the Devil having already suggested in the heart of Judas, son of Simon Iscariot, that he betray Him, Jesus, knowing that the Father had put everything into His hands and that He had come from God and was returning to God, got up from the table, took off His cloak, and took a towel, which He put round His waist. Then He put water into a washbasin and started to wash His disciples' feet and dry them with the towel around His waist. When He reached Simon Peter, he said to Him: "Lord, are you going to wash my feet?" Jesus answered Him: "You do not understand now what I'm doing, but very soon you will understand." Peter answered Him: "I will never consent to You washing my feet." Jesus answered Him: "If you don't let Me wash you, you will not be one of Mine." "Lord, Simon Peter said to Him, but also my hands and head." Jesus answered Him: "Whoever is clean only needs his feet washed, because he is all clean, and you are clean, though not all of you." He knew who was going to betray Him; because of this He said: "You are not all clean." After washing their feet, taking His cloak and sitting down again, they said to Him: "Do you understand the fullness of what I've just done to you? You call me Lord and Master, and you do so correctly, because I am: I have given you an example so that you do the same as I have done to you[1] I say to you with certainty: The slave is not greater than his master, nor is the envoy greater than the person who

---

1. Jesus wanted to give His apostles an example of humility and charity by washing their feet, a task proper to servants. He, who was infinitely superior, made Himself the last.

sent him. Since you know these things, you will be happy if you put them into practice."

The traitor: John 13, 18-30; Mat 26, 21-25 (Luke 22, 21-23; Mark 14, 18-21)

"I don't refer to all of you; I know those whom I have chosen well; but it is necessary for the Scripture to be fulfilled: «He who eats bread with Me lifted his heel against Me» (Sl 40,10). I say to you now, before it happens, so that when it does happen you will recognise who I am. I say to you with confidence: Whoever welcomes Him who I shall send, welcomes Me, and whoever welcomes Me, welcomes Him who has sent Me." Having said these things, Jesus was moved within, and He revealed it by saying: "I say to you with certainty that one of you will betray Me." «They, utterly saddened, started to ask Him, one after the other: "Maybe it's me, Lord?" He replied: "Whoever puts his hand on the plate with Me, will be the one to hand Me over. The Son of man is going, as is written about Him; but woe on him who hands over the Son of man! Better that he had never been born[1]»." The disciples were looking at each other, not knowing whom He was talking about. One of the disciples, Jesus's favorite[2], was reclining next to Jesus's chest. Simon Peter hinted by signs: "Ask Him whom He's talking about." The former, reclining as he was next to Jesus's chest, asked Him: "Lord, who is it?" It is him to whom I shall give the morsel which I am going to moisten." And, moistening a morsel[3], He gave it to Judas, the son of Simon Iscariot. After the mouthful Satan entered Him. Jesus said to him: "What you're going to do, do it soon." «Then Judas, the traitor, asked Him: "Perhaps it is me, Master?" "You have said it",» replied Jesus. None of the diners understood why He was saying this. As Judas had the purse, some thought that He had said to him: "Buy what you need for the feast, though

---

1. Jesus' sentence was condemnatory.
2. The apostle John.
3. Giving a morsel to a fellow-diner was a sign of distinction. It was the last call to his heart, but he closed himself off to love.

give something to the poor." He, having eaten the morsel, went out. It was already night.

Eucharist and Order: Mat 26, 26-29 (Mark 14, 22-25; Luke 22, 19-20)

Whilst they were eating, Jesus took bread and recited the blessing; He broke it and gave it to His disciples, saying: "Take and eat, this is My Body «which will be given up for you; do this in memory of Me".» Afterwards, He took a chalice and, giving thanks, gave it to them, saying: "Drink, all of you, because this is My Blood, the blood of the alliance, which will be spilled for everybody, «for you,» for the forgiveness of sins[1]. Do this in My Memory[2]."

New commandment: John 13, 31-35

When He had left, Jesus exclaimed: "Now the Son of man has been glorified and God has been glorified in Him. Since God has been glorified in Him, God will also glorify Him in Himself, and very soon. My sons: I am amongst you for a short while; you will search for Me; but, as I have said to the Jews: Where I am going, you cannot go, I also say it to you now. I give you a new commandment: Love each other, as I have loved you; that is how you must love each other. Then everybody will know that you are My disciples, because you show each other charity."

Prediction of denials: John 13, 36-38 (Luke 22, 31-34)

Simon Peter asked Him: "Master, where are You going?" Jesus answered him: "Where I'm going you cannot follow Me now, you will follow Me later." Peter insisted: "Lord, why can't I follow You now. I would give my life for You." Jesus replied to him: "You would give your life for me? I assure you with certainty: You will deny Me three times before the cock crows

---

1. As He had promised, Jesus changes bread and wine into His Body and Blood, really, not symbolically, and institutes the Holy Eucharist and the priesthood.

2. Love yourself as I have loved you.

three times. «Simon, Simon, think that Satan has looked for you to sieve you like wheat; but I have prayed for you so that your faith does not waver, and you, when you have come back to yourself, comfort your brothers[1].»

Way, Truth and Life[2]: John 14, 1-11

"Do not trouble your heart: As You believe in God, believe also in Me. In My Father's house there are many mansions: if it were not so, I would have told you; for I am going to prepare a place for you. After having left and prepared you a place, I shall come again to take you with Me, so that wherever I am, there also you will be. And you already know the way to go where I'm going." Thomas said to Him: "Lord, we don't know where You're going, how can we know the way?" Jesus answered Him: "I am the way, the truth and the life: nobody goes to the Father except through Me. If you know Me, you will also know My Father. But from this moment you do know Him and you have seen Him." "Lord, Philip exclaimed, show us the Father and that is enough for us." Jesus answered him: "Philip, I've been with you such a long time and aren't you saying: Show us the Father? Don't you believe that I am in the Father and that the Father is in Me? I do not pronounce the words that I say to you on My own account; the Father who dwells in Me is the one who acts. Believe it, I am in the Father and the Father in Me, at least believe this through the works themselves."

Great promises: John 14, 12-22

"I say to you with confidence: Whoever believes in Me, will also realize the works that I realize and will also realize greater ones, because I shall go to the Father. And whatever you ask for in My name, I will realize it, so that the Father is glorified in the Son. If you love Me, you will fulfill My commandments. I shall pray to the Father and He will give you another Advocate to

---

1. Peter's presumption had its punishment with the triple denial.
2. The way, the Commandments and Evangelical Counsels, the Truth of His revelations, and the Life of Grace recovered.

always remain with you, the Spirit of truth, whom the world cannot receive, because he neither sees him nor knows him. You know him because he dwells in you and is always with you. I shall not leave you orphans, I shall return to your side. In a little while, the world will not see Me; you will see Me, because I shall continue living and you will live. Then you will know that I am in My Father and you in Me and I in you. Whoever respects My commandments and follows them, that is somebody who loves Me. And whoever loves Me will be loved by My Father, and I will love him and reveal myself to him." Judas (not Iscariot) asked Him: "Lord, how can it be that You are going to make Yourself known to us and not to the world[1]?"

Peace of Christ: John 14, 23-31

Jesus answered Him: "Whoever loves Me, will fulfill My word and My Father will love Him and will come to Him and put His dwelling within him. Whoever does not love Me, does not observe My words. I come saying these things to you whilst I remain with you. The Advocate, the Holy Spirit, whom the Father will send Me in My name, will make you understand and remember everything I have said to you. I leave you peace, I give you My peace. The peace that I give you is not like the one given by the world. Do not trouble your heart or panic. You have listened to what I have said to you: I'm leaving, but I'm coming back to you[2] If you love Me, you would be glad that I'm going to the Father, since the Father is greater than Me. I have said it to you now, before it happens, so that you believe when it does happen. I shall not talk much to you, because the master of the world is going to come, but He has nothing against Me. But it is necessary for the world to know that I love the Father and that I am acting in accordance with what the Father has commanded Me[3]."

---

1. Jesus confided intimately in His Apostles, and He announced that He would send them His Holy Spirit, the advocate and consoler.
2. Your sadness will turn to delight.
3. They got up from the table and He continued the talk.

Remain in Me: John 15, 1-8

"I am the true vine and My Father is the vine-grower. He cuts away every branch that, joined with Me, does not give fruit; and He cleans every branch which gives fruit so that it gives more. You have now been cleaned by the word which I have addressed to you. Remain in Me and I will remain in you. In the same way that the branch does not give fruits on its own if it does not remain on the vine[1], so neither will you if you don't remain in Me. I am the vine, you are the branches. Whoever remains in Me and I in him gives a lot of fruit, because without Me you can't do anything. Whoever does not remain in Me is thrown out, just as they collect the dried-up branch, toss it on the fire and it burns. If you remain in Me and My words remain in you, you will ask for whatever you want and it will be granted you. My Father will be glorified if you give many fruits and are My disciples."

Law of love: John 15, 18-25

"This is My commandment: Love one another as I have loved you. A man's supreme love consists in giving up his life for His friends. You are My friends if you follow what I have commanded you. I do not call you servants, because the servant doesn't know what his master is doing; I have called you friends, because I have brought to your attention whatever I have heard from my Father. You did not choose Me; it is I who have chosen[2] you and I have destined you to walk and give fruit and your fruit will be long-lasting, so that everything you ask the Father in My name will be conceded you. What I command you is that you love one another."

---

1. Grace unites us with Christ, like the sap in the vine, by means of the Sacraments. It is only broken with mortal sin.

2. He has called us and predestined us to His love, so that we give fruits of virtues and good works, and grow in His love.

Hatred of the world: John 15, 18-25

"If the world loathes you[1], bear in mind that it loathed me first: If you were of the world, the world would love you as its own kind; but, as you are not of the world, because I've taken you out of it, the world therefore loathes you. Remember what I've told you: The servant is not greater than his master. If they have persecuted Me, they will also persecute you. If they have welcomed My word, they will also welcome yours. But they will do these things against you because of My cause, because they don't know Him who has sent Me. If I had not come and had not spoken to them, they would not have sin; but now anybody who loathes Me also loathes My Father. If I had not performed deeds, some of which nobody else has ever performed, they would not have sin, but now they have seen them, and yet continue hating My Father and Me. But in this way the word written in His law is fulfilled. They have hated Me without any reason» (Sl 24, 19)."

Assistance of the Holy Spirit: John 15, 26-27; 16, 1-4

"When the Advocate comes, which I shall send you on behalf of My Father, the Holy Spirit, which comes from the Father, He will declare on My behalf. And you will also declare, because you are with Me from the beginning."

Work of the Holy Spirit: John 16, 5-15

"It is better for you that I go, because if I don't go, the Advocate will not come to you; but if I go, I shall send Him to you. And when He comes, we will make plain to the world sin, holiness and judgement; sin, in fact, because they don't believe in Me; justice, because I'm going to the Father and you will not see Me; judgement, because the master of this world has already been judged. I have many things to say to you, but you cannot understand them now. When He, the spirit of truth, comes, He will lead you to the fullness of truth[2]; because He will not speak

---

1. Because the world only loves pleasures, honors and riches.
2. The Holy Spirit will fill them with His gifts and will explain everything to them.

on His own account, but will speak of what He has heard, and He will proclaim to you what is going to happen. He will glorify Me, because He will receive what is Mine in order to reveal it to you."

Eternal joy: John 16, 16-22

"In a short while you're not going to see Me; but within another short while you will see Me[1]." Then some disciples said to each other, "what does it mean when He says to us: In a short while you're not going to see Me, but within another short while you will see Me? And, I'm going to the Father?" So they said: "What is the meaning of this short while You're talking about. We don't know what it refers to." Jesus understood what they wanted to ask Him, and He said to them: "You're wondering why I have said: In a short while you're not going to see Me, but within another short while you will see Me? I say to you with confidence: You will weep while the world rejoices; you will be saddened, but your sadness will turn to joy."

I am going to the Father: John 16, 25-30

"I have come from the Father and I have come into the world; now I leave the world and I'm going to the Father." "Now we know that you know everything and that you don't need anybody to ask. Because of that, we think that you have come from God."

Priestly prayer: John 17, 1-5

Jesus said these things; afterwards, raising His eyes to heaven, He exclaimed: "Father, the time has come; Glorify Your Son so that Your Son glorifies You, so that You transmit, according to the power which you have given Him over all Creation, eternal life to everybody whom You have entrusted Him. Eternal life consists of this, where they know You, the only true God, and He who was sent by You, Jesus Christ. I

---

1. After the night of the Passion they will see Him again, brought back to life, and their hearts will be gladdened.

have glorified You on earth, I have finished the work which You entrusted Me; and now, You, Father, glorify Me along with You with the glory which You had at your side before the world existed[1]."

I pray for them: John 17, 6-19

"I have let Your name be known to the men which You gave Me out of the world. They were Yours and You entrusted them to Me and they have observed Your word. I pray for them, I don't pray for the world[2], but for those whom You have entrusted to Me, because they are Yours and all that is Mine is Yours, as all that is Yours is Mine; and I am glorified in them. Now I'm not remaining any longer in the world; but these are remaining in the world, whilst I'm going to You. Holy Father, guard them in Your name, those whom You have given Me, so that they may be one like us. Whilst I was with them, I guarded them in Your name; I have guarded those You have entrusted in Me and none of them has perished, except for the son of damnation. Thus the Scripture has been fulfilled. But now I'm going to You, and I talk of these things that are in the world, so that they have the fullness of My rejoicing within them. I have transmitted My word to them, and the world has hated them, because they are not of the world, just as I am not of the world. I don't ask you to take them out of the world, but to keep them from evil. They are not of the world, as I am not of the world. Consecrate them in the truth. Your word is truth."

That they may be one: John 17, 20-26

"I don't pray only for them, but also for those who must believe in Me through their word; so that all may be one[3]; just

---

1. Jesus leaves this world to receive from His Father the same divine glory which He had in the Kingdom of Heaven.
2. Jesus's last prayer in this world is for the priests who will pursue His mission in the bosom of the Church.
3. The unity of His disciples, united to the Church by the bonds of charity, is one of the principal charges which Jesus gives them, so that they see that God sent Him.

as You, Father, are in Me and I in You, may they also be one in Us, so that the world believes that You have sent Me. And I have given them the glory that You have given Me so that they may be one as We are one. Father, I want those that You have confided in Me to be there where I am, to contemplate My glory, which You have given Me, because You have loved Me before the creation of the world. Righteous Father, the world has not known You, but I have known You. I have revealed You to them and I will reveal Your name, so that the love with which You have loved Me is in them and I in them."

RELIGIOUS PROCEEDINGS

Way of the Orchard: Mat 26, 30-35 (Mark 14, 27-31; John 18, 1; Luke 22, 39)

After having recited the hymn, they went to the Mount of Olives. «Towards the other side of the river Cedron.» «According to custom.» Then Jesus said to them: "Tonight you will all see in Me a reason for abandoning Me, for it is written: I shall wound the Shepherd and the sheep of the flock will disperse (Zac 13, 7). But after I have revived I shall go before you to Galilee[1]."

Agony in Gethsemane: Mat 26, 36-46 (Mark 14, 32-42; Luke 22, 39-46; John 18, 1)

Then Jesus arrived with them at a place called Gethsemane «where there was an orchard[2], which He and His disciples entered,» and He said to the disciples: "Sit down here, whilst I go over there to pray. «Pray that you don't fall into temptation»." And taking Peter and the two sons of Zebedee, «James and John,» with Him, He started to experience sadness and anguish. Then He said to them: "A mortal sadness has

---

1. Jesus says to them that everybody will be shocked by Him that night and will abandon Him, but after The Passion He will meet up with them again in Galilee, now brought back to life.

2. Where He used to withdraw to pray, a place known to Judas.

seized hold of Me. Stay here and keep watch with Me." And, advancing a little «He fell face down in the ground like a stone being thrown,» «on the earth» and prayed like this: "My Father, if it is possible, pass this chalice from Me; but may not My will be done, but Yours." He came back to His disciples and found them sleeping, «tired through sadness,» and He said to Peter: «Simon, are you asleep?» How have you not resisted so as to keep watch for an hour with Me? Keep watch and pray that you don't fall into temptation because the spirit is willing, but the flesh is weak." He went away again and started praying for the second time, saying: "My Father, if this chalice cannot pass without Me drinking from it, Let Your will be done." He went back again and found them sleeping; because their eyes were heavy, «and they didn't know how to answer Him.» He left them and went away again and prayed for a third time, repeating the same words, «and an angel appeared from heaven to comfort Him. And, beset with anxiety, He prayed more intensely. And His sweat turned into drops of blood, which fell down to the floor[1].» Afterwards He returned to His disciples and said to them: "Sleep now and rest! The hour has come and the Son of man will be handed over into the hands of sinners. Get up! Let's go! Now He who will hand Me over is approaching."

Treacherous kiss: John 18, 2-3 (Mat 26, 47-50; Mark 14, 43-45; Luke 22, 47-48)

Judas, the one who was due to betray Him, knew the place, for Jesus had assembled His disciples there many times. So Judas arrived, bringing a bunch of soldiers and agents of the chief priests and the Pharisees, with lanterns, torches and arms.

The traitor had given them a signal: "The one whom I kiss, that's Him; arrest Him. «And be sure to take Him well»." And he immediately went up to Jesus and said: "Hail, Master." And

---

1. Causes of His mortal agony could have been: the pains of His Passion, humanity's sins which He had assumed, and the usefulness of His blood for many that were due to be condemned.

he kissed Him[1]. Jesus said to him: "Friend, you have come to this! «Judas, you hand over the Son of man with a kiss?[2]»"

Who are you looking for?: John 18. 4-9

Jesus, conscious of everything which was to befall Him, went forward and said to them: "Who are you looking for?" They answered Him: "Jesus Nazarene." Jesus replied: "It is I." Judas the traitor was also with them. So, when He said to them "it is I", they retreated and fell to the ground[3]. He asked them again: "Who are you looking for?" They answered: "Jesus Nazarene." Jesus replied: "I have told you that it's Me. If, then, you're looking for Me, let these go." Thus the word which He had said was fulfilled: "I have not lost any of those whom you have entrusted Me."

Arrest: Mat 26, 50-56 (John 18, 10-11); Mark 14, 46-53 (Luke 22, 49-53)

Then they approached, laid hands on Jesus and arrested Him. «And those with Jesus, seeing what was going to happen, said. "Lord, is it necessary to wound with the sword?"» Then, one of those who was with Jesus, «Simon Peter, drew a sword which he had,» putting His hand to his sword, drew it and wounded a servant of the pontiff, cutting his «right» ear; the servant was called Malchus, «and Jesus said. "Calm down, that's enough." And, touching his ear, He cured it.» Jesus said to him: "Put your sword back in its place; «sheath it,» because all those who take up the sword will die by the sword. Do you think that I can't ask my Father to immediately put more than twelve legions of angels at my disposition? «Why don't I go and drink the chalice which the Father has given Me?» How, then, will the Scriptures be fulfilled, according to which it is necessary for this to occur in this way?" At that moment Jesus said to that group of people: "You have come to arrest Me like a thief, with swords and

---

1. His perfidy went to the extremes of delivering Him with a kiss.
2. Despite this, Jesus called him friend, offering him the last chance.
3. Jesus shows His power and hands Himself over freely.

staffs. I've been teaching among you in the Temple every day, and you didn't arrest Me." Then the disciples all abandoned Him and fled. «Then the gang, the tribune and the Jews' agents overcame Jesus and tied Him up.» «Only one youth[1] followed Him, wrapped in a sheet over his naked body. They grabbed him; but he left the sheet behind and escaped naked.»

Annas: John 18, 13-14; 19-24

And they took Him first to Annas[2], father-in-law of Caiphas, who was high priest that year; Caiphas was the one who had given this advice to the Jews: "It is better that one single man dies for the people." The high priest interrogated Jesus[3] about His disciples and His doctrine. Jesus answered him: "I have spoken in public to the world; I have always taught in the synagogue and in the temple, where the Jews congregate, and I haven't said anything in private. Why do you ask Me? Ask the listeners what I have said to them. They know very well what I have said to them." When He said this, one of the agents present there, struck Jesus a blow, saying; "Is that how you reply to the Pontiff" Jesus replied: "If I have spoken badly, show me where; if good, why do you hit Me?" Annas sent Him, tied up, to the high priest, Caiphas.

Caiphas: Mat 26, 57-68 (Mark 14, 35-65; Luke 22, 63-65)

The people who detained Jesus led Him to the house of Caiphas, the high priest, where the scribes and men of social standing were assembled. «All the chief priests.» The chief priests and all the Sanedrin were looking for a false testimony against Jesus to be able to condemn Him to death. But they did not find it, even though many false witnesses appeared. «Many presented false accusations against Him, but their declarations did not agree.» Finally two presented themselves, who made this declaration: "This man has said: I can destroy the temple of

---

1. Jesus did not need human defenses.
2. He must have been the son of the owner of the orchard and of the Cenacle, John Mark, the Evangelist.
3. This interrogation was illegal, it fell to the Sannedrin.

God and rebuild it in three days[1]." Then the high priest got up
and said to Him: "Don't you have any reply to those who are
testifying against you?" But Jesus kept His silence. The high
priest addressed Him in these terms[2]: "I entreat you by the
living God to say whether you are the Christ, the Son of God."
Jesus answered Him: "You have said it[3]. «Yes I am; and you
will see the Son of man seated at the right hand of the Power
and coming from heaven on the clouds»." Then the high priest
tore His clothes, exclaiming: "He has blasphemed! Why do we
need witnesses now? Look, you've just heard the blasphemy.
What does it seem to you?" "Sentence him to death", they
replied. Then they spat in His face and punched Him; others
struck Him, «and, blindfolding Him, they asked Him.»
"Prophesy, Christ, who was it who hit you[4]?" «And they hurled
many other insults at Him[5].»

First denial: John 18, 15-17 (Luke 23, 54-57; Mat 26, 58-69-70; Mark 14, 54-66-68)

Simon Peter and another disciple[6] followed Jesus «at a
distance to the high priest's palace». This disciple was known to
the high priest, and so went into the Pontiff's atrium at the same
time as Jesus. But Peter stayed outside, at the gate. But the other
disciple, known to the Pontiff, went out, talked to the
gate-keeper and brought Peter in. The gate-keeper confronted
Peter: "Aren't you one of this man's disciples too?" "No, I'm
not", he replied. «He sat down with the servants to see what
would happen.» «Having arrested Him, they took Him and

---

1. Jesus's reply was noble, and a lesson in legal procedure. The winesses have to
   be questioned, not the offender. Although the evidence of witnesses was
   unnecessary, for the sentence had already been decided.
2. Caiphas broke the *impasse*.
3. Before these grave words, Jesus spoke and declared Himself the Son of God.
4. In this way they avenged themselves for the countless times that He had
   defeated them. Disgraceful spectacle in a tribunal.
5. The condemnatory sentence was for the blasphemy of claiming to be the Son
   of God.
6. John the Evangelist.

brought Him to the High Priest's palace. Peter was following Him, a long way off.»

Second denial: Mat 26, 71-72; John 18, 18-25; Mark 14, 69-70; Luke 22, 58

«The servants and agents who were there had made a fire and were warming themselves, as it was cold. Peter was also with them and was warming himself... They said to Him: "Aren't you also one of His disciples?" He denied it, saying: "No, I'm not."»

Third denial: Luke 22, 59-62 (Mat 26, 73-75; Mark 14, 70-72; John 18, 26-27)

«A little later on the people there approached Peter and said to him: "Surely you're also one of them; because your manner of speaking gives you away[1]." Then he started to swear[2].» «I don't know this man whom you're talking about."» «One of the High Priest's servants, a relative of the one whose ear Peter had cut off, added: "But didn't I see you in the orchard with Him?" Peter denied it once more[3].» And at that very moment, as he was still yalking, the cock crowed. And the Lord turned round and looked at Peter, who remembered the Lord's word, as He had said to him: "Before the cock crows today, you will deny Me three times." And he went out and wept bitterly.

Before the Sannedrin: Luke 20, 66-71; 23, 1 (Mat 26, 60; Mark 15, 1)

And, when it was day, the people's Senate, the chief priests and scribes[4] assembled «against Jesus to put Him to death» and took Him to their tribunal. And they said to Him: "Tell us if you

---

1. The Galileean accent betrayed Him.
2. Poor Peter, in this tight corner, could not deny any more, remembered Jesus and a cock crowed.
3. Peter's presumption had the punishment of three denials.
4. The meeting was called to save legal formalities, but the defendant had already been sentenced.

are the Messiah." He answered them: "If I say yes, you won't believe Me; and if I ask you, on the other hand, you won't answer Me. From this moment the Son of man will be seated at the right hand of the Power of God (Dn 7, 13)." They all asked: "So you're the Son of God?" He answered them: "You're saying it, not Me." They said. "What need do we have of witnesses? We've heard it ourselves from His own mouth[1]." Then the meeting closed and they took Him (Mat) bound, to the Governor, Pilate[2].»

Judas: Mat 27, 3-10

When Judas the traitor learned that He had been condemned, he was overcome with remorse and returned the thirty silver coins to the chief priests and men of position, saying: "I've sinned by handing over innocent blood." They answered: "What is that to us? That's your affair!" Then he cast aside the silver coins in the temple, and went away and hanged himself. The chief priests collected the silver coins and said: "They can't be put into the temple's treasury as it's blood money." And, after consultation, they bought the potter's field with them, as a burial ground for pilgrims. That is why that field is called the Field of Blood until this day. Thus the prophet Jeremiah's oracle was fulfilled: "and they took the thirty silver coins, the price the sons of Israel fixed for him, and they gave them in exchange for the potter's field, as the Lord had commanded Me[3]"» (Jr 32, 6-10; Zac 11, 12-13).

Public accusation: John 18, 28-32; Luke 23, 2

They took Jesus from the house of Caiphas to the Pretorium[4]. It was daybreak; but they didn't go in, so as not to pollute themselves, because they had to celebrate the Passover.

---

1. They condemned Jesus for blasphemy, without any prosecution witnesses, because He had claimed to be the Son of God.

2. The Roman governor of Palestine.

3. Judas's despair for what he had done was not like the distress of Peter. If he had repented, Jesus would have forgiven him.

4. Governor's Residence.

Pilate came out, went to them and said: "What accusation are you bringing against this man?" They answered him: "If he wasn't an evil-doer we would not have brought him." Pilate said to them: "You take him, and try him according to your Law." The Jews replied to him: "We are not allowed to put anybody to death."

And so the word which Jesus had spoken on the kind of death which He had to undergo was fulfilled. «And they started to accuse Him[1]:» "We have found this man stirring up our people and prohibiting the payment of tributes to Caesar, and passing himself off as the Messiah, the King[2]."

Private interrogation: John 18, 33-38; Luke 23, 3 (Mat 11; Mark 15, 2-3)

Pilate went back into the Pretorium and, calling Jesus, said to Him: "Are you the King of the Jews?" Jesus replied: "Do you say that on your own account or because others have said it about Me?" Pilate answered: "I'm hardly a Jew. Your people and the chief priests have delivered you to me. What have you done?" Jesus replied: "My kingdom is not of this world. If My kingdom were of this world, my agents would have fought so that I would not be handed over to the Jews. So, then, My kingdom is not here." Pilate said to Him: "Then you are a king[3]?" Jesus replied: "You are saying it; I am a king. I was born for this and I've come to the world for this, to be a witness to the truth. Everybody on the side of truth listens to my voice." Pilate asked Him: "What is the truth?" And, having said this, he went out again to the Jews and said: "I don't find any guilt in Him."

---

1. The condemnation for blasphemy by the Sannedrin was not valid for Pilate.
2. They accused Him of being a rabble-rouser and claiming to be King of the Jews.
3. Jesus is indeed a king, but unlike those of this world, rather the eternal King of Heaven and earth.

New interrogation: Luke 23, 4-7 (Mat 27, 12-14; Mark 15, 4-5)

Pilate said to the chief priests and to the spectators: "I don't find any crime in this man." «And although the chief priests and men of position were accusing Him» «of many things,» «He gave no response.» «Pilate asked Him: "Have you no reply? Look how many things they're accusing you of." But Jesus still gave no response, to the extent that He inspired admiration in Pilate.» They stubbornly insisted: "He's been stirring up the people by teaching, from Galilee, passing through all of Judea, before arriving here." When he heard this, Pilate asked if He was Galileean. And having ascertained that He was under Herod's jurisdiction, he sent Him to Herod, who was also in Jerusalem in those days.

Herod: Luke 23, 8-12

When Herod saw Jesus he was extraordinarily glad, because he had wanted to see Him for a long time, since He had heard many things about Him, and was hoping to see Him perform a miracle. He put many questions to Him, but He didn't reply to any of them[1]. The chief priests and scribes were there, obstinately accusing Him. Herod, along with his personal guard, poured scorn on Him and mocked Him, put a brightly-colored cloak on Him and handed Him back to Pilate. That very day, Herod and Pilate, previously enemies, became friends.

Pilate: Luke 23, 13-17 (Mat 27, 15-19)

Pilate then convoked the chief priests, the men of position and the people, saying to them: "You have presented this man to me as a trouble-maker, but, look, I have interrogated him in your presence and I've not found any of the crimes which you're accusing him of. But neither did Herod, since he sent

---

1. Herod Antipa, the one who killed John the Forerunner. He was a lecherous and petty king. Jesus did not want to satisfy the curiosity of that bad king.

him back to us; in short, nothing meriting his death has been proved against him[1]."

Jesus or Barrabas: Mat 27, 15-19; Mark 15, 6-10; John 18, 19

The Governor had the custom of freeing one prisoner, chosen by the people, for the feast. There was then a famous prisoner, called Barrabas, «who was a thief,» «imprisoned along with the rioters who had committed a homicide in the uprising. And the crowd came up and started to ask that this custom be granted them.» When they were all assembled, Pilate asked them. "«You have the custom that I set one person free for you at the time of the Passover.» Whom do you want me to put at liberty: Barrabas or Jesus, «the king of the Jews», called Christ[2]?" Because he knew that they had handed Him over out of envy. He was sitting on the tribunal, and his wife sent word to him: "Do not trouble with that righteous man, because today I have greatly suffered for His cause in my dreams."

Barrabas: Luke 23, 18-25 (Mat 27, 20-23; Mark 15, 11-15; John 18, 40)

«But the chief priests and men of position persuaded the crowds to ask for Barrabas and let Jesus perish. They were to blame for stirring up the people against Jesus[3]. The Governor, taking up the word, asked them again: "Which of the two do you want me to let go?"» All the people started to shout as one: "Barrabas." The one who had been imprisoned for a mutiny that had occured in the city, and for a homicide. Pilate, wanting to release Jesus, addressed them once again. "What shall I do, then, with Jesus, called Christ?" But they shouted: "Crucify him! Crucify him!" He said to them for the third time: "But what wrong has he done? I've found in him no crime punishable by death. So, after punishing him, I shall set him

---

1. Pilate recognises His innocence.
2. Pilate was unjust, having declared Him innocent.
3. They had turned the people against Jesus.

free." But they pressed him at the top of their voices, demanding that He be crucified, and their voices became more and more aggressive. And Pilate, «wanting to contain the mob[1]», gave out the sentence which they wanted. He put at liberty, as they had asked, the one who had been imprisoned for sedition and homicide, and left Jesus to their whims.

Flagellation: Mat 27, 27-30 (Mark 15, 16-19; John 19, 1-3)

Then the Governor's soldiers led Jesus to the Pretorium and gathered all the cohort around Him. They stripped Him of his clothes, they whipped Him, put a scarlet cloak on Him and, plaiting a crown of thorns, put it on His head, and a staff in His right hand. Then they knelt before Him and made fun of Him, saying: "Hail, king of the Jews!" (John) «And they slapped His face.» And they spat at Him, took the staff and struck Him on the head[2].

"Ecce Homo": John 19, 4-7

Pilate went out again and said to them: "Look, I'm going to bring Him out so that you may see that I have found Him totally blameless. So Jesus went out, wearing the crown of thorns and the purple robe. And Pilate said to them: "Here is the man[3]." When they saw Him, the chief priests and agents shouted: "Crucify him! Crucify him!" Pilate retorted: "Take Him yourselves and crucify Him. Because I find no fault in him." The Jews answered Him: "We have a Law, and according to that Law, He must die, because He has passed himself off as the Son of God[4]."

---

1. Pilate gave way to the uproar of the populace.
2. The soldiers lashed Him cruelly, and tortured Him and ridiculed Him as the mock king of the hated Jews.
3. Thinking to move them to compassion and release Him. But they got more excited.
4. According to the Law He had to be stoned, but they wanted Him crucified to satisfy their hate and hypocrisy.

Pilate's fear: John 19, 8-11

When Pilate heard this phrase, fear entered Him; he went into the Pretorium again and questioned Jesus: "Where do you come from?" Jesus did not give him a response. Pilate said to Him: "Don't you talk to me? Don't you know that I have the power to give you liberty or have you crucified?" Jesus answered him: "You wouldn't have any power over Me if it hadn't been given you from above; therefore, whoever handed Me over to you has the greater sin."

Crucify him!: John 19, 12-15

From this moment on, Pilate searched for the way to put Him at liberty. But the Jews shouted: "If you set this man free, you are no friend of Caesar. Anybody who considers himself a king goes against Caesar." When Pilate heard these words, he ordered Jesus to be taken out, and sat down on the tribunal, in the place called the Pavement, or Gabbatha in Hebrew. It was the eve of the Passover, at about midday, and he said to the Jews: "Here is your king." But they shouted: "Out, out! Crucify Him!" Pilate reprimanded them: "Am I going to crucify your king?" The chief priests replied: "We have no other king but Caesar[1]."

DEATH

Condemned to death: Mat: 27, 24-25; John 19, 16 (Mark 15, 15; Luke 23, 25)

When Pilate saw that he wasn't achieving anything, and that the tumult was getting louder and louder, he asked for water to be brought, washed his hands[2] in front of the people and said: "I am innocent of the blood of this righteous man. You will see."

---

1. Pilate thought that He was their king. Not being a friend of the Emperor was falling into disgrace, and he gave in.

2. This was a hypocritical and cowardly gesture.

All the people replied: "May his blood fall on us and on our children[1]. «Then he handed Him over to be crucified.»

Calvary: Mat 27, 31; John 19, 17; Luke 23, 26 (Mat 27, 32-33; Mark 15, 21-22)

After having mocked Him, they took off His cloak, dressed Him and took Him to be crucified. And He went off, carrying the cross Himself, to the place called Calvary, or Golgotha in Hebrew. «When they were taking Him, they grabbed a certain Simon of Cyrene,» «the son of Alexander and Rufus, who came from the country.» «And they forced Him to carry the cross.» «And they burdened him with the cross so as to carry it behind Jesus.»

Crucifixion: Mark 15, 23-25; 27-28 (Mat 27, 34; Luke 23, 33; John 19, 18)

They crucified Him in the mid-morning. They crucified two thieves with Him, one on His right and the other on His left, thus fulfilling the prophesy which says: «He was counted amongst the evil-doers[2]» (Is 53, 12).

INRI: John 19, 19-22 (Mat 27, 37; Mark 15, 26; Luke 23, 38)

And Pilate ordered a notice with "the cause" to be written and put on the cross; "over his head" was written: Jesus Nazarene. King of the Jews. Many Jews read this notice, since the place where Jesus was crucified was near the city and the notice was written in Hebrew, Latin and Greek. The Jews' chief priests said to Pilate: "Don't write King of the Jews, but what he said: I am the King of the Jews." Pilate answered: "What I have written, is written."

---

1. The people's response was horrifying!
2. The most innocent of men was dubbed a delinquent.

Clothes: John 19, 23-24 (Mat 27, 35; Mark 15, 24; Luke 23, 38)

Having crucified Jesus[1], the soldiers took His clothes, and made four lots, one for each soldier; then they took the tunic. The tunic was not sewn and had been woven in one piece from top to bottom. Because of this they said to each other: "Let's not tear it, instead let's draw lots to see who'll win it"; and so the Scripture was fulfilled: «They divided up My clothes and drew lots for My tunic» (Sl 21, 22-19).

Forgive them[2]!: Luke 23, 34-35

And Jesus said: "Father, forgive them, because they don't know what they're doing." The people were there to watch; the chiefs were also mocking Him, saying: "He's saved others, let him save himself, if he's the Messiah of God, the Chosen One."

Insults[3]: Mark 15, 29-32 (Mat 27, 39-44; Luke 23, 36-37)

The people passing by there cursed Him and moved their heads saying: "Look what's happened to the man capable of destroying the temple and rebuilding it in three days! Save yourself and come down from the cross!" In the same way the the chief priests made fun of Him amongst themselves and with the scribes, saying: "He saved others and can't save Himself. Let the Messiah, the King of Israel, come down from the cross now, so that we may see Him and believe!" And even those crucified with Him insulted Him. «The soldiers also ridiculed Him, by going up to Him and offering Him vinegar, and saying: "If You're the King of the Jews, save yourself":»

---

1. Forty years later Jerusalem paid for the deicide. It was destroyed; according to Flavio Josepho a million Jews died, there were not enough crosses, and the rest were sold as slaves.

2. His first filial word on the cross was of forgiveness and excuse for His enemies.

3. The mob followed the example of the chiefs by mocking Jesus.

Mother and Son[1]: John 19, 25-27

Jesus's mother Mary and her sister, Mary, mother of Cleophas, and Mary Magdalene, were beside His cross. When Jesus saw His mother, and alongside her the favorite disciple, He said to His mother: "Woman, here is your son." Afterwards He said to His disciple: "Here is your mother." And from that moment the disciple welcomed her into his house.

Good thief: Luke 23, 39-43

One of the evil-doers who were crucified insulted Him thus: "Aren't you the Messiah? Save yourself and us." But the other reprimanded Him, saying: "Don't you even fear God when He's undergoing the same torture? We're doing it justly, for we're receiving the just punishment for what we're doing; but He hasn't done anything wrong." And he said to Jesus: "Remember me when You're in the Kingdom." And He answered him: "I assure you that without doubt you will be with me today in Paradise[2]."

My God, my God!: Mat 27, 45-47, 49

There was darkness over the earth from midday until three in the afternoon. At about three o'clock He let out a very loud cry: Eli, Eli, lema sabactini?", that is, My God, My God, why have You abandoned Me[3]? Some of those who were there said, when they heard Him: "He's calling Elias." But others said: "Let's see if Elias comes to save him."

I'm thirsty: John 19, 28-29

Then, when Jesus knew that it had all been fulfilled, according to the Scripture, He said: "I'm thirsty." There was a

---

1. Jesus gave us Mary as a mother.
2. The repentance of the Good Thief was so profound that he went directly to Paradise.
3. This was the most painful torture for Jesus, the Father's abandoning Him as a man.

jar full of vinegar; they put a sponge soaked in vinegar on a hyssop stick and put it to His mouth.

All finished: John 19, 30

When He had had the vinegar, Jesus exclaimed: "Everything has been fulfilled."

Death of Jesus: Luke 23, 46; John 19, 30

Jesus exclaimed: "Father, I commend My spirit to Your hands." And, having said this, He passed away.

And, inclining His head, He offered up His spirit[1].

Strange phenomena[2]: Mat 27, 51-54; Luke 23, 48-49

Then the veil of the temple was torn in two from top to bottom; the earth shook and the rocks cracked[3]; the sepulchres opened and many saints' corpses came back to life. And, coming out of their sepulchres after Jesus's resurrection, they came to the holy city and appeared to many people. When the centurion and those who were with him keeping guard over Jesus saw the earthquake and what was happening, they were panic-stricken and said: "This truly is the Son of God." And when all the people who witnessed this spectacle considered the things which had happened, they came back giving themselves blows on the chest. All his acquaintances and the women who had followed Him from Galilee were there, watching these things at a distance.

Joseph of Arimathea: Luke 23, 50-52; Mark 15, 44-45

And then a man called Joseph, a native of Arimathea, a member of the Sannedrin, a good and righteous man, who had not given his consent to the others' decision to scheme for execution, and who awaited the Kingdom of God, presented

---

1. The New Alliance was sealed with the blood of Jesus between God and men. Sin is erased and Grace restored.
2. Nature herself went into mourning over His death.
3. Even today the split in the Calvary rock can be seen.

himself to Pilate and asked for Jesus's body. «But Pilate was surprised that He was already dead, and, summoning the centurion, asked him if He was indeed dead. And when the centurion had reported to him, he agreed to concede the corpse to Joseph.»

Spear thrust: John 19, 31-37

As it was Parasceve, the Jews asked Pilate for their legs to be broken and for them to be taken away, so that the bodies wouldn't remain on the cross during the Sabbath, since this Sabbath was a solemn day. So the soldiers came and broke the legs of the first man who had been crucified with Him, and then those of the other. Then they went up to Jesus; seeing that He was already dead, they didn't break His legs, but one of the soldiers opened up His side with a spear, and straight away blood and water came out[1]. And he who was there records it thus; and his record is trustworthy, and he knows that he is telling the truth in order for us to believe. With these things the Scripture was fulfilled: «No bone will be broken» (Ex 12, 46). And in another passage: "They will see Him whom they pierced» (Zac 12, 10).

Sepulchre: John 19, 38-42

When these things had occured, Joseph of Arimathea, who was Jesus's disciple, though in secret out of fear of the Jews, asked Pilate to let him take away Jesus's body. Pilate agreed; so he came and took away Jesus's body. Nicodemus also arrived, the one who had earlier gone to meet Jesus at night, bringing one hundred pounds of a mixture of myrrh and aloes. So they took Jesus's body and wrapped it in aromatic cloths, according to Jewish burial customs. There was an orchard in the place where He was crucified, and a new sepulchre in the orchard,

---

1. The Holy Fathers have seen in the mystery of the blood and water the symbol of the Baptism and the origin of the Eucharist.

where nobody had as yet been put. They deposited Jesus there, as the sepulchre was nearby, because of the Jews' Parasceve[1].

Holy women: Luke 23, 54-56

It was the day of Parasceve and the Sabbath was going to begin. The women who had come with Him from Galilee followed Him, to inspect the sepulchre and see how His body had been placed. And then they went back and prepared aromas and perfumes; and during the Sabbath they rested, in accordance with the precept of the Law.

Soldiers on guard: Mat 27, 62-66

On the following day, the day after the preparation for the Passover, the chief priests and the Pharisees[2] assembled in Pilate's house and said to him: "Sir, we have remembered something that impostor said when he was alive: 'After three days I will come back to life.' So, give orders for the sepulchre to be safeguarded until the third day, so that the disciples don't come and steal him and say to the people. 'He has come back from the dead.'" This imposture would be worse than the first one. Pilate said to them: "You have a guard at your disposition; go and take the security measures which seem best to you." So they went and safeguarded the sepulchre, sealing the stone and placing a guard[3].

Earthquake: Mat 28, 2-4

Then, there was a great earthquake: The angel of the Lord came down from heaven, removed the stone and sat on it. His appearance was like that of a lightning flash; his clothes as white as snow. The guards trembled with fear before him and fell down as if they were dead[4].

---

1. The Jew's cemeteries were only for pilgrims and the poor.
2. They had their doubts about the resurrection of Jesus on the third day, put a guard and sealed the stone.
3. In this way the Resurrection was more patent.
4. And the sepulchre remained open.

RESURRECTION

Empty sepulchre: Mark 16, 1-4; John 20, 1; Mat 28, 1; Luke 24, 1-2

Once the Sabbath was over, Mary Magdalene, Mary, mother of James, and Salome, bought perfumes to go and anoint Jesus's body. And on the first day of the week, they went to the sepulchre very early, with the sun barely out. They were saying to each other as they went: "Who will move the stone away from the sepulchre for us?" But when they looked carefully, they observed that the stone, which was truly enormous, had already been moved away[1].

Magdalene's notification: John 20, 2

She went running to Simon Peter and Jesus's other favorite disciple and said: "They've taken the Lord from the sepulchre and we don't know where they've put Him."

Announcing angels: Mark 16, 5-7; Mat 28, 5-7; Luke 24, 3-8

When they entered the sepulchre[2] they saw a young man seated on the right hand side, wearing a white tunic, and they were terrified. He said to them: "Don't be afraid. Your looking for Jesus Nazarene, the crucified one. He has come back to life, He is not here. This is the place where they put Him. But go and say to His disciples, above all Peter, that He will go ahead of you to Galilee. (Luke). «Remember what He said to you when He was still in Galilee. Of how the Son of man had to be delivered into the hands of the sinners and be crucified and come back to life on the third day." And they remembered His words.» They fled, running from the sepulchre, since they were overcome by fear and amazement.

---

1. Once the Sabbath was over, which had to be kept, they could now go to the sepulchre.
2. The other two Marys.

Incredulity: Luke 24, 9-11 (Mark 16, 8; Mat 26, 8-11)

They went away from the sepulchre and went to tell the eleven, and all the others, about it. They were: Mary Magdalene, Joanna and Mary, the mother of James. All the other women who were with them related this incident to the Apostles. But these accounts seemed pure fantasy to them and they did not believe them.

Peter and John: John 20, 3-10

Peter and the other disciple[1] left[2] in the direction of the sepulchre. The two ran together, but the other disciple ran faster than Peter and arrived first at the sepulchre, and, leaning in, saw the cloths on the ground, but did not go in. Peter then arrived straight after and went into the sepulchre, and saw the cloths on the ground, and the shroud which had been on His head, not on the ground with the cloths, but rolled up to one side. Then the other disciple, who had arrived first at the sepulchre, also entered; he saw and believed; but they had still not understood that, according to the Scripture, He was due to come back from the dead. Then the disciples returned home.

Jesus appears to the Magdalene: John 20, 11-16; Mat 28,9

Mary was weeping outside, next to the sepulchre[3]. She was there weeping and leaned into the sepulchre, and saw two angels dressed in white, one seated at the head of the place where they had put Jesus's body, and the other at the foot. They asked her: "Women, why are you weeping?" She replied: "Because they have taken away my Lord and I don't know where they have put Him." On saying this, she looked behind her and saw Jesus standing, but did not realize that it was Jesus. Jesus said to her: "Woman, why are you weeping? Who are you looking for?" She, thinking that he was the gardener, said to Him: "Sir, if you've taken Him, tell me where you've put Him

---

1. John.
2. Because of the Magdalene's announcement.
3. Mary went back to the sepulchre and remained in the entrance.

and I'll take Him with me[1]." Jesus said to her: "Mary!" She turned round, and she replied in Aramaic: "Rabboni!" (which means Master[2]).

Let go of me!: John 20, 17-18

Jesus said to her: "Let go of me! for I still haven't gone up to the Father; go and meet My disciples and say to them: I'm going up to My Father and your Father, to my God and your God." Mary Magdalene went to notify the disciples that she had seen the Lord and that He had said these things to her.

Bad faith: Mat 28, 11-15

Whilst they were on the road, some of the soldiers from the guard came to the city and told the chief priests everything that had happened. The latter confered with the men of position and gave the soldiers a big sum of money with these instructions: "You must say this: His disciples came in the night, whilst we were asleep[3], and stole him. And if this comes to the knowledge of the Governor, we shall convince him and save you." They took the money and acted according to the instructions they had received. And this lie has been divulged amongst the Jews until today.

The road to Emmaus: Luke 24, 18-32; Mark 16, 12-13

That same day, two of the disciples were travelling on the road to a village called Emmaus, sixty furlongs from Jerusalem. They were discussing these occurences. And whilst they conversed and argued, Jesus himself approached them and started walking with them. But their eyes had been made unable to recognise Him. He said to them: "What observations are you making as you walk?" They, saddened, stopped. And one of

---

1. Overcome by grief, she didn't know what she was saying.

2. Then she recognised Him.

3. They were the ones asleep. The body could not have been taken without breaking the Sabbath. The stone of the sepulchre was enormous. If the soldiers were asleep, how could they be witnesses to the theft? And, if not, how did they let Him be taken away?

them, called Cleophas, took up the word and said to Him: "Are you the only stranger in Jerusalem who hasn't heard about what's gone on there these days?" He asked: "What has gone on?" They said to Him: "The matter of Jesus of Nazareth, who had revealed Himself before God and all the people as a powerful prophet in words and deeds; and how the chief priests and our authorities handed Him over and got Him condemned to death and crucified. We were hoping that He would be the one to liberate Israel. However, this took place three days ago. The truth is that some of our women have alarmed us; they went very early to the sepulchre, and, not having found Jesus's body, they came back saying that some angels had appeared to them, assuring them that He's alive. And some of us went to the sepulchre and found the things as the women had said. But they didn't see Him." And He said to them: "Oh, ignorant and dull-witted men to believe everything that the Prophets said. Is it necessary for the Messiah to suffer these things in order to enter in His glory? And, starting with Moses and following with the other prophets, He interpreted all the passages from the Scripture that refered to Him." When they arrived near the village where they were heading[1], He made as if to continue ahead. But they insisted, saying to Him: "Stay with us, since it's already late and the day is ending." And He went in stay with them. And He was with them at the table, and, taking bread, recited the blessing and, after breaking it, gave it to them. Their eyes were opened and they recognised Him[2], but He disappeared from their view. Then they said to each other. "Isn't it true that our hearts were burning when He spoke to us on the road and explained the Scriptures to us?"

Great news: Luke 24, 33-45

They immediately returned to Jerusalem and found the eleven and their companions assembled, saying: "It's a reality! He's come back to life and appeared to Simon." And they, in

---

1. Emmaus is 12 kilometers from Jerusalem.

2. It was the same act as at the Last Supper, when He instituted the Eucharist.

their turn, refered to what had happened on the road, and how they had recognised Him when He broke the bread.

Gift of peace: John 20, 19-23

When it was already late that afternoon[1], the first of the week, and the doors of the place where the disciples were being closed, Jesus appeared in person. Putting Himself in the center[2], He said to them: "Peace be with you." And, having said this, He showed them His hands and side; then the disciples rejoiced on seeing the Lord. He said to them again: "Peace be with you. Just as the Father sent Me, so I am sending you." Having said these words, He breathed and said to then: "Receive the Holy Spirit. Whoever's sins you pardon, they will be pardoned; whoever's you retain, will be retained[3]."

Thomas, the unbeliever: John 20, 24-29

But Thomas, one of the twelve, surnamed Didymus, was not with them when Jesus arrived. So the other disciples said to Him: "We have seen the Lord." But He answered them: "If I don't see the mark of the nails on His hands, and put my fingers where they were, and my hand in His side, I shall not believe." Eight days later, the disciples were again to be found inside, Thomas among them. The doors being closed, Jesus appeared in person; He put himself in the center and said to them: "Peace be with you." Afterwards He said to Thomas: "Bring your finger here and look at My hands; hold out your hand and put it in My side, and don't be incredulous, but believing." Thomas answered Him: "My Lord and My God!" Jesus answered Him: "Have you believed because you have seen Me? Blessed are those who have believed without having seen[4]."

---

1. The same Resurrection Sunday.
2. It is proper to glorified bodies to be visible or invisible. Clarity. Agility. Impassibility.
3. He thus instituted the Sacrament of Penitence.
4. Faith is more deserving.

Miracles to believe: John 20, 30-31

Jesus performed many other miracles in the presence of the disciples, which are not written in this book. These have been written so that you believe that Jesus is the Messiah, the Son of God, and so that by believing you have life in His name.

Appearance in Galilee: John 21, 1-14

After this, Jesus appeared again to the disciples next to the sea of Tiberias[1], in this way: "Simon Peter and Thomas, surnamed Didymus, were together; Nathaniel, from Canaan in Galilee; the sons of Zebedee and two other disciples. Simon Peter said to them: "I'm going fishing." They replied: "we'll go with you too." So they left, and got into the boat; but that night they did not catch anything. At daybreak, Jesus appeared to them on the bank; but the disciples did not realise that it was Jesus. Jesus said to them: "Boys, do you have anything to eat?" They answered Him: "No." He answered them: "Cast the net over the right side of the boat and you will find something." So they cast it and could hardly haul it in because of the quantity of fish. Then Jesus's favorite disciple[2] said to Peter: "It's the Lord!". When Simon Peter heard: "It's the Lord", he tied his outer garment round his waist, for he was naked, and threw himself into the sea; the other disciples arrived with the boat dragging the net with fishes, for they were only some two hundred cubits from the shore. When they jumped onshore they saw fires ready with fish on top, and bread. Jesus said to them: "Bring some of the fish which you've just caught." Simon Peter boarded the boat and dragged ashore the net, which was filled with one hundred and fifty fishes and three big ones. And, in spite of having so many, the net did not break. Jesus said to them: "Come and eat." None of the disciples dared to ask Him: "Who are You?" For they knew that He was the Lord. Jesus approached, took the bread and gave it to them; He did the same

1. Just as the Angel had said to the Marias.
2. John.

with the fish. This was now the third time that Jesus had appeared to His disciples after having come back from the dead.

Peter's primacy: John 21, 15-19

When they had eaten, Jesus said to Simon Peter: "Simon, son of John, do you love me more than these?" He answered Him: "Yes, Lord, You know that I love You." He said to Him: "Pasture My sheep."

He asked him a second time: "Simon, son of John, do you love Me?" "Yes, Lord, he answered Him; You know that I love You." He said to him: "Pasture My sheep[1]."

He asked Him for a third time: "Simon, son of John, do you love Me?" Peter was saddened because He asked him a third time: "Do you love Me?" And he answered Him: "Lord, You know everything, You know that I love You." Jesus answered him: "Pasture my sheep."

"I say to you with absolute certainty: When you were young you girdled yourself and went wherever you wanted. But when you are old you will hold out your hands, and somebody else will girdle you and he'll take you where you don't want to go." He said this to insinuate with what class of death he would glorify God. Afterwards He added: "Follow Me[2]."

Mission of the Apostles: Mat 28, 16-20; Mark 16, 14-20; Luke 14, 44-49; John 20, 21

The eleven Apostles set off to the mountain which Jesus had pointed out to them. When they saw Him, they worshipped Him. Some, however, doubted. Jesus approached them and addressed these words to them: "I have been given all power in heaven and on earth. Go, then, and convert all nations into disciples, baptizing them in the name of the Father, Son and Holy Spirit; and teaching them to observe everything I have

---

1. He had promised him it and now He puts it into effect. But first He had to retract the three denials.
2. He confered on the Primacy government, sanctification and teaching. To Peter and his successors, the Popes, up to the present day.

commanded You. I am constantly with you until the end of the world[1]."

Last appearance: Luke 24, 41-48; Mat 28, 18-20

As they were still hesitating and had not emerged from their astonishment because of their joyfulness, He said to them: "Do you have anything to eat?" They presented Him with part of a broiled fish; and, taking it, He ate it in their presence[2].

And they said to Him: "These are the things which I was talking to you about when I was still with you, when I stated that everything concerning Me that is written in Moses, in the prophets and in the Psalms, must be fulfilled." Then He cast light on their understanding so that they would understand the Scriptures. And He added: "It is written that the Messiah had to suffer and come back from the dead on the third day, and that penance and the forgiveness of sins had to be preached in His name, starting with Jerusalem. You are witnesses to these deeds."

Coming of the Holy Spirit: Luke 24, 49

"And pay attention: I am going to send the one promised by My Father; stay in the city until you are clothed in the force from on high[3].

Ascension: Mark 16, 14-20; Luke 24, 50-53; Mat 1, 1-11

Finally He appeared at eleven o'clock when they were at the table. And He said to them: "Go all over the world to preach the Gospel to all creatures. Whoever believes and was baptized[4], will be saved; but whoever does not believe will be condemned."

---

1. Moreover, He has promised His presence and attendance to the Church until the end of time.
2. Thus they could say: "We have eaten with Him", it was not a ghost.
3. Cenacle.
4. This is the mission of the Church: to preach the Gospel to everybody. Whoever does not want to be believed will be condemned.

So, then, after talking to them, the Lord Jesus was taken up to heaven and is seated at God's right hand.

They went to preach everywhere, the Lord's virtue working with them, and confirming His doctrine with the signs accompanying it.

Final testimony: John 21, 24-25

This same disciple is the one who is witness to these things, and has written them down, and we know that his testimony is trustworthy[1] There are many other things which Jesus did. If they were narrated one by one, I don't think that the whole world could contain the books which could have been written.

---

1. Scripture and Tradition are the two sources of the Revelation. Saint John told us that not everything has been written down.

ACTS OF THE APOSTLES[1]

INTRODUCTION

Last instructions and Ascension[2]. And when He was with them at the table, He told them not to leave Jerusalem, but to wait for the Father's promise, "which you have heard from Me; because John baptized with water; but you will be baptized with the Holy Spirit a few days from now, you will receive the strength of the Holy Spirit, who will come down on you, and you will be My witnesses in Jerusalem, in all Judea, in Samaria and until the ends of the earth.

When He had said this, they saw Him being taken up; and a cloud hid Him from their view. And whilst they were looking intently at the sky as He was going, two men[3] in white clothes appeared, who said to them: "Men of Galilee, why do you continue to look at the sky? This Jesus, who has been taken up from you into heaven, will come in the same way as you have seen Him go into heaven[4].

Persevering prayer. Then they returned to Jerusalem from the mount of Olives, which is near Jerusalem, a Sabbath day's journey away. And when they got there, they went up to the

---

1. These are like the continuation of the Saint Luke's Gospel. They are both by the same author.
2. Jesus appeared to the Apostles for 40 days until His Ascension.
3. Angels.
4. In the second Coming at the end of time.

upper room, where they customarily lodged[1]. There were Peter and John, James and Andrew, Philip and Thomas, Bartholomew and Matthew, James the son of Alpheus, Simon Zelotes and Judas, brother of James. They all stayed united in prayer, with the women, and with Mary, the mother of Jesus, and with her brothers.

THE CHURCH IN JERUSALEM

Pentecost. When the day of Pentecost came[2], they were all together in the same place, and suddenly a noise came from the sky, like an impetuous wind gusting by, which filled all the house in which they were. Tongues of fire appeared to them, and divided up and positioned themselves on each of them, and they were all filled with the Holy Spirit, and started to talk in strange tongues, as the Spirit moved them to express themselves[3].

Now, there were pious men from all nations under the sun living in Jerusalem; when they heard the noise, the crowd assembled and were astonished, because each one heard them speaking in his own language. They were all amazed and full of wonder, and said. "Aren't the men speaking all from Galilee? Then, how is it that each of us hears them in our own maternal language. Parthians and Medes and Elamites, and inhabitants of Judea and Cappadocia, Pontus and Asia, Phrygia and Pamphylia, Egypt and the regions of Lybia and Cyrene, and Roman, Jewish and proselyte strangers, Cretes and Arabians, we have heard them speak of the greatness of God in our own languages[4]." So they were all amazed and perplexed, saying to each other: "What does this mean?" But others, mocking, said: "They're full of new wine."

---

1. In the Cenacle of Jerusalem.
2. Fifty days after the Resurrection.
3. The Holy Spirit communicated to them His gifts and charismas. Gift of Miracles, etc.
4. 17 representative nations.

St. Peter's sermon. Then Peter[1], standing up with the Eleven, raised His voice and addressed these words to them: "Men of Israel[2], hear these words: Jesus of Nazareth, a man approved before you by God through miracles, prodigies and signs which God made through Him amongst you, as you know; handed over according to the counsel and foresight of God, you killed Him, crucifying Him with evil hands; but God brought Him back to life, breaking the chains of death, because it was impossible for it to reign over Him, since David says of Him: You will not abandon My soul in Hell, nor will You allow Your Saint to see corruption[3].

This is what you see and hear. Because David did not go to heaven, but he says: 'The Lord said to My Lord: Sit at My right until I put your enemies under your footstool.' Rest assured, then, all the house of Israel, of the certainty that God made this Jesus, whom you have crucified, Lord and Christ."

First conversions. When they heard this, their hearts were torn, and they said to Peter and the other disciples: "What must we do, brothers?" And Peter said to them: "Repent, and may each one of you be baptized in the name of Jesus Christ, for the remission of your sins; and then you will receive the gift of the Holy Spirit[4]. The promise is for you and your children, and for all those from afar, as many as the Lord, our God, calls." And he exhorted and testified with many other words, saying: "Save yourselves from this perverse generation[5]." And those who acknowledged his words were baptized, and some three thousand souls were added that very day. They persevered in the teaching of the Apostles, in the communion, in the breaking of bread and in prayers.

Cure of a lame man. Peter and John went up to the Temple to pray at the ninth hour. And a man crippled from birth was

---

1. As Primate, he speak in the name of the Apostles.
2. Before they hid themselves, now they leap into the market squares. Ignorant before, they preached the crucified Jesus, full of wisdom and eloquence.
3. Place of the dead.
4. Two things are needed to enter the Christian community: to repent and be baptized.
5. John the Forerunner announced the true baptism of water and fire of the Spirit.

taken every day and placed at the gate to the Temple, called Beautiful, to ask for alms from those who went in. When he saw Peter and John going in, he asked them for alms. Peter, looking at him fixedly, with John as well, said. "Look at us." He looked at them, hoping to receive something from them. But Peter said: "I have neither gold nor silver; but what I do have, I give to you: In the name of Jesus Christ, the Nazarene, walk." And taking him by the right hand, he raised him up; and at that moment his feet and ankles became whole, and with one jump he stood up and walked, and went into the temple with them, walking, leaping and praising God. All the people saw him walking and praising God; and they realised that he was the one who customarily sat down next to the Beautiful gate and asked for alms; and they were filled with amazement and awe at what had happened.

Peter's new sermon. When Peter saw this, He said to the people: "Men of Israel, what amazes you in this, or why are you staring at us, as if we could have made this man walk through our own power and pity. The God of Abraham, of Isaac and Jacob, the God of our fathers, glorified His son Jesus, whom you handed over and denied before Pilate, who had decided to let Him go; but you denied the Holy and Righteous, and asked for the grace of a murderer, whilst you killed the Author of life, whom God brought back from the dead. And through faith in His name[1], He strengthened this man whom you see and know; and the faith which comes through Him gave this man complete wholeness in your presence. Now, brothers, I know that you were acting out of ignorance[2], in the same way as your chiefs. But God fulfilled in this way what He had announced beforehand through the mouth of all the prophets: that His Christ had to suffer. Therefore, repent and convert so that your sins are erased, for when the time of freezing comes from the Lord and He sends the Christ destined for you, to Jesus, of whom God spoke out of the mouths of His prophets since antiquity."

---

1. As when he fished, Peter always acted in the name of Christ.
2. Peter excuses those who crucified Jesus as He had done from the cross.

Peter and John in prison. While they were talking to the people, the priests[1] and the Temple Official, and the Sadducees appeared, annoyed that they were preaching to the people and proclaiming Jesus's resurrection from the dead; they arrested them and buried them until the following day, for it was already late. But many of those who heard the sermon believed; and the number arrived at some five thousand[2]. The following day the town chiefs, elders and scribes assembled in Jerusalem: There were Annas, the High Priest; Caiphas, John, Alexander and all the offspring of the High Priests. They put them in the center and asked them: "With what power or in whose name have you done this?"

Peter's defence. Then Peter, filled with the holy spirit, said to them: "Leaders of the people and elders of Israel. Since you are asked by a benefit done to a sick man to see how he has been healed, you and all the people of Israel should know that this man is sane on Christ, the Nazarene's account, whom you crucified and God brought back from the dead. He is the rock which you builders have despised, and he has come to be the cornerstone. And he is the only salvation, for no other name has been given to mankind from heaven for our salvation[3]".

The Sannedrin's threat. Thinking, on the one hand, of Peter and John's safety, and understanding, on the other, that they were unlearned and uncultured men, they ordered them to go to the Sannedrin, and they started to deliberate amongst themselves, saying: "What shall we do to these men? Because they have really performed a remarkable miracle, for all the inhabitants of Jerusalem to see, and we cannot deny it. But so that it is not divulged any more amongst the people, let's threaten them not to speak to anybody in that man's name." They called them and ordered them not to speak or teach in Jesus's name. But Peter and John answered them: "Judge for yourselves whether it is right before God to obey you rather than obey

---

1. Isaiah and others.
2. The town chiefs and elders were alarmed by so many conversions.
3. These miracles were performed on Christ's behalf.

God[1]. We can't lay aside what we've seen and heard." But they took their leave, threatening them again, without finding any way of punishing them, because of the people[2].

The Church's prayer. Set free, they went to their people and reported what the pontiffs and elders had said. After listening to them, they raised their voice as one, saying: "Sovereign Lord, You are the God who has made heaven and earth, the sea and everything in them. Now, Lord, look at their threats and grant Your word, holding out Your hand to cure and make signs and prodigies in the name of Your holy servant Jesus." When their prayer was over, the place where they were assembled trembled and they were all filled with the Holy Spirit, and they freely announced the word of God[3].

Union of the faithful. The crowd of believers had one sole heart and soul, and nobody called any possession their own, rather they had all their things in common. And the Apostles testified to the Resurrection of the Lord Jesus with great energy, and everybody enjoyed a singular grace. There were no poor people among them, because all those that had estates or houses sold them and brought the money from the sale and laid it at the feet of the Apostles; and it was distributed according to each person's needs. Joseph, whom the Apostles called Barnabas —which means son of consolation—, a Levite and native of Cyprus, had a field, sold it, brought the money and put it at the Apostles' feet.

Increase in the Church. Many miracles and prodigies were performed at the hands of the Apostles, and everybody congregated at Solomon's porch; and they even took the sick to the squares and put them on beds and barrows, so that, when Peter passed by, His shadow at least might touch some of them. Crowds from the cities nearby also came to Jerusalem, bringing sick people, and those possessed by unworldly spirits, and they were all cured.

---

1. Without the corner stone, Christ, everything tumbles down.
2. Peter and the other Apostles were not the same.
3. The primitive Church was a model of unity and charity, with a perfect communion of spirit and brotherhood.

New persecution. Then the Pontiff intervened with all those from his party —the sect of the Sadducees—. Full of jealousy, they arrested the Apostles and put them into the public jail. But an angel of the Lord opened the the prison gates at night, took them out and said: "Go to the Temple and courageously announce to the people all the words of this Life." When they heard this, they entered the Temple in the early hours of the morning and started to teach.

Meanwhile the Pontiff and his supporters summoned the Sannedrin and all the elders of the sons of Israel, and sent word to the jail to look for the Apostles. The constables went, but didn't find them in the prison; they returned and reported this, saying: "We found the prison carefully closed and the guards beside the gates; but when we opened it we didn't find anybody inside."

When they heard this, both the Temple prefect and the pontiffs were perplexed when they thought of what could have become of them[1]. But somebody arrived and said to them: "The men whom you imprisoned are in the Temple teaching the people." Then the prefect set off with the constables and led them away, but without violence, because they feared that the people would stone them; and having led them away, they presented them to the Sannedrin. And the Pontiff asked them: "Didn't we solemnly order you not to teach in that man's name? And look how you've filled Jerusalem with your doctrine and want to make his blood fall on us."

Then Peter replied with the Apostles: "God must be obeyed before men. Our forefathers' God has brought Jesus back to life, Him whom you killed by hanging Him from a bit of wood. God has exalted Him with His right hand as Chief and Saviour to give Israel repentance and forgiveness of sins. We are witnesses to these things, as also is the Holy Spirit whom God has given to those who obey[2]."

---

1. Those Sadducees and Jewish authorities did not believe what they saw.
2. Nobody could match the wisdom and courage of those poor illiterates, because they were filled with the Holy Spirit.

Stephen, before the Sannedrin. Stephen[1], for his part, full of grace and power, performed great prodigies and miracles among the people. But some people emerged from the synagogue, which is called that of the Libertines, the Cyrenians and Alexandrians and the people from Cilicia and Asia, and they started to argue with Stephen, but they could not resist the wisdom and spirit with which he was speaking. Then they bribed some men to say: "We have heard this man utter blasphemies against Moses and against God"; they thus stirred up the people, the elders and the scribes, who threw themselves on him, arrested him and took him before the Sannedrin. Then they presented false witnesses, who said: "This man does not cease to utter words against this holy place and against the Law; for we have heard him say that Jesus, the Nazarene, will destroy this place and change the customs which Moses has passed down to us." Then everybody who was seated in the Sannedrin stared at him and saw his face like that of an angel.

Stephen's sermon. The Pontiff asked: "Is this true?" And he said: "Brothers and fathers, listen: The God of glory appeared to our father Abraham when he was in Mesopotomia, before he lived in Charran, and He said to him: 'Leave your land and your family, and come to the land which I shall show you.' Then he went to the land of the Chaldeans and lived in Charran. And there, after the death of his father, God moved him to this land in which you now dwell, and He didn't give him any property in this region, not even one foot of earth. But He promised to put it in his possession, and in that of his descendants.

What prophet was not persecuted by your forefathers? They killed those who foretold the coming of the Just One, of whom you are now betrayers and murderers. You have received the law from the angel's ministery but have not keep it."

Stephen's martyrdom. When they heard this their hearts were inflamed with rage, and they gnashed their teeth against him. But he, full of the Holy Spirit, his eyes fixed heavenwards,

---

1. He was one of the seven Deacons which the Church created to tend to the poor and widows, whilst the Apostles devoted themselves to the ministry of the Word and Prayer.

saw the Glory of God and Jesus at God's right hand, and said: "I see the heavens open, and the Son of Man standing on God's right." They yelled loudly and stopped their ears, and threw themselves on him as one, and, throwing him out of the city, began to stone him. The witnesses left their clothes at the foot of a young man called Saul. Whilst they were stoning him, Stephen prayed thus: "Lord, Jesus, receive my spirit." And, on his knees, he shouted loudly: "Lord, do not impute this sin against them." And saying this, he went to sleep. And Saul verified his death[1].

Persecution in Jerusalem. On that day a great persecution against the Church of Jerusalem was organized, and everybody, except for the apostles, scattered around the regions of Judah and Samaria. Some pious men buried Stephen and mourned him. Saulo, on the contrary, attacked the church entering through the houses and imprisoned men and women.

PROPAGATION OF THE GOSPEL OUTSIDE JERUSALEM

Philip's prediction[2]. As for those who had been dispersed, they went everywhere announcing the word. Philip, going down to Samaria, preached to them about Christ. The crowds paid attention to Philip's words, seeing and hearing as one what he said and the miracles he performed[3]. Because impure spirits left, screaming, many possessed people. And many paralytics and lame people were cured. And because of this there was great joy in that city.

The Holy Spirit. The Apostles who were in Jerusalem, knowing that Samaria had received the word of God, sent Peter and John; who went down and prayed for them to receive the Holy Spirit; for He still had not descended on any of them, and

---

1. Saul, the future Paul.
2. One of the Deacons, like Stephen.
3. The charisma of miracles and cures received from the Holy Spirit gave credit to the messengers of the Gospel.

they had only received baptism in the name of the Lord, Jesus. Then they lay hands on them, and received the Holy Spirit.

Baptism of the Ethiopian. The Angel of the Lord said to Philip: "Walk until midday along the desert road which goes down from Jerusalem to Gaza[1]." And he set off. And there was an Ethiopian eunuch[2], a minister under Candace, queen of the Ethiopians[3], superintendent of all her treasures, who was coming back from Jerusalem, and was sitting on a cart reading the prophet Isaiah. The Spirit said to Philip: "Come here, next to this cart." Philip ran and said: "Do you by any chance understand what you're reading?" And He said: "And how can I, if nobody guides me?" And he asked Philip to get up and sit with him. The Scriptural passage which he was reading was this:

"He was taken like a sheep to the slaughterhouse, like a lamb
    silent before the shearer, and does not open his mouth."

Then the eunuch said to Philip: "I'm asking you to tell me who this prophet is talking about. About himself, or another?" Then Philip took up the word and, starting with this passage in the Scriptures, taught him about Christ. Continuing on the way, they arrived at a place with some water, and the eunuch said: "Look, here's some water, what's preventing me from being baptized?" And Philip said: "If you believe[4] with all your heart, it can be done." And he replied: "I believe that Jesus Christ is the Son of God." And he told him to stop the cart. They both got into the water, Philip and the eunuch, and he baptized him: Having got out of the water, the Spirit of the Lord swept Philip away, and the Eunuch didn't see him any more, and continued happily on his way. Philip found himself in Azotus, and went round evangelizing all the cities until he reached Caesarea.

---

1. Port city in South Palestine.
2. Queen's favorite and minister.
3. Region of the Nile Valley in the South of Egypt between Sudan and Abyssinia.
4. Faith opens the bridge of Baptism.

Saul's conversion. Saul, for his part, still breathing threats and death against the disciples of the Lord, presented himself to the High Priest, and asked him for letters for the Synagogues of Damascus, to see if he could bring to Jerusalem, chained up, any men or women who followed this road[1]. They were on the road, and already nearing Damascus, when suddenly a light from heaven enveloped him[2], and, falling to the ground, he heard a voice which said to him: "Saul, Saul, why are you persecuting Me?[3]" And he asked: "Who are you, Lord?" And He: "I am Jesus, whom you are persecuting. But get up and enter the city and you will be told what you have to do." And the men who accompanied him stood in amazement, hearing the voice, but not seeing anybody. Saul got up from the ground, and, although his eyes were open, he couldn't see anything; and taking him by the hand they took him into Damascus. And he remained three days without seeing, or eating or drinking.

There was a disciple in Damascus called Ananias, to whom the Lord said in a vision: "Ananias!" And he answered Him: "I am here, Lord." And the Lord to him: "Get up and go to the street called Straight[4], and look for a certain Saul of Tarsus in the house of Judas; for he's praying, and saw in a vision a man called Ananias, who came in and laid hands on him to see." But Ananias replied: "Lord, I have heard many people talk about this man and say how much evil he has committed against Your saints in Jerusalem; and he's here with the full authority of the High Priests to arrest whoever invokes your name." But the Lord said to Him: "Go, because he is My chosen instrument, to bear My name to Gentiles and kings, and to the sons of Israel. I'll show him how much he has to suffer for My name." Ananias then went and entered the house, put his hands on him and said: "Saul, my brother, the Lord Jesus is sending you, He who appeared to you on the road when you were coming, so

---

1. Generic name for religion, Christianity, the Gospel.
2. Which knocked him off his horse and blinded him.
3. Saul (Paul) was not directly persecuting Jesus, but the Christians representing Jesus.
4. Still in existence today.

that you may see and be filled with the Holy Spirit." And immediately something like scales fell from his eyes, and he recovered his sight, got up and was baptized; and, eating something, he was comforted. And he stayed a few days with the disciples who were there in Damascus.

He preaches at Damascus and is persecuted. And then in the synagogues he preached that Jesus Christ was the Son of God. The people who listened to him were amazed and said, "Is he not the one who pursued in Jerusalem those who invoked that name and brought them here to deliver them chained to the High Priests?" But Saul was taking heart and confused the Jews living at Damascus, showing that Jesus was the Messiah. Some days afterwards, the Jews plotted to kill him. But Saul knew about the plot. The Jews watched the gates night and day, but his disciples got him down a wall into the night.

Saul in Jerusalem and Tarsus. When he arrived in Jerusalem, he tried to meet the disciples; and they all feared him and did not believe he was a true disciple. Then Barnabas[1] took him with him and brought him to the Apostles; and he related to them how Saul had seen the Lord in the road, that He had spoken to him and how he had boldly preached in the Name of Jesus in Damascus. And he was with them in Jerusalem, coming and going, speaking freely in the Name of the Lord. He spoke and debated with the Hellenists, who tried to kill him. But the brothers knew about this and led him to Caesarea[2] and they got him to leave for Tarsus[3].

Vision and Cornelius's embassy. Peter explained what had happened. The Apostles and brothers who were in Judea knew that the Gentiles had also received the word of God. And when Peter went up to Jerusalem, the Jews[4] argued with him, saying: "Why have you entered into the house of uncircumcised men and eaten with them?" Then Peter started to explain to him by

---

1. (Hebrew = Son of prophecy) He introduced Paul to the Apostles and accompanied him on some journeys.
2. Capital of Roman Palestine.
3. Paul's homeland in Asia Minor.
4. In the house of Cornelius, centurion from the Italian cohort.

order, saying: "I was in the city of Joppa[1], praying, when I had an exstatic vision: An object like a big piece of canvas came down, suspended from the four points of the sky, and reached me. I stared at it, examining it, and saw the quadrupeds of the earth, and the beasts, the reptiles and the birds of the sky[2]. And I also heard a voice which said to me: 'Get up, Peter, kill and eat.' But I said: "Absolutely not, Lord; because nothing profane or impure has ever entered my mouth.' But the voice from the sky replied for a second time. 'Do not call impure what God has purified.' This was repeated three times, and everything was again snatched out of the sky. And then they came to the house where I was staying, three men sent from the Cesarea. And the Spirit told me to go with them without doubt. The six brothers came with me and we entered the house of the man in question. And he told us how he had seen and angel standing in his house, and that the angel had said to him, 'Sent Jope to fetch Simon, whose surname is Peter, who will tell you some words by which you and your family will be holy.' And when I started to talk, the Holy Spirit came down upon them, as it had done before upon us. And I remembered these words of the Lord, 'John baptized with water, but you will be baptized with the Holy Spirit.' So God gave them the same gift that He gave to us because they believed in the Lord Jesus, how could I oppose him?" When they heard my words they remained silent and glorified God, saying, "Therefore also the gentiles have been granted penitence in life by God."

The Church of Antioch. Those who had been dispersed by the persecution which arose regarding Stephen, arrived as far as Phenice and Cyprus and Antioch, preaching only to the Jews. But amongst them there were some Cypriots and Cyrenians[3], who also addressed the Greeks when they arrived in Antioch, proclaiming the Lord Jesus. The hand of the Lord was with them, and a great number believed and were converted to the Lord. This came to the attention of the Church in Jerusalem, and

---

1. Palestinian city on the coast.
2. Animals prohibited by the Law.
3. From Cyprus and Cyrene, in Northern Africa.

they sent Barnabas to Antioch. When they arrived and saw the grace of God, he rejoiced and exhorted everybody to persevere with a firm heart, faithful to the Lord; because he was a good man and full of the Holy Spirit and of faith; and a great crowd were united with the Lord. He went to Tarsus in search of Saul, and, having found him, he took him to Antioch. And they were in that Church for a whole year, and instructed many people; and it was in Antioch where the disciples first received the name of Christians[1].

Herod Agripa persecutes the Church[2]. In those times King Herod arrested some of the Church members in order to mistreat them. He had James, John's brother, put to the sword. And seeing that the Jews were pleased about this, he also had Peter arrested. They were the days of the unleavened bread. And once he had been arrested, he imprisoned him and ordered him to be kept in custody, intending to make him appear before the people after the Passover. Whilst Peter was in custody in this way, the Church prayed to God for him without respite.

Peter's liberation. The same night that Herod was going to make him appear, Peter was asleep between two soldiers, tied with chains, and the sentinels kept guard on the prison door. And behold, the Angel of the Lord appeared, with a shining light in the room. The Angel touched Peter on the side, woke him up, saying: "Get up right away." And the chains fell from his hands. The Angel said to him: "Gird yourself and put on your sandals." This he did. And he added: "Wrap yourself in your cloak and follow me." Peter went out and followed him; and he didn't know whether what the angel was doing was real, or whether he was taking part in a vision. They went by the first guard, and the second, and arrived at an iron gate which gave on to the city, which opened by itself. They went out and went down one street, and suddenly the Angel left him.

Then Peter, coming back to his senses, said: "Now I really know that the Lord has sent his Angel, and has snatched me

---

1. Followers of Christ.
2. He lived scandalously, and had links with a secret organization opposed to Christian expansion.

away from the hand of Herod, and from everything the Jewish people was hoping for." And, after reflecting, he went to the house of Mary, John Mark's mother[1], where many were congregated in prayer. At daybreak there was a big commotion amongst the soldiers about what had come of Peter.

PROPAGATION OF THE GOSPEL AMONGST THE GENTILES

SAINT PAUL'S FIRST JOURNEY

Election of Saul and Barnabas. There were prophets and doctors in the Church of Antioch: Barnabas and Simon, who was called Niger, Lucius of Cyrene, Manaen, who had been raised with Herod the tetrarch, and Saul. Whilst they were celebrating the cult of the Lord and fasting, the Holy Spirit said: "Take aside Barnabas and Saul for the work for which I have called them." Then, having prayed and fasted, they put their hands on them and took their leave[2].

In Cyprus. Therefore they, sent by the Holy Spirit, went down to Seleucia, from where they sailed to Cyprus. And when they came to Salamin, they preached the word of the Lord in the synagogues of the Jews.

In Antioch in Pisidia[3]. Having set sail from Pasphos, Paul and his companions arrived at Perga in Pamphylia. But John[4] left them and returned to Jerusalem. They continued their journey and from Perga they went to Antioch of Pisidia. On the Sabbath they entered the synagogue and sat down: After reading from the Law and the Prophets, the Synagogue chiefs sent for them to say: "Brothers, if you have any word of exhortation for the people, speak."

---

1. The Cenacle. John Mark was related to Barnabas, Paul's companion. He was Saint Paul's secretary in Rome and wrote his Gospel.
2. This liturgical rite seems to be a customary blessing for missionaries setting off on Apostolic journeys.
3. From Paphos, in Cyprus, to Perga in Asia Minor.
4. John Mark.

Paul stood up and, making the signal of silence with his hand, said: "Israelites and those who fear God, listen[1].

Brothers, children of the lineage of Abraham, and those who fear God; this word of salvation has been sent to you. Because the inhabitants of Jerusalem and their chiefs have, without knowing it, fulfilled the words of the prophets which are read every Sabbath; and without having found any reason for his death, they condemned Him and asked Pilate to kill him. And thus was fulfilled what had been written about Him, they took Him down from the wood and put Him in the sepulchre. But God brought him back from the dead;He appeared for many days to those who had gone up with Him from Galilee to Jerusalem, who are now witnesses before the people. And we are proclaiming the Good News: The promise made to our fathers. Know, then, brothers, that by means of Him the remission of sins is announced to you, and whoever believes in Him, is justified by the Law of Moses."

And when they left, they requested him to continue speaking on the same subject on the following Sabbath. Once the meeting was dissolved, many Jews and proselytes who feared God followed Paul and Barnabas, who spoke with them and exhorted them to remain in the grace of God. The following Sabbath almost all the city attended to listen to the word of God.

They preach to the Gentiles. When they saw the crowd, the Jews were filled with jealousy and opposed what Paul was saying with blasphemies. Then Paul and Barnabas said with total freedom: "The word of God has to be announced to you before anybody; but if you reject it, or do not consider yourselves worthy of eternal life, we will go to the Gentiles. That is what the Lord commanded us[2]. When the Gentiles heard this they rejoiced and glorified the word of the Lord, and they believed they were all ordained for eternal life. And the word of the Lord was disseminated over the whole country. But the Jews stirred up the noble and devout women and the principals of the

1. Paul always started off by announcing the Gospel amongst the Jews, in the synagogues.

2. From then on they preached to the Gentiles.

city, and provoked a persecution against Paul and Barnabas and threw them out of their territory[1].

In Lycaonia, Iconium, Lystra and Derbe. In Iconium they also went into the Synagogue of the Jews, and spoke in such a way that a large crowd of Jews and Gentiles was formed. But the Jews, who did not want to believe, excited the Gentiles and set them against the brothers. And as a riot was produced by the Gentiles and the Jews, in league with their rulers, they took to harassing them and stoning them; but they took note and went in search of shelter in the cities of Lycaonia, Lystra and Derbe and their surroundings, where they began to announce the Good News.

In Lystra there was a man crippled in the feet, sitting down; lame from birth, he had never walked. He heard Paul speaking, who looked at him fixedly and, seeing that he had the faith to be cured, said loudly: "Get up and stand up on your feet." And he jumped into the air and started to walk. When they saw what Paul had done, the crowds started to shout in Lycaonian: "The gods, in human form, have come down to us." And they called Barnabas Jupiter and Paul Mercury, because he was the most eloquent. The priest of Jupiter who was at the entrance to the city put bulls adorned with garlands in front of the gates, and, in league with the throngs, wanted to offer a sacrifice[2]. When the Apostles Barnabas and Paul knew, they tore their clothes and threw themselves into the midst of the crowds shouting: "Friends, why are you doing this? We're also men, just like you." Even with these words they only succeeded with great difficulty in preventing the crowd from offering a sacrifice to them.

Then Jews came from Antioch and Iconium who won over the crowd. They stoned Paul, and dragged him out of the city, believing him dead. But, as the disciples had surrounded him,

---

1. The Mosaic Law did not forgive sins like the Law of Grace of the New Alliance, and the Resurrection was the nucleus of their preaching.

2. The cure of the congenitally disabled man awoke a great enthusiasm among the Gentiles and they considered them gods.

he got up and entered the city. The following day he set off for Derbe, accompanied by Barnabas[1].

After having evangelized that city and having made a good number of disciples, they returned to Lystra, Iconium and Antioch, and raised the spirits of the disciples, exhorting them to remain in the faith and telling them that we have to undergo many tribulations to enter into the Kingdom of God. Crossing Pisidia they arrived at Pamphylia; they preached in Perga and disembarked at Antioch.

Return to Antioch in Syria. From there they sailed to Antioch, from where they had set off, commended to the grace of God for the work they had carried out. When they arrived, they congregated the Church and told of everything that God had done through them, and that the door of faith was open to the Gentiles. And they stayed a long time with the disciples.

Council in Jerusalem. But some of those who came down from Judea taught the brothers: "If you are not circumcised according to the rite of Moses, you can't save yourselves." After an altercation and no small discussion, with Barnabas and Paul against them, it was decided that Paul and Barnabas and some of the others would go up to Jerusalem to the Apostles and elders to deal with this matter.

After a long debate, Peter got up and said to them: "Brothers, you know that a long time ago God chose me from amongst you so that the Gentiles would hear the word of the Gospel through my mouth, and believe. Now then, why are you tempting God to put a yoke on the neck of the disciples which neither our fathers nor ourselves have been able to bear? But we believe we are saved by the grace of the Lord Jesus in the same way as them." The whole crowd grew quiet and listened to Barnabas and Paul who related all the prodigies and miracles which God had performed through them amongst the Gentiles.

When they finished, James spoke, saying: "Brothers, listen to me, Simon has related how God wanted from the beginning to take a people for His name from amongst the Gentiles. The

---

1. They returned and encouraged those whom they had won over for Christ and went back to Antioch in Syria.

words of the apostles agree with this. Because of this I consider that we should not trouble those Gentiles who have converted to God, but write to them that they abstain from contaminating idols, from fornication, from strangling and from blood."

Council decree. Then the Apostles and the elders, with all the Church, decided to choose some of them and send them to Antioch with Paul and Barnabas. They wrote to them "Because we and the Holy Spirit have decided not to impose any burden on you greater than these necessary ones: Abstain from sacrifices to idols, from blood and strangled animals and fornication; you will do well to keep away from these things. God be with you." The delegates went down to Antioch, where they gathered the crowd together and delivered the letter. And having read it, they were happy with this message. Paul and Barnabas remained in Antioch, teaching and evangelizing the word of the Lord in association with many others.

SAINT PAUL'S SECOND JOURNEY

Barnabas and Paul separate. After a few days, Paul said to Barnabas: "Let's go back and visit the brothers in all the cities in which we proclaimed the word of the Lord, to see how they are." Paul chose Silas and set off, commended by the brothers to the grace of the Lord. And He crossed Syria and Cilicia, confirming the Churches.

Timothy. He arrived at Derbe[1] and then at Lystra, where there was a disciple called Timothy, son of a Jewish believer and a Greek father. The brothers of Lystra and Iconium gave good testimony of him. Paul wanted him to leave with him. So he took him and circumcised him because of the Jews that were in those places; for they all knew that his father was Greek. And as they went passing through the cities, they recommended them to keep the decrees given by the Apostles and the elders of Jerusalem. The Churches strengthened themselves in the faith and grew in number daily.

---

1. In Asia Minor.

Paul called to Europe. They crossed Phrygia and the territory of Galatia, prevented by the Holy Spirit from announcing the word in Asia. And when they arrived in Mysia, they tried to enter Bithynia, but the Spirit of Jesus did not allow them to. And leaving Mysia on one side, they went down to Troas[1]. And during the night Paul had a vision: A Macedonian, standing, beseeched him: "Come to Macedonia and help us." Immediately after the vision we tried to go on to Macedonia, persuaded that God had called us to evangelize them.

In Philippi. So, setting off from Troas, we went straight to Samothracia, and the following day to Neapolis, and from there to Phillipi, the first city of this part of Macedonia[2], a colony where we remained for a few days. On the Sabbath we went outside the gates, beside the river, where we thought the praying ground was. We sat down and spoke to the women who had assembled. A woman called Lydia, a seller of purple, from the city of Thyatira[3], which feared God, was listening to us. The Lord opened her heart so that she would heed the the things which Paul was saying. After having been baptized with all her family, she begged us: "If you have considered me faithful to the Lord, come and stay in my house." And she obliged us to do so.

The crowd rose up against them and the pretors ordered their clothes to be torn and them to be beaten with sticks. After having rained many blows on them, they put them in the jail, and charged the jailer with guarding them carefully; when he received these orders, he put them in the inner dungeon, and he secured their feet in stocks.

Around midnight, Paul and Silas were praying, singing hymns to God; and the prisoners were listening. And suddenly an earthquake occured, so great that the prison's foundations were shaken, all the doors were immediately opened and all

1. Port on the Aegean Sea, opposite Greece. There he had the vision of the young Macedonian.

2. Greek cities.

3. Roman colony in the region of Lydia. Industrial and commercial centre of Asia Minor.

their chains were loosened. The jailer woke up and, seeing the doors open, thought that the prisoners had fled and drew his sword to kill them. But Paul shouted to him: "Don't hurt yourself, we're all here." He asked for a light, entered and threw himself trembling before Saul and Silas, took them out and said: "Sirs, what must I do to save myself?" They said to him: "Believe in the Lord Jesus and you and your family will be saved." And they announced the word of God to him, and everybody who was in his house. And at that very hour of the night he took them with him, washed their wounds and he and his family were immediately baptized. And taking them up to his house, he put out the table and rejoiced with all his family for having believed in God.

When day broke, the pretors sent the lictors[1] to say to the jailer: "Release these men." The jailer addressed these words to Paul: "The pretors have ordered that you be released. "Leave, then, and go in peace." They left the prison and went into Lydia's house; they saw the brothers, consoled them and went.

In Thessalonica. Passing through Amphipolis and Apolonia, they reached Thessalonica[2], where the Jews had a Synagogue. Paul, according to his custom, introduced himself to them, and debated the Scriptures with them over three Sabbaths, explaining and proving that Christ had to suffer and come back from the dead, and "Christ, he said, is the Jesus that I'm announcing to you." Some of them were convinced and joined up with Paul and Silas, as well as a large crowd of God-fearing Greeks, and a good number of noble women. But the Jews, envious, took hold of some infamous and perverted individuals and provoked disturbances which unsettled the city.

In Berea. The brothers immediately arranged for Paul and Silas to leave during the night for Berea, and as soon as they arrived, they went into the Jews' Synagogue. They were nobler than the ones in Thessalonica and they received the word with all promptness, and examined the Scriptures every day to see whether all these things were true. And many of them believed,

---

1. Ministers of justice.
2. Capital of the province of Macedonia.

as well as some distinguished Greek women and a good number of men[1]. Those who accompanied Paul took him to Athens, and they returned at once with the commission for Silas and Timothy to join up with him as soon as possible.

In Athens[2]. Whilst Paul was waiting for them in Athens, his Spirit was indignant when he contemplated the city full of idols. He debated in the synagogue with the Jews and with those who feared God; and each day with those who were in the market place. Some Epicurean philosophers and Stoics conversed with him, and some said: "What does this charlatan mean?" And others: "He seems to be a preacher of foreign divinities, because he's announcing Jesus and the resurrection." They took him and brought him to the Areopagus, saying: "Can we know what new doctrine you're teaching? Because you're bringing strange things to our ears. And we want to know what it is concerned with." All the Athenians and foreigners who were there entertained themselves by merely uttering or hearing novelties.

Paul in the Areopagus[3]. Paul, standing in the middle of the Areopagus, said: "Athenians, I see that you are the most religious in everything. Indeed, touring your city, and contemplating your sacred monuments, I also found myself in front of an altar with this inscription: 'To the unknown God'. Well then, what you venerate without knowing, is what I am going to proclaim to you. The God who made the world and everything in it, does not, as Lord of heaven and earth, dwell in Temples built by the hands of man[4]. Neither is He served by human hands, as if He needed anything, He who gives life, breath, everything, to all of us. He has made all mankind from one single man, to live on all the earth's surface, pre-establishing the times and frontiers of their Dwelling, so that they seek God; and to see if, gropingly searching for Him, they

---

1. After an initial success, they had to abandon the city, and they took them to Athens, the goal to which Paul aspired.
2. In Athens, empire of knowledge and the arts, he saw that its streets were full of idols.
3. The Areopagus was a place or centre where philosophical novelties were discussed. Tribune coveted by Paul.
4. May the Creator be known by his works.

could find Him; although He is not far from each and every one of us, since we live, and move in Him and are in Him[1]; as some of your poets have also said: 'Because we are of his lineage'. But if we come from God's lineage, we mustn't think that divinity is like gold or silver or stone, or sculpture made by the art and ingenuity of man. So God, passing over times of ignorance, is now communicating to men that everybody, everywhere repents, since a day for judging the universe has been set by means of a man, whom He has designated and accredited to everybody by bringing him back from the dead." When they heard him talking about the "resurrection of the dead", some poked fun and others said: "We shall hear about this another time." And so Paul took his leave of them. Some, however, joined him and believed, among them Dionysius the Areopagite and a woman called Damaris, and others.

In Corinth[2]. After this Paul left Athens[3] and went to Corinth. There he met a Jew called Aquila, a native of Pontus, who had just arrived from Italy with his wife Priscilla, because Claudius had decreed that all the Jews should leave Rome. Paul made friends with them, and, as they had the same work, he stayed and worked in their house; for they devoted themselves to making tents. Every Sabbath he debated in the Synagogue and won over Jews and Greeks. But when Silas and Timothy arrived from Macedonia, Peter dedicated himself exclusively to preaching the word and testifying to the Jews that Jesus was the Messiah. As they contested this and blasphemed, he shook them by their clothes and said to them: "May your blood fall on your heads; I am clean; from now on I will go to the Gentiles." He departed from there and went to the house of somebody called Titus Justus, a God-fearing man, whose house was next to the Synagogue. Crispus, the chief of the Synagogue, and all his family believed in the Lord, and many of the Corinthians who had heard Paul believed, and were baptized. One night the Lord said in a vision to Paul: "Don't fear, speak and don't hold your

---

1. That He lives amongst us, not in idols, and that He sent His son Christ.
2. A very flourishing city, the capital of Achaia, to the south of Athens.
3. In Athens he understood that human wisdom was foolish in the eyes of God.

tongue, because I am with you, and nobody will try to make you commit evil, for I have numerous people in this city." And he stayed there a year and six months, teaching the word of God among them[1].

Return to Antioch in Syria. They arrived at Ephesus. He disembarked in Caesarea and went up to greet the Church, and then went down to Antioch.

He was there for some time and again toured the territory of Galatia and Phrygia, giving strength to all the disciples.

SAINT PAUL'S THIRD JOURNEY

Paul in Ephesus[2]. And while Apollos[3] was in Corinth, Paul arrived in Ephesus, after having toured the mountain regions.

He preaches to the Gentiles. Paul went into the Synagogue, where he spoke with total freedom for three months, debating and straining to convince them about the Kingdom of God. But, as some of them were hardened and did not want to believe, he drew apart from them, separated the disciples and went to teach daily in the school of Tyrannus[4]. This lasted for two years, in such a way that all the inhabitants of Asia, both Jews and Gentiles, heard the word of God.

After these events, Paul proposed crossing Macedonia and Achaia and going to Jerusalem. After going there, he said: "I must also visit Rome." He sent two of his collaborators, Timothy and Erastus, and he stayed some time in Asia.

Across Macedonia and Greece. After Paul called the disciples and exhorted them, he said goodbye to them and set off for Macedonia. He toured those regions exhorting them with many words. After that he arrived in Greece, where he spent three months. When he was going to embark for Syria, the Jews set a trap for him, and he decided to return to Macedonia.

In Miletus. Going ahead in the ship, we went to Assos, where we had to collect Paul; the following day we arrived in

---

1. And working with his hands.
2. Ephesus was an Ionic city, an opulent sea port in Asia.
3. Alexandrine Jew, brilliant orator and scholar.
4. Public school.

Miletus. Because Paul had resolved to go past Ephesus, so as not to waste time in Asia, for he wanted to hurry to be in Jerusalem for the day of the Pentecost, if it was possible. From Miletus, he sent a message to the elders of the Church in Ephesus[1].

Sermon to the priests of Ephesus. When they arrived, he said to them: "You know how I behaved with you at all times, from the first day that I came to Asia. Serving the Lord in all humility and with tears, in the middle of so many trials which have befallen me due to the Jews' traps. I never refrained from announcing and teaching you in public and in private, wherever I could be useful, testifying to Jews and Greeks on conversion to God and faith in Our Lord Jesus. And now, look, I am going to Jerusalem, chained by the Holy Spirit, without knowing what will happen to me there, only knowing that the Holy Spirit testifies to me that prisons and trials await me in every city[2]. But I do not bother about my life, nor do I consider it noteworthy, apart from finishing my career and following the ministry which I have received from the Lord Jesus, of proclaiming the Good News of the grace of God. And now I know that none of you through whom I have passed preaching the Kingdom will see me again.

Keep watch over yourselves, and over the entire flock, of which the Holy Spirit has made you like bishops to pasture the Church of God, which He has acquired with His own blood. I know that after my departure cruel wolves will insinuate themselves amongst you, and they will not pardon the flock[3]. And that men will emerge from amongst you yourselves, teaching perverse doctrines in order to drag the disciples away with them. Because of this, keep watch, remembering that for three years I have not ceased to exhort each one of you with tears. And now I commend you to God and the word of His grace, to Him who can build and give you the inheritance with

---

1. Passing through on the way to Jerusalem, to bid farewell.
2. Taking leave of them definitively, he made the final recommendations.
3. The most affecting for Paul was the foreseeing of false brothers who would lead many astray.

all the sanctified ones. I have never desired silver, gold or clothes from anybody. You know very well that these hands have satisfied my needs and those of my companions. I have always shown that you must work this way to help the weak, remembering the words of the Lord Jesus, for He said, 'There is more blessing in giving than in receiving.' After saying this, he kneeled down and prayed with them. They bursted into tears and embraced Paul. They kissed him, so sad did they feel because of his leaving. And they accompanied him to the ship[1]."

Paul in Jerusalem. When we arrived in Jerusalem, the brothers welcomed us joyfully. The following day Paul went with us to James's house, where all the elders were congregated. After greeting them, he related, one by one, all the things which God had done among the Gentiles by means of his ministry.

PAUL IN PRISON IN JERUSALEM, CAESAREA AND ROME

Paul in prison. When seven days had almost gone by, the Jews from Asia, having seen him in the Temple, stirred up all the mob, and grabbed hold of him, shouting: "Israelites, help us; this is the man who goes preaching everywhere and to everybody against the people, against the Law, against this place[2]." Whilst they were trying to kill him, the tribune[3] of the Cohort[4] was informed that all Jerusalem was rioting; he immediately took some soldiers and centurions and ran down towards them; and then they stopped harassing Paul when they saw the tribune and the soldiers. Then the tribune approached him and seized hold of him.

---

1. They sailed from Milet to Rodhe. They turned round Cyprus and headed for Tyrus, where they greeted their brothers. Then Ptolemaida and Cesarea, Roman capital of Palestine.
2. And he had introduced his Greek companions into the temple.
3. The tribune was Claudius Lisia, who had 2,000 soldiers under his command in the Antonia Tower.
4. A Cohort was one-tenth of a Legion, or rather 6 hundred.

When he reached the steps he had to be carried on the soldiers' backs as a consequence of the violence of the rabble. Because all the people came behind, shouting: "Kill him!"

The Jews' fury. The Roman citizen. "Take this man away from the world, because he is not worthy to live[1]." As they continued shouting and grabbing his clothes and throwing dust in the air, the tribune ordered him to be put into the fortress, and told them to punish him with lashes to find out why they were shouting against him in that way. But when they were going to bind him with thongs, Paul said to the tribune who was there: "Is it lawful to whip a Roman citizen without even judging him[2]?" When the centurion heard this, he went out to tell the tribune, saying: "What are you going to do? This man's a Roman." The tribune went and said to him: "Tell me, are you a Roman?" Paul replied: "Yes." And the tribune answered: "I attained this right of citizenship with a great sum of money." And Paul said: "I have it from birth." At that very moment those who were going to torture him, backed away. And the tribune was afraid when he realized that he was Roman and that he had chained him up. The next day, wishing to ascertain what the Jews accused him of, he untied him and ordered the High Priests and all the Sannedrin to convene. Then he brought Paul down and made him appear before them.

Before the Sannedrin. Paul, knowing that one part of the Sannedrin were Sadducees and the other Pharisees, shouted like this: "Brothers, I am a Pharisee, the son of Pharisees; I am judged by the hope and the resurrection of the dead[3]." When he said this, a debate sprung up between the Pharisees and the Sadducees, and the crowd was divided: Because the Sadducees say that there is no resurrection, nor angel, nor spirit, whilst the Pharisees accept these things. This caused a great uproar. Some scribes who supported the Pharisees got up and energetically

---

1. The hatred that they had for Paul as a traitor, exacerbated by religious fanaticism, had reached paroxysm. If the tribune had not intervened they would have torn him apart.

2. Paul appeals as a Roman citizen, who could not be condemned without having been judged beforehand.

3. Paul divided them.

affirmed: "We don't find any wickedness in this man, and what if the spirit or an angel has spoken to him?" As the tumult grew bigger and bigger, the soldiers were ordered to come down, take him out of their midst and lead him to the fortress, out of fear that they would tear Paul apart.

Plot to kill Paul. The following night the Lord appeared to him and said to him: "Be encouraged, for as you have given testimony about Me in Jerusalem, it is fitting that you do the same in Rome." At daybreak, the Jews called a meeting, in which they commited themselves under oath not to eat or drink until they had killed Paul. But the son of Paul's sister, who knew about the plot, appeared, entered the fortress and warned Paul. Paul called one of the centurions and said: "Take this youth to the tribune, because he has something to inform him about." He took him with him, took him to the tribune and said: "The prisoner Paul has called me and requested me to bring you this youth, who has something to say to you." The tribune, taking him by the hand and drawing him aside, asked him: "What have you got to say to me?" And he said: "That the Jews have decided to ask you to bring Paul down to the Sannedrin tomorrow, with the pretext of of examining his case in greater depth. Don't believe it, because more than forty from amongst them are setting a trap for him, and they've sworn not to eat or drink until they've killed him; and now they're prepared and only await your promise." And the tribune dismissed the youth and ordered him: "Don't tell anybody that you've revealed this to me."

Paul and the procurator Felix. Then he called two centurions and said to them: "Prepare two hundred soldiers, seventy horsemen and two hundred lancers for the third hour of the night, to go to Caesarea." And they also provided them with horses to take Paul, on horseback, safe and well to the procurator Felix[1]. Felix, who had detailed knowledge of things refering to the Way[2], defered the case, saying: "When the

---

1. The procurator was the governor of a minor Roman province which posed special difficulties, like Judea: They were Pilate, Felix and Festus.

2. Way = Christian religion.

tribune Lysias comes down, I shall examine your case in depth." And he ordered the centurion to keep him in custody, permit him some liberty and not forbid any of his people from tending to him. After two years, Porcius Festus succeeded Felix, and, wanting to ingratiate himself with the Jews, Felix left Paul in prison.

Paul, judged by Festus. Festus went up from Caesarea to Jerusalem, three days after having arrived in the province. The High Priests and Jewish chiefs presented themselves to accuse Paul, and asked for him, as a favour, to be brought to Jerusalem, whilst they laid traps for killing him on the road. But Festus replied that Paul was in custody in Caesarea, and that he himself had to leave shortly. "Therefore, let the foremost among you come down with me and accuse him, if there is any crime in this man." And Festus did not stay any more than eight or ten days among them; afterwards he went down to Caesarea; the following day he sat on the tribunal and ordered Paul to be brought. When he appeared, the Jews who had come down from Jerusalem surrounded him, making many serious accusations which they could not prove; while Paul defended himself by saying: "I have committed no offence, against either the Jewish Law, or the temple, or Caesar." But Festus, wanting to ingratiate himself with the Jews, asked Paul: "Do you want to go up to Jerusalem and be judged before me there for these things?" And Paul said: "I am before Caesar's tribunal, where I must be judged[1]. I have done absolutely no injury to the Jews, as you very well know. If I have committed some injustice or done something worthy of death, I do not refuse to die; but if there's nothing in what these people are accusing me, nobody can hand me over to them. I appeal to Caesar." Then Festus, after having spoken to the council, replied: "You've appealed to Caesar; to Caesar you will go."

Sailing to Rome. When it was decided to embark for Italy, they handed Paul and some other prisoners over to a centurion

---

1. The Roman citizen could not be punished and judged except by the Emperor, to whom he had the right to appeal as a supreme court.

called Julius, from the Augusta cohort. And we boarded a ship from Adramyttium[1], which was heading for the coasts of Asia.

The storm. And a south wind having arisen, they thought that the conditions were appropriate for putting their plan into effect; they weighed anchor and passed close by Crete. After a short while a hurricane was unleashed on the island, the so-called Euroclydon[2]. The ship was caught up and, not being able to resist the wind, we let her drive, and we were caught up in such a strong storm that we now had no hope of coming out of it alive.

But they struck a salient beaten by the water on both sides, the ship ran aground, and the prow lodged itself there and did not move, whilst the stern broke up due to the violence of the waves.

In Malta. Once we were saved, we knew that the island was called Malta[3]. The natives treated us with an uncommon humanity. They gave us many honors as tributes and, when we left, they provided for our necessities.

After three months we embarked in an Alexandrine ship, and we headed for Rome in this way[4]. The brothers from Rome, notified of our arrival, came to meet us as far as the Apii Forum and the Three Taverns[5]; when he saw them, Paul gave thanks to God and took heart. When we entered Rome, Paul was allowed to stay in a private house, with a soldier who kept guard over him.

Paul stayed for two years in a rented house, and welcomed all those who came to him; he preached the Kingdom of God and taught of things concerning The Lord, Jesus Christ, with complete liberty and without any obstacle.

---

1. Small port in Misia, Asia Minor.
2. Which would sweep them westward.
3. Malta, halfway towards Rome, was the site of the shipwreck.
4. They sailed along the Italian coast.
5. Outpost and inn on the Via Appia, 48 kilometers from Rome.

EPISTLES OF SAINT PAUL

LETTER TO THE ROMANS

INTRODUCTION

Thanksgiving. He reveals his desire to go to Rome. Firstly I give thanks to my God through Jesus Christ for all of you, because your faith is known throughout the world[1].

DOGMATIC PART

Corruption and punishment of paganism[2]. And so God delivered them to the concupiscences of their hearts, to impurity, until they dishonored their own bodies, bartered truth for lie, and worshipped and gave homage to creatures rather than the Creator, who is blessed throughout the centuries. Amen.

And as they did not endeavour to have complete knowledge of God, God delivered to them depraved minds to do unfitting things, full of all injustice, malice, perversity, covetousness, evil; covered in hate and homicide, abhorrers of God, insolent,

---

1. The knowledge of God through the works of the Creation implies the obligation to serve Him.
2. And so God punished them for having strayed from Him with idolatry.

disdainful, arrogant, inventors of evils, disobedient to their parents, insensitive, unloyal, without love and without pity; those who know God's righteous decree and do such things are worthy of death, and not only do these things, but take pleasure in anybody else who does them[1].

The Gentiles have the Law, by which they will be judged. Because it is not those who hear the Law who are righteous before God, but those who comply with the Law who will be justified. So when the Gentiles who have not got the Law, naturally practice the things of the Law, not having the Law, they are in themselves the Law, showing the work of the Law written in their hearts[2], as will be seen on the day when God judges the secrets of men, according to my Gospel, through Jesus Christ.

The Jews who break the Law bear the greatest blame. But if you call yourself a Jew and trust in the Law and glory in God, and know His will and know how to discern what is best, instructed by the Law, and you presume to be a guide for the blind, a light for those who are in darkness, an educator of the ignorant, a teacher of children, having, in the Law, the norm for the science of the truth; you, then, who teach others, do you not teach yourselves. Because "the name of God is blasphemed amongst the Gentiles because of you", according to what is written.

Abraham justified by faith without the works of the Law[3]. What will we say, then, that our father Abraham obtained, as regards the flesh? Yes, indeed, Abraham was justified by virtue of the works of the Law, and glory is due to him, but not before God. What, then, does the Scripture say?: "Abraham believed in God[4] and this was computed as justice."

---

1. They did not comply with the Lord of God and He deliveeed them to their baser insticts and to corrupt customs.
2. The pagans have the Commandments of the Law of God written in their hearts.
3. The Mosaic Law comes after Abraham. He is not justified by the Law, but by obedience to God. By his faithfulness.
4. Practical faith: he believed and obeyed.

The work of Adam and of Jesus Christ. Therefore, in the same way as sin entered the world through a man, and through sin, death, and in this way death passed on to all men, because they all sinned[1]... So sin was already in the world prior to the Law; but sin is not imputed when there is no Law; however, death reigned from Adam to Moses even on those who hadn't sinned, in accordance with Adam's transgression, who is the figure for the one who was to come...

But the gift was not like the crime; because if everybody died as the result of a single man's crime, much more so did the grace of God and the gift through grace of one single man, Jesus Christ, superabound in everybody.

If, then, due to one single man's crime, death reigned because of this individual's conduct, much more so will they who receive the superabundance of grace and the gift of justice reign in life by means of a single individual, Jesus Christ.

Dead to sin, let's walk with new life, living united with Christ through baptism[2]. What will we say, then? We went, then, sepulchred along with Him by baptism in death, so that, as Christ was brought back from the dead by the glory of the Father, let us likewise also walk in a new life.

But if we have arrived to be one and the same life with Him through a death like His, we shall also be it through a similar resurrection. We know this, that our old man has been crucified with Him so that the body of sin may be destroyed, in order that we may not be slaves of sin, since whoever dies remains free of sin. And if we die with Christ, we believe that we shall also live with Him, knowing that Christ, brought back from the dead, does not now die; death now has no dominion over Him. In reality, he who died in Him, died to sin for once and for all, but he who lives, lives for God. Thus consider yourselves also dead to sin, but alive for God in Jesus Christ.

---

1. Through original sin.
2. We are dead to sin through Baptism and will come back to the supernatural Life of Grace, which makes us children of God, brothers of Jesus Christ and inheritors of Heaven.

The Christians free from the Law of Moses[1]. O brothers, do you not know —for I speak to those who know the Law— that the Law has dominion over man whilst he lives? For when we are in the flesh, the passions of sins, by means of the Law, they were working in our members to produce fruits of death. But now we are disconnected from the Law of death to which we were bound, in order that we serve in the novelty of the spirit and not in the old age of the letter.

Opposition between the flesh and spirit[2]. As I want to do good, so I find this law: that evil puts itself before me; because I delight in the Law of God according to the inner man; but I see another law in my members which struggles against the law of my reason and enslaves me to the law of sin which is in my members. Unlucky me! Who will free me from this body of death? Let thanks be given to God by Jesus Christ our Lord. In the same way that I myself serve the Law of God with my reason, but the law of sin with my flesh.

Spiritual life as opposed to that of those who follow the flesh. Now there is no damnation for those who are with Jesus Christ. For the Law of the Spirit of Life rid you of the Law of Sin and Death. Certainly, what was imposible for the Law, for she was weakened by the flesh, God did it sending his own Son in flesh similar to the flesh of sin and damned because of sin, the same sin in flesh, so that the justice of the Law was fulfiled in us, those who walk guided by spirit, not by flesh. For those who follow the spirit think about the spirit, and those who follow the flesh, think about the flesh; the thought of flesh is death, but the thought of the spirit is life and peace. Those who life following the flesh cannot please the Lord, but you do not follow the flesh, but the spirit, if God's Spirit is in you; for the one who does not have it, is not His. And if the Spirit that resuscitated Jesus from among the dead lives in you, he will give life alto to your mortal bodies by means of his Spirit that is

---

1. The Mosaic Law, the Cult, the Sacrifices, all has expired before the Law of Grace, of the New Alliance.
2. The law of the flesh, with its concupiscences, fights against that of the spirit, but with the Grace of God we triumph.

in you. Therefore, brothers, we depend on the Spirit, not on the flesh, for if you follow the flesh you shall die, but if you follow the Spirit you will kill the works of the body and therefore you will live.

The Christian is the son of God and inheritor through the Spirit of God. Indeed, whoever are guided by the Spirit of God are God's children, because you did not receive the spirit of slavery to fall once more into fear, you rather received the spirit of adopted children which makes us exclaim: Abba! Father! The same spirit gives testimony with our spirit that we are the children of God. And, if they are children, they are also inheritors[1]: inheritors of God, co-inheritors of Christ, if it is the case that we suffer jointly with Him, so as to be also glorified jointly.

Hope of the children of God and all creation. I consider, in effect, that the sufferings of the present time cannot be compared with the glory which is to be revealed in us[2] because creation is waiting in earnest expectation the revelation of the children of God, since creation was subject to vanity, not of its own will, but for he who subjected, with the hope that creation will be freed from the slavery of corruption to be admitted to the liberty of the glory of the children of God[3].

We know, in effect, that all creation groans and has labor pains up to the present moment, and not only creation, but also we who have the news of the Spirit groan within, waiting for filial adoption, the redemption of our body, because we were saved in hope.

The help of the Holy Spirit and predestination. The Spirit likewise also comes to the aid of our frailty, because we do not know what to ask for in order to pray fittingly; because the same Spirit intercedes for us with ineffable groans.

And we know that God orders all things for the good of those who love Him, for the good of those who have been called

---

1. If we remain Children of God, we are inheritors of God and will live with Him for ever.
2. It is necessary to join our pain to Christ's suffering.
3. Creation itself, subject to a curse by Original sin, will also be liberated.

according to His design. Because He also predestined those whom He knew beforehand to be consistent with the image of His Son, so that He may be the first-born of many brothers; and He also called those whom He predestined; He also justified those whom He called; He also glorified those whom He justified.

Securitty of salvation. What will we say, then, to this? If God is for us, who is against us[1]? He who did not even pardon His own Son, but handed Him over for all of us, how will He not freely give us everything with Him? Who will bring an accusation against the children of God? As it is God who justifies, who will be the one who condemns? Jesus Christ, the one who died, or rather came back to life, is the one at God's right hand, and the one who intercedes for us?

Who will separate us from the love of Christ? Tribulation or anguish, persecution or hunger, or nakedness or danger or the sword? It is written accordingly: "For your cause we are delivered to death all day long; we are considered as sheep destined for the slaughterhouse."

But we emerge triumphant in all these things by means of Him who loved us.

Paul's feelings for the Jews. I say the truth in Christ, I do not lie, and my conduct in the Holy Spirit gives testimony with me of how great is my sadness and continuous the pain in my heart[2]. For I myself would wish to be anathema for Christ in favour of my brothers, inherent to me according to the flesh, who are Israelites, of whom are filial adoption and glory and alliances and legislation and the cult and promises, of whom also are the patriarchs and those who proceed with regard to the flesh of Christ, who is above all things[3], may God be blessed throughout the centuries. Amen.

Neither will the reprobation of Israel be perpetual. For, brothers, I do not want you to be ignorant of this mystery —so that you are not presumptuous about yourselves—: that a

---

1. If God has freed us from sin and death, He will glorify us.

2. Paul's heart is Christ's heart.

3. Love of Christ is above everything and unites us to Him.

toughness has come to a part of Israel, to such an extent that the majority of the Gentiles have entered; and so the whole of Israel will saved, as is written:

"The Liberator will come from Zion, will banish the impieties
    of Jacob.
And this will be My alliance with them, when I erase their
    sins[1]."

As for the Gospel, they are enemies for your good, but as regards the election, they are loved in the sight of their parents, because the gifts and vocation of God are irrevocable.

Profundity of God's judgement. Hymn to His wisdom. Oh profundity of the richness and wisdom and knowledge of God! How incomprehensible are His judgements and inscrutable His ways!

MORAL PART

Compendium of the Christian life. And so I beseech you, brothers, by the mercy of God, to offer up your bodies as living, holy sacrifice, pleasing to God: this is the cult which you must offer. And don't adapt yourselves to this world; on the contrary, reform yourselves for the renovation of your understanding so that you know how to distinguish the will of God; the good, the pleasing to Him, the perfect.

Charity with everybody. Let love be without hypocrisy; hating evil, apply yourselves to good; loving each other with brotherly love; progressing towards mutual esteem; do not be lazy in the fulfillment of duty; be fervent of spirit, serving the Lord; joyful in hope, suffering in trials, constant in prayer; attending to the needs of the saints, endeavoring to practice hospitality.

Bless those who persecute you; bless and don't curse. Rejoice with those who rejoice, cry with those who cry. Be unanimous amongst yourselves in your feelings; not arrogant,

---

1. Thanks to them, we obtain forgiveness for our sins and the Lord's mercy.

but accomodating to the humble. "Don't be wise in your opinion." Don't repay anyone evil with evil: "trying for good before all men[1]". If it's possible, as far as it depends on you, be at peace with all men. Beloved, don't avenge yourselves, rather give way to God's punishment, for it is written: "Vengeance is mine. I shall pay, says the Lord." In such a way that if your enemy is hungry, give him something to eat; if he's thirsty, give him something to drink, so that if you do this you will pile up lighted firebrands on his head. Don't let yourself be overcome by evil; on the contrary, overcome evil with good.

Love, the plenitude of the commandments[2]. Don't owe anybody anything, except mutual love; for he who loves his neighbor, fulfills the Law. Because: "You will not commit adultery; you will not kill; you will not steal; you will not bear false witness; you will not covet", and if there is any other precept, it is reduced to this thought: "You will love your neighbor as yourself." Love doesn't harm the neighbour; and so the plenitude of the Law is love.

Mutual duties between the strong and weak in faith. Because none of you lives for himself alone, and none of you dies for himself alone. For if we live, we live for the Lord; and if we die, we die for the Lord. And so, live or die, we are of the Lord. Because Christ died for this and came back to life, to reign over the living and dead[3].

But you, why do you judge your brother? or why do you despise your brother? We all have to present ourselves before God's tribunal. Therefore, each one of us will give an account of himself to God.

Mutual tolerance or comprehension of Christ's example. We, the strong, must suffer the deficiencies of the weak and not be pleased with ourselves. Each one of us endeavours to please his neighbor, for his benefit and edification.

---

1. Paul presents us the Christian renovation program, basing it on love for and service to others.
2. Christian charity obtains its plenitude in the love of God.
3. We are of God in life and death.

For whatever things were written before, were written to teach us[1]; so that we conserve hope through the patience and consolation of the Scriptures. And may the God of patience and consolation grant the same opinion in Jesus Christ, so that you can give glory to God, the Father of our Lord Jesus Christ, with one heart and one voice.

EPILOGUE

The Apostle's personal news. Excuses for having written. For my part I am convinced, brothers, that you are full of good intentions and all kinds of knowledge to enable you to notify each other.

Projects for voyages to Jerusalem and Spain. This has prevented me many times from coming to you, for I have wanted to visit you for many years, and when I go to Spain[2] I hope to pass by and see you, and to be accompanied there by you, after having enjoyed your company for a while.

Now, however, I'm going to Jerusalem to help the holy, because Macedonia and Achaia have resolved to make a collection among those holy men in Jerusalem who are poor. And they have decided this because they consider themselves in debt to them, for if the Gentiles have participated in their spiritual goods, they must in their turn serve them with material ones. And so, once this is finished, when the collection made has been delivered to them, I shall go to Spain, and pass through. I know that if I come to you, I shall come with the fulness of Christ's blessing.

He asks for prayers. Brothers, I ask you, by our Lord Jesus Christ and the love of the Holy Spirit, that you fight with me, praying to God for me, so that I can defend myself from the unbelievers in Judea, and so that the mission which I'm taking to Jerusalem proves gratifying to the holy men.

May the God of peace be with you all. Amen.

---

1. Whatever things have been written, are done so for our good.
2. The Apostle could fulfill his wish to come to Spain when He was set free, as tradition assures.

Exhortation that they take precautions against false doctors. Greetings of those who are with him. And, brothers, I beseech you not to lose sight of those who cause divisions[1] and scandals against the doctrine which you learnt, and draw away from them; because they do not serve our Lord Christ, but their stomachs, and they deceive the hearts of the simple with sweet and pleasant words.

My collaborator Timothy, and my relatives Lucius, Jason and Sosipater, greet you.

---

1. The holy Apostle alerts his disciples against the false doctors and prophets who wreak havoc in the Church.

1st EPISTLE TO THE CORINTHIANS

PROLOGUE

I give thanks to God continually for you due to the grace of God. He will keep you irreproachable until the end, on the day of our Lord Jesus Christ. God is faithful, for which reason you were called to the communion of his Son, Jesus Christ, our Lord.

HE REPROVES ABUSES

Parties in Corinth[1]. I exhort you, brothers, in the name of our Lord Jesus Christ, to have the same language and have no divisions among you, but to conserve harmony in thought and opinion. Because, my brothers, the people from Chloe have mentioned discords among you. I refer to what each of you say: "I am from Paul, I'm from Apollus, I'm from Cephas, I'm from Christ." Is Christ divided[2]? Was Paul crucified for you, or have you been baptized in my name? For Christ did not send me to baptize, but to evangelize, not with literary artifices in order not to devalue Christ's cross.

---

1. Corinth was the capital of Achaia in Greece, famous in antiquity for its commerce and corrupt customs.
2. From the beginning they had already formed sects. Jesus Christ founded one single Church.

The wisdom of the world and of God. Because the language of the cross is madness for those who perish; but for us, who are saved, it is the power of God. Because the Jews are asking for miracles, and the Greeks are looking for wisdom; but we are preaching the crucified Christ, a scandal for the Jews and madness for the Gentiles; but the power and wisdom of God for those who have been called, Jews or Greeks[1]. For the madness of God is wiser than men, and the weakness of God stronger than men.

If not, brothers, consider your vocation: there are not many wise men according to the flesh, nor many powerful ones, nor many noble ones; but God chose the foolishness of the world to confuse the strong, the evil, the despicable, which is nothing, to annul what is, so that nobody glorifies himself before God[2] You are in Jesus Christ through Him, who became wisdom, justice, sanctification and redemption for us on God's behalf, so that, as is written, "he who glorifies himself, let him glory in the Lord."

Saint Paul's preaching. Brothers, when I came to you, I announced the mystery of God, not with sublimity of word or wisdom; for I have never boasted among you of knowing any other thing apart from Jesus Christ, and Him being crucified. I presented myself amongst you weak, with great fear and great trembling. And my word and my preaching are not based on persuasive discourses of wisdom, but on the demonstration of the spirit and and of power, so that your faith should not be based on human wisdom[3], but on the power of God. We preached wisdom amongst the perfect, not of this world, nor of the princes of this world, who are wiped out.

We preach a divine, mysterious, hidden wisdom, which God predestined for our glory before the centuries[4], and which none of the princes of this world knew. Because if they had known it, they would not have crucified the Lord of glory. And God

---

1. The power of God is infinitely greater than the power of men.
2. The neophytes were coarse.
3. The wisdom of men, in comparison, is foolishness in the eyes of God.
4. We have to carry out the mystery of the Passion and death of Jesus in life, by dying to sin and living the life of Grace.

revealed this to us by means of His Spirit, for the Spirit scrutinizes everything, even divine profundities. What man, indeed, knows the intimate parts of man, except for the spirit of man which is in him? And we have not received the spirit of the world, but the spirit which comes from God, so that we know what God has freely given us.

We are also talking of this, not with language learnt from human wisdom, but learnt from the Spirit, expressing spiritual doctrines in spiritual terms. But the material man does not accept the things of the Spirit of God; they are madness for him and he cannot understand them, since they have to be judged spiritually. The spiritual, on the other hand, judges everything and nobody judges him. Because, who knew the thought of the Lord to be able to teach it? But we possess the thought of Christ.

Dignity and obligations of the preachers. I planted and Apollus watered, but God was the one who caused growth. The ones who plant and water are nothing, without God, who causes growth. [1] The one who plants and the one who waters are the same, and each one will receive his reward according to his work. Don't you know that you are temples of God and that the spirit of God dwells in you. If somebody destroys God's temple, God will destroy him, because the temple of God, which you are, is holy.

True wisdom[2]. Nobody deceives himself. If anybody amongst you thinks that he is holy in the eyes of the world, let him become a fool in order to become wise. Because the wisdom of this world is foolishness before God, as is written: "Surprise the wise men in their astuteness." And furthermore: "The Lord knows how vain are the thoughts of the wise." Therefore, don't let anybody glorify themselves among men, for everything is for you: the world, or life, or death, or the present, or the future, everything is yours, yours from Christ, and Christ from God[3].

---

1. The one who gives life is God.
2. God dwells in us through the mystery of Grace.
3. Everything is yours, but you are from God.

Christ's ministers. Let men have us for ministers of Christ and dispensers of the mysteries of God. Now then, what is requisite in dispensers is faithfulness. It hardly troubles me if I am judged by you or by a human tribunal. Not even I myself judge myself. I don't feel guilty of anything; but I am not justified by this, because the one who judges me is the Lord. So, then, don't judge anything before its time, until the Lord comes, who will illuminate the hiding-places in the darkness and will declare the intentions of hearts[1], and then each will receive the praise due to him from God.

Ay, you're already satiated! You're already rich! You have come to be kings without us! May you reign, so that we reign with you[2]! For I believe that God has presented us, the Apostles, the last, those condemned to death, because we have come to be the spectacle of the world, of the angels and of men. Us, idiots through Christ, you wise in Christ; us weak, you strong; you honest, us despised. Up to now we are suffering hunger, thirst and nakedness. We are beaten and go wandering, and we get tired working with our hands. Insulted, we bless; persecuted, we endure it; defamed, we respond with affection. Until now we have been like the garbage of the world, like everybody's scrap.

Fatherly exhortation. I do not write this to you in order to make you ashamed, but to admonish you as my sons and my beloved. Because even if you had ten thousand teachers in Christ, you would not have many fathers[3], for by means of the Gospel I will engender you in Jesus Christ. I beseech you therefore to imitate me.

The Christians and the pagan tribunals. Or do you not know that the unrighteous will not inherit the Kingdom of God[4]? Do not deceive yourselves; neither fornicators, nor idolatrors, nor adulterers, nor the effeminate, nor sodomites, nor thieves, nor misers, nor drunkards, nor slanderers, nor bandits will inherit the Kingdom of God. And you were some of these,

---

1. Because there is only one judge, Christ.
2. Saint Paul treats his conceited detractors ironically. We are nothing.
3. What is clear is that we only have one father.
4. Dissensions between brothers must be settled.

but you were washed and sanctified and justified in the name of our Lord Jesus Christ and in the Spirit of our God.

Malice of dishonesty. The body is not for fornication, but for the Lord[1], and the Lord for the body. And God brought the Lord back to life and will also bring us back to life with His power. Don't you know that your bodies are members of Christ? And shall I, taking the members of Christ, make them members of a prostitute? Never! Don't you know that whoever joins himself to a prostitute becomes a single body with her? The two wil be —He says— one flesh. But whoever joins himself to the Lord is one single spirit with Him. Flee from fornication: Oh, don't you know that your body is the temple of the Holy Spirit, who dwells in you, the Spirit you received from God and is not yours? They were bought at a high price. So, glorify God in your body.

SOLUTION OF VARIOUS QUESTIONS

Matrimony and virginity. I come now to what you have written me. It is good for a man not to touch a woman; but to avoid fornication, let each one have his wife, and each woman her husband[2]. Let the husband give the wife what is her due, and the wife the same to the husband. The wife is not the mistress of her body, it is the husband; likewise the husband is not the master of his body, it's the wife. Do not abstain from each other for a certain period, if it is not by common agreement to dedicate yourself to prayer, and afterwards go back as before, so that Satan does not tempt you for your incontinence. I say this affably, not as a command. For I would like all men to be like me; but each one has his own grace from God; some in one way, others in another. I say to the celibates and the widows: "It is good for them to stay like me. But, if they cannot keep continence, let them get married. It is better to get married than to get burnt. It is not I, but the Lord, who commands married

---

1. Our body is not ours: it is of the Lord, who created it: It is a member of Christ and will come back to life some day. God must be served in body and soul.

2. It's a duty of the state.

couples that the woman should not separate from her husband[1] —but, if she does separate, then she must not marry or she must reconcile with her husband— and the man must not repudiate the wife.

Virginity is more excellent than marriage[2]. On the subject of those who are virgins, I don't have any precept from the Lord; but I give my advice as somebody who has obtained trustworthiness through the mercy of the Lord. I think it is good for the present need for a man to remain like that. Are you bound to a wife? Don't look for her. But if you do marry, don't sin, and if a young girl gets married, don't sin; but they will experience the tribulationsof of life which I wanted them to be spared. I say to you, then, brothers, that time is short, for it passes on the stage of this world. I want you to be free of preoccupations. The celibate worries about the things of the Lord, and how to please him. The married man worries about the things of the world and how to please his wife; so, he is divided. The unmarried woman and the virgin worry about the things of Lord, and how to be holy physically and spiritually. But the woman who is married worries about the things of this world, and how to please her husband. I say this to you for your own good, not to tie a knot around you, but looking at what is the most perfect and at what facilitates familiarity with the Lord.

Legality of second marriages. The wife is bound for as long as her husband lives; but if the husband dies, she is free to get married with whoever she wants, but in the Lord. But, in my opinion, she will be happier if she stays as she is; and I think also that I have the Spirit of God.

The example of Saint Paul. And so the lord also ordered those to whom He announced to live from the Gospel. But I made absolutely no use of this. For, woe to me if I did not evangelize! If I did this of my own will, I would deserve recompense; but if I do this under command, I fulfill a commission which has been entrusted me. What, then, is my

---

1. Marriage is indissoluble.
2. Virginity is more perfect than marriage for the kingdom of God. It is not a command but a counsel of the Lord to those whom it has been given.

recompense? That, preaching the Gosdpel, I do it freely, without evaluating my rights for evangelization[1]. Free as I am, in fact, of everything, I made myself a servant to everybody so as to gain everything. And with the Jews I became a Jew; with those that are under the Law, I became somebody under it, without it being so, to win those who are under the Law; with the lawless, I became a lawless person, to win them over, I myself not being without the law of God, but under Christ's law. I became weak with the weak, in order to win over the weak; I became all things to all men, in order, in every case, to win over some of them. I do everything for the Gospel, to participate in its goodness.

Don't you know that those who run in the stadium all run, but only one wins the prize. Run so as to win it. But the athletes abstain from everything, and do so to obtain a corruptible crown, but ours is incorruptible. I run, then, not for adventure; I fight, not like somebody who strikes the air, but I discipline my body and enslave it, so that, by preaching to others, I am not disqualified.

Lessons from the history of Israel. Therefore, whoever thinks he stands firm, take care that you don't fall. No temptation has overcome us which is not supplied. God is faithful, and will not allow you to be tempted beyond your strength, but with the temptation He will give you the strength to overcome it.

Imitate me, as I imitate Christ.

Institution of the Eucharist[2]. In effect, I received from the Lord what I conveyed to you: That on the night He was handed over, the Lord Jesus took bread, and, having given thanks, broke it and said: "This is my Body, which is given up for you; do this in My memory." And also, in the same way, with the chalice, after dining, saying: "This chalice is the New

---

1. Those who preach the Gospel and those who serve others, do so disinterestedly as somebody who does God a service in the person of the poor and needy.

2. Paul knew about the Institution of the Eucharist through personal revelation, and from the Apostles themselves.

Testament, in My blood; whenever you drink it, do it in My memory." So, whenever you eat this bread and drink this chalice, announce the death of the Lord until He comes. For this reason, whoever eats the bread and drinks the chalice of the Lord unworthily, will be an offender against the Body[1] and Blood of the Lord[2]. Examine the man, then, and then eat the bread and drink from the chalice. Because whoever eats and drinks without discerning the Body, eats and drinks his own condemnation. Therefore there are many sick and feeble among you, and many die. If we examine ourselves, we would not be condemned. But when we are judged, the Lord corrects us, so that we are not condemned with the world.

Spiritual gifts. Brothers, I don't want you to be ignorant as regards spiritual gifts. There is a diversity of spiritual gifts, but the Spirit is the same; a diversity of ministries, but the same Lord, and a diversity of operations, but the same God who operates everything in everybody. The revelation of the Spirit is given to each person for the common good. And so the spirit gives to one person the word of wisdom; to another, the word of knowledge, after the same Spirit; to another, faith, in the same Spirit; to another, the gift of healing, in the one Spirit; to another, prophecy; to another, discernment of spirits; to another, diversity of tongues, and to another the interpretation of the one and same Spirit, distributing to each one in particular according to His wishes[3].

The body and the members. In the same way that the body is one although it has many members, and all the members of the body, even though there are many, form one body, such is the case with Christ. Because all of us, Jews and Greeks, slaves and freemen, were baptized in one single Spirit to form one single body. And we have drunk from the same Spirit. The members are many, but only one body. The eye cannot say to

---

1. Whoever does not know how to distinguish, or receives it unworthily, in sin, becomes an offender against the Lord's body.
2. Therefore it must be received with a soul clean from sin. Repent, and confess if it's serious.
3. The charismas are supernatural gifts, miracles, cures, for the edification of others.

the hand: I don't need you; nor the head to the feet: I don't need you. Furthermore: the apparently weakest members are the most necessary, and those that seem the basest, we surround with more honor. And it is the case that God formed the body, giving the greatest honor to the least noble, to avoid divisions in the body and so that all the members have mutual concerns. So if one member suffers, all the members suffer with him; if one member is honored, all of them take pleasure.

The mystical body of Christ. Now then, you are the body of Christ, and its members, each one for his part[1]. And so God put the Apostles in the Church in the first place; in the second, the prophets; in third, the doctors; then those who have the power to perform miracles; afterwards, those with the gifts for healing, care, government, for speaking a variety of tongues[2]. Are they all Apostles? Or all prophets? Or all doctors? Do they all have the power to perform miracles? Do they all have the gift of healing? Do they all speak in tongues? Or all interpret them? Aspire to higher gifts[3]. I am going to show you a very much better way.

Hymn to charity. Even though I spoke the tongues of men and angels, if I didn't have charity, I would be like a bronze which resounds or a cymbal which tinkles. Even if I had the gift of prophecy and knew all the mysteries and all science, and even though I had so much faith that it moved mountains, if I didn't have charity, I'd be nothing. And even though I distributed all my goods amongst the poor and delivered my body to the flames, if I didn't have charity, it would be of no use to me.

Characteristics of charity. Charity is patient, is kind, it is not envious, it does not flaunt itself or become conceited; charity does not offend, does not search its own interest, does not get irritated, does not take evil into account; charity does not rejoice at injustice, but rejoices at the truth; it excuses

---

1. We are members of the Mystical Body of Jesus Christ, each one according to the gift received for the edification of others.
2. The charismas are not a sign of saintliness.
3. Without charity we are nothing.

everything, it believes everything, it awaits everything, it tolerates everything.

Eternity of charity. Charity never passes away. Prophecies will disappear, tongues will cease and science will come to an end. Our science is imperfect and so is our prophecy. So, when the perfect arrives, the imperfect will disappear. When I was a child, I spoke like a child, I understood like a child, reasoned like a child. When I grew to be a man, the childish things disappeared. Now we see confusedly, through glass, then, we shall see face to face. Now I know imperfectly, then I shall know as I am known. Now these three virtues remain: faith, hope and charity, but the greatest of these is charity.

So you who also aspire to spiritual gifts, endeavour to abound in them for the edification of the Church.

The resurrection of Christ. Brothers, I appeal to the Gospel which I preached to you, and in which you are persevering, and by which you are saved, if you retain what I preached to you, for in any other way you would have believed in vain. Of course I conveyed to you, in the first place, what I received in my time: that Christ died for our sins, according to the Scriptures; that He was entombed and came back to life on the third day, according to the Scriptures, and that He appeared to Peter and then to the twelve. He also appeared to more than five hundred brothers at one time, of which the majority are still alive, and others have died. Then He appeared to James, afterwards to all the Apostles and after everybody He also appeared to me, as somebody born out of his due time[1]. Because I am the least of the Apostles, unworthy of being called Apostle through having pursued the Church of God. But I am what I am through the grace of God, and the grace of God was not sterile in me, for I have worked more than the rest; but not I, but the grace of God with me. Well, then, both them and I, this is what we preach and what you have believed.

Union between the resurrection of Christ and ours. If it is preached, then, that Christ came back from the dead, how do

---

1. The Resurrection of Jesus Christ is a rigorously historical event, vouched for by more than 500 witnesses who saw Him when He appeared.

some of you say that there is no resurrection of the dead? Because if there is no resurrection of the dead, then neither did Christ come back to life. And if Christ did not come back to life, our preaching is in vain and our faith is in vain. We would even be false witnesses to God, for we weould be testifying against God that He brought Christ back to life, whilst He would not have done so if the dead don't come back to life. Because if the dead don't come back to life, neither did Christ. And if Christ didn't didn't come back to life, our faith is in vain; and you are still in your sins, and therefore those who died in Christ are condemned. If we await Christ only in this life, we are the most miserable of men.

The resurrection of Christ, pledge for our own. But look how Christ came back from the dead as the first fruits of those who die. Because as death came as for a man, so did the resurrection of the dead for a man. And as everybody dies in Adam, so will everybody live again in Christ. But each in its turn: the first fruits, Christ; then, at the time of the Parusia[1], those of Christ. The end will finally come when He delivers the kingdom of God the Father, after having destroyed every principate, every power and every force[2]. For it is necessary for Him to reign "until He puts all his enemies under His feet": The last enemy destroyed will be death: becasuse "he put it all under His feet".

Confirmation of the resurrection. If the dead do not come back to life "we eat and drink, for tomorrow we shall die[3]". Don't allow yourselves to be deceived: "bad conversations corrupt good habits". Be discriminating and don't sin, for some of them are greatly ignorant of God. I say this for your own shame.

Mode of resurrection. But somebody will say: how will the dead come back to life? And with what body? Fools! What you sow does not germinate if it doesn't die. And what you sow is

---

1. Second Coming.
2. If the head came back to life, so also would the members.
3. This is the outcome for fools, according to the Scripture. We should do good whilst we have the time, says Saint Paul.

not the body which is due to be born, but a simple grain, of wheat, for example, or some other seed. And God gives it the body which He wants, and a body proper to each seed. So also for the resurrection of the dead. It is sown in corruption and brought back to life in incorruption. It is sown in baseness and comes back to life in glory. And as we wear the terrestrial image, we shall also wear the celestial one. Now I'm going to declare a mystery to you. We shall not all die, but we shall all be transformed[1]. In a moment, in the opening and closing of an eye, at the sound of a final trumpet, for the trumpet will sound, the dead will come back to life incorrupt and we shall be transformed. Because this corruptible must be dressed in incorruptibility, and this mortal in immortality. When this corruptible must be dressed in incorruptibility, and this mortal in immortality, then what is written will have been fulfilled: "Death has been absorbed by victory. Death, where is your victory? Death, where is your sting?" But thanks to God who gives us the victory for Our Lord Jesus Christ. Therefore, my dear brothers, stand firm, unshakeable, always superabounding in the work of the Lord, knowing that your weariness is not vain in the Lord.

EPILOGUE

Greetings. The churches of Asia greet you. Aquila And Priscilla greet you warmly with the church which is in their house. All the brothers greet you, Paul. If somebody does not love the Lord, let him be anathema. MARAN ATHA[2]. The grace of the Lord Jesus be with you. I love you all in Jesus Christ.

---

1. Glorified as the body of Jesus. The grain of wheat rots and an ear is born.
2. Hebrew = Come, Lord.

2nd EPISTLE TO THE CORINTHIANS

PROLOGUE[1]

Thanksgiving. Blessed be the God and Father of our Lord Jesus Christ, Father of mercies and of all consolation, who consoles us in our tribulations, so that we can console whoever has tribulations, with the consolation which we ourselves receive from God. And so the sufferings of Christ abound in us, as our consolation abounds, through Christ.

DEFENSE OF HIS APOSTOLATE

Superiority of the New Testament over the Old. Therefore invested mercifully in this ministry, we are not discouraged, nor do we proceed with cunning nor do we falsify the word of God, and we recommend[2] ourselves to all human conscience before God with the manifestation of the truth. If our Gospel is still uncovered, it is still so for those who are lost, for the incredulous, whose intelligence blinded the god of this century so that that the brilliance of the Gospel of the glory of God, which is the image of God, does not shine. Because we are not

---

1. Having sent Titus to inform him, Saint Paul knew that not everything in the community was going well. The Judaizers were stirring everything up and some were questioning his authority.

2. Paul is not preaching to himself. In his Gospel there is no duplicity or deceit.

preaching to ourselves, but to Jesus Christ, the Lord; we are your servants through Jesus. Through the same God who said: "The light shines out of the darkness, lit up our hearts so that the knowledge of the Glory of God shines, shining in the face of Christ."

Sufferings and hope of the apostolic ministry. But we carry this treasure in clay vessels[1], so that it appears clear that this extraordinary vigor comes from God and not from us. We are grieved in everything, but not beaten; perplexed, but not desperate; persecuted, but not abandoned; cast out, but not destroyed; we always carry in the body, wherever we go, the sufferings of Jesus's death, so that the life of Jesus is also revealed in us. Because, living, we are all exposed to death because of Jesus, so that the life of Jesus may also reveal itself in our mortal flesh. And in this way death acts on us, but life does so on you. But, having the same spirit of faith, according to what is written: "I believed, therefore I spoke", we also believe and therefore speak, convinced that He who brought Jesus Christ back to life, will also bring us back to life in your company. Because everything is for you, so that grace, more and more abundant, multiplies the thanksgiving for the glory of God. For this reason we do not faint, for although our outward man is being lost, our inner man is renewed from day to day. For the light, momentary weight of our tribulations produces an eternal weight of glory, beyond measure, for those who do not look at the things which are seen, but rather at those which are not seen, for the visible is temporary, and the invisible, eternal[2].

We know, then, that if our tent in which we dwell on earth is destroyed, we have another house which is the work of God[3], an eternal dwelling in the sky, not built by the hands of men. Therefore, present or absent, we yearn to be pleasing to Him, for we must all appear before Christ's tribunal so that each may receive what he deserved during his mortal life in accordance with what he did, good or evil.

---

1. Conscious of his human frailty, he feels strong with the Grace of God.

2. The Christian looks and judges with the eyes of Faith.

3. Our House in Heaven.

Charity, stimulus of the apostolic ministry. Knowing well the fear of the Lord, we try to convince men, for we are well known to God, and, I hope, also to your consciences. We are not trying to recommend ourselves again, but to give you the occasion to glorify yourselves from us, so that you can answer those who glorify themselves on the outside and not in the heart. Because Christ's charity rewards us[1], thinking that if one died for many, then everybody has died; and He died for everybody so that those that live, do not live for themselves, but for Him who died and came back to life through them. In such a way that he who is in Christ is a new creature; the old has now passed away and the new one has appeared. Everything comes from God, who reconciled us with Him by means of Christ, and entrusted in us the mystery of reconciliation[2]. For God reconciled the world in Christ, and did not impute it its sins and entrusting us with the mystery of reconciliation. We are, then, ambassadors of Christ, as if God was exhorting for us.

He made sin Him who did not know sin, in our place, so that we may be the justice of God in Him.

Christian saintliness. Do not mix with the pagans, for, what has justice have to do with injustice, and what do light and darkness have in common? What harmony between Christ and Belial, or what does the faithful have to do with the pagan? What relationship between the the temple of God and the idols[3]? Because we are temples of the living God. As God said: "I shall live and walk in the middle of them and I shall be their God and they will be my people." Therefore: "Don't touch anything impure, and I will receive you, and I shall be Father for you, and you will be sons and daughters for me", says the Omnipotent Lord.

So, by taking such promises, let us purify ourselves from any stain on the flesh and the spirit, by obtaining sanctification in the fear of God.

---

1. Zeal for the Glory of God and the salvation of souls.
2. The Apostles pursue the work of Jesus.
3. Paganism and idolatry are the kingdom of the devil. Do not contaminate oneself with the impurities of the world.

PAUL REFUTES HIS ENEMIES

Saint Paul's disinterest. I have kept myself, and I shall keep myself from being vexatious with you. And what I do, I shall continue doing to cut every pretext from those who seek the occasion to find how to boast of being like us. These are false prophets, deceitful workers disguised as Apostles of Christ. Which is not surprising, for Satan also disguised himself as the Angel of light[1]. It is of no significance, then, that his ministers disguise themselves as ministers of justice; but their end will correspond to their deeds.

Saint Paul's impressive record. I repeat: Nobody takes me to be fatuous, allow me to boast a little as well[2]. They are Hebrews? So am I. They are Israelites? So am I. From the lineage of Abraham? So am I. Are they ministers of Christ? —I speak like a madman—, I more so than them. More in works, more in prisons; in wounds, immensely more. I received thirty-nine lashes from the Jews five times; I was beaten with staffs three times, stoned once, shipwrecked three times; I've passed a day and a night in the depths of the sea; countless journeys with dangers from rivers, dangers from bandits, dangers from those of my race, dangers from pagans, dangers in the city, dangers in the deserts, dangers in the sea, dangers from false brothers. In works and tiredness, in frequent vigils, in hunger and thirst, in constant fasting, in cold and nakedness. And moreover my daily obsession: care for all the churches. Who suffers depression, and I don't suffer it? Who is offended, and I don't burn? If boasting must be done, I shall boast of my weakness. God, the Father of the Lord Jesus, eternally blessed, knows that I'm not lying. In Damascus the governor under King Aretas kept the city from the Damascenes in order to arrest me, and I was lowered through a window in a basket and thus I escaped from their hands.

---

1. The false apostles affect spirituality. And they sift through and distort Biblical texts to support their errors and theories.

2. His detractors obliged him to defend himself.

Visions and revelations. Is it necessary to boast? Although it's not really fitting, I shall move on to the visions and revelations of the Lord. I know a man[1] in Christ who, fourteen years ago —whether in the body or out of it, I don't know, God knows— was snatched up to the third heaven. And I know that this man —whether in the body or out of it, I don't know, God knows— was snatched up to Paradise and heard ineffable words that man cannot express. I shall boast of this man, but of myself I shall only boast of my frailties. If you tried to boast of me, I would not play the fool, for I would tell the truth; but I abstain so that nobody considers me any more than what they see in me or hear from me. And so that I don't become conceited by the sublimity of the revelations, my flesh was administered a sting, an angel of Satan who beats me so that I don't become arrogant.[2] I beseeched The Lord three times on this matter, that He draw away from me, but He answered me: "My grace is sufficient for you, for my power triumphs in frailty." With pleasure, for I shall boast of my weaknesses so that the power of Christ may rest on me. I therefore take pleasure in my frailties, in reproaches, needs, persecutions, in anguishes for Christ, for when I am weak, then I am strong.

Saint Paul's denial. I've played the fool, but you've obliged me. For you must praise me, since I am behind the most senior Apostles in nothing. The characteristic of the true Apostle has been verified before you; constant patience, signs, prodigies and miracles. In what have you been less than the other churches, except that I have not been burdensome to you. Forgive me this wrong!

See that for the third time I am on the point of coming to you, and I shall not be burdensome to you, for I'm not looking for your things, but for you yourselves. Because sons mustn't hoard treasure for parents, but parents for sons. And I shall

---

1. Paul himself.

2. We don't know whether it's a bodily illness, wounds received, spiritual temptation: What we do know is that God does not allow us to be tempted beyond our strength.

gladly spend and be spent for you. Why is it that, the more I love you, the less I'm going to be loved by you?

Saint Paul's worries. It will appear to you that we have been justifying ourselves to you for some time. We speak before God and in Christ; all, beloved, for your edification. For I fear that whenever I do go I shall not find you as I would wish, and you will find me as you would not wish; I fear that there are fights, envies, animosities, ambitions, discords, detractions, murmurings, vanities, riots, and that when I arrive My God will humiliate me because of you.

Exhortations and threats. What we ask for in our prayers is your perfection[1]. Therefore I write this in my absence, so that, when I am present, I won't have to work harshly in accordance with the power which the Lord gave me to build and not to destroy.

EPILOGUE

Final recommendations and farewell. For the rest, brothers, rejoice, perfect yourselves, console yourselves, share one opinion, live in peace, and may the God of charity and peace be with you. Greet each other with the holy kiss. All the saints greet you. May the grace of the Lord Jesus Christ, the love of God and the communion of the Holy Spirit be with you all.

---

1. The epistle is written in a tone of correction, but he finally softens his words in a tone of friendship.

EPISTLE TO THE GALATIANS[1]

PROLOGUE

There's only one true Gospel: that of Christ. I am astonished at how rapidly you have passed from the Gospel which called you through the grace of Christ, to another; and it is not the case that there is another, but that there are people who stir you up and want to pervert Christ's Gospel. But even when we or an angel from heaven proclaim to you a Gospel different from the one we have proclaimed, it is anathema[2].

As we have said before, so shall I say it again now. If somebody announces to you a gospel different from the one you've received, it is anathema. Now, then, do I look for the favor of men or of God? Or is it that I seek to please men? Even if I had tried to please men, I would not have been a servant of Christ.

APOLOGY OF PAUL'S APOSTOLATE

The Gospel of Paul is that of Christ. Because I am making you know, brothers, that the Gospel preached by me does not come from men; for I did not receive it nor did I learn it from any man, but through the revelation of Jesus Christ. You have

---

1. Galatia was a country originating from some tribes in Galia installed in Asia Minor, and evangelized by Saint Paul.

2. It was the Judaizers who were stirring up the community.

heard, in effect, of my conduct in other times in Judaism; to
what extremes I pursued the Church of God and devastated it,
and how I excelled in Judaism over many of my age in my
nation, being extremely zealous of the traditions of my fathers.
More so when it pleased Him who chose me from my mother's
womb and called me for His grace, to reveal His Son in me, in
order that I should proclaim Him amongst the Gentiles.

JUSTIFICATION OF FAITH

The Law[1] cannot justify us. Oh senseless Galatians! Who
has bewitched you, before whose eyes the figure of the crucified
Jesus Christ was presented? I only want to know this of you:
Did you receive the Spirit through the works of the Law or
through the faith which you had heard? Are you that stupid?
Having started in the Spirit, now you finish in the flesh? Have
you experienced so many things in vain? If so, it would be in
vain. For He who gives you the spirit and performs miracles in
you, does He do so through the works of the Law or through the
faith which you had heard?

**The Law does not contravene the promise, but prepares
for Christ.** Now then, before faith came we were locked in,
under custody of the Law, waiting for the faith which was due
to be revealed. There is no Jew nor Greek, there is no slave nor
free man, there is no male nor female, for you are all one in
Jesus Christ, and if you are of Christ, then you are of Abraham,
inheritors according to the promise[2].

Situation of men before Christ. I say, then: Throughout all
the time that the inheritor is a child, he doesn't differ from the
servant in anything, even though he is the lord of everything,
but he is under tutors and administrators until the time

---

1. Saint Paul always speaks of the Mosaic Law and opposes it to Faith. Faith and
   works of the Commandments is what saves, not Faith alone. That would be
   presumption.
2. The new Law of the Gospel is not only for the Jews disseminated throughout
   the world, but for all men, as Jesus died for all of them, without any
   distinction.

established by the father. And so we also, when we were minors, were enslaved under the elements of the world; but in the fullness of time, God sent His Son, born of a woman, born under the Law, in order for us to receive the adoption of children, and because you are children, God has sent your hearts to the Spirit of His Son, who cries out: Abba, Father, what luck that you are not a slave, but a son; and if you are a son, you are also an inheritor from God.

Saint Paul's memories and anxieties. I beseech you, brothers, to be like me, because I am also like you. In such a way that I am your enemy when I tell the truth? You are zealous, not for good, but they want to distance you from me so that you love them with zeal. It is a good thing to be loved with zeal provided it is to the good, and not only when I am present amongst you, my sons, for which I suffer labor pains once again, until Christ is formed in you. For I would like to be present now amongst you and change my tone of voice, because I am in doubt about you.

MORAL CONSEQUENCES

Christian liberty. Christ freed us to enjoy freedom; so, remain firm and do not tie yourself again to the yoke of slavery[1]. Look, I, Paul, tell you that if you are circumcised, Christ will not profit from you at all. And I declare again that all men who are circumcised remain obliged to follow all the Law. Those who want to be justified by the Law have become untied from Christ[2]; you have fallen apart from grace. A little yeast makes all the dough ferment.

Liberty, not libertinage. The works of the spirit are different from the works of the flesh. Brothers, you were indeed called to liberty; but strive so that freedom[3] is not a reason to serve the flesh, rather serve each other through

---

1. Slavery of the Mosaic Law and sin.
2. Separated from the Grace which Christ has won back, we are excluded from the Kingdom of God.
3. Don't let your freedom be libertinage.

charity. Because all the Law is summed up in one sole precept, in that: "You will love your neighbor as yourself." But if you bite yourselves and devour each other, take care that you don't destroy each other.

The works of the flesh are: fornication, impurity, lechery, imagery, sorcery, foes, quarrels, jealousy, anger, divisions, heresies, envy, murder, drunk people, gluttony, and similar. I warn you to keep of these thinks, as I said before, for those wo do such things will not inherit the Kingdom of God.

On the contrary, the fruits of the Spirit are: charity, joy, peace, long life, goodness, uprightness, faith, meekness, abstinence. There is no Law against such things. Those who are Christ's crucified the flesh with passions. If we live by our spirit, let us walk by spirit too. Let us not desire fame, by quarreling with each other because of envy.

Various counsels and applications. Brothers, if a man was surprised in some fault, you, the spiritual ones, correct him in a spirit of meekness, keeping watch on yourself, unless you also may be tempted.

Give mutual assistance to each other with your burdens, and you will thus fulfill the Law of Christ, because if somebody imagines himself to be something, he's deceiving himself, because he's nothing. Don't deceive yourselves: God will not allow Himself to be mocked; for man himself will reap what he sows; because whoever sows his own flesh, will harvest corruption of the flesh; but whoever sows in the spirit, will harvest eternal life.

Let us not get tired, then, of doing good, because in due course we shall reap, if we are not faint-hearted. Consequently, whilst we have time, let's do good to everybody, and especially to the brothers in the faith.

EPISTLE TO THE EPHESIANS[1]

The apostle's greeting. Paul, Jesus Christ's apostle for the will of God, to the holy and faithful who are in Ephesus.

THE MYSTERY OF CHRIST[2]

Blessing, and divine election, filiation and predestination. Blessed be the God and Father of our Lord Jesus Christ, who blessed us in Christ in heaven with all the fortune of spiritual blessings, in as much as He chose us in Him from the end of the world to be holy and immaculate before Him, predestining us through love to the adoption of His sons through Jesus Christ in Himself, in accordance with the consent of His will, which was proposed in Him, in the economy of the fullness of times by recapitulating all things in Christ, those of the heavens and those of the earth.

Redemption through Christ and recapitulation in Him. We have redemption through his blood, the pardon of sins, according to the wealth of his grace, which he poured upon us with all his wisdom and gentleness, so that we knew the mistery of his will according to his wishes when He recapitulated all

---

1. On his third apostolic journey, Paul founded a flourishing Christianity in Ephesus, the capital of Asia Minor.
2. The mystery is the Incarnation of the Word, whose purpose is the reunion of all things in Christ.

things within Christ, those things from heaven and from the earth.

Union and equality of Jews and Gentiles in Christ. He is indeed our peace; He who made two peoples one, knocking down the dividing wall, enmity; annuling the Law of the commandments formulated in decrees in His flesh, to create in Himself one new man from these two, making peace, and reconciling both in one single body by means of the cross, destroying enmity[1] in Himself, and with His coming He proclaimed peace to those of you who were a long way off and peace to those who were nearby, because through Him each of us has access to the Father in one same Spirit; so that you are not strangers and guests, but citizens of the holy and familiars of God, built on the foundation of the Apostles and the prophets, the cornerstone being Jesus Christ himself, on which the entire building, well constructed, rises up to form a temple holy in the Lord, in which you yourself are also built through the Holy Spirit to be the room of God.

The ministery announced by Paul. It is for this reason that I, Paul, am Jesus Christ's prisoner through loving you Gentiles... because you had certainly come to know, as God has dispensed my the grace of the apostolate, that which He had confered to me on your favour, when I was given knowledge of the mystery by means of a revelation, as I briefly outlined before.[2] This mystery consists in the Gentiles being co-inheritors and members of one single body, and participants in the Gospel, of which I have been made minister through a gift of the grace of God which has been conceded me according to the efficacy of His power. This grace was given me, the lowest, the last of all Christians, for evangelizing to the Gentiles the incalculable richness of Christ, and shedding light on those for whom the dispensation of the mystery was hidden for all the centuries in God[3], the creator of all things, so that the incredible

---

1. He erased the frontiers between all peoples with His blood.
2. The mystery of love.
3. All the blessings which we have received as children of God derive from this mystery of love of men.

wisdom of God may be known now by means of the Church to the principates and potentates on high in the heavens, in accordance with the eternal plan which He undertook in Jesus Christ.

NORMS OF CHRISTIAN LIFE

Exhortation to unity. So, I —who am a prisoner for the cause of the Lord— exhort you to walk in a manner worthy of the vocation with which you were called, with all humility and meekness, with forbearance, supporting each other with charity, being diligent in preserving unity[1] with the tie of peace, for there is no more than one single body and one single spirit, as likewise one hope to which you have been called by your vocation, one single Lord, one single faith, one single baptism and one single God, Father to everything, who is above everything, through everything and in everything.

Diversity of gifts[2]. But grace has been given to each of us in accordance with the measure of Christ's gift. He made some apostles, others prophets, some evangelists, others shepherds and doctors, in order to perfect Christians in the work of His ministry and in the edification of the body of Christ, until we acquire unity of faith and complete knowledge of the Son of God, and the state of the perfect man by means of Christ's age of plenitude, so that we may not in any way be hesitant children and allow ourselves to be cunningly blown away by any wind of doctrine into the whim of men, who induce in us the machination of error, before, on the other hand, we grow, versed in the truth, in the love of all things up to He who is the head, Christ.

Renew oneself in Christ, stripping oneself of the old man. So, I say this to you, and I exhort you in the Lord that you don't now go as the Gentiles do, in accordance with the vanity of their thoughts, with their reason obscured, separated from the

---

1. The unity desired by Christ is a tie of peace and friendship.
2. Each one has to serve God and the brothers with the gift which I have received.

life of God by the ignorance within them due to the hardening of their hearts, which, having been made senseless, will be delivered to impurity, to work avidly on all kinds of dissolutions.

But you, you must strip yourselves, through looking at your past, of the old man[1], who is corrupted according to the depraved desires of error, and renew yourselves in the spirit of your mind and clothe yourselves in the new man, the one created after God in true justice and holiness.

Christ's example. Be, then, imitators of God, like much loved children. Live in love, following the example of Christ, who loved us and delivered Himself to God for us as an offering and sweet-smelling sacrifice[2].

Flight from impurity. As regards fornication and all kinds of impurities or avarice, don't even name them amongst yourselves, as is fitting to holy people; nor obscene words, vulgarities or vile deeds, unfitting things, but rather thanksgiving.

Because understand well that no fornicator or impure person or miser —which is the same as worshipping idols— will inherit the Kingdom of Christ and God. Don't let anybody deceive you with vain discourses, since because of them the wrath of God will descend on the children of the disobedient. So, don't take any part in them[3].

The conduct of God's children. You were indeed darkness at one time, but now you're light in the Lord; walk like children of the light. (Because the fruit of light consists in goodness, justice and truth), judging by experience, which is what pleases the Lord, and don't take part with them in the fruitless works of darkness; on the contrary, condemn them openly, because it is shameful to say the things which they do in secret, and all these

---

1. We must strip ourselves of bad habits and reclothe ourselves in the spirit of Jesus.
2. He showed the measure of His infinite love with His great sacrifice.
3. Great punishments of God decended on men because of corrupt customs.

things are reprimanded once they are revealed by the light, and everything which is revealed is light[1].

Therefore it is said: "Wake up, you who are sleeping, and get up from the dead, and Christ will illuminate you."

Prudence and sobriety. Look, then, with diligence, as you go, don't be like fools, but like wise men, taking advantage of time, because the days are bad. In consequence, don't be senseless, but endeavour to know the will of the Lord, always giving thanks for everything to Him who is God and Father in the name of our Lord Jesus Christ, being equally submissive to each other in the fear of Christ.

Reciprocal duties of married couples. Women should be as submissive to their husbands as if he were the Lord, because the husband is the head of the woman, in the same way that Christ is the head of the Church, His body, of which He is the Saviour. But as the Church is subject to Christ, so also must women be so in everything. Husbands, love your spouses as Christ loved the Church and handed Himself over for it, in order to sanctify it and purify it in the baptism of water with the word which accompanies it, so as to present this, His glorious Church, before Him, without stain, nor wrinkle, nor such like, rather holy and immaculate.

Thus husbands must also love their wives like their own body. Whoever loves his wife loves himself, because nobody ever hates his own flesh, but, on the contrary, feeds it and cares for it, as Christ does the Church, for we are members of His body. "For this reason man will leave his father and mother and will attach himself to his wife and the two will become one flesh." This mystery[2] is great; but I say it with regard to Christ and the Church. But, as far as it concerns you, let each man love his wife as he loves himself, and may the wife revere the husband in her turn[3].

Duties of children and of parents. Children, obey your parents in the Lord, because this is righteous. "Honour your

---

1. The obscenities and impurities of the darkness will be revealed some day.
2. Mystery, or rather sacrament, reflects the Church through its own significance.
3. Marriage is not only indissoluble but its holiness comes to it from Christ.

father and mother", which is the first commandment with promise), "so that you are happy and have a long life on earth." And you, parents, don't enrage your children, but raise them in the discipline and correction of the Lord.

EPILOGUE

The Christian's arms[1]. To sum up, comfort yourselves in the Lord and the strength of His power. Dress yourself in God's armour so that you can resist the temptations of the Devil, because our fight is not against flesh and blood, but against principates and potentates, against the dominators of this obscure world, against evil spirits. Therefore, receive God's armour[2] so that you can resist evil by day and be perfect in everything. So, be firm, your loins girded with the truth, wearing the breastplate of truth and shoes on your feet, ready to announce the Gospel of peace. On all occasions take up the shield of faith with which you can render useless the burning darts of Evil.

Take also the helmet of health and the sword of the Spirit which is the word of God. Praying in the Spirit at all times, with all kinds of prayers and supplications, and keeping watch for this purpose over all the holy ones with every perseverance and supplication, and over me, so that appropriate words may be given me when I open my mouth with courage to proclaim the mystery of Christ, whose ambassador and prisoner I am, so that I may dare speak freely of Him, as is fitting.

Final greeting. May peace and charity, as well as faith, be conceded to the brothers on behalf of God the Father and the Lord Jesus Christ.

---

1. The Christian is a militant.
2. The spiritual arms of the Christian are: Faith, the sword of the word of God, justice and truth, soon to proclaim the Good News to the rest.

EPISTLE TO THE PHILIPPIANS[1]

Thanksgiving and supplications. Whenever I remember you I give thanks to my God, and I always make joyful supplications for you in all my prayers for your participation in the progress of the Gospel.

Feelings of Christ's prisoner. Brothers, I want to know that the things which have occured to me have come to favor the progress of the Gospel, until the point where it is well known in the pretorium and in every place that I bear chains for Christ, and the majority of brothers, encoraged in the Lord by my chains, prove to be more intrepid as they fearlessly proclaim the word of God[2]. It is true that some people preach of Christ in a spirit of envy and competition, but others do it with an honest intention; the latter moved by charity knowing that I am ready to defend the Gospel, the former by rivalry, preaching Christ in the belief that the are adding tribulation to my chains[3]. But, at the end of the day, what does it matter? However Christ is proclaimed, hypocritically or sincerely, I am happy and I shall be happy. Since for me life is Christ and death is something gained, and although continuing to live is for me the fruit of the apostolate, I don't know which to choose. I feel pressed on both sides; on one, I yearn for death to be with Christ, which is best

---

1. Phillipos was a Roman city in Macedonia, Greece, and a sea port. It was evangelized by Saint Paul on his second Apostolic Journey.

2. He seems to be writing from Rome, and Faith was being propagated.

3. Paul was not lacking in envious people, but God made use of them to proclaim the Gospel.

for me; on the other, for continuing to live, which I consider more necessary for you. I am convinced that I will remain and stay with you for your progress and delight in faith, in order that your glory grows in Jesus Christ through me when I come to you for a second time.

Worthy life against enemies. Above all, I beg you to live a life worthy of Christ's Gospel, so that, whether I go and see it, or hear about it in my absence, you persevere firmly in one single spirit, fighting with one single soul for the faith of the Gospel, without letting yourself be intimidated in the slightest in front of your enemies; that which is for them a sign of damnation will for you, on the contrary, be one of salvation[1], and this through the work of God. Since grace is granted you, not only from believing in Christ, but also from suffering for Him, you have to sustain the same combat which you saw in me before and which I now hear of in you.

Christ, an impressive example of abnegation. Endeavour to have the same feelings as Jesus Christ, who, having the glorious nature of God, did not consider maintaining Himself equal to God as a covetable treasure, but humbled Himself by adopting the nature of a servant, and making Himself like other men; and in his condition as man He humiliated Himself by making Himself obedient until death and the death of the cross[2]. Therefore God highly exalted Him and gave Him a name, so that the celestial beings, and those from the earth and Hell, bend their knee at the name of Jesus, and every tongue confesses that Jesus Christ is Lord for the glory of God the Father.

Exemplarily Christian life. So, then, my beloved, as you have always been obedient not only during my presence but also, and much more so, when I was absent, work for your salvation with fear and trembling; for it is God who works in you[3] both to will and work according to His pleasure. Do it all without murmurings or disputes, so that you may be

---

1. He exhorts his Christians to fidelity; Christ is always a sign of contradiction.
2. Our only master and model will always be Christ.
3. The Church teaches us that we cannot save us without the Grace of God. Faith and Deeds with the Grace of God.

irreprehensible and without malice, sons of God irreproachable in the middle of this perverse and deviant generation, in the middle of which you shine like asteroids in the universe, keeping the word of life firm so that it can boast of me on the day of Christ that I have neither run nor worked in vain. And even if I had to spill my blood as a libation on the sacrifice and service of your faith, I delight and rejoice with you all. You also, be joyful for the same reason and rejoice with me.

Warnings as regards the Judaizers[1]. As for the rest, brothers, rejoice in the Lord. It does not trouble me to write the same things to you, and it is useful for you. Be careful with dogs, careful with evil-doers, careful with the circumcised ones! We are the true circumcision, those who who worship wearing the spirit of God, and we rejoice that Jesus Christ does not put our trust in flesh, although I could put my trust in flesh. If someone thinks of being able to trust the flesh, I more so. I was circumcised on the eighth day, from the lineage of Israel, from the tribe of Benjamin, a Hebrew, the son of Hebrews, and, as regards the Law, a Pharisee, and as for zeal under the Law, a persecutor of the Church, as regards the justice which comes from fulfilling the Law, irreproachable.

Paul has sacrificed everything for Christ. But whatever things I then had to my advantage, I now consider harmful for Christ; but I still consider everything I have as harmful compared with the sublime knowledge of Jesus Christ, my Lord, for whom I have sacrificed everything, and I consider them trash to gain Christ, and find myself in Him not in possession of my justice, which comes from the Law, but of that which is obtained by faith in Christ, the justice of God which is based on faith; in order to know Him and the virtue of His resurrection and the participation in His sufferings, which fashioned me at His death to achieve the resurrection of the dead[2].

---

1. Paul alerts us against Judaizers everywhere.
2. Saint Paul considers as nothing titles and human greatness, in comparison with the love of God.

The imitation of Paul. We are citizens of heaven.
Brothers, all of you, be my imitators and observe those who
behave themselves according to the model which you have in
us, for many move amongst you, of whom I have said many
times and now have to repeat to you with tears in my eyes, that
they are enemies of the cross of Christ; their end will be
damnation, their god is their belly, their glory that which
dishonors them, their heart being turned to things of the earth[1].
Our fatherland is in the heavens from where we are waiting for
the Saviour and the Lord Jesus Christ, who will transform our
body full of miseries so that it is like His glorious body by
virtue of the power which He has to make all things submit to
Him.

So, then, my much loved brothers, my joy and my crown,
remain resolute in the Lord, much beloved.

Joy and peace. Always rejoice in the Lord; I repeat, rejoice.
May your benignity be as notorious to all men. The Lord is
near. Do not worry about anything, but rather present the Lord
your necessities with thanksgiving in all prayers and
supplications. And the peace of God[2] which surpasses all
intelligence will guide your hearts and your thoughts in Jesus
Christ.

Paul's gratitude to the Philippians. I have experienced a
great joy in the Lord because you have revived your feelings for
me; you feel them, but have not had the occasion to make them
apparent. I do not say this induced by my destitution, for I have
learnt to be happy with my lot. I know how to do without
necessities and to live in abundance; I have been taught each of
these things, to be full and to be hungry, to swim in abundance
and suffer shortfalls. I can do everthing in Him who comforts
me. You have done well, however, to assume my tribulation. I
havev everything I could need and still more; I have to excess
after having received your assistance from Ephroditus[3], a

---

1. Enemies of the cross of Christ who look for pleasures and shun all sacrifice.
2. The gift of peace. "God alone is sufficient", said Saint Theresa.
3. Paul never accepted anything for the services of his ministry. He made an
   exception with his beloved Philippians.

sweet-smelling offering, an acceptable sacrifice, pleasing to God. My God, in His turn, will abundantly provide for your indigence according to His riches in glory in Jesus Christ. Glory to God and our Father for the centuries of centuries. Amen.

LETTER TO THE COLOSSIANS[1]

THE MYSTERY OF CHRIST

Excellence of the person of Christ:

a) In the creation of the world. He is the image of all creation, because all things were created by Him himself, those of the heavens and those of the earth, the invisible and the visible, both thrones and dominations, principates and potentates; absolutely everything was created by Him and for Him; and He himself exists before all things and they all subsist in Him[2].

b) In the Church. He is also the head of the body of the Church, being the beginning, the firstborn among mortals to thus occupy the same position before all things, the Father wanted all plenitude to dwell in Him.

Christ's work and the sufferings of the apostle. Now I take pleasure in my sufferings for you, and in compensation I complete in my flesh what is missing from the tribulations of Christ through His body[3], which is the Church, of which I was made a minister according to the mission which God gave me

---

1. Colossas was a city in Phrygia in Asia Minor. Paul charged Epaphras with the foundation of a Christian community there. And he corrects the errors which had been introduced.
2. Christ in the creation and in the Church.
3. With our suffering we compensate for what is missing in us, the Passion of Christ.

for your good, with the aim of fulfilling His divine message, the mystery hidden for centuries and for generations and now revealed to His saints, to whom God wanted to disclose the richness of this mystery among the Gentiles, which is Christ among you[1], the hope of glory, which we proclaim by warning and instructing all men in all wisdom, to present them perfect in Jesus Christ, whereupon I labour by struggling according to His actions which work powerfully in me.

THE CHRISTIANS' NORMS

New life in Christ. In consequence, if you have come back to life with Christ, look for the things of above, where Christ is seated at God's right hand; delight in the things of above, not in those of the earth. You really died and your life remains hidden with Christ in God. When Christ reveals Himself, He who is our life, then you yourself will also appear with Him in glory.

Flight of ancient vices[2]. Don't live in mutual deceit, but divest yourself of the old man with all his bad actions, and reclothe yourselves in the new, who renews himself successfully until he acquires full knowledge in accordance with the image of He who has created it, in which there is no distinction between Greek and Jew, circumcision or uncircumcision, barbarian, slave, servant, freeman, only Christ, who is everything, in everything[3].

The Christian virtues. Therefore, as God's chosen ones, holy and loved, reclothe yourselves in a compassionate, bountiful, humble, meek, magnanimous heart, helping each other and mutually forgiving each other whenever somebody has a reason for complaint against another. In the same way that the Lord forgave you, so must you pardon each other. But above all reclothe yourself in charity, which is the knot of perfection. May the peace of Christ likewise reign in your hearts

---

1. Suffering with Christ is sharing our Redemption with Him.
2. The Resurrection of Christ must be the beginning of a more Christian life.
3. If we live with Christ, the same Spirit which brought Jesus back to life will also bring us back to life.

in which you were called to construct a single body; and be grateful. The word of Christ lives richly among you, teaching you and warning you mutually by means of all wisdom, with psalms, hymns, divine canticles, singing and pleasing God in your hearts. And whatever word or work you undertake, do it in the name of the Lord Jesus[1], giving thanks to God the Father for his intercession.

Family duties. Wives, submit to your husbands as is fitting in the Lord. Husbands, love your spouses and do not get angry with them. Children, obey your parents in everything, because this pleases the Lord. Parents, don't arouse your children to anger, so that they don't become discouraged.

Prayer and prudence. Masters, carry out justice and equity with the servants, since you know that you also have your Lord in heaven. Persevere in prayer by doing it watchfully and with thanksgiving, also praying for ourselves at the same time, so that God opens the gate of the word to reveal the mystery of Christ —for which I also am in chains—. And look for the favorable occasion to reveal it to the Gentiles. Behave wisely with those that are outside, profiting from auspicious occasions. May your conversation also be agreeable, seasoned with the salt of grace, so that you know how you must respond to each one.

Final greetings[2]. I put down the greeting with my own hand, that of Paul. May grace be with you. Amen.

---

1. Whatever you do, do it in the name of Jesus, offering Him your works and deeds of each day to His intention.

2. He sends greetings from the prison in Rome to the Colossians on behalf of Epaphras and his doctor Luke the evangelist.

1st EPISTLE TO THE THESSALONIANS[1]

Paul's Apostolate in Thessalonica. We know very well, beloved brothers of God, that you have been chosen. Because our evangelical messasge was not conveyed to you merely in words, but also with portentous works under the action of the Holy Spirit and, for our part, with a deep commitment.

Indeed, you know that our acting amonst you was for our good. And you have behaved like imitators of us and of the Lord, receiving the preaching with the delight of the Holy Spirit, even in the middle of great tribulations; to the point of becoming models for all the believers in Macedonia and Achaia, so that we have no need to talk about it.

As regards ourselves, everybody talks about the welcome you gave us, and how you converted from idolatry to God, to serve Him, the only living and true, awaiting His Son Jesus, who will come from the heavens and whom He brought back from the dead and who is due to liberate us from the wrath that is coming.

---

1. Thessalonica, present day Salonika, was the capital of Macedonia, situated on the coast of the Aegean Sea. It was evangelized on his second Journey.

PAUL'S BEHAVIOUR IN THESSALONICA[1]

The Thessalonians' faith and patience. Because of all thi sour thanksgiving to God is continuous because, once the word of God was received from our preaching, you embraced it not as the word of man, but like what is truly the word of God, which remains vitally active in you, the believers. Indeed, brothers, you have made yourselves imitators of the churches of God in Christ Jesus Christ, which are in Judea; for you have suffered at the hands of your fellow citizens, the same as them with the Jews, who put the Lord Jesus and the prophets to death and have persecuted us and displease God, being enemies to all men, by preventing us from preaching to Gentiles, so that they may be saved. In all this they exceed the measure of their sin. But wrath will fall heavily on them.

Timothy to Thessalonica. So then, not being able to resist any more, we resolved to stay on our own in Athens, and we sent Timothy, our brother and minister of God in Christ's Gospel, with the mission of comforting you and inspiring you in your faith, so that nobody is left downhearted by these tribulations. During our stay amongst you, we foretold you that you were now due to have tribulations, as in fact occured. You know this well. Therefore, not now being able to resist anymore, I sent him to inform me about your faith; whether Satan had now tempted you and our work had proved barren.

EXHORTATIONS

Holiness, of life, charity and work. Finally, brothers, I beg and exhort you in Jesus Christ that you progress still further in your way of life, in pleasing God, as you learned from us and as you now behave. You well know what instructions we gave you in the name of the Lord Jesus. Now then, this is the will of God: your sanctification; that you flee from impurity; that each of you

---

1. His first mission was to put himself on guard against the Jews who stirred up and harassed the small community.

knows how to treat your own body with dignity and holiness, without allowing yourself to get carried away by passion, as do the Gentiles who don't know God. That nobody injures his brother, with violence or deceit, because the Lord is the avenger of all that, as we have also told you and emphasized. And the point is that God has not called us to impurity, but to live in holiness. Therefore, whoever despises all this, does not despise a man, but God, who gives you His Holy Spirit.

On the subject of brotherly love, you do not need it written down for you, because you have learned personally from God how you must love each other. And indeed this is what you are doing with all the brothers in all of Macedonia. However, we want to exhort you, brothers, to progress still further, and to strive with maximum effort to live in peace, busying yourselves with your tasks and working with your own hands, as we have recommended you to do. Thus you will live decorously in the eyes of the non-Christians, without needing anything.

The fate of dead Christians at the Parusia[1]. Brothers, we don't want to leave you in ignorance about the dead, so that you are afflicted in some way, like others who have no hope. Because, if we believe that Jesus has died and comes back to life, so will He also reunite those who have died in Jesus with Him. So see what we are saying to you as the word of God: We the living, who are still in the time of the Lord's coming, will not precede those who are dead. Because the Lord himself, on the signal given by the voice of the Archangel and the sound of God's trumpet, will come down from heaven, and the dead in Christ will come back to life first. Then we, the living, those who are so until the coming of the Lord, will be snatched away along with them, by air currents between the clouds, to meet the Lord. And we shall be with the Lord for ever. So, console yourselves mutually with these words.

---

1. The destiny of the dead was worrying the Thessalonians. The Parusia is the Second Coming of the Lord at the end of time. When the Lord judges the world and confirms the particular sentence of each one at the time of our death. Eschatology = final destinies.

Uncertainty of the Parusia. As for the exact time, brothers, we do not need it to be written down. You know perfectly that the day of the Lord will come like the thief in the night. They will go along saying: "Peace and Security", and then, out of the blue, damnation will surprise them, like the labor pains of a pregnant woman, and they will not be able to escape. But you, brothers, do not live in darkness, so that that day may surprise you like the thief. You are all children of the light and children of the day; you are not children of the night or of darkness. Therefore let's not sleep, like the others, but let's keep watch and be sober, so that, living or dead, we may always live with Him. Therefore, encourage each other mutually and fortify each other, as you are already doing.

Special recommendations. Brothers, I beseech you to defer to those who work amongst you and direct and admonish you in the Lord. Reciprocate their watchfulness with an ever growing love. Live in peace amongst yourselves. I also beseech you, brothers, to correct the undisciplined, encourage the pusillanimous, support the weak and be patient with everybody. Don't let anybody return one evil with an other, but always have good as your goal, both among yourselves and everybody else. Always be joyful. Pray without respite.

EPILOGUE

Votes and greetings. May the God of peace sanctify you completely and may your entire being —spirit, soul and body— be unreproachably preserved for the coming of our Lord Jesus Christ. He who has called you is faithful and will do the same. Brothers, pray for us. Greet all brothers with the holy kiss. I entreat you by the Lord that you read this letter to all the brothers[1]. The grace of our Lord Jesus Christ be with you all.

---

1. The epistles of Saint Paul were usually circular. They were passed from one Christian community to another.

2nd EPISTLE TO THE THESSALONIANS

Thanksgiving. Brothers, we must, as is fitting, continually give thanks to God as regards you, for the great advances in your faith and for the increase in the mutual charity amongst yourselves, and your faith in all the persecutions and tribulations which you have to endure[1].

This is a manifestation of God's righteous judgement, to make you thus worthy of His kingdom, for which you are suffering.

For it is proper to divine justice to repay tribulation to those who inflict it, and to give you, who are suffering it, repose in our company, when the Lord Jesus appears in heaven with the angels in His power, between fiery flames, to take vengeance on those who don't know God and don't obey the Gospel of our Lord Jesus.

All these will suffer the punishment of eternal damnation, far from the face of God and His splendid glory, when the day comes to be glorified in His saints and admired in all those who believed.

---

1. The hounding of the persecutors, for both epistles deal with this. The apostle comforts and consoles them, in preparation for the eternal reward for those who persevere in the Faith.

THE LORD'S PARUSIA[1]

The Parusia and the Antichrist. As regards the coming of
our Lord Jesus Christ and our reunion with Him, we beseech
you, brothers, not to let yourselves be so easily impressed in
your spirits nor to be alarmed by any revelation, word or epistle
which induces you to think that the day of the Lord is imminent.
Let nobody deceive you in any way, because firstly the
Apostasy[2] has to come, and the ungodly Man, the one Destined
for damnation, the Adversary, who will rise up against
everything called God or having a religious nature, until he
comes to sit in God's sanctuary, passing himself off as God.
Don't you remember that I have already told you this, when I
was still amongst you? You know very well that this is what is
holding Him back now, preventing Him from appearing in His
time. Really, the mystery of iniquity is already in action; all
that's missing is that he who is holding Him back be pushed
aside. Then the Evil One will be revealed, whom the Lord Jesus
will make disappear with the breath of His mouth and will
destroy with the splendour of His coming. The coming of
the Ungodly one, with regard to Satan's activity, will be
accompanied by all kinds of prodigies, signs and deceptive
portents, and by all the seductions proper to evil, for those who
will end up in damnation, for not having accepted the love of
truth, which would have saved them. For this very reason, God
sends them a deceitful power, which pushes them into believing
the lie, so that all those who not only resisted believing the
truth, but also others who took pleasure in iniquity, will be
condemned.

Exhortation to perseverance. But we must continually give
thanks to God for you, beloved brothers of the Lord, because
God has chosen you from the beginning, to save you through
the sanctifying action of the Spirit and faith in the truth. For

---

1. He speaks again of the Parusia. Perhaps his teachings were adulterated or
   misunderstood.
2. He is saying that the second Coming will precede a general apostasy and the
   Antichrist.

precisely this reason He called you for our preaching of the Gospel, so that you attain the glory of our Lord Jesus Christ.

WORK AND OBEDIENCE

Work and order. Brothers, I command you, in the name of our Lord Jesus Christ, to keep your distance from any brother who lives a life of leisure, contrary to the teachings which you have received from us[1]. You well know your duty to imitate us. We did not live idly amongst you, we didn't eat anybody else's bread for nothing, but we worked day and night, with sweat and toil, so as not to be superior to anybody, and not because we didn't have the right, but because we wanted to give you an example in ourselves to imitate. Indeed, when we were still amongst you, I gave you this maxim: "Whoever doesn't work, doesn't eat." However, we have learned that some of you live in idleness and do no work apart from snooping around. Well then, we exhort them and admonish them, in the Lord Jesus Christ, that they eat the bread they earn through disciplined work. But, brothers, don't tire of doing good. But if somebody does not obey the instructions in this epistle, point it out to him and avoid all contact with him, so that he feels ashamed. However, don't look on him as an enemy, but correct him as a brother.

EPILOGUE

May the Lord of peace Himself give you peace, always and by all means. May the Lord be with you.

---

1. There must have been some idlers in the community who were giving rise to unrest amongst the others; he will give themr a word of warning, and the example of working with their hands to earn their bread.

PASTORAL EPISTLES[1]

1st EPISTLE TO TIMOTHY

Greetings. Paul, apostle to Jesus Christ by the order of God, our Saviour, and of Jesus Christ, our hope, to Timothy, a true son in faith: on the part of God the Father and Jesus Christ.

Attitude to false doctrines[2]. When I set off for Macedonia I asked you to remain in Ephesus so as to order certain people to abstain from teaching strange things and to not pay attention to fables and interminable genealogies, more appropriate for promoting arguments than for realising God's plans, which are based on faith. The purpose of these orders is the charity of a pure heart, of a good conscience and a sincere faith, from which some have deviated by losing themselves in vain words, claiming to be doctors of the Law without understanding either what they're saying or what they are categorically stating. For we know that the Law is good if it is put to legitimate use, aware as we are that the Law is not for the righteous, but for cursed rebels, the ungodly and sinners, the irreligious and the perverse.

---

1. This is the name for those epistles addressed to his disciples Timothy and Titus, whom Paul had left as bishops in Ephesus and Crete respectively to give them norms of good government.

2. Vigilance.

Recommendation to Timothy. This is the recommendation that I'm making you, my son, Timothy, in compliance with the prophecies to which you were subject at another time, so that, having given them eyes, you may free the good fight, maintaining faith and good conscience. Some of them shipwrecked on faith when they had abandoned it.

The liturgical prayer. May everybody be saved. This is good and agreeable to God, our Saviour, who wants all men to be saved and come to know the truth[1]. Because there is one God, and also only one mediator between God and men, Jesus Christ, also Man, who handed Himself over for the redemption of everybody; a testimony given in its own due time, for the promulgation of which I have been made herald and apostle —I tell the truth, I don't lie— a doctor to the Gentiles in faith and truth.

Attitude which Timothy has to observe. You will be a good minister of Jesus Christ if you teach these things to the brothers, feeding your spirit with the teachings of faith and the good doctrine, like the faithful disciple you have proved yourself to be. On the other hand, reject profane fables and old wives' tales. Exercise yourself in piety, for bodily gymnastics are of little use, for piety is useful for everything[2], having promises for the present life and the future one. This doctrine is worthy of faith and all acceptance. So, for this reason, we strain and struggle, because we have put our hope in the living God, who is the Saviour of all men, above all the believers.

You must prescribe and teach these things. Let nobody scorn you for your youth, but be, rather, an example to the faithful in word, behaviour, charity, faith, chastity. Persevere in these things. Working like that you will save yourself and those who listen to you[3].

Conduct with different kinds of people. Don't reproach an old man harshly, rather exhort him like a father; young people

---

1. Magnificent declaration by Saint Paul of God's will to save all men who come to know the Truth. Ephesus was a cosmopolitan city.

2. Special recommendation of piety.

3. Timothy was young and had to gain prestige with an exemplary life.

like brothers; old women like mothers; young ones like sisters, with all purity.

Conduct for priests. The priests who govern well are doubly honored, especially those who busy themselves with preaching and teaching. I entreat you before God and Jesus Christ, and the chosen angels, that you observe these things impartially, without getting carried away by human appreciations. Do not lay hands on anybody without due consideration, don't be made to participate in other people's sins. Keep yourself pure.

· The sins of some men are known even before the judgement; those of others at the time. The same is the case with good deeds; some can be seen, and those which are not will not be able to remain hidden.

Avarice and frugality. Truly, we have brought nothing to this world, nor can we take anything from it. Let us be content with having food and clothing. For anybody who wants to get rich falls into temptation, in snares and much senseless and baneful covetousness which drown men in ruin and damnation, because avarice is the root of all evil, and some who have been carried away by it have strayed from the faith and inflicted much pain on themselves.

Final warning. Oh Timothy! Guard the deposit of faith which has been entrusted to you, avoiding vain and empty words and the contradictions of a false science. Some have lost their faith by bragging about this. May grace be with you.

2nd EPISTLE TO TIMOTHY

Strength in the preaching of the Gospel. For this reason I caution you to revive the grace of God, which was confered on you by laying on hands. For the Lord has not given us the spirit of fear, but that of strength, charity and prudence[1]. So, then, don't be ashamed of the testimony of our Lord, nor of mine, of His prisoner, but support with me the works through the Gospel with the aid of the power of God, who saved us and called us with a holy vocation, not by virtue of our deeds, but according to His blessing and the grace which has been given us in Jesus Christ for eternity, and now revealed by the appearance of our Lord, Jesus Christ, who destroyed death and made life and immortality shine through the Gospel, of which I have been made herald, apostle and doctor. I suffer these things for this cause, but I am not ashamed, for I know in whom I have put my trust and I am persuaded that He has the power to keep my deposit for that day.

Fight like a good soldier of Christ. So you, my son, strengthen yourself with the grace of Jesus Christ, and confide the things which you have heard from me, before many witnesses, to faithful men who are capable of teaching others. Bear trials with me like a good soldier of Christ. Whoever enlists as a soldier does not devote himself to a life of commerce, in order to please the person who enlisted him. And the athlete is not crowned if he does

---

1. He exhorts him so that the grace of the vocation which he has received and communicates to the others may not be in vain.

not fight according to the rules. The exhausted worker must be the first to partake of the fruits. Think on what I'm saying, for the Lord will give you understanding of everything.

Suffer with Christ to reign with Christ[1]. Remember Jesus Christ, brought back from the dead, from David's lineage, according to my Gospel. I suffer for Him, to the point of being in chains, as if I was an evil-doer, but the word of God is not chained. I support everything for the chosen ones, so that they attain the salvation which we have in Jesus Christ with eternal glory. This word is worthy of all faith: if we die with Him, we shall also live with Him; if we suffer with Him, we shall also reign with Him; if we deny Him, He will deny us. If we weren't faithful to Him.

Practice the virtues, especially meekness. Flee from the passions proper to youth and pursue justice, faith, charity and peace with those who invoke the Lord with a pure heart.

Difficult times will come. Know this, that difficult times will come in the last days. For men will be selfish, friends of money, arrogant, proud, blasphemous, rebellious against their parents, ungrateful, ungodly. Stay away from them.

Resolute perseverance in the example of the Apostle. You, on the other hand, remain faithful to what you have learnt and of what you are convinced, knowing for whom you have been instructed; for since childhood you have known the Holy Letters, which can give you the wisdom which leads to salvation through faith in Jesus Christ. For all divinely inspired Scripture is useful for teaching, for arguing, for correcting, for teaching in justice, so that the man of God may be perfect, and prepared for all good work.

Unconquered faithfulness to the ministry. I entreat you before God and Jesus Christ, who has to judge the living and the dead, through His coming and through His kingdom; preach the word, insist opportunely and inopportunely, argue, reproach, exhort with every patience and doctrinal preparation. For there will come a time when men will not tolerate the healthy

---

1. The union with Christ through Faith and Love makes us run and achieve the same fate as Christ, His Passion, Death, Resurrection and Glorification.

doctrine, but, carried away by passions and the urge to hear novelties, they will gather a crowd of masters around them, and will divert their eyes from the truth and go back to the fables[1]. But show yourself as vigilant in everything, support the work, perform the task of evangelist, fulfill your ministry with perfection.

Paul, ideal apostle[2]. I am now going to be offered as a libation, and the time of my departure is very close. I've fought the good fight, I've finished my career, I've kept my faith. And now the crown of justice is prepared for me, and the Lord, the just Judge, will reward me with it, and not only me, but also everybody else who has awaited His coming with love.

Nobody helped me in my first defense, rather everybody abandoned me. Let this not be taken into their accounts! But the Lord helped me and strengthened me so that, through me, preaching may be done and be heard in all nations, and I was freed from the mouth of the lion. The Lord will deliver me from all evil deeds and will save me for His heavenly kingdom[3]. Glory to Him for the centuries of centuries. Amen.

The Lord Jesus be with your spirit. Grace be with you.

---

1. This is a prophecy repeated by Saint Paul, currently topical in the many sects derived from the "Free Examination" or Protestant free will.
2. Victory cry of the old Paul.
3. In the evening of his life, and in chains, he sees his mission fulfilled and already has the eternal prize within his grasp.

LETTER TO TITUS[1]

Introductory greeting. Paul, servant of God and apostle of Jesus Christ to bring God's chosen ones faith and knowledge of the truth which leads to piety, with the hope placed in eternal life, to Titus, my true son in our common faith; grace and peace on the part of God the Father and of Jesus Christ, our Saviour.

The bishop priests. I left you in Crete to put in good order to what needed to be ordered, and so that you might ordain priests throughout the cities, in accordance with the instructions which I have given; may the candidate be irreproachable, married once, may his children be believers, who cannot be imputed with libertinage or indiscipline. It is essential that the bishop be irreproachable, as he is a steward of the house of God[2].

Conduct with false doctors. For there are many insubordinates, charlatans and swindlers, above all amongst the circumcised, whose mouths it is necessary to cover. Entire families go round teaching what they shouldn't, carried away by a covetousness of dishonorable winnings. Everything is clean for the clean, but, for the contaminated and those who have no faith, nothing is pure, because they have their minds and consciences contaminated. They profess to know God, but they

---

1. Titus, converted to the Faith by Paul, gave him good service, and Paul ordained him bishop of Crete.
2. Saint Paul advises celibacy. In the beginning married men were admitted to the priesthood, out of necessity; even then, only exemplary widowers.

deny Him with their deeds, being abominable and rebellious, incapable of any good deed[1].

Regenerated by Christ. For we were also foolish sometimes, disobedient, led astray, dominated by concupiscence and all kinds of pleasure, living in evil and envy, abhorrent, mutually hating each other. But when the kindness and love from God to man was revealed, our Saviour saved us, not through the righteous works which we may have done, but through His mercy, through the regenerative and renovating washing of the Holy Spirit, which spilled over us in abundance through Jesus Christ, our Saviour, so that, justified by His grace, we may come to be participants in eternal life, as we had hoped.

Good works and healthy doctrine against error. This word is worthy of faith and I want these things constantly inculcated so that those who have believed in God stand out in good works. These are good and useful for men. Draw away from the heretic, after admonishing him once and then again, knowing that he is perverted and is condemning himself through sin.

---

1. The Judaizers were also declared enemies of the Christians. They will receive their payment, just like the pseudoprophets.

EPISTLE TO PHILEMON[1]

Greeting and addressees. Paul, prisoner of Jesus Christ, and Timothy, the brother, to Philemon, our beloved collaborator, to Apphia, the sister; to Archippus, our companion in hardships, and the church which is congregated in their house. Grace and peace to you on the part of God the Father and the Lord, Jesus Christ.

Thanksgiving and praise for Philemon. I give thanks to my God, always remembering you in my prayers, because I hear of the charity and faith which you have for the Lord Jesus and all the saints, so that your participation in the faith proves to be efficacious in you for the glory of Christ, through the knowledge of everything good within you for the glory of Christ. I've received great joy and consolation from your charity, because the hearts of the saints have been comforted by you, brother.

Petition in favor of Onesimus[2]. Wherefore, although I have total freedom in Christ to send you what is your due, I beseech you rather in the name of charity, being Paul, an old man, and now, moreover, a prisoner of Jesus Christ; I beseech you for my son, Onesimus, whom I engendered in the faith in my prison, who was not useful for you at one time, but is now very useful to you and to me. I send him to you, that is, my own entrails. I wanted to have him at my side so that he might help me in your

---

1. He is a patrician, a rich citizen of Colossus, converted by Paul.
2. Onesimus was a slave who had escaped from his master and converted to the faith in Rome. He is sending him to him and is asking for his liberty.

place in my prison through the Gospel, but I have not wanted to act without your consent, so that you might do me this good deed, not out of force, but out of good will[1].

Perhaps for this reason he separated from you, so that you might always have him, not now like a slave, but like a beloved brother, who means a great deal to me, much more for you, both in the flesh and in the Lord! If you consider me a colleague, welcome him as you would welcome me. If he has offended you in anything, or owes you anything, put it on my account; I, Paul, sign it with my hand and writing, I shall pay; although I would say that you yourself owe me. Yes, brother, may I obtain this of you in the Lord; give this counsel to my heart in Christ. I have written to you, trusting in your obedience, knowing that you will do more than what I tell you[2].

Commission and greetings. Prepare a lodging for me at the same time, because I hope that through your prayers I shall be restored to you. Greetings to you from Epaphras, my companion in captivity in Jesus Christ; Marcus, Aristarchus, Demas, Luke, my collaborators. The grace of the Lord Jesus Christ be with your spirit. Amen.

---

1. The delicacy with which he intercedes for a brother slave, already in the Faith, is admirable.
2. The Church made this so deep-rooted plague on humanity disappear, not with violence, but with love.

EPISTLE TO THE HEBREWS

PROLOGUE

God, after having spoken many times and in different ways to the Fathers by means of the prophets, in those days, which are the last, has spoken to us through the Son, whom He has made heir to all things, through whom He also made the universe.

EXCELLENCIES OF THE NEW TESTAMENT

I. Christ, natural Son of God, greater than the angels[2]

Test of Scripture. To which of the angels, in effect, did God at any time say: "You are My Son, I have engendered you today"? And furthermore: "I shall be His Father and He will be My Son." And again, when He introduced the Firstborn into the world, He said: "Let all God's angels worship You." "Your throne, oh God, endures for ever", and "the sceptre of Your throne is the sceptre of equity". "You have loved justice and hated iniquity; because of this, God, your God, has anointed you with the oil of joy in preference to your companions." Still more: "It is You, Lord, who, in the beginning, laid the

---

1. Saint Paul addressed this epistle to the converted Jews, from Rome.
2. The Jews had not yet assimilated the New Doctrine and the Christian realities, and missed the liturgical splendor of the cult of the Temple of Jerusalem, different from the New Alliance.

foundations of the earth and the heavens are Your handiwork. They shall perish, but you remain." And to which of the angels did He ever say: "Sit at my right hand until I put Your enemies as a footstool for you[1]"? Aren't all these spirits charged with one ministry, sent to the service of those who must inherit salvation?

Exhortation. For this reason we must stick more diligently to the teachings received, so as not to go adrift. Because if the word promulgated by the angels was guaranteed to the point where every transgression and disobedience received its just punishment, how could we escape if we fail to look after such a great salvation?

The redemption carried out by Christ. It was fitting, in effect, that He through whom and for whom everything was made, wanting to bring to glory a great number of children, made perfect, through suffering, the chief who was to guide us to His salvation. Because the sanctifier and the sanctified all have the same origin. Therefore do not be ashamed of calling them brothers[2], saying: "I shall proclaim your name to my brothers; in the middle of the assembly I shall sing you hymns." And furthermore: "I shall put my trust in him." Still more: "Behold me and the children which God has given me."

Israelite incredulity and our faith. Therefore, as the Holy Spirit says: "Today, if you hear His voice, don't harden your hearts, as occured in the rebellion, the day of the temptation in the desert, when your fathers tempted me, by putting me to the test, and they tested my deeds for a period of forty years[3]. Because of this I became angry with that generation and said: 'His heart always goes lost; they never know my ways'. And I swore in my indignation: They will not enter my repose." Take care, brothers, that there is not amongst you a heart so bad and incredulous that it draws away from the living God. Rather, mutually encourage each other every day that this "today" lasts,

---

1. Jesus, the Son of God, is seated on the Father's right. Saint Paul argues with texts from the Bible to deal with the Jews.
2. Jesus was made our brother to save us.
3. The time in which they wandered through the desert.

so that none of you becomes hardened by the seduction of sin. Because we have come to be participants in Christ, if we continue to keep our initial faith unyielding until the end.

And as, on the one hand, it is true that some must enter his repose, and, on the other, that the first ones who received the good news did not enter because of their disobedience, God again fixes a day, a "today", saying through David, after such a long time, what has already been said: "Today, if you hear his voice, don't harden your hearts..." But if Joshua had procured the repose for them, David would not later have spoken of another day.

For there is a repose reserved for the people of God. For, whoever enters the repose of God will rest, he too, from his works, like God from His. Let's strive, then, to enter this repose so that nobody succumbs, imitating this example of disobedience[1].

The word of God is Christ the priest. For the word of God is alive and efficacious and sharper than a double-edged sword: it penetrates to the division of the soul and the spirit, of the joints and the marrow, and is capable of distinguishing the feelings and thoughts of the heart. There is no creature who is hidden before it, but everything is naked and laid bare to the eyes of Him to whom we must give account[2].

Therefore, having a high priest, sovereign, who entered heaven, Jesus, the Son of God, let us remain firm in our faith. For we do not have a high priest who is not able to forgive our weaknesses, for he was tested in everything, as we were, except for sin. Let us come near to the throne of grace then, so that we can get mercy and the grace of help.

Jesus Christ, the true pontiff. Because every pontiff, taken from among men, is ordained to intervene on behalf of men in their relations with God and offer gifts and sacrifices for sins. Capable of showing compassion to the ignorant and lost, since he is also surrounded by weakness, and he must offer sacrifices

---

1. The place of repose for the Hebrews wandering through the desert was the Promised Land. For us Christians it is the land of Heaven.

2. All consciences are patent and diaphanous before God.

for his own sins, as well as for those of the people. And nobody can assume this honor if he is not called by God, like Aaron. And so Christ also did not attribute to Himself the glory of being ordained high priest, but he received it of the one who said to Him: "You are My Son, I have engendered you today"; as He also says in another place: "You are a priest for ever, according to the order of Melchisedec." He who, in the days of His mortal life, having offered prayers and supplications with intense cries and tears to Him who could save Him from death and having been listened to because of His piety, although He was the Son, learned obedience through what He suffered; and, made perfect, He became for all those who obey Him the origin of eternal salvation[1].

Superiority of the cult, the sanctuary and the mediation of Christ the priest[2]. The key point of what we are saying is that we have a high priest who is seated at the right of the throne of Majesty in heaven, as a minister of the sanctuary and the true tabernacle erected by the Lord, not by man.

But now Christ has obtained a ministry both more excellent and better than the alliance, of which He is the mediator[3], and with more advantageous promises on which it is founded. Because if the first alliance had been perfect, there would have been no need to look for a second one. However, He says to them in a tone of recrimination:

"Look at the days to come, says the Lord, and I shall conclude
a new alliance with the house of Israel and with the
house of Judah.
This is the alliance which I shall make with the house of
Israel, after those days, says the Lord; I shall put My
laws in their minds, I shall record them in their hearts,
and I shall be their God and they will be My people.

---

1. He received the supreme priesthood directly from His Heavenly Father, but selected by the man whom He represents. He is in harmony because He has previously suffered.
2. Jesus Christ is at the Father's right hand to intercede for us.
3. Jesus is the most perfect Mediator, because He is God and a true man who represents all men for us.

Because I shall pardon their iniquities and will not again
remember their sins[1]."

When He spoke of the "new alliance", God declared the first
one antiquated. So now, what is old and antiquated is on the
point of disappearing.

Need for Christ's death. For this reason He is the mediator
of a new alliance, in order that, by contributing His death to
redeem the transgressions committed in the first alliance, those
who are called may receive the promised eternal inheritance.
Because where there is a testament it's necessary for the death
of the testator to be proven. A testament is only valid in the case
of death; because it does not come into force whilst the testator
is alive. Therefore, not even the first alliance was inaugurated
without bloodshed. Because Christ did not enter into a
sanctuary built by the hands of man, a copy of the real thing, but
into heaven itself, to present himself now before the face of
God, in our favor. Not to offer Himself anymore, as does the
high priest who enters the sanctuary every year with somebody
else's blood, because he had to suffer, in another way, many
times since the creation of the world; but now he has been
revealed one time only, at the end of time, to abolish sin through
His sacrifice. And in the same way that it is established for men
to die one time only, and afterwards there is a trial, in the same
way Christ also, after having offered himself up one time only
"to remove the sins of the world", will appear a second time,
without sin, to give salvation to those who await Him.

Christ, offered as a voluntary victim[2]. Therefore, when He
entered this world, Christ said:

"You have wanted neither sacrifice nor oblation; in exchange
You have formed a body for Me.
You have taken no pleasure in holocausts or in sacrifices for
sin;

---

1. Mediator of the New and definitive Alliance with His new People, the Church.
2. Jesus Christ is Priest, Victim and Altar of the only sacrifice, that of the Cross,
which is repeated on all our altars.

Then I said: Behold; I am coming, as is written of Me in the
    volume of the Book, to do Your will, Oh God."

Saying firstly: "You have taken no pleasure in sacrifices,
oblations, holocausts, or in sacrifices for sin", which are offered
according to the Law, and adding afterwards: "Behold; I am
coming to do Your will", He repeals the first regime in order to
found the second one. And because of this will we are sanctified
ourselves, once and for all, by the oblation of Jesus Christ's
body[1].

Efficacy of Christ's sacrifice. Such is the alliance which I
shall make with them after these days, says the Lord:

"I shall put My laws in their hearts and record them in their
    minds.
I shall not again remember either their sins or their iniquities."

NEED FOR FAITH AND DEEDS

Exhortation to perseverance. Let's firmly maintain the
hope which we profess, for He who has promised is faithful,
and let us look to each other to stimulate ourselves in charity
and good works.

Danger of apostasy. Since whoever breaks the Law of
Moses "is irredeemibly condemned to death by the testimony of
two or three witnesses", how much greater a punishment do you
think will be fitting for anybody who has abused the Son of God
and has treated as something profane the blood of the alliance,
by which He was sanctified, and has outraged the Spirit of
grace? Because we know Him who has said : "Vengeance is
mine; I shall repay." And also: "The Lord will judge His
people." It is terrifying to fall into the hands of the living God[2]!
Remember, on the other hand, those days in which, after having
been illuminated, you withstood great struggles full of

---

1. The New Alliance has annulled the old one; the Cult and the Mosaic Law have
    expired with the New Law of the Gospel.

2. He who breaks the old Law was punished, how much more will it be deserved
    by anybody who disobeys the New Law!

suffering[1]; now exposed publicly to opprobiums and tribulations, now showing solidarity with those who were treated in this way. Because, in effect, you have taken part in the penalties of the prisoners; you have accepted with joy the plundering of your goods, aware that you possess a better and permanent wealth. So don't lose your certain hope, which has a great reward. You have, then, the need to persevere, so that, satisfying the will of God, you obtain what is promised you. "Because still a little, very little time, and He who is coming will arrive and He will not delay[2]. But My righteous man will live by the faith[3], but, if he retreats like a coward, My soul will not take pleasure in him." We, however, are not of those who retreat like cowards, for damnation, but men of faith for the salvation of the soul."

Christ's example, courage in the struggle. We also, for precisely this reason, wrapped as we are in a great cloud of witnesses, must free ourselves of everything which is a burden for us, and of sin which easily seduces us, and run with perseverance in the trial which is proposed us, fixing our gaze on Jesus, the author and consumer of the faith, who, to obtain the glory which was proposed to Him, supported the cross, valiantly accepting ignominy, and He "is seated to the right of God's throne". Think continually, then, of Him who supported such a great contradiction on the part of sinners, so that you don't faint from getting discouraged. You still haven't resisted the spilling of blood in the fight against sin.

The two alliances. You, on the other hand, have approached Mount Zion, the city of the living God, the celestial Jerusalem, the myriads of angels, the festive assembly, the congregation of the first-born who are written in the heavens, and God, the universal judge, and the spirits of the righteous which have been

---

1. The persecutions.
2. The second Coming of Jesus Christ.
3. The Christian lives from faith, which has its solid foundation on the Word of Christ, who, as God, is unable and unwilling to deceive us. It is the Word of God.

made perfect, and Jesus, the mediator of a new alliance, and the blood of aspersion, who speaks more eloquently than Abel.

Last recommendations. Persevere in brotherly love. Do not forget hospitality, for, thanks to it, some people housed angels. Remember the prisoners as if you were within their bodies. Let matrimony be held in great honour and the conjugal bed be without blemish, for God will judge the adulterous and those who fornicate. Let your behaviour be free from greed. Be pleased with what you have, for God Himself has said,

"I will not forsake you not abandon you", therefore we can say, "The Lord is my help, I shall not be afraid. What can men do to me?"

Faithfulness in the follow-up to Christ. Remember your chiefs, those who proclaimed the word of God and, considering the end of His life, imitate His faith. Jesus Christ is the same yesterday and today, and He will be so for always. Do not allow yourself to be seduced[1] by different and strange doctrines; because it is better to strengthen the heart with grace than with foodstuff that doesn't do any good to those who stand by it. For this reason Jesus Christ suffered outside the gate, to sanctify the people by His own blood. Let's go out to meet Him, then, outside the camp, bearing His opprobium. Because we don't have a permanent city here below, but we are looking for the future one. Through Him, we ceaselessly offer to God "a sacrifice of praise", that is, "the fruit of the lips" which confess His name. Don't forget about beneficence and mutual aid, because God takes pleasure in such sacrifices. Obey your chiefs and be submissive to them; because they keep watch over your souls, of which you must give account, so that they do it joyfully and not with groaning. Because that would not be advantageous to you.

---

1. He puts the newly converted on their guard against the intrigues and deceits of sects, sowers of tares, and beseeches them to unite in mutual love for Jesus Christ.

EPILOGUE

May the God of peace[1] who brought back to life the great Shepherd of the sheep, Our Lord Jesus, through the blood of the eternal alliance, make you fit to fulfill His will in all kinds of good deeds, working in you what is agreeable for Jesus Christ, to whom there is glory for the centuries of centuries. Amen.

---

1. To help and serve the brothers is to love the Father.

EPILOGUE

CATHOLIC LETTERS[1]

JAMES'S EPISTLE[2]

Address and greetings. James, Servant of God and of the Lord Jesus Christ, to the twelve tribes of the Diaspora, greetings.

Counsels for the testing time. My brothers, consider the various tests to which you could be subjected as a supreme joy, knowing that faith tested produces constancy, but that constancy is accompanied by perfect deeds, so that you are perfect and irreproachable, without leaving anything to desire. Blessed is the man who endures the test; because if he has overcome it, he will receive the crown of life, which God has promised to those who love Him.

Temptation and grace. Let nobody say that He is tempted by God in temptation. Because God cannot be tempted to evil, nor does He tempt anybody. But each of us is tempted by his concupiscence, which attracts and seduces him. Once consented to, concupiscence afterwards engenders sin and sin, once committed, produces death. Don't deceive yourselves, then, my beloved brothers. Every excellent gift and every perfect

---

1. So called after Origenes and the holy Fathers, through being more universal, for those of Saint Paul were addressed to specific churches.

2. James the Younger, Jesus's cousin, was bishop of Jerusalem and died a martyr in the same city.

donation comes from on high, from the Father of the lights, in whom there is no change, or hint of variation.

There is no true faith without deeds[1]. Brothers, what does it serve somebody to say that he has faith, if he has no deeds? If a brother or sister are naked, and they're lacking their daily food, and one of you says: "Go in peace, warm yourselves up, and feed yourselves", without tending to their bodily necessities, what good is that? Faith is the same: If it has no deeds, it is dead within.

Patience in the wait for the Lord. Have patience, therefore, brothers, until the coming of the Lord. See how the worker waits for the precious fruit of the earth, waiting patiently until the early and late rains fall. You too, wait pastiently, raise your spirits, because the coming of the Lord is close[2].

Extreme Unction. Is one of you afflicted? Pray. Is he joyful? Intone Hymns. Is one of you sick? Call the priests from the Church and pray for him, annointing him with oil in the name of the Lord. The prayer of faith will save the patient, and the sins which he had committed will be pardoned him[3].

The conversion of the sinners. My brothers, if any of you deviates from the truth and somebody else converts him, know that whoever converts a sinner from his wayward path, frees his soul from death and will hide a multitude of his sins.

---

1. Faith without deeds is dead. Living faith is demonstrated in deeds; if it is not practiced, it dies, like any other work or profession.
2. Then he will confirm, in the Universal Judgement, the destinies and sentences received on the day of our transit or death.
3. The Sacrament of Extreme Unction for the sick.

1st EPISTLE OF SAINT PETER

HEADING

Peter, Christ's apostle, to the pilgrims in foreign lands, in Pontus, Galatia, Cappadocia, Asia and Bithynia, chosen according to the prescience of God the Father to be sanctified by the Spirit, to obey Jesus Christ and be sprinkled with His blood: May grace and peace abound in you[1]!

Hymn of praise. Blessed be God, Father of our Lord Jesus Christ, who has, through His great mercy, made us be born anew through the resurrection of Jesus Christ from the dead to a living hope, an incorruptible inheritance, uncontaminated and imperishable, which is reserved in heaven for you whom, by means of faith, are guarded by the power of God in sight of the salvation which is soon to be revealed in the final days. Be glad about this, since although at the moment you see yourselves obliged to undergo various trials so that the purity of your faith, (much more precious than gold, which, although pure, is corrupted by fire), may appear worthy of praise, of glory and honor whenever the revelation of Jesus Christ takes place; whom you love without having seen, in whom you now believe without seeing Him and rejoice with ineffable and glorious

---

1. This is a circular letter for all those in the diaspora, from Rome "the Babylon", to confirm them in the Faith. At his side he has John Mark, the Evangelist amanuensis, and Luke.

delight, secure of welcoming the object of your faith, the salvation of souls.

GENERAL EXHORTATIONS

Exhortation to a holy Christian life. Wherefore, gird the loins of your spirit, remain impeturbable and put all your hope in the grace which will be granted you on the day of Jesus Christ's revelation[1].

Exhortation to brotherly love. So, reject all wickedness, deceit and all kinds of hypocrisy, envy or slander, yearn, like new-born children, for unadulterated spiritual milk[2] so that, feeding on it, you may grow in an orderly way to salvation, and taste how good the Lord is. When we come to Him, a living stone, cast out by men but chosen and appreciated[3] by God, we play our part as living stones to be built in a spiritual house and holy priesthood to offer spiritual victims acceptable to God through the mediation of Jesus Christ, for the Scripture says: "Behold, in Zion I place a cornerstone, chosen, precious; he who believes in it will not be confused." Honor, then, devolves upon you, the believers. For the unbeliever, on the other hand, the stone cast out by the builders has come to be the head cornerstone, causing errors and scandals. They blunder precisely because they refuse to believe in the Gospel for which they have been destined. You, on the contrary, are "the chosen lineage, the royal priesthood, the holy nation, the special people", to aproclaim the greatness of Him who has called you out of the darkness to His marvellous light; you who once were not the people of God, have now come to be His people, and, in other times excluded from mercy, you have now attained it.

---

1. Saint Peter begins his exhortations for the neophytes and catechumens.
2. Spiritual milk is the doctrine of the Gospel.
3. We are all the living stones out of which the building of the Church is put together.

SPECIAL EXHORTATIONS

In the midst of the pagans. Dearly beloved, I exhort you as the pilgrims and foreigners that you are to abstain from the carnal appetites which fight against the soul. Behave exemplarily in the midst of the pagans so that when they see your good deeds they will glorify God[1] for the day of your visit in the same way that now they they now slander you as evil-doers.

Subject to all authority. This is the will of God, that we reduce the ignorant to silence with our exemplary conduct. Being free, as Christians, use freedom, not as a pretext to conceal evil, but knowing that you are God's servants[2]. Respect everybody, love the brothers, fear God, honour the king.

Christ's example[3]. Furthermore, this is your vocation, for Christ also suffered for you and left you an example so as to follow in His footsteps. He, in whom there was no sin and on whose lips no deceit was found; He who, when insulted, did not reply with insults; when mistreated, did not threaten, but abandoned Himself into the hands of Him who judges with justice; He who expiated our sins in His own body on the cross, so that, dead for sin, we might live for justice: "you were cured with His wounds." For you are like lost sheep, but now you have come back to the shepherd and keeper of your souls.

To wives. You, wives, likewise live in submission to your husbands so that if some of them prove themselves resistant to the Word, they will be led to faith by your conduct, when they see your respectful and chaste behaviour. May your adornment not be external, made of curls and plaits, of gold and clothes, but internal, rooted in the integrity of a sweet and quiet soul; this is what has value before God.

To husbands. Likewise, you, men, treat your wives conscientously like weaker beings, honoring them as

---

1. He counsels detachment from fleeting things, because we are only passing through here on the way to the Fatherland.
2. The abuse of liberty turns into libertinage.
3. The imitation of Christ, who is our model.

co-inheritors of the life of grace, so that your prayers are not obstructed.

ESCHATALOGICAL EXHORTATIONS

Proximity of the Parusia. The end of everything is approaching, be temperate and vigilant in prayer. Insist above all in mutual charity, for charity covers a multitude of sins.

Be hospitable to one another without grumbling. Put to the service of others each gift received, as is fitting in good stewards of God's various charismas: if someone has the gift of the word, let him use it as befits the oracles of God; if somebody has a ministry, let him practice it as God's agent, so that God may be glorified in everything through Jesus Christ, to whom power and glory is due for the centuries of centuries. Amen[1].

Before the persecutions. You are lucky if you are insulted in Christ's name, for the Spirit of glory, which is the Spirit of God, rests on you[2]. None of you is obliged to suffer through being a murderer, thief, evil-doer or through meddling in other people's affairs, but suffering on account of being a Christian is not shameful, rather it glorifies God because it bears this name. For the time has come for God's judgement by the house of God to begin! And if the judgement starts for us, what will be the end awaiting those who have rebelled against God's Gospel? For if the righteous man saves himself with great difficulty, where will it end for the ungodly one and the sinner? So, then, let even those who suffer through divine will commend their souls to the faithful Creator and continue to practice good.

To shepherds and the faithful. And when the supreme shepherd appears you will receive the imperishable crown of glory. In the same way, you youths, live in submission to the elders: dress yourselves in mutual humility because God resists

---

1. Service to God must be in accordance with the gift which each has received.
2. God permits persecutions in life to test our virtue and to be able to reward us for it.

the arrogant and gives His grace to the humble. Humiliate yourselves, then, under the powerful hand of God so that He may praise you in His time. Unload your troubles on to Him, for He takes care of you. Be temperate and alert! Your enemy, the Devil, stalks like a roaring lion, looking for somebody to devour[1]. Resist him, resolute in faith, knowing that your brothers scattered over the world are enduring the same suffering. God of all grace, who called you in Christ to His eternal glory, He himself will perfect you after brief suffering, He will confirm you, strengthen you and consolidate you. Glory and power to Him for the centuries of centuries. Amen.

The church of Babylon[2], chosen by God the same as you, and my son Mark, greet you. Greet each other with the kiss of charity. May the peace of the Lord be with you all, those who are in Christ.

---

1. The call is for everybody. In order to attain complete knowledge of God and gain His favor and friendship.
2. Rome, capital of paganism and idolatry. There was a small community.

2nd EPISTLE OF SAINT PAUL[1]

HEADING

Simon Peter, Jesus Christ's servant and apostle, to those who have attained one faith, no less precious than ours, through the justice of our God and Saviour Jesus Christ. May grace and peace abound in you through the knowledge of God and our Lord Jesus.

EXHORTATIONS AND THEIR MOTIVATION

Divine gifts. Since His divine power has granted us what is necessary for life and piety through knowldge of Him who has called us for the manifestation of His own glory and virtue, and for having poured on us precious and rich promises for this end, in order to make us participants of the divine nature, once we have escaped from the corruption which exists in the world because of concupiscence.

Consequently, brothers, make more and more effort to assure your vocation and election[2] in this way, you will never stumble. And the gates of the eternal Kingdom of our Lord and Saviour Jesus Christ will open two by two.

---

1. Saint Peter addresses the Jews in general, as Primate of the Apostles, so that they may grow in Faith, and he insists against those who mocked the Parusia. The Nicholaitans, Gnostics, etc.

2. The vocation, like Grace, must be cultivated so that it doesn't die.

The future coming of Christ. However much you now know them and are even secured in the present truth, I shall never cease to remind you of these things, for I consider it a duty to stimulate you with with my exhortations whilst I live in this tent[1], which I shall soon abandon, according to the revelation received from our Lord Jesus Christ. Because we did not give you to know of the power and coming of our Lord Jesus Christ on the basis of artificially combined fables[2], but as eye witnesses of His majesty. He received the honor and glory of God the Father when this voice was made to come from the grandiose glory: "This is my beloved Son in whom I have all my pleasures[3]." We ourselves heard this voice which came down from heaven, when we were with Him on the holy mount, and it is confirmed even more in the prophetic word. Knowing above all that no Scriptural prophecy is subject to personal interpretation, since men spoke on God's behalf in times past, prompted by the Holy Spirit, and their prophecies were not proffered by human will[4].

WARNING AGAINST THE LOOSE-LIVING HERETICS

There will be false doctors. As there was false prophets within the people, there shall also be false doctors, who will introduce sects of perdition, the will deny the Lord who redeemed them and bring upon them disaster. Many people will follow them, and the ways of truth will be cursed on their account. Taken by greed they will make business with you with lies, but damnation is threatening them, and perdition is not asleep.

---

1. Mortal body.
2. They are not stories.
3. The Transfiguration.
4. Private interpretation cannot be done without falling into many mistakes. This is the origin of the sects. Because of this the Church orders notes to be put in the Bible.

Their punishment is certain. If God did not forgive the angels who had sinned but threw them to hell, to the prisons awaiting their judgement, nor forgave the ancient world, from which he only saved eight people, amongst them Noah, as a baluart of justice. He sent the flood upon the world of the impious and destroyed and burnt up the cities of Sodom and Gomorrah so that they could be an example to all the impious people in the future, and spared Lot the upright. The Lord spares the pious ones from temptation and the impious he keeps for their punishment in the day of the judgement.

THE SECOND COMING OF CHRIST IS CERTAIN

Dearly beloved, this is the second epistle which I'm writing to you. My purpose is the same in both: to excite your healthy intelligence with my exhortations. Remember the words foretold by the holy prophets and the Lord and Saviour's commandment conveyed by your apostles. Dearly beloved, one thing, however, is not hidden: one day is like a thousand years to God, and "a thousand years like a day". The Lord is not delaying the fulfillment of the promise, as some who accuse Him of tarrying believe, but uses patience with you, for He doesn't want anybody to perish, only for everybody to achieve repentance. The day of the Lord will come like a thief[1]; then the heavens will disintegrate with a great uproar, the burnt-out elements will dissolve and neither will the earth and everything in it escape.

If everything has to disappear like this, what kind of person must you be in holy customs and works of piety, whilst you wait for and accelerate the coming of the day of God when the molten heavens will disintegrate and the burnt elements will dissolve? But according to His promise we are awaiting new heavens and a new earth, wherein justice lives.

---

1. He will come soon, and out of the blue, when we least expect it. For each of us the coming of the Lord is the hour of our death.

FINAL EXHORTATION

Wherefore, dearly beloved, as we await these things, let us make the effort to find ourselves without stain, without blame and in peace in the Lord's presence. Take the patience of our Lord as medicine and rescuer, as our much loved brother Paul has already written to you, in accordance with the wisdom granted him. In fact, in all the epistles, whenever this subject is brooked, it is expressed like this. It is true that some difficult points are to be found in them, which the ignorant and unstable distort for their own perdition, as they do with the rest of the Holy Scripture[1]. Dearly beloved, you, however, be on guard, forewarned, so as not to fall away from your own resoluteness, led astray by the error of the licentious. Rather believe in the grace and knowledge of our Lord and Saviour Jesus Christ. Glory to Him now and until the day of eternity!

---

1. The Bible is difficult, we need the Church's teaching for its correct interpretation.

1st EPISTLE OF SAINT JOHN

Exordium. What was from the beginning, what we have heard, what we have seen with our own eyes, what we have contemplated, what our hands have touched, of the Word of life, yes, life has been made manifest, we have seen it, we bear witness to it and proclaim eternal life to you, which was next to the Father and has been made manifest to us; we proclaim to you what we have seen and heard so that you are in communion with us. Our communion is with the father and with His Son Jesus Christ. I write all this to you so that your pleasure may be complete[1].

Divine communion and sin. This then is the message which we have heard of Him and which we proclaim to you: God is light and there is no darkness in Him. If we say that we are in communion with Him, and walk in darkness, we are lying and not dealing with the truth. But if we walk in the light, as He is in the light, we are in communion with each other, and the blood of Jesus, his Son, purifies us of all sin. If we were to say that we have no sin, we would be deceiving ourselves and the truth would not be with us.

My sons, I am writing these words so that you do not sin. But if some of you does, we have an advocate by the father, Jesus Christ, the Just One. He was the victim for our sins; not only for our sins, but for everybody's.

---

1. The apostle Saint John wrote to the churches in Asia Minor from Ephesus, around the year 98, to defend them from the heresies which denied the divinity of Jesus. They were the Gnostics.

Divine communion and the commandments. We know that we know Him if we keep His commandments. Whoever states that he knows, but does not keep His commandments, is a liar and the truth is not in him. But whoever keeps his word, the love of God is truly perfect in him. We hereby know that we are in Him; whoever states that he remains in Him, must behave as He behaved.

Love of the world and of God. Don't love the world, if somebody loves the world, the love of the Father is not in him. Because everything that's in the world, concupiscence of the flesh, the concupiscence of the eyes and pride in riches, does not come from the Father, but from the world[1].

Truth and the Antichrists. They have emerged from amongst us, but they were not of us. Because if they had been ours, they would have remained with us. But this has occured so that it should be made manifest that all those were not ours. I have written to you about those who want to seduce you. But ensure that the unction, which you have received from Him, remains in you; and you don't need anybody to teach you. And now, sons, remain in Him, so that when He comes, we shall be able to sit down in safety and not be ashamed of finding yourselves far from Him when He comes. If you know that He is righteous, recognise too that whoever practises justice has been born from Him.

Rights and duties of the children of God. Look at how great a love the Father has given us by causing us to be called children of God, and indeed we are[2]. If the world does not know us it's because it hasn't known Him[3]. Dearly beloved, from now on we are children of God, and what we shall be still has not been revealed. We know that when it is revealed, we shall be like Him, because we shall see Him like He is. Whoever has this hope in Him, is purified in himself, as He is pure. But whoever

---

1. It is not the material world, but the mundane spirit corrupted by vices, errors, scandals and sins, because the universe and nature are beautiful.

2. Our divine filiation through Grace makes us brothers of Jesus and inheritors of Heaven.

3. The worshippers of that pagan world are dazzled by pleasures, honors and riches.

sins, practices iniquity, and sin is iniquity. Children, don't let anybody seduce you. He who practices justice is just; whoever sins is from the Devil, because the Devil is a sinner from the beginning. The Son of God has been made manifest to destroy the works of the Devil. Because this is the message which you have heard from the beginning: Let them love each other.

Don't be amazed if the world hates you[1]. We know that we have passed from death to life, because we love the brothers. Whoever hates his brother is a murderer and you know that no murderer has eternal life permanently within Him. Then we have known Love because He has given His life for us. And we must also give our lives for our brothers. If somebody has goods in this world and sees his brother in need, and closes his own heart to him, how can the love of God be in him? Let's love each other not with words nor tongues, but with deeds and truth. We shall receive everything we ask of Him, because we keep His commandments and do what pleases Him.

The spirit of truth and the spirit of terror. The one who is with you is the greatest one in the world. They are the world and therefore they speak up for the world, and the world listens to them. But we are God's. The man who knows God listens to us, and the man who is not his, he does not listen to us. In this we see the spirit of truth and the spirit of terror.

Love of God and love of the neighbour. Dearly beloved, let us love each other, because love is from God. Then the love of God was made manifest through us, because He has sent His only Son to the world so that we live through Him. His love consists of this: It is not us who have loved God, but God who has loved us[2], and He has sent His son as a propitiatory victim for our sins[3]. Dearly beloved, if God has loved us in this way, we must also love each other. Whoever confesses that Jesus is the Son of God, God dwells in him and he in God. We have known the love which God has for us and we have believed.

---

1. This world is the enemy of God and our soul.
2. God loved us before we existed. In the God's thought we were already existing from all eternity, because everything is present in God.
3. Jesus Christ, the Son of God.

God is love and whoever is in love is in God and God in him.[1] The perfection of love in ourselves consists of this, that we have absolute confidence in the day of judgement; because as He is, so also are we in this world. There is no fear in love; on the contrary, perfect love casts out fear, for fear supposes punishment and whoever fears is not perfect in love. As for ourselves, let us love each other, because He loved us first. If somebody says that he loves God and hates his brother, he is a liar. Whoever doesn't love his brother, whom he sees, cannot love God, whom he doesn't see. This is the commandment which we have received from Him, that whoever loves God also loves his brother.

Faith in Jesus Christ. Whoever believes that Jesus is the Christ was born in God. Then we know that we love the children of God and keep His commandments. Because the love of God consists in keeping His commandments. Because everything born of God conquers the world. And this is the victory which has conquered the world, our faith. Whoever does not believe in God has made Him a liar, because He does not believe in the testimony which God has given from His Son. This is the testimony which God has given us, eternal life and this life is in His Son[2]. Whoever has the Son, has life; and whoever doesn't have the Son of God, does not have life. I write you this, so that you know that you, who believe in the name of the Son of God, have eternal life.

Prayer and sin. This is the security which we have in God, that if we ask something according to His will, He listens to us. And if we know that He listens to us in everything which we ask of Him, we also know that we now possess what we have asked for. If somebody sees his brother commit a sin, which does not merit death, pray, and God will give him life; this for those who sin without meriting death. There is a sin which deserves death[3]; I don't say that they ask for this one. All

---

1. He is the source of love. Whoever loves according to God is in God.
2. Faith is based on the word of Christ, who does not want, nor is able to deceive us, because it is good and knows everything.
3. The one which deserves eternal death; it is mortal sin.

injustice is a sin, but there are sins which don't merit death. We know that whoever has been born of God does not sin.

2nd EPISTLE OF SAINT JOHN[1]

Greetings and commendations. I, the Presbyter to the Chosen Woman[2] and her children, whom I love in the truth —not only I, but also all those who have known the truth.

Exhortation to brotherly love. I rejoiced greatly when I found your children walking in the truth, in accordance with the commandment received from the Father. Love consists of walking according to His commandments. And this commandment, as you have received it from the beginning, is that you walk in love. Because many seducers have burst into the world, who don't confess to Jesus, as the Christ incarnate. Here you have the Seductor, the Antichrist. Watch over yourselves, so that you don't lose the fruit of your deeds, but so that you receive a full reward.

Conclusion. I have many things to write you, but I haven't wanted to put them down with ink and paper, for I hope to come to you soon and speak to you in person, so that your joy may be complete. The children of your Chosen sister greet you.

---

1. Saint John (Presbyter = elder) is the principal of the Churches of Asia.
2. The Chosen Woman is an unknown community threatened by the doctrines of false doctors.

THE EPISTLE OF SAINT JUDE

3rd EPISTLE OF SAINT JOHN

Greetings and commendations. I, the Presbyter[1], to the beloved Gaius, whom I love in the truth. Dearly beloved, I hope all your things are prospering and that you enjoy good health in body and soul. I greatly rejoiced when the brothers arrived and testified to your truth, that is, to how you walk in the truth. Dearly beloved, you work faithfully in everything which you do for the brothers, even though they are foreigners; they have born witness to your charity before the Church. You will do good work by getting them ready for the journey in a manner worthy of God. I have written something to the Church, but Diotrephes, who craves pre-eminence, does not receive us[2].

Conclusion. I have many things to say to you, but I don't want to do it with pen and ink. I hope to see you soon and we shall speak in person. May peace be with you. Your friends greet you. Greet the friends by name.

---

1. John was called Presbyter, a title reserved for heads of communities.
2. The Apostle contrasts the exemplary conduct of Gaius with the insubordinate and ambitious Diotrephes.

EPISTLE OF SAINT JUDAS

Address, greeting and reason for the epistle. Judas, servant of Jesus Christ, brother of James, to those who have been called, loved in God the Father and preserved for Jesus Christ; may mercy, peace and charity be copiously given you[1]. Dearly beloved, I had a great desire to write to you about our common salvation and I have been obliged to do it to exhort you to fight for the faith, which has been transmitted to the saints once and for all. Because some ungodly men have furtively been introduced amongst you[2], as had already been foretold in the past that they would be condemned in this way, and they have turned the grace of our God into libertinage, and deny our sole master and Lord, Jesus Christ.

They are dissatisfied gossips, who live at the whim of their passions; their mouths proffer bravado, and they praise people out of their own self-interest.

Exhortation to the Christians. But you, dearly beloved, remember the words with which the apostles of our Lord Jesus Christ prophesied to you. It is these sensual men, deprived of the Spirit, who provoke discords. You, on the other hand. dearly beloved, build on your holy faith, praying in the Holy Spirit; preserve yourselves in the love of God, keeping the mercy of

---

1. Judas Thaddeus, brother of James the Younger, the bishop of Jerusalem, and Jesus's cousin, writes to the Christian Jews.
2. Thaddeus warns them that some subversive elements have infiltrated certain Christian communities.

our Lord Jesus Christ for eternal life. Convince those who hesitate; save others, pull them out of the fire[1].

Doxology. Conclusion. Glory, majesty, sovereignty and power to Him who has the power to keep you from sin and present us faultless with joy before His glory; to the sole God, our Saviour through Jesus Christ Our Lord, before all time, now and forever. Amen.

---

1. He incites them all, with great apostolic zeal, to persevere and help the brothers to gain the Eternal Kingdom.

APOCALYPSE[1]

LETTERS TO THE SEVEN CHURCHES OF ASIA

Preparatory vision. I, John, your brother and companion in tribulation, in the kingdom and in constancy, in Jesus. I found myself on the isle of Patmos, because of the word of God and the testimony of Jesus. I fell into ecstasy on the day of the Lord and I heard behind me a voice as loud as a trumpet, which said: "Write what you see in a book and send it to the seven Churches, to Ephesus, Smyrna, Pergamos, Thyatira, Sardis, Philadelphia and Laodicea." I turned round to see the voice which was speaking to me, and hardly had I turned round, when I saw seven golden candlesticks[2] and in the middle of the candlesticks, somebody like a Son of man[3], dressed in a large tunic and girded with a golden sash round his chest. His head and hair were white as white wool, as snow; his eyes, like a fiery flame; his feet, like brass when it is purified in fire; his voice, like the noise of many waters. He had seven stars in his right hand and a sharp double-edged sword came out of his mouth; his face was like the sun which shines in all its radiance.

---

1. Apocalypse means revelation. The historical framework is one of confusion and the violent persecution of Nero. John himself, the author, emerged unscathed from the martyrdom. His message is "Jesus will come" and his esoteric language will enable him to elude the investigations of the persecuters. The Church is immortal, it will triumph.

2. The 7 Churches.

3. Jesus.

The seven stars are the angels of the seven Churches and the seven candlesticks are the seven Churches.

Letter to the Church of Ephesus. Write to the angel[1] of the Church of Ephesus: I know your deeds, your trials and your constancy. I know that you can't tolerate the wicked; that you have put to the test those who call themselves apostles, without being them, and have found them to be liars; that you are constant and that you have suffered for my Name without fainting. But I have this against you; you have lost the charity of the beginning. Remember, then, from where you have fallen, repent and go back to working as before. Because, if you don't convert, I shall go to you rapidly and take the candlestick away from you. Whoever has ears, let him hear what the Spirit says to the Churches.

Letter to the Church of Smyrna[2]. Write to the angel of the Church of Smyrna: Thus says the first and the Last, He who died and came back to life. I know your tribulation and your poverty (although you are rich) and the calumnies on the part of those who call themselves Jews, without being so, for they are more like a Synagogue of Satan. Don't be afraid of what you are going to suffer. The Devil will imprison some of you; he is to put you to the test, you will undergo a test of ten days. Be faithful until death and I shall give you the crown of life. Whoever has ears, let him hear what the Spirit says to the Churches. The conqueror will not be wounded with the second death[3].

Letter to the Church of Pergamos. Write to the angel of the Church of Pergamos: This is what He who has the sharp, double-edged sword says. I know where you're living. The throne of Satan is there; but you remain faithful to my Name and have not denied my faith. But I have something against you: you also have adepts of the doctrine of the Nicholaitans[4]. Repent, for if you don't, I shall go to you directly and fight

---

1. This is the bishop of each church.
2. City in Asia.
3. The eternal one.
4. Heretics with libertine and unchecked customs.

against you with the sword from my mouth. Whoever has ears, let him hear what the Spirit says to the Churches. I shall give hidden manna[1] and a white stone to the winner. And I shall write a new name on the stone, only known to the one who receives it.

Letter to the Church of Thyatira[2]. Write to the angel of the Church of Thyatira: This is what the Son of God, who has eyes like a flame and feet like brass, says. I know your deeds, your love, your faith, your service, your constancy; your last deeds are more numerous than the first ones. But I have this against you: You allow Jezebel, that woman considered a prophetess, to teach and seduce my servants[3]. I shall give to the conqueror, to Him who remains faithful to my service until the end, power over nations, and he will pasture them with a rod of iron, as clay pots break.

Letter to the Church of Sardis. Write to the angel of the Church of Sardis: This is what he who has the Seven Spirits of God and the seven stars, says. I know your deeds. You pass as living, but you are dead. Keep watch and reaffirm what remains and is on the point of perishing. Because I have not found your deeds perfect before God. Remember how you received and heard the word; keep it and repent. Because, if you are not vigilant, I shall fall on you like a thief, without you knowing at what time I'm going to surprise you. But you still have some people in Sardis who have not contaminated their clothes. They will walk with me with white clothes, because they are worthy of them. The conqueror will be dressed in white clothes[4], and I shall never erase his name from the book of life and I shall confess his name before my Father and the angels. Whoever has ears, let him hear what the Spirit says to the Churches.

Letter to the Church of Philadelphia[5]. Write to the angel of the Church of Philadelphia: This is what the Saint, the

---

1. The food of eternal life.
2. City in Asia Minor.
3. Jezebel, the depraved wife of King Achab.
4. Symbol of purity and victory.
5. Hellenistic city in Lydia.

Truthful one who has David's key, He who opens and never closes, He who closes and never opens, says. I know your deeds. Here is a door which I have open before you, which nobody can close[1]. Because, despite your weakness, you have kept my word and you have not denied my Name. My coming is close. Keep what you have so that nobody removes your crown[2]. I shall make the conqueror a column in God's temple, and he shall not leave any more. I shall write the name of my God on him, the name of my God's City —the New Jerusalem, which comes down from my God's heaven— and my new name. Whoever has ears, let him hear what the Spirit says to the Churches.

Letter to the Church of Laodicea[3]. Write to the angel of the Church of Laodicea: Here is what the Amen, the faithful and truthful testimony, the beginning of God's creation, says. I know your deeds: You are neither cold nor hot. If only you were cold or hot, because you're lukewarm, and you are neither cold nor hot, I'm going to vomit you out of my mouth. You are saying: I am rich, I've gotten rich, I don't need anything; and you don't know that you are wretched, miserable, poor, blind and naked. I reproach and punish the one I love; be zealous, then, and repent. Here I am at the door, calling you. If somebody hears my voice and opens to me, I shall enter his house[4]; I shall dine with him and he with me. I shall place the conqueror on my throne with me, in the same way as I, who have conquered, have sat with my Father in his throne. Whoever has ears, let him hear what the Spirit says to the Churches.

THE SEVEN SEALS

God's throne and the heavenly court. After this I had a vision. Behold, a gate was opened in the sky; and the first voice,

---

1. Open door to the apostalate.
2. For the value demonstrated in the Jewish persecution.
3. City in Phrygia.
4. Calling at the gate of conversion.

which I had heard speaking to me as if with the sound of a trumpet, said to me: "Come up here and I shall show you what's going to happen directly". At that moment I fell into ecstasy. And, behold, there was a throne in heaven and somebody seated on the throne[1]. He who was sitting on the throne had the appearance of a jasper and sardine stone. The throne was surrounded by a rainbow resembling emerald. Around the throne there were twenty-four thrones, on which were seated twenty-four elders[2] dressed in white, with golden crowns on their heads. Lightning, voices and thunder came out of the throne. Seven fiery lamps (which are are the Seven Spirits of God[3] burned before the throne. Before the throne there was a sea of glass, like crystal. In the middle of the throne and round about, four animals covered with eyes, in front and behind. The first resembled a lion; the second, a bull; the third has a face like a man's and the fourth, like an eagle which flies. Each of the four animals has six wings, and inside they were full of eyes. And they repeat, day and night, without respite: "Blessed, Blessed, Blessed is the Lord God, the Omnipotent, He who was, He who is, He who is coming". Evert time the Animals give glory, honor and thanks to Him, who is seated on the throne and who lives for the centuries of centuries[4], the twenty-four elders prostrated themselves before Him who was seated on the throne, worship Him who lives for the centuries of centuries and cast their crowns before the crown, saying: "You are worthy, Lord, Our God, of receiving glory, honor and power. Because you have created all things, and they exist and have been created by your will[5]".

The book of the seven seals. I saw, on the right hand side of Him who was seated on the throne, a book written on the inside and outside, sealed with seven seals. I saw a powerful angel, who was exclaiming loudly: Who is worthy of opening the book

---

1. Somebody seated: the Sovereign of the Universe.
2. These elders exercise priestly and royal functions, so they wear crowns. Their number perhaps corresponds to the 24 priestly classes.
3. Angels, living beings.
4. Derived from Ezekiel (1,5 ss and 10, 12 ss).
5. The 4 living beings support the throne of the omnipotent God.

and breaking the seals? And nobody in heaven or on earth could open the book and read it. I wept a lot, because nobody had been found who was worthy of opening the book and reading it. One of the Elders said to me: "Stop crying. Behold the Lion who has conquered the tribe of Judah, the scion of David, who'll manage to open the book and its seven seals." Then I saw a lamb, standing as if slaughtered, betwee the throne and the four Animals on one side and the Elders on the other. He had seven horns and seven eyes (these are the Seven Spirits of God sent throughout the world). He approached and took the book from the right hand of Him who was seated on the throne. When he had taken the book[1], the four animals and the twenty-four Elders prostrated themselves before the Lamb[2], each holding in their hands a harp and gold cups full of perfumes (the prayers of the saints). They sang a new canticle: "You are worthy of taking the book and opening its seals, because you have been slaughtered and with your blood you have rescued the men of all tribes, tongues, peoples and nations for God. You have made a Kingdom of Priests reigning on earth for our God." Afterwards I saw and heard the voice of a multitude of angels, who were around the throne, and of the Animals and Elders. In number, myriads and myriads and millions and millions. And they said in a loud voice: "The slaughtered lamb is worthy of receiving the power, richness, wealth, strength, glory and praise."

Opening of the first four seals. Horses and horsemen[3]. I immediately had a vision in which the Lamb opened the first of the seven seals. I heard the first of the four Animals shouting, as if with a voice of thunder: "Come". I saw a white horse appear. The rider had a bow; he was given a crown and left as a conqueror. When the Lamb opened the second seal, I heard the second animal shout: "Come". And another, red, horse came out; his rider was given the power to take peace from the earth,

---

1. The Book of the seven Seals. A roll of parchment containing divine decrees.
2. Christ, the Lamb of God, indicated by the Forerunner.
3. The 4 horses (Zac. 6, 1-7). The white one: victory and salvation. The red: war and justice. The black: hunger. The dun-colored: death.

to cause men to be slaughtered; he was given a big sword. When the Lamb opened the third seal, I heard the third animal shouting: "Come". And I saw a black horse appear, whose rider had scales in his hand. And I heard a voice in the middle of the four Animals, which said: "Two pounds of wheat for a penny, but don't touch the oil and wine." When the Lamb opened the fourth seal, I heard the shout of the fourth animal: "Come". And behold, there appeared a dun-colored horse, whose rider was called Death. He was given power over one quarter of the earth to kill with the sword, with hunger, with plague and with the beasts of the earth.

Opening of the fifth seal[1]. The prayer of the martyrs. When the Lamb opened the fifth seal, I saw under the altar the souls of those who had been slaughtered because of the word of God and for the testimony which they had given. They shouted loudly, saying: "Until when are You, the Master, the Saint, the Truthful one, going to wait to do justice and avenge our blood on the inhabitants of the earth?" And each one was given white clothing and was told to have patience for a little while more, until the number of their companions in service, and their brothers who had to be killed like them, was complete. When the Lamb opened the sixth seal[2], a violent earthquake occurred, the sun darkened like a horsehair sack, the moon became all bloody, and the stars in the sky fell to earth, just as a fig tree drops its green figs when shaken by a strong wind. The sky disappeared like a volume which is rolled up, and all the mountains and all the islands were removed from their places. The kings of the earth, the princes, the tribunes, the rich, the powerful, all the slaves and all the men hid in the caves and in the rocks of the mountains. And they said to the mountains and rocks: Fall on us and hide us far from the face of Him who is seated on the throne, and far from the wrath of the Lamb.

---

1. The fifth seal are the martyrs who ask for justice. The white clothes are a symbol of purity.

2. Cosmic upheavals.

Because the great day of his fury has come, and who will be able to endure[1]?

The sealed ones. After this I saw four angels standing on the four corners of the earth, holding back the four winds of the earth so that the wind should not blow either on the earth, or on the sea, or on any tree. Then I saw another angel who was coming up from the East and carried the seal of the Living God, and who shouted loudly at the four angels, to those who had been given the power to damage the earth and sea: "Don't touch the land, nor the sea, nor the trees, until we have sealed the foreheads[2] of the servants of our God". And I heard the number of the sealed ones of all the tribes of the sons of Israel, one hundred and four thousand.

The chosen ones. After this I saw a great crowd appear, which nobody could count, of every nation, tribe, people and tongue[3]. They were standing in front of the throne of God and in front of the Lamb, dressed in white clothes and with palms in their hands[4]. They were shouting loudly, saying: "Hail our God, who is sitting on the throne, and the Lamb." All the angels were standing around the throne, the Elders and the four Animals. They fell headlong before the throne and worshipped God, saying: "Amen. Blessing, glory, wisdom, thanksgiving, honor, power and strength to our God, for the centuries of the centuries. Amen."

One of the Elders took the word and said to me: "These people dressed in white, who are they and where have they come from?" I replied to him: "Sir, you know that." He said to me: "These are the ones who come from the great tribulation and have washed their clothes and whitened them in the blood of the Lamb. Because of this they are in front of the throne of God and they serve him day and night in his Temple.

The seventh seal. When the Lamb opened the seventh seal, there was a silence in heaven for about half an hour. Then I saw

---

1. Desperation of the wicked.
2. The sign of the chosen ones.
3. That is to say, everybody.
4. The white clothes and palms are a symbol of victory and triumph.

the seven angels, standing on foot in front of God; and they were given seven trumpets[1]. Afterwards, another angel came, who stopped and stood next to the altar, with a golden censer. They were given many perfumes, so that they could offer them together with prayers to all the saints, on the golden altar placed in front of the throne. And the smoke from the perfumes went up from the angel's hand, with prayers to the saints.

The woman and the dragon[2]. A great sign appeared in the sky: A woman dressed in the sun, with the moon under her feet and a crown of twelve stars on her head. She was pregnant and shouted with birth pains and the anguish of giving birth. Another sign appeared in the sky: A dragon, the colour of fire, with seven heads and ten horns; on his heads, seven diadems. His tail dragged along one third of the stars of the sky and threw them on the earth. Then there was a battle in heaven. Michael and his angels fought against the Dragon[3]. The Dragon and his angels fought, but couldn't prevail, and there was no place for them in heaven. And the great Dragon, the former Serpent, who is called "Devil" and "Satan", the seductor of the whole world, was flung out and his angels were flung out with him. I heard a loud voice in the heaven, which said: "Now salvation has arrived, the power, the kingdom of our God and the sovereignty of his Christ, because the accuser of our brothers, the one who, night and day, used to accuse them before our God, has been flung out. They have conquered them through the blood of the Lamb and through the words of their testimony and they have scorned their own life to the point of suffering death. Therefore, rejoice, oh heavens, and you who live in them. Cursed be the land and sea, because the Devil has come down on you with great fury, knowing that he has little time left." The Serpent spewed a river of water from his mouth, behind the woman, so that it might take her away. But the land came to the woman's assistance, opening its mouth and swallowing the river

---

1. Number 7 is undefined in the Bible.
2. The woman announced in Genesis 3,15.
3. God put his angels to the test and some of them, the dragon and his angels, were insubordinate; and they were cast out to Hell, converted into demons.

which the dragon had vomited out of his mouth. The dragon got angry with the woman and went to wage war against the rest of her descendants, those who keep God's commandments and have the testimony of Jesus[1].

The Lamb and the virgins. After I saw the Lamb, who was standing on Mount Zion, accompanied by one hundred and forty-four thousand people who had His Name and the Name of His Father written on their foreheads. I heard a voice which came from heaven, similar to the voice of great waters and the noise of a great thunderclap. The sound which I heard was like that of harpists when they play their instruments. They were singing a new canticle in front of the throne, in front of the four Animals and the Elders. Nobody could learn the canticle, apart from the one hundred and forty-four thousand rescued from the earth.

These are the ones who have not soiled themselves with women, because they are virgins; they were rescued from among men as novelties for God and for the Lamb; no lie has been found in their mouths: They are irreproachable[2].

The three angels. I saw another angel who was flying in the middle of the sky, and he had eternal good news to proclaim to the inhabitants of the earth, to all nations, tribes, tongues and peoples. He said loudly: "Fear God and give him glory, because the time of his judgement has come; worship Him who has made the heaven and earth, the sea and the springs of water." And a second angel followed him, shouting: "Babylon's fallen, fallen, the Great one, which drenched all peoples with the wine of his burning lewdness." I heard a voice which came from the sky and said[3]: "Write: Blessed from now on are the dead who die in the Lord. Yes, said the Spirit, so that they rest in their works, because their works accompany them."

---

1. The Messiah and his Mother triumphed from His Immaculate Conception. Now the dragon fights against His children.
2. The virgins sing a new canticle, and they will accompany the Lamb everywhere.
3. The angel announces the end and the triumph. The fall of pagan Rome, symbol of the end of the world.

The Son of man. Afterwards I saw a white cloud and on the cloud was seated One like the Son of man[1], with a golden crown on his head and a sharpened sickle in His hand. Another angel came out of the Temple shouting loudly at Him who was seated on the cloud: "Take your sickle and reap, because harvest time has come, for the cornfields of the earth are dry." Still another angel came out of the altar, the one who had power over fire, and shouted loudly at the one which had the sharpened sickle in his hand: "Take your sharpened sickle and gather the bunches from the vine, because the grape is mature." The angel cast the sharpened sickle down to the earth and gathered the vine from the earth, and threw the grapes into the big winepress of the wrath of God. The winepress was downtrodden outside the city and blood came out of the winepress, reaching even the horses' bridles, for a distance of one thousand six hundred furlongs.

After this I heard the voice of a great crowd in heaven saying: "Hallelujah! Salvation, glory and power to our God, because His judgements are true and just." Afterwards they continued, saying: "Hallelujah! His smoke rises for the centuries of centuries." Then the twenty-four Elders and the four Animals[2] prostrated themselves and worshipped God, who is seated on the throne, saying: "Amen. Hallelujah!" And a voice which came out of the throne said: "Sing to our God, all His servants who fear Him, big and small[3]." Then I heard the voice of a big crowd and like a voice of many waters, and like a voice of powerful thunder, which said: "Hallelujah! Because the Lord, Our Omnipotent God, has established His kingdom. Let us be happy and joyful and let's give Him glory, because the wedding of the Lamb has come; His spouse is already prepared, and He has been given fine, clean and pure linen to wear." (The fine linen are the works of justice of the saints.) And the angel said to me: "Blessed are the guests to the Lamb's wedding banquet." And he added: "These words of God are

---

1. Jesus Christ.
2. Some relate these to the 24 Patriarchs and Prophets, and the 4 creatures to the the 4 Evangelists.
3. The song is a triumphal hymn of the victory of the blessed.

true." I fell at his feet to worship him, but He said to Me: "Refrain from doing that; I am a servant with you and your brothers, who have the testimony of Jesus; worship God."

Extermination of the Beasts. Then I saw that the sky was open, and a white horse appeared. The horseman is called the Faithful, the True, and he judges and fights with justice. His name is the Word fo God[1]. And the heavenly armies accompany him riding white horses, dressed in white and clean linen. From their mouth a sharpened sword comes out to wound the nations. He will use them steadily, he threads the press of wine of God Almighty's wrath. Upon his cloak and tight a name is written: "King of Kings and Lord of Lords."

FINAL HAPPENINGS

The last judgement. I saw a great white throne and the one seated on it. The sky and earth fled from his presence[2], without finding their places. I saw the dead, big and small, on foot before the throne; and the books were open[3]; and another book was open, the Book of Life. And the dead were judged according to the contents of the books, each one according to his deeds. The sea returned the dead that it had been guarding; Death and Hades[4] returned the dead that they had been guarding, and each one was judged according to his deeds. Death and Hades were cast into the pool of fire —the pool of fire is the second death— and anybody who was not written into the book of life was cast into the pool of fire[5].

Heavenly Jerusalem. Then I saw a new heaven and a new earth, for the former heaven and the former earth have disappeared, and the sea no longer exists[6]; and I saw the Holy City, the new Jerusalem, which was coming down from heaven

---

1. Jesus Christ, the supreme judge.
2. They will disappear.
3. That of mens' actions and the Book of Life with the names of the chosen ones.
4. Hades, the Jewish name for the place of the Dead.
5. Hell.
6. Man's renovation involves the renovation of all nature corrupted by the Original Sin.

by God, as a bride dressed for the bridegroom. And from the throne a sound voice came out, "This is the home of God among men. He will live among them; they will be his people, and God will dwell among them. They will not weep again, and there will not be more death, mourning or suffering, for the former world has vanished." And He who was sitting on the throne said, "I make all things anew." Then he said to me, "Write down that this words are true and certain." Still, he said, "Done and over with. I am the Alpha and the Omega, the Beginning and the End: the thirsty shall drink free out of the spring of life. The winner will inherit all these things; I shall be his God and he shall be my son. But cowards, unbelievers, those degraded, murderers, those who fornicate, sorcerers, image-worshippers, and liers shall inherit the burning pool of fire and brimstone —this is the second death."

I saw no Temple in it, for the Temple is the Lord, God Almighty, and the Lamb. The City does not need sun, its light is the Lamb. Nations shall walk according to its light, and the kings of the earth will bring their glory to her[1]. Her gates will never be shut, for there is no darkness in her. The glory and honour of nations shall come to her. Nothing impure shall enter her, nor the one who committs abomination and lie, but only those whose name has been written in the book of life, the Lamb.

God's throne and the Lamb will be in the city, and God's servants shall worship him, they will see his face and his Name will be on their forefront. There will be no more night, they will not need light or lamps, not even the sun, for the Lord God will give them light. And they will rule for centuries.

Epilogue. And he said to me: "These words are certain and true. And the Lord God of the spirits of the prophets has sent his angel to show his servants what is going to happen now. I will come back son. Blessed be the one who keeps the word of the prophesy of this book."

---

1. The new heavenly city and the Kingdom are not like those in this world, and the bodies shall be glorified as Jesus was resuscited. The new Jerusalem is our home in heaven.

I, John, have seen and heard all these things. When I heard them and saw them, and prostrated before the angel who had shown them to me to worship him. But he said to me, "Do not do that, for I am a servant, like you and your brothers the prophets and those who keep this book. Worship God." And he said, "Do not seal the words of the prophecy of this book, for Time is coming near. Let the sinner go on sinning, and the wicked do their abominations; but also let the upright do justice and the holy man remain in his holiness. I will come soon and bring your reward, which I will distribute according to everyone's deeds. I am the Alpha and the Omega, the First and the Last One, the Beginning and the End.

I, Jesus, have sent my angel to witness all these things regarding the Churches. I am the root and descendancy of David, of the morning shining star. The Spirit and the Bride said, "Come." Let those who listen say, "Come." Let the thirsty come, and everyone who wants to do so come and drink from the water of life. I bear witness to all those who listens to the words of the prophesy of this book. The one who states these things says, "Yes, I am coming soon." Amen. Come, Lord Jesus! Lord Jesus' Grace be with the Saints. Amen.

INDEX

OLD TESTAMENT

NEW TESTAMENT